DOING EVERYDAY LIFE

DOING EVERYDAY LIFE

Ethnography as
Human Lived Experience

Edited by

Mary Lorenz Dietz
University of Windsor

Robert Prus
University of Waterloo

William Shaffir
McMaster University

Copp Clark Longman Ltd.

ISBN: 0-7730-5405-7

Executive editor: Jeff Miller
Managing editor: Barbara Tessman
Editing: Susan Wallace-Cox
Design and typesetting: Sharon Foster
Cover illustration: Pierre-Paul Pariseau
Printing and binding: Metropole Litho Inc.

Canadian Cataloguing in Publication Data

Main entry under title:

Doing everyday life

Includes bibliographical references.
ISBN 0-7730-5405-7

1. Social groups.   2. Subculture.   I. Dietz, Mary Lorenz.   II. Prus, Robert C.   III. Shaffir, William, 1945–

HM131.D65 1994   305   C94-930901-X

Copp Clark Longman Ltd.
2775 Matheson Blvd. East
Mississauga, Ontario
L4W 4P7

Associated companies:
Longman Group Ltd., London
Longman Inc., New York
Longman Cheshire Pty., Melbourne
Longman Paul Pty., Auckland

Printed and bound in Canada

1 2 3 4 5   5405-7   98 97 96 95 94

Table of Contents

To my mother and friend, Evelyn Highlund.
—MARY LORENZ DIETZ

To Greg and Wendy, Marshall and Jordan.
—ROBERT PRUS

To my wife, Rivka; children, Yael, Elichai,
and Ariel; and sister, Chave.
—WILLIAM SHAFFIR

Preface

This book originated as the three of us were discussing a number of the very interesting papers delivered at a series of conferences on symbolic interaction and ethnographic research. As we talked with others about assembling a package of materials along these lines, we encountered much enthusiasm concerning the utility of having a collection of articles of this sort available for classroom use. There was also considerable enthusiasm expressed about the desirability of providing readers with a conceptual and methodological framework for comprehending and approaching the ethnographic study of human lived experience.

Accordingly, in approaching this book, we assumed two objectives. First, we wanted to compile a series of articles that would convey some of the vitality and richness of ethnographic research conducted in the Chicago style of symbolic interaction. Second, we wanted to provide readers with a theoretical viewpoint and a set of concepts that they could use both to synthesize the ethnographic material presented in this volume and to facilitate their own understandings of the social worlds around them.

We think we have accomplished the first objective in developing this volume. While we have been able to include only a small portion of the highly insightful and compelling works that fall under the rubric of Chicago style interactionism, we expect that readers will find the articles in this volume to be diverse, interesting, and highly relevant to a fuller understanding of the ways in which people accomplish everyday life. The papers presented here are slices of larger studies of people's experiences in a variety of settings, but they still generate considerable insight into participant viewpoints, involvements, identities, activities, and relationships. Thus, in particularly valuable manners, these papers indicate the ways in which human group life is accomplished in practice.

The second pursuit was that of introducing readers to a conceptual frame for approaching the study of human lived experience. To this end, the first article, "Approaching the Study of Human Group Life: Symbolic

Interaction and Ethnographic Inquiry," lays out the major thrusts of an inter-actionist approach for such study. As well, it introduces readers to the methodological practices characterizing interactionist research. The conclud-ing statement, "Generic Social Processes: Intersubjectivity and Trans-contextuality in the Social Sciences," pursues these same themes by delineating a set of "generic social processes" pertinent to ongoing concep-tual develoments in interactionist research. Representing a means of synthe-sizing and dialoguing with much of the vast array of research falling within this style of research, these trans-situational or transcontextual social processes also constitute the frame around which the studies in this volume were organized.

The collection of articles in this volume have been arranged with the introductory-level student in mind. We have tried to ensure that the materials are highly readable and devoid of complex jargon that often serves as a stum-bling block to those unfamiliar with the theoretical framework within which the materials are cast. In short, we have aimed to provide an understanding of, and appreciation for, the organization and practice of social life across a variety of settings. In this respect, especially, the volume is suitable not only for courses in social psychology and social interaction, but also for introduc-tory courses in sociology.

We wish to thank those who contributed to this volume. Although the individual chapters reflect considerable variation of style and emphasis, we appreciate the efforts these scholars made both to meet our deadlines and to adapt their writing style and conceptualization of the subject matter to meet our specific requirements. We imagine that all those who read this volume will have their particular favorite articles, reflecting their own circumstances and past experiences, or perhaps even their own curiosities and fascinations. In all instances, though, we anticipate that people reading this collection of articles will develop a better understanding of "the generalized other" (Mead 1934) as a consequence of these situated examinations of the ways in which human lived experience is accomplished on a day-to-day basis in a wide variety of contexts. Hopefully, too, readers will envision ways in which they could apply the insights generated here to any variety of other situations. Indeed, we would consider this volume especially valuable should the people reading these statements be sufficiently stimulated that they feel encouraged to embark on research of this sort on their own—for it is only in pursuing intimate familiarity with the lived experiences of others that one may develop more profound appreciations of both the intriguing features of one's own circumstances and the ways in which community life is constituted more generally.

We would like to acknowledge the support of the Universty of Windsor, the University of Waterloo, McMaster University, and the Social Sciences and Humanities Research Council of Canada (SSHRCC). As well, we are very grateful to all those who participated in the Ethnographic/Qualitative

Research Conference over the years. Although we've used only a small portion of the many stimulating papers presented by these scholars, we've appreciated the collegiality and enthusiasm of all those who participated in this conference. It was from this impetus that this volume was developed.

We would like to thank Janice Drakich for her helpful readings and comments of earlier drafts of this manuscript and Sue McGilveary for her invaluable assistance in putting this manuscript into publishable form.

Finally, we would very much like to express our thanks to Jeff Miller, Barbara Tessman, and the other members of the Copp Clark Longman team for their enthusiasic support of this project. We've very much enjoyed working with them and consider ourselves most fortunate to have become partners with them in producing this ethnographic venture.

Introduction: The Study of Everyday Life

Platform or stand-up magic is a more versatile form of magic. You might do some close-up magic and then do a small stage show, say for fifty people. The idea is to "pack small and play big" to produce very obvious effects with small props, like rolled up newspapers, for instance. You have to be more versatile, and you have to be able to connect with people both ways, with both stage or close-up magic, depending on how you're working at the time.... Usually, though, people have different strengths or different appeals, when they work from stage or in close-up.... You can do the very same tricks, the same magician doing the same tricks, and for some, it will come across better off the stage and for others, it will be much better in a close-up situation.... Like this one guy, [name], he just does not feel very warm when he's doing close-up right next to you, but when he's working on stage, you don't feel the lack of warmth or see the deadness of the eyes. On stage, you just don't see these failings. It depends entirely on your distance from the other person.... Some people are very good at close-up magic, but stand-up is a different mode and they can't project the same qualities. Like you might be very warm in close-up, but not be able to bridge the gulf on stage. Having charisma at two feet and having charisma at a hundred feet is a completely different thing! The audience sees different things in you. It's not just the performer. It's something going on with the audience and how they react to you! (Prus and Sharper 1991, 224–25)

Doing Everyday Life: Ethnography as Human Lived Experience is a book about human lived experience. It focuses on the "what and how" and "here and now" of human group life. It is not intended as a source of advice or a set of prescriptions that tells people how they ought to live. Instead, the emphasis is on the ways in which people accomplish their activities on a day-to-day, moment-to-moment basis.

While there are a great many ways of approaching the study of human group life, this volume takes the viewpoint that if anyone wants to understand people, then it is necessary to become intimately familiar with their life-worlds: to see how people make sense of the situations they encounter in their daily routines and how they deal with these situations on an ongoing basis. Thus, in contrast to those who send out questionnaires to people or run them through sets of experiments, the approach taken here concentrates on achieving in-depth familiarity with the life-worlds of the people being considered by venturing out into these life-worlds. This means talking to people about their experiences and activities, as well as observing their behavior and inquiring into their meanings, concerns, and practices, and, wherever feasible, participating in those same situations ourselves.

In many respects what one does as a field researcher or ethnographer in these settings is not so different from what people do whenever they enter into new settings and attempt to make sense of these settings and the people they encounter therein. Certainly, many of the same sorts of social skills that people use to relate to others on a day-to-day basis are fundamental to ethnographic inquiry or field research.[1] The implication, too, is that people who are interested in others and who are able to communicate easily, fluently, and intensively with others have considerable potential to become good field researchers.

Although some people may be prone to dismiss an approach that is built on commonplace forms of association as somehow unscientific, this view is quite mistaken. A fuller examination of this volume and the methodology employed herein strongly refutes this contention. Indeed, as will be indicated later, any approach to the study of human behavior that does not attend to human lived experience may itself be challenged for its lack of scientific authenticity. To approach the study of any phenomenon scientifically means to subject it to close, sustained examination and ongoing conceptual (re)appraisal. And this is precisely what we do with the study of human lived experience.

In some ways the methodology we employ is akin to that of the natural biologist. And just as the natural biologist studying wolves or geese, for instance, would want to spend as much time as possible in the natural environments of these species, so do we insist on becoming intimately familiar with the ways in which people deal with their natural life-worlds on an ongoing basis. The difference, however, is that researchers studying people are dealing with symbol-using, reflective life-forms and need to attend to these human qualities in approaching the study of human group life. If people (symbolically) interact with one another, using language forms to communicate and can develop selves and take themselves into account in developing their lines of action, then it is essential that researchers respect these human essences and incorporate them into their theories of human behavior. To overlook, dismiss, or ignore these central features of the human condition would be an irresponsible position for anyone wishing to develop a viable "social science" to take

Further, since people can only know the world as they experience it, we insist on the necessity of attending to human lived experience as our primary reality and data base. This data, or knowledge about the other, can only be obtained through extended association with those about whose life-worlds we wish to learn. In this regard every person who attempts to make sense of his or her community and the activities that go on therein, may be seen as a social scientist of sorts. Thus, some citizens may become remarkably astute students of human behavior without ever having taken any formal studies in the area.

What differentiates our approach from that of others who constitute the general public and in particular the more astute "naïve" social scientists among them (who may develop a most impressive stock of knowledge in their own right) is largely a matter of the resources, insights, and practices that develop over time through a sustained community focus on the study of human lived experience.

If one were able to tap into, assess, and systematize all the insights that various people may have had over the years, our social science would likely be much richer as a consequence. However, as long as these insights remain fragmented, isolated, and fail to transcend the life spans of particular individuals, there is little hope of developing a more extensive social science. It is here, then, that a community of people dedicated to the pursuit, acquisition, and assessment of insights pertaining to the nature of human lived experience is so consequential. It is here, too, that the development of resources of a conceptual, methodological, substantive, and analytical nature becomes so vital in sustaining and pursuing a science of human group life. Without this ongoing academic community; without this focus on understanding human group life; without activities explicitly directed toward this objective; without the relationships that both ethnographic inquiry and scholarly exchanges entail; and without the substantive and conceptual materials developed and acquired over the years, we would have very little to pass on to subsequent generations of students.

Of the various approaches to the study of human behavior developed in the social sciences, only some have attended to the *interpretive* (or hermeneutic) features of human group life. One of the academic communities that has pursued the task of studying human group life as it is accomplished on a day-to-day or here-and-now basis is that of the symbolic interactionists. *Symbolic interactionism* is most readily associated with the works of George Herbert Mead and Herbert Blumer. Although it is one of several somewhat inter-related interpretive sociologies, symbolic interactionism has maintained and developed a unique emphasis on the necessity of building a social science through studies grounded in human lived experience. While interactionism has incorporated a number of insights from phenomenological sociology, ethnomethodology, reality construction theory, and the new sociology of science, symbolic interactionism is the most theoretically coherent and methodologically informed of the interpretive approaches to the study of human lived experience.

"Approaching the Study of Human Group Life: Symbolic Interaction and Ethnographic Inquiry" outlines the basic thrusts of an interactionist or social constructionist approach to the study of human group life. Here, we draw attention to the necessity of studying human group life as ongoing activity and of examining the ways in which people define situations (and themselves) and work out lines of action in conjunction with one another. The emphasis is very much on the ways in which people produce or formulate activity on an ongoing basis and, in so doing, how they take themselves and others into account. In addition to laying out the sorts of assumptions that characterize symbolic interaction and ethnographic research, this article also considers the ways in which researchers go about conducting ethnographic inquiry. Thus, some attention is given to the procedures people use in gathering ethnographic data and pursuing co-operation on the part of those they study.

"Field Research as Social Experience: Learning to Do Ethnography," examines some of the processes and problematics of "doing" field research. Building on their own experiences as ethnographers and those of others working in this tradition, Shaffir, Dietz, and Stebbins discuss the objectives, obstacles, and tactical dilemmas that social scientists encounter when they research people. In reading this paper, we develop a fuller appreciation of the task of "interpreting the interpreters." Focusing on the basic practices in which ethnographers engage as they attempt to learn about, depict, and analyze data gathered through participant-observation, general observation, and extended, open-ended interviews, this paper provides a valuable background statement to the materials following.

Part 2, "Studying Everyday Life: Ethnography in Process," is divided into five subsections, providing readers with a rich assortment of ethnographic inquiries focusing on human lived experience. Building on data acquired through participant-observation in particular settings and extended open-ended interviews with participants, as well as an assortment of observational materials, this collection of ethnographic statements offers readers a body of literature, depicting the ways in which human group life is accomplished in practice.

Focusing on *ethnographic research* (or studies that examine the way of life of a group of people), this material is organized around five "generic social processes." These concepts (*getting involved, acquiring perspectives, achieving identity, doing activity,* and *experiencing relationships*) are termed "generic" because they seem applicable to any group context. The notion of "social process" draws attention to the interpretive, interactive, and emergent nature of human experience. These processes are central to understanding people's participation in community life.

The studies featured here detail people's experiences in a wide variety of contexts and provide readers with opportunities to examine a number of life-worlds from the points of view of the participants. By attending to the trans-situational, transcontextual, or generic features of human association, however, we not only learn things about people in other situations by examining their life experiences, but we also have the means of more carefully comparing and contrasting people's experiences across a wide range of situations. Thus, for instance, we consider the experiences of people *becoming involved* in ballet, shuffleboard, and political parties. We compare the ways in which people *acquire perspectives* as deaf children, as parents, or as feminists. Similarly, we examine the *identity work* of medical students, ill people, and people getting tattooed. In like manner, we observe how comedians, students studying for tests, and people working in human service agencies go about *co-ordinating activities*. Focusing on basic social processes, we also consider the ways in which *relationships* are developed with respect to drug dealing, outlaw bikers, and the integration of mental patients into the community. In each case we pursue *intimate familiarity* (Blumer 1969b) with our subject matter by drawing upon people's lived experiences in particular contexts. We gain a sense of their viewpoints and dilemmas, their uncertainties and risks, their practices and negotiations, and their friendships, conflicts, and animosities. However, by attending to the generic features of human association, we also have a means of achieving a fuller appreciation of human experience across a range of settings.

Attending to the necessity of building a social science around the concept of intersubjectivity, the two articles in Part 3 conclude the volume. While Elvi Whittaker discusses the relevance of Herbert Blumer's work on symbolic interaction for anthropologists doing ethnographic research, the implications of Blumer's approach to the study of human group life extend to the social sciences more generally. Indeed, her paper draws attention to the necessity of clarifying one's assumptions about the nature of human group life and developing a conceptual thrust more clearly grounded in action. These issues are pursued more generally by Robert Prus wherein the notion of generic social processes is used as a means of achieving intersubjectivity and transcontextuality in social science research. Like other concepts, generic social processes enable us to abstract general patterns from particular cases. Here, however, we refer more specifically to process-oriented concepts that enable us to transcend particular social settings. Thus, for example, concepts such as "becoming involved," "developing relationships," and "co-ordinating activities" are relevant to understanding social behavior regardless of whether one is discussing juvenile delinquency, dating relationships, welfare agencies, or sports teams. This statement on generic social processes not only provides a foundation for ordering the ethnographic studies in this volume, but also constitutes a framework that students may use to conceptualize, assess, and synthesize ethnographic research more generally.

As you examine the contents of this volume, we very much encourage you to assess all of these materials against your own situations and experiences. A science of human behavior ultimately must be adjusted to the behavior of human beings and not vice versa.

NOTES

1. The term *ethnographic research* is often used more or less synonymously with interactionist research, qualitative research, naturalistic inquiry, participant-observation, interpretive inquiry, grounded theory, Chicago school sociology, the subcultural tradition, and the reality construction or negotiated reality approach. Additionally, strong affinities may be noted with what has also been termed the dramaturgical approach, labeling theory, *verstehen* sociology, phenomenological social science, hermeneutics, existential sociology, ethnomethodology, and some varieties of "humanist" social science.

PART 1

Getting a Foundation: The Interpretive/ Ethnographic Tradition

The two articles in this part focus attention on an essential conceptual framework for the study of human behavior and on the dynamics involved in conducting ethnographic research. Neither paper is meant to provide a truly comprehensive account of the theoretical and methodological issues surrounding the study of social life, but each aims to flag some of the more salient dimensions and aspects involved.

The first selection by Robert Prus establishes the theoretical and methodological thrust of this volume. Building on the work of those involved in developing Chicago-style interactionism, Prus contends that symbolic interaction and ethnographic inquiry offer the most credible means available with which to analyze social interaction. Drawing upon the specific contributions of George H. Mead and Herbert Blumer, Prus specifies the assumptions underlying the interactionist framework. He suggests that the focal point of ethnographic research must center on activity and the manners in which human group life is accomplished in practice.

While the first article is primarily focused on the conceptual underpinnings of symbolic interaction and ethnographic research, the contribution by William Shaffir, Mary Lorenz Dietz, and Robert Stebbins attends to the social processes shaping ethnography. Examining a number of issues that have arisen in the literature with respect to fieldwork methods, the authors claim that the very nature by which ethnographic research is accomplished requires an active awareness of the relationship of the researcher's personal involvements and the task of data collection and management. Learning to do ethnography requires an appreciation of field research as process, and the authors examine a variety of social features that shape and affect ethnographic inquiry.

Along with the two concluding articles at the end of this volume, these introductory statements provide a conceptual frame for the ethnographic studies that follow. While alerting readers to the human nature of ethnographic inquiry, these articles also generate a great deal of conceptual coherence for those interested in pursuing the study of human lived experience.

Approaching the Study of Human Group Life: Symbolic Interaction and Ethnographic Inquiry

Robert Prus

A self without an other, or an outer without an inner—these are merely sense-less words. All this finally boils down to the fact that there is no such thing as an "enclosed self" from which the other or the outer could arise. (Dilthey in Ermarth 1978, 101)

Language is itself a form of social behavior, one of the latest achievements of evolution, and as indispensable as the brain itself to the higher kinds of life. Its function is to define, organize, and guide the subtler forms of human activity, and it is natural that social science, which aims to extend and perfect this function, should find in language its main instrument. (Cooley 1928, 316)

The study of human behavior is first and foremost a study of *ongoing community life*, for only through interaction with others does one develop a capacity for *language* and only in the process of achieving these sets of shared symbols can people make sense of themselves or any other object of their awareness. Indeed as Wilhelm Dilthey contends, it makes no sense to speak of "a self without the other."[1] And, as Charles Horton Cooley observes, language is as indispensable for appreciating human conduct as is the possession of a brain, for only through language is the world of human beings intelligible.[2]

Language may be seen to consist of words, gestures, and other shared symbols or indications that people make with respect to one another, along with any rules or patterns of usage they may establish in invoking these communications. Still, the significance of language for human behavior can only be appreciated when one recognizes its potential for *intersubjectivity* (obtaining a shared understanding of the other), *self-reflectivity* (developing a sense of self, interpreting, conversing with oneself), and *meaningful activity* (anticipating, performing, interacting, accomplishing, or doing things). Quite simply, without language, there would be no world as we know it. Furthermore, without language, we would have no basis for even trying to imagine what a world without language would be like. Still, while language is essential for the human condition, it is important that we not elevate language beyond the level of human group life, for language is itself a product as well as a medium of human association. Human interchange cannot be reduced to linguistics, for language itself is part of the much larger realm of ongoing human enterprise and accomplishment embodied in the concepts of action and community life.

The human capacities for intersubjectivity, self-reflectivity, and meaningful activity do more than merely differentiate humans from non-humans, for purposes of inquiry or study. They point to the necessity of developing a conceptual framework and a set of methodological practices that are attentive to these fundamental features of the human condition. In this article we first present a rudimentary overview of symbolic interaction, an approach to the study of human group life that is attentive to intersubjectivity, self-reflectivity, and meaningful activity as basic human essences.[3] This is followed by a brief discussion of the ways in which *ethnographic research* (or the study of the way of life of a group of people) is pursued. These materials are of an introductory nature, but should provide students with fundamental understandings of theory, methods, and conceptual themes.

Symbolic Interaction

Symbolic interaction rests in the last analysis on three simple premises. The first premise is that human beings act toward things on the basis of the meanings they have for them.... The second premise is that the meaning of such things is derived from, or arises out of, the social interaction that one has with one's fellows. The third premise is that these meanings are handled in, and modified through, an interpretive process used by the person in dealing with the things he encounters. (Blumer 1969b, 2)

The term *symbolic interaction* sometimes seems a little overwhelming to people when they first encounter it, but there may be no better shorthand way of depicting the fundamental essence of human group life than describing it as symbolic interaction, a term suggested by Herbert Blumer in 1937.

While symbolic interaction is only one of several interpretive approaches in the social sciences, it is *the* interpretive approach which has been most attentive to the necessity of developing a social science rigorously grounded in the study of human group life as it is accomplished on a day-to-day basis.[4]

At a base-line level, symbolic interaction centrally acknowledges the human capacity for communication through a sharedness of gestures and the resultant sense of reality that emerges as people interact with one another. Human communication depends most fundamentally on people's abilities to make indications to one another and to work out some sort of shared meanings for those gestures, symbols, or indications so that one might interpret particular conversations of gestures in the manners in which the other intended and viceversa. It is not possible within the confines of this article to present a detailed statement on symbolic interaction, but an introduction to the works of George Herbert Mead and Herbert George Blumer is essential if one is to acquire even a rudimentary appreciation of this perspective.

George Herbert Mead

> The principle which I have suggested as basic to human social organization is that of communication involving participation in the other. This requires the appearance of the other in the self, the identification of the other with the self, the reaching of self-consciousness through the other. (Mead 1934, 253)

Although George Herbert Mead (1863–1931) taught in the philosophy department at the University of Chicago, he was to have a profound influence on what was to become known in sociology as *symbolic interaction*. Mead published little of his own work on social psychology, but three books on this subject—*The Philosophy of the Present* (1932), *Mind, Self, and Society* (1934), and *The Philosophy of the Act* (1938)—were published posthumously by students working primarily with notes from his classes. Of these volumes, *Mind, Self, and Society* clearly has had the greatest impact on the sociological community.

Mead's thinking appears to have derived much inspiration from ongoing interaction with other pragmatists in the early 1900s (particularly John Dewey, Charles Horton Cooley, and William James),[5] but it was Mead who provided the major conceptual foundations with which students and faculty (most notably, Ellsworth Faris and Herbert Blumer) at the University of Chicago forged a unique interpretive tradition, *symbolic interaction*. Thus, as a means of comprehending symbolic interaction, it is essential to consider the *social behaviorism* of George Herbert Mead.

One finds very few references to the German social theorist Wilhelm Dilthey in Mead's published works, but Mead conducted some doctoral studies with Dilthey (Joas 1985). Hence, while Mead played a central role in the development of American pragmatism (Morris 1970), it is worth noting that the social psychology that Mead developed is remarkably parallel with Dilthey's hermeneutic social science in several key respects. Like Dilthey (Ermarth 1978; Prus, forthcoming), Mead's notions are *intersubjective* (interactive and interpretive) to the core, with a strong insistence on recognizing the inter-relatedness and irreducibility of *mind, self,* and *society.* For both scholars, as well, *language* is considered absolutely fundamental to the human essence.[6] Although both a product and a process of human expression, language, or the symbolic means of achieving a sharedness of perspectives, is envisioned as *the* medium that makes interaction possible and accounts for the development of mind, the dynamics of self, and the production of action. Viewed thusly, mind, self, and society are rooted in, and sustained through, symbolically mediated interaction. To better provide readers with an appreciation of Mead's thoughts, the discussion following builds on some central themes from *Mind, Self, and Society.*

For Mead, the concept of *mind,* (or an internalization of the perspective(s) of the [interactive] community in which one is located), is viewed as an ongoing process by which one makes sense of the world as encountered. Although the mind provides a basis for organizing one's experiences, Mead does not accept the idea of the mind as a given. It is a symbolic or linguistic essence and arises out of, and takes its (emergent) shapes from, the communication process, through interaction with others. Thus, Mead spends considerable time establishing the centrality of the *shared gesture* or *significant symbol* as the foundation for human communication, conceptualization, and reflection. A gesture can only become shared or attain the status of a significant symbol when it can be used to invoke in the other a sense of the world experienced by oneself. At that point, it becomes "language" and it is only through the acquisition of language that thinking or an internalized conversation with the self is possible.

From Mead's viewpoint, reality is a *symbolic* (or intersubjectively accomplished) experience. Realities are created and transmitted in the course of human interaction through the development of shared sets of symbols. Thus, while individually possessed, minds are, according to Mead's theory, community products that are more or less continuously in the making as people interact with others.

Mind is not simply a passive receptacle from Mead's viewpoint. Mind involves an active sense of participation in the community of others. Hence, the ability to make meaningful indications to self and to others is essential for even rudimentary notions of "minded behavior."

If the mind can be viewed as an emergent, interpretive frame, which develops as people interact and work out lines of action with each other with respect to the objects to which people attend in this or that manner, a stronger, fuller sense of the mind becomes apparent with the recognition of the *self* as an object of one's own awareness. Like the mind more generally, people's images of the self are predicated on interaction with others and involve taking the role or adopting the viewpoint of the other. As with mind, interaction (made possible through language) is essential if people are to develop a sense of self. For Mead, the self arises in the process of social (symbolically mediated) experience and activity.

Mead clearly recognized the initiative capacity of humans for action, which he terms the "I." However, the more social self, or the focused or contextually meaningful self, is predicated on the recognition of oneself as an object (the "me") in a world of other symbolically mediated objects.[7] Self-reflectivity, or the recognition of self as an object, only comes about by taking the role or viewpoint of the other. Thus, there can be no self without a prior recognition of the other.

Humans may be born with the physiological capacity for thought, but thinking (interpreting, defining, contemplating, assessing, selecting, creating) is a reflective process which develops only by attending to the other and envisioning the self as an object from the viewpoint of the other.

The reflective essence of self is rooted in a community of others, or what Mead termed, "the generalized other." Self develops and takes its shape as people take the role or assume the perspective of the community at large, and this is done most fundamentally or essentially as people acquire the shared language of the community and attempt to fit their lines of action into those of others in that community.[8]

Further clarification of the notions of mind and self emerge when Mead focuses more squarely on society. *Society* (or community), from Mead's viewpoint, consists of people interacting with one another in ways made meaningful as a consequence of shared symbolic representations of the generalized other. Human societies consist of communities of minded individuals who possess selves and who act and interact with one another in reflective, meaningful manners.

As people develop minds and selves and indeed begin to realize the potential for thought and creativity by taking the viewpoint of the other, they also acquire and internalize notions of the moral orders of the communities in which they participate by taking the role of the other. It is with respect to the generalized other that people develop moral viewpoints and begin to assess their own behaviors and that of others.

A fuller appreciation of Mead's work hinges on the notion of *action*. So integral is action to Mead's formulation of social behaviorism that his book might have been better retitled, *Mind, Self, and Society in Action* because Mead envisioned human behavior taking place in process terms, as people make symbolic indications to themselves and others on an ongoing basis.

Herbert Blumer

Herbert George Blumer (1900–1987) very much envisioned himself as a student of George Herbert Mead and continually emphasized the importance of Mead's work for the social sciences. However, in the process of elaborating upon the theoretical and methodological implications of symbolic interaction for the study of group life, it is Blumer who most cogently and forcefully emphasized the intersubjective foundations of human group life in twentieth century social science.

Blumer's work may epitomize symbolic interaction better than anyone else's,[9] but it should be appreciated that symbolic interactionism became established as a tradition in the sociology department at the University of Chicago through the efforts of a number of people who worked along more or less related lines. Thus, in addition to the efforts of Herbert Blumer, it is essential to acknowledge the contributions that scholars such as W.I. Thomas and Florian Znaniecki, Robert Park and Ernest Burgess, Everett Hughes, and their students made to the more general enterprise of studying the ways in which human group life was accomplished in practice.[10]

Still, it was Herbert Blumer who, deriving central impetus from Mead and Cooley, would play the pivotal role in synthesizing interpretive social theory with ethnographic research in what has come to be known as *Chicago-style interaction*. Although Blumer directly embarked on a relatively small amount of research that could be defined as ethnographic in nature (Blumer 1933; Blumer and Hauser 1933; Blumer 1967), he was to become the central author and intellectual spokesperson for this tradition as well as the dominant source of challenge to mainstream social science with its emphasis on "causes" and "factors" purporting to explain human behavior.

Whereas mainstream social science assumes a "positivist" cast with its emphasis on causation, quantification, and objectification, Blumer argues for the necessity of an interpretive social science that would respect the human condition. Blumer observes that, in its quest to predict and control human behavior, positivist social science has erred by trying to reduce human behavior to a series of sociological and psychological variables or factors. What is missing in formulations of these sorts, Blumer contends, is an attentiveness to the essential features of human lived experience. Thus, despite attempts to be "scientific," most positivist approaches in the social sciences ignore or disattend to the most central features of human group life. They ignore the ongoing production of human action or the socially constructed nature of the human life-world; they disattend the diverse and shifting meanings that people attach to objects; they dismiss the self and people's capacity for self-reflectivity; they overlook the ways in which people interact with one another; and they ignore the ways in which people sustain and change the ways in which they associate with one another over time. Thus, Blumer asks whether approaches to the study of human behavior, which so extensively ignore or disattend to central features of human group life, ought to be considered scientific even though its proponents may invoke images of "scientism" in their presentations. In contrast, he proposes a social science that is thoroughly and rigorously grounded in the lived experiences of people, an approach that is explicitly focused on the ways in which people go about their activities on a day-to-day basis.

In discussing symbolic interaction, Blumer (1969b, 6–20) delineates several root images central to this perspective. An abbreviated version of his presentation will be used to provide readers with a preliminary overview of his position.

First, Blumer stresses the point that human groups exist *in action*. People act individually and in combination with others, but society consists of people doing things and fitting their activities together with those of other people in their settings.

Second, society consists of people *interacting* with one another. Social interaction takes place between people, not between factors. Further, this interaction is mediated by the use of symbols as people make indications toward one another and establish shared meanings of objects. Sharedness of meanings develop as people take the role of the other or make indications to themselves from the standpoint of the other. As such, interaction is an ongoing interpretive, adjustive process, consisting of people making indications to one another, interpreting the indications that others make, and adjusting one's own definitions and behaviors to these interpretations.

Third, human beings live in a world of *objects*. An object is anything to which some reference may be made.[11] The human world or environment consists only of those objects that humans recognize and know. The meanings of objects are formed, learned, and transmitted through an interpretive, interactive process. Objects do not have inherent meanings, but they assume particular qualities by virtue of the ways in which people define those objects and act toward them.

As with other objects, people may make indications toward themselves. Like other objects, an awareness of the *self as an object* arises when people define themselves as objects. The self emerges as people begin to take the viewpoint of others with respect to their own being or begin to make indications to themselves as an object of their own awareness. The human being becomes a "social being" when it is able to take itself into account in formulating lines of action. At this point, one achieves a sense of agency, intentionality, or purposiveness of one's own conduct that transcends attempts to explain human behavior by virtue of some factor or set of factors purportedly acting on people.

Human action thus entails ongoing (minded) construction or *reflective* enterprise as people take objects (including oneself and others) into account in formulating lines of action. People do not merely respond to situations, but interpret, anticipate, act, assess, and adjust to the socially meaningful situations in which they find themselves.

According to Blumer's theory, human group life consists of, and exists in, people fitting their lives together with others. This notion of *joint activity* is contingent on somewhat shared (or intersubjectively acknowledged) sets of understandings. A great deal of interaction or joint activity takes the form of recurrent patterns and reflects mutually aware, pre-established understandings on the part of the participants. Still, while people may generally acknowledge, act upon, and otherwise sustain these conventional meanings and practices, it is essential to recognize that each instance of human activity needs to be constituted anew. Even highly repetitive, long-established activities are subject to ongoing definition and adjustment on the parts of the people involved. Thus, existing practices remain viable only so long as people continue to acknowledge them as appropriate and continue to act accordingly. Should people start to define these situations differently or encounter new concerns, then the precarious nature of these human dependent practices becomes markedly apparent.

Blumer also uses the notion of joint activity to alert us to both the *contextual* (situated or horizontal) and the *temporal* (longitudinal or historical) dimensions of human behavior. In the first instance, we become more cognizant of the interlinkages of people's activities in organizational routines and practices. Organizations or institutions do not function automatically, but achieve their essences because people "do things" at particular points in time and co-ordinate their activities in this or that manner. Although organizations at times may appear to "do things," organizational practices cannot be understood apart from the activities of the people therein who, like others in society, are engaged in an ongoing series of interpretive, interactive, adjustive processes. Used in Blumer's terms, joint activity sensitizes us to the necessity of examining the social (interactive, reflective) processes by which people shape the nature of organizational life both on a more situated basis and over time.

The concept of joint activity also draws our attention to the necessity of attending to the vertical or historical interlinkages of people's present activities with their previous practices and understandings. Although human behavior is situated within a current (or here-and-now) context, it is built on previous instances of here-and-now practices, with these earlier arrangements providing backgrounds for envisioning and developing the now current lines of action. Thus, we would want to be attentive to the emergent, ongoing formulation of human association; to examine the ways in which human action is built up over time, both among the same sets of interactants and among those whose associations effectively denote community life over longer periods of time.

Ethnographic Implications

When people speak about embarking on ethnographic research, they assume the tasks of thoroughly examining the life-worlds and practices of those whose situations are being studied. Indeed, this is most basic and yet, from the researcher's viewpoint, there is much more to ethnographic inquiry than simply going out to attend the world of people's lived experience in this or that setting. In their quest to be careful and thorough, as well as to be able to communicate the information and insights they acquire to others, researchers are apt to find that ethnographic inquiry also encompasses concerns with clarifying one's assumptions and accessing worlds of human lived experience,[12] as well as analyzing the material and dialoguing with the other ethnographic literature. It is to a consideration of these matters that we now turn.

Clarifying Ethnographic Assumptions

In order to provide readers with a better sense of fieldwork practices, it may be instructive to specify a set of assumptions that people working within an interactionist/interpretive tradition normally make (sometimes explicitly, sometimes implicitly) as they approach the study of human lived experience.

1. Human group life is (multi) perspectival. This premise acknowledges that people act toward objects in terms of the meanings those objects have for them and tend to alter the meanings they attribute to objects over time. People develop meanings for objects as they interact with one another and develop styles of relating to those objects. Rather than assume that objects have fixed or inherent meanings, it is posited that both the meanings attached to objects and the earlier identification of things as "objects" are problematic. When people establish consensus on the existence and meanings of particular objects, they tend to envision these definitions as "real" or "objective." Thus, while the interactionists see different people's worldviews as denoting multiple perspectives or realities, they also attend carefully to the realities of the groups they study, since these worldviews represent the paramount realities for understanding people's participation in the situations at hand. Thus, people are seen to operate in versions of multiple realities which they share, albeit imperfectly, with others at an intersubjective level. The alternative assumptions are: (a) there is a singular reality; and (b) the recognition of a multiplicity of perspectives is irrelevant to the study of human group life.

2. Human group life is reflective. People have the capacity to become objects of their own awareness. They attribute meanings to their own essences and develop lines of action which take themselves (and others, via role-taking) into account. People become self-reflective or develop a sense of self awareness through a process of interacting with others and taking the viewpoint of the other with respect to oneself. Denoting the abilities of people to become objects unto themselves or to be able to converse with themselves, the acquisition of reflectivity enables people to assume initiative (human agency, enterprise, intentionality) as they develop their activities in manners which take themselves into account. As reflective entities, people may pursue activities on their own and may also resist unwanted impositions. It is not assumed that people will always act wisely or be successful in their undertakings. The alternative assumptions are: (a) reflectivity does not exist—it is a figment of the imagination (as self-contradictory as that might seem); and (b) reflectivity is inconsequential in the study of human group life.

3. Human group life is negotiable. This assumption further acknowledges the abilities of people to resist the influences of others. Thus, notions of co-operation, competition, conflict, and compromise are recognized as central to human interaction, as are other forms of influence (accommodation and resistance). Although all matters of interaction may be quite uneven, some element of mutuality, sharedness, or intersubjectivity is evident in the ways in which people attempt to attend to and/or shape the behavior of others. The alternative assumptions are: (a) people do not influence each other in any direct sense; and (b) concepts such as those of negotiation, influence, bargaining, and the like, are irrelevant to the study of human group life.

4. Human group life is relational. People develop bonds and selectively associate with others. This premise attends to the identities that people attach to one another and to the loyalties, disaffections, and other interactional styles that emerge within human interaction. People do not exist as random or undifferentiated entities within the context of everyday life. The activities in which people engage are made meaningful and thus shaped by the others to whom they attend on a day-to-day basis. Definitions of objects, definitions of self, and negotiations of reality (including language) all depend centrally on people's participation or embeddedness in a community of others. The alternative assumptions are: (a) humans mix without regard to distinctions, preferences, obligations; and (b) relationships are inconsequential for the study of human group life.

5. Human group life is processual. Human lived experiences are viewed as emergent or ongoing social constructions or productions. The emphasis is on how human group life is shaped by people as they go about their activities at this, that, and other points in time. While notions of perspectives or worldviews, reflectivity, negotiated interchange, and relationships are all central to the ways in which the interactionists approach the study of human lived experience, so, too, is the matter of *process*. Referring to the emergent or ongoing nature of group life, process is basic to an understanding of these other themes. *Perspectives* (or the meanings that people attach to objects) develop, are implemented, and change over time. Likewise, reflectivity is not only a product of ongoing association, but assumes its significance as people go about their activities. It becomes expressed as instances of definition or interpretation, and intentionality or purposiveness, in process. Negotiation or interchange also assume a processual dimension as people define situations (and selves), work out tentative lines of action, make indications to others, interpret the indications of others, and make ensuing adjustments in the form of subsequent definitions, plans, and indications. Relationships, as well, are best understood in processual terms (or as having natural histories) with respect to their emergence, intensification, dissipation, and possible reconstitution, as people define themselves and attempt to deal with those with whom they associate over time. The implication is that all aspects of group life should be studied with respect to this emergent or dynamic notion of human enterprise. The alternative assumptions are: (a) the emphasis should be on outcomes and factors associated or correlated with particular outcomes; and (b) an appreciation of the formative process of human action is inconsequential to the study of human group life.

These assumptions place ethnographers very squarely in the interpretive or *hermeneutic* (after the Greek messenger [interpreter] god, Hermes) tradition.[13] From this viewpoint, all inquiry implies interpretation on the part of those involved. However, since social scientists observe people who differ from other objects of study by virtue of their interpretive and interactive capacities, ethnographers need to be sensitive to the *double hermeneutic* (or interpreting entities which themselves interpret the worlds they experience).[14] The *objects* (people) that social scientists study not only interpret other aspects of their worlds, but also exchange and recast their interpretations as they interact with others. Further, not only may people try to make sense of researchers' attempts to study them, but they may also react to researchers by withholding co-operation and engaging in purposive deception or other types of playful or evasive action. In contrast to those studying non-interpreting objects, we require a methodology which is thoroughly sensitive to the human capacity for symbolic interaction.

Viewed thusly, human behavior is a socially contextualized, ongoing, interactive process. To ignore any of the preceding features of group life (perspectives, reflectivity, negotiability, relationships, and processes) is to violate central qualities of our subject matter. If researchers are to try to be true to their subject matter (human group life), then they should be attentive to all these aspects of human association.

The research implications of these assumptions are highly consequential. It means that social scientists should attend to: (1) the viewpoints of those whose worlds they purport to examine; (2) the interpretations or meanings that people attach to themselves, other people, and other objects of their experiences; (3) the attempts that people make to influence (as well as accommodate and resist) the inputs and behaviors of others; (4) the bonds that people develop with others over time and the ways in which they attend to these relationships; and (5) the natural histories or sequences of encounters, exchanges, and events that people develop and experience.

The study of human group life is the study of lived experience. It is an examination of the ways in which people make sense of their situations and work out their activities in conjunction with others. Human experience is not to be dismissed as subjective, epiphenomenal, or non-factual. Since people know the world only as they experience it, and people experience the

world in an intersubjective manner, then this realm of inquiry (human experiences within a world of others) becomes the paramount reality to which
researchers should attend in their investigations of human group life.

Pursuing Ethnographic Inquiry

In their attempts to achieve intimate familiarity with the life-worlds of those
they study, ethnographers rely primarily on three sources of data: *observation, participant-observation,* and *interviews.*

Observation encompasses not only those things that one witnesses
through one's visual and audio senses, but also any documents, diaries,
records, and the like that one may be able to obtain in a particular setting.
While materials thusly gathered can be valuable, it is imperative to recognize
that the worth of any observation (or artifact) is contingent on researchers'
abilities to achieve clear and accurate definitions of how that phenomenon or
aspect of the situation was experienced and constructed by those participating in the situations under consideration. Observational material on its own
is an inadequate basis on which to build an ethnographic study because one
would have to make extensive inferences regarding people's meanings and
intentions. However, observational materials can be very valuable in helping
researchers formulate questions to be pursued in interviews as well as in providing a means of assessing and contextualizing the information one obtains
through interviews and participant observation.

Participant-observation adds an entirely different and vital dimension to
the notion of observation. Although this practice has often been dismissed as
subjective by positivist critics, and while researchers employing this strategy
of research would want to be cautious about any claims they make about
others based on their own experiences, the participant-observer role allows
the researcher to get infinitely closer to the lived experiences of the participants than does straight observation. Like those doing straight observation,
researchers engaged in participant-observation normally try to remain fairly
unobtrusive or non-disruptive in the setting being studied. However, this
research strategy entails a more active and interactive role as researchers
attempt to fit into the settings at hand. Insofar as participant-observation
allows researchers to experience on a firsthand basis some aspects of the life-
worlds of the other, it offers to those who are able and willing to assume the
role of the other in a more comprehensive sense, a unique and instructive
form of data. Additionally, since it typically puts researchers in close, sustained contact with others, participant-observation generates further opportunities to gain insight into the viewpoints and practices of the other through
ongoing commentary and other interactions. Participant-observation thus
provides a doubly privileged form of contact with the other.

Interviews represent the third major method of gathering ethnographic
data and, under some circumstances, may provide the primary source of data

for field researchers. While those conducting interviews become participants of sorts in the life-worlds of the other, interviews alone should not be considered substitutes for extensive involvements as participant-observers. At the same time, when researchers are able to establish a good working rapport with the other and can generate extended trust and openness, they may be able to obtain a great deal of information about the life-situations of the other through extended conversation. Ethnographers sometimes develop fairly extensive interview formats, but these normally take shape in the field as researchers learn more about the situations and the participants involved. The ethnographic interview is characterized by careful and receptive listening, open-ended queries, and extensive probing. It reflects a generalized curiosity about the situation of the other, and sets of questions develop as the researcher spends more time in the setting and the company of the other. Researchers in the field vary greatly in the ways and extent to which they pursue interview materials, but a fuller openness to the other or greater receptiveness to letting the other "talk back" to the researcher is fundamental in achieving a more viable sense of intersubjectivity. Indeed, without this opportunity to uncover, ascertain, and qualify the meanings that others hold for objects in their life-worlds and the ways in which people go about accomplishing their activities in practice, it would make little sense to talk about studying human lived experience.

While each setting is somewhat different from the next (as is each encounter with the same person), and may necessitate some change in researchers' practices, there is little doubt about the generally enhanced quality of the data one may obtain by spending more time in the setting and more fully participating in the life-worlds of the other. When researchers are able to gather observational, participant-observation, and interview data on a more or less simultaneous basis, this generally leads to a more complete understanding of the other. Researchers who become more immersed in the setting are not only more apt to be exposed to a wider and more intricate range of materials, but they are typically in a much better situation to inquire about, pursue, and assess incoming information gleaned in all of these manners.

Making Contacts with the (Ethnographic) Other

Since the subjects of ethnographic research are people, researchers face the problem of making contact with others. There are four major options one may use: (a) draw on one's own experiences; (b) access mutual settings; (c) find sponsors; and (d) make "cold calls." Researchers in any given setting may find that one or other means of making contact predominates, but as with the three methods of gathering data, researchers using all of these methods are apt to be advantaged over those not doing so.

When one has been, or is presently, involved in a particular situation, one of the easiest methods of generating descriptive material is to examine one's own experiences. Of course, extensive accounts of one's own lived experiences are more valuable than fleeting commentaries. It is also crucial that one be attentive to the need to generate materials that describe (rather than moralize), and that openly and honestly depict one's own activities. One strives for accounts that are thorough, careful, and brutally honest. A self-observer who is patient, willing to tolerate a great deal of ambiguity, open to everyone in the setting, and meticulous in maintaining detailed accounts of situations will fare much better overall. This mode of data collection denotes an ongoing interview with oneself, and the same concerns apply to gathering data on (or from) oneself as from others. As with probing in an interview with another person, the more contextual the material provided in one's own journals, the more valuable that material is. Thus, for instance, while one may describe a particular encounter in considerable detail, it is also very valuable to discuss any reservations one might have had along the way, as well as other lines of action contemplated as the encounter developed, and any adjustments or reflections made after the encounter. It is also helpful to indicate how this encounter might have differed from, or been similar to, others in which one had been involved.

A second type of contact situation that nicely lends itself to ethnographic inquiry is that in which one has "natural contact" with people whose worlds one would like to study. Any setting can lend itself to research, and in "mutual contact" situations, one is typically able to build on one's own experiences in the setting as well as on an existing set of contacts in a given community of others. Thus, for instance, people who have friends, associates, or family members involved in this or that lifestyle may ask these acquaintances to help them with their research. Since these other people already know and presumably feel comfortable with the researcher, they are often willing to provide a great deal of inside information as well as other opportunities to learn more about the situation at hand. These settings not only offer genuine advantages in terms of time expediency, but also offer the advantages of substantive familiarity and minimized stage fright. As well, insofar as these settings often are ones in which people may be doing jobs to earn their livings, or may be enjoying particular activities and associates, the situation may well offer the researcher an opportunity to benefit doubly from the research application—that is, by doing the job at the same time as enjoying doing the research.

"Sponsors" denote people who in one way or another facilitate the researcher's contacts with those they would like to access. Sometimes people offer to serve as sponsors for researchers embarking on particular lines of inquiry, but other times researchers may approach particular people as a means of making contact with others. On some occasions, sponsors may be formal gatekeepers of sorts who provide permission and entry into certain research sites. In other cases they may be friends or associates who introduce researchers to those with whom they wish to make contact. Some sponsors are very strong (helpful and well connected) and may also serve as key informants themselves, while others may provide researchers with an introduction or a name of another contact, possibly without much enthusiasm at all for the project.

Cold calls represent a fourth means of making contact with people. The term *cold call* is commonplace among salespeople who present themselves to relative strangers at their homes or places of business. The notion of cold calls is most applicable to field research as well, because field researchers are often concerned with the tasks of initiating contact, managing stage fright, and obtaining an opportunity to present one's proposals to the other. Because of the outreaching nature of this enterprise and the uncertainty of the reactions of the people being approached, cold calls put the initiator in a more vulnerable situation. However, because cold calls put salespeople or researchers in direct contact with people with whom they wish to make contact, they can be extremely valuable. Thus, even when researchers have good overall contacts in the field, they are apt to find it productive to approach those they do not know as well. While some people may be reluctant to participate in the project once it is explained to them, others may turn out to be excellent sources of information and contacts.

Managing Oneself in the Ethnographic Context

In contrast to those who work with questionnaire or experimental data, people doing ethnographic research very much put themselves on the "front lines." Not only do they deal with people and all the uncertainty that human interaction entails, but they are also highly dependent on these others for their co-operation and overall well-being.

Encounters with strangers and others upon whom one is dependent may engender some stage fright on the part of field workers. Even though many of their reservations may later prove to be unfounded, researchers do not know how receptive others will be when approached for assistance on various matters or how extensively they will pursue these matters with the researchers over extended periods of time.

Ethnographers have found that a concerted role-taking or empathizing effort is essential to obtaining in-depth materials, as is patience and perseverance when one depends on others for co-operation and information. Much more important than the specific questions researchers ask is the development of trust and openness between the participants and the researcher. Indeed, it is essential that participants be given opportunities to elaborate on their positions in full and open manners.

To be a good listener is vital, as is open-ended and non-judgmental inquiry. Thus, the interviewers most likely to obtain extensive materials and information are those who are chameleon-like in their demeanor and who intensively pursue elaboration and clarification. The interview is an ongoing exercise in fitting activities together with those of others and requires continuing adjustments both to the situation and to the other. It entails sustaining participants' interests in the discussions at hand. It necessitates a degree of sympathetic understanding, but it also requires that the researcher invoke some distance; that is, that one not be *too* understanding or helpful so that the other is encouraged to detail the events being discussed. In this respect, a very "helpful" interviewer can effectively destroy an interview by taking things for granted or assisting the respondents in summarizing their positions on things.

In addition to encouraging a sense of enthusiasm on the part of respondents, researchers are also faced with the task of maintaining their own sense of enthusiasm for the project at hand. Ethnographic inquiry is often interesting and may be quite fascinating at times, but it can be very gruelling in many respects. In addition to overcoming any stage fright one might experience along the way, as well as managing any difficult or disquieting situations that might emerge, one must deal with a great deal of ambiguity and have a willingness to put the outcome of one's study in the hands of others. Researchers never really know how projects will work out in the end, how much work will be entailed, or when their projects might be considered completed. This sense of "open-endedness" is further complicated by a realization that beyond the efforts one might be willing or able to devote to a project, one is inevitably dependent on the schedules and willingness of others to participate in this endeavor.

Ethnographic research is also complicated by an awareness that in some respects, one is always "on" while in the field. The other people in the setting may attend to the researcher in manners paralleling those of the researcher attending to them. Thus, although researchers may find themselves relaxing in this or that setting, it may be at some cost to the overall project. As well, comes the realization that the typically massive amounts of material emerging from ethnographic inquiry tend to complicate rather than simplify the researchers' understandings. And, unlike questionnaire or experimental data, which can be readily slotted into variable analysis, the expansive type of data that ethnographic research entails does not lend itself to highly distilled sets of findings for analyses and eventual publication. This is mentioned not to discourage people from doing ethnographic research, but rather to assure them that these sorts of experiences are quite typical.

Conclusion

This chapter began with what seems a very simple premise, that the study of human behavior is the study of human group life. Although this statement can do little more than introduce readers to symbolic interactionism and ethnographic research, it is hoped that it has provided a starting point for acknowledging the fundamentally and thoroughly intersubjective, or community-based, nature of human lived experience.

As Mead and Blumer indicate, by virtue of this intersubjective essence, the study of human behavior requires a theoretical and methodological orientation that respects this unique, but fundamental, feature of human group life. Thus, in contrast to those who would reduce human behavior to causes (factors, variables) and effects or outcomes, the interactionists insist on building a social science that is attentive to the community dimensions of human lived experience.

Recognizing that language is both a product and the medium of human association, these scholars draw our attention to the centrality of symbolic communication not only for people achieving a sense of the world (and other people therein), but also for acquiring *any* sense of self. Society may be seen as consisting of selves interacting with other selves, but people's capacities for possessing "selves," their abilities to think, and their notions of reality are fundamentally community products. They are contingent on ongoing interactive processes. Further, it is only as reflective entities (or objects of their own awareness) that people may (linguistically, mindedly) anticipate, act, and adjust to other (minded) people and other aspects of the situations they encounter.

People may attend to any variety of objects, including some that quantitative researchers label "factors," but as Blumer (1969b) observes, people are *not* merely mediums for the expression of so-called psychological or sociological factors. "Factors" or "variables" do not exist as inherent features of human group life, but achieve their existence as social constructions of particular researchers and those they can convince to accept these models. "Objects" do not have inherent meanings. Indeed, as Weston La Barre (1947) illustrates in a review of the anthropological literature on gestures and emotions, different peoples may vary remarkably in the ways and extent to which they recognize, define, evaluate, and act toward objects. Thus, instead of envisioning people's behaviors as determined by some factor or set of factors, human behavior is seen as denoting an ongoing formulative process on the part of minded interacting beings who possess selves and are able through symbolic communication to take the role of the other and adjust their activities accordingly. The claim is not that people will act rationally or wisely from this or that perspective, for these notions, too, reflect particular perspectives. Rather, the inference is that human behavior denotes a realm of human agency and enterprise rooted in an awareness of the intersubjective other.

Appreciating the fundamental human essences of intersubjectivity, reflectivity, and activity, Blumer (1969b) argues for a methodology that is attentive to the ways in which human group life is accomplished on a here-and-now basis. Whether one refers to this methodology as ethnographic inquiry, interactionist research, field research, participant-observation, or sympathetic introspection, the emphasis, according to Blumer's approach, is on achieving *intimate familiarity* with one's subject matter. In contrast to those who assume or profess that their research is empirical because they are "counting something," Blumer emphasizes that for the research to be empirical means that one must examine one's subject matter in a close, sustained manner. Likewise, being empirical means more than purporting to be scientific. If the outcome of one's research is to be empirical or endeavor to be scientific, one ought to respect the fundamental essences of one's subject matter. And, in the case of human beings, this means developing a methodology that is attentive to intersubjectivity, reflectivity, and ongoing activity. It means studying human group life as it takes place, as it is experienced by the people involved in its ongoing production. It means attending to the ways in which people "do" everyday life, on a day-to-day moment-to-moment basis.

In the studies that follow, many instances of these objectives are put into practice. Far from claiming that these are perfect illustrations of ethnographic inquiry, the researchers whose works are represented in this volume are very much aware of the problems associated with accessing and comprehending the other, sorting and analyzing the data collected, and conveying central aspects of these life-worlds to readers. Affording a window to people's ambiguities, dilemmas, strategies, and resourcefulness as well as a host of other experiences, ethnographic research tends to be interesting in many respects, but it is also challenging, laborious, and downright frustrating at times. Still, there is no viable substitute if we are to pursue an open, sincere, and informed understanding of the world of the other, and ourselves.

NOTES

1. For a fuller appreciation of Dilthey's contributions to the hermeneutic or interpretive social science, see Ermarth (1978) and Prus (forthcoming). Prus, especially, draws the linkages of Dilthey's work with the development of symbolic interaction.

2. See Prus (forthcoming) for a more detailed consideration of Cooley's contributions to symbolic interaction. Also, see Cooley (1909, 1926, 1928, 1964).

3. In addition to Blumer (1969b) who provides the single most valuable statement on symbolic interaction, readers are referred to Mead (1934) and a variety of other sources, including, Meltzer, Petras, and Reynolds (1975), Karp and Yoels (1979), Hewitt (1991), Charon (1992), Reynolds (1993), and Prus (forthcoming).

It should be noted that the version of symbolic interaction presented here is sometimes referred to as "Chicago" or "Blumerian" vs. "Iowa" interactionism. Chicago symbolic interactionism is much more attentive to the interpretive, processual, ethnographic aspects of the study of human group life, while Iowa (Manfred Kuhn) interactionism has traditionally been more structural, causally oriented, and quantitative in its thrust. See Meltzer and Petras (1972), Reynolds (1993), and Prus (forthcoming) for fuller elaborations of the similarities and contrasts between these two positions.

4. For an elaboration of other interpretive approaches in the social sciences and their affinities with symbolic interaction, see Prus (forthcoming).

5. It is difficult to provide an accurate shorthand definition of American pragmatism. As a group of scholars, however, these people were oriented toward an investigation of the ways human

group life might be accomplished on a practical (i.e., day-to-day) basis. They were concerned with the ways in which people made sense of their worlds and how they went about accomplishing their daily routines. Of the early pragmatists, it is Charles Horton Cooley who most explicitly proposed a method (*sympathetic introspection*) for doing social science. In formulating symbolic interaction, in which he draws the linkages of pragmatist philosophy and ethnographic research, Herbert Blumer draws particular inspiration from Cooley. Those interested in pragmatism are more generally referred to Konvitz and Kennedy (1960), Rucker (1969), Morris (1970), Scheffler (1974) and Reynolds (1993).

6. Despite the great importance they attached to language, neither Mead nor Dilthey were willing to divorce language from its *intersubjective* (ongoing community) context. Mead seems quite unwilling to separate language from the human formulation of action (and interaction); indeed, language was very much a part of this process. Language, for Dilthey, somewhat similarly, was a part of the historical-cultural mediated context that defined intersubjective reality.

7. Mead's (1934, 173–178) discussion of the "I" and the "me" is much more complex than implied here. In part these terms draw our attention to the dialectic, acting nature of the self: as an actor ("I") and an audience of one's own actions ("me"). Acknowledging people's abilities to be both objects unto themselves (as the "me") and active participants or agents (as the "I") in their presently unfolding situations, Mead envisioned the self as involving a process unto itself whereby people may sequentially and simultaneously attend to themselves and the lines of action they are developing along the way.

8. In practical terms "the generalized other" is often more situated or contextualized than implied here. Thus, in addition to the community at large, to which people may attend, people may also take the role of the other on a more delimited or localized basis. Here, one attends to the perspectives of some more immediate set of others (e.g., the other players on a baseball team, the other people in a classroom, or the other members of one's family). As well, one can also assume the viewpoint of particularized others, such as one's mother, one's friend, or one's immediate supervisor. Even in taking the role of an immediate other, however, one's understanding typically reflects one's familiarity with the (wider sense) of the generalized other for one can only make sense of specific others within the context of one's more general perspectives.

9. The bibliography at the end of this book provides a good starting point for appreciating Herbert Blumer's contributions to symbolic interaction and the social sciences more generally. Also see Prus (forthcoming) for a fuller statement on the role that Herbert Blumer assumed in developing and pursuing an interpretive social science along with references to other sources addressing other aspects of his work. Elvi Whittaker (in this volume) provides an indication of the centrality of Blumer's work in her delineation of his contribution to anthropology.

10. For a more detailed, conceptual, and historical statement on the development of symbolic interaction and ethnographic inquiry and the role that these scholars and others played in the process, see Prus (forthcoming). It is worth emphasizing, too, that although interactionist ethnography may have derived some inspiration from anthropological inquiry, there was not much sustained anthropological ethnographic research on which to build at the time sociological ethnography was taking shape. Ethnography in the two disciplines thus developed somewhat concurrently but also rather independently of one another, despite some seemingly notable links (see Prus, forthcoming).

11. An object is any item, distinction, concept, or image to which people may refer (i.e., become aware of, attend to, point to, acknowledge, consider, discuss, or otherwise act toward).

12. Readers are referred to Shaffir, Dietz, and Stebbins (in this volume) for a more extended statement on the problematics and processes of conducting ethnographic research. For other accounts of life in the field, see the collections of articles in Shaffir, Stebbins, and Turowetz (1980) and Shaffir and Stebbins (1991). Readers should also consult Taylor and Bogdan (1984), Lofland and Lofland (1984), and Jorgensen (1989) for other valuable statements on field research.

13. Wilhelm Dilthey (Ermarth 1978) is best seen as the founder of a hermeneutic social science.

14. See Blumer (1969b), Giddens (1973), and Prus (1992) for elaborations of these notions as they are applicable to the social sciences.

Field Research as Social Experience: Learning to Do Ethnography

William Shaffir, Mary Lorenz Dietz, and Robert Stebbins

Field research or what is called *participant-observation, qualitative research,* or *ethnography* refers to research in which the researcher personally observes, discusses, and records the words and actions of people engaging in social interaction.[1] In Chicago, where field research for sociologists was developed most extensively, researchers were at first simply instructed to go out among the people whose cultures were being studied. It was generally understood, however, that doing ethnographic research was different from doing journalism and literature. There were no guidelines at that time telling how this observation, recording, and analysis could or should be accomplished. Accuracy was considered to be important, but it was also clear that separating the perspectives of the researcher from the members of the community being researched was of paramount importance. Critics alleged that this type of research, by its nature, could not be objective and field researchers were defensive about this criticism.

Field research has now moved from an oral tradition, passed on in the mentor-student relationship, to a methodology increasingly examined, codified, and communicated in published form. This development helps meet the "need for working students in sociology to communicate the procedures and strategies of field research they have found consequential in their own studies to the less instructed or less experienced" (Habenstein 1970, 1). At the same time, field researchers know that there is no single best way of conducting field research. Field research experiences are unpredictable and approaches must be adapted to any particular research problem and setting. The interactional, situational, and volatile character of fieldwork roles and relationships mitigates the development of exact procedures. Hence the difficulty of delineating the "do's" and "don'ts" and "ropes" (Geer, Haas, Vivona, Miller, Woods, and Becker 1968) of social research.

In recent years field research seems to have enjoyed a renaissance as evidenced by the amount of published work on the subject. As late as 1960, in one of the very first attempts at codifying the problems and practices of field research, Junker (1960, 32) observed that field researchers had not published much about the processes they had experienced. Subsequently, both for the neophyte and for the experienced field researcher, numerous texts are available, outlining the organization and structure of this methodological approach (for example, Van Maanen et al. 1982; Emerson 1983; Lofland and Lofland 1984; Whyte 1984; Strauss 1987; Gubrium 1988).[2] Such texts, however, offer little more than the sometimes simple, but often intricate, mechanics of the methodology. Merton (1962) observed that the literature on scientific methods is primarily concerned with what social scientists *ought* to think, feel, and do, and fails to draw necessary attention to what they *actually* think, feel, and do. As if in response to Merton's observation, more than a few researchers have by now provided personal chronicles of their research. In these accounts attention is focused on the process of interaction between the researcher and the community members and on the personal considerations affecting both the organization and outcome of their research activity (Kirby and McKenna 1989; Prus and Sharper 1991). The early arguments surrounding field methods were primarily concerned with accuracy, objectivity, and ethics. This resulted, in many cases, in a reporting style that made it appear as if the researcher was a neutral, unobtrusive presence. The researcher's thoughts and actions were scrubbed out of the finished product other than in the occasional note (for example, Polsky 1972). Still, those who did this type of research were convinced that actually viewing, talking to, and being a part of a studied community[3] produced more accurate understanding than did what they viewed as sterile surveys, counts, and statistical manipulations. Field researchers began publishing in two major aspects of their method: how to do the research—the research process; and how to deal with the massive and often seemingly disorganized data that were collected (Shaffir, Stebbins, and Turowetz 1980; Spradley 1980; Lofland and Lofland 1984; Jorgenson 1989). But they also returned even more strongly to the subjective experience of doing field research, of being a part of the experience they studied, and re-examined ways in which they could and should account honestly for their own experiences in the field. More and more, there was recognition that the groups and peoples studied were collaborators and even friends. The Adlers draw attention to this very point by focusing on an emergence, begun in the 1980s, of new thinking about subjectivity. They contend that researchers, in a variety of disciplines, are increasingly unwilling to divide themselves into two distinct parts: the human role wherein the researcher interacts with members and establishes relationships, and the research role aimed at data collection. According to the Adlers, however, such bifurcation did not actually occur during the fieldwork itself. They write:

> Most fieldworkers ... have followed their social instincts in interacting with members. They knew that the structure of the setting and the personalities of the individuals involved were the most critical determinants of the role the researcher would take.... In recounting their experiences, though, they cast them into the style of then current epistemology: that is to say, they suppressed their membership by analyzing their material from the outside perspective and emphasizing detachment. (1987a, 85)

Generally, such chronicles have focused around the ongoing relationships established in the field and how these influence the data collection process and the research results. More specifically, they focus on "the intimate connection between the investigator,... methods of investigation,... results, and ... [the researcher'] own future intellectual development" (Vidich and Bensman 1964, vii).

In contrast to other methodologies, the very nature of field research requires investigators to talk about themselves. Indeed, some personal involvement must be conveyed in order to generate closeness to the situation as a warrant for the argument (Lofland 1967). The researcher is required by the nature of fieldwork and canons of fieldwork evidence to describe personal involvement in the research. The researcher, however, in the past typically presented accounts that steered away from self-indulgent narration of personal experiences and feelings, theories about people, fantasies, embarrassments, and the like. Fieldwork accounts potentially use self-reflection and must deal with the trickiness of self-presentation, while other methods may rely more strongly on the assumed neutrality of "scientific talk."

A presentation of the personal and human reactions to fieldwork reflects the ever-present reality that the characteristics of the researcher may indirectly and inadvertently (or directly and advertently) affect the process of the research (Warren 1988; Gurney 1991).[4] The personal and social dynamics of the field research adventure must, and has, come under increasingly closer scrutiny as researchers have focused on expectations and feelings as these affected their study and became part of the research process (Kleinman 1991).

Marginality

The one especially well-suited adjective that describes the social experiences of field research is marginality.[5] Once in the field, all participant-observers, if they are known as such to their subjects, are more or less marginal to their subjects' world. As Hughes (1960, ix) argues, even when sociologists report observations made as a member of the group under study, their attempts to be objective in their reporting make them something of a stranger in the group. In a similar vein, Freilich (1970, 2) cautions against the common desire among researchers to become a native pointing out that no matter how good the researcher becomes at playing roles or handling relationships or rituals he or she is still marginal. Based on his own research among hustlers, beats, and other persons classed as criminals, Polsky draws attention to the problematics of becoming "one of them" and explicitly cautions against this approach:

> In doing field research on criminals you damned well better pretend to be "one of them," because they will test this claim out and one of two things will happen: either you will ... get sucked into "participant" observation of the sort you would rather not undertake, or you will be exposed, with still greater negative consequences. You must let the criminals know who you are; and if it is done properly ..., it does not sabotage the research. (1967, 124)

Accounts by sociologists attest that marginality inheres in the field research process. However successfully they might integrate into the social setting, the fundamental and irreconcilable difference between them and insiders is that their presence is strategically organized around their research objectives (Heilman 1992). Indeed, we would define "going native" as losing the sense of research purpose that brought the researcher to the field in the first place. However, a number of exceptions to being or becoming a member of a community as a research strategy are available in the literature. The Adlers (1987a) cite several examples which they situate in the "complete membership role." One can point to Barrie Thorne's (1979) research on the draft resistance movement in the 1960s where she shared the values, beliefs, and goals of the participants as well as much of their behavior; or Burke Forrest's (1986) research on spiritual groups in Southern California where she became inducted into mediumship as a result of her years of involvement. Heavy involvement in the setting, *per se*, is not inimical to research, so long as the researcher can still write about that setting in a way that is informative even to the people who live or otherwise function within it. In other words, the researchers should never lose their capacities to shed new light on the setting under study.

The theme of marginality is sometimes connected to *culture shock* which refers to a syndrome "precipitated by the anxiety that results from losing all your familiar cues, which includes frustration, repressed or expressed aggression against the source of discomfort, an irrational fervor for the familiar and comforting, and disproportionate anger at trivial interferences" (Golde 1986, 11). It results from an inadequate set of meanings that interfere with our ability to understand others' behavior but, as she indicates, "the concept includes the notion of threat to one's own system of meanings and values, and consequently to one's own identity" (1986, 12). The experience is generally most intense during the initial period of the field research in an unknown setting. In her account of her research experiences among a small group of Eskimos, whom she first met by being flown to their camp in a single engine plane that the government chartered to service the remote camps and villages of the Canadian Arctic, Jean Briggs (1970) recounts her initial reaction to her introduction to the community:

> It was only as the hum of the motor faded into the snow-heavy clouds that I fully realized where I was. Realization came in the form of a peculiar sense not of loneliness but of separateness, of having no context for my existence. With the plane had vanished the last possibility of access to my familiar world until the strait froze in November, and as yet no bond of language, of understanding, or of shared experience linked me with the silent Eskimos behind me. (1970, 23)

Shaffir's initial foray into the Hasidic community similarly points to his anxieties at the very beginning:

> During my first visit ... the Hasidic area appeared deserted. The enclave was located at the end of a narrow dirt road and there were two poorly maintained structures which served both as synagogues and *batei-midrashim* (study halls) for the Satmarer and Kausenburger.... A handful of Satmarer children played on a nearby bridge throwing stones into a stream and a few *bakhurim* (teenage yeshiva students) were standing on the porch of the synagogue. As I came closer, the youngsters stopped playing. They noticed my skullcap, which made it obvious that I was Jewish. I had intended to enter the synagogue, but I suddenly became apprehensive and walked past without talking to anyone, all the while berating my cowardice. When I came back on the following morning, I could hear voices chanting. Walking closer to the synagogue, I saw a room filled with some forty teenage boys; they all had flowing earlocks and were dressed in long black coats, black trousers, white shirts, and black hats.... It took me but a moment to recognize how uncomfortable I would feel standing among them dressed in white jeans and a multi-coloured sports jacket. And what would I do once inside? Pray with them? Perhaps. Participation in prayer, however, would require feigning familiarity with the chronology and rituals of the prayer service. I decided to begin the research on the following day. On my third trip to the Hasidic colony, I took the plunge and entered the synagogue. Nothing happened. At first, no one acknowledged my presence. Finally, a few youngsters and *balebatim* (married men) nodded to me and offered me a place to sit. Then everyone stared, especially the younger children, who positioned themselves close to me and waited to see whether I donned my *tefillin* (phylacteries) correctly and recited the appropriate prayers. I felt anxious and entirely out of place. (1985)

Junker believed the problem of marginality to be inherent to field research and characterized it as the tension resulting between the role of the member (participant) and stranger (observer and reporter). In his view, the dialectic cannot be completely resolved "for to do good social observation one has to be close to people living their lives," but the researcher also has to live his or her life and must also report observation (1960, x). Such experiences of dislocation will be shaped by the degree to which the new norms, values, and behavioral expectations conflict with the researcher's own values, emotional profile, and sense of self.

Field Research as Process

As is commonly acknowledged, field research is an ongoing, dynamic, interactive process. For purposes of better understanding the method's social components, as well as signaling the actual mechanics in gathering the data, attempts have been made to identify the dimensions, stages, or phases of the experience. Thus, for example, Junker (1960) discusses the problems and challenges of "getting-in," "staying in," and "easing out," and Berg (1989) conceptualizes the ethnographic process in terms of "accessing the field setting," "becoming invisible," "watching, listening, and learning," and "disengaging and getting out." Along similar lines, Shaffir and Stebbins (1991) have focused their ordering around "getting in," "learning the ropes," "maintaining relations," and "leaving and keeping in touch." In each of these attempts at characterizing the dimensions of the field research adventure, the authors have also pointed out that the dimensions are distinguishable for analytical purposes only since, in actuality, they are interwoven and interconnected in the execution of the research. The following discussions examine some of the considerations and social contingencies confronting researchers at various points of the research process. The reader may also wish to examine several excellent accounts that detail other features of ethnographic inquiry such as recording and analyzing field notes, and writing research reports (Glaser and Strauss 1967; Lofland and Lofland 1984; Taylor and Bogdan 1984).

Getting In

A central problem shared by all field researchers is getting in, or gaining entry to a particular setting. It is difficult for a researcher to gain intimate familiarity without being in close touch with group members.[6] Far from being a straightforward procedure, gaining access typically involves processes of negotiation and renegotiation which occur throughout the research and which influence the kind of investigation that can be completed.

Despite unwarranted expectations that research settings are equally accessible, successful entry is influenced by the possible combinations of "investigator relationship to the setting, the ascriptive categories of the researcher and researched, and the specific nature of the setting" (Lofland and Lofland 1984). Gaining access is shaped by the social contexts within which the research is evaluated, as well as by the nature of the relationships established between the researcher and the researched. The chances of one's research being accepted are increased when the researcher's interests appear to coincide with those of the people being studied. For example, members of the group may believe that the research will report favorably on an issue they wish publicized. As Wax (1952, 34–37) claims, groups may wish to know not only what the researcher is up to, but also what they stand to gain by co-operating. Rejection and opposition are most likely to occur when the people being approached do not understand what the researchers are doing and what they wish to know, or when the subjects do not want anyone to know what they are doing.

As field research accounts inform us, access is often shaped by the cultural and ascriptive differences or similarities between the field researcher and the researched. Where these differences are minimal, access and even acceptance are likely to be enhanced, but where the differences are large, participation opportunities may be severely constrained and even eliminated.

Gender

The influences of sex and gender on field research are increasingly well-documented, focusing mainly on how being female or male influences the roles expected of the researcher, which may affect access to particular situations (Golde 1986; Warren 1988; Wax 1979). Early ethnographers, not unlike other social and physical scientists, were unaware of the insidious effects of patriarchal mind sets on their observations and reporting. In recent years researchers have been more sensitive to the ways gendered society affects both the researcher and researched. Joan Neff Gurney's (1991) experiences suggest that the disadvantages of being female in conducting short-term research are relatively minimal but that, by contrast, the long-term experiences of being a female in a male-dominated setting prove to be more significant sources of discomfort and anxiety. The exclusiveness of sex as engendering observational limitation was encountered by Shaffir (1974) in his studies of Hasidic sects as he was forced, due to differential access, to accept different orders of data for males and females; and Wax (1971) describes the exclusiveness of sex categories she encountered as a woman scientist who has worked in several different groups. Elenore Bowen's anthropological account of her research experiences in *Return to Laughter* highlights the saliency of gender to access:

> I should have been content, and I was.... My dissatisfaction lay wholly in the part I was being assigned.... I had been identified with the women: unless I could break that association, I would leave the field with copious information on domestic details and without any knowledge of anything else. (1964, 79)

Race and Ethnicity

Suttles' (1968) study of a Chicago slum and Liebow's (1967) research among black, street corner men indicate how ethnicity and race constrained access to the research participants. Although such social and identity categories affect access, they must not be over-emphasized, for one need not be identical to those one studies. Many studies offer convincing testimony to a researcher's capacity to transcend gender, age, ethnic, and cultural differences. As an example, Van Maanen (1991) argues that the success of his research on the police was influenced less by his cultural and ascriptive characteristics than by his ability to adopt a variety of research roles and the reciprocal relationship that evolved between the police and himself.

Gatekeepers

Access to a research setting is sometimes controlled by gatekeepers—those individuals in the organization who have the power to grant or to withhold access to people or situations for purposes of research (Taylor and Bogdan 1984). More accurately, however, it is unusual for the researcher to negotiate with a single gatekeeper to secure access to all facets of the setting. A more realistic assessment involves multiple points of entry into the setting and, consequently, negotiations with gatekeepers who can grant permission for, or facilitate, specific kinds of access. As Geer (1970) observes, research access is not merely granted or withheld at one particular point in time, but may be an ongoing contingency. However, there are settings without any official gatekeeper from whom formal permission for the research is sought. Numerous studies can be identified where the researcher befriended an individual or number of individuals who sponsored them into the group (for example, Whyte 1955; Gans 1962; Liebow 1967; West 1980).

Research Bargains

Successful entry is also shaped by the bargain struck between researcher and subjects. Research bargains are agreements and commitments that result from negotiating the research access and use. Ideally, the researcher wishes to complete the work without interference, but securing a free hand is not always easy. Research accounts have shown that the nature of the bargain may constrain maneuverability within the setting, sometimes undermining the research or even terminating the project (Diamond 1964; Haas and Shaffir 1980). The formal bargain is likely to differ from the day-to-day reciprocities between researcher and group (Habenstein 1970, 5). As fieldworkers have sometimes painfully discovered, completing a successful bargain with the gatekeepers is no guarantee of full co-operation from the group members or even the gatekeepers themselves. Typically described as a series of mutual obligations agreed upon at the outset of the research, the bargain should more accurately be represented as a continuing process of negotiation in which promises between the various parties may shift and even change over time, and that does not end until the research is published (Geer 1970, 85). Although the formal requirements are usually negotiated at the outset, getting in involves a continuous effort to establish, maintain, and cement relations.

Research Settings

The organization of the research setting may also influence the effort to secure access. In formal settings such as public bureaucracies or business corporations, permission is typically granted by those with authority and power (see Miller and Holstein, and Emerson on bureaucracies, and C. Wolfe and D. Wolf on the less empowered in this volume). In contrast less formally organized settings such as ethnic groups and deviant subcultures usually lack such authoritative positions and the researcher is less dependent on obtaining permission to enter the community from a gatekeeper (see Miller and Holstein, and Emerson in this volume).

In addition to the above considerations, entry also hinges on the personal judgments made of the researcher. Wax (1971, 365) observes that researchers will be judged more by their lifestyle and how they treat members of the community than by anything they say about themselves or the research. This emphasis suggests that entering the field and cultivating rich relationships are related to the researcher's personal attributes and self-presentation and to others' judgments of him or her as a human being. Evaluating his research experiences among the ultra-Orthodox Hasidic Jews he studied, Shaffir writes:

> Co-operation depends less on the nature of the study than on the perception informants have of the field researcher as an ordinary human being who respects them, is genuinely interested in them, is kindly disposed toward them, and is willing to conform to their code of behavior when he or she is with them. In short, the skills in using commonplace sociability ... are as much a prerequisite in conducting field research as they are in managing our affairs in other settings and situations unrelated to our professional work. (1991a, 80)

Although it is impossible to outline a set of procedures which, if followed, will automatically procure access, the experiences of many field researchers suggest that entry can be facilitated if the researcher can provide a credible and plausible account justifying his or her research interests, has some connection to the persons in the setting, and is perceived by those to be researched as a personable and decent human being (Lofland and Lofland 1984).

Learning the Ropes

In studying a social world the researcher must learn to appreciate the distinctive concerns and ways of behaving that he or she is observing and "to comprehend and to illuminate the subject's view and to interpret the world *as it appears (to the subject)*" (Matza 1969, 25). The process of acquiring such a sense of the meanings attributed to objects and events in a given society has been observed by Wax as follows:

> The student begins "outside" the interaction, confronting behaviors ... [that are] bewildering and inexplicable: the actors are oriented to a world of meanings that the observer does not grasp ... and then gradually ... [the student] comes to be able to categorize peoples (or relationships) and events. (1967, 325)

Whereas getting in is designed to secure access to the setting and its participants and lays the groundwork for achieving trust and rapport, learning the ropes involves attaining an *intimate familiarity* with a sector of social life. Learning the ropes begins as soon as the researcher sets out to learn: (a) about the subjects and their activities in the research setting; and (b) about his or her relationship to the setting and its people, and it continues until he or she exits from the field. Doing field research requires an understanding of the interpretive process that shapes and guides human behavior (Wax 1971, 3). Fieldworkers believe that since "to understand a people's thought one has to be able to think in their symbols" (Evans-Pritchard 1974, 79), data must be collected "within the mediums, symbols, and experiential worlds which have meanings to [their] respondents" (Vidich 1955, 354). Data collection preferably involves participation "in the daily life of the people under study,... observing things that happen, listening to what is said, and questioning people, over some length of time" (Becker and Geer 1957, 28). In his discussion of learning the ropes in a variety of research settings, Gubrium (1991) stresses the importance of both learning the meanings that permeate the setting, and learning to become sensitive to its local culture. Such learning does not include a pre-determined sequence of steps, but requires an ongoing appreciation of how the local culture is defined and organized by spatial and temporal variations.

Much like getting in, learning the ropes is affected by the characteristics of the research setting, the interpersonal styles of the investigator, and the group members' feelings and responses to the researcher and the project. The elements to be learned and the timing involved are as varied as the settings selected. For example, based upon her study of working-class women in Birmingham, England, Griffin (1991) considers how such issues as race, sex, and gender influenced the research process. As well, she discovered that the social and political organization of the research setting helped determine which particular ropes would have to be learned.

While learning the ropes involves the gradual acquisition of insights into the meanings that experiences hold for the researched, it also concerns a series of more mundane issues. For instance, however different the social groups or social worlds may be, common to each is a native (or secret) language—an argot—consisting of expressions and phrases that help members assess their experiences and organize their behavior (Maurer 1964; Letkemann 1977; Katz 1988). In addition the researcher must become familiar with the basic norms and rules governing specific situations of the group. The research reported by Wallis (1977) and Barker (1984), on Scientology and the Moonies respectively, as well as Grills' (in this volume) work on the Christian Heritage Party, address the specific group expectations that researchers were required to learn and incorporate into their self-presentation when in contact with members of those groups.

While there are no magic formulas for learning the ropes, the researcher must begin by participating in the subjects' daily life—talking to them, observing what they do, and listening sympathetically to what they say. This very point is emphasized in Prus's (1989a, b) research regarding vendor activity and the marketplace. By attending trade shows and exhibitions, as well as becoming involved in a craft enterprise for three years, Prus acquired a deeper understanding of the social world he studied than could have been gained from interviews alone. In research reported in this volume, Dietz, Shaffir, Sanders, Adler and Adler, and Daniel Wolf all studied aspects of groups as participating members.

Research Roles

As the accounts of seasoned field researchers attest, learning the ropes takes place as researchers "hang around." It is clear that by definition "learning the ropes" means that the researcher is ignorant of how people should act and how they will react under some conditions. During this period different research roles are assumed and shift as the research progresses. The particular roles that are claimed and/or to which the researcher is assigned, are critical for learning the ropes. While the range of research roles is theoretically unlimited, role alternatives available to the researcher are circumscribed by the nature of the research setting and its participants as well as by the personal characteristics of the observer (Sanders 1980; Padavic 1991). In a rather innovative attempt at constructing a taxonomy of researchers' relationships with their settings and their subjects, the Adlers introduce the category of "the membership role," and analyze some salient comparisons and differences among different "schools" for studying social life. The *peripheral, active,* or *complete* membership roles in which researchers may become involved may evolve or change over time "depending upon changes in the members, the setting, or the researcher" (1987a, 34).

Closeness or Distance

In learning the ropes, a basic problem revolves around the delicate balance required between involvement and attempts to acquire an insider's perspective, and the possibility of "going native" (Miller 1952), and the danger that excessive involvement may thwart the possibility of conducting meaningful research. The problem of going native has often been conceptualized as one of over-involvement. In the context of discussing the Chicago School's field researchers efforts to seek a balance between over-involvement and remaining objective and detached, the Adlers write:

> Defined in a broad sense, going native brings specific dangers to the research and researcher and must be avoided. First, going native involves developing an over-rapport with the research subjects that could harm the data-gathering process. Becoming too closely aligned with one group in the setting may prevent the researcher from gaining access to the perspectives of the other groups in the scene.... Over-rapport may also bias researchers' own perspectives, leading them to accept uncritically the views of the members (or one group of members) as their own. (1987a, 17)

As argued by Hammersley and Atkinson, the greatest danger of going native results in the loss of one's analytical perspective:

> There can be no question of total commitment, "surrender," or "becoming." There must always remain some part held back, some social and intellectual "distance." For it is in the "space" created by this distance that the analytic work of the ethnographer gets done. Without that distance, without such analytic space, the ethnography can be little more than the autobiographical account of a personal conversion. (1983, 102)

It is important to note that it is against this very position of distance that increasing numbers of researchers have recently spoken. Rather than contending that sound and credible ethnographic research must be characterized by a healthy measure of objectivity and separation of the researcher from the research subjects, they claim, instead, that such separation is artificial and necessarily results in incomplete research.[7] It must be recalled that many sociologists develop research out of serendipitous contacts in their real lives so they are "native" already (see M. L. Dietz on ballet and D. Wolf on biker gangs, both in this volume, and Becker [1953] on jazz musicians).

The literature indicates that field research is characterized by a combination of engrossment and distance (Thorne 1979; Karp and Kendall 1982), both of which are necessary to gain an appreciation of the actor's perspective. Fundamentally, the problem relates to the nature of the rapport that is established with the subjects of the research. While the advantages of rapport are commonly assumed, it can also work to the disadvantage of the investigator. Miller has reported a study in which excessive rapport between himself and members of a local union leadership impeded his ability both to maintain objectivity and to collect certain kinds of data:

> Many personal things were told to me in a friend-to-friend relationship; undoubtedly I gained information because of this relationship which would not have been available to me in any other way. On the other hand, once I had developed a close friendship to the union leaders I was committed to continuing it, and some penetrating lines of inquiry had to be dropped.... Friendship connotes an all-accepting attitude; to probe beneath the surface of long-believed values would break the friend-to-friend relationship. It may also be that development of a friend-to-friend relationship between the leaders and the participant observer was a means used by the former to limit the observer's investigations and criticisms. (1952, 97–99)

In an insightful comment on the problem of closeness and distance in fieldwork based on his research experiences with proselytizing groups, David Gordon argues that, quite paradoxically, field research relationships are most successfully maintained when the researcher clearly establishes the differences between him or herself and those who are being studied:

> Thus, "getting close" (i.e., creating rapport and maintaining relationships) is accompanied by "staying distant" (i.e., highlighting differences between the observer and the observed). I will call this approach "empathic disagreement," suggesting that disagreement does not necessarily conflict with empathy or rapport in fieldwork. (1987, 269)

In anticipation of being rebuffed, field researchers who are not a part of the researched community, often mistakenly strive to become completely immersed in the world they are studying, hoping to master the ropes by striving to gain immediate and total acceptance. Indeed, sometimes, researchers delude themselves into believing that their presence in, and involvement with, the group is tantamount to being one of them (Wax 1971, 47). Recalling his study of Boston's North End, W. F. Whyte states that early in his research, in an attempt to enter into the spirit of his friends' small talk, he blurted out a string of obscenities and profanities. His friends stopped to look at him in surprise. Doc, shaking his head, said: "Bill, you're not supposed to talk like that. That doesn't sound like you." Recounts Whyte: "I tried to explain that I was only using terms that were common on the street corner. Doc insisted, however, that I was different and that they wanted me to be that way" (1955, 304).

Whyte realized that "people did not expect me to be just like them; in fact, they were interested and pleased to find me different" (1955, 304). This example suggests, as Wax wisely advises, that the field researcher should "aim to maintain a conscious respect for him or herself and for his or her hosts' identities as well" (1971, 48). William Stringfellow's study of a Harlem slum also emphasizes the importance of remaining true to oneself as opposed to immediately altering one's identity. In that way, he believed, others would also be free to be themselves (1966, 24–25). David, one of Dietz's informants on felony homicide, acknowledged her different attitudes toward rape as he explained doing a rape during the robbery of a dope house. He said, "Well, it was O.K. She wasn't like you. She was the dope man's woman." To David this meant that the victim was accepting different standards and risks and that David should not be judged in the same way he would be had the victim been a "civilian." His comment also acknowledged that he recognized the researcher could understand and accept that he had different "rules" without supporting or accepting those "rules" for herself (Dietz, Field notes, 1981).

Researchers who show respect for those studied and a willingness to consider their views and claims very often discover that others are prepared to teach them the ropes. Learning involves assuming research roles that can be modified as new relationships are established and as rapport is enhanced. Fetterman, an anthropologist, draws attention to the importance of personal attributes that characterize the successful field researcher, including curiosity, a lifelong commitment to learning, patience, sincerity, and honesty, that he considers essential for analyzing and understanding a group's culture (1991). Clint Sanders (in this volume, 204) talks about his personal qualifications for fieldwork in this volume:

> I find that I possess a certain ability to interact comfortably with a fairly wide range of people. Doing this sort of "lone-ranger" fieldwork in the kinds of social settings I tend to choose has always provided me with a certain measure of adventure and allowed me to escape legitimately from the narrow confines of academia.

Feminist researchers, for example Kirby and McKenna (1989), take the position that the people who are sharing information are collaborators and that the discussions between them are interactions rather than one-sided interviews as is suggested by earlier research models. They admonish researchers to be honorable in their relationships with the people they deal with, but to also recognize that these are autonomous people who are not under the control of the researcher nor should they be.

Approaches to learning the ropes will require modification and revision as the research unfolds: such adaptations, if they are met successfully, are largely determined by the personal qualities of the researcher. Learning the ropes is a continuous process, integral to field research, and not something done before the "real work" begins. The investigator aims to learn the ropes of the setting for purposes of developing trust and rapport and establishing relationships.

Maintaining Relations

To facilitate in the collection of data, the researcher chooses from an availability of research roles. The basic typology of such roles was devised by Gold

(1958, 217–23) in which he distinguished four "ideal typical" field roles: the *complete participant*, the *participant as observer*, the *observer as participant*, and the *complete observer*. In the *complete participant* identity, the observer attempts to become a full-fledged member of the group under investigation, although his or her scientific intents are entirely concealed. A classic example is the study of Festinger and his colleagues (1956) of a small group of persons who predicted the destruction of the world. The authors believed that, given the nature of the group, if they presented themselves as researchers, entry would be denied, so they posed as persons genuinely interested in the group's outlook and soon were able to penetrate its boundaries and become full-fledged members. Another classic study along this line was Humphreys' (1970) research that investigated impersonal sexual encounters in public restrooms. Looking for a role with which to justify his presence, Humphreys, who did not make his identity as a sociologist known to the participants, assumed the role of a lookout in these public facilities. Jorgensen provides the argument for the complete involvement position as follows:

> The methodology of participant observation rejects the conventional conception of and distinction between subjectivity and objectivity. Gaining access to the *subjective* reality of everyday life—the world as it is experienced and defined by insiders—is required for accurate and truthful findings. Objectivity, defined as truth, cannot be achieved without coming to terms with the insiders' world. The most direct route to truth is for the researcher to experience the phenomenon of interest—to "become the phenomenon." (1989, pp. 27–28)

There have been continual arguments among field researchers regarding the ethics of doing concealed research. Burgess (1984, 186–209) provides a general discussion of the ethical problems involved, particularly in covert observation. There does seem to be general consensus that deception should be avoided if possible and that any type of exploitation of communities being researched should be avoided as well. As Denzin has pointed out, "The problems of ethics, organized research, responsibility to subjects, value positions, informal demands on the investigator, and misconceptions of the subject are issues that lie at the heart of doing sociology and science in general, yet they are not adequately treated in most methodology texts" (1989, 250).

Unlike the complete participant role or identity, the *participant as observer* makes his or her presence as a researcher known and attempts to form a series of relationships with the subjects. The role is frequently employed in community studies. While the observer may be relieved of the tensions arising from role pretense, problems of locating informants, establishing and maintaining relationships, and not "going native" must still be negotiated. Researchers employing this strategy discuss the several phases that are passed through in the course of conducting the research (for example, Olesen and Whittaker 1968, 273–81).

In the third type of research role, *observer as participant*, the investigator typically includes a single visit with the respondent during which an interview is conducted. The nature of the contact is brief and devoid of attempts to establish any enduring relationship.

The *complete observer* is the fourth researcher identity and is best seen in experiments where observations are recorded mechanically or carried out through one-way mirrors in a laboratory.

Researcher as Chameleon

In the sense that field research is similar to playacting (Wax 1971, 49), the enactment of particular roles evolves as the dynamics of the research unfold. At various times specific roles may be highly confining while others, as Whyte has observed, "can offer the fieldworker rich opportunities to gain a broad range of experiences and observations as well as considerable depth" (1984, 27–28). Despite the evolution of social and research roles over the course of the study, however, the initial role that is adopted is usually the one that remains fairly permanent throughout the study and to which successive research roles are connected. It is this initial role that so dramatically shapes the field researcher's self-presentation and the subjects' reaction to him or her, thus setting the stage for the kinds of relations that follow. This should not, however, suggest that the researcher is impervious to change during her or his experiences in the field.

At first the matter of getting along with the people in the field may appear to be of little scientific interest. Such an outlook, however, is quite unwarranted. The validity of the data hinges, in part, on achieving that delicate balance of distance and closeness that characterizes effective research—the establishment and maintenance of rapport. Whatever else it may include, rapport, basically, is a blend of the interactional ingredients of day-to-day involvement. When rapport is established, the participants show a willingness to co-operate in achieving the goals of the study and trust the researcher to handle personal and sensitive information with tact and objectivity.

Relations with members may be strengthened or weakened during the research project at various points. One of these is the discussion or observation of sensitive topics, behaviors, or events. For example, Junker (1960, 34) points out how researchers develop a sensitivity to the many kinds of distinctions subjects make about public versus private events. An inability to take the role of the subjects may cause researchers to treat this information inappropriately, resulting in soured relations with people on whom he or she depends. Dietz and Callaghan (1985) report the experience of collecting data on prison-visiting in the prison setting, and then continuing to see informants after they were paroled. Callaghan found that the rules that had governed relationships in the secure prison situation did not hold on the street. She relates the following experience:

When I got to Slim's at about 8 o'clock, he was pretty strung out.... He said, "Come on, let's go. I have to get straight." ... We got pretty close to YOUNG BOY'S territory when he said, "Pull over." He said, "Okay, you got some money?" I said, "No,... I'm not wasting my hard-earned money on this shit." He was silent. He just looked out the window. I started the car again. He turned to me and yelled, "Look, bitch, it's about time you learned who the motherfuckin' boss is around here. I need money and you are going to give it to me." (Dietz and Callaghan, 1985, 11)

Eventually he took her money and bought his dope after threatening to take her car and leave her in a very dangerous area of the city. This account illustrates the problems that can occur while a researcher tries to maintain and negotiate or renegotiate research relationships. It demonstrates that both rules and relationships can change during the course of the research. The research bargain that had been struck between the two was not honored on this occasion. Although the bargain had been made at the beginning of the study, time had passed, circumstances had changed, and more importantly, the setting had changed dramatically. The researcher had to make a decision on the spot to preserve her own safety even though she was attempting to maintain what had obviously become an obsolete research bargain.

Research Trade-Offs

Another strategic point in the maintenance of field relations is the offering of assistance to some or all of the subjects. This does not mean giving advice, professional or otherwise; rather, the researcher does something useful such as serve as "watch queen" in a homosexual tearoom (Humphreys 1970, 26–28), convey messages or materials among members of a Gamblers Anonymous chapter (Livingston 1974, 11), or provide transportation and money for a group of urban blacks (Liebow 1967, 253). This way of maintaining relations involves reciprocity with one's subjects. In partial repayment for their co-operation, the researcher lends a hand with an appreciated form of help. Yet another strategic point in maintaining relations involves living up to the bargains field researchers often have to strike with their subjects in order to gain access to them and to the field setting. One such bargain involves causing little or no disruption to organizational or group affairs. As well, confidentiality of detailed interview and observational data may be an implicit or explicit bargain that is crucial during the field research. However, even though the researcher is willing to guarantee secrecy, if he or she is not in the same vulnerable position as the member, there are certain topics that respondents may not wish to discuss. For example, Dietz found that unionized veteran urban lumberjacks freely criticized their bosses, but that non-unionized ballet dancers at all levels were very reluctant to discuss their current bosses (artistic directors). The dancers were much more willing to discuss those who had power over their careers with another dancer. Dietz's son, also a dancer, was perceived by the other dancers to be as vulnerable to career penalties as they might be if they revealed insider secrets about the dance hierarchy. They therefore felt more comfortable discussing their boss with him, rather than with Dietz herself. Even though Dietz had nothing to lose, her son did, and it was therefore assumed that any discussions would be handled in a discrete manner (Field notes 1988; 1990). When a researcher defaults on a bargain, smooth relations with subjects, as well as rapport, are threatened (Haas and Shaffir 1980). This is equally true when the collaborator defaults on the research bargain as illustrated in the Dietz and Callaghan example above.

Achieving Rapport

Maintaining field relations can be a challenging task. For one thing, rapport sometimes becomes the basis for deeper friendships, stronger identification with the group under study, or both. This "over-rapport" (Miller 1952) or "going native" (Paul 1953, 435) could destroy the delicate balance of external and internal considerations so painstakingly achieved in ideal field relations by allowing the latter to predominate (see Kirby and McKenna [1989] for an alternate view). Yet, the field researcher can also err in the opposite direction by trying to function in an atmosphere of under-rapport. Here, a number of factors may combine to chill social relations. One of these is a desire to rush the interviews or cut short the observation sessions in an attempt to complete the project quickly; another is a reluctance to consider suggestions from subjects on how to conduct the study.

The cultivation of rapport and sound relations requires some attention to commonsensical practices of sociability. Investigators who refuse to spend time discussing aspects of daily life that researcher and subjects have in common and who avoid participating in the subjects' activities when it is possible to do so, may lose valuable opportunities to gain rapport and promote good field relations. Likewise, insensitivity to subjects' routines, observing and scheduling interviews in ways that violate the local code of etiquette, airs of superiority, obnoxious personal mannerisms, and other characteristics contribute to under-rapport and hence ineffective field research. In Lofland's (1976, 13) words: "Many of those who populate the social science disciplines are temperamentally unsuited for the less than traumatic mucking around in the real world outside the academy."

In sum, maintaining relations through sustained rapport involves keeping the goals of the study in mind while pursuing them in ways that gain subject co-operation and trust. In working toward this end, one must often tactfully remind well-intentioned subjects that these very goals prevent such forms of participation as giving advice, taking sides in a dispute, and engaging in certain tasks and activities. To complicate matters further, the

goals may change during the course of the study, requiring further explanations to the subjects most directly affected.

Managing Contacts Following Data Collection

When turning to another area of field relations, concerns with maintaining
relations with subjects may extend well beyond the data collection phase of
the project. One of the common bargains reached with gatekeepers, and frequently with others who participate closely in the study, is to give them a
report of the findings. The writing of this report may require occasional
consultation with some of them to maximize accuracy and readability.
Moreover, field research projects tend to raise more questions than they
answer, driving some investigators back to the original setting to do more
work or simply to see what changes have taken place over the intervening
years. These enduring research interests are accompanied at times by friendships that have sprung from the initial contact between researcher and
subject. By means of telephone calls, personal visits, or letters, the field
researcher maintains contact with members of the focal group and thus
remains informed about at least some of the developments that bear on his
or her professional interests (Miller and Humphreys 1980).

The importance of establishing and maintaining relations relates both to
the quality and quantity of data that become accessible to the researcher.
Recounting their experiences in conducting research among drug traffickers
and a top-ranked college basketball team, the Adlers (1991) point to the ebb
and flow of field relations. Drawing on their experiences in studying these
two different groups, one unorganized and the other organized, their analysis
shows how their roles in the two settings influenced the kinds of relations
they could maintain in the respective settings. Their experiences illustrate
how the choice of roles may be constrained by the demands and expectations
imposed by the setting itself.

It is equally important that the researcher learn to "get along" with him
or herself as well. While a considerable body of literature has been addressed
to relations with the research population, as well as relations with colleagues,
the emotional stresses accompanying field research can impede both the
kinds and degrees of relationships with others in the field. Reflecting on her
study of a holistic health center, Kleinman (1991) emphasizes that her relations with the subjects of her research were influenced by her feelings about
the people she studied. She also discovered that her own understanding of
herself was important in shaping her reactions to the settings and to the participants in her study. Thus, the dynamics of maintaining relations in the
field require not only careful attention to the demands and sensitivities of
the setting's participants, but continuous introspective examination by the
researcher of his or her feelings and emotions and how these influence the
process by which the research unfolds.[8]

The maintenance of effective relations with subjects and collaborators is central to the social experience of field research. As much as the researcher may try to ensure that life in the field is orderly and manageable, the dynamics of field research are unpredictable. As Lofland and Lofland observe:

> New problems continually arise; new solutions are continually necessary. Cooperative people may turn nasty. Uncooperative people may become superior sources of data…. Quiescent difficulties may erupt at any time. Expected difficulties may never materialize. (1984, 31)

Leaving and Keeping in Touch

While much attention has been given to the relationship between the researcher's entrance and presence in a particular setting and the resulting constraints for data collection, the researcher's departure from the setting deserves attention as well. In a comprehensive piece on the topic, in which he draws on his ethnographic experiences with a Buddhist movement in America, Snow (1980) organizes the discussion around three general issues: *informational sufficiency* or when the researcher believes that enough data have been collected to answer the questions posed by the research; *extraneous precipitants*, which may be institutional, interpersonal, or intrapersonal in character; and *barriers* that pull on the researcher to remain in the field, such as the attitude of the group studied toward the withdrawal of members or the intensity of the established relations. Maines, Shaffir, and Turewetz have proposed that the process of disengaging from the field is related to the commitment structures formed during the course of the research. Specifically, they conclude that "the leaving process is an aspect of an ongoing interplay between field circumstances and the way in which the researcher negotiates social relationships and a workable identity" (1980, 273). Wolf's (1991b) account of his research experiences offers an interesting case in point. A lengthy association with the Rebels motorcycle club preceded his attempt to secure permission for the research. In fact, the intimate nature of his clandestine involvement with the club almost compelled him to disengage from the research setting as circumstances made it awkward for him to request support for the study. Berg, too, has addressed disengaging from the field, and observes:

> Exiting any field setting involves at least two separate operations: first, the physical removal of the researchers from the research setting, and second, the emotional disengagement from the various relationships developed during the field experience. In some situations *getting out* is described as a kind of mechanical operation, devoid of any (personal) emotional detachments…. However, negative repercussions can occur in the forms of possible effects on the group(s) as a whole, or the possible reception future field investigators might expect. (1989, 78)

Basic to an understanding of the process of disengagement is the review of the field researcher's experience. More often than not, researchers' accounts fit within the boundaries of how research *should* proceed and fails to address how, as a result of both foreseen and unforeseen contingencies, it is *actually* executed. Such contingencies might include mistakes in participant-observation, fractious relations with respondents, or the betrayal of confidences. It is precisely these contingencies and their handling by the researcher that help to shape and define the problem of leaving the field. Stebbins (1991), for example, addresses several of these contingencies in his review of his various field research studies. Specifically, in reflecting on his experiences surrounding the leaving stage in his ethnographic studies on amateurs and professionals, he concludes that the researcher never leaves completely as a result of secondary involvements that are established during the course of the study. At the same time, ways of remaining in the field vary according to the nature of the relationships that were formed. Along a similar line, Taylor (1991) addresses and identifies several considerations of this dimension of the research process which, he maintains, are related to the implicit bargain struck between himself and those he studied. His discussion helps us realize that while the researcher may leave the field in a physical sense, he or she may remain there indefinitely both in terms of maintaining friendships and in contending with the human issues generated by the research.

In some instances the process of exiting and remaining in touch is a stage in the ongoing interplay between the researcher and the subjects of the research (Altheide 1980). Kaplan (1991), based on her research on fishermen and fishing communities, points to this dimension, which can be easily overlooked; specifically, the extent to which such behavior is routinely accepted by the setting's participants. Just as coming and leaving were a natural part of the fishermen's lifestyle, so, too, could they appreciate the researcher's decision to leave and to return.

In some sense then, leaving the field may mean completing the research but remaining a part of the community, while in other types of research, the researcher actually must physically leave the site and end research relationships.

How the Researched Group Views the Ending of the Research

Another consideration in leaving the field is the way in which the members of the community have perceived the research. In some cases members have been less than enthusiastic about being studied. For a variety of reasons, they may not share the researcher's excitement about the study. As they see it, they stand to gain little, if anything, from research findings. While researchers may not be perceived as a direct threat, they might be seen as nuisances since they occupy people's time.

Such a situation is both discouraging and despairing to the researcher. Convinced that the research will shed light on a particular problem or may make a special contribution to the discipline, he or she seeks ways to pursue the study. Although the researcher is familiar with the potentially disruptive consequences of becoming personally involved with, and obligated to, the subjects, he or she may be prepared to temporarily abandon such warning in order to solicit their help. In those situations where the researcher's involvement extends beyond the expected academic requirements, leaving the field becomes even more problematic.

The Impact of the Researcher's Identity on Leaving the Field

Another area of concern, which underscores the complex nature of the leaving process, deals with the misrepresentation of the researcher's identity. Qualitative research studies often illustrate the intimate relationship between the researcher's academic and personal involvement with the subjects (Whyte 1955; Milner and Milner 1972; Wolf 1991a). Although the majority of researchers are honest and aboveboard in the conduct of their research, it is suspected that a number of cases go unreported in which researchers intentionally and deliberately misrepresent their interest in, and commitment to, the research activity and to community members. As a result of researchers' activities, no matter how clearly they present themselves, subjects may expect them to continue to live up to previously made commitments permanently. On completing the research, however, commitment often subsides and is overshadowed by other considerations shaping the researcher's day-to-day life. When subjects become aware of diminished interest in their lives and situations, they may come to feel cheated—manipulated and duped.

Just as there are no sure ways to handle the problems associated with gaining access, learning the ropes, and maintaining field research relations, there are no infallible strategies for leaving the field and keeping in touch.[9] For some, leaving the research setting is as much a personal problem as a tactical one as when Roadburg (1980), for example, was overcome with feelings of guilt and alienation when his project with the professional soccer team ended.

The relationships made in the field and how they will be maintained presents a serious problem for any ethical researcher. In some communities it is common for people to enter, remain for a short while, and leave; in others, leaving the community is regarded as betrayal or, at the very least, rejection or exploitation. The researcher does not always know, going into a research setting, how easy or difficult it will be to either end or maintain relations after the research is done. As in every other aspect of field research, there are more questions than answers; however, it is clearly important that researchers in the field must handle both their hellos and goodbyes with respect and sensitivity.

Conclusion

Although descriptions and analyses of the various dimensions of the field research experience have become more plentiful recently, the social aspects underlying and shaping researchers' experience have only begun to receive sufficient attention. These social aspects, which include feelings of self-doubt, uncertainty, and frustration, are inherent in field research and are also the "basic stuff" of which this methodology consists.

Field research is accompanied by a set of experiences that are, for the most part, unavailable through other forms of social scientific research. These experiences are bound together with satisfactions, embarrassments, challenges, pains, triumphs, ambiguities, and agonies, all of which blend into what has been described as the field research adventure (Glazer 1972). It is difficult to imagine a field project that does not include at least some of these features, however skilled and experienced the investigator. Numerous accounts are available testifying to the anxiety and uncertainty experienced by the researcher both prior to, and even after, entering the field. Thus, for instance, E. C. Hughes admits that "I have usually been hesitant in entering the field myself and have perhaps walked around the block getting up my courage to knock at doors more often than almost any of my students" (1960, iv). And Gans has written:

> Despite my success in gaining entry, the process is for me one of great anxiety.... Until I feel that I have been accepted, the research process is nerve-wracking; I lack the personal security to banish rejection or anxieties, to feel free to observe fully, and to take in as much data as possible. (1968, 310–11).

While other research methodologies can be described in terms of specific rules and procedures that guide the research and must be carefully observed, the same cannot be said for field research. While attempts have been made to identify the stages of the field research process, and to specify the types of observer identities that can be assumed (Gold 1958; Junker 1960; Denzin 1989), the intricacy and variety of observational procedures—the forms they take, and their relationship to specific objectives of the research—militate against the presentation of systematic steps that ensure the success of the field research study. Wax draws attention to the complexities inherent in understanding the ways of an alien people and suggests that while the description of fieldwork or participant-observation is simple, its practice is not. In her view, while it is possible to identify some of field research's most salient issues, a researcher cannot simply learn a few basic "rules of fieldwork" (1971, 15). Whatever else it concerns, field research involves the adoption of a role, or series of roles, and the cultivation of varied relationships with those we wish to study. By its very nature, field research requires some measure of role-playing and acting. In order to be granted access to the research setting and to secure the co-operation of his or her hosts, the researcher learns to present a particular image of him or herself. The proffered image cannot be determined in advance but, instead, reflects the contingencies encountered in the field. Moreover, as fieldwork accounts attest, the kinds of roles that are assumed are hardly static, but are evolving constantly. As Wax has observed, the researcher eventually discovers that the value of any particular role is best measured by the vantage point it gives to the observer or participant who plays it. In this respect Wax's contention that well-executed fieldwork is analogous to playacting, fittingly underscores the drama inherent in this methodological approach. Stressing that field research requires a process of resocialization for the researcher, Wax advises:

> The student who expects to be told precisely how to construct this kind of field relationship would do well to read a number of the available descriptions carefully. If ... [the researcher] has the wit to be a good fieldworker,... [he or she] will perceive how different were each of these situations and ... [he or she] may also understand why honest and experienced fieldworkers frequently tell beginners that there is not much they can tell them because each situation differs from every other. (1971, 20)

Along similar lines, Junker's caution, presented some thirty years ago, continues to be pertinent—that while there may be some useful ways of thinking about a particular field situation, "There can be no simple set of do's and don'ts for fieldworkers generally" (1960, 33).

NOTES

1. As Lofland and Lofland (1984) have observed, social science is a terminological jungle. Such terms as field methods, field research, qualitative social research, fieldwork, ethnographic research, naturalistic interactionism, the Chicago school of ethnography, and naturalism are all used, although *qualitative social research* seems most general and all encompassing. We would like to thank Bob Prus and Janice Drakich for their editorial help and thoughtful comments.

2. In one of their research procedures series, Sage publishers have developed an entire series on doing fieldwork which they continue to expand.

3. As Blumer (1969b, 37) put it, field research on another way of life consists of "getting closer to the people involved in it, seeing it in a variety of situations they meet, noting their problems and observing how they handle them, being party to their conversations and watching their way of life as it flows along."

4. Although the influential role of the researcher has been seen as most important in field research, there is no question of researcher effect in other research methods as well (Rosenthal 1966; Friedman 1967). Golde (1986) points out growing recognition of social science research being viewed as process and product of the interaction between the observer and the observed.

5. A recent book on field methods by Kirby and McKenna (1989) draws attention to marginality by including in the sub-title, "Methods from the Margins."

6. The fact is that most researchers only have a limited number of sub-cultures or groups to which they have personal or easy access. Many of the groups we would like to study have very clear reasons for keeping us out. Examples of these are organized crime groups, secret societies, the very rich, or unethical political groups.

7. As Ellis (1991, 30) points out "Some ethnographers already see themselves as part of the situation they study (Caughy 1982; Adler and Adler 1987; Van Maanen 1988) and many openly acknowledge looking to their own thoughts, feelings, and personal experiences as legitimate and insightful data."

8. Ellis contends that "Sociologists ... can generate interpretive materials about the lived experience of emotions by studying their own self-dialogue in process. Who knows better the right questions to ask than a social scientist who has lived through the experience? Who would make a better subject than a researcher consumed by wanting to figure it all out?" (1991, 29–30).

9. It may well be that leaving the field is rarely discussed in the literature because it is taken for granted as the natural and routine way of ending researcher-subject interaction. The work of several researchers (for example, Letkemann 1980; Altheide 1980), however, suggests that social scientists should attend to the processes of disengagement, for these form an integral dimension of the field research adventure whose execution may affect the efforts of future investigators in the same or similar research milieus. In Dietz and Callaghan's (1985) discussion of attempting to end research relationships with dangerous felons when continuing those relationships involved the researchers in unacceptable levels of legal, professional, or personal risk, they pointed out that although the researchers had "cooled out" the friendships and minimized the contacts, they felt obligated to try to help when their research confederate was in trouble. In most cases, they were able to maintain their contacts at a much reduced level of interaction.

PART 2

Studying Everyday Life: Ethnography in Process

This section, "Ethnography in Process" represents the core of this volume. It is organized around five generic social processes (GSPs) or basic interactional dimensions of human group life. Focusing on people's participation and experiences in this or that aspect of community life, attention is given to the ways in which people: *get involved* in this or that situation; *acquire perspectives* pertinent to that social context; *achieve identities* in particular settings; *do the activities* characterizing that subcommunity; and *develop relationships* with the others participating in that setting.

These processes seem basic to any notion of community, subculture, or group life. Human life is an ongoing set of *involvements* in social settings; people get in and out of situations involving others. Human group life becomes distinctive as a consequence of the *perspectives*—world views, frames of reference, or interpretive frameworks that develop over time as people interact with one another; it is in this respect that we speak of human behavior as "minded," for it is informed by the perspectives shared with others. Human behavior entails *identities*—some cognitive or categorical differentiation of self and others; indeed, achieving a sense of self requires that one be able to make indications both toward the other and toward one's own being as an object of one's own awareness. Human *activity* denotes human agency or enterprise; people do things in ways that they find meaningful with respect to their notions of perspective and their self-other identities. But, action is much more than that and entails a sense of purposive effort and accomplishment. Further, while people may do things by themselves or in co-ordination with others, it is only within the realm of the intersubjective other that people's activities are meaningful. Human behavior is also *relational* in its essence—since people's lives become meaningful only as a consequence of others, they want to be attentive to the sorts of bonds, affiliations, or associations that people develop with one another and the ways in which they work out the aspects of their lives in conjunction with one another.

Although these processes very much overlap each other in actual practice, we have broken human group life up into these analytical themes because these processes represent unique dimensions. By focusing more explicitly on one generic social process at a time, we are able to develop a much fuller appreciation (contrasts and similarities) of these processes across multiple settings. In this way, by examining human behavior in an assortment of contexts, we achieve a fuller sense of the varieties and viabilities of these processes as we push toward more refined notions of these concepts.

As well, we recognize that in human group life everything more or less happens at once. Although each line of involvement or participation in group life can be seen to develop over time or assume a historical dimension with a past, present, and a future, matters pertaining to perspectives, identities, activities, and relationships within the group setting take place more or less simultaneously. But since one cannot examine or discuss all of these processes at once, they have been presented in a particular sequence for organizational purposes. These concepts (and the ethnographic materials they encompass) could be presented in any variety of orders, and instructors and researchers may find it advantageous on many occasions to alter the sequence used in this volume.

"Studying Everyday Life: Ethnography in Process" begins with the generic social process of *getting involved*. Although people's involvements centrally reflect perspectives, identities, activities, and relationships, we have started with this broader concept not only as a means of introducing each of the other generic social processes, but also to emphasize the holistic nature of human lived experience. That is, while perspectives may imply unique substantive features of particular groups or communities of people, perspectives are only more fully appreciated or realized by people as they achieve a sense of identity, as they act (and interact), and as they develop bonds with others. Likewise, notions of identity, activity, and relationships very much hinge on sharper notions of perspectives, and so forth. Involvements, thus, draw our attention to all of these features of human lived experience, for it is only through involvements with others that people's experiences can be achieved or made meaningful. While all of the other articles in this volume focus on aspects of involvement, we have asked the contributors addressing the other four generic social processes to concentrate their papers in one of those more specific realms (perspectives, identities, activities, relationships). Here, as well, however, readers should appreciate that all papers, regardless of the specific generic social process addressed, will invariably contribute to understanding the other generic social processes en route.

Getting Involved: Initial Involvements, Continuities, Disinvolvements, and Reinvolvements

Becoming involved in some aspect of community life draws our attention to a most central feature of human group life, namely that people conduct their lives in conjunction with other people. Thus, only in these community contexts (or subcultural settings) can we make sense of people's activities. The concept of "career" emphasizes the emergent or temporal dimension of people's involvements in particular lines of activity, while the notion of "inter-related careers" alerts us to the ways in which people's lives intersect with those of others as they go about conducting their activities in this or that setting. Rather than ask, "why" people do this or that or "what made them" do something, we attend to the natural histories of people's participation in particular settings. Thus, we consider the ways in which people initially became involved and the manners in which they take others into account along the way.

The term "subculture" is used to refer to any group within a larger community. Although the term is often employed in reference to deviance (for example, the thief, drug, or biker subcultures), it is most instructive also to envision people involved in ballet, shuffleboard, baseball, political parties, stamp collecting, scientific inquiry, or student life as participating in subcultures of sorts. Likewise, one may envision work groups, play groups, families, roommates, and other such groupings as also denoting subcultures of sorts, since the people interacting with one another in these settings also develop viewpoints, identities, practices, and relationships that serve to differentiate them from the larger communities in which they are embedded. Subcultures vary greatly in size, formality, exclusivity, duration, and such, but minimally, they entail some degree of interaction, continuity, and distinctiveness from the larger community. Units described as "formal organizations" may also be seen as subcultures of sorts. The participants may develop more explicit and detailed sets of perspectives or world views; they may become more attentive to insider and outsider definitions of members; and they place more emphasis on establishing proficiency at particular activities, but it is essential to appreciate the centrality of human interchange in these settings as well. Without these interchanges, formal organizations would be nothing more than empty shells.

While individual participants may be at varying stages of involvement in this or that subculture, and some people may never progress beyond initial inquiries (or solicitations to join), we want to be attentive to these generic or trans-situational social processes with respect to all group involvements. We will be developing a processual analysis of everyday life, but since human lived experience is also contextually based, we want to be particularly attentive to this aspect of human group life as well.

Acquiring Perspectives: Interpretive Frames

Perspectives (also symbolic realities, worldviews, orientational frameworks, conceptual paradigms, cultural viewpoints, ideologies) refer to the interpretive frameworks that characterize particular communities or subcultures within. Rather than assume a singular objective reality and contend that people are either correct or mistaken in their perceptions of that reality, we adapt Schutz's (1962) notion of *multiple realities*. In other words, reality is viewed as an ongoing social construction, and there are as many views of reality as there are audiences attempting to make sense of the situations in which they find themselves. Some of these notions of reality may be more widely shared and *objectified* (characterized by higher levels of agreement or intersubjective consensus within a community), while other viewpoints might be shared by only a few people possibly to the point of representing the views of a single person.[1] Regardless of their degree of sharedness, however, perspectives are extremely important, for they serve to provide contexts in which human experience is made meaningful. This is why an appreciation of language is so very central to the interpretive tradition. It is through language that images of reality are formulated, shared, and transformed. It is through linguistic communication with the other (symbolic interaction) that people develop ways of looking at, and acting toward, any and all objects of their awareness. As human beings in a community of others, we live and act in a world of linguistically meaningful symbols or images. Identities, activities, involvements, and relationships are all made meaningful as a consequence of symbolic communication with the intersubjective other.

Achieving Identity: Self-Other Definitions

Identities (or people's definitions or typifications of self and others) are also central to an interactionist analysis of human lived experience. Insofar as people act toward objects as they define (assign meanings to) those objects, the meanings that people attribute to objects (including oneself and others) have a vital bearing on the ways in which people act toward one another. As reflective entities, or objects of their own awareness, people can also attempt to project particular images of themselves to others and, thus, encourage others to define and act toward the self in more desired manners. Goffman (1959) uses the term "impression management" to refer to this aspect of identity work in his discussion of *The Presentation of Self in Everyday Life*. As well, though, since people recognize that others may selectively present themselves to this or that audience, they may attempt to ascertain the authenticity of those projected images. Human lived experience, consequently, represents a forum of ongoing identity work as people anticipate, project, define, interpret, assess, accept, resist, and modify images of self and others over the course of their encounters with one another.

Doing Activity: Accomplishment in Process

Activity (or doing things) represents another fundamental feature of human group life. It is in doing things or working things out over a period of time that human lived experience is accomplished. In contrast to those approaches to the study of human behavior that concentrate on causes and outcomes, we attend to the ways in which people go about conducting, assembling, constructing, forging, or shaping their activities on an ongoing or emergent basis. Viewed thusly, action incorporates aspects of people's senses of past, future, and present. While activity may be performed in the present (or the here-and-now), it is built on people's sense of the past and is conducted mindful of the future. It is in this respect that notions of anticipation, accomplishment, assessment, and adjustment are so consequential for the study of human lived experience.[2]

It is in reference to activity, as well, that we see human agency or human enterprise and co-ordination (human interchange or joint activity) at work. Human behavior is not something that is emitted or extruded; it is built up as people take themselves, one another, and other objects into account and attempt to make these linkages more meaningful by adjusting their lines of action accordingly. This is not to imply that people's behavior necessarily will appear wise, rational, or even comprehensible to others, but rather to acknowledge the human capacity for the reflective, minded, or purposive "doing" of activity. As objects unto themselves, people may act toward themselves in solitary manners (consider getting dressed, reading a book, going for a walk), but even these actions are best understood within a community context (consider how people learn to dress, read and walk; how they make decisions about what to wear, what to read, and where to walk).

In developing a capacity for reflectivity, we also learn to take the other into account, and much of our activity involves co-ordinating our doings or practices with those of others in the settings in which we operate. These joint, or mutually constructed, endeavors are not only worthy of attention in themselves (as we ask how people conduct conversations, go shopping together, play a baseball game or a game of tag, or co-ordinate a wedding or a corporate takeover), but they also serve to make other activities, which we appear to do on our own, meaningful. Thus, if we refer to the earlier mentioned activities of dressing, reading, and walking, we start to see how the meanings of each particular instance of these activities are defined by the social contexts to which the participants attend. Someone may get quickly and casually dressed, read a textbook until the afternoon, and then walk hurriedly to a classroom to write an exam. Another person may dress more stylishly, read a book on photography to fill some time, and then walk over to a date's home. A third may dress very conservatively, read a book on "making sales," and walk from a parking lot to the purchasing office of a plastics manufacturer. The options and combinations are endless; the point being that activities are oriented toward, and made meaningful because of, the ways in which people incorporate them into their own particular situations. It is also in the doing of things that people experience stage fright and confidence, happiness and disappointment, intimacy and distancing, fun and frustration, pride and shame, and so forth. Human lived experience is very much bound up in action, and it is for this reason that we put such a heavy emphasis on the necessity of attending to people as thinking, acting, interacting, and adjusting beings.

Experiencing Relationships: Bonds, Networks, Communities

Relationships (or bonds, affiliations, associations, or networks) further emphasize the intersubjective essence of human lived experience. Relationships always take place within contexts and as such imply perspectives, identities, and activities. However, we can focus more specifically on the ways in which relationships are initiated and rebuffed, continue and become intensified, as well as become disrupted, dissolved, and possibly reconstituted over time. Relationships also imply selectivity and rejection, but there is much more to people's relationships than simply identifying those with whom one associates. Indeed, we need to consider the ways in which people: (a) approach others (mindful of their attractions, reservations, and other anticipations); (b) fit their lines of activity together; and (c) begin to organize their routines with respect to these particular sets of others. As well, we should examine the ways in which people attend to others over time with respect to their opportunities for involvements in this or that setting, the perspectives they develop, the identities they attribute to themselves and others, and the activities in which they engage. Thus, as we consider the following set of studies, it is instructive not only to ask what we can learn about involvements, perspectives, identities, activities, and relationships in this or that setting, but also what insights we might gain into people's lived experiences in other settings by close, intimate examinations of people's participation in these settings.

NOTES

1. As self-reflective entities, people may arrive at unique interpretations or versions of "reality." At the same time, however, it is essential to appreciate that even the most individualized notions are rooted in the views (perspectives) and expressions (languages) these people developed through their earlier associations with others in the community. Individuals cannot arrive at completely unique views of reality on their own (i.e., in the absence of pre-existing cultural frames.)

2. In developing this discussion of "action," our indebtedness to Blumer (1969b) is of considerable magnitude.

Getting Involved:
Initial Involvements,
Continuities,
Disinvolvements, and
Reinvolvements

The first section of ethnographies contains four studies on entry into very different social worlds or subcultures. As you study the processes that describe how people become involved in various social worlds, you may ask yourself, "Are these worlds available to everyone?" You may wonder how certain people seem to be sought after, while others are ignored. We ourselves may have become involved in these worlds or activities if circumstances had been different. As you read these ethnographies, you will begin to see how people have had different opportunities for involvement. You will learn how, in some cases, people seek out these opportunities and in others, how they are influenced or convinced to join. These studies also show how some people persist and others simply drop out. You will therefore begin to understand the processes of continued involvements and disinvolvements. As you read further in the book and examine other processes, you will be able to apply these understandings. You will recognize that, in some cases, people become eligible to participate in social worlds and to take on identities without having a motivation to do so, such as deaf or ill persons. Although the ethnographies in this first section deal with persons who chose to become involved by their own actions or because they have been recruited by others, it is useful to remember that the entry processes occur, in all cases, where people become a part of a new community voluntarily or involuntarily.

The first article in this section deals with entry into the professional ballet world. Most professional ballet dancers enter this world as children often taking their first steps toward this career path in recreational dance classes. Ballet is a short career in which participants may turn professional in their teens and may often end their dancing activities in their thirties. The activities and involvements during this short career are usually intense, and members of this world are frequently isolated from other contacts due to the activities required of them, the hours and the travel. Most of the dancers who speak to us from these pages see themselves as privileged to have been able to enter and sustain a career in dance. They view themselves as a chosen few who have entered a world to which many aspire. As the professional dancers in "On Your Toes: Dancing Your Way Into the Ballet World" describe their entry into the ballet world and the continuities of a ballet career, we are able to view their profession and their activities from their own perspective.

In "Getting Involved in the Shuffleboard World," Eldon Snyder describes entry into a post-retirement social world. This contrasts with the entry into professional ballet, which concentrates on the very young. Involvement in the leisure time career of competitive shuffleboard occurs serendipitously for retirees who have selected a particular lifestyle for their retirement. In this selection we are able to view varying degrees of involvement in the world of shuffleboard and to see how this activity becomes a central focus around which social interactions and relationships are built. Although there are obvious differences in the skills of participants, the seekership and recruitment processes that can be observed in ballet or sports, based on physical assets and abilities, take on much less significance. "Shuffling" is a much more home-based activity and is characterized, in Snyder's work, by inclusivity rather than the exclusivity we find in some of the other social worlds studied.

The final two articles in this section describe recruitment into two very different social worlds. Scott Grills' "Recruitment Practices of the Christian Heritage Party" examines the processes of recruitment in a small Canadian federal political party. Most of us have some familiarity with involvement in major political parties, but we rarely have the privilege of understanding how people come to enter the less well-known parties that tend to emerge so frequently in societies dominated by two- or three-party political systems. While all of the papers in this section deal with initial involvements into groups or activities, political recruitment is described as dealing with deep-seated values to a much greater extent than the other social worlds that are entered. In his study of the Christian Heritage Party, Grills, like Snyder, pays close attention to existing and continuing personal relationships as keys to the involvement in this activity. Party affiliation can continue throughout life along with other occupational and recreational involvements. In studying entry into the Christian Heritage Party, attention is drawn to concerns for reputation, performance, and for trust and secrecy—concerns that are also reflected in the recruitment of elite athletes. Grills pays particular attention to both personal and religious relationships, drawing our attention to the importance of these relationships on the decision to enter into this and other social worlds.

In "Being Recruited: The Experience of 'Blue Chip' High School Athletes," Dietz and Cooper view the process of recruitment of elite high school athletes into college sports programs from the perspective of the athlete. Because this type of recruitment is based on evaluations of skills and potential performance, the recruit must place a value on her or his abilities as must the recruiter. The process of recruitment of highly valued persons into highly valued situations involves negotiations and a much clearer sense of the necessity for evaluating the match between the potential member and the group than we find in entry into other worlds. In the study of recruitment of Blue Chip high school athletes, the time frame for the recruitment is much more restricted and the decision-making process much more formal. We can see very clearly that entry into highly competitive college sports is based on the recruit being both a seller of him or herself and a buyer of a particular program. Dietz and Cooper trace the process of recruitment within this context and provide some insight into the stress and self-evaluation that is involved in being recruited as an elite high school athlete.

After reading the selections in section 2.1, it should be obvious that entry into different social worlds is extremely variable. It can be relaxed and take place over an extended period or it can be intense and occur within a restricted time frame. In some cases, entry into a social world can be a decision that will make major life changes and, in other cases, it may have only a small impact on the life of the neophyte. In either case, it is a complex process that we all experience throughout our lives.

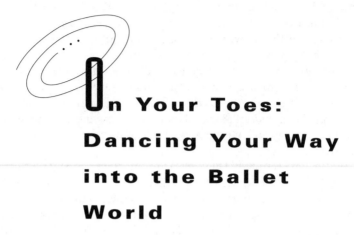

On Your Toes: Dancing Your Way into the Ballet World

Mary Lorenz Dietz

Typically envisioned as an art form and a kind of entertainment, the world of professional ballet can be cruel and demanding. Indeed, there may be no other occupation that takes so much from its participants and gives so little visible reward in return. Further, the small band of survivors in this profession live in a world apart—aliens and strangers to the "real" world that most of us inhabit.

Like many specialized occupational worlds, the back regions or underlife of the ballet world is unknown to most of us. Even aficionados have little knowledge of the dancer's day-to-day life. In the broader occupational field of dance, professional ballet is the most isolated, the most demanding, and requires the most dedication. While it shares some affinities with other forms of dance, the training, selection, limitations, and stakes are very different. In this paper I will examine the processes and activities involved in becoming a professional ballet dancer.[1] First, the entry into ballet as an occupation is examined. After achieving entry into the professional track, the major consistent activities of dancers including classes, auditions, rehearsals, and performances are discussed from the perspective of professional dancers.

Theoretical Considerations

Prus (1984) has written on the concept of career contingencies, discussing not only four central processes of initial involvement, continuities, disinvolvements, and reinvolvements, but also the careers of people's identities, worldviews, commitments, and relationships that accompany their role involvements. He suggests that his model could be applied to a range of involvements in group life, particularly in areas of sport and leisure, but also in other deviant and non-deviant careers. The nature of the ballet career involvement is such that this approach is particularly useful.

Prus's concepts of stages of involvement enable us to focus on seekership and recruitment at the early stages of the ballet career and provide a conceptual framework for viewing parental involvement, a major consideration in professions where career choices are made in childhood. Being aware of worldviews, identities, activities, commitments, and relationships is of even greater importance in this closed, competitive, "total institution-like," environment (Goffman 1961). The constant critical evaluation by teachers, choreographers, peers, critics, and especially, continual self-appraisals, is such a crucial aspect of the ballet world that the looking-glass self (Cooley 1964) and mirrored self-reflection have become standardized in the ballet classroom. In fact the mirrored-self becomes a vital part of the ballet dancer's self-concept and provides the basis for self-criticism through interactions with the dancer in the mirror, as Hall (1977) has pointed out.

Although extensive literature is available on myriad occupations, the literature dealing directly with dance as a career, especially ballet, is just beginning to develop. Most notable among works dealing with dance are Federico's (1968; 1983) examinations of the ballet career and particularly the problems of facing retirement, which highlight the intensity and compressed time frame of the career. Also important is Hall's (1977) work on the advanced ballet class as a vehicle for the study of dancers' self-concepts and status systems. The most extensive work on dance has been Hanna's (1983; 1987; 1988), which provides an in-depth analysis of dance as non-verbal communication, and thoroughly examines the intricate relations between dance, culture, and gender. As well, Gordon's *Off Balance: The Real World of Ballet* (1983) and Gelsey Kirkland's *Dancing On My Grave* (1986) provide intimate glimpses of the troubled ballet world. All of these writers have had personal involvement with dance and all agree that ballet dancers constitute a unique occupational category. Not only have some very peculiar practices developed in the back regions of this work, but it is also difficult to resist labeling the participants, especially ballet dancers, as anorexic, masochistic, addicted, neurotic, obsessive, and unrealistic. Indeed, they often label themselves in just these terms. In brief, the world of ballet provides the sociologist with an outstanding example of how an isolated social world, under ideal conditions, can obscure the realities of a larger society.

The fact that more and more people (Gordon 1983) are seeking the few poorly paid positions in this profession may suggest a trend worth looking at. It may be that the tightly controlled environment and rigid discipline of the ballet world provides something that is missing in the permissive home and school worlds, something that adolescents and even adults find comforting. As one young dancer recalled: "The first guy I studied with was Romanian and he was a very strict disciplinarian. Whether I knew it or not I needed that right then." Another also spoke about the attraction of the disciplined lifestyle:

> That's exactly what I needed. You know, my whole childhood had been completely invisible from day one. I grew up, fed myself, did everything, because of my father's drinking,... the way he isolated us ... so I had no discipline, the thing, the only discipline that I had was that I was grown up by the time I was six years old. [Ballet] it's a very disciplined thing that you get into, and it's almost addictive for those of us who have those real lonely type attitudes.

Methods

In addition to twenty extended interviews with professional ballet dancers in New York, Detroit, and several southeastern dance companies, this study was supplemented by fifteen years of observation and participation in the community of professional and student ballet dancers. In ten years of literally supporting my son's professional dance career, I was involved in forming and administering a dance support group for a local semi-professional company; doing dance video and still photography exhibits on dance; observing classes from beginner's to master class levels; and, attending numerous recitals, auditions, rehearsals, and performances. I have spent many hours talking and listening to ballet dancers at all levels as well as to teachers, ballet masters, choreographers, and ballet parents. Although I am not a dancer, these other forms of participation provided a viable base from which to study the dance world. The twenty extended formal interviews with dancers significantly under-estimate the store of knowledge gathered through hundreds of conversations about the world of dance.

Initial Involvements

The initial involvement in ballet is usually parent-sponsored as an educational or cultural experience. Since dance is both a leisure activity and a profession, it is similar to some sports, but unlike occupations such as engineering or economics, which are rarely pursued as a hobby or leisure activity. Many parents enrol their children in dance classes with little attention being paid to the children's interests or abilities. They consider this training (primarily for girls) to be a "normal" part of their education, similar to scouting or music lessons. Generally speaking, there seems to be little expectation that the child will consider the activity as a career. Most dancers are signed up for dance classes by their parents although some children seek it out themselves. The following are three different initial involvements:

> My mom ... got us involved in different things. Like I took piano lessons and I played on a softball team. We had tap and ballet and tumbling ... and I really liked the ballet part of it. (Interview, Karri 1991)

> Before I was dancing I was playing the piano and I was in a child's acting class.... I don't know why, if it was something my parents wanted me to do or because I decided to do it. (Interview, Michael 1991)

> I just started when I was a little girl and I wanted to dance. I used to beg my mom, it was like, "Can I take ballet class?" (Interview, Evie 1991)

Many local dance schools start children of age three to five years in ballet class the first year, in tap the second year, and continue this rotation for several years. This is a common procedure for neighborhood dance schools that are not professionally oriented. Children frequently take five to ten years of classes. Classes normally meet once a week during the school year with summers off. If the novices become particularly interested in dance, they may enrol in two or more classes per week, depending on the parents' finances and time constraints. Presently group classes usually cost five or more dollars while private lessons can reach fifty dollars per hour.

Sometimes around the age of nine or ten, the child may develop a special interest in dance and want to increase class time. Here the child might ask to have a practice barre installed in the home and may show a diminished interest in other activities. In other cases, parents, not necessarily seeing ballet as a career, but wanting their children to excell in all activities, will encourage the child and increase their own involvement in the school, hoping that their children will receive lead roles in recitals. Those parents who are labeled "ballet parents" are seen as pushing their children into greater and greater involvement, admonishing them to practice and take additional classes. While many parents may be supportive, it is "ballet parents" who invade and manipulate their child's career decisions.

Dance teachers also centrally involve themselves in the recruitment process. When they have especially talented students, they will ask parents to increase the number of classes the child is taking. Teachers will also begin to talk to these children about the possibility of a dance career and to actively discourage them from taking part in other activities, such as sports, that interfere with their dance involvement or that may cause injury. Teachers will recommend private lessons for advanced or talented students and indicate to the parents that the child may have a successful career in dance. If the parents are not affluent, most teachers will also give free lessons to talented students or exchange free lessons for their help with lower level classes. Eddie describes an influential teacher as follows:

He took time out which is very important to me. He took time out and worked with me by myself on things that I needed in my body.... He fixed a whole lot of things that I'd been trying to find.... He made me more confident in the way I moved. (Interview 1991)

Another dancer also gives us a glimpse of the importance of the teacher for the student:

[He] was the kind of person who knew how to get respect from the dancers ... everyone worked the hardest in his class, paid the most attention, and really had the most respect for him. [He] ... could promote the desire to dance in other people and live out his dreams through a different body. He was always enthusiastic for other dancers. He was very demanding yet he didn't frustrate the students. He was encouraging yet strict. (Interview, Melanie 1991)

Technique and Status

During the stages of initial involvement, both career and non-career oriented students begin their indoctrination into the technical and social aspects of ballet. Technical training involves learning movement to music, basic dance forms such as foot, arm, and body positions, and dance movements; French dance terminology such as *plié*; and the importance of practice. On the social side, the young dancer is initiated into the ballet status hierarchy with which dancers must comply and accept. A dancer, in describing one particular company, points out:

You know one of the things about [company name]. I think it's their ability to take away your dignity with that caste system they believe so strongly in. (Interview, Denny 1991)

Young dancers are taught that independence, autonomy, and egalitarianism have no place in the ballet world. Tiny dancers line up at the end of each class and genuflect in front of the teacher to symbolically thank their teacher for the privilege of being in class (in spite of the fact that, in most cases, that privilege was paid for):

In ——— School of Dance, the instructor trained her students in every class to respond to her question, "Who was the greatest ballet teacher of all time?" The children joined their hands together in prayer fashion, bowed their heads, and in unison replied, "Maestro Ceccetti," at which time the teacher asked them, "And who was MY teacher?" Again, in unison, "Maestro Ceccetti." (Field notes 1976)

Status degradation ceremonies (Garfinkel 1956) begin with the requirement that students attend class in ballet uniform—black leotards and ballet-pink tights for the girls and black tights and white tee shirts for the boys.

The standardization of appearance is further extended for girls who must also wear their hair pulled back and fastened into tight buns. Status degradation ceremonies are also built into the classes wherein students learn that they are inferior both to the teacher and to the "great ones" of ballet. Melanie comments: "I think they act that way toward their dancers because that's how they were treated when they danced" (Interview 1991).

It is during this period that the young dancers are initiated into the ritual of public shame and humiliation, and to the knowledge that praise is as rare as perfection itself. As Anne describes it:

> I hate it when teachers say you're too heavy or something. And that you won't get into a company because you are too heavy. She pulled that kind of stuff. (Interview 1991)

> The only teacher I really hated ... actually I don't really think she was that negative, I think she just criticized me a lot. And like all at once. And she didn't really like the way I danced. And she just basically told me everything I was doing was wrong. (Interview, Karri 1991)

This aspect of socialization is extremely important as it serves to screen out students who are very poor at dance as well as those who are not temperamentally suited to living with daily public criticism. Testing and criticism of "rookies" is well documented in sport and in other professions. Haas and Shaffir (in this volume) discuss this aspect of the life of medical students. The continual criticism is not an ongoing part of career activity as is true in ballet. As Denny points out:

> I see a dancer's life, I see a lot of dancers with problems. Because they're surrounded in a world where they're never good enough in it.... Instead of a world where you are accepted just as you are ... dancers are never good enough. (Interview 1991)

It also builds up some tolerance to the criticism, but creates a desperate desire to do sufficiently well to avoid being singled out and publicly humiliated. One dancer points out:

> There are just people in this business who are willing to do anything to get a part. Or who are willing to do anything to better themselves at no matter the cost to other people. (Interview, Richard 1991)

This constant focus on the body and execution creates a self-concept that is characterized by low self-esteem, and many dancers develop a "me" that is negative and hypercritical. Continual comparisons of one student to another make it difficult to form solid relationships with others who are continually shown as competitors. This divisiveness also creates greater dependence on the instructor whose power is continually being demonstrated:

He was so belittling in his correction. Like "Did your first teacher tell you that you needed to do this?" "How long have you been dancing?" And he was funny, but it was in the way he slashed your throat as everybody laughed. (Interview, Denny 1991)

More advanced students come to want the attention of criticism, or "correction" as they call it. Or as one dancer puts it, if the instructor "gives you corrections he thinks you are worthwhile." He said that he felt most sorry for the student who was ignored.

Moving into the Professional Track

By the time they are in their pre-teens or early teens, students considering a career in ballet must have personally made a commitment to such a career. Because of the relatively young age of these students, most parents remain heavily involved both emotionally and financially. Students who have made a ballet career commitment often decide (with the parents) to change teachers or go to a school that teaches ballet exclusively. In some cases instructors may recommend an apprenticeship into a company school (a school that has a performing company connected with it). Elli describes her experience:

I went to SAB when I was nine and there's a certain point that you reach at SAB where you just have to think of it as a career because you are missing so many other things.... From a young age you think about wanting to be in a company. (Interview 1991)

I can remember a couple of occasions being in the locker room, and seeing girls maybe eight or nine years old looking at themselves in the mirror. And I remember this one day this little girl turned to the other one and said, "I feel so bad, I had ice cream today." I thought this is just tragic. This kid is nine years old and she is freaking out because she had ice cream.... And you know that just typified ——— or the dance world generally to me. (Interview 1991)

A number of students stop attending academic classes entirely at this time, but some finish through correspondence or by taking high school equivalency tests:

It costs about $78,000—the equivalent of a college degree and part of a master's—to produce a dancer. For a child of six or seven, parents must spend about $400 a year for lessons, plus $30 for shoes, $60 for tights and leotards, and $30 for dance slippers. As the child grows, the sums grow too. From a class once a week when she is six, the budding dancer moves to daily classes when she is ten or eleven. Then the annual bill may come to $900 for classes, $110 for pointe shoes, $90 for tights and leotards, and $40 for leg warmers. (Gordon 1983)

Of course, all of these prices have increased since the early 1980s. Both the financial and social cost of becoming a dancer can be prohibitive for those who are not totally dedicated, and many aspiring dancers drop out of dancing when they recognize how costly it can be. As Denny says:

> Make sure that you always love it. That you love what you are doing because there is really no other reason to get involved in something that is as painful, emotionally and physically, and pays so little. (Interview, Denny 1991)

Several dancers remarked on the social status and wealth of serious dance students, commenting that the parents of these students all seemed to be doctors, lawyers, or had their own business. It should be noted, too, that while both parents tend to support women dancers, most of the men interviewed suggested that their fathers were silent or discouraging. Two male dancers remark on their fathers' attitudes:

> Me and my dad didn't get along. He wanted me to be an accountant. I was an athlete because of him. (Interview, Jerry 1991)

> Yes, my dear father has tried to discourage me. He gave me a speech about being 5'8" and trying to get into the NBA.... It was a very discouraging talk. (Interview, Eddie 1991)

Dancers at this level are expected to make a *total* commitment to the life. Being a ballet dancer means giving up all other activities. By the time the student moves to this stage, both the student and the family have already made tremendous investments of time and money into a possible career. One mother told me that:

> In addition to the two classes a day, six days a week, that her daughter was taking, she was also paying for two private lessons per week, transportation, tights, leotards, pointe shoes, and spending money. She said that the entire earnings from her own full-time job went into her daughter's dance expenses. (Field notes 1982)

Career Continuities: Life Is Dance

To move to the apprenticeship level in ballet means that the student has moved into the professional stream, although apprenticeship does not insure making it as a professional. As pointed out by Gordon (1983), many young dancers have never seen a sports event nor attended a rock concert. We are misled when we see a superstar like Baryshnikov at Hollywood events or in the gossip columns. These activities may be a part of his lifestyle now, but most dancers' apprenticeships do not include external social activities. Karri describes how she handled her social life:

> In high school, because I went to a performing arts high school, I was really dedicated. It just started being a lot more important to me than anything else

and people asked me to do things and I'd say "No, because I have to dance, you know, because I'm a dancer. I have to go to class." (Interview 1991)

Melanie describes a similar recognition of the need for an early and total commitment in her high school experience:

> In the ninth grade, when I was probably fourteen, at that time a lot of my friends were trying out for cheerleaders and I had to make the decision whether I was going to devote more time to ballet and be very serious with it or if I was just going to keep it as an outside activity and have other activities ... at that point I decided ballet was what I wanted to do and so I had to sacrifice other things for ballet. (Interview 1991)

André echoes the feeling of many young dancers: "I didn't have an ambition to do anything else. Throughout my adolescence I considered other options but I just wanted to be a dancer" (Interview 1991).

Most ballet dancers, at this stage, do not even read the newspaper and most have few friends or relationships outside the dance world. They rarely date, except other dancers, because their practice and rehearsal hours make dating non-dancers so difficult. Obviously, commitment in this occupation is total and all-encompassing:

> There's a deep, deep satisfaction that I couldn't exactly put my finger on. It's a very elusive thing that I'm sure every ballet dancer knows about. A deep sense of, I don't know, I guess of accomplishment and pride despite all the obstacles you have to overcome. (Interview, Denny 1991)

Most apprentices do not even see their families as they often live away from home. When they do live at home, they leave early in the morning and return late at night:

> I didn't go out a lot at all and then they just, after awhile, they just stopped asking me because I would never go. (Interview, Karri 1991)

> I think dancers are awfully limited. They limit themselves.... So many of them are so intensified. Ballet! Ballet! Ballet! They go, they rehearse, then they go take class at night. (Interview, Michael 1991)

> I haven't read a book in two, no three years. (Interview, Jerry 1991)

Family relations are sharply curtailed and there is little parent-child contact unless parents have some dance involvements or see their children during travel time, until the dancers are old enough to drive or take the subway alone. In some cases, parents, usually those known as "ballet mothers," leave the rest of their family and move out of town with the child to continue to support the child's career, but it is more common for the child to leave home early and to return rarely. Relationships with parents often decline early in the dancer's life and may be substituted by relationships with parent figures in the dance world. Whether or not the mother-child relationship is continued, the dancer must accept the idea that the parental role has been transferred to the artistic director, choreographer, and ballet master/mistress. As Michael describes this relationship: "They were like parents. They adopted a lot of us" (Interview 1991). But others describe the people who assume the parental role as "bad" parents:

> When I went in the first year I was very upset because it was my first year away from home, you know, and he pulled me in there after a month and I refused to cry, but I was looking down and the tears started to form. But I wasn't going to bawl, because I just wouldn't do it.... I think he was irritated that I didn't.... He stood up, "I can't believe you'd have the nerve to contradict me. Young dancers, blah, blah, blah." (Interview, Maria 1991)

> I went to (company school name) for like ten years. Madame ——— was the director there. You know I saw her every single day and she saw me, yet she never said "hello" to me in the hall or anything.... I was the only one who showed up and she never treated me politely. I was right there and she didn't ask me. It was like I was a non-person. (Interview, Evie 1991)

These relationships will continue to dominate the dancer's life until retirement. One dancer describes her relationship with the artistic director:

> Every time I get in there he treats me like I'm about five years old.... He scares me.... He's kind of psychotic, you know, I mean I've heard stories about him actually hitting girls and it scares me. (Interview, Maria 1991)

The dancer-teacher relationship forces a kind of emotional dependency and makes the dancer appear "child-like" with respect to other relationships. Several dancers commented on power relationships:

> I think it's scary that someone has so much power. It needs to be distributed. Nothing should be like that. (Interview, Annie 1991)

> I don't think he cares about ballet, I think he cares about money and power and that's not ballet. (Interview, Jerry 1991)

> I mean the power to pull someone in your office and within two minutes to have them in tears, I think its a kind of sickness ... because it can ruin people. (Interview, Melanie 1991)

Many dancers view their lives as having been manipulated and distorted. One describes it as follows:

> That comes from always feeling that you are not good enough. I mean it's like pathological that we kind of breed that. You get somebody at a young and impressionable age of seventeen in a professional company and for the next ten or twenty years they are constantly told every day of their lives how they are not good enough. (Interview, Denny 1991)

Dancers who do not accept this domination are likely to find their careers ended or ruined if they continue to try to be independent. To refuse to accept the patronage of those in power is essentially to give up the opportunity to dance. For most dancers, refusal is not an option because the "dancer" identity becomes so central to the individual that the thought of not being able to dance is unbearable.

Activities in a Dancer's Life

Dancers' lives are centered around the basic activities of *classes, rehearsals, auditions,* and *performances.* These dance-related activities consume their lives, dominating what they do and what they talk about.

Classes

Ballet dancer's take *class* throughout their professional careers. Companies like the American Ballet Theatre or the Royal Ballet of Canada have company classes every day before rehearsal, even when they are on tour. For the apprentice dancer, the number of classes depends on the level to which he or she has progressed. Most take at least one advanced class and a partnering class, but dancers may take up to four classes a day if they are not in rehearsal.

Class consists of warm-up, which students do in a ritualistic and individual manner as they prepare for class by stretching and doing movements. They are expected to be in class and warmed up by the time the instructor arrives. In some schools, students who arrive late are not allowed into class. Even major stars are expected to apologize if they arrive late and disrupt the class. Michael describes his feelings about classes:

> Most people would think going to class for an hour and a half is kinda like the way I view it,… it's drudgery. But I still get enjoyment occasionally with it. But basically I'd rather get on with the meat of the story, then start rehearsing, and then get on stage, that's where I want to be. But a dancer's very disciplined. (Interview, Michael 1991)

Classes begin with instructors running through some basic movements. Movable barres are placed in the room and classes are accompanied by a pianist, although in smaller schools, tapes may be used. The instructor calls out *"plié, plié, demi-plié"* moving quickly through the more simple movements to the more complex and difficult. The instructor walks among the dancers, often physically poking and prodding, moving their feet, hands, and bodies into proper position and alignment. As they do this, they frequently make comments about the physical flaws they see in the dancer's bodies or positions. One dancer described someone being singled out his first day in class:

> A new apprentice came into class and took his place near the back of the class, demonstrating that he recognized that at that point within the company he

was a low-status person. The director watched him for a short while, then he stopped the class and said "Class look at Mr. Smith, those are the worst feet I have ever seen in my life. Show the class your feet, Mr. Smith. Isn't that disgusting class?" (Interview, Loki 1984)

A female student kept her short plastic sweatpants on after class started. The ballet master said, "Stop class. We have to wait for Miss Blake to be dressed properly for class. What is the proper attire for a dancer, Miss Blake?" The student answered "a leotard and tights." The ballet master said, "Oh, you do know the proper attire for class, then tell the class why you do not dress properly. Have you gained weight? Did you think no one would notice?" (Field notes 1982)

After the class has gone through the initial phases and corrections, the portable barres are moved to the side of the room and the class is arranged into smaller groups while the instructor calls off combinations of eight or ten movements, which the students perform in their groups. The instructor often gives minor corrections (criticisms) as they move across the floor. Any student who performs the combinations incorrectly or cannot remember the combinations is then singled out as shown in this observation of an advanced class:

The ballet master said, "Mr. Lawrence, Mr. Samson seems to be unable to execute a double tour. Perhaps you will be kind enough to show him how to do it properly. Mr. Samson, pay close attention and perhaps you will learn the double tour. You know you will never dance an important role if you cannot do it. Alright, Mr. Samson now you will have a chance to show if you have been paying attention. Again. Again. Again." (Field notes 1981)

The apprentices or the students often leave class in tears saying, "He hates me!" or, "I'll never get a part!" But soon they learn that the people who receive attention, no matter how unpleasant, are acceptable. After each class, no matter what goes on in class, class members, who may include known professionals from other companies, applaud the instructor and often the accompanist as well.

Classes are a stabilizing element in the lives of dancers. Most dancers feel uncomfortable and out of condition if they do not take classes throughout their careers from student through apprenticeships and as professionals.

Rehearsals

An important part of the apprenticeship period is the opportunity dancers have to learn and perform in the traditional ballets that are included in the repertoires of most companies. Even before apprenticeship, most young dancers have taken part in annual performances of "The Nutcracker," which is performed by most companies both on national and regional levels. In their participation in these performances of "The Nutcracker," dancers begin to learn the rigors and requirements of *rehearsals*, which will remain with them throughout their careers. Although "The Nutcracker" has been recorded and is on videotape in many versions, each company varies the ballet, depending on the quality of dancers available, the sets and costumes the company has, and the interpretation of the choreographer or artistic director. One professional dancer describes how she worked her way from the baby parts in this ballet, through her apprenticeship, until she finally won the role of the sugarplum fairy as a professional:

> I danced first in "The Nutcracker" when I was just a baby, first in the children's corps roles as a doll, or a child, then as a mouse or a soldier doll. At [company name] dancers followed a natural progression although everyone didn't progress. The artistic director wanted us to know all the parts because that's how it was done in his country. All the girls had to do "friends" and "pages" and the corps roles for "flowers," "mirlitons," and "parents." We all wanted to dance "Clara" because it was a lead. We usually had to bring a boy in to do "Fritz" because we didn't have any small boys that were any good. But the girls, if they were small, were still doing "Clara" in their twenties (if they were lucky enough to do it at all). We all had to audition for "Chinese," "Russian," and "Arabian," and for "Pas de Quatre," "Snow," and "Mirliton" solos. We always knew in advance who would get the parts, so the competition, if you were a soloist, was to get the best parts for the most nights or just the most nights because that's how you could tell who was on top. The top male and female dancers got to understudy the "Sugar Plum" and "Cavalier" because we always brought them in from another company. Sometimes they weren't even as good as us, but they got the star treatment because they were in a bigger, more well-known company. Some nights we had to do four or five, sometimes even six different, hard roles and costume changes. Anybody who complained so the artistic director could hear it, they could always be replaced. (Interview, Paula 1980)

Rehearsals involve not only running through all or parts of the ballet, but also the rehearsing of solos and practicing *pas de deux* with different sets of partners. Each dancer has individual characteristics, so partners must make adjustments for differences in height, weight, strength, and speed, and prepare to deal with their partner's weaknesses and strengths. A male dancer describes his rehearsals and their results:

> When we rehearsed "Corsaire," I partnered both Paula and Karin. Karin was always hurt so she missed as much rehearsal time as possible. Backstage we fought all the time; she was always such a bitch and she thought the world revolved around her schedule, but she wanted to dance with me so she could only go so far. She was much shorter than Paula and easier to handle on the lifts. On the final lift where the girl is carried off sitting on my hand, over my head, I was always really tired because the solo is hard. If the girl didn't jump,

she was likely to wobble. You have to have your hand right in their crotch to balance right. Even though Paula and I rehearsed every day, I still blew the lift on opening night and had to catch her with my other hand as we went off. I thought it was her fault because she didn't jump and I was mad. She was already crying when we went out to take our bows. (Interview, Loki 1982)

Apprentices, if they are lucky enough to be chosen, must also understudy principal roles so that they are prepared to go on in case someone has an injury. Therefore, by the time dress rehearsals start, all the dancers are tired and feeling frazzled. Often, half the cast is not talking to the other half, and any number of people may be concealing serious injuries. One dancer describes how he was injured and his decision nòt to report it:

When he [artistic director] told Jane that she was going to dance "Arabian," she was so excited. Kevin and I looked at each other and groaned and he shook his head. Jane weighed over 140 and, even figuring her to lose ten pounds during rehearsals, lifting her was going to be tough. The ballet master tried Kevin first because he wanted him to dance "Arabian" because he's black. When Jane stepped into Kevin's hand for the first behind the back lift, he dropped flat on the floor. He said, "I guess I'm just not strong enough." Jane was only sixteen and self-conscious about her size, and she had a big crush on me. I knew if I didn't do it she would be dropped from her big chance so I made up my mind I would partner her. We were O.K. until about two days before the dress. The ballet master was running me about eighteen hours a day and I was over-tired. When I dropped her into a fish during rehearsal, I felt my groin muscles tear. I danced every night but it took the groin muscles six months to heal and I still have problems. Kevin thought I was a real asshole to do it at all. (Interview, Loki 1983)

Rehearsals go on, as do classes, even on performance nights. They cannot be missed without special permission, especially for beginning dancers, because there is always the fear, and the very real chance, that the role will be given to someone else.

Auditions

When students move from the student to the apprenticeship or professional status, they will be expected to *audition* for the school or company. Depending on how well they do, they may be allowed to take classes at the school, they may be offered a partial or a full scholarship, they may be taken on as an apprentice or as a full member of a company:

I auditioned a lot of places before I came here. In Europe, I was in Europe for thirty-one days and I auditioned for twenty-eight companies. Got some good responses from some people. (Interview, Denny 1991)

Once in a company, all but the top performers may have to audition for every part in every ballet including, in some companies, the *corps de ballet* (a group of dancers acting under common direction) parts. In some companies, even if they do not want to dance the role, or if they are not going to dance it, some ballet masters require that they audition for the role. If they are in a school that does not have an attached company or if they want to change companies, again they have to audition:

> I picked out a few places and I decided, "Alright, if I get in these places, I'm going to go. And if I don't, I'm going to quit." And I auditioned and I didn't get in. And I just couldn't quit. I just wasn't ready. (Interview, Evie 1991)

Auditions put people's identities on the line and can be so personally devastating that even dancers with years of criticism behind them, may have difficulty facing auditions. As dancers go from audition to audition, they expose themselves to continued criticism and rejection:

> I've done tons of auditions. I don't like them. I mean the more you do, I guess the more comfortable you become with them, but they're never a fun experience for me. (Interview, Evie 1991)

When dancers first begin to audition for apprenticeships or for professional companies, they often naïvely believe that if they audition well they will be selected for the company. They often feel like total failures the first few times, especially if they are dismissed immediately (after one or two combinations):

> We got taken in there ten people at a time. And the first thing they made us do was walk across the floor and they cut eight of the ten. (Interview, Eddie 1991)

Eventually, most dancers learn more about the reality of auditions and, at the same time as they are learning the art of dancing, they are also learning the art of rationalizing that will ultimately allow them to continue to pursue their career:

> The first time I auditioned for a company, I didn't make callbacks. I felt my life was over. They didn't want me. I thought I must be terrible. I realized it hadn't been an especially good audition, but still I thought they should see something good about me. After a few more auditions I began to realize that I was doing good if I made callbacks. Eventually, I came to know that some companies were only holding auditions so they could be eligible for government grants and they had no intention of hiring anyone. In other cases, they were looking for someone the right size for their costumes, or that would look good with one of their principals. I still get a little down when I don't get the role or the job that I'm auditioning for, but now I don't always automatically think that it's because there's something wrong with me. (Interview, Loki 1985)

> There are a lot of tricks that people use during auditions to help make the companies notice. Since most of them require standard colors, it's important to get their attention because everyone looks a lot alike. The best thing is to

rehearse something you do really well during warm-ups. Of course, they may not even be looking then. People scramble and push their way into spots where they are visible, they always think that helps. I guess it does sometimes, but mostly you have to be what they are looking for. It doesn't hurt if your teacher is promoting you either. (Interview, Kyle 1984)

Of course, auditions can help build confidence as well. Dancers who are repeatedly singled out from a large group of dancers can maintain hope and begin to see themselves as one of the best:

I have these weird delusions of grandeur sometimes. And they make me audition for people that I don't really need to audition for. You ever had that feeling that you take a class and somebody is in class and you think, that person is watching me and I'm the only fucking person in the room? (Interview, Eddie 1991)

Performances

The end result of all the classes, practice, rehearsals, and auditions are the *performances*. Performances begin in early years at recitals and continue through the apprentice years with *corps* parts and occasional solos. Most dancers love to perform:

That's the beauty of a lot of performances. Everybody will act themselves and it should be different. It shouldn't be a generic copy. (Interview, Michael 1991)

Performing is why I'm dancing. When I perform ... I want the audience to feel something.... It gives me such a feeling of satisfaction to be on the stage. (Interview, Annie 1991)

A performance season for a major company, such as the New York City Ballet, may involve a month of performances six nights a week with Saturday and Sunday matinees. A season such as this would include the performance of a full-length major ballet and several short ballets or segments of longer ballets. For the New York City Ballet, a company of over 100 dancers would perform up to forty ballets. Usually this type of season would include one or two premiers of new pieces, several traditional ballets, and a number of lesser known or infrequently performed ballets. Touring companies will usually perform fewer ballets with a much smaller troupe. Larger companies may remain in a major city for a week or ten days, while smaller companies may be booked for one or two days with only two to four performances. Regional companies may have only two or three performances per year. In major cities, four or five well-known companies may be performing on a given weekend during the winter or spring season. Other cities may have six to eight companies in for a weekend series, while still others may have a touring company only once or twice a year. The performances of major companies are reviewed by dance critics for the local papers as well as in dance magazines.

The performance is the activity on which the dancer and the company is judged and the activity for which they are paid. It is during the performance that the dancer is able to demonstrate his or her technique and ability to influence the audience. While it is only the soloists and principals who are mentioned by name in a review, the performance of the *corps de ballet*, whether it performs well or not, is always mentioned in the review. Dancers who are highly skilled, but do not have stage presence or the technique to affect an audience do not become star attractions:

> Basically I think people do perform kind of for themselves, but it is a giving thing too. I just don't think when you are out there you are thinking, "Oh, I'm giving this to everyone." (Interview, Jill 1991)

Professional Status

A professional is someone who earns the majority of his or her pay doing a particular activity. People who dance in small or regional companies often have a semi-professional status. The companies usually have a very small budget so only a few of the dancers are paid; they are often contracted for a limited number of performances and rehearsals. Even if they dance with several companies, these semi-professionals do not make enough money to survive without additional, non-dance employment. Apprentices are also paid, but they receive very low salaries and often must supplement their income with part-time jobs or money from their families. Many of the smaller professional companies have very short contracts and, between contracts, dancers add to their incomes by appearing as a guest performer, by teaching, or by taking short-term jobs. One dancer sees this as part of the attraction, saying: "I always liked the idea of being a gypsy. I like moving around, I like seeing other places, I like being unencumbered" (Interview, Eddie 1991).

Some dancers accept contracts with European countries as well. The dancers that work on a full-time professional basis are relatively few in number and are, for the most part, the best and the most dedicated. Although most of them at one time had dreams of being a soloist or principal in a major company, many are content just to be dancing:

> To be a professional dancer … I never really planned that far because I thought that I was being really hopeful even hoping to be in a dance company. And that was like my goal that I was working towards all my life, just to get in. (Interview, Karri 1991)

> I can be in the corps of a company and be perfectly happy if I'm in a situation where I can work to my full potential. I want to get into a company that's not mediocre. (Interview, Kim 1991)

> I always wanted to just dance. Dance and get paid. I'd be happy just dancing in the corps. (Interview, Evie 1991)

The professional career tends to be quite short for most, although there have been such notable exceptions as Dame Margot Fonteyn, Rudolf Nureyev, and Natalia Makarova. A dancer about to retire comments on his career:

> I had what I guess a lot of people consider the true dancer ideal. To have a long career, do a lot of roles, perform for a lot of people ... and feel fairly fulfilled. (Interview, Michael 1991)

These extended careers are rare and many dancers move into teaching while they are still in their thirties. Dance companies, with few exceptions, do not have good benefits in terms of health insurance or retirement. In many companies, contracts are for only one or two years with little guarantee of renewal, especially as the dancers age beyond their twenties. Dancers view their world as hard and challenging, but worth almost any sacrifice that allows them to dance:

> You have to be a warrior to be a dancer.... There are some of us that fight everyday. (Interview, Eddie 1991)

> You're never not a dancer, you're always a dancer in everything you do.... It comes out in the way you act, in your whole life. You're always thinking about it...you're always dedicated. (Interview, Melanie 1991)

> Dancers sort of live their work more. You have to be totally involved to be a dancer. (Interview, Karri 1991)

> I don't know how I would exist not dancing.... That's always been everything that I am.... I don't have anything besides me and dancing. That's all I have. (Interview, Kim 1991)

Disengagement

Although the actual career in ballet is very short, between ten and twenty years, most dancers do not leave the profession completely unless they quit early in their careers. Not unlike compulsive gamblers, dancers become addicted to the routine of the constant motion and attention to themselves and seem unwilling to give it up. People have suggested that as a group they are dependent and immature people. Most, however, seem to be able to step into the demanding roles of choreographer, teacher, or artistic director without too much difficulty once they are faced with the prospects of not being able to dance anymore. The dancers who start very young often have to retire by the age of thirty because of arthritis caused by the ballet positions that distort their young bones and joints, and the thousands of jumps on hard floors, as well as the nutritionally inadequate meals many of them eat, because of both poverty and the constant attention to their weight. One dancer describes his pain:

> But those shoulders are the big thing because its no more synovial fluid between the bone. It's bursitis, bone on bone now. That's from all the partnering I've done. I've done so much lifting that the sack is gone. I mean it's a constant click. They grind and click every time I move.... I'm twenty-eight and it's going to hurt. It is hurting. It has always hurt, but now it's hurting more. (Interview, Denny 1991)

Most ballet dancers have little knowledge of anything other than ballet, so they cannot find work outside of the dance world in any case. The rare ones with more education, or who have learned other skills along the way, may still be reluctant to leave the one love that has been their entire life from childhood (Federico 1983):

> It's very short, it's a short career. Pray that you'll be lucky and your body will be able to withstand the rigors of it. (Interview, Michael 1991)

> Other art forms have longer lifespans. Of all the arts it's the lowest on the totem pole and probably the most refined. With all the work it took you to get there, nobody can just jump in and do it. I certainly think we're all crazy. (Interview, Michael 1991)

Conclusion

The majority of ballet dancers that I have spoken with would not change their career choices. They are well aware of the problems they face in being involved in such a competitive and difficult profession. Most recognize that they have missed out on many things that others have experienced and yet, even with their knowledge and complaining, they believe they are able to do something that only a select few people have the ability, determination, and ambition to attempt. No dancer I have spoken with ever said they were sorry they chose a career in professional ballet.

We can look at the involvement of ballet dancers in their profession and recognize that this type of activity does not involve only one aspect of their lives, but requires a total commitment and involvement. In many ways it is like professional sport, but does not have the protections that huge salaries and players' associations provide. Also, because it involves activities that the public does not understand or participate in, to the same degree that they do in sport, it is a more separate and isolating experience. The dancer identity is one that engulfs and overwhelms all other aspects of their life. Further research needs to be done to discover what combination of skills and motives combine in developing the dancer identity and how this identity survives the transformation when dancers can no longer dance.

NOTES

1. This research has been supported by a grant from the University of Windsor. I would like to thank Bob Prus, Janice Drakich, and Debra Matheson for reading this paper and for their suggestions. I especially want to thank Leif Lorenz for sharing his expertise and for his help with interviewing.

Getting Involved in the Shuffleboard World

Eldon Snyder

Research in recent years has focused on leisure as a phenomenon in its own right rather than as a mere complement to, or compensation for, work. Kelly (1981) notes that the meanings associated with leisure are often *relational*, that is, they center on primary social relationships. Presumably, this increased attention to the social context of leisure reflects the fact that for many people leisure activities are not a residual or something left over; rather, they are a primary source of self-fulfillment and a "central life interest" (Dubin 1979; Stebbins 1982). Although a case can be made for viewing leisure as a problem, particularly for retirees whose identities remain fixed on a diminished occupational role, it is, for many older adults, a source of social integration.

Research shows that many older people manifest low levels of leisure activity. For example, in a study of leisure activity across the life span, Gordon, Gaitz, and Scott (1976) report that the youngest respondents (age twenty–twenty-nine) were almost four times more likely to participate in leisure activities than the oldest respondents (seventy-five years and over). The irony of these findings is that the aged often are released from the occupational obligations of their earlier life and have more time to pursue leisure activities, assuming that they are in good health. Furthermore, as Unruh (1983, 17–18) has noted, the aged are a collection of people who often find that integration into society in general is problematic. Thus, leisure activity as an expressive pursuit, is a particularly significant source of collective involvement for the aged.

Earlier research has ordered leisure activities on a continuum of increasing intensities, complexity, and meanings. For example, low-intensity forms of leisure include attending movies, reading, visiting museums, television viewing, and watching athletic events. A more intense and complex participation in leisure social worlds is described by Irwin (1977) and Unruh (1983). The notion of *social worlds* has been used to understand collective responses to such leisure activities as art (Becker 1982; Gilmore 1990), surfing (Irwin 1977), rock climbing (Donnelly 1980), karate (James and Jones 1982), and running (Nash 1979). Unruh (1983, 14) defines a *social world* as "an extremely large, highly permeable, amorphous, and spatially transcendent form of social organization wherein actors are linked cognitively through shared perspectives arising out of common channels of communication." A social world incorporates a large number of people from several geographical regions who have common practices, meanings, events, procedures, and forms of communication. Furthermore, a social world facilitates integration among its participants and is a means of self-expression in that gratifications are intrinsic to the social activity itself rather than instrumental for future objectives.

In these terms shuffleboard is a leisure activity that is a distinct social world for many senior citizens. In Florida approximately 60,000 people are registered members of 430 organized shuffleboard clubs. There are 11,000 members representing 220 clubs in the California Shuffleboard Association, and shuffleboard organizations and local clubs are flourishing in several other states, including Texas, Arizona, Ohio, Michigan, Indiana, North Carolina, Colorado, and New Jersey. Furthermore, competition is promoted by the International Shuffleboard Association. Many times this number of official club members play the game on a casual basis, especially in retirement communities in Florida, Texas, Arizona, and California.

Many of these players are senior citizens who look upon shuffleboard (or in the argot of these players, *shuffling*) as a meaningful and central part of their daily lives. Participants offer characterizations such as the following: "We sure have a lot of fun shuffling"; "Time doesn't hang heavy on our hands"; "It's a way of keeping busy"; "It gives you something to get up for"; "You get to know a lot of people"; "When you retire you can't just sit in a rocking chair—that will take ten years off your life"; and "There is so much strategy and challenge to the game." In short, playing shuffleboard is a leisure activity that is a meaningful part of the lives of these senior citizens.

Within the shuffleboard social world, the intensity of involvement varies widely. Some seniors become engulfed by the activities surrounding shuffleboard; for others, involvement lacks intensity and they remain on the periphery of the social world. The pattern of involvement may also be viewed as stages through which individuals pass. In essence, the sequence of stages represents a career line. Subjectively, one can observe the way a person changes in identity, interprets, and gives meaning to the sequence of events as he or she moves from one stage of involvement in the social world to the next (Stebbins 1970a). Yet it should be noted that an increasing depth of involvement in the social world of shuffleboard is not inevitable. Indeed, there are a variety of contingencies that may enhance or hinder a continuation from one stage to the next. These contingencies are based in part on the costs involved, and on the perceived satisfactions and rewards that result from participation in this leisure activity (Becker 1960; Ritzer and Trice 1970; Prus 1984).

In summary, this article examines the social world of shuffleboard among senior citizens. Attention is given to the activity as an expressive leisure activity and the attendant contingencies that may enhance or detract from a commitment and integration into this social world. Secondly, aspects of the shuffleboard subculture (normative patterns, values, argot) will be highlighted.

Setting and Method

The data for this article were collected over a period of several years. Initially, informal conversations were held with shuffleboard players as I participated in social games with friends and family. This participation and observation led to a more systematic collection of data. Subsequently, field notes were collected and semi-structured interviews were conducted with players, their spouses, and non-tournament players who were attending and watching the Ohio State and National Shuffleboard Tournaments at Lakeside, Ohio. Additional interviews and notes were taken in Florida at the St. Petersburg and Lakeland Shuffleboard Clubs. This material was supplemented by observations, photographs, and informal discussions among players as they were waiting for court assignments, during coffee breaks, and while they were watching matches from the spectator seats. Some of these findings were originally published in *Urban Life* (Snyder 1986). The present paper is a revision of this study. The majority of the participants interviewed were retirees who play in a number of club, county, and district tournaments during the winter in Florida or Texas and in northern tournaments during the summer months. More men than women participate in these tournaments; usually about sixty percent of the tournament entrants are men. However, in terms of local club membership, in which the competition is less serious, the number of men and women is about equal.

Initial Involvement

The general pattern of involvement in the social world of shuffleboard begins at retirement when a couple moves to a retirement village—usually a mobile home park—where shuffleboard courts are available. Many of these retirement settings provide the appropriate opportunity structure for learning the game—beginner lessons and informal local club and *potluck* (doubles competition in which the partners are randomly drawn) tournaments. Often the initial involvement is promoted by other players, who provide a form of sponsored recruitment for the beginner. Socialization into shuffleboard reflects the generic processes that are evident in socialization into other sports and leisure activities (Snyder and Spreitzer 1989, 78–98). This process of involvement is illustrated in the following comment by a female player:

> We [my husband and I] didn't know anything about shuffleboard when we moved to Florida. Because we were into boating, we went to a particular park because of the opportunities for boating. There were so many activities in this park we didn't have time for the boat. Then we got involved in shuffleboard. At first we just went to watch, then my husband refereed, and pretty soon he was playing. Then I was keeping score, and the next thing I knew I was playing. From there we went to one tournament and we placed second in the consolations. From then on we were hooked; he gave up golf, we gave up square-dancing and bowling. We had all kinds of activities going and we gave up everything for shuffleboard. That's just about what happens to everybody.

When asked how he became involved, one man gave the following response, which seems to be a typical description of how many seniors come to take up the sport:

> We moved to a mobile home park in Texas for the winter. At the park they had some shuffleboard courts and I would go over and watch. One day they were one player short for doubles. I filled in and have been shuffling ever since.

The wife of another player provided the following account of how her husband became involved in the game:

> My husband used to play golf all the time. Then he saw some good shuffle-board players and he became intrigued with why the players didn't try to score; they just tried to keep the board clear. He started talking to shufflers and found out there is a lot of strategy in the game. Then he gave up golf completely. He plays shuffleboard all the time.

In short, the primary factors that players associated with their initial involvement in shuffleboard are the availability of courts, social influence of friends, and the intriguing aspects of the game itself.

In our society, shuffleboard is perceived as a game for the elderly, and the stigma associated with being old (Hochschild 1973; Matthews 1979; Unruh 1983) may be transferred to shuffleboard. Thus, some senior citizens refrain from playing because they say, "It's an old person's game and too tame," or "When I get too old to play golf or tennis, I'll take up shuffleboard." As one player noted, "Whenever the news media cover a tournament, they take pictures of the oldest player—usually a woman—to illustrate a shuffle-board player." One Florida player commented, "I always shied away from shuffleboard because I figured that I would play shuffleboard when I had a cane in one hand and a cue in the other. I figured it was strictly for old folks. Now I regret I didn't start when I was about fifty."

All shuffleboard players are aware of this negative connotation associated with the game, however, they often find ways to overcome this negativism by providing positive justifications for their participation. Justifications are verbal accounts whereby a person admits there may be a negative aspect to an activity, but, at the same time, attempts to justify it by redefining it as more positive than negative (Scott and Lyman 1968; Snyder and Spreitzer 1979; Stokes and Hewitt 1976). Thus, shuffleboard players frequently turn the age factor into a very positive factor and will point out that one of the advantages of the game is that it is suitable for people of all ages. One grandmother said "It's a great game to play with your grandkids when they come to visit." Another player noted, "In our (mobile home) park there are six to eight people who are over nintey years old and they are very good players." Also, players will often identify elderly shufflers in their club and attribute their longevity and vitality to an active participation in the game. These justifications—to be involved in a healthy, challenging social activity—are often cited by players as the rationale and legitimation for their initial and continued participation.

Degrees of Involvement

Numerous comments from shufflers indicate that after retirement they moved to a mobile home park and were involved in several activities such as golfing, bowling, and boating and then became primarily interested in shuffleboard. The following story was told by one player: A man who had never watched shuffleboard went to a park in Florida. His friend said, "You mean you have never seen shuffleboard." He answered, "No." The friend's reply was, "Then turn around and leave, otherwise you'll become addicted to it."

The changes in relationships and activities surrounding shuffleboard over time constitute elements of what was earlier defined as stages of a career. That is, initially it is a form of casual leisure activity and is usually one of several leisure activities that retirees engage in. However, if participation moves to a more intense level, increased skills, knowledge, experience, and associations may promote a progression toward more encompassing involvement through tournament competition.[1]

Social Players and Tournament Players

In the shuffleboard social world a career, in an objective sense, is defined by the distinction between a *social player* (sometimes called a "fun player") and a *serious* (or tournament) player. Social players approach the game casually and non-competitively, generally playing only at their local courts. Most mobile home parks provide a variety of leisure activities, including checkers, card games, dancing, and billiards, and social players generally participate in several of these activities. However, if a social player becomes a serious player, shuffleboard becomes the central life interest and a major part of his or her daily routine. If the weather permits, serious players usually play every day for several hours and compete in a number of tournaments—often several tournaments a week within a radius of 75 to 100 miles (120 to 160 kilometers).

Furthermore, serious players' social lives and friendship networks primarily involve other tournament players. They frequently travel to tournaments in vans with other players—usually as couples—and much of their social life and conversations are related to shuffleboard. As one player noted, "Our best friends are shufflers, we're closer to them than our own relatives." When another player was asked about social relationships in shuffleboard, he said, "Oh yes, most of our friends are also shufflers." When asked if they talk about shuffleboard, he replied, "You better believe it. We often go with three other couples to eat out and they also shuffle. When we get together it's, 'If I had made this shot or if I had made that shot.' I guess we have to cry on each others' shoulders." Another serious shuffler said, "Shuffling is where you make your friends. That's the nice part of shuffling. You go out and make friends here in the South, then go North and play tournaments and meet your old friends, and then go back to Florida and there are your friends again." Informal conversations of tournament players at coffee breaks and at refreshment tables (when waiting for pairings and games to be posted), in the spectator stands, and at tournament social events reinforce this affective dimension. Similarly, when tournaments begin and end, one can observe that greetings and farewells often are accompanied by hugs and kisses, as might be expected of close friends or relatives.[2]

Because many tournament opponents are close friends who are seriously competing against one another, there are a variety of deference rituals displayed that serve to protect these relationships and the participants' egos. Thus, tournament matches are conducted with a decorum of politeness, personal consideration in the form of compliments ("good shot," "you really played well," "I was lucky"), handshakes, and overall humility and self-control. Although players may show disgust with their own performance, there is little negative emotion displayed toward the opponent. These deference rituals protect friendships in highly competitive tournament contexts in which the game strategies, discussed in the following portion of this article, would be viewed by social players as "too competitive" and "in poor taste." Among tournament players these highly competitive strategies are defined as "part of the game."

Variations in How the Game is Played

The distinction between social and tournament players is perhaps most evident in the approach toward the game by players in these levels of involvement. For example, the tournament player is often ridiculed by the social player as being too serious—"they play for blood," and "it becomes too much like work." One tournament player explained, "The *locals* (social players who play only in their local mobile home park) dislike playing with us because they feel we are too aggressive." This aggressive play is displayed by trying to "keep the board (the court) clear" (or clean) of discs that might otherwise be hit by one's opponent into the 10–off area (a kitchen shot). Keeping the court clear is accomplished by hitting one's opponent's discs off the court; however, one's own discs should not be left on the court either (that is, they should not "stick") in order to eliminate the probability of having one's opponent bump them into the kitchen.

Frequently, the "clearing game" requires hitting the discs hard, but not squarely. The clearing game is also based on scoring with the "hammer shot"—the last shot in the sequence. If one does not have the hammer, the strategy involves attempting to situate a disc in the front part of the court to block another disc that may be in a scoring area. Of course, in this case one's opponent, who has the hammer shot, is trying to keep the board clear of discs and score with the hammer. Additional strategies are based on one's score, the opponent's score, the position and number of discs on the board, and so on. In general, these strategies are disdained by the social players, who are likely to play a "board game," that is, put their discs on the court (board) and count up the scores without using the tactics they define as too aggressive and which they associate with tournament play. One serious player said the local club players want to play a "footsy game," while some local clubs in Florida have signs that read, "No hard shooting."

For the serious player, the advanced level of competition, strategy, and overall challenge provide the intrinsic rewards that promote continued involvement in the game. For the uninformed, the goal of shuffleboard appears simple—push the discs down the court and score points. However, as noted above, this description is too simplistic. Universally, tournament players characterize shuffleboard as a game of skill and strategy. One player noted, "This game is so challenging, you can lose points as well as score; this makes it even more challenging."

The differences between social and tournament players are also apparent in the serious way tournament players prepare for a game. Many tournament players take notes on the conditions of each court prior to the match; these notes include information about the *drift* (tendency for a disc to slide off-center due to a slant in the court) and *speed* (smoothness) of the court. Players frequently refer to their notes during a game as they prepare for a shot. Likewise, prior to a game, some players ritualistically examine the edges and bottoms of the discs and mark them with chalk according to the order in which they will shoot them. Discs may vary somewhat in smoothness; players will therefore take this into account when the disc is played. Marking the discs and consulting one's notes during the game are manifest actions that are indeed functional to the game outcome, but they also create the impression that the player is prepared, knows the court, and has poise. These actions thus represent forms of posturing and image management that may have a "psyching out" or intimidating effect on less-experienced opponents.

Interestingly, the degree of seriousness and levels of play seem to vary according to the region in which the game takes place. These differences are evident in a portion of an interview with a tournament player from Texas:

> PLAYER: When we play, we play more for fun. Here [Lakeside, Ohio], these people from Florida don't want you to say a word when they shuffle. They want to concentrate. To me it's too much like you're out for blood. I like to have fun.

> INTERVIEWER: You think there is a difference between the type of play in Florida and Texas?

> PLAYER: Yes, that's right in terms of seriousness; everybody likes to win but we're not out for blood.

> INTERVIEWER: I notice that some players, as the lady over there, mark their blocks [discs].

> PLAYER: That's a Florida lady. They number their blocks 1, 2, 3, 4. They also make notes on how the blocks play. They're really out for everything they can get.

It is evident from these accounts that the social and tournament players approach the game differently. These variations include the overall time and energy devoted to shuffleboard, skill, competitive orientation, and degree of personal identity invested in the game.

Ranking Structure

Among tournament players, there is a ranking system based on tournament performances of the past year. These performances and point totals are published in the state shuffleboard association yearbooks. Players who have won major tournaments may accumulate a sufficient number of points to be reclassified from amateur to professional status (in some states the professionals are termed "experts"). Some tournaments are open to both amateurs and professionals; other tournaments are limited to one classification or the other. Professionals receive money rather than trophies for their successes in tournament play. The money received for winning a tournament varies—often fifty to one hundred dollars. The symbolic value is, however, more significant than the amount of money. Additionally, the top professionals in men's and women's categories are classified as "masters." Thus, the classification system or typology of players on the shuffleboard career line includes the social players and serious players; then, based on tournament competition, the serious players are amateurs, professionals, and masters.

On the subjective level, the ranking system within shuffleboard, as in other forms of competition, may help establish a sense of career accomplishment, identity, and status among players. One player interviewed at the Lakeland Shuffleboard Club proudly pointed out his name on the bulletin board as one of the top professional players in the Florida Shuffleboard Association. And the following comments by a woman player illustrate her sense of identity, well-being, and accomplishment that are anchored in the shuffleboard social world:

> Here in Ohio I'm classified as an expert. I've just been elected to the Shuffleboard Hall of Fame. I'm so thrilled over that. I've won the nationals, singles and doubles, and the Ohio singles and doubles. You have to do a lot of winning. You have to qualify and be nominated by a club. The Akron club nominated me. The committee voted for me according to my record. Not everyone gets in, only the best. There are a lot of great players in the Hall of Fame. Some have passed on, but their pictures remain in there.

The ranking system and the feelings of self-esteem associated with successful tournament competition represent an aspect of extrinsic satisfactions associated with the game. The extrinsic dimension, evident in all forms of competition, includes the symbols of success in the form of victories, trophies, medals, money, recognition, and prestige that are personally satisfying and provide a continued motivation to participate. These rewards were illustrated by a player who proudly produced for the interviewer two lists of tournaments that he and his wife had entered in the past year. The lists included notations about their performances along with a photograph of the trophies they had won.

Disinvolvement

Involvement in the shuffleboard social world may be diminished when the contingencies of commitment such as the social influence of friends, intrinsic and extrinsic satisfactions, and legitimating reasons for participating no longer exist. For social players commitment and involvement in the social world is minimal, perhaps based only on the social dimension of the game itself, and they are likely to maintain a variety of other leisure activities. However, serious tournament players are deeply embedded in the structure of shuffleboard and to leave this source of identity and social integration is likely to be stressful. Indeed, for some tournament players shuffleboard has replaced the satisfactions they previously received from their occupations. The sentiments of many players are reflected by one player in answer to the question: "If you didn't have shuffleboard, what would you do?" His reply was, "I'll tell you, I don't know what I would do; I would really miss it. I would be very bored down here [in Florida] without it."

A number of respondents were asked about players who have given up shuffleboard. Typically, they were unable to think of tournament players who had done so, except when forced to by declining health:

INTERVIEWER: Do people ever drop out of shuffleboard?

PLAYER: Some people do for health reasons. They wouldn't otherwise.

INTERVIEWER: What happens when a husband or wife dies?

PLAYER: There are a lot of women who are still coming [to tournaments] after their husbands die, and husbands who have lost their wives eventually come back. They stay away for a little while because it's hard to face people, but they come back. It keeps them occupied and their friends are in shuffling.

Another elderly lady player gave the following poignant account:

My husband died over here on court 11 in 1976. There was no warning; it was instant. We used to travel all over Florida to tournaments. We'd leave after church on Sunday afternoon and be gone a couple days, then return home, and maybe there would be another tournament on Thursday and Friday. I don't travel to tournaments as much as we used to, but I still play in tournaments. These were our friends and they are still my friends.

In general, involvement in the shuffleboard social world among tournament players continues until the infirmities of age force a disengagement. However, this process is often gradual and, as ill health or age forces them to reduce their participation, shufflers often continue to play in smaller tournaments within their own locality. This limited form of disengagement is illustrated by a ninety-year-old shuffler at Lakeland, Florida, who gave the following description of his playing career:

I've played shuffleboard for thirty years. I was an amateur and won thirty trophies. Then I became a professional, but now I don't play the big tournaments anymore; yet I still play in the local tournaments and I help out here at the club—organizing play and supervising the courts.

Conclusion

Among senior citizens, leisure activities may be a primary source of life satisfaction. This article has focused on the participation of senior citizens in the social world of shuffleboard. Involvement in shuffleboard serves as a socially integrating process. Levels of involvement are represented by two extreme types of participants: social players and serious tournament players. The latter may be further subdivided into amateurs, professionals, and masters. In reality, of course, these types of players reflect a continuum of shuffleboard ability and commitment. The processual emergence of involvement in the shuffleboard social world is determined by the contingencies that include the perceived justifications and benefits of participation, social support from friends, and a variety of intrinsic and extrinsic satisfactions. Negative factors that may detract from progressing to the high levels of involvement include distaste for the competitiveness of tournament play, the stigma of the game being viewed as an old person's game, and the time and energy necessary to become a tournament player. For the most serious players, shuffleboard often becomes an engulfing central life interest that provides personal fulfillment, enhancement of identity, and self-expression. An analysis of the shuffleboard subculture and the career progression provides a generic model of leisure that may be generalized to other spheres of leisure activity. This knowledge is particularly important for understanding and promoting the happiness and well-being of the senior citizens in our society.

NOTES

1. This career line in shuffleboard is similar to the steps described by Nash (1979) and Altheide and Pfuhl (1980) in a "running career." That is, among runners there are distinctions between casual (sometimes called joggers) and serious runners. Objectively, this process can be observed in the lowering of running times and increased participation in road races. Subjectively, runners report that running, as reflected in their level of performance, has a significant impact on their self feelings.

2. Other studies have also noted the importance of age-peers—persons with similar values, interests, and experiences for the morale of older people (Blau 1973; Wood and Robertson 1978). In this regard, Wood and Robertson (1978) report data from a sample of grandparents that indicate friendship relations are of greater importance than kinship interactions in the maintenance of morale and life satisfaction.

Recruitment Practices of the Christian Heritage Party[1]

Scott Grills

The concept of recruitment has proven useful for examining the question of how actors "get involved" in a range of social careers. As a processually grounded concept, recruitment is responsive to the dynamic nature of social life. This paper examines some of the implications of interpreting recruitment as complex social action in its own right, involving themes of negotiation, emergence, perspectives, self indications, and social process. Such an approach encourages us to reject overly simplified notions such as "peer pressure" or "my friends wanted me to," as explanations for initial involvement. Viewing recruitment as joint action (Blumer 1969b), this paper examines the promotion of political involvements as a practical activity. Specifically, I examine recruiter concerns relative to issues of *trust* and *security, reputational dynamics,* and *performance competencies.* In addition, I discuss various associational and relational qualities which may serve to facilitate or hinder one's initial involvements in political campaigns.

"Telling" of Recruitment

In *Culture and Truth* Rosaldo writes, "The ethnographer, as a positioned subject, grasps certain human phenomena better than others…. By the same token, so called natives are also positioned subjects who have a distinctive mix of insight and blindness" (Rosaldo 1989, 19).

The task of the ethnographer is to balance the tension of the member's intimate familiarity with local cultures while not substituting audience perspectives for explanation. The ethnographer draws upon the activities and accounts of participants selectively, utilizing these materials as the data upon which claims are grounded. The ethnography is a systematic "juggling" of blind spots—an attempt to construct a rich account of social process and social life. Hence, Silverman's (1989) caution to utilize qualitative data as a point of departure for analysis, rather than as a substitute for it, is an essential requirement of successful field study.

If we were dealing with equations, or barometric pressure, the principle would be a simple one. We are not to confuse the data with an analysis of the data. But for the ethnographer the line is not so easily drawn. The materials that make up the data are the actions and arguments of lively actors who are engaged in making sense of their worlds. The ethnographer enters that world, albeit on something of a unique footing. The data are not something distant from the researcher, but are part of the lived experience of the ethnographer. For example, Whyte's (1981) actions held direct implications for Doc's place within his community, Prus and Sharper (1991) confronted the impact of their performances on the hustling activities of others, while Haas and Shaffir (1987) became intimately familiar with the personal concerns and fears of medical students.

It is within this context that the ethnographer must struggle with the careers of involvement of participants. If we are interested in the question of how people become marijuana users (Becker 1973), prostitutes (Prus and Irini 1980), or gun collectors (Olmstead 1988) we may *ask* them, and their responses inform us how members *think* they ended up where they are. Participants frequently point to the influences of friends, family, and others—to the sociological notion of recruitment. We find similar themes expressed in a range of substantive materials such as entering the shuffleboard subculture or obtaining a tattoo:

> We moved to a mobile home park in Texas for the winter. At the park they had some shuffleboard courts and I would go over and watch. One day they were one player short for doubles. I filled in and have been shuffling ever since. (Snyder in this volume)

> We were up in Maine and a bunch of us were just talking about getting tattoos—me and my friends and my cousins. One time my cousin came back from the service with one and I liked it.... The only place I knew about was ———'s down in Providence. We were going right by there on our way back home so we stopped and all got them. (Sanders 1991, 42)

In his essay "Grief and a Headhunter's Rage," in *Culture and Truth: The Remaking if Social Analysis,* Rosaldo (1989, 1–21) struggles with the apparent oversimplicity of participants' accounts of head-hunting in much the same way we confront the deceptively simple accounts of recruitment.[2] Ethnographic data on involvements emphasizes the associational nature of the memberships we come to share. Our friends and families seem quite capable of "getting us into" a range of initial involvements that might otherwise have remained outside of our experiences.

As a positioned subject, the recruited actor can share with us just that— that they were recruited. The recruited are often the targets of prior social constructions, which they may have had no direct hand in producing. They have at best limited, and, in many cases, no access to prior activities directed at facilitating recruitment. Therefore, to gain a more complete account of the processes of recruitment and the joint action that encourages initial involvements, it is essential for the ethnographer to examine the activities of recruiters.

By attending to the activities of recruiters as well as the recruited, we construct a fully social model of recruitment. Family, friends, and others become lively actors attending to a range of contingencies in their recruitment endeavors—contingencies and problematics which the recruited actor may be unable to share with us, but which are essential to an appreciation of recruitment as social action.

Recruitment in a Community Context

While recruitment reflects generic aspects of the career contingencies of involvement, it nevertheless occurs within a specific cultural context. The problematic nature of recruitment takes on its "full value" given specific involvements, and the accompanying hindrances and limitations to participation. There are few involvements where *any* person would serve as an acceptable recruit. Even voting in a democracy requires one to possess appropriate credentials of age, mental stability, and residency. Reflecting such concerns over the relative suitability of potential recruits, we find recruiters attending to various dimensions which serve to qualify some people as potential recruits and to disqualify others. These hindrances to recruitment might be profitably cast as: *trust/secrecy* concerns, *reputational/identity* concerns, and *performance* concerns.

Trust/Secrecy Concerns

Prus (1989a, 104) views trust as "a quality attributed to persons by others; it denotes an anticipation that these persons will act in manners consistent with one's own interests." Trust is something of an interpersonal gamble. To identify another as trustworthy is to place expectations upon acts that have yet to be accomplished. To trust is to engage in risk-taking activity with stakes that may vary greatly.

When community members perceive themselves to be at risk through the nature of their involvements and activities, their recruitment activities may reflect this threat by prioritizing concerns related to *trust* and *secrecy*. To promote the membership of others is to admit them to the "secrets of the tribe": performance elements often concealed from audience members, and possibly stigmatizing information which holds the potential to discredit (Goffman 1959; 1963). Sharing in the potential of disclosure, members hold a unique power, which once expended, is lost (Simmel 1950). As Teft (1980) demonstrates, the influence of the "secret to be kept" is experienced cross-culturally, whether one is confronting a secret society or a society of secrets. In such settings recruitment is an activity that exposes the community to the additional risk of disclosure. Therefore, members may be selective in encouraging the participation of others, or in revealing their own involvements to others.

As one might expect, the extent to which recruiters attend to trust/secrecy concerns is variable. My research on recruitment within fourth-party politics provides for an example of such diversity. Within the same political party, we will find some members utilizing rather elaborate means to conceal their involvements from family and employers, while others will publicly display their involvements through the use of bumper stickers and the like. In addition, recruiters may attend to the extent to which encouraging involvements might place the community at risk. The following material illustrates this theme in a political context—one respondent speaking of the experiences of the Communist left, another of the Christian right:

> Security is important, but you can't be paranoid about every person who walks through the door either, but you can't be too careful. We are threats to the bourgeoisie, and we will be more of a threat to them in the future than we are now. So if we aren't careful, if everyone knows everyone else, if your records are public, then when the time comes, we will be very easy to neutralize. The bourgeoisie will move in and capture everyone. But as it is, we have been careful, we all have party names and real names and many of the names you have heard here are party names (party member, Communist Party of Canada, Marxist-Leninist).

> If you walk up to the average Canadian and say "Christian" they say, "Phew Phew, Jimmy Swaggart, Jim Bakker, Blech." ... Even before we got started we gave ourselves a weight to carry and yet we didn't mind in a way because the Lord said, "My yoke I have given you is light." ... Society is not ready to accept the rules so every time we go forward we risk the tribulations. There are a lot of people who do not want us doing what we are doing so every time you make a public statement, you ask for support or membership you risk that (national executive, Christian Heritage Party).

Reputational Concerns

Recruiters may also attend to how the participation of others may degrade or tarnish the established identity of the collective enterprise, given the antici-pated response of some audiences. As Goffman (1959, 85) notes in his exam-ination of teams, "the object of a performer is to sustain a particular definition of the situation." Yet the performers we encourage to join in our joint acts hold the potential to challenge the very bases of the "local cultures" we have constructed (Gubrium 1991).

As Gubrium (1991, 132–33) has noted, "locally meaningful differences have been noted in what may appear to be formally similar establishments." In research on political party formation (Grills 1989), I found that while riding[3] associations shared in their structural relations to the national party organization, they nevertheless developed unique local cultures. These cultures varied relative to such themes as the prioritization of ties relative to national, provincial, or local boundaries, the inclusivity of membership, policy position, and organized support to executive membership in the national organization. These differences are important, as it is from the col-lective experiences arising out of shared action that we develop notions of what we are undertaking and the purposes and value of our involvements. Through such activities, local cultures develop reputations amongst their various constituencies and participants' identities are influenced by such asso-ciations. Such *reputational concerns* (and by implication, audience dynamics) hold import for recruiters when considering the potential involvements of others. Whether or not the other is seen as the "right kind of person" for the established local culture may play a part in recruitment efforts.

In the "perception is reality" world of federal politics, reputational concerns may be particularly important in recruitment decisions. Such is the case with the Christian Heritage Party (C.H.P.), a Canadian federal political party which nominated sixty-three candidates in the federal election of 1988 and received just over 100,000 votes. During my field research with the C.H.P. (1987–89), the recruitment of general membership was marked by what might be termed "entry level" concerns over such themes as the reli-gious orthodoxy of potential members, as well as any previous discrediting political involvements.[4] In contrast, when recruiting potential candidates, reputational concerns extended to such themes as gender, occupation, eth-nicity, integrity, regional representation, previous convictions (criminal and/or other), and adherence to key party policy:

> We have to be very careful that the people we place in control are not people
> who have different ideas in regards to the way a Christian party should behave
> and should act. [In] fact, we have recognized this early on in the party—that
> we had to have something like the integrity analysis in place. Basically, you
> could bring anybody into a political party, but the fact is, when you bring

people in you are accepting their world view.... I mean what is the point in doing what we've done, investing the time and money and effort we have put into this to have some bozo come out of left field and say, "Hey, homosexuality is fine." (national executive)

Performance Concerns

Reflecting the problematic nature of the recruitment of others, *performance concerns* may overlap with reputational concerns. Reputational concerns focus on the question of "who we are," while performance concerns focus on the question of "what we do together." Performance concerns prioritize the anticipated ability of the potential recruit to "fit in" to the activities and performances undertaken by the collective. In settings where there is little diversification of performance possibilities, the distinction between reputational and performance concerns may prove less than helpful. For example, membership in organized, competitive sport implies participation. If who we are is a "winning baseball team," and what we do together is "play baseball," there may be little room for the person who loves the game but lacks the range of desirable performance qualities of running, hitting, throwing, catching, or coaching.[5]

In settings with higher levels of role diversification, however, reputational concerns over admitting the other as a member may be distinct from concerns over the performance competence of the member. The relative importance of being perceived as "solid," "trustworthy," or "one of us," varies, relative to performance concerns which prioritize the techniques and motives necessary for participation within a local culture (Sutherland, Cressey, and Luckenbill, 1992). For example, Prus and Sharper's work illustrates the importance of developing a "larceny sense" among card and dice hustlers:

> The position they take is that "You can't have feelings on the road." And it is true, if you start saying to yourself, "Well maybe I better not beat this guy or that guy," you would soon be out of business or at least you would really cut down on your profits. (Prus and Sharper 1991, 49)

In the C.H.P., performance concerns tend to occupy a secondary place relative to reputational and identity concerns. This reflects the diversity of the practical tasks confronting a developing political organization. Where personnel needs run the range from envelope stuffers to party leader, there is little basis to disqualify a potential member on performance grounds. Therefore, unlike settings where performance qualities of actors serve to disqualify them from membership, within the C.H.P., we find performance qualities serving to enhance the desirability of some recruits relative to others, particularly those with valued political experience and/or an extended "power base."

As national and provincial organizers have emphasized, the successful recruitment of those who have been previously politically active is a high priority. Such individuals bring an established familiarity with the political process and provide insight and contacts relative to the "opposition." The practical constraints on a new party dictate that if they are seeking a politically experienced candidate, riding executive, policy chair, or leader, that experience will have had to be gained elsewhere. To bring these people "on board" requires something of a political conversion which, in and of itself, is problematic. The following quotations, gathered several months apart, speak to the dual concerns of the desirability of recruiting the politically experienced actor and concerns that may accompany distancing oneself from previous commitments:

> Sometimes you have to be willing to go the extra mile to get the people involved you want. Take H. K. for example. R. and I really had to be persistent. We had to argue with him, to convince him. He had no intention of joining us but we knew he was interested, and it is not every day you have a chance to bring on side a former M.P., a member of the ——— government, and former ——— [title identifies specific parliamentary responsibility]. (provincial executive)

> Changing my politics was a little like changing my church. It takes time. You have to admit to yourself that you were barking up the wrong tree.... J. and B. were by the house twice before I gave it a really serious thought.... Then they said, "How about you? Are you coming along with us on this?" My reaction was no, no way this thing won't work. I'm known for my politics around here, I'm not going to jump horses now. I decided staying put served myself, not my country or my God. Once I decided that, I didn't have a choice left. I'm telling you that signing that membership form was not one of the easiest things I have done in my life. (local organizer)

Recruitment and Associational Dynamics

In the preceding, I have argued that recruitment is problematic activity and have examined some dimensions to which recruiters may attend when designating appropriate targets for their activities. However, my understanding of recruitment also attends to the emergent and negotiated qualities of human action. Therefore, an examination of the *associational* and *relational* dynamics which accompany recruitment activities is essential. The following data primarily address identity and performance concerns of membership recruitment within the C.H.P. Reflecting recruitment as one aspect of "relationship work," I contextualize recruitment tasks relative to common avenues of political recruitment—through a knowledge of personal history and through shared affiliations.

Recruitment Within an Extended Personal History Context

Hunting-and-gathering and other small-scale societies are unique, in part, relative to the level of familiarity that members share with one another (Marshall 1976; Service 1979; Brymer 1984; Raybeck 1984). The life circumstances of those who live in such communities is such that a wide range of information and experiential evidence of others is readily at hand. By sharing a full range of experiences with others, fairly complete personal histories are constructed. Of course, access to such extended personal histories is not limited to comparatively isolated or strictly bounded communities. In larger scale associations members are capable of constructing fairly complete dossiers on a range of significant "others". As such, we come to know our intimates as complete actors who are identified by a range of qualities and are therefore not as easily characterized by some singular dimension or deviant social status (Lemert 1951).

Recruiters may utilize such personal histories to identify likely "targets" for their recruitment efforts. Given the more complete information that extended personal histories afford, recruiters possess a fairly high degree of certainty in their ability to identify those who are likely to be receptive to their message and, conversely, to anticipate those less likely to share their enthusiasm. The personal relationships established between actors may, at times, have more bearing on the initial success of recruitment efforts than do qualities strictly associated with the party:

> I don't know how to explain it to you. Look at the membership form, I couldn't even ask my father to sign that. He couldn't, that's it. But my brother is a completely different story, I showed it to him, now he is starting to get things going [where he lives]. You just know, this is for M. I've got to get him signed up. He would want to be signed up. (party member)

> To be absolutely honest with you I am not here tonight for the Christian Heritage Party. I am here for [J.]. I have never seen him throw himself at anything quite like he has taken on this. His father and I went to school together, I've known him since he was up to here [indicates about "knee high"]. One night he got up the courage and came by the house.... I told him to put all the papers away and that I had two questions for him. The first one was "Did he believe that this would be a better thing for Canada?" He said "yes" as firmly and as clearly as he could. The next question was "Where do we sign?" I have never known [J.] to try and pull the wool over anybody's eyes. If he believed in what he was doing enough to ask for my help, then he's got it. (party member)

Recruitment via Shared Affiliations

Rarely are relations to those with whom we share our worlds so complete as to provide for an extended personal history. More often than not, we share fairly selective parts of our lives with others. It is upon these shared experiences that we construct generalized and typified notions of others (Schutz 1962). For those who attempt to recruit others into the C.H.P. "fold," such generalized notions of those more or less likely to be responsive to their message serve to identify networks of affiliation upon which recruitment efforts can be based. Whereas extended personal histories aid in identifying specific others who are more likely to get involved, an attentiveness to shared affiliations focuses upon the generalized other (Mead 1934). Thus, recruitment efforts tend to be directed toward audiences and networks of association considered valuable by recruiters for contacting likely members. A review of data on this theme emphasizes the party's utilization of three complementary yet distinct networks of contact as sources of potential recruits. Specifically, these are *church affiliations, political affiliations,* and *complementary crusading affiliations.*

Recruitment and Church Affiliation

Churches provide a comparatively rich ground for party recruitment activities. This should be less than surprising. Like the C.H.P., selected Christian churches represent the few associations which may require similar statements of belief from their members. Recruiters know in advance that members of certain churches *can* sign their name to a profession of belief in the trinity and the inerrancy of the Bible. Given the party's emphasis on recruiting only those with a certain system of belief, various Christian churches provide a network of association through which "believers" can be accessed.

Those who actively undertake church-based recruitment speak of the process in mixed terms. Working within one's own faith group is not necessarily easy or non-problematic. Aspects of these activities may prove unsettling as successes arise from unexpected "allies" and assumptions of the relative unity and like-mindedness of "believers" are challenged:

> The way I will know if this thing is going to go anywhere is when I look at the members of our local executive. When I started, I knew everyone from somewhere else. Now there are people there that I have met only through the C.H.P. It is a good thing. If you had told my wife five years ago that I would be over at the Roman Catholic church meeting with the priest asking for his help on anything, she would have laughed you right out of the house. But I was there. We had a good talk. There was a lot we agreed on. Now one of his people sits on our executive. He has brought a whole new group of people to us. That is the way this thing will grow. Next week I have a meeting with a Baptist committee. (local organizer)

> There are some though that I just can't get. It bothers me too. Like if you don't sign up, what should it worry me? But these people are in my church. If they don't think the Lord has a place in politics, where else do they think He

doesn't belong? That bothers me. That really bothers me. Some nights when I come home I have prayed for the ones who wouldn't become members. (local organizer)

Church-based recruitment is accomplished with varying degrees of formal sanction from church officials. At times a congregation is "worked" for membership exclusively by the laity within the group. On other occasions clergy have become relatively active in the process of promoting the "well-being" of the C.H.P. within their congregation. During the course of this research, clergy have led their congregations in prayer calling for a divine blessing upon the party's endeavors, have turned their sanctuaries over to party promoters to provide the sermon during regularly held services of worship, have personally endorsed the C.H.P., and have called on their congregations to vote Christian. Such "clergy sanctioning" activities were observed within a range of denominations—from Roman Catholic to Canadian Reformed to churches of the Pentecostal Assemblies of Canada. The relative importance of clergy involvement should not be undervalued. However, congregation members and clergy alike express a range of concerns over direct clerical involvement in party promotion:

> I stop just short of telling my congregation to become members of the C.H.P. I do tell them that it is time for them to become politically active. I tell them that if they don't, there may not be a church left for their children to worship in.... Inside my church we set our spiritual lives straight and ask the Lord for his guidance. But it can't stop there. It is time to roll up our sleeves and get to work. I for one am not above that. (clergy/party member)

> I was worried about what would happen tonight. I took a big risk you know. Letting these people into my church. I have never held a political discussion like that in the sanctuary. I prayed about my decision a lot. It came down to this, if there ever was a time when God's buildings needed to be made political—you know—it is now. This election coming up is crucial. I wish these people well. They are standing up for what a lot of us believe. But this is the end of the road for me. I can't stick my neck out any further. If this is going to go any further, one of the people in the church who heard them tonight is going to have to take over. (clergy/membership status unknown)

Recruitment and Political Affiliation

Hall (1972, 98) suggests that "there exist multiple collective goals which when implemented require political behavior for implementation." However, an understanding which posits a relationship between desired ends and the necessity for politically oriented action is not something that party recruiters assume all potential recruits share. For example, denominational affiliation may indicate a prior commitment to the faith claims of the C.H.P. Yet this commonality of faith provides no assurance that members will see their religious beliefs as requiring political action of them and may serve to generally challenge the appropriateness of secular activity. In contrast, those who are politically active have demonstrated a commitment to political process as an agent of change. Therefore, those with prior involvements in political campaigns comprise a "target group" for recruitment activities in that they tend to share in a general level of politicization—a common "faith" in the relevance and importance of political involvement.[6] As one local organizer put it:

> You build a party like this slowly. I have been talking to some of [the incumbent's] people. I know that they aren't all happy with him. There are some very strong Christians who worked to get him elected that I know through my church. I took them aside and tried to politely show them that they had been let down. It didn't take too much convincing. But once we got them with us, it was time to ask them to get us in touch with people that were involved with his campaign last time around to see if they would be willing to give us a hand. We don't get a lot of members that way but we do get some of our most important ones.

Recruitment via Complementary Crusades

As Blumer (1971) has demonstrated, the process by which any given issue is established as a social problem is an uncertain. Those who come to see a particular feature of everyday life as problematic and requiring action may construct very different plans of action and forms of association to address their concerns. While some, like those who have become involved in the C.H.P., may prioritize federal political involvement, others may choose to address concerns through a range of activities such as education campaigns, lobby groups, and direct action initiatives. Such associations, which share a common definition of the problem and yet have chosen divergent means though which to address issues of concern, I refer to as complementary crusades.

Such enterprises are complementary in that participants view their endeavors as contributing toward a common definition of the appropriate. To suggest that crusades are complementary should not be taken to imply that relations between those who are a part of such endeavors are exclusively cordial. In fact, complementary crusades are frequently in competition for membership, financial resources, and media attention. While participants may recognize a commonality of purpose, perceived differences may influence the degree of co-operation present between such enterprises.

Nevertheless, perceived commonalities of purpose have provided a basis from which C.H.P. promoters have engaged in policy-based recruitment. Such endeavors mirror key party policy by attending specifically to like-minded groups. Most notable here are recruitment efforts within the extended anti-abortion movement (Alliance for Life, Birthright), the traditionalist family-oriented lobbies (REAL Women, Family Forum), and Christian business associations (Reformed Christian Business and Professional Association, and the Christian Farm Federations). Effective policy-based recruitment hinges on demonstrating to the members of these various interest groups that the C.H.P. is the political party that represents their concerns:

> The two most important issues for us in this election are going to be daycare and abortion. They are the ones that distinguish us from the other parties. There are a lot of pro-life people out there with nowhere for their vote to go. The people who join Alliance For Life are our people. We have to get our message to them and let them know that they finally have a federal party that they can join with a clear conscience and vote for without swallowing hard first. (local organizer)

Conclusion

Recruitment is the process by which initial involvements are encouraged by others (Prus 1987, 276). As such, it is, in and of itself, a human activity appropriate for processual analysis. A more complete understanding of the process of "getting involved" requires that we be willing to move beyond the accounts of the recruited to include examination of the activities and perspectives of those engaged in the practical activity of recruitment. By so doing we view recruitment as joint action in the fullest sense of the term. Utilizing such an approach, I have examined some aspects of political recruitment undertaken in the context of party formation. The unique and particular features of the C.H.P. are central to understanding their activities.

We can also examine the relevance of this essay to the processes of recruitment more generally. In the first and last instance, the people I have examined are undertaking an activity which, in many fundamental ways, is similar to the everyday activities of those who have an interest in promoting the involvements of others. The themes I have examined—*trust, performance,* and *reputational concerns,* as well as *relational* and *associational* dynamics— impinge upon the recruitment activities of those with diverse interests. C.H.P. recruitment holds much in common with the activities of vendors, sports teams, biker gangs, university admissions officers, car club members, or conceivably, any other context where members are engaged in the social process of encouraging involvements. By attending to the fully social qualities of recruitment, we gain a clearer understanding of the extent to which our initial involvements are a part of the practical accomplishment of everyday life.

NOTES

1. Author's Note: I wish to thank Robert Prus and William Shaffir for their comments on earlier drafts of this paper. The financial support of this project by SSHRCC, McMaster University, and Augustana University College is much appreciated.

2. The Ilongot notion that the "rage of bereavement" could be released through the head-hunting celebration (and the activities which would facilitate the commencement of such festivities) seemed, initially at least, shallow and incomplete. In response, Rosaldo (1989) "confesses" to forcing his ethnographic data into an exchange model—head-hunting as retribution for loss. Rosaldo thereby grounded his explanation "in the literature" despite the consideration that the elements of exchange were not supported in the community's everyday or ritualistic life.

3. "Riding" is equivalent to a "precinct" as a geographical voter boundary.

4. I refer specifically here to perceived associations with the "hate right" (Westin 1964; Barrett 1987). The C.H.P. is making a concerted effort to distance its position and membership from "supremacist" associations.

5. For example, Adler and Adler's (1987b) study of an NCAA basketball team was facilitated in part by adopting the role of "team sociologist," which allowed for the study of "an institutionally lodged group with extreme sensitivity to the insider-outsider distinction" (Adler and Adler 1991).

6. The data collected over the duration of this project suggest that C.H.P. members have experienced a range of previous political involvement. It would be inaccurate to attempt to depict C.H.P. membership as resulting from mass defections from one existing party or another. All of the (former) "Big Three" in Canada—the Progressive Conservatives, the Liberals, and the New Democratic Party—have lost supporters to the C.H.P.

Being Recruited: The Experiences of "Blue Chip" High School Athletes

Mary Lorenz Dietz and Michael Cooper[1]

Recruitment of elite high school athletes—especially young men—is the kind of adventure that inspires Hollywood movies. "Blue Chip"[2] high school athletes are given royal treatment by big name colleges and universities, complete with jet planes, fancy restaurants, and talk of riches beyond their belief. Sports fans are familiar with the recruitment process of star athletes since ratings, predictions of choices, and interviews may be found in newspapers and sports magazines for each of the major sports. Every year the selection of top college athletes by professional sports teams is televised, complete with reporters doing live coverage of the athletes waiting with friends and family members to receive a call from the team that selected them in the draft. Sports segments of TV news shows picture athletes receiving team jerseys, and provide sound bites that let fans know how pleased or disappointed the athletes were at their level of selection. Not that the round they are selected in, or the team that chooses them, is very much of a surprise since reporters have speculated, ranked, and sought insider information for weeks before the draft. The draft into pro sports is just another milestone in the career of high-level athletes. Their lives have been and will, as long as they are successful, continue to be marked by highly public speculation, recruitment, selection, evaluation, and public scrutiny of every success and failure in both their occupational activities and their private lives.

Outstanding athletes begin to experience the rumor, recruitment, selection, and adjustment to new teams and locations very early in their lives. Some start receiving outside notice in elementary school and Little League. Recruitment of star athletes is at its peak when the Blue Chip high school athlete begins the process of selecting a college. At this point recruitment is not controlled by draft, although it is controlled by NCAA (National College Athletic Association) rules. As well, the recruitment and choice are handled directly by the athlete and recruiters, rather than agents. In sports, from the earliest stages, players become used to being publicly evaluated and compared to others. Although the rest of us are compared to some degree by grades and honors, nowhere in our academic or professional lives are our accomplishments listed in the newspaper or reported on television in the same comparative manner as sports stars. In the everyday life of most people, we may be invited to audition or try out for entry into various groups or occupational venues, but most of us do not experience an all-out barrage by a wide variety of groups doing whatever they can to get us to join their organizations. This, however, *is* the experience of the Blue Chip athletes as they make their college selections. It is on these processes of recruiting Blue Chip athletes that this paper will focus. This paper first examines the experience of being recruited from the perspective of the athlete. Then the strategies of recruits and recruiters used to secure and confirm commitments will be discussed.

College Sports as Big Business

College sports, at least high revenue sports like football and basketball, are big business for universities. These sports bring in a great deal of money and increase the visibility and success of marketing the university itself. However, in order for sports to be productive and bring in revenue and publicity, they must be successful. That means they must have winning teams. It is toward the creation of these winning teams that recruitment of Blue Chip athletes is directed in an activity that is as competitive as the sport itself. In major universities, athletic directors and head coaches are paid enormous salaries. They have large staffs working for them and big budgets that include a number of full four- or five-year scholarships for the athletes they recruit.

Because these particular sports activities are a part of university life and the athletes are required to be students as well, the process is even more complicated. In order for college athletes to compete in their sport, they must be registered as full-time students who are passing their courses. This would not be a problem for most college athletes except that while attending classes, they must also spend a great deal of time practicing, playing, and traveling. For many years it has been argued that big-time sports have no place in universities, however, the counter argument has been that, in addition to the revenue, many athletes who would otherwise not be able to do so have an opportunity to attend college.

Method

Data for this paper were gathered in a number of ways. Unlike many areas that sociologists examine, a great deal of information about recruitment is provided by the public media. Interviews about recruitment with elite athletes in football, basketball, hockey, and baseball are supplemented with newspaper commentaries on recruiting. Although not at this elite level, we ourselves have been involved in sport as players, coaches, managers, and also as sports fans. We were therefore able to use our personal experiences to provide insights into the processes involved in the complicated process of recruiting. Recruitment can be studied from a number of viewpoints, including that of specific organizations or programs. This paper makes no attempt to be comprehensive, but rather tries to describe the process of recruitment within the limited framework of the athlete's perceptions.

Research on Recruitment

Recruitment is a social process, but it is only one way that a person may come to be a part of a particular group or organization. In discussing processes of entry, we often separate them into recruitment and seekership depending on which—the group or the individual—seems most desirous of making the alliance. The period prior to becoming a member of a fraternity or sorority is clearly labeled "rushing." This label is an indicator that the fraternities and sororities are going all out to get the best members possible during the designated joining period. Blue Chip athletes go through a period of "rushing" by college recruitment teams, but the period in which it is done is much longer than the few weeks allotted to fraternities. Much of the literature on recruitment is subsumed under the categories of initial involvements, initiation, or conversion. For example, in a classic study, Becker (1963) describes the process of becoming a marijuana user. Indeed, much of the literature does describe the process of being recruited into deviant activities, usually in a much more informal manner than occurs in big revenue college team recruiting. Such studies as Miller (1978) describe friends and family as informal recruiters for involvement in the rackets. We have seen similar patterns of involvement of an athlete's social network in sports recruitment as well. Dubro (1985) provides some insight into recruitment and initiation into the mafia; Johnstone (1983) discusses recruitment into street gangs; Dietz (1983) describes how individuals are recruited into murder as an occupation; Rooney (1961) details recruitment into skid row bottle gangs; and Prus and Sharper (1991) show how people become involved in card hustling. Each of these studies adds to the understanding of how recruiting is carried out. A number of studies describe ways in which both male and female prostitutes are recruited (Milner and Milner 1972; Prus and Irini 1980; Luckenbill 1985; Visano 1987). Other studies follow the procedures of recruitment into religious groups (Wallis and Bruce 1982; Shaffir 1983) or political parties (Grills in this volume). By comparing these diverse types of groups, we are able to recognize recruitment as a generic social process. The work of Griff (1964) on recruitment into the arts, for example, finds many parallels to recruitment into sports, particularly in that the greater the ability, the greater the efforts to recruit which, in turn, increases the impact of the recruitment itself in reinforcing the artist's identity. There are very few studies about sports recruiting aside from Curtis and McTeer (1981), Scott (1981), and Cooper (1988). Sports recruiting is best described in James Rooney's (1980) *The Recruiting Game*, although this offers little in the way of sociological insight. What can be best learned from recruitment literature is that both recruit and recruiter have something to gain and lose in the transactions. Some forms of recruitment, such as religious groups or political parties, are able to offer only future and non-material advantages, whereas recruiting into businesses such as those described by Prus and Frisby (1990) on home party recruiting, or into criminal activities, as well as college sports, may offer financial and lifestyle benefits. In any case, in most types of recruitment there seems to be the following characteristics:

1. **Involvement** of family, friends, and other known and trusted persons as sponsors;

2. **Impact** of the recruitment process itself on the recruit's identity, related to the activity for which he or she is being recruited;

3. **Changes** in the way the recruit values particular abilities as they are discussed and evaluated during recruitment;

4. **Bargaining** for benefits based on recruit characteristics and recruiter assets.

Ratings: Rankings by Self and Others

In Peter Golenbock's *Personal Fouls*, an exposé of basketball problems at North Carolina State during the tenure of Coach Jim Valvano, Golenbock tells the following story about Blue Chipper, Chris Washburn:

> Chris Washburn knew at an early age that he would go to college and ulti-mately to the pros—at age nine to be exact. That's when he got his first letter of college recruitment. From that time on, he was the target of hundreds of colleges, even though all along he displayed a marked lack of interest in doing any schoolwork. (1990, 45)

Washburn was an exception because his size and skill were visible early. Still, another teammate, Andy Kennedy, also a recognized standout, was recruited from the ninth grade on (1990, 72). What is clear is that these elite athletes were aware of external appraisals of their ability as early as elementary school. These early appraisals shaped their identities as athletes and as persons who would be able to choose from a number of colleges and types of programs. These experiences help athletes to learn to view themselves not only as preferred persons, but also as persons inseparable from their identities as athletes. For the majority of athletes at this stage of their career, there are still many doubts on how highly they will be rated. Most of them begin to suspect that even though they are highly talented, their final ranking, which will influence recruitment, will involve politics at the high school and league levels, and may be influenced by unpredictable injuries, team quality, coaches, and a myriad of other factors. Since there are so many sources of information about athletes, it is not until the honors are passed out and the ratings are complete that most athletes can be sure of their standing. One high school coach describes how the process is initiated at the coaching level:

> The colleges, every year they send out forms and on the form they'll ask you, they would like to have your best players on that. "Do you think this player could play for us?" And "Who are the best players in your league?" And that is how the contact is initiated. And then the colleges will send letters back to these ball players.

He went on to describe what happened when one of the athletes received the initial form from one of the colleges:

> Kid comes to me and says so and so sent a letter. They sent a question-naire ... they send a questionnaire out to everybody, you know, anybody who is anybody. They like to tell their friends, "Look I got a letter from Michigan or from here or from there."

Even the questionnaires, which are recognized as the lowest level of interest, are still described as going out to "anybody who is anybody" or, in other words, a select group. In many cases, the questionnaire is sent to those who win honors early in their high school careers, but they also may be initiated by an alumni or a scout or by opposing coaches or players. The following is an excerpt from a letter to a talented softball player:

> Dear Maggie,
> You have been identified as an outstanding high school softball player, with the potential to play at the college level. As the head softball coach at Midwest College, I would be very interested in initiating contact with you. Please fill out the enclosed questionnaire and return it to me as soon as possible. This will supply me with important information and allow me to include you among my list of recruits. I will start making personal contacts this winter.

A Blue Chip football player received the following contact letter:

> We at Big Ten U. have recently learned of you and your athletic accomplishments. Hopefully, we can find out more about you and your interests. Enclosed are two questionnaires for you and your coach to complete and return to me. These will enable us to begin to compile information about

you.... Our format of evaluation is based on several items: grades, overall transcript, playing film, personal interviews, etc. Primarily, it all begins with this questionnaire.

In each of these letters the recruiters indicate that they are already aware of the athlete's accomplishments and have begun to narrow down their recruiting to those playing at the same level who have managed to stand out in some way from others. Indeed, many of these high level athletes have been followed in their sports careers beginning with Little League. They have been observed at camps and discussed and tracked long before the initial college letters are received. The initial contacts are exploratory, but they either initiate or reaffirm, for the athletes, that they are indeed being considered as college prospects. This evaluation is combined with many others as the athlete attempts to assess his or her chances for the big-time universities and for extending a high school career at least as far as college. Both the *quality* (in terms of the reputation and league level) and the *quantity* of contacts are important in this self-assessment. As discussed by Prus (1984, 14), recruitment plays an important role in determining life chances. The impact of receiving the initial recruiting letters and calls is reflected in the comment of a Big Ten football player:

That was when I started to realize that I was a pretty good athlete and that I was valuable to some people.... I got a lot of media attention but I mean that only tells you so much, I mean when you start to find out that you are a good athlete is when the colleges start to recruit you.

The athletes rank themselves on the basis of how they are recruited and by whom, but they also use the standard ways of indicating outstanding athletes in their self-descriptions. Athletes discuss their own recruitment with recognition of the kind of awards that place them among the elite. One describes himself as follows:

I was All American, All Stater. A big thing that I made was Parade All American. That is one of the top All American teams you can make. You get a lot of notoriety from that.

Another describes himself this way: "I was first team All State and I was in the top 100 Blue Chip athletes in the states." Thus the athletes themselves seek out independent corroboration that they are really among the top recruits. These rankings combine with the recruiters' contacts and rhetoric to influence the way the athletes value themselves as well as how they are valued by others. At the same time, recruiters are making and juggling a series of lists which include Blue Chippers, very good athletes, and so on, or A, B, and C lists. Still, many of these athletes have coaches and parents who try to keep them in touch with the vagaries of the collegiate recruitment process. A high school coach describes how coaches try to get athletes to view themselves in a realistic manner:

The head coach will sit down with them and he'll ask the kids at the end of the season, "Do you want to play college ball?" Now if a kid says "Michigan, Michigan State, Southern Cal," and all that, he'll tell the kid, "No, you have to be more realistic." And he will get a list of different schools and he will send films to the different schools to see if they are interested.

High school coaches are aware that usually a very small number of their outstanding athletes, if any, will be regarded as Blue Chip prospects and recruited by major programs even if they have campaigned for them to be considered among the elite. They also understand that colleges only have a limited number of scholarships and that they are recruiting all over North America. Most coaches are aware that, even with the outstanding athletes, other considerations may influence who is going to be recruited. The "outstanding" athlete is rare and, even among the stars at high school level, some will not have the size or skill to advance to big-time college sports. One Blue Chipper discussed his strategy at the initial stages of recruitment and how he took into account his father's advice:

> And also during my junior year when the schools did send letters, I sent all of the questionnaires back no matter what school it was from. I mean even small schools, I sent everything back. My junior year I didn't turn anyone down ... I mean I filled everything out, sent it off. Right, like my father was telling me, you never know what is going to happen. The big schools may change their minds and you may have to fall back.

Thus as the recruitment is going on, the athlete's identity as "outstanding" is being negotiated up or down against an ever stronger and more competitive group. At each stage of the recruitment process, the athletes begin to develop more and more sophistication about the process. Even though they are high school stars, some Blue Chippers begin to wonder if they may have to look to smaller schools because they do not seem to be getting as much attention as they expected from schools in Big Ten, Pac Ten,[3] or other major conferences. The more fortunate ones have advisors who understand the system and who prevent the athlete from narrowing choices too soon or from overestimating or underestimating college potential. When the recruiting actually starts, many highly rated athletes have to face the fact that it is not only their playing that is being rated, but also their grades and scores on college admissions tests. *The Detroit News* reported the following, not unusual, story:

> Terry Harvey wishes he could go back in time. Not a long time. Just long enough to give himself a better opportunity. A chance to prove himself in the classroom as well as on the football field. Harvey's situation has become all too familiar to some high school athletes. The senior from Detroit Denby is rated No. 13 on *The Detroit News* Blue Chip list. No university has questioned his athletic ability.... What has kept most universities from recruiting Harvey

is his inability thus far to pass the American College Testing (ACT) entrance examination.

Even making the Blue Chip lists is not a guarantee that athletes will be recruited by a major program or that they will continue to be recruited once college entrance scores are made known.

Deciding Which Schools to Visit and other Ways of Narrowing Choices

Athletes are only allowed to make five formal visits to different universities. It is important for them to narrow down their choices to the schools they are really considering and that are likely to offer them some type of scholarship. Only a very limited number of athletes are sufficiently good that they can choose freely from any school. Frequently, when athletes are asked later in their careers why they did not attend a particular school in their geographic area, they will answer that the particular school did not really seem to be interested. For the Blue Chip athlete, both the number and type of contacts by recruiters takes on significance in their self-evaluations. Whether the recruiting is done by assistant coaches, alumni, or the head coach is an indicator of how interested the university is in a particular recruit. The recruits also begin to sort out whether or not they have been individually singled out for some personal treatment or whether what they have experienced is the same treatment given to all of the top athletes. It is also important to athletes to see how the recruiter relates to other members of his or her family.[4] One star athlete was recruited by the head coach and visited by an assistant. His former coach describes how they treated him:

> When they recruited Sammy, they sent in a head coach and an assistant coach.... The assistant coach stayed in our office for two months. One day it was Sam's birthday and the assistant had a present for him. Anything he wanted, the assistant was like his little gopher. The man actually lived in town for two months to recruit that guy. They sent a private plane and took him there. The mayor and the governor met him personally at the plane.

The visit by the head coach and the treatment by the assistant coach were indicators to both the coach and the athlete that this team considered him to be a most important recruit. The parent of another athelete describes how a personal visit by a high profile coach influenced his son's status as a recruit and how the father viewed this visit by the head coach:

> And the head coach only goes out for who? The superstars! I mean everything is already set up. The head coach flew a private jet in to see James and had a car take him from the airport to his high school. Flew in to see James. When the big man comes in, it makes all the difference.

A visit by the head coach, especially a coach who is regarded as a star himself, gives the recruit the opportunity to envision him or herself as a member of that coach's team not just as a dream, but as a realistic possibility.

Campus Visits and Their Impact on Recruits

Coaches, alumni, and other persons who recruit for colleges, call the athletes, send them postcards, birthday cards, and school paraphernalia. They contact them before and after visits, but the campus visits are a highlight for the athletes. Many of the athletes have not been out of state before nor have they flown on a plane. On the visit, they meet other potential recruits as well as members of the team. Athletes remember their visits to certain colleges long after they have signed a declaration or are playing with another school. As a result of his campus visits, one athlete describes how he thought of himself: "I thought of myself as being in the big time, you know. Flying all over the place every week." A college football player recalls his sense of importance as he describes his experience on a recruiting trip:

> They had a private jet for me. That Saturday they took us out to this big ranch that was owned by one of the alumni. We did skeet shooting, horseback riding, A.T.V. riding—those three wheelers—archery. All the food we could eat. We had a good time.

On the first visit, the athletes are usually overwhelmed by the flight and the red carpet treatment that they receive. As they continue to make visits, they begin to compare one situation with another. One top recruit describes his trip:

> When I went down to Miami, they set us up with a girl, that was kind of neat. A honey. Oh, yeah, she was like 25 years old, beautiful girl. I was just 17, in my glory. They did, they set me up on a date. That was it, nothing happened. It was a drag. Believe me, we tried. That was the first time I had a roommate ... the other schools I went to, they gave me my own room.

The major universities usually provide the top recruits with parties, dates, and in the above case with a sexual opportunity, although the athlete reported regretfully that he had not been able to take advantage of that experience. After each visit, the athletes try to assess the way they were treated so that they can attempt to figure out how badly the school wants them. They also consider their impressions of the university itself, their potential teammates, the coach, and many other factors that will influence their decision. During campus visits, athletes try to get a sense of the academic demands, perks, treatment of new players, opportunities for playing time, and other key points. They may seek advise from other athletes already in the program, from assistant coaches, and from other people they meet. They want to test the offers and promises made by recruiters against the realities experienced by those already in the program. During the visits "special" offers of spending money, cars, or other things may be made, or they may hear of others being offered those benefits. As they learn of the amount of money and support made to certain athletic programs, athletes begin to develop ideas of the possibilities of benefits for top recruits at different universities.

Following up the Campus Visits

Both before and after the campus visits, the athletes and their families and high school coaches are in negotiations with the recruiters. The very act of selecting a school to visit is an indicator that the school and the athlete have narrowed down their considerations. After the campus visits, there are still usually a number of major universities competing to sign the star athletes. The recruit knows that the school is still interested when follow-up calls and messages are received. The high school softball player received the following letter from the head coach after her initial visit:

> Dear Maggie,
> I hope you enjoyed your visit to Big East and the east coast. I'm sorry we didn't have better weather for you, but I haven't figured out how to control that! As of April 10 there is a moratorium on communication between coach and athlete. Although I cannot contact you, feel free to call me with the news. I hope your visit with your brother was enjoyable. Also please tell your mother I enjoyed meeting her.

In this type of letter, the coach is able to personalize the contact even more. References to family members and planned activities indicate to the player that the coach was paying attention and knows exactly who the player is. A personalized follow-up indicates continued interest in the athlete attending the particular school. The top athletes are not only contacted by mail, but there are increased numbers of phone calls and visits as the recruiters pressure them for a commitment.[5] In many cases, it is difficult for the athlete to decide among the top schools because they all sound attractive. One college football player describes his experience:

> The head coach was supposed to come over to our house for dinner, and the position coach, the defensive back coach, he even came over a couple times.... [He] was at my house waiting for me when I came home from school and he had been talking to my ma. He knew I was really close to my ma, and so he was trying to get with her, get close to her, and she really wanted me to go [there], she really did.

This period is very difficult for both the parents and the athletes because in a sense both are being recruited. A Junior A hockey player reported how his parents were contacted:

My parents had met them [recruiters] at various tournaments. They called my parents as well. They talked to my parents somewhat towards the end because my parents just didn't want me to get shafted.

The indicators that a particular school is interested in a recruit, how the recruit is rated, and whether or not that recruit is leaning toward a particular choice are reported almost daily on local newspaper sports pages. While the attention paid to the young athletes is exciting and self-gratifying in the early stages of recruitment, by the time the signing days draw near, most of the Blue Chippers simply want to make a decision and get the whole process over with. They are tired of the endless visits and phone calls. *The Detroit News* reported the following comment from the 1992 number one basketball prospect in the state of Michigan:

> I'm glad I play basketball. When I'm out on the court, it's relaxing. It helps take my mind off recruiting. It's not really so bad. I don't lose any sleep at night. I've been on the telephone for three and a half hours with calls from reporters and recruiters. Actually it's an honor to be asked so many times where I'm going. Heck, they want to know as much as I do.... Even my class-mates will give me advice. And the teachers, too.

Eventually, they are no longer happy when friends and even strangers give them advice. Mostly, they are afraid that they will make a wrong decision that will hurt them in the future. They are afraid that if they commit too early they will get a better offer later, but if they don't commit soon enough the school will sign someone else. They are afraid to trust the recruiters, who they often describe as "bullshitters," but they are equally afraid that their family and friends really do not know the score. And they are afraid of responding to the pressure of hard-sell recruiters. As one football player said: "Oh, my God, the coach at Florida. Every minute, 'Are you going to sign with us?' 'Why don't you sign with us now?'" Another top football recruit described it this way:

> They visit your school, they may even visit your home. They call you ... every night. It gets to where they really push you, they have only got so much time to sign you. They are salesmen. It really gets busy, a lot of phone calls, a lot of letters. I had one guy come to see me every week, sometimes twice a week just to see me. Talk to me. "How are you doing?" ... So right away it was hectic.

The recruiters promise playing time, tutoring, money, stardom, and many other things, but the ultimate responsibility for deciding where their best prospects are rests with the athletes themselves. They may begin to distrust everyone and wonder if their assessment of their abilities has been over-inflated. By the time the signing date comes around, the Blue Chip athletes have experienced being courted and desired in a way few other people have. One could consider signing a "commitment" as analogous to a marriage.

Like everyone else who joins a group or becomes a part of a relationship, these athletes may still have some worries about how the "marriage" will work out.

What Athletes Want and how They See Recruiting Strategies

The kinds of things that the athletes finally decide they want vary somewhat. They begin to consider: (a) the type of evaluations they have received; (b) whether they have a realistic opportunity for a professional sports career; (c) the advice they have been hearing from parents, high school coaches, and other advisors; and (d) other more mundane things like whether or not their current girlfriend/boyfriend will attend the same school, wait for them, and so on. Essentially, most athletes have a list of desires/demands that they will try to negotiate for, including:

1. a "full-ride" scholarship that will give them four years eligibility, five years to graduate, and scholarship continuation if they are injured;

2. sufficient playing time to demonstrate their abilities;

3. knowing ahead of time if they will be *red-shirted* (not begin their playing time in their first year);

4. knowing how many players are on the squad or are being recruited at their position;

5. what will be possible and expected of them academically, what kind of academic assistance they can expect;

6. what kind of perks they can expect in terms of extra money through gifts, real or pretend jobs, living arrangements, home or family visits, or other miscellaneous advantages.

Although this is not an all-inclusive list, it covers the major concerns that the athletes express. While Blue Chip athletes have received considerable attention by the time college recruitment begins in earnest, they are still only sixteen or seventeen years of age. Although they have been inundated by the media and recruiters, most are aware that playing sports in major universities represents the expectations for much higher level play than they have previously been involved in. The recruitment process itself gives them a sample of what to expect in terms of scrutinization in all aspects of life and not just on the playing field. Naturally, different athletes respond to the recruitment situation in different ways. Some are supremely confident after having starred in elementary and high school level sports; they expect to continue through college and, in many cases, on into the pro leagues. Others, however, worry about the competition, about their future, about academic pressures, and about being away from home. All of these areas are discussed with recruiters as well. For many athletes, much of what the recruiters are doing is not only making them feel wanted, but is also reassuring them in areas where they have doubts or, in effect, bargaining with them by guaranteeing that their problems will be taken care of. For example, one athlete being recruited by a school with an outstanding academic reputation talked about his doubts: "I was still hesitant, so to speak. I didn't know what to expect at all. Like they say you will have tutors and all that, but I was still scared." Much of what the recruiter did to ensure that this athlete would commit to his school was to give reassurances that the athlete would receive help with his school work and that he would have time to keep up with his studies so as not to become ineligible. The reputation of the university is used by recruiters as a selling point, but the recruiting process involves negotiating the concerns each recruit has and recognizing that each one is different. Most athletes feel that some recruiters and some schools depersonalize the prospective athletes and this turned them off. One athlete described a recruiter who treated black athletes differently from whites:

> One time he said "If you need help with drugs or whatever, like if you have a drug problem, I can help you with that too." ... He thought being black you would probably have a drug problem.

The recruits all tended to be sensitive to any treatment that suggested that they were all alike. A Junior A hockey player remembered: "A few schools, even when they talked to me they didn't really seem personal. It felt a little bit like I was just going to be a number." A football player had this to say about his perception of being treated impersonally:

> If they start talking about their school and then their football team then you should consider putting them in the top three. Because they are not trying to taunt you towards football, they are trying to get you to go to their school for an education, that makes it sound like they care about you. The other way around you are just a hunk of meat.

Other athletes are worried about being homesick if they go too far away. Recruiters often take this into account because every year some very good prospects leave in their first semester. One athlete reported discussing the distance with his brother who had gone away to a distant school. He said:

> Also really I thought about the location of the school because my brother ran track at the Naval Academy. He ran track and he was really successful at that, but he told me that the only thing he hated was that after a big meet, he would look up into the stands and my parents weren't there. He talked to me about that and I guess that kind of touched me because my family is very close.

Each of these recruits had considerations that all athletes and students have, but each consideration weighs differently on the decision to sign with a particular team. Some of the athletes mentioned that they were more concerned with actually getting on the field to play rather than the reputation or location of the school. One football player stated:

I was looking to start playing football right away. I didn't want to sit around and not play for two or three years. I wanted to come in and play right away, so I was looking for a school that was looking for linemen. I wanted to find out if they had a lot of linemen, young linemen or whatever, or if they had a lot of guys graduated.

In many cases the athlete is controlling the recruiting by not pursuing schools that do not meet his or her interests. In the last example, the athlete is unlikely to select a school that has a large portion of its team returning the next year, no matter what they have to offer. The recruiter, even if it is the head coach, can only promise an opportunity to play, but, in many cases, the recruit remains skeptical. While recruits may be young and unsophisticated about college life, most understand very well how athletes achieve playing time in sports. It is important to recognize that being recruited is *not* a passive activity in which the athlete simply sits back and waits to see what will happen. Even at this age, many athletes recognize that their chances for a pro career are limited. One athlete indicated his concern for future plans as he mentioned meeting alumni during his campus visits:

I was really impressed with the alumni. When I went to that banquet, that is, all that was sitting around me, doctors, engineers, dentists, I mean some very smart people.

He went on to say how he evaluated various schools and on what basis he was making decisions:

Oh, you have to pay attention to the alumni because they have been there and like most of the people were like doctors, engineers, and I looked at that and I went, "Hey, you know, they would probably help me out once I got out of school." Maybe they would help me with a job or something.

It is obvious that, in many ways, being recruited involves the same kind of decision-making and comparisons that any job or college selection does. However, it differs considerably from the experience that most people have in that when we make decisions, we do not often have the pressure of trying to make a decision and choose from a large number of highly competitive and attractive offers. Most of us rarely experience the types of inducements that these athletes do.

Recruit (Target) Strategies

Elite high school athletes often develop a number of strategies for dealing with recruiters and recruitment as the process continues. Recruits also learn to recognize and negotiate according to the various recruitment strategies used on them. Some allow their parents and their high school coaches to handle most of the contacts and negotiations. They use a "You had better talk to my mom" strategy. Others depend heavily on their ratings and write-ups in the media to emphasize their desirability, using a "Read my clippings" strategy. Still others maintain control over the contacts and the negotiations so that they can respond to any questions or doubts on the part of the recruiter by emphasizing their desire, their work ethic, and their knowledge of the sport. These use a "Here is what I can do for you" kind of sales pitch. Problems might arise when the recruits believe that they can choose any school they want or do not recognize that a program may decide that they are not worth the effort.

Recruiting Strategies

The recruitment of Blue Chip athletes is not only a career decision for the recruits, it also has considerable impact on the career of the recruiter. Recruiting successes bring about winning teams and may foster future recruiting as well. Failure to recruit strong players or recruiting too many athletes who have legal problems, are injury prone, or who are not able to stand up to the rigors of big-time college sports may put the recruiter's career in jeopardy. This is particularly true if he or she is a new coach or an assistant who has not established a solid reputation. Even for the well-established coach, poor recruiting may result in job loss.

While the emphasis varies for different recruits, recruiters, and programs, most of the recruits described strategies that were quite similar. The following are some of the major strategies that recruits described:

1. I will make you a star. Most of the Blue Chippers, even those who see themselves as stars already, look forward to college stardom and a possible chance at the pros. Some recruiters are able to use their past experiences such as having Heisman trophy[6] candidates, arranging national TV appearances, and the school's winning records to emphasize that they have done this for others.

2. You will get a good education. This often appeals particularly to parents, but the academic reputation of the university and graduation rates of athletes can be generally attractive.

3. We will build our team around you. This tactic is more apt to be used by smaller schools or schools that lack a strong record. It is especially effective for those athletes who are concerned with playing time.

4. We will take care of everything. Athletes have all of the normal fears of going away from home, finding living arrangements, and the like. Many are tempted by recruiters who offer to handle all details for them.

There are many other strategies tailored to particular concerns or problems of the athletes. The basic problem of recruiters is to establish a trusting relationship with the recruit and family members. The actual personal feelings recruits have for the recruiter cannot be minimized. Beyond that, the recruiter works with what the school has to offer and the degree to which he or she is authorized to provide additional inducements either within or outside the NCAA rules.

Conclusion

Being recruited to a program, team, or activity is an experience that most people have during their life. Being recruited in the way that Blue Chip athletes are is an experience that very few people have. This type of recruitment moves from the level of ego enhancement or ego deflation to the level of identity transformation. The athletes' own evaluation of themselves as "outstanding" and "desirable" for their sports ability may be confirmed, and their identity as athlete becomes an even more entrenched master status as a result of being recruited. While all of us have our qualities and characteristics examined and scrutinized as we enter into new arenas of activity with different groups and on different levels, we rarely have these qualities and characteristics printed in newspapers and magazines to be debated by experts. In most of the professions, there are no listings that proclaim certain practitioners to be among the top 100 in the field. Even "star" scholars, choosing between several scholarships or job offers, rarely face the type of sales pressure that is found in sports recruiting. Thus, while being recruited is something many people experience, recruitment of Blue Chip athletes can be said to illustrate an extreme case.

An important follow-up to this research could examine how this intense recruitment affects the subsequent satisfaction of the recruit. It seems almost inevitable that the recruit, who has learned during this period to view him or herself as "one of a kind," will have problems adjusting to being "one of many" as practice begins. After building up such an exceptional self-concept during the recruitment period, the reality of being simply a member, and not necessarily the most outstanding member, of a team may require some reconstructive identity work. Moving from the status of "highly desired star" to "rookie" would appear to maximize the adjustment required to begin any new venture. Further research would be useful in finding out how recruitment expectations of self and others influence entry into the group.

In summary, being recruited as a Blue Chip high school athlete is the extreme end of the combination of courtship and sales that makes up the recruitment process. Being recruited at this level and with this intensity underlines the kinds of self-evaluation and decision-making that goes into entering any group or activity. Because the recruitment involves so much evaluation of personal skills, character, and lifestyle both by the self and by others, recruitment of elite high school athletes is in itself an identity transforming process that we as sociologists need to examine in even closer detail.

NOTES

1. Data for this paper were collected for Michael Cooper's Master's thesis, "The Recruitment Process: Sport Recruitment as a Case in Point," University of Windsor, 1988. Some of the data was used in a paper of the same title presented at the Qualitative Research Conference, Hamilton, Ontario, 1987. We would like to thank Janice Drakich for her editorial help.

2. The blue chip in poker is the highest value, thus when people refer to the highest valued stock, athlete, or other asset, they are referred to as "Blue Chip."

3. The Big Ten football conference includes ten mid-western U.S. colleges and universities. The Pac Ten conference is the U.S. Pacific Coast conference.

4. Cooper (1988) found that recruiters were very aware of parents and that many of them focused their recruiting as much on the parent as on the athlete (117–18).

5. The work of Prus (1989a) on marketing activities offers a number of useful insights on interactions between salespersons and customers.

6. The Heisman trophy is awarded to the top American college football player each year.

Acquiring Perspectives: Interpretive Frames

The four articles in this section examine how people come to adopt the perspectives held by the social worlds to which they belong. Every social world develops a culture which includes its unique ways of viewing the world. People, as members of a subculture, undergo conversions in the ways they view themselves and other objects as they become a part of the group they belong to. The meanings held by group members and their interpretations of situations are what ethnographers seek to discover as they study social worlds. Learning these perspectives is an essential aspect of becoming a member of any group or community, as well as in understanding any social world. In some groups there is a period of deliberate teaching of new members, as we often see in apprenticeships and in the educational period before members are fully initiated into religious communities. Other social worlds are less formal in initiating members into new perspectives, and the prospective members seek out new understandings themselves.

Donald Evans, in "Socialization into Deafness," helps us to realize that deaf people need to learn how to understand and see the world from their perspective as a "deaf person." For many of us this is a startling revelation—we have taken it for granted that people who are deaf somehow automatically know how to interpret the world as a deaf person. Evans, however, uses his observations at a State School for the Deaf to illustrate how deaf children are socialized into understanding that they are non-hearing persons in a hearing world. We are able to understand that, for deaf people, a deaf self is socially constructed. Deaf children learn to view themselves as others view them. Adopting the perspective of the deaf world is an important part of the socialization of non-hearing persons and one that gives objects and activities such as music and conversation, specialized meanings.

The second selection in acquiring perspectives describes the group experiences of women who have come to interpret and re-interpret the world from a feminist perspective. Charlotte Wolf uses the insights of this small feminist community to demonstrate how both past and present lived experiences come to be viewed differently as the perspective is more deeply appreciated. In the process of changing, or being converted to a new perspective, there is also a perceived change in identity as the women come to see themselves as feminists. During the process through which the women come to adopt new perspectives, they experience a series of "reality shocks," that is, the recognition that the way in which they interpreted their experiences in the past has had an impact on their lives. Their new perspectives result in changes being made in other areas of their lives and progressing toward a commitment to a feminist viewpoint and identity. Just as the deaf were socialized into a deaf view of the world in Evans' study, the women in Wolf's study were resocialized into a new perspective that also changed their lives.

In "Learning Meanings From the Fashion World" we journey with Fred Davis over a number of years as he develops different meanings in his own understanding of fashion. He begins with his introduction to an understanding of fashion from the perspective of a sociologist rather than a lay person. In this revealing selection, we are able to follow Davis as he struggles with various meanings attributed to fashion both in sociology and in the fashion world. It is enlightening to recognize that each of the perspectives that are adopted allow Davis, and the reader, to interpret fashion in a different manner. We are able to follow how a naïve or common sense knowledge of a particular social world can become transformed by developing and refining a sociological perspective through which it can be interpreted.

Finally, Kerry Daly's "Uncertain Terms: The Social Construction of Fatherhood" traces the changes in the way fatherhood is socially constructed. In this selection, as in that of Charlotte Wolf, we are able to view people while they are still in the process of changing one perspective for another. Daly allows us to understand how traditional and important meanings that we have learned, are the perspectives that we carry with us when we enter a new identity or social world. It is clear that for Daly's fathers, the perspectives through which they will view the world of fatherhood are emerging and changing as they experience fatherhood themselves. Daly emphasizes the importance of the father identity and the importance of others in influencing the perspectives that we adopt.

The processes by which we develop perspectives and interpret our worlds are described in this section. The importance of these perspectives and the fact that they are learned throughout life emphasizes the impact that they have on the way we view and interpret everyday life. It is clear that new perspectives and new social worlds are a continuing part of our lives and are not fixed in any way, collectively or individually, as we continue to interact as social beings.

Socialization into Deafness[1]

Donald Evans

"The Limits of My Language Mean the Limits of My World"
—LUDWIG WITTGENSTEIN

Sociologists believe that an individual is a group product, something of a social artifact, a veritable social construct. This premier idea was stated long ago with unparalleled eloquence by John Donne (1980, 254), the famous poet, who penned, "No man is an island entire of itself; every man is a piece of the continent, a part of the main." Apart from the world of poetry there are, in fact, a few individuals who are islands cut off from the main, from language, knowledge, and culture.

This paper focuses upon one type of human island—deaf children who literally begin life dramatically cut asunder from the everyday talk of their group. Simply put, deafness is a paramount problem of language, socialization, and knowledge.[2] This is a topic of great interest to the social sciences— that now and then some individuals do begin life with little or no symbolic interaction and sometimes grow up without attaining even the "thin veneer of civilization."

Most deaf children do become socialized, and it is the specific aim of this paper to present research findings that help explain the processes whereby some children with little or no hearing "become deaf people."[3] I do not, of course, refer to their becoming physically deaf, but rather to their becoming sociologically, behaviorally, and cognitively "deaf" people.

In a related study more than two decades ago, Scott (1969) wrote about the way blind children are "made," and how "the sensory basis of language for the blind person and the sighted person is different, and to that extent all common ground of shared meanings between them is different" (1029). He goes on to say that, like a deaf child, a blind child "is seriously hampered in developing knowledge and experience about the world" (1029) and that a blind child has a great problem developing "a clear impression of non-self," and self is very slow to emerge (1032). A sighted (and hearing) child soon begins to share meanings with others, but a blind (or deaf) child "diverges ... toward an inordinate egocentricity" (Scott 1969, 1033; Evans and Falk 1986, 193). In both cases, experience provided by conversations or gestures between child and parents gets lost since sight and hearing are needed to help give meaning to the gestures.

Blind children develop *blindisms*, or peculiar patterns of behavior (Scott 1969, 1034), and deaf children develop *deafisms* (Evans and Falk 1986, 150). Blindness and deafness both interrupt the play process whereby "a child learns to internalize the behavior of others" (Scott 1969, 1034). The content of role behavior, the "recipe knowledge" (Berger and Luckmann 1966) of everyday life is not very accessible to these children. As teacher after teacher at SSD (State School for the Deaf) complained, "We have to teach them *everything!*"

We learn all our symbols from others via the social process of language acquisition. Those deaf people without symbols, Leslie White (1949, 22) once said, "are not human beings" because human behavior is dependent on symbols. "One thing we are not in the dark about, and that is the role of language in making man quintessentially human" (Becker 1971, 14). The main idea here is that, without language, we would be unable to attain culture and therefore would remain at a basic animal-stimuli level in terms of cognitive processes (Becker 1971, 5–7).

For many readers the preceding characterization by White is too strong. Nevertheless it helps sharpen the point that I want to emphasize in this paper, namely that a newborn infant, an isolate, a feral child, and people like Helen Keller (before she learned to fingerspell English words) are cultural *tabulae rasae*; they live almost completely outside the symbolic universe of humanity. The human world as compared with the animal world is, above all, a world of socially constructed and socially shared symbolic images. For animals without language, and this includes prelingual deaf children (and even prelingual adults), the world is basically a place of signs and stimuli.

Charles H. Cooley had similar thoughts when he "envisioned each life history as containing a stream and a road; he discerned the stream as heredity ... [and] the road as 'communication or social transmission,' including language, interaction, and education" (Collins and Makowsky 1978, 164–65).

In more contemporary language, Cooley's "road" refers to culture. If we actually apply this idea, then most deaf children enter school with virtually no road (no culture) because, at this point in time, they have no language. If we push this point of view, we can also say that these children possess neither mind, nor self, neither community, nor intersubjectivity. Remember that mind and self, for symbolic interactionists, are symbolic processes; they are verbs, not nouns. The brain, on the other hand, is literally a physical entity. This distinction helps clarify the notion that, while one is born with a brain, mind and self are acquired via social-linguistic interaction. In other words, "Language is as indispensable as the brain itself is to the higher kinds of life" (Cooley 1928, 316).

What about cognitive community? When one speaks to an other using shared language and the other comprehends the ideas that are transmitted, there is intersubjectivity; there is community by communication. Mind touches mind. It seems likely, therefore, that a deaf person without language would stand outside all of these uniquely human acts. He or she would be *in* the world, but not *of* the world. As a hard-of-hearing person, I spend many Sunday evenings alone in a den filled with children and grandchildren whose chatter remains a few decibels too low for my range of hearing. I am alone in a crowd.

George H. Mead correctly saw language as the source of mind, self, and society; his distinction between a stimulus and an object is really useful here. The former has no meaning, while the latter has meaning conferred upon it by a group of languaging persons. With symbols, one lives in a world of both physical and social objects.[4] Without symbols, a deaf child lives in a world of physical objects. A diamond ring given to a chimpanzee or to a languageless child, for example, is merely a stimulus without socially ascribed meanings of monetary value and social prestige.

In this paper I apply the theories and concepts of Mead to prelingual deaf children (and, to some extent, to postlingual deaf children because their languaging processes are relatively shortened). So it was in a "Meadian laboratory" at SSD that I looked at the effects of the double dosage of spatial and linguistic isolation, at processes of language deprivation, minimized acquisition of symbolic capital, and very parochial socialization. Again, I was not concerned at all with eardrums, decibels, speech therapy, nor any other physiological and clinical matters. From the outset, this research was about the role of language, social interaction, and segregation in the unique process of learning to be a "deaf" person.

The research findings presented here derive from a body of ethnographic research some of which appeared first in my doctoral dissertation (Evans 1982) and was eventually published as a book, *Learning to be Deaf* (Evans and Falk 1986).

Methods

In the present study I attempted to observe, discover, analyze, and conceptualize, at the microscopic level of analysis, the social processes at SSD that *create* deaf children. This study is qualitative research; it "grounds" (Glaser and Strauss 1967) its findings and subsequent theoretical statements in close-up observations, participant-observation in classrooms, lunchrooms, playgrounds, bus trips, and dormitories. The field technique and approach used was that of Cooley's (1964) *sympathetic introspection* by which I collected information by doing face-to-face interaction with deaf children on a daily basis for four months in 1981 at a state residential school for the deaf.

I used both structured and unstructured interviews (see Lofland 1971, 75–92) to gain access to students' frame of reference or world view (Kearney 1984). In all, I interviewed thirty-two students from high school, middle school, and the vocational school at SSD. In addition, I interviewed twenty-three teachers, five administrators, eleven staff members, and six houseparents. I also interviewed seven hearing townspeople from the nearby village.

My access to the *social world* (Shibutani 1978) or *lifeworld* (Schutz 1967b) of this very segregated group of young people was further implemented by a document analysis of secondary data, including books, student files, school manuals, school annuals, school newsletters, and the many mimeographed articles/studies on deaf children available in open stacks in the main administration building at SSD.

The Setting

The *social world* for this study was a large state residential school for the deaf located in the southeastern part of the United States. The school is located in an idyllic mountain town with a population of only one thousand people. It is a social world surrounded by verdant mountains dotted with church steeples, house trailers, cows, and ubiquitous cedar trees.

I have used the pseudonym "Doubletown" (Evans and Falk 1986) for this social world to refer to the actual *vis-à-vis* coexistence of the hearing and deaf worlds whose physical proximity was essentially nullified by a linguistic gulf that prevented all but a modicum of intersubjectivity between the two groups.

In terms of everyday talk and interaction, SSD is a world of pictures and icons (Cicourel and Boese 1972) because ASL (American Sign Language) is a language with a substantial element of *iconicity*[5] when compared to any spoken language.

Upon arrival at SSD, children who have been diagnosed and labeled as deaf pass through the portals of the school and fall into the enormous and all-embracing grip of a place superbly conceptualized by Goffman (1961, xiii) as a *total institution*. Goffman describes total institutions as "places of residence and work where a large number of like-situated individuals, cut off from the wider society for an appreciable period of time, together lead an enclosed, formally administered round of life."

The Findings

It seems almost axiomatic that any study of human beings who are deprived of language acquisition would be confronted at the outset with a "sociology of knowledge." Indeed, the emergent and nagging question for me was a simple one: What could one *know* with little or no language? And the query was soon met by a felicitous, but powerful statement written by Wittgenstein (1973), "The limits of my language means the limits of my world."

At SSD administrators and teachers are keenly aware of the profound consequences of symbolic deprivation upon children. They know that:

> Most children learn [language] between the ages of one-and-a-half and two. We [at SSD] are at a disadvantage. Children come in knowing nothing. Can you imagine? A two-year-old hearing child may have a vocabulary of 250 words. Our children come not knowing that they have a label, that they are called by a name, that they are "Ronny" or "Donny." They don't know that their primary caretaker is called "Mama." They just don't know the labels for things. They don't know that the red thing they just ate is an apple. They know that liquid is to drink and food is to eat, from past experience, but they don't know the names for things like that. (Evans and Falk 1986, 55)

In this observation a young pre-school teacher repeatedly referred to what a child without language cannot *know*. In addition, however, she appropriately noted in the last line that these children could know some things by experience.[6]

The Babies at SSD

Solo Boy: The Process of Learning to Cry

Children without language enter SSD as young as two-and-one-half years of age, and once inside the embrace of that powerful institution, they begin to learn moment-by-moment to be deaf people. This means that almost immediately upon arrival they begin to learn the manual sign language of the deaf world—a language system that would bring to all newcomers a flood of thoughts, values, and norms peculiar to the deaf world at SSD.

A good case in point is Solo Boy, age four, who first entered SSD with numerous sores and was placed immediately in the school infirmary for treatment. There, I observed a frightened child all alone in a room for a few days, clutching first a plush mouse and then a stuffed monkey. Several times as I moved away from him toward the door, he would vigorously wave, "bye-bye." His uneasy facial expression and shrinking posture indicated to me that the gesture was an invitation for me to leave the room. He feared the unknown, and *everything* that day was unknown.

Later, a nurse said to several of us seated in the infirmary lobby, "I wonder *what* he [Solo Boy] thinks. I wonder *where* he thinks he is."[7] "After all," she added, "his parents just dumped him here. [When he arrived] he had long sleeves on [in August] and later we found that he had many sores on him. That's why he's here [in the infirmary]." Seated nearby, a nurse's aid offered to further define the frightened boy by using medical model (Ritzer 1986, 416–20) language, that is, by using psychological, mental terms: "He's here [in the infirmary]," she declared, "because of 'emotional problems.'" This was a hint of the orientation that would characterize the socialization process yet to come.

How *would* a child respond to such a new experience of lostness? A disconcerted night nurse at the infirmary described his initial reaction: "He screamed loud all afternoon! The look in his eyes scared me! This [sort of thing] upsets me!" As an afterthought, she noted something of great interest—that all human babies have to learn to cry. "His cry tells me that he may have some [residual] hearing." "You mean babies learn *how* to cry?" I asked with surprise. Indeed, they do, several nurses agreed. They explained that profoundly deaf babies produce tones and pitches different from those of other babies who can hear some or all sounds. The socially acquired animal-to-human cry, therefore, and its fine qualities, its pitches, tones, and volumes, are things learned from daily social interaction with others who hear and cry. That very process has been aptly conceptualized by George Mead as a "conversation of gestures" (Mead 1934).

The Process of Reality Construction Via Coercion, Colors, Signs, and Words

For maximum insight into the *tabula rasa* condition of a languageless child, I first went to the pre-school program at SSD. In that classroom there were only three children, two little girls and—there he was again—Solo Boy! It was a rare social situation where the usual power of language to direct thought and behavior was completely stymied because the "babies" had none.

In that room a young teacher and her aid daily resorted to gentle physical coercion in order to accomplish a simple request. Daily I observed the very dawning of a social construction of reality, indeed the first weary sparks in the gradual fabrication of mind.

The generic process I observed was not only an imposition of social order, but also a prefatory indexing of certain concrete attributes of things; it was the ordering of colors, shapes, and names (signs) for physical objects. At this level of socialization, the paramount goal of the teacher was to convey to symbol-less "babies" the first rumblings of language, the principal tool by which humans segment nature (Whorf 1962).

Since there was no common language system available to the teacher and children, the teacher and her aid reverted to physical ways of transmitting thoughts about the world and about proper behavior. My field notes reflected often "The teacher holds the child in order to control him (or her)." Without language a teacher cannot persuade, threaten, or beg a child to comply with processual classroom expectations. Physical coercion was even used to begin the language acquisition process. These acts were some of the first moments in the long process of "becoming deaf."

One day when one of the little girls correctly executed a task, the teacher took the child's hand and physically forced her to make the sign for "good." Unlike a hearing-talking child who cannot be forced to speak, an attempt at achieving a first language in this case was literally (and physically) projected into the child's great symbolic void. Moreover, this was the beginning of a value system where these tots would soon *know* that some behavior is "good" and some is "bad." So it was, by means of push-and-pull social interaction and physically coerced symbols, that the first chisel blows to the rock of reality had commenced. Mind, hence self and society, were on the way. And for a long time afterward, most teachers agreed, the deaf mind would rigidly conceive of the social world in bipolar terms.

In the meantime, Solo Boy (age four with no language) was difficult to manage. "Solo Boy," I wrote in field notes, "sits now with his head on his arms [on the floor] while a girl puts [multi-shaped wooden] blocks through the holes [of a board]."

> TEACHER TO GIRL: "He is homesick. That means he misses his mommy and daddy." [As a new class activity begins] Solo Boy sits down, head on arms and cries. The teacher and TA [teacher's aid] ... tell [both] girls, "[Solo Boy] is crying. He's homesick." Soon he looks up to see what's happening.

> TA: "It's just time for him to show sadness" and [the TA] laughs with the teacher who agrees.

Initial sessions of reality-making with languageless children were very concrete and short-lived. Within fifteen minutes of class time, a fifth activity had begun, something the teacher called, "sense training." In that moment-by-moment process where vision was paramount to sound, the "three little blank slates" were shown how to match pictures, how to begin thinking in the context of categories: place a rooster next to another rooster, a cat to a cat, a pig to a pig, and a house to a house. One little girl, who had some residual hearing, was learning to match English words to pictures. In Helen Keller's words, the phenomenal lesson here was that "everything has a name" (Keller 1902, 36). Some deaf children never go to any school and therefore never enter, to any significant degree, the actual process of mind construction. At home these children certainly experience crude, homemade, gesture communication with parents and siblings. They develop gestures for basics like "eat," "sleep," "bathe," and so forth.[8] If anything, this propensity to attain intersubjectivity is the salient mark of human uniqueness, but having said that, it must be emphasized that such communication is extremely low level and concrete. In such social settings, mind and self might barely develop just above point zero.

The Social Construction of a Deaf Self: The Process

At SSD, children with late language acquisition must learn so much. For example, there was evidence that prelingually deafened children did not understand at all why people moved their lips. Sound itself, especially sound of a voice, was something beyond comprehension. This paucity of sound knowledge was colorfully illustrated in an unexpected account described by a deaf staff member at SSD. She told how as a child, she and another little girl, about age four, entered the institution, learned some signs, and one day came to realize for the first time, why some hearing people at SSD moved their lips. "Look at them. How pitiful," the little girls signed to each other. "These poor people can't sign, can't communicate to each other." It seemed obvious to the girls that some people could only wiggle their lips. For these two girls, the world of physical-manual sign language was all there is. Ethnocentrism, we may discover, is a twin to one's emergent symbolic system.

During the daily interaction process, of course, deaf children did eventually learn that non-deaf people are, in fact, talking with sound-based words. Related to this learning process, is another hard lesson: they learn from the dominant group (family or school) that they are different, less valued, and they begin to wonder why.[9]

The process of the self-discovery: "I am deaf and different," and the flood of subsequent explanations for this are often painful to the only deaf person in a family. This process is illustrated by a rare incident involving a hearing parent whose entire family had moved to the community in which SSD was located in order to be near their deaf daughter. In the interview outlined below, the mother gives some insight into the social process that gradually helped her teenage deaf daughter to learn from the larger group, the generalized other, that she was deaf:

> DON: Can you briefly tell your experience of raising a deaf child?
>
> MOTHER: It's been a struggle. It's been rewarding.... We've learned to adjust to many situations because of her deafness ... like going out in public and being stared at because you're signing to a child—which never bothered me all that much—but it bothered Erin.... Then for a while she didn't want to talk with signs anymore in public. She didn't want to be different.

In response to the emerging definition of Erin's atypical selfhood, the mother frequently told Erin who and what she was: "It's all right to be *different*.... I can hear, but you can't, but that's all right. Don't be ashamed that *you're deaf*" (emphasis added). But Erin was an outsider in her own family as well as her own society and she kept the hard questions coming (Higgins 1980).

"Why," she wanted to know, "am I deaf and Josh [a brother] can hear?" In this daily process of self construction, no pedagogue is formally teaching Erin that she is sociologically deaf; she is observing that very fact herself. For Erin, Cooley's mirror may have been cracked, but it still communicated to her and all the others that they were not like family and neighborhood children.

Another facet of the daily social process where one learns to be deaf, to take on the content of that ascribed status, occurred when teachers at SSD and Erin's mother began to teach and emphasize speech-reading (also known as lip-reading) skills to deaf students. This process denoted, first, that speech and speech-reading are primary characteristics of the dominant social world and, second, that the deaf person cannot do them well, and hence must be taught to be like those of us who hear and speak. For these awkward children, the "moral entrepreneurs" (Becker 1963) never seem to stop defining reality in their own terms.

School and family processes help children learn a hidden curriculum (Jackson 1968)—that there are two worlds and two symbol systems, that their parents and siblings are outsiders in a deaf world in the very same way that hearing people tend to see deaf people as outsiders. The gap between the two universes is inordinately deep and wide.

To leave campus is to leave one's culture, one's soul-place. At the encouragement of her mother, Erin, age eighteen, took a summer job cleaning tables and washing dishes. Her mother recalled how the social world of work was another universe and the message was overwhelming:

> They have meetings at work. Well, [at those meetings] she's *just there.* And if she is lucky enough to sit close enough, she might catch a word now and then.... So this guy that's in charge ... takes [written] notes and then sits down and goes over them with Erin.

Erin had a language and the workers had a language, but the twain never met. In the words of an American Indian writer (Highwater 1981, 3), "The greatest distance between people is not space but culture" (and, we would add, language).

Many deaf people are *in,* but not *of* the crowd. One day in Baton Rouge, I had Sunday dinner with a twenty-five-year-old deaf man whose parents and sisters talked all afternoon without signs. I saw his isolation so I asked him if he became bored sitting with, but not of, the family (for him intersubjectivity was virtually nil). "No," he shrugged. "I'm used to it." What one never knows, it seems, one may never miss.

One final example of the unintended, all-embracing "hidden" process that creates and maintains deaf status was given by a deaf teacher at SSD who said, "Often I go into the teacher's lounge at break time and ninety percent of the time the hearing teachers (who totally dominate in numbers) are talking without signs." And what does he do? "I just sit there."

The Social Construction of a Deaf Person: The Product

The truism holds: "Birds of a feather flock together." When one is deaf, the school psychologist said, "You tend to seek out those who can communicate with you and those who know what your world is about. And that [fact] automatically limits you." For most deaf children, SSD becomes the incubator of life, the umbilical cord to language, knowledge, community, and security. Language becomes the mother creator of mind and self. Perhaps the finest declaration of having learned to be deaf was given by the school's most popular high school student at the time:

> A short time [from now] I will graduate and go out. Can't come to school again. Truly, I like school. That's all. Truly, I hate to leave school because I like staying many years [here] because I like to see my best friends in SSD. [It is] more interesting, friends interacting with each other … more fun, pleasure and joy. When I leave school truly very disappointed if go to work, work, work for a long time living. My friends [will be] gone out and gone away and dispersed and I can't meet them, my best friends. Maybe my friends will move to another State and I want to meet them so I know where they live. Really, I'd like to stay in school. I truly want to stay in school until I die. I wish I could because I like to see my best friends.... I wish to see them before they die. I want to remain with friends so that I can see them every [time of] interaction [or association] with friends. So I can visit and talk.... I truly don't want them to die and to be absent.... I wish they would stay and keep living forever. (Evans and Falk 1986, 161)

Discussion

Even a hearing child can learn to be deaf if the child has little opportunity to interact with other hearing people. As one author put it:

> A boy with normal hearing but with deaf parents who communicated by the American Sign Language was exposed to television every day so that he would learn English. Because the child was asthmatic and was confined to his home, he interacted only with people at home, where his family and all visitors communicated in sign language. By the age of three he was fluent in sign language, but neither understood nor spoke English. (Moskowitz 1978, 94–94B)

At SSD deaf children typically arrive as cultural *tabulae rasae* and they, too, learn to be deaf. Unlike other young children with normal hearing, they arrive with virtually no language, no self, no mind, and no symbolic knowledge. Initially, the school has no foundation on which to build. Across town, a hearing child, age seven, enters school with a strong and powerful (average) vocabulary size of 2600 words (Moskowitz 1978, 94D). In this frame we may say with confidence that young deaf children at least approach the magnitude of symbolic deprivation and crippled socialization experienced by the more dramatic cases mentioned below.

Sociologists have long shown interest in rare cases where individuals are deprived of language and/or social interaction. Many introductory sociology textbooks include accounts of three little girls without language and socialization: Anna, Isabelle (Davis 1949), and Genie (Curtiss 1977). These three children were literally reared in isolation apart from any group of human beings. Psychologist Harlan Lane (1976) also wrote a fascinating account of an eighteenth century "wild boy of Aveyron." For these children the social construction of mind, self, and society was totally lacking. They were found to be animal-like in behavior. In the literature, they are known as isolates and ferals, respectively.

Beyond isolates and ferals, we have focused here upon another much neglected group of children who experience profound and long-lasting socialization problems. They truly constitute an uncharted area of research, a social situation where hot questions blister the mind: If mind and self are symbolic constructs, does a symbol-less, languageless deaf child mentally attain some degree of mind and self? What social structure is possible for them? I suppose they have no "inner voice," no "internal conversation" (Berger and Luckmann 1967).

The children of this study are unique in that they belong to the only group of disabled people in the world that has its very own non-verbal language system. While they are generally thought of as "handicapped" people, sociologically speaking, the deaf community is precisely the same as an ethnic or subcultural group—a group with its own language, churches, theaters, and clubs. And the State School for the Deaf is the incubator where most deaf people—deaf minds, deaf selves, deaf cultures are made. As expected, one finds that, like many other subcultural groups, the deaf group is ethnocentric. It is also *endogamous*—that is, deaf people marry each other.

Language is the birth canal of humanity and the tie that binds. Unlike braille, which uses our alphabet, ASL is a *foreign* language. This creates a distinctive socialization process in that most deaf children and their parents do not speak the same language! This fact, in itself, pre-empts the traditional socialization process and the pre-eminent parental role in the transmission of culture and knowledge from one generation to another.

When does significant *symbolic* interaction between deaf children and their families take place? The socialization process at SSD is a narrow one and is virtually monopolized by the State institution. Deaf children who attend residential schools get a double measure of social and symbolic segregation and deprivation. First of all, their families, churches, and other sources have contributed little to the creative, formulative process of mind development and then when parents place them in a State School for the Deaf as early as age four, they are physically and spatially removed from family and community.

Second, sign language acquisition is very late. Some say that most deaf children who enter SSDs have already passed the optimal period of time when language should have been successfully learned. Further, even when they learn sign language, it is a symbol system not shared by the contiguous communities in the immediate area nor by society at large. It is a language that works well for a very small community, but has minimal external utility in the larger community. In short, language is the key ingredient to self: "Deafness as indicated primarily by 'signing' is the *master status* for these outsiders" (Higgins 1980, 131).

Social Interaction: A More Specific Definition

I think we cannot over-emphasize that social interaction, as sociologists conceptualize it, is much more than a person having physical proximity with other people; it is much more than moving bodies. Essentially and primarily, *social interaction* is a process where one attains intersubjectivity with others by linguistic/symbolic means (Charon 1979, 3).

Whenever people interact with conventional gestures, their minds connect and they establish a good degree of *isomorphism*—that is, symbolic interaction, the real stuff of human life. In the dominant hearing world, most deaf people experience a good degree of daily *body communication* (facial expressions, head nods)—that is, a good amount of physical interaction and a small amount of linguistic interaction.

Conclusion

Language is the vehicle upon which self and cultural knowledge ride, in particular, it is "language-based ... knowledge ... that constitutes the essence of humanity" (Evans 1988, 237). Language is "the bridge to humanity and 'human' is something symbolic both cognitively and behaviorally" (Evans 1987, 168). For White, "All human behavior originates in the use of symbols ...," and "human behavior is symbolic behavior; symbolic behavior is human behavior. The symbol is the universe of humanity" (1949, 22). To say it yet another way, "Knowledge of language is knowledge of [socially constructed] reality" (Israel 1979, xiv).

Without language, Huxley (1962) thought, one's world would be like the world of monkeys and dogs. As I have noted previously, "Without language, without words or even signs, reality remains raw, holistic, and continuous, similar to the worlds of non-languaging animals and human infants" (Evans 1987, 160). Starke (1992, 145) recently reported that a child in Seattle who had been deprived of language and social interaction "could not speak intelligibly, crawled rather than walked, and barked like a dog when people approached him."

In this paper I follow Berger and Luckmann (1967) and take *everything* that passes for knowledge in society (like religion, art, morals, law, myth, science, and even "recipe knowledge") to be knowledge. In a classic work, Weston Labarre (1947), painstakingly presented a veritable collage of human emotions and contextual gestures that one learns by means of social interaction and language. Acts like nodding the head for "yes," pointing with one's forefinger, smiling, laughing, crying, gestures of greeting, spitting, urinating, kissing, and so on are learned from one's own group and have different meanings cross-culturally. In short, "There is no 'natural' language of emotional gesture" (Labarre 1947, 55), and deaf children without language live outside the ocean of meanings that get attached to smiles and handshakes. Young deaf children who enter school with little or no language at ages four, six, ten, or even later, experience "reality gaps." For example, some of the teens said Superman was real, some deaf boys wanted to join the army, some deaf girls planned to be nurses, and two high school seniors insisted that one of them was "rich" because he had more than one hundred dollars in a bank (Evans and Falk 1986; Evans 1988, 241).

Finally, self is a creature of social interaction that includes languaging. The youngest children just entering SSD have no self, no mind, and no world (no social objects, no symbolic universe). Even many high school students were unable to self disclose when I asked them to "Tell me five things about yourself." Was my sign language making sense? Whenever I failed to get more than frowns and rolling eyes squinted (as if in deep thought), I asked *deaf* teachers to use their way of signing to the deaf students, but the result was the same! Selfhood was, presumably, in the making, but not yet to the fore. It must be true that, "In the Word was the Beginning ... the beginning of Man [and Woman] and of Culture" (White 1949, 22). And, I would add, of *mind, self,* and *society.*

NOTES

1. I want to thank my colleague, Dr. Leona Kanter, whose enthusiasm and editorial comments were truly helpful.

2. Some deaf children at SSD (ages 4, 8, or older) did not know nor could they even think that a family was divided into parents, siblings, grandparents, uncles, aunts, etc. They certainly may experientially know that individuals are different but, beyond that, people at large—including intimate ones—are neither tagged, valuated, nor categorized. Some children at SSD of different races said they were "brothers" because they were from the same home town.

3. All deaf people do not use ASL. Some children learn oral methods of communication instead of signs and this paper is not about them at all. For 200 years in America there has raged a war between these two philosophies, the "manuals" and the "orals." This paper discusses the manuals who lived at SSD.

4. The physical environment for all children without a symbol system is a holistic, unsegmented chunk of "physical objects" as opposed to discrete, clearly defined, and labeled "social" objects.

5. All languages have verbal (sound) and written forms which are arbitrary (i.e., neither the sounds nor the written symbols have any resemblance to the referents). The spoken or written word for "tree" has absolutely no likeness to the actual physical tree itself. The American Sign Language hand-arm configuration, however, does look somewhat like a tree and this correspondence between a sign and its referent is called *iconicity*. "Although there are definite distinctions between regular ASL signs and the spontaneous mimetic representation characteristic of pantomime, even many regular ASL signs clearly exhibit traces of mimetic properties" (Klima and Bellugi 1979, 21). Many signs, like spoken symbols, are arbitrary and yet, "the vocabulary of ASL ... is a great deal more iconic than are the morphemes of spoken languages" (21). Just what the effect of this unique quality of iconicity means in terms of ASL being a language fully capable of equal abstract communication is a topic of debate (see Schein 1984, 28, who downplays the significance of iconicity). Research also indicates that iconic signs are not necessarily transparent to nonsigners. That is, nonsigners cannot understand signed words even though they are somewhat iconic. An important question for me is whether or not ASL, with its iconic tie to many referents is as abstract as spoken languages.

6. See Kottack 1991, 37 for a good distinction between (a) individual situational learning, (b) social situational learning, and (c) cultural learning. For our purposes here, I would prefer to call (c) "symbolic" or "linguistic" learning.

7. It seems reasonable to assume that Solo Boy had no idea at all where he was nor why his parents had left him in a strange place where people wore white clothes, white hosiery, and white shoes. Of course he did experience the physical place, but without a symbol system he did not know, for example, that he was in the Northern part of the state at an "infirmary" of a "State School." In short, no one could convey complex symbolic-linguistic knowledge or information to him. Why his parents waved "bye-bye" to him and drove away that morning could not be explained to him. They could not say to him, "We will return in a few weeks to visit. We are not abandoning you, we love you!" In a word, he was alone and without any significant degree of intersubjectivity with any other human being.

8. One administrator at SSD told me about two very poor illiterate deaf brothers without language who used a very unusual sign for "car." They would raise both arms skyward with hands cupped in a gripping configuration. After several visits to their home, the SSD administrator observed one boy faithfully holding up the hood of his father's automobile while father worked on the engine, hence the origin of the sign!

9. Three profound realizations were made by these developing children: first, family members typically cannot sign; second, family members attended public schools; and third, their family talks with their voices and tries to teach the deaf child to do so. It could not be more clear: family members do not belong to the deaf world at all. They are not one of us. The global social process of being taught sound-based symbol systems and speech reading skills are experiences that help construct and confirm one's deaf self. Like the walls of a great womb, the self-mind definition process is ubiquitous.

Conversion to Feminism

Charlotte Wolf

Commencing in the 1960s and continuing on into the subsequent decades, the embers of the early-twentieth-century feminist movement were again fanned into life. Books and papers about women's status—a subject that in the previous few decades had seldom been discussed—were once more being written, and for a growing audience. Meetings were called and women came together to talk over their situation; feminist groups were created, both as a bridge between individual response and institutional context, and as a mechanism for mediation and change.

To become a member of such a group and to become sympathetic with feminist ideas was, in fact, to assert the validity of an alternative set of categories, those which involved not just different interpretations of reality—of a woman's life situation, of the social world around her—but which could eventuate in her conversion into a feminist. The course these changes took was multi-dimensional, having both personal, interpretive components and social, contextual components. Thus, it is the concern here to examine the processes by which the evaluation of past experience, growing commitment to the women's liberation movement, and conversion and resocialization into a feminist takes place, and in this regard, to touch on the relationship of feminist organization and personal change. It is suggested that the feminist organization provided a supportive social world, a universe of discourse in which cognitive frameworks could be re-interpreted and individual identities transformed.

Theoretical Framework

The framework for this analysis is based on symbolic interactionist theory and on ideas and research dealing with identity conversion and commitment. Years ago, Anselm Strauss (1959), in writing about identity transformation, discussed "turning points" as a component of this process, these being usually accompanied by an underlying belief in identity continuity. Tamotsu Shibutani (1961), and later Orrin Klapp (1969), expanded this set of ideas by suggesting that identity change could be related to conversion; and Peter Berger and Thomas Luckmann (1966), in continuing this discussion, proposed that there are three ways by which identity might change: *resocialization, alternation,* and *conversion.* In noting these distinctions, however, Richard Travisano (1970) stressed that alternation and conversion represent two very different sorts of identity transformation: although alternation might be simply a sequence of identities, conversion signals "a radical reorganization of identity, meaning and life" (600). Taking this a step further by shifting levels of analysis, Zurcher and Snow (1981), and later Ralph Turner (1983), stated that identity change could be critical to the development and success of social movements.

Other studies relevant to the question of identity transformation include: Barkun's (1972) discussion of the characteristics of followers; the work of Heirich (1977), who mentions the importance of friendship networks and social encapsulation to the conversion process; Greil and Ruby (1984) who emphasize the type of organizations or "social cocoons" necessary for supporting identity transformation; the discussions of Snow and Phillips (1980) regarding the importance of intensive interaction in contributing to this process; and, in the same vein, Stark and Bainbridge's (1980) discussion of the importance of networks in recruitment of members to a conversion-type organization.

Much of the literature, however, has been on religious conversion. William James (1902; 1911), many years ago, prominently mentioned conversion as a basic aspect of religious experience. More recently, the research on conversion has been extensive, including, for example: the work of Lofland and Stark (1965); Lofland (1966); Lebra (1972); Gordon (1974); Bromley and Shupe (1979); Richardson (1980); Lofland and Skonovd (1981); Biermans (1986); and Fichter (1987).

The idea of commitment has often been used in conjunction with conversion concepts. Some work that has defined the area includes the following: Howard Becker (1960; 1970a) suggests that commitment permits situational adjustment during periods of change; and Rosabeth Moss Kanter (1972a; 1972b), in studying commitment in communes and utopias, discusses the importance of this process in welding members together and in building and strengthening a community. Other research that could be profitably mentioned is that of Kornhauser (1962) on political commitment, Gerlach and Hine (1970) on social transformation movements, and Killian

(1973) on social movements. Micossi (1970) and Green (1979) have both focused on the women's liberation movement as a context in which a change of consciousness has been fostered, and both Carden (1974) and Friedan (1976) have emphasized the importance of commitment in feminist organizations. These ideas on conversion and commitment, as related to this paper, imply that, at the end of the change process, the individual would ordinarily see herself as a feminist and would likely be committed to the women's movement. In discussing the process of becoming a feminist, Chow (1987) insists that gender consciousness precedes feminist consciousness and commitment to the movement; Rowbotham (1974) emphasizes that such changes ultimately make for a revolutionary consciousness; and, in widening the net, Stoll (1974) says that changes in feminist consciousness are necessary prerequisites for effecting social change in women's situation.

Definitions and Directions

Definitions of a feminist or of feminist beliefs usually include the following points: the understanding that women are "a caste or class, linked together by their sex" (Hymowitz and Weissman 1978, 350); the presumption that women and men are equal, and the view that they are "committed to the goals, beliefs, and values of the women's movement" (Green 1979, 359). Cott (1987) similarly suggests that the three essential features of feminism are: (1) opposition to all forms of stratification based on gender; (2) a belief that biology does not consign females to inferior status; and (3) a sense of common experience and purpose in working to effect change.

It is proposed in this paper then that feminist ideas, by delineating a different world and encouraging an alternative set of expectations, tend to be instilled in the process of conversion and come to order and to provide interpretations of women's experiences. However, the social climate of the 1970s, while conducive to attracting some women to the movement, was also one in which feminist beliefs were not generally acceptable. It is possible that the external hostility to feminism that was encountered by interested women strengthened and astringently tempered the conversion process, contributing to the building of a cohesive, supportive community of like-thinking feminists outside the family and friendship groups in which these women had usually operated (Simmel 1950, 369).

Furthermore, the strong feelings and identity changes, which it is suggested here were manifested by the women studied, might represent a mini-social revolution from the midst of a very unlikely group—middle-class, middle-aged, educated, conventional, and mostly conservative women, without experience in revolutionary ethics, philosophy, or tactics. That such restlessness and desire for change should explode into a radical shift from the staid and prosaic center might have made this a somewhat different conversion group that put its own stamp on the conversion process.

Methodology

This study is part of a larger work focusing on the members of a metropolitan chapter of a feminist organization in which both participant-observation and interview methods were used. Thirty-three women, who had been executive board members, chairpersons, and organizers of task forces and committees during the 1970s, were asked to reminisce about their pre-movement, movement, and after-involvement feelings and experiences. All of them had been highly active in the organization at the city or state level and had represented both its early or charismatic phases and its later more administrative, but overlapping, phases.

In the 1980s, at the time of the in-depth interviews, these women were no longer deeply involved in the women's movement, having passed their leadership roles on to more active and younger women. Retrospection on their experiences for these women, while sharpness and spontaneity were now blunted, permitted them a sense of distance and analysis in their reconstruction of the events. The willingness of these women to be interviewed and to speak openly about their involvement in the women's movement stemmed from knowing the researcher, who had also been a member of the organization during the same period.

The interview group consisted of thirty Anglo women, one Black woman, and two Hispanic women, ranging in age from their mid- or late-thirties into their fifties. Most (88 percent) of these women had received at least one college degree, and twelve of them held professional degrees (three PhDs, two MDs, two JD degrees, and five MSW or MA degrees), and the remaining group of women had some college training. Most of these women were middle-class and at the time of the interviews, twenty-eight of them (82.4 percent) were employed full-time, working in professional or managerial positions. Of the total, seventeen (52 percent) were married; thirteen (39 percent) were divorced; and three women (9 percent) were single.

The primary purpose of this paper then is to describe the process of becoming a feminist from the point of view of these women, and to illuminate the analysis by repeating in their words how they remembered their experiences.

Process of Identity Change

Initial indicators of identity change include major steps such as: joining a women's liberation organization; undergoing resocialization activities; the advent of turning points; changes in cognitive frameworks and interpretations; changes in life patterns, in friends, in social and political affiliations, in the old supports with attendant costs of occasional hostile response; and in living for a time, what seemed to them, embattled lives. These major life changes were combining with an emergent sense of commitment and dedication to the women's movement.

Joining

Before joining the organization, many of the women recalled that they were restless and discontented with their lives, believing that something was wrong with them. For example, one woman said:

> First of all, I was aware that I had some unresolved anger in me that didn't seem to fit situations. You know, when I studied psychology and social work, I studied Freud, and I kept trying to figure it out in those kinds of terms. And I couldn't. There were things that seemed unfair to me. But my tendency was to think that I was crazy, to think that I was wrong because I didn't fit.

Other women also recalled a growth of awareness, sometimes dating it to college years, but sometimes even earlier. For example, one woman discussed how different she had felt being a girl raised among boys:

> It basically started when I was a little girl, in that I was the oldest of six and I had a very difficult relationship with my father. I was often angry because my two little brothers got everything. I resented it. I thought it was wrong.

By the time the chapter of the women's organization was formed in 1970, many of these women knew about the national organization from newspapers, magazines, radio, and television, or they had heard about it from friends, and out of curiosity and possibly pique with their own lives, they had determined to go to a meeting. However, one women told of her fears of violating the gender norms of being a proper, middle-class female, and it was with a great deal of trepidation that she went to a meeting:

> I remember reading one article on this strange group of people with NOW [National Organization for Women] that was formed and it was the scariest thing I ever did, going to that first meeting. I just had visions in my mind that it was going to be all these people not wearing bras, and wearing old dirty T-shirts, all about twenty. And when I got there and saw all these lovely women of all different ages, I thought, "I don't believe it. These are all women just like me."

Several other women also expressed a sense of relief on finding women at these meetings who were just like themselves—that is, middle-class and mostly middle-aged.

And so the membership grew from the requisite chapter size of ten people to over one hundred within a couple of months. Other than newspaper announcements of meetings and the telephoning of friends, no organizational effort was made to recruit new members. As a matter of fact, the organization had grave problems with the rapid expansion and with the lack of procedures to socialize people to function as effective members. Interest and some awareness, of course, were part of the self-selection process before joining the organization. However, for the conventional middle-class women of that time, joining a feminist organization was a very large first step toward commitment to a new perspective.

Resocialization Processes: Consciousness-Raising Groups

Consciousness-raising groups, while perhaps not deliberately constructed to be as radical a mechanism of change as they became (Carden 1974, 35; Cassell 1977; Hartsock 1981, 598–99; MacKinnon 1982, 17–29; Deckard 1983, 463), were basic organizational means or tactics for changing perspectives and indirectly, identities, and were important to the conversion process. Women got together, talked over their experiences, their past, their hopes for the future, within the agreed-upon rules of as much honesty as could be mustered by the individual and with the support and understanding of other members in the circle. A woman, who had organized some of the small consciousness-raising groups in the organization, discussed the responses she had noted:

> Well, I ran into two kinds of women in these groups, and both of them were legitimate. It was either the "poor me" syndrome or "I'll get the son-of-a-bitch" syndrome. And I'd give them a year to get over it, because they had every right to that after being discriminated against for thousands of years.

Although anger and rage frequently exploded in these sessions, as well as emotional depression and confusion, elation and relief were also expressed. Yet these consciousness-raising group meetings marked, for many women, a major step toward cognitive restructuring of their worlds. A middle-aged white woman, in summing up how she had felt in these sessions, said: "There were lots of confrontative things. I was scared to death. But I got so I just said, 'I believe this is right. Do it!'"

The experience for minority women was somewhat different. Although they were keenly aware of what discrimination was like, they had not defined their problems as similar to those of majority women. Thus, consciousness-raising for them had the double edge of identifying themselves as members of two oppressed groups; that is, as members of a minority ethnic group and also as women. A minority woman described how this had happened to her:

> They didn't have to teach me too much about discrimination because I knew exactly what they were talking about. But I hadn't seen myself as a woman. I had seen myself as being part of a family, which was the Hispanic family, and discrimination was against all Hispanics. But NOW taught me to think of myself as a woman. And I just ate it all up.

In this climate women came to define sexism, to become sensitive to it, to gain insight into their own problems, and to see that their experiences were not singular, but were class-related experiences of an oppressed group. Consciousness-raising, then, became a ritual of purification, a stripping away of the unsatisfactory, and sometimes even of the satisfactory aspects of the old life. And out of the seemingly endless stories of hard times, fruitless efforts, limited futures, failures, humiliations, joblessness or lack of job success, of being defined as sex objects or being sexually harassed, and so on, a means was provided by which to examine the outlines of the individual's life and to relate it to other women's lives. Hence, such a group-based method represented an extraordinarily powerful tool for redefining personal experiences within an ideological framework. It gave these women what they had lacked: a *weltanschauung* of understanding.

Turning Points and Reality Shocks

Anselm Strauss (1959, 93–100) suggested that there can be turning points in people's lives, when through evaluation, new alignments, and commitments, old identities are shucked aside, permitting a conversion to a new identity. The idea of "reality shock" (Schutz 1962; Wolf 1975) further illuminates the disruption that an extraordinary event or threat to previous suppositions can present to one enveloped in everyday life. The individual, brought abruptly face-to-face with a new and shocking interpretation, or with sudden aware-ness of other formerly unperceived aspects of life, might fall into uncertainty, conflict, and cognitive crisis over their meanings.

For some, a reality shock followed by a turning point, came at home with family relations and was more than simply reflective, but integral to the emerging interactive relations, as well. For example, one women recalled:

> I knew that other women were being discriminated against, but I didn't think it had anything to do with me. As a matter of fact, I thought I was very privi-leged. One Saturday, after working all week, I wasn't able to go downtown with the rest of the family because I had to do "my laundry." I really wanted to go. I was picking up dirty clothes—men's and teenagers' underclothing, dish-towels, family tablecloths, and sheets when suddenly it hit me: "My laundry! Why *my* laundry?" The words rang in my head as I threw the whole load down to the basement, got my coat, and walked out the front door.

Another woman told of a work situation that had provided a reality shock for her:

> I was a social worker, and I had a supervisor who was a divorced woman who was raising two kids. And the top administrator, a man, who was also a social worker and all for civil rights and all the things everybody was for in the '60s, actually made this comment to her, in front of me: that women really didn't need to be paid as much because they didn't have the responsibility for raising children. And he was looking her straight in the eye, and he knew she was divorced and raising children.

For some women, turning points came from reading feminist books or from talking to friends or in their consciousness-raising groups; for others, the turning point came from joining the feminist organization, as illustrated by these comments from a middle-aged teacher:

> I had always felt totally displaced, totally out of sync all the time. I was on the fringes, which my father always said. I was the girl who didn't know her place. And then I joined NOW and immediately the tensions got better and I felt the bondage. Immediately I felt a very common ground.

Regardless of how it occurred, for most women, there was some turning point or reality shock that was a critical juncture in their lives.

Identity Dissonance and the Agonistic of Change

These experiences took place within a social context that, to some of these women, appeared to be hostile and disapproving. Many of them were being labeled with what was perceived as negative epithets such as "feminists," "bra-burners," and "women's libbers," sometimes at work and sometimes at home. These were pressures that caused a few women to drop out, but most did not. Conflictual feelings between anger and the desire to be a feminist and yet to be feminine and remain respected in the gender role took hold of their lives. One of the leaders described it this way:

> Sometimes I was tempted to try for both worlds—have a man protect and support me, and also have the respect due to being a self-supporting, independent person.

Another woman, who later became a political leader in the state, said: "I had been a Barbie doll, and it was so hard to change."

Conversion was often signalled by intense inner conflict: it could be said that this conflict was between the old and the new self. And for a time, there was an adjudication between old and new identity demands. As one woman said, "I wished I could go back to my old life. I had been so comfortable, but I knew I couldn't have stood it if I did." Another woman from a minority ethnic group described this process similarly:

> Because I was Hispanic and poor, I'd never felt I belonged to the mainstream of society. So I just sat back and dreamed about what it would be like. But being around feminist leaders, I knew I just couldn't sit back any more. That was painful. But it was painful to change, too.

For many women a sense of *identity dissonance* (Wolf 1975) arose, and attempts to bring reconciliation between the past definition of self and the newly emerging definition of self became a problem. There was the fear that new identities might be branded as "masculine," or "aggressive," or "lesbian." There was the fear of being called unfeminine, not a lady, and thus a generalized fear of entering into unknown territories of identity. There were deep fears of not being accepted by old friends, of being disapproved of and cast out by one's husband or family. Witness how one woman responded to this identity tug-of-war:

> I became an angrier person. And the injustices that I saw around me were ones I thought I had to work on and had to do something about. And every chance I had I went out and talked and worked. Meanwhile, though, a psychological war was going on at home; and outside was easier than in the house.

What occurred with these feminist leaders was that gradually they began to change their lifestyle, sloughing off people who did not agree with them, changing toward a more consensual universe of discourse within the feminist group, concentrating their interests and group memberships, and ultimately making feminism their central concern, the major integrating factor in their lives. Changes in costume, in language, in jobs, and returning to school for further education marked this transition. Mostly, for the first time in their lives, these women began to seek out and read books and articles *about women*. The sharply new importance of reading or hearing about women was attested to by the remarks of one of the leaders who, with the kind of encouragement that came from reading that women were intelligent and capable, had started law school in her late forties:

> I was just a non-person; and NOW was like a light going on. I started reading; and, you know, I just ate it up because it felt so good to read about us being persons and able to do thus and so. I just devoured books as though I was going down for the last time in the ocean, and that was my straw that was going to keep me afloat. I just couldn't get enough of it.

Changes in attitudes toward other women were usual. One woman said that she had thought that women were "dull and stupid," but she, as well as others, now felt a growing sense of respect and liking for them. As part of this, came a distinct change in attitudes toward their mothers. An older woman stated that her relationship with her mother had always been "angry, bitter, and hostile," but that had changed since she had become a feminist and now tried to understand her mother as a human being. Another woman described her relationship with her mother as going from "fair to good to excellent." Remembrances of mothers' and grandmothers' acts of independence and strength of character permitted a strong sense of identity continuity. A rooting of reference groups and location of self within the generations of women occurred in conjunction with this. Part of this extension of time back into the generations of women and the thrust into the future included the often fictional construction of identity as a feminist. Such statements as, "I was born a feminist" or "I have always been a feminist" were frequent, denoting the constructed continuity of identity. Comments like the following are illustrative:

> I think I was always basically a feminist, which is awful because I went through cheerleading and I was the prom queen. All that kind of stuff, you know, was very "in" in the 1950s.

Thus, past behavior became explained as being superficial to the real feminist self beneath, and the conversion process in attitudes was continued by engulfing the past as well as the present.

Almost all of the women made changes in their home lives and sought a redistribution of household responsibilities. Often this was set with conflict and alarm. One married woman said that when she had demanded that her husband recognize that she was becoming a different person, he treated her as if she were an unruly child:

> It was a battle, really. I was a real warrior. It was very frightening for me. My husband and I had terrible problems. I think I finally had to recognize that in a structure of an authoritarian marriage, husbands respond to you within that structure. My husband kept saying, "Oh, you'll get over this," like I was sick or something. But you can't go back to a blissful state of ignorance.

In trying to put her feminist ideas into practice at home, another woman told of the problems she had had with her teenage children, as well as her husband:

> NOW was the hardest thing I ever did after I got married. And my family had a hard time coping with it. There was a lot of conflict about sharing the household chores. One day, though, I came home and told everybody, "I cooked for fifteen years, and I quit." I also quit grocery shopping. I didn't like that job. They all felt rejected, and they thought Mama had gone crazy and a whole bunch of other things. The conflict lasted for about two years.

Yet, husbands and children were sometimes supportive, and along with accepting the changes in the wife or mother, they also began sharing some of her feminist ideas, as well as the household duties. However, if the marriage was shaky or the renegotiation of gender roles did not meet with sufficient success, new arrangements, including divorce, became more possible. A few women chose alternative paths such as living in an all-woman family or small group, or perhaps establishing a lesbian relationship. As one woman said, "The Movement allowed me to face my lesbianism openly and gratefully."

Commitment

Commitment to the organization commenced with joining the group, paying dues, and going to meetings. Core members accepted the early responsibilities for heading task groups or working on the executive board level or in some action-directed way. To give talks or speeches was a part of organizational activity and an important step toward commitment. With this involvement came the sense of obligation, of "faithfulness" (Simmel 1950, 384–85), of devotion to one another and to the group. As part of the feminist ideology, the term "sisterhood is powerful" exemplified these feelings, having both personal and political effects (Yates 1975, 101; Brownmiller 1970, 154–55) and idealistically underlying the thrust toward commitment.

Although not all "sisters" such as poor women and minority women had flocked to join this feminist organization, the principle of sisterhood was one that these women came to acknowledge. Several women from minority groups became leaders in the organization, yet within their own ethnic groups, they had the double problem of being seen as having transgressed both feminine and racial roles and were chided on both counts. As one woman recalled: "Friends told me that I was going into the white women's bag, and that I wasn't being true to my race."

During the 1970s, however, if a woman became known as a feminist, which either swiftly or at least ultimately occurred, regardless of race, she was forced into defending it. By becoming a target for curiosity and hostility, her commitment to the movement tended to become accentuated and the boundaries of the group more highly delineated. To be known as a feminist during this period meant that at parties, meetings, work, and school, it was necessary to defend feminist ideas. Witness how this woman, who said she had been shy and quiet, described how she changed, doing things she had never thought she would do, defending points that she had never before thought about, and, in short, under the cloak of the committed crusader, becoming quite a different person:

> Not only at NOW meetings, but I become an activist and played quite a role in the company where I worked. I became "*the* feminist." They had thought they were all out there on the East Coast and all out there on the West Coast; and, my God, they had one right there in their midst, doing picketing, the full thing, and quite colorful, too. I tend to be quite flamboyant when I'm really moved; and when I was fully into it, it was quite a scary thing for the company. Was I afraid I'd lose my job? Not really. I rather thrived on it. I came to like confrontation.

The longer people remained in the movement, the more radical they tended to become. The tendency was for them to move away from conservative politics and passive personal behavior, as this woman's statement makes clear: "It horrified me at first, but I realized that sometimes you have to push things over the brink. You just have to use confrontation politics." A radical shift, then, away from the conservatism of their status as middle-class women was part of the conversion and commitment process, as this woman attests:

> I think the thing that changed my attitudes most was the day we marched, because I'd never had the privilege of being able to do that. It was a very big

step to go out on the streets with women and march for something in which I believed. It was just so liberating.

Another woman provided a rationale for radicalization, stating strongly: "I didn't perceive myself as radical. No, I felt very comfortable. Is it radical to do things that are right? Is equality radical?"

Thus, the sense of solidarity with "sisters," of being morally right in their feminist beliefs, of being radically involved in a crusade against injustice were salient features of the commitment process. As one woman, who had expressed how important the community of "sisters" and the meetings were to her and how they had provided a bulwark against an inimical social climate, said:

> I'd come to a meeting, and these were my family, these were my sisters. But I'd leave this room, and it was a different world out there because people didn't think the way I did and the way we did.

The feminist group and organization came to be a community of significant others, providing a micro-world in which the agonistic of identity conversion could play its way out, a place in which to resolve identity dissonance, and thus the new identity could be made meaningful, socially validated, objectified, and reinforced within a social context. Being in a group of like-others yielded to its members a variety of bonds and so the organization and the network of women came to stand as an island of identity legitimation, a social mirror by which to tentatively come forth in the garments of a transformed self.

Conversion

The end result of the conversion process was that women thought themselves to be feminists, and they believed that what they had gone through had changed them permanently in this direction. One woman described this as "a total change of awareness. It is in every single area of my life." When asked to compare their transition into feminists with that of religious conversion, most of them said there was little difference. However, an older woman, who was both politically astute and analytical about the feminist movement, believed this was not quite the case: "I grew up in the deep south. Southern revival meetings—that's an emotional thing. It's hysterical. Feminist conversion is different." Still, she went on to say, there were similarities:

> People who have been born again, in a religious sense, perceive everything that happens and everything they see in a religious way, and they put it into their religious context. I think that every women who goes through the feminist conversion then perceives everything they see and do in a feminist sense.

The women's passage through the stations of conversion had been frequently painful yet often euphoric; however, the transformation process for some had been more extensive, the conversion more complete than for others. Thus, there were differences in levels of commitment, in the extent of linkage of feminist perspectives to their lives, in the amount of social change that each felt would necessarily have to occur. On these bases, these women could be divided into roughly three subgroups: *gradualists, reformers,* and *radicals.* Of course, there was often a moving in and out of categories by individual members, and in regard to issues, lines were frequently blurred.

Gradualists defined themselves as feminists with a level of involvement that was occasionally tenuous, and a degree of pervasiveness of conversion that was limited. Feminism was not their primary base of identification, nor did they express interest in seeing such deep or extensive changes in women's status as did the other women. Making up a minority of the leadership cadre, their influence on the directions the organization took was slight.

Reformers made up the bulk of the group. They strongly recognized how important feminism had become to them and how their attitudes and politics and even their careers had changed. Yet overall they were moderate in their views on how deep social changes would have to be in order to effectively bring about gender equality. Tinkering, but not destruction, of the social system was seen as appropriate. One woman, who worked on national boards of both religious and family planning organizations, stated:

> I believe the only way to accomplish change is that women have to organize with their allies to bring it about. I think we have to be much more sacrificial in what we give and definitely examine where we are giving money, and give only to candidates who advance women's causes.

Radical points of view were expressed by about seven women in the study group. They felt that they were highly committed to feminism and had attempted major changes in their personal lives. Conflictive interpretations of gender relations were frequently made, for example:

> I think that the white male system is out to get us. And I don't think we will really ever be able to change the system because we are out of power, and as long as we have no power, we cannot change it. Everything is run by a small group of wealthy, powerful, white males who work only to continue the system. You know, my theory is that women are, in a way, in a Renaissance period with new and enlightened ideas, new consciousness, new outlooks. And men are still in the medieval period, fighting with armor and chains and all those crazy axes. Unfortunately, they have all the power.

Another woman believed that drastic changes would have to come in gender relations because "relationships between men and women now are nearly impossible, there is so much underlying hostility in men toward women." And she went on to state her feminist worldview: "Everybody would have an equal share. It's a very small-community sort of perspective, very communal and sharing." Other views of this genre were less sanguine, but still as broad in their scope of criticism and demands for social change:

> The capitalistic society, the way it is today in Western civilization, perpetuates the submission of groups of people.... It must do this in order to exist. It must have a secondary poverty level, a dependence level.... I think there have to be lots of changes here in values, and Western civilization absolutely must change.

Conclusions

Conversion to a feminist identity was signaled by a radical reorganization of meaning and of everyday life, of how a woman saw herself and her situation. The pervasiveness of conversion for these leaders tended to expand situationally and definitions of past and present identities and experiences were brought into greater or lesser congruence as outside contacts become less satisfying and commitment to feminism grew.

Transformation therefore meant that a partial or more or less complete dissociation with the old self had occurred. However, changes in identity had gradations. It is suggested that the compass of identity change or the depth of conversion experience was indicated by the extent of commitment to the feminist cause and the linkage of feminist perspectives to the woman's life.

A basic factor in this process was the feminist community in which the shared outcast status of these women and the ideology of feminism provided the struts of a protective identity-affirming social world. It is proposed that the external context of hostility as perceived by these women tended to increase the solidarity of the group. Yet as these conflictual currents appeared to abate and the antipathy toward feminism became moderate, sharp differences between the feminist community and the social context also diminished, and the boundaries of the feminist community became less distinct.

It is further suggested that this was a revolution from the center; that for middle-class, middle-aged, educated women to cross normative lines of proper behavior required changes in personal life and self. Possibly acceptance of a feminist framework occurred because of the uniqueness of the conversion dynamic: first came the intellectualized interpretations of gender discrimination, and only subsequently was this followed by ideological fervor and closure.

This odyssey of conversion and movement involvement was not without cost—exhaustion, loss of jobs and old acquaintances, expenditures of time and energy. Still, with the catalyst of the women's movement, it was recognized that their views of "woman's place" and of the world itself had changed. All of those interviewed said: "I could never go back." For that matter, it is possible that the radical re-integration of the self that comes with identity conversion makes reversion to the earlier self difficult, and perhaps unlikely.

Time has passed for these women and there has been an attenuation of ties to each other and, for a few, there has been a lessening of commitment. The hostility of the outside world has dissipated to some extent, but this is not surprising since many feminist ideas have been accepted, and sometimes co-opted or deflected, and thus differences between the two worlds have become more difficult to define.

Learning Meanings

from the

Fashion World

Fred Davis

How does the sociologist of everyday life—and what people wear, furnish their homes with, watch on TV, and listen to in music certainly counts for everyday life—acquire an analytical perspective on something so complex, elusive, and ephemeral as fashion? Even restricting one's purview to fashion's most familiar domain, that of clothing, does one simply look at what people on the street are wearing today, and then, by way of trying to extract some larger cultural meaning from dress, compare this to the way they dressed last year, five years ago, a decade ago, or even a century ago? Would one then seek to supplement the analysis of findings from such a comparison by asking a sample of clothes wearers (how many? drawn from what populations? at what interview sites?) why they wear what they do? What if their statements agree with your preliminary analysis? What if they disagree? And what would such agreement or disagreement mean for the soundness of your inquiry? Or, assuming there are some long-term historical factors at play in the symbolic evolution of modern dress—an assumption many a cultural scientist is bound to entertain—would it be better to place one's own immediate impressions on ice and turn instead to books on costume history for a sense of the whither and whence of contemporary dress? Or, in accordance with the accepted practices of empirical science, should one again dispense with one's own impressions and intuitions, but this time, rather than turning to historical works, look instead to what leading sociological theorists such as Veblen, Simmel, Tarde, Sumner, and Blumer have written on fashion. One would then extract testable hypotheses from their writings and subject them to one or another experiment or test. (What these might conceivably be is by no means obvious or straightforward.) From the resulting data, appropriately abstracted and statistically transmuted, the investigator could, or so it is alleged by those partial to this methodology, determine which theory or combination of theories is correct.

Depending on which social science the student is trained in, although nowadays literary theory offers its own methodologies for the study of everyday life (de Certeau 1984), and on the epistemological leanings of the student's teachers, one or another of the above strategies—there are yet others I have not considered—is likely to be seriously recommended as the preferred way to acquire a perspective for studying some circumscribable segment of everyday life. Although each strategy, from "first blush" on-the-spot comparisons of this year and yesteryear, to sample surveys, to extended historical inquiry, to theory-derived testing of hypotheses, has its important place in research, it is not for that of "acquiring a perspective." To understand where these strategies fail or miss the point, we must first grasp what it is to have a perspective and what acquiring it entails.

The first poses no particular difficulty. A dictionary definition (Webster's Third New International) suffices: "*perspective* ... 2a: the interrelation in which parts of a subject are mentally viewed: the aspect of an object of thought from a particular standpoint ... b: capacity to view things in their true relation, relations, or relative importance." Clearly, whatever words are used to define it, what we are dealing with is some everyday notion of seeing things in a particular light; or being able to relate parts of a subject to each other and to the whole from some consistent standpoint; or securing guidance in our approach to a phenomenon through interpretative rules or standards that allow for categorical assignments and evaluations. On a mundane level it would seem that, however acquired, perspective is necessary if we are not to be continually thrown into a dither and victimized by what so often strikes us as the buzzing confusion of everyday life.

What it means to acquire a perspective, however, and how this is done cannot so easily be reduced to the conveniences of a dictionary definition. Whatever value one may attach to one or another of the more formal approaches to the perspective-acquisition process I touched on above, my own conviction is that the researcher's conscious sense of possessing a perspective occurs considerably later in the process than earlier. (That possession of a perspective is desirable and perhaps even inevitable, I take to be a given.) I say this because of the peculiar epistemological relationship we as researchers bear to the everyday life we mean to study. Unlike the phenomena studied by the astronomer, physicist, chemist, or for that matter, the anthropologist working in a remote culture, we sociologists of everyday life are *prima facie* as much a part of that everyday life as are those whose everyday activities, attitudes, and practices we wish to comprehend in some systematic way. From the very outset, therefore, we cannot, short of pretending to be a martian (Davis 1973), but help bring some perspective (call it prejudice, ideology, paradigm, taken-for-granted outlook, whatever!) to the everyday domain we wish to study. True, it may be—indeed is likely to be—a nascent perspective different from that held by some or even many of those whose activities we observe and inquire about. But, however crude, incomplete, and inconsistent our research later reveals it to be, that it is a perspective cannot for a moment be doubted; moreover, it is a perspective that was formed and developed in the course of *our* everyday life experience in the domain under study, much as were the perspectives of the persons with whom we conduct our study.

Thus, in a certain sense, the problem for the sociologist of everyday life is, initially at least, less one of acquiring a perspective than of critically scrutinizing the pre-formed "everyday" perspective brought by him or her to the topic at hand. And, such scrutiny can, if properly reflexive and probing, not merely dispel prejudice and error, but it can also serve as a rich source of insight and conceptual breakthroughs.

In these pages I wish to offer what I trust is a useful example of the process whereby the sociologist's lived-in-the-world, lay perspective on some facet of social life interacts with other perspectives. These "other" perspectives are mainly those engendered by his or her more deliberate and reasoned reflections on the topic as well as the more formal, conceptually anchored perspectives students are heir to by virtue of their disciplinary attachments. In keeping with the central theme of this volume, I view this process as one in which, through a kind of dialectic, our own lay and refined-through-reflection perspectives come, both to be modified and to modify those perspectives proffered us by our scholarly discipline, sociology. I shall try to illustrate this by recounting some of the conceptual twists and turns I have encountered over my almost life-long fascination with the notoriously "fickle and frivolous" Dame Fashion.[1]

I shall divide the discussion of the process into four successive phases: *native view, engagement, resolutions and riddles,* and *finding answers.* I should emphasize that this four-part division is mainly for the sake of discussion. In principle there could just as well be three or eight phases. Moreover, to the extent that the designation of sequential phases can felicitously reflect something of what the researcher experiences in the course of acquiring and refining his or her perspective, it must at the same time be understood that in actuality, life offers us no such neat categorical or temporal divisions. The on-the-ground researcher is constantly moving between and among what I have here arbitrarily delineated as successive phases. Yet—and this perhaps ultimately justifies the resort to a phase-type analysis—for all of the confusion, contradiction, and indeterminacy, one thing is certain: a process is in play and its end points are clearly different from its beginnings. However we approach it, therefore, we must try to describe as best we can how this came to pass.

Native View

By native view I mean to refer to the "natural" lay person's drawn-from-the-culture perspective I brought to the topic at about the time it first occurred to me (as it probably would not have were I not a sociology graduate student at the time) that one could seriously study so sociologically marginal but, for me, intriguing a phenomenon as fashion.[2] The occasion for this realization— its legitimation, if you will—was a number of lectures on fashion given at the University of Chicago in 1948 in a course titled "Collective Behavior" by the late Professor Herbert Blumer and his then graduate student assistant, Tamotsu Shibutani (Davis 1991a).

My own native perspective on the topic was one greatly influenced by my upbringing in New York City during the depression and early World War II years as the son of immigrant Jewish parents, both of whom had, as young immigrants, worked in the New York City garment trades as had many of my relatives. Theirs was a first and second generation, almost ghettoized, bilingual (Yiddish and English), working-class milieu whose members strove, quite successfully it turned out, for middle-class status. As seems to have been characteristic of many urban European immigrant groups in North America at the time, this was also a milieu whose members, while not preoccupied with fashion *per se*, attached great value to clothing, to how well it was made and worn. My mother, for example, would speak admiringly, as did many of the people I knew in my youth, of someone who was, to quote her, "a good dresser."

The perspective itself was a grab bag of attitudes, impressions, prejudices, and inchoate beliefs (some half-baked, some conceptually promising) to the effect that fashion, among other things: (a) dealt mainly with clothes; (b) concerned women more than it did men (though men who were too involved in it tended to be effeminate); (c) changed often; and (d) was economically wasteful, but nonetheless, worth attending to if you wished not to look strange or old fashioned. Moreover, it kept many people employed and sometimes made a lot of money for merchants, manufacturers, and designers with foreign sounding names quartered in Paris, France. (Dior, whose 1946–47 "New Look" had recently swept Western womankind, giving rise to much collective protest along the way, was the most famous of these.) I might here note that it was only in retrospect many years later I realized that this jumble of fragmented and ill-assorted ideas contained within it, in embryonic form, nearly every major social science theory of fashion I was to encounter in my subsequent research. I note this if only to underscore a point made earlier, namely, that lay perspectives on some domain of everyday life can too quickly be dismissed in toto by the trained social scientist as "biased," "prejudiced," "self-serving," "stereotyped," "distorted," and so forth. Doubtless they are just this in some respects, but because they are shaped by the very same everyday life they purport to describe and make sense of, they may also contain the conceptual seeds for a more ordered and far-reaching comprehension (Schutz 1962).

Engagement

There were other strains in the cacophony of thoughts and sentiments on fashion that sounded in my head, which I have omitted from the above listing. Two in particular deserve special mention both because of their resonance with much of what Blumer and Shibutani lectured on and because of the strategic place they (or, more accurately, their subsequent transmutations) came to occupy in my thinking on fashion. One of these was my fascination with the "magic" of fashion—how some new fashion which looked awful and out of place when first seen could, within a matter of months, come to look "just right," even beautiful. (I had recently experienced this when a woman I dated made the quick switch from the rather masculinized women's styles of the immediate postwar years into the exaggeratedly feminine contours of Dior's "New Look.") If, as I was then inclined to believe, beauty and ugliness had something of the absolute and eternal about them, how could such a thing happen? Why did it happen?

The other vagrant intuition presented itself to me in the form of a paradox, one which eventually would prove exceptionally productive as time and again it came up against the fundamental question of what the stylistic changes of fashion "meant" to those who created them, to those who adopted them, and to society-at-large. It was my sense that, whereas on the surface these changes made no real sense, they were perhaps deeply and elusively related symbolically to the changing moods and dispositions of modern peoples, to the cultural meanings that guided their lives, and to the societal state they found themselves in. This is what I found most intriguing about fashion: it led millions upon millions of people to engage in what felt subjectively like highly individual acts of deviation, or even rebellion from established clothing norms, yet all would be doing so at more or less the same time. Surely there was something about the constitution of social and cultural life that might account for this, as well as for the fact that fashion change appeared so cyclical with one wave succeeding another for as far back as the thirteenth century. What could this "something" or, perhaps, "somethings" be?

It was especially in this latter connection that I found the lectures of Blumer and Shibutani so exciting and illuminating. Blumer had studied fashion in Paris in the early 1930s and was, to my knowledge, the only living sociologist who had written seriously on the subject. (Veblen and Simmel had long since passed on.) Fashion was, he argued, inseparable from the modern condition, an expressive social movement (to be distinguished from political or religious movements) that affected ongoing symbolic adjustments and realignments between people's dispositions and the ever-changing technological, organizational, and cultural demands of modern life. Some sense of the tenor of his argument can be gleaned from a passage in a later article of his (Blumer 1969a):

> the movement of fashion represents a reaching out for new models which will answer to as yet indistinct and inarticulate newer tastes. The transformation of taste, of collective taste, results without question from the diversity of experience that occurs in social interaction in a complex moving world. It leads, in turn, to an unwitting groping for suitable forms of expression, in an effort to move in a direction which is consonant with the movement of modern life in general.

Here at last was some suggestion of what that "something" might be, a suggestion, which in its intellectual breadth and analytical texture reached well beyond the commonplace explanations of fashion I had so far come upon—that it relieved boredom, that it had mainly to do with the sex or social class of people, or with the profit motive, and so on. I also discovered that Blumer's argument went beyond the few extant scholarly theories on fashion put forth by certain of Blumer's predecessors in the field, namely, Tarde, Veblen, Simmel, and Sapir.

True, there was much that Blumer's fashion theory did not explain or even touch on. I was, for example, even then aware that it left unexplicated the actual symbolic dimensions of fashion change, an omission that much later was to strike me as strange coming as it did from he who is commonly regarded as the father of symbolic interactionism (Davis 1982). But, for a budding sociologist groping for a more comprehensive and integrated perspective on the subject than the one he brought with him, Blumer's perspective was oriented, I was convinced, precisely in the right direction. In any case it was his theoretical fix on the topic that launched me into the ongoing dialectic of conceptual confrontation, refinement, and integration that has brought me in time to the perspective I currently hold on what is still for me a somewhat enigmatic Dame Fashion.

In retrospect I also see that, stemming largely from my own native view, I tended unwittingly to attribute more of a *zeitgeist* (spirit of the times) flavor to Blumer's perspective than was actually the case, or than may even be inferred from the above quotation. Blumer, I learned subsequently, was highly critical of *zeitgeist* theories of fashion—that is, those that claimed to find in fashion a rather direct symbolic expression of the "spirit of the times" as when, for example, commentators attribute a turn to dark and somber clothing to economic recession or a taste for more masculinized women's clothing to the movement for women's liberation. Indeed, both scholarly and popular explanations of fashion positively brim with notions of *zeitgeist* causality, especially when all other explanations fail. Blumer criticized such explanations, as have others, for their tautological, *post hoc, ergo propter hoc* quality—the commentator claims to discern in a certain fashion, expressions of some societal condition and then goes on to claim that the condition caused the expression. This is logically akin to inferring that a person whose nose is running, has a cold, and then asserting with no further proof that the cold causes the running nose. Blumer, for his part, preferred to locate explanations of fashion in the intensive social interaction that marks the general condition he termed *modernity*. It is in the nature of such interaction that the taste and stylistic changes that flow from it are essentially unpredictable and incapable of being reduced in a single conceptual leap to some abstract societal condition inferred by the theorist.

My incorrect *zeitgeist* attribution to Blumer notwithstanding, I now regard as a "strategic misreading," akin to what the literary critic Harold Bloom (1973) has written of the history of poetry. Though wrong, it allowed me to continue to draw on Blumer in a way that enriched my investigation of what was as much a core question for me as it had been for him: What exactly is the relationship between the symbolic movements of fashion and the everyday lives of persons in society?

Resolutions and Riddles

My initial engagement with Blumer's views on this issue helped resolve a number of naïve and not so naïve questions encompassed in my native view of fashion. It also helped answer yet other questions that had, up until then, not occurred to me. Foremost was Blumer's strong, at times scathing, critique of the several "theories" of fashion found in the scholarly literature and popular thought of the time (Blumer 1968, 1969a), among them, Veblen's (1899) and, less extreme, Simmel's (1904) analyses of fashion as originating in the invidious distinctions of a class-stratified society; related Marxist notions of fashion change, emanating from a kind of clothier's conspiracy designed to fuel the profit-driven engines of a capitalist based consumer economy; theories that located the *raison d'être* for fashion in sexuality (Flugel 1930), or ego enhancement (Sapir 1931), or relief from boredom. For all such theories, Blumer was able to cite historic instances or universal conditions that belied the theory in question. Even more persuasive was Blumer's ability to draw on his own field research in Paris in the 1930s to underscore how far the postulates of some theory departed from what he had observed and recorded at first hand.

Blumer also brought into sharper focus an aspect of fashion I had been crudely aware of, but had not paused to probe sufficiently with a view to uncovering certain generic features of the phenomenon. (Sometimes referred to as serendipity, a facet of a phenomenon that at first strikes us as minor or peripheral will, upon sustained probing, be found to contain the analytic clues that reveal its essential character.) This had to do with the breadth of fashion in modern life. As indicated above, my native fix on the topic was confined mainly to clothing. Yet one could not help but be cognizant of fashion's presence in numerous other realms as well: in interior decoration, auto styling, popular music, children's names, dog breeds, religious beliefs, and possibly even science and sociology as well. Is fashion everywhere? And, if so, is its power and its manifestation the same in all cultural spheres? If not, what might the differences tell us about the underlying conditions of its activation?

Blumer, whose own field research dealt with fashion in clothing, nonetheless gave more than casual attention to these issues. His sustained concern for what he termed the generic features of fashion led to the insight—still far from fully realized by me, however—that one, perhaps, could ultimately learn as much about the significance of fashion in dress from its appearance or absence in other cultural domains as from that in dress alone.

Yet, despite how much my perspective on fashion had been enlarged by Blumer, there remained dark corners, obscurities, and omissions that the critical apparatus he brought to bear on the topic failed to illuminate. (He, I am sure, would not have thought this amiss; it is part and parcel of the ongoing quest for meaning striven for in the symbolic exchanges of the social interaction of which he constantly spoke.) Certainly, it is true, as he held, that fashion is overwhelmingly symbolic, that it is somehow intimately related to the modern temper (although precisely what this is and how far back in history it goes is not altogether clear), and that the processes which propel it through a population are collective in character—hence, more akin to the spontaneous behavior found in social movements, religious conversions, and expressive crowds than in the structured role behaviors of organizations and institutions.[3]

But what were the symbolic shifts affected by fashion about; what, in short, was being communicated in the displacement of one symbolic complex by another? And inasmuch as the "symbols" of clothing fashions (fabric, hue, texture, color, shape, silhouette, and so forth) were different from those employed in speech and writing, how did they come to acquire the meanings they did? How widely were such meanings shared? What brought about not infrequent changes in meaning as, for example, when around 1900 the color pink gradually ceased to be thought of as appropriate for boys and came increasingly to be viewed as the exclusive color for girls? Moreover, if, as Blumer maintained, the shifts in fashion were tied somehow to the moods and sentiments abroad in society at large, be this a *zeitgeist* or some other collective disposition, through what means and processes did the collective psychological state come eventually to translate itself into fashion motifs? And while he certainly did not rule out its importance, Blumer had little to say about the role of the fashion industry (the designers, publicists, manufacturers, merchandisers, and retailers) in the creation and propagation of clothing fashions. It seemed on the face of it inconceivable that this vast and complex industry (in which my immigrant forebears found their identity as Americans on arrival to these shores) simply responded to, or was merely wafted aboard, the waves of searching, collective unrest of which

Blumer spoke. Without attributing conspiratorial fashion determinacy to it, surely the industry had much to do with the direction, velocity, and duration of fashion change. But what and how?

These were the principal riddles I pondered in the years following my engagement with Blumer's thought and with that of other scholars of whom Blumer had made me aware. While the circumstances of my career caused me for many years to set aside my fascination with fashion, when I returned to the topic in the early 1980s, it was these questions I grappled with.

Finding Answers

Although I set out with no specific research program in mind, I found myself turning first to the question of *what* a new fashion concept communicated and *how* it was being communicated. If, as our everyday folk knowledge of social life instructs us, there is some vital connection between clothes-wearers identities and what their clothes "say" about them, how do the collective expressive changes signalled by fashion alter what is being said or, at very least, the terms on which it is said. What, for example, did the hippie styles of the late 1960s or punk styles of the 1970s (both of which managed to "travel up" the social structure, albeit in modified form, well beyond their stations of origin), say about the lives of persons who adopted them?

In both the popular fashion press and scholarly treatments of fashion there is, to be sure, no shortage of interpretations of what is being communicated by such changes. And remarkably, there tends to be considerable consensus among commentators, including even lay observers, on what these fashions "mean." (Attributions of heightened or muted sexuality, greater or lesser formality, gender conservatism or adventurism, and so on are the staple of such interpretations.) In light of such widespread consensus, there must then be some operative thing approximating a visual "language" that encodes the meaning elements whereby the "message" of a new fashion, or for that matter some previous or future fashion, is understood by clothes wearers belonging to the same clothes-wearing community. But how to describe and explain the code? (Davis 1985; 1992).

When I came finally to seriously address this matter in the early 1980s, some thirty years had passed from the time my contacts with Blumer had set the stage to even raise the question. By then the field of semiotics, which describes itself as the science of signs and symbols, had begun to exercise a small influence in sociology and it was to that I turned for guidance on understanding clothing and, accordingly, fashion communication.

Although semiotics provided me fewer answers than I would have liked, concerning *what*, and *how* clothing communicates—its analytic scheme suffers, in my opinion, a taxonomic rigidity that greatly impoverishes its depiction of what people actually see and feel when they view clothing—at least it offered a conceptual framework for approaching the problem. At that it made one much more conscious of how clothing meanings are encoded in such things as shapes, colors, patterns, and textures than could ever have been gleaned from Blumer's circumscribed collective behavior approach to fashion.

A heightened appreciation of the role of clothing symbols (in effect, meanings) in fashion change made it possible to consider what the symbolic apparatus of contemporary clothing typically dealt with. While it was soon evident there was hardly any aspect of the self, from boudoir proclivities to barricade loyalties, that clothing was incapable of alluding to, there nonetheless were some identity issues that, in Western society, had, over the centuries, preoccupied clothing. These placed such constant demands on clothing's symbolic resources as to repeatedly and, in cyclical manner, subject it to the play of fashion. As one might have anticipated, I came to see that these preoccupations had mainly to do with issues of gender, sexuality, social status, and age, about which Western culture or, more exactly, the value milieu in which we live, is decidedly ambivalent. Do we, via our dress, wish to present ourselves as sexy or modest? well-heeled or humble? authoritative or demure? youthful or mature?

With respect to nearly all of these culturally encoded issues of identity, one typically finds secular-hedonistic and status-elevating preferences counterposed to more modest, pietistic, and egalitarian affirmations (Davis 1988, 1989, 1991b). The extent to which fashion feeds on the resultant tensions, forever shifting in its symbolism from one pole to the other or simultaneously melding symbols from both, helps account for its continuous presence in Western society for some eight centuries now. The concept of *cultural ambivalence* (the value tensions we experience within ourselves and are likely, because we live in the same society, to share with many others) thus came to occupy a central place in my thinking and writing on fashion.

I felt that this concept of cultural ambivalence was a definite advance in my understanding of fashion's symbolic structure. Still to be clarified, however, was fashion's market structure, the role of the apparel industry in the creation and propagation of fashions. Did the industry, broadly conceived, originate fashions? dictate them? or perhaps, merely reflect or elaborate upon styles that would have come to pass in any case—the argument being that "the culture was ready for it anyway"? Having become strongly committed to an ethnographic approach from my earlier researches in sociology, the only sensible way I could think of to tackle these questions was to ask "the industry" itself, as it were. I embarked on this formidable challenge despite my recognition that the very breadth and complexity of the fashion diffusion process (beginning with an idea in a designer's head and ending, ultimately, with different realizations of the finished product on the racks of J.C. Penny and Nieman-Marcus) would in the end defy any simple or sure formulation of the process. Still a partial, empirically grounded idea of how the fashion industry processed fashions would be better than none at all.

Over the course of the next several years, therefore, in addition to reading widely on the question, I set aside time for sporadic bouts of fieldwork in San Diego, Los Angeles, New York, and Paris to interview, when I could, designers, clothing manufacturers, fashion journalists, buyers, retailers, and so forth. I also attended fashion shows and observed sales interactions in the showrooms of clothing wholesalers and retailers.

As with my venture into semiotics, the findings I came away with were far from definitive or comprehensive. While too many and too contingent to set forth here (Davis 1992), they nonetheless advanced the dialectic initiated in the encounter of my native view of some year's back with Blumer's fashion theory.

That theory, in marked opposition to the leading ones in sociology at the time, placed preponderant emphasis on the interaction of collective taste, that is, the developing and shifting tastes of fashion consumers, for the emergence and symbolic articulation of new fashions. The conviction I came away with from my field research was that whereas the collective taste of fashion consumers—their "unwitting groping for suitable forms of expression"—had a great deal to do with inspiring and adjudicating fashions, it was the producers of fashion, the industry in the complex interplay of its many subworlds (from Paris design houses, the fashion press, multi-national apparel manufacturers, department store buyers, all the way down to neighborhood boutiques), that set the fashion agenda for consumers by offering them the style alternatives, sometimes many, sometimes few, from which they would choose. Clearly then it was neither a case of the industry dictating fashions nor of its being the passively receptive vessel for symbolic emanations arising from the miasma of modern collective life. A central task for future students of fashion, therefore, will continue to be that of better delineating how the fashion industry and its component parts not only apprehend popular moods but also shape and channel them.

Conclusion

It is obvious that the perspective on fashion I have acquired over the years is far from that naturally confused, native view I harbored when I first encountered Herbert Blumer's seminal thinking on the topic. Yet fragments of that early reaching-for-understanding can still be detected and although transfigured, they still exert their force; for example, the 1930s depression-borne, cynically tinged, belief that profit and public manipulation are somehow important in the comings and goings of fashion or, from another facet of my upbringing, the fascination with the symbolic power of clothing and the uses to which it is put. But as is true of social experience generally—whose truths were for Blumer the overarching object of his intellectual quest (see Blumer 1969b)—what happened to these views and where they have come to rest, albeit still uneasily at times, is the product of a long, dialectically framed, interactive process, aspects of which I have tried to sketch here.

Put simply, my perspective on fashion changed and was constantly being reformulated (though almost never overhauled) as I encountered the perspectives of others. In retrospect the changes and the reformulations can be seen to reveal both continuities and discontinuities, but at the time of their occurrence there typically is, at best, only partial awareness of what is changing and what remains in place. Interestingly, it is this symbolically negotiated process which, at a level of abstraction removed, is the hallmark of the sociological perspective Blumer came to term *symbolic interactionism*, a perspective whose analytic powers can, I believe, be as revealing of the processes of scientific inquiry as it is of the mundane affairs of everyday life.

NOTES

1. The ironic reference to Dame Fashion is intended to underscore one such "twist" met up with very early in my career that has pursued me ever since, as it would nearly anyone in the social sciences interested in studying fashion. Put bluntly, fashion as a topic of serious intellectual inquiry was and is more than slightly *infra dig* (Latin contraction for *infra dignitatem* meaning undignified) among cultural scientists. In common with the not unfamiliar everyday, Puritan-tinged attitude it echoes, the phenomenon of fashion is, by its very nature, seen as frivolous and inconsequential; hence, unworthy of "serious" study. To make it one's major research interest is something young scholars wishing to make a career for themselves should think about twice. I, for one, kept my interest in fashion on a backburner for many years before I felt I could commit myself professionally to its study.

2. Like the member of a minority group who identifies in some part with the prejudices directed at him or her by the majority, I myself was not wholly above the discipline's patronizing attitude toward fashion as a topic for research. Much as it fascinated me, if challenged I probably would have conceded that it hardly merited the same serious attention as did such areas in sociology as race relations, class conflict, social movements, etc.

3. As I have previously pointed out (Davis 1991a) and as I shall touch on again in these pages, this is, perhaps, the major limitation of Blumer's conception of fashion, i.e., its near total dependence on the collective behavior paradigm developed in French and American sociology in the late nineteenth century up to roughly the Second World War.

Uncertain Terms: The Social Construction of Fatherhood

Kerry Daly

Feminist scholarship has focused on making women's voices heard in social science research (Westcott 1979). This stems from a long patriarchal tradition where women have had "no more than marginal voices" in "the intellectual, cultural, and political world" (Smith 1987, 1). Although men's voices have typically dominated throughout history, there is one sphere where their voices have been but a murmur—their everyday experience of fatherhood.

This is a study that was designed to listen to men's voices regarding what it means to be a father. Two incongruous trends appear to characterize our current understanding of fatherhood. First, there are studies which examine the amount of time that men spend in various activities related to fatherhood. The conclusion here is that men have not changed much: their participation in housework and childcare has increased only marginally in spite of increased numbers of women in the paid labor force (Meissner, Humphreys, Meis, and Scheu 1975; Geerken and Gove 1983; Harvey and Elliott 1983; Armstrong and Armstrong 1984). The second theme in the literature on fatherhood is that men have changed a great deal: their commitment to the identity has intensified in recent years so they are now a new breed of fathers known as "nurturant fathers" (Giveans and Robinson 1985). In light of this apparently contradictory evidence, what does it mean to be a father? How have men changed as fathers or to what degree are they changing?

The answer to these questions are further muddled by research that suggests that men are clearly performing an increasing proportion of a couple's total family work (Pleck 1983; 1985). This may reflect a shift in the balance of occupational and family commitments for men. Where once the emphasis was on the centrality of the "good provider" role (Bernard 1983), there is now an increasing emphasis on the psychological commitment to fatherhood (Cohen 1987). At the same time, other research challenges the presence of "new" fathers suggesting that the "nurturant father" may be based more on rhetoric than empirical evidence (Lewis and O'Brien 1987). For example, research that focuses on behavioral indicators of how men father (Lamb 1986) suggests that the "new" father is not radically different from fathers of days past. Furthermore, Sidel (1989) suggests that the stories of househusbands and paternity leave are just not representative of men as a whole, but rather reflect the experiences of a relatively few highly educated upper-middle-class men. As evidence of this, one of the few research studies done on househusband fathers was based on a sample of men where 85 percent reported some college education and 46 percent had reached graduate level studies (Lutwin and Siperstein 1985). In a more cynical vein, Backett (1987) argues that couples create a belief in the "involved father," that serves to maintain gender inequalities within the family.

These discrepancies in the literature mirror a cultural ambiguity about how men "contend with the cultural content" (Prus 1987, 274) that shapes society's thoughts on what it means to be a father. It suggests that perhaps only one trend is really clear—the cultural meaning of fatherhood is in transition and, as a result, the social construction of fatherhood rests on a set of "uncertain terms."[1] Parke (1985) suggests that in order to adequately research fathers during this time of great change, "continuing pictures need to be taken across time." This research provides one such portrait of what it means to be a father.

Theoretical Perspectives

Several theoretical approaches have historically dominated the analysis of fatherhood identity: *socialization* theories, *psychoanalytic* explanations, and *developmental* theories. In its most rigid form, socialization theory is represented by the work of structural functionalists such as Parsons and Bales (1955) who suggest that becoming a father involves the internalization of a set of role prescriptions and requirements for what a father *should* be. These prescriptions are rooted in cultural values and stereotypes which have reinforced the breadwinner role of fathers with their families. Although structural functionalist explanations have at least partially fallen into disfavor, notions of "instrumental" roles and the "provider" function continue to have a residual impact on our way of thinking about fatherhood.

Psychoanalytic explanations of fatherhood identity gained a resurgence of momentum with Chodorow's (1978) feminist writings which focused on the inadequacy of fathering role models and the corresponding power that women have in shaping male identity. The consequences for the fatherhood identity are profound: "Women come to mother because they have been mothered by women.... By contrast, that men are mothered by women reduces their parenting capacities" (Chodorow 1978, 211). The psychoanalytical approach suggests that men are handicapped in their effort to become committed fathers by the absence of early identification experiences with their own fathers.

Developmental theorists have examined the role of fathers in shaping the development of their children. Early studies focused on the question of whether fathers were as able as mothers to "bond" with, or become attached to, their children. This research (Lamb 1976; 1977; 1981) supports the fact that infants attach to their fathers as well as their mothers and that fathers are as sensitive to infant cries as mothers (Boukydis and Burgess 1982). Nevertheless, this research often says more about the development of the child than the identity of the father (Lynn 1974).

The proposed research will address some of the issues arising from these theoretical approaches, but will do so within a symbolic interactionist theoretical framework. In accordance with the fundamental premise that identity is an ongoing process of social construction (Berger and Luckmann 1966), fatherhood will be examined as it is interpreted and negotiated from situation to situation. Hess and Handel (1959, 8) convincingly argue that patterns of family action can never be complete "since action is always unfolding and the status of family members is always undergoing change." In this regard fatherhood is an emergent identity that is continuously being reshaped and re-interpreted as one encounters new circumstances, challenges, or obstacles. In light of the changing nature of men's roles, Turner's (1962) notion of "role-taking" is an appropriate concept for examining the social construction of fatherhood.

This is in distinction from the socialization and psychoanalytic views that emphasize identity as *product*, that is, in varying degrees of success shaped early on. Nevertheless, the interpretation and re-interpretation of these modeling influences are an important dimension in the process of socially constructing the fatherhood identity. Hence, participants in this study were prompted to discuss who the salient actors were in their ongoing construction of fatherhood. They were asked to identify the situations when the fatherhood "identity work" was most evident. They were asked to talk about commitment, relationships, the salience of activities, and the distribution of time as they defined their role as fathers.

Approaching the study of fatherhood in this way is not to deny the importance of social structural influences which shape the fatherhood identity. Occupation, education, culture, and family structure are important variables for fully understanding family experience. In fact a major trend in the literature has been to examine how structural forces have had an impact on the fatherhood role (Hood and Golden 1979; Benokraitis 1985; Pleck 1985; Moss and Brannen 1987). For example, how do political and economic trends such as the increased labor force participation of wives, continued occupational constraints, the industrialization of housework, or the availability of daycare affect the amount of time that men spend in the fathering role? As this research suggests, fathers from both traditional and non-traditional families continue to encounter a variety of institutional constraints that interfere with their commitment to fatherhood (Lewis and O'Brien 1987). These structural conditions will be examined in the present research in terms of how they become part of the dynamic negotiation process that is involved in the construction of fatherhood reality.

This research then is fundamentally concerned with acquiring the perspectives of men who father. These perspectives can be examined from three vantage points: *individual, interactive,* and *structural.* On an *individual* level, how do they make sense of the world and "develop images" (Prus 1987) of fatherhood? *Interactively,* to whom and how do they talk about being a father? As part of this, how do they deal with the generational inconsistencies that exist with respect to the pattern of fathering? At a *structural* level, how do they resolve dilemmas that arise between their changing commitment and unchanging structural constraints? Approached in this way, this research can contribute to a conceptualization of fatherhood that is less deterministic than the traditional socialization or psychoanalytic models. It also has the potential to contribute to the empirical literature on fatherhood by focusing on the way that fathers interpret and make meaningful the contextual influences that shape this identity. As Richards (1982) has suggested, what is lacking in the literature is the male equivalent to the now extensive feminist literature on the institution of motherhood. Finally, this research has the potential to provide practical insight into the conflicts, strains, and rewards that fathers encounter in reconciling their own role models with current attitudes and constraints.

The Sample

A sample of thirty-two fathers from intact families was obtained through two sources, a children's recreational program and a large corporation. Only two criteria were used in the selection of the sample: first they had to be in an intact family (in order to avoid issues of step-parenting or divorce), and second, they had to have at least one child who was age six or under. The second criteria was intended to create some homogeneity in the sample with respect to the fathering experience. This is in keeping with Goffman's (1974) notion of "framing" a time period in order to define some experiential boundaries. The young age of the children was chosen on the assumption that the process of constructing the fatherhood identity would be more salient at this early stage of the parenting career than later on. Although the sample is non-random and therefore limited in its generalizability, the goal of this qualitative research is not to discover how many, or what kind of people share a fatherhood characteristic, but rather it is to capture the complex assumptions, meanings, and contradictions that enter into the process of experiencing and constructing the fatherhood identity.

The two different recruitment methods used to gain access to these fathers had very different outcomes; one approach was an abysmal failure, while the other was a dramatic success. In recruiting through the children's program, the organization agreed to distribute a letter of invitation to all families who had children six or under, participating in their programs. This approach was taken because they did not wish to have the researcher present at the programs (too much interference), and they did not wish to release the names of the parents. Of the approximately eighty letters that were distributed, only three men responded using the form and the stamped envelope addressed to the researcher. These three were asked to recommend a friend for participation, which resulted in another two men being involved.

The other approach involved contacting the vice-president of personnel at a large corporation. Working with the Employee Assistance Program staff, letters were sent to all employees who were eligible to participate. The letter invited employees to attend an information session on company time. During this session I had an opportunity to describe the goals of the research and what would be involved for their participation in the study. At the end of the session I distributed a request-to-participate form. All who were present agreed to participate. Using this approach, twenty-nine men were eligible and interviews were completed with twenty-seven. The two who were not interviewed did not show up for the information session and no reason was given.

Men have typically been difficult to recruit in social science research. The first recruitment method was a shocking reminder of that. However, what appears to be critical for successfully recruiting men is to have sponsored, face-to-face contact between the researcher and eligible participants as part of the recruitment. This approach appears to have lessened the anxiety that eligible participants felt in response to the invitation. Not only did the company encourage their participation, but they also provided time during working hours for the researcher to do a "sales pitch." This gave the researcher an opportunity to pique the fathers' curiosity, to give them some reasons to participate, and to establish a relationship with them before the fathers had to commit themselves. These efforts appeared to be important in light of the fact that fatherhood is not a topic that men have traditionally spoken about and that face-to-face interviews may have appeared to be intimidating and time-consuming.

The average age of the sample group was thirty-four. Participants were married for an average of eight years. Fifty-six percent had two children,

31 percent had one child, and 12 percent had three or more children. The sample represented a good range of educational and occupational experiences. Sixteen percent held a Master's degree, 28 percent a Bachelor's degree, 28 percent had attended community college, 25 percent had completed high school, while 3 percent had not completed high school. In terms of occupation, 25 percent held senior management or semi-professional positions, 22 percent held a middle management position, 25 percent were in skilled trades, 25 percent were laborers, and one participant was a student. Nineteen percent worked shifts. Most wives were employed outside the home. Forty-one percent worked part-time, 28 percent worked full-time, while 31 percent worked in the home.

Methodology

Following the qualitative research principles of grounded theory and comparative analysis (Glaser and Strauss 1967), this research focuses on identifying the most salient dimensions of the fatherhood identity as defined by fathers themselves. In keeping with this method the data were categorized and analyzed for emergent themes. Although in its purest form, a grounded theory approach involves suspending preconceived notions about what to expect in the data, the reality is that the researcher's experience with the phenomenon in question and the existing literature give some shape and direction to the interview. In this study my experience as a father of two children ages six and five has had a strong impact on my motivation to do the study and my way of thinking about fatherhood. This experience has both positive and negative implications for the research. On a positive note it is a source of "theoretical sensitivity" that stimulates the generation of concepts and their relationships (Strauss and Corbin 1990). Conversely, such experience can also be seen as having a biasing effect on the research. Inasmuch as I would like to say that my awareness of this bias is sufficient for controlling it, the reality is that it will shape the process of selection and interpretation in many ways.

The interviews were audio tape-recorded and later transcribed verbatim. The researcher conducted all the interviews between the fall of 1990 and the spring of 1991. All interviews started out in a general, non-directive way. Questions were asked about how the fathers decided that they wanted to have children, what was important about being a father, what they disliked about being a father, what it meant to be a "good father," and how important fatherhood was to them in relation to other identities. Following from these, the interview was organized into four general classes of questions. These classes are suggested by *identity theory* and include the role of significant others, perceptions of time, situations, and relationships. For example, with respect to significant others, questions were asked about whether they talk to others about what it is like to be a father, who they talk to about it, what they talk about, whether they compare themselves to others, or who their role models are.

Providing some structure to the interview beforehand has the pragmatic advantage of "diminishing the indeterminacy and redundancy" of unstructured interviews, thereby making the data-gathering process more efficient (McCracken 1988). However, consistent with the qualitative aim of discovering the participant's view and avoiding the "passive-compliance" that stems from a highly structured interview format (Cicourel 1967, 58), questions within these broad classes were as non-directive as possible. Furthermore, the researcher was quite happy to wander into areas that were outside of these general classes.

Discussion

Although the intention of this study was to listen to men's voices of fatherhood, there was considerable reluctance on the part of men to have their voices heard. For some this was expressed through their outright refusal to participate. For the others who did participate, there was frequently a cautious attitude. One father explains how he felt vulnerable as a result of having agreed to the interview:

> I was a little bit nervous about it, but I see it as, not a challenge ... or maybe it is on a personal level. A sort of challenging need to come to terms—do you really know what you see, how you see your role? You're worried that you won't have a formed opinion on it, and you'll feel inadequate as a father. There's always a worry that...well I know you're not going to be judgmental on it ... but there's always a worry that somebody will make a comment that will bother you.

As this passage would suggest, fatherhood represents an important, but private, experience that is difficult to discuss. The voices that follow reflect a sense of risk that seems to permeate the discussion of what it means to be a father.

Three themes are explored in this paper. These themes focus on the meaning and importance of the fatherhood identity, the influence of significant others, and the perceived impact of structural factors on the social construction of fatherhood.

The Meaning and Importance of the Fatherhood Identity

With only rare exceptions and minimal equivocation, men ranked fatherhood as the most salient identity within their identity hierarchy (Stryker 1980). This is consistent with Cohen (1987) who reported that 90 percent of his sample of men defined their marital or parental roles as their most important social roles. Ralph's response was typical:

I think that fatherhood is the most important. I was off work for six months and things got pretty tense, but the fact that I had my family and being a father is what's most important. Making money and things to support the family isn't as important as being the father to my children.

As the most important identity in the salience hierarchy, fatherhood lessened the importance of all other identities. As Jefferey points out, fatherhood precipitates a re-arrangement of priorities:

Oh, I'd have to put it [fatherhood] first. I think it's certainly re-arranged some priorities for me.... Work used to be a higher priority for example, and I used to spend more time at work, more time thinking about work or worrying about work.... Probably education has dropped down as a lower priority. We used to like to travel, business travel in particular.... I used to spend a lot more time on fitness kinds of things. I used to do some running. I don't seem to have that high of a priority with it now.

Although the men in this study ranked fatherhood at the top of the salience hierarchy, its importance took on a different meaning when placed up against motherhood. Consistent with the literature (Geerken and Gove 1983), which indicates that men do not see themselves as the primary caregiver, the men in this study often saw themselves as marginal caregivers in relation to their wives. Dan, for example, talks about what is most important about being a father:

I think first and foremost of being supportive to my wife because she's home with the child, she's really the primary caregiver. So I felt right from pregnancy to when he was born, that anything I could do to help—because I really think that's a tough role for "the mom." So anything I can do to help, housework wise, support wise, emotional, anything, was certainly a primary concern.

Dan continues on and explains this marginalization in a way that is consistent with Firestone's (1970) arguments about the importance of biology for understanding women as primary caregivers:

Yea, I feel a bond there but I also think that because of the time and effort and because of the birthing experience, that I wouldn't have any difficulty reconciling that my wife would sense that she would have a greater bond than I would. That doesn't trouble me, because it's such an overwhelming experience for the woman.

Perhaps the most obvious manifestation of this marginalization is the tendency of men to see themselves as "filling in" or being "Mr. Mom" when their wives are absent. In a sense men are alienated from their own labor with their children. As the following passage from Alan would suggest, work with children, done in the absence of mothers, is not identified as fathering, but is identified as mothering:

INTERVIEWER: Some people who I have talked to, have talked about that time when you get home, either as work time—it feels like a different kind of work that you move into—or others describe it as a play time for themselves. How does it feel for you, when you come home at the end of the day and are with your kids?

FATHER: Depending on what activities are available to do, I generally enjoy it now. When I did find it was like work, for a while my wife was working every weekend so she would look after the kids and be mom during the week while I was at work; all weekend I would be mom and look after the kids, and I didn't enjoy that. Because I found that I never had a break, at that point I did feel like hey, I'm working seven days a week and the wife did that for four or five months straight and it seems we never had a weekend.

INTERVIEWER: You mentioned that when she was working weekends you felt like "mom" all weekend. Can you tell me why, or using that phrase what that means for you.

FATHER: I would be doing the traditional mommy type things. I'd look after the kids, cook the meals, do the dishes, clean the house all that type of stuff, that's the traditional mom's role. So I found that I was behaving more as mom on the weekends.

The discrepancy between the high salience of fatherhood and the sense of marginalization is also a reflection of the competing commitments of work and family roles. For the men in this study, there was a strong undercurrent of guilt that they would never be able to spend enough time with their children. The continued sense of marginalization might also be accounted for by "provider anxiety" (Osherson 1986), which kept interfering with their full commitment to fatherhood. Jim talks about the financial pressure he feels in preparing for his children's future:

You know, the way the economy is ... I feel a little pressured for looking out for their education and their future, as far as trying to plan now for that so that when we get to that point, we are not hit with it all of a sudden. We don't want to force the kids to go and finance an education totally by themselves, and not that I'm going to hand it to them, or am going to be in any position to hand it to them on a silver platter, but I'd certainly like to help out.

For other men it is not "provider anxiety" that is the issue, but "success anxiety." When comparing himself to his own father, Edward suggests that the struggle is the same, but the issue is different:

I have challenges and situations that I have to address, whether it's my career or whether it's [pause] well you know it's not an issue of putting bread on the table. Its a very different kind of issue. He [his father] had very different issues to face.... I'm building my career. I have those same challenges in terms of making sure that I find the appropriate balance between work and family.

The discussion of the salience of fatherhood must also acknowledge that there are strong norms of social desirability that suggest that men should say fatherhood is the most important, especially when the research focus is fatherhood. For Ted, fatherhood was expressed as the most important identity in his life, yet children are referred to as "obstacles" to other activities. As this would suggest, fatherhood may be the most important because of what is demanded of them, not necessarily because it is freely chosen.

> If I didn't have kids I probably would work a little bit longer but not as long as I would if I was single because I would like to spend time with my wife as well. So I see those two as the, I shouldn't call them obstacles, but the factors preventing you from spending more time as an individual yourself or at your work.

As these responses would suggest, the fatherhood identity is rife with contradiction. At the same time that they place fatherhood at the top of the salience hierarchy, there are a number of indications which suggest that their role performance is something less than primary. Specifically, these fathers tend to see themselves as marginal in relation to the central mothering role; they tend to define their role in intensive parenting situations as "mothering"; and their commitment to work continues to compete with their commitment to "fathering."

The Role of Others in the Social Construction of Fatherhood

Stone (1962) has argued that the construction of identity involves two stages—the *identification of* and the *identification with*. This is based on the premise that social actors first discern what it means to play out a role by identifying in others what is involved in that role, and then trying out those actions as part of one's own role repertoire.

For the men in this study, one of the resounding themes was the absence of a role model to "identify with." Nevertheless, their own fathers emerged as the main influence in their construction of fatherhood. However, their process of *identification of* focused not on what they valued in their own father's behavior, but rather, on those elements of their father's role that they hoped to actively avoid in their own fatherhood identity. In this regard their own fathers served as a kind of antihero or negative role model:

> I don't want to be like him as far as his parenting goes…. It's not that I don't love him, and I respect him as a father, but he's not a family person. I guess, he brought us up in an era too where the father was the breadwinner and, you know, he came out with the major discipline if mom couldn't handle that type of thing, but at the same time he feels that children are to be seen and not heard. We don't want to bring our kids up that way. I don't really think of him as a father, in my interpretation of a father. He's someone who was there,

brought the paycheck home and, you know, did things around the house. I just don't feel close to him. We never had a closeness.

At the same time that they sought to reject the influence that their own fathers had on their role, the men expressed a belief that this was an influence over which they had little control. Their own fathers had a strong residual presence in their own fathering role:

> FATHER: I was very different from my father and I would say "I'm absolutely not going to do those things like that when I grow up," but despite that, in the last few years, I started noticing doing certain things, little things.... I started finding myself displaying certain attitudes and behaviors and noticing that "this is what my father used to do."

> INTERVIEWER: Any specific examples you can think of, behaviors that you recognize in yourself that are like your father?

> FATHER: Yeah, being very unemotional.... He didn't use to display his emotions and he used to worry about certain things really bad, really bad but he would just close to the outside world, keep to himself. He would display a very distant attitude which is like "I don't want anybody around me and then eventually he would get out of it and he would open up again and that was his way of dealing with it and as I said, the last few years I've started doing that a little bit and then noticed it very quickly so I am trying to break that.

Chodorow (1978) suggests that the absence of father models results in men shaping their identity based on an identification of their mother's behavior. Consistent with this, the men in this study suggested that their wives, as a kind of mother figure, were a particularly salient influence on the way that they shaped the fatherhood identity. Second only to the negative modeling of their own fathers, wives were very influential in shaping the fatherhood identity:

> The way my father was, I wouldn't take that as a role model simply because of his character and probably mostly because of the generation.... I really didn't have a lot of people around me—at least when I was growing up or before I became a father—to really stick in my mind to say "Yeah, I'd like to be a father like this one." My fatherhood was influenced more by the bad examples I had around me than good, so I knew what to avoid. Second, my wife's ideas about being a parent are more centred around kids than mine so she is even more focused on raising the kids. Her standards, her expectations are higher and ... those things influence me.

Although these men saw their wives as playing an important role in shaping their own fatherhood identity, they typically had difficulty seeing themselves from their wife's perspective. The typical first response to the question "How do you think your wife sees you as a father?" was "Gee, I've never thought about that." In this regard the "looking glass" (Cooley 1967) was blurred. This runs contrary to what one would expect from identity theory. One would expect that the most salient influence on identity comes from those with whom one has frequent interaction.

When the men were able to articulate how they thought their wives saw them as fathers, they tended to express it in general non-specific terms such as "she thinks I'm a good father." In this respect they saw their wives evaluating their performance against that of other fathers in a way that is similar to the process of *comparison level* in exchange theory (Thibaut and Kelley 1959). Tony explains:

> INTERVIEWER: How do you think your wife sees you as a father?
>
> FATHER: Well she has told me, and at times when we've had our quiet times together in talking about this and that, that she thinks I'm a very good father. Looking at some of our friends who are fathers and stuff, she has said she thinks I'm doing more with my child than some of our friends are and spend more time and do more things with her than they do. I don't think she's being terribly critical: it's just an observation she made.

Although men talked about the people who were closest to them as having the main impact on their formation of identity, others who were more distant also played a role. These included acquaintances, strangers, or people who appeared on television. Although somewhat embarrassed to admit it, one father talked about the effect of TV on his sense of identity:

> I can't say there was a figure that influenced me. Mind you, I should admit it, Cosby show, the Bill Cosby show itself, the way he handles things does have an influence. I hate to admit that I am influenced by shows I watch on TV but some of the things I think are very carefully planned, written and I think they are made to convey certain messages and I feel they are very powerful.

"Non-specific" others also played an important role by serving as a reference point for evaluating their performance as a father. From this perspective, fathers tended to be aware of a group of faceless others who were there to judge their success or failure. As David describes in the following passage, "everybody" potentially stands in judgment of his role as father:

> If my daughter runs away from home or gets in trouble with the law, it will reflect badly on me. One side of me says it wouldn't matter, that's her, that's not me, it's not important, it might not affect me. On the other hand, everybody is going to say "what a jerk this father is." I guess in some sense, I feel like there is kind of a judgment—your kid has turned out great—you must be a terrific parent. If your kids have a problem, no matter what it is, it's kind of a veiled indictment of your ability to manage or lead or whatever else. I probably wouldn't lose a ton of sleep over it. I'm probably more worried about what's happening with my kid than what other people thought.

A major theme to emerge was that "talk" was not an important mecha-nism in the social construction of fatherhood. Few men talk about what it means to be a father. When they do talk to each other, it tends to focus on the child's activities and interests rather than the father's identity. Jacob provides some insight into why this may be so:

INTERVIEWER: Do you ever talk about how it feels to be a father to other people?

FATHER: Not usually. That's something that men don't often talk about being a father, and the relationship to the children. We talk in generalities about raising the children, rather than use specific instances. How many sports they want to take, and how you should treat that, and which ones are the best—we won't talk about a certain experience with a sport, or with disciplinary tech-niques—it's funny, because men just don't seem to talk about it.

INTERVIEWER: Why do you think that is the case?

FATHER: I think men get hung up a lot on the traditional idea that child-rearing is something left to the women, and I think that a lot of men get caught up [with this] when you talk to them. Usually you enquire about their job, how they're doing, how are their finances—they're supposed to be the provider. That's normally what you talk about, you don't often talk about, it seems, I don't know why, it seems you fall into the role and that's what you talk about.

As this would suggest, there is an apparent anomaly between the expressed salience of the fatherhood identity and the very limited amount of interac-tion that focuses on the discussion of fatherhood. In this regard a central hypothesis in Stryker's (1980, 84) *identity theory* is not supported: the more salient an identity is, the more likely one is to seek opportunities for its enactment. For fathers, there appears to be little effort expended in the search for "father talk." This, however, may not necessarily be a failure of the theory, but rather, it may again point to a discrepancy between their psycho-logical and behavioral commitment to fatherhood.

Structural Influences in the Social Construction of Fatherhood

In addition to the interpersonal influences on the construction of father-hood, there was also a structural shaping of who these men felt they were *supposed to be* as a father. In this regard ideological beliefs and societal norms and practices regarding fatherhood had an impact on the piecing together of the identity.

One of the dominant themes to emerge with respect to the fatherhood ideology was that the norms and expectations were in flux. This idea of fatherhood in transition arose through a series of questions about how they had perceived that fatherhood had changed. Like John, most fathers acknowledged that parenting in this generation is different from their parents where "dad was supposed to work and mom was to look after the kids," for now "dads *are supposed* to participate in raising a kid." Ray elaborates on the implications of this:

> I think there is a greater expectation for fathers to be in more dimensions than they have been in the past to go beyond say the primary caregiver routine—to participate in caregiving and time spent at home and feeding and all those things that maybe in the past the male delegated and abdicated participation in. But now with both spouses working, it's really not as clear anymore, and really both are playing that role of changing diapers etcetera and I think it's—I don't know if it's pressure.

Not only were norms about fatherhood identified as being in flux, but the expectations were seen as having an inherent contradiction. *Contradiction* in families is a structurally rooted concept that is defined by Morgan (1975, 96) as "the simultaneous affirmation and negation within a system," which results in the unavoidable demand that one act in two opposite ways. For the men in this study, there was a contradiction between the social expectation to be fully available to children and the social and political mechanisms that are in place to support it. Brian, who works in personnel, provides some insight into the nature of this contradiction:

> INTERVIEWER: Would you say that one of you is the main parent?
>
> FATHER: The parent at home, which definitely is the mother. In fact, our benefits government structure really makes that happen, doesn't it?... We're seeing that with the paternity benefits, there's still a stigma to it, you know. I mean, I bet dollars to doughnuts, if I called the UI people and asked how many males participated in the paternity benefits, it would be less than one percent. Why is that?... My own perspective is that men really are there, but they need to have the other things in place to convince them—whether it's ego trips or whatever, I don't know, but they need to see that what they're thinking is okay, and it's reinforced by the fact that their employer says, "You want to take six months off to care for your newborn child, the government is going to provide you some support, so that you can do it with dignity." I think there really are a lot of guys out there that, given the opportunity, would get off the fence.... I think the interest is there, but I don't know if it's part of the way men are, but we tend to need to have everything in place, and it kind of reinforces those that were on the fence that we should stay there, cause there's nothing else to support us getting off it, other than it might feel like what we need to do. But I think as males, like I don't know if it's just my own sample of one here, but I'm not a psychologist or anything, but as males, we tend to be less, tend to make decisions less on the basis of emotion than logic, even though emotionally we feel the same way. We've got those same needs, things aren't really all that different between males and females, but females would say, "hey, it's a crock, I'm doing it because it's right," but a guy would say, "well, you know, guys at work would think I'm a wuss or can't afford it."

The contradiction between the expectation that men participate in paternity leave and the absence of support, largely among men themselves, results in a feeling of inertia. The perceived stigmatization and lack of incentives for change results in men continuing to "sit on the fence" and provides further insight into "why men resist" (Goode 1982). James provides a concrete example of how this contradiction was introduced very early on in his parenting career:

> INTERVIEWER: Do you think that the responsibilities that you carry as being a father are acknowledged at your work place?
>
> FATHER: No, I don't think so maybe because my boss is, like most older people. The old generation—their kids are grown up. When Sarah was born and in the hospital, they wanted to use her for the demo baby for the bath. The fathers were welcome to come. Well I'm excited of course, I'm up on cloud 9-1/2. I say to my boss "I'm taking Friday morning off,"—it was a Friday morning off as vacation time. I did give a reason (which I don't any more) because I'm going to see my child getting bathed because she's the demo baby and I want to see how it is supposed to be done. Well he just thought this was the funniest, biggest joke in the whole wide world—"We never had this and that and everything else!" When I happened to mention this to my co-worker that I was taking a morning off this past week to go see her get her eyes tested he said, "For God's sake don't tell the boss because it was like four months and that's all we heard of." He just couldn't believe you would be going, a man would be going to see how the baby is being bathed. Maybe you feel the same way, I don't know, but that's my opinion and I wanted to be part of it. Okay, so like I say, no one at work appreciates it; I don't really think so.

Social policies and attitudes appear to serve as real barriers for men in their process of reshaping the fatherhood identity. Although the message is clear that they are supposed to be different from their own fathers and spend more time with their children, they continue to be constrained by the opportunities to do so and the apparent lack of support from their male peers.

Conclusion

The dominant theme that reverberates through this analysis is *contradiction*. As the data strongly suggest, men as fathers are in a period of transition. Perhaps the strongest manifestation of those changes was the prevalence, throughout the interviews, of mixed messages and apparently contradictory findings. In this regard men's voices reflected a complex web of meanings for the fatherhood role. Furthermore, it was not always clear that men were in fact aware of the contradictions in their own lives.

The major contradictions to surface in the analysis have to do with the primary salience of the fatherhood identity and the subjects' experience of marginalization as fathers; the absence of strong fatherhood role models and the expectation that they be strong, committed fathers themselves; a strong importance attributed to fatherhood and yet little talk about it with others; and finally, a perception that they should be highly involved fathers and yet a set of structural barriers ranging from work policies to non-supportive peers.

As these contradictions would suggest, the work of "role-taking" for fathers is one of reconciling competing demands. If this research is to represent a snapshot of fathers at one point in history, it is perhaps best characterized as a struggle between a set of residual norms that are grounded in the previous generation and a set of present expectations that demand change in their commitment to family roles. This struggle is the "private transcript" (Hess and Handel 1959, 1) of their lives as fathers whose challenge is to negotiate the ongoing uncertainty of change.

NOTES

1. As I was growing up, my father used to use the expression "in no uncertain terms ... [e.g., will you stay out past 11 o'clock]" when he was being stern with me. The clarity of the terms then, compared with now, struck me as an appropriate metaphor for the changes in the experience of fatherhood between his generation and mine. Hence, credit for the title goes to Dad.

Achieving Identity:
Self-Other Definitions

The first article in this section by Jack Haas and William Shaffir focuses on the professional socialization of medical students. Contending that the professionalization process involves the initiation of not merely an alteration of self, but also an ideological and psychological transformation, Haas and Shaffir pay particular attention to a dimension of the conversion experience involving an emphasis on self-presentation and impression management. Identities are dramatically transformed as neophytes envelop themselves in a "cloak of competence," which is ultimately aimed at learning to assume an appropriate professional stance. The authors' analysis also examines the related processes of the transformation of student idealism as well as the adoption of the symbols of professionalism in an attempt by the medical profession and students to convert the layperson into the role of physician.

In the next selection, Clinton Sanders, relying on his own experiences as a tattooed person and as a participant-observer in the social world of tattooing, examines how the acquisition of this form of personal adornment becomes a component of the individual's "identity kit." Sanders considers not only the motives underlying this activity, but also focuses on how the wearing of a tattoo influences one's interactions with others. An important dimension of this activity is that in choosing to permanently alter their bodies, tattooed persons voluntarily shape aspects of their social identities in contrast to other aspects that are determined and over which they exercise little, if any, control.

The connection between self and identity is next illustrated in Karen March's study of adoption reunions. Much like Sanders' tattooees who alter their identity, the adoptees interviewed by March seek to redress gaps in their identity by attempting to accumulate missing biographical information. Experiencing social discomfort and even a sense of stigma, resulting from their adoptive status, the adoptees take pains to achieve greater control over their presentation of self by initiating and organizing reunion contacts in order to manage what they perceive to be discreditable. By focusing on the importance of ascertaining aspects of their biographical past, March's analysis draws attention to the connections between identity and social action in general and to the link between biographical discontinuities and social identity in particular.

In the last selection in this section, Kathy Charmaz discusses how chronically ill people manage identities reflecting their self-perceptions. Her paper, which is part of a larger study about experiencing chronic illness, focuses on the effects of illness upon identity. In examining the chronically ill, Charmaz analyzes conditions contributing to an awareness of a changed self. In particular, her analysis considers the altering definitions and meanings of self as well as the conditions underlying the creation of fictions about oneself as people attend to their chronic illnesses. By demonstrating how chronic illness might undermine notions of self and personal identity, her analysis points to the importance of viewing self as a process consisting of continuous interpretations of self made by the individual as she or he interacts with others and mentally converses with self. Indeed, the importance of others in the formulations of self-concept and identity is a theme underlying each of the selections in this section.

The Development of a Professional Self in Medical Students

Jack Haas and William Shaffir

Professionalization involves the moral and symbolic transformation of a layperson into an individual who can take on the special role and status claimed by the professional—a process that Davis (1968) labels *doctrinal conversion*. In order for individuals to make such significant status changes, they must undergo public initiations or *rites de passage* that prepare them for adoption of their new role. A would-be professional must undergo a process of mortification, of testing and ritual ordeal, before they can be elevated to the special status and role accorded by a profession. This ritual ordeal is important to the professionalization process because, on the one hand, it fosters an image of participants having worked to achieve special competence and, on the other, it requires people taking on an appropriate professional image.

Renée Fox (1957) aptly refers to the newcomer's problem as one of "training for uncertainty." Student anxiety is common in studies of socialization into various professions (Mechanic 1962; Orth 1963; Lortie 1968; Olesen and Whittaker 1968; Bucher and Stelling 1977), but this is especially true of medicine (Fox 1957; Merton, Reader, and Kendall 1957; Becker, Geer, Hughes, and Strauss 1961; Simpson 1972; Bloom 1973; Fredericks and Mundy 1976; Coombs 1978; Haas and Shaffir 1987). In becoming members of the medical profession, students experience ritual ordeals of uncertainty (Lortie 1968; Haas, Marshall, and Shaffir 1981) and perceive that professionalization involves successfully taking on a symbolic role that meets others', sometimes exaggerated, expectations. Doctors do, after all, often deal directly with matters of life and death and their clients often compound this responsibility by demanding that doctors display exceptional competence, sometimes even casting physicians into the role of demigods.

The professionalization process (Haas and Shaffir 1978; Kamens 1977), like the deviance process (Garfinkel 1956; Goffman 1963), involves dramatic rituals which symbolize the transformation of "the called" into "the chosen."

As students are professionalized, they are initiated into a new culture wherein they gradually adopt those symbols that represent the profession and its generally accepted authority. These *symbols* (language, tools, clothing, and demeanor) establish, identify, and separate the bearer from outsiders, particularly from client and paraprofessional audiences.

Becoming professional involves not only this symbolic alteration of self, but also an ideological and psychological transformation. In medical school the ideology of psychological separation from clients is presented to the neophyte as a part of professionalization. This is necessary for: learning from the material (patients); developing a trustworthy competence; practicing the profession effectively and competently by presenting an image of *affective neutrality* (relationshhips between professionals and clients that prohibit personal feelings); and protecting the professional from feelings of transference.

Student idealism is thus fated to change to "objective" affective neutrality as the incumbents perceive and adapt to professionalizing expectations. The taking on, and manipulation of, professional symbols and ideas reinforces the neophytes' self-separation from lay culture and further inhibits identification with clients because of "professed" differences. The constructed inequality of the professional-client relationship undercuts newcomer idealism. As newcomers become separated distinguished bearers of moral authority, they adopt both inner and outer shields. The outer shield of symbols and ideology protects them from any audience perceptions that "the emperor has no clothes." The psychological separation protects the performer from emotions between equals and from unprofessional feelings.

Our analysis[1] describes the related processes of the transforming of student idealism, assuming a professional stance, adopting the symbols of professionalism, and the general art of impression management, reflecting professionalization or alteration of the lay person into the role of physician.

The Transformation of Idealism

In many, perhaps all, fields, professionalization entails a radical reorientation of people's pre-existing and stereotypic notions of the goals and methods of the work involved. There is a shedding of prior, often lofty conceptions of how professionals ought to work and a concomitant adoption of the ways in which they actually behave and think. This attitudinal and behavioral shift is accompanied by the neophytes' symbolic conversion to the special status of professionals. The change, inner and outer, is particularly apparent among medical students, who generally enter medical school with high hopes of achieving a humanistic, caring approach to patients, but who emerge from their classroom and clinical experiences demonstrating, both by their actions and words, that pragmatism and affective neutrality are in their own and their patients' best interests (Becker and Geer 1958; Olesen and Whittaker 1968; Simpson 1972).

Students soon learn that a basic problem for medical practitioners is personal control and functioning in the face of highly emotive situations. Given their idealism, neophytes, in particular, must learn to distance themselves from clients by covering and controlling their emotions. Although students initially express considerable anxiety about achieving this adaption, they need not search far to recognize a collective solution (Becker, Geer, Hughes, and Strauss 1961); it is provided by the very profession for which they are being trained. They learn that their sense of idealism is noble, but that their progress through medical school requires objectification of the patient. This sense of distancing and depersonalization is one of the major accommodations they must make to the system of organized medicine.

The accommodation is generally made in two steps. The first is primarily a response to situational demands and many students regard it as temporary. The second is the true conversion that is demanded of students as part of the transformation to a professional self.

The primary context for learning about professional objectivity is in the clinical skills sessions of hospital settings. Early in their program students encounter striking examples of the way in which the profession subjugates patients' needs, rights, and dignities to the clinical tasks at hand.

Initially, students are often dismayed by the way in which physicians and other hospital staff members treat patients. More often than not, however, the students are reluctant to challenge their evaluators and legitimators:

> They hardly talked to the patient at all. We'd get in there and he'd hold the speculum and we'd all take a look and we would just herd right out again into another room and have a look and herd out again. I thought the dehumanization was awful,... I didn't tell the doctor how I felt at the time, but when I left, other people felt the same way.... And we sort of bitched to each other how rough it was and how we're going to do something about it and we never did. We let it slide by. (Interview, Second year)

Over time, students come to accept the idea that patients are objects— material to learn from. They learn that this is necessary, at least temporarily, if they are to learn clinical symptoms and pathology and add to their medical knowledge and competence:

> I think you realize there is a structural problem, and there are a lot of demands made on you and you are forced to act in certain ways just to accomplish your work. But right now in the training phase, I find if the

clinical preceptor takes me around to listen to six patients with heart murmurs and I only have five minutes with each patient, I don't get concerned if I'm not getting it on with the patient, because I'm trying to learn about heart murmurs. (Interview, Second year)

The dominant concern with learning medicine leads students to focus their time and energy on studying efficiently. They soon find that they have little time for the frills of emotional involvement and quickly learn to shut down feelings that interfere with their work (Lief and Fox 1963) and with immediate productivity. As one student says:

You can't function if you think about things like that [death and dying].... Everything you see sort of gets in there and turns about in your mind and you aren't productive. The reason you have to shut it off is because you won't be productive.... I think that my prime objective is to learn the pathology. (Interview, Third year)

Thus, striving for competence is the initial professionalizing rationale for avoiding or shutting off emotional reactions and treating patients as objects (that is, the "pathology" from which to learn):

When you see someone who is going to die, especially when you're still learning, you're really cut off from the personal level. You just clue into the pathology. You really shut off. You sort of turn it out of your mind and this person is going to die. You just look at the pathology.... You don't really think, "What about the family?" What they must be going through.... You can't fall to pieces because you find your patient is going to die in three months or is rapidly going downhill. You have a role to play here. (Interview, Third year)

Assuming a Professional Stance

A critical factor influencing the pace at which students realign their idealism and change their perception of the profession and its practices, is the realization that their best interests are served by conforming to the demands and expectations of faculty members—the profession's gatekeepers, models, and control agents. Many hints are dropped from the outset, suggesting to students that some form of accommodation will be required to reconcile the discrepancy between the idealized and actual realities of the medicine:

[The Dean] said when we first came here we would be as idealistic as we would ever be, and we would see many abuses and problems in medicine, but that by the time we graduated we would accommodate ourselves to the system of organized medicine. (Field notes, Second year)

Quickly or slowly, reluctantly, or otherwise, students learn that they do not have time for both learning and caring, and they must stifle their feelings because of the higher value their legitimators place on a "professional" approach of affective neutrality (Parsons 1951; Daniels 1960; Kadushin 1962; Emerson 1970; Coombs and Powers 1975). The following is a typical view of most students:

> Look, as I see it, you can't afford to care too much. You keep your feelings at a distance because we have a phrase for it—we call it being professionally responsible.... You can't allow your feelings to interfere. (Field notes, Third year)

Students discover that a posture of affective neutrality is a routine feature of the hospital setting, regularly accepted by the medical profession. They heed the reminders that their primary objective at this stage of their careers is to absorb as much pathology as possible. They also observe that a physician's high case load precludes attending to anything but the patient's medical condition. In due course the students adopt the profession's rationale that detachment from patients is in the latter's best interests, that patients themselves prefer such a response from the physician. A student expresses this view:

> Now there are really very few people, very few patients who want their doctor to be the one who is going to sit there and cry over them, because really they are looking to get out of this predicament they're in.... Most patients would be very uncomfortable if they saw you in that state. (Interview, Third year)

As they advance through the program, students continually observe doctors' working habits, listen to their philosophies of medical practice, take note of their competencies and incompetencies, and reflect upon the nature of their own present and future relationships with patients. The physicians with whom they practice their clinical skills become models after which students pattern their own beliefs and behavior:

> Certainly there are people who impress me ... certain aspects of their personality that I would want to incorporate in some way in my practice. It is easy to model yourself after people you see on the wards.... You don't know anything and you start watching them and before too long you find yourself in a position where you tend to model yourself after these people.... (Interview, Third year)

Through observation, role-playing, and practice, students begin to identify with the organization and practice of the medical profession. As students observe and experience the problems of medical care and practice, they learn to identify with the profession and the means by which its members confront their problems. As they assume increased responsibilities and make medical judgments (for which they may be made to account to a variety of professionals), they develop an increasingly sympathetic outlook toward their future profession. The following examples illustrate this point. These conversations center around clerkship, when students actively engage in various medical rotations, and how this phase of the program alters their view of the medical profession:

> I think it does from the point of view that you can more or less see other people's situations much more because you're in their boat.... I agree with that. Having been in it [medicine], I can see why patients are dealt with quickly, perhaps. (Interview, Second year)

> I remember when we were back in Phase II and Phase I, we would go see a patient with a clinical skills preceptor, and he might have said something to the patient that seemed rude and I'd get all very indignant about it and say, "My God, you're not being very sensitive." While that may have been justified, now that I'm on the ward I can see that in a way it's a bit silly to take that one episode, because what you're seeing is one episode in a long history of the relationship between that patient and his doctor. You're taking this totally out of context and it's really not relevant to criticize unless you really know the relationship. Now I'm much less free with those sorts of criticisms.... (Interview, Second year)

The transformation from an idealistic phase to what they believe is a more realistic one occurs as students begin to take on the responsibilities and identity of doctors. A student describes this transition:

> First of all, the exposure to what really goes on.... You sort of keep your eyes open and you really get an idea of the real world of medicine.... The other part of it is when you're allowed responsibility ... and you really become involved with patients. (Field notes, Second year)

Advanced students are less vocal in their questioning and criticisms of the medical profession. They attribute many of their earlier concerns to naïveté and argue for a more sympathetic view of doctors and the profession:

> You go through a sort of stage of disillusion in which you sort of expect doctors to be perfect, and the medical profession and treatment and everything else to be perfect. And you find out that it's not. So you sort of react to that. I think now, after about two years, I'm starting to get to the phase now where I'm quite pleased with it really.... Part of the flack that you hear about medical doctors and malpractice suits, and about things that go wrong, are partly due to the fact that doctors tend to look after themselves and examine their own profession very carefully. (Interview, Third year)

In brief, the students' shift, from an idealistic perspective to one more closely aligned with the realities of professional practice, is accompanied by a change in the way they view and treat patients. Their priorities change as they learn how to negotiate their way through the program successfully and as they adopt the profession's rationales for defining patients as objects.

The Symbols of Professionalism

The professionalization of medical students is facilitated and intensified by the adoption of professional symbols. Possession of these symbols announces to both insiders and outsiders how the students are to be identified. During the first weeks of their studies, students begin wearing white lab jackets with plastic name tags which identify them as medical students. Since, from the beginning, clinical skills sessions are included in the curriculum, students participate in a variety of settings with the tools of the doctor's trade carried on their person. Their attire clearly identifies students to participants and visitors of the hospital/school setting. Equipped with their new identity kits, students also begin to learn and express themselves in a new symbol system, the medical vernacular, sometimes referred to as "McBabble" or "medspeak." Distinctive dress, badges, tools, and language provide the student with symbols which announce their role and identity, and significantly contribute to a changing identity and view of self.

The significance of these symbols to the professionalization process and changing perception of self is critical. The symbols serve, on the one hand, to identify and unite the bearer as a member of a community of shared interests, purpose, and identification (Roth 1957), and on the other hand, they distinguish and separate their possessors from lay people, making their role seem more mysterious, shrouded, and priest-like (Bramson 1973). The early manipulation of these symbols serves to heighten identification and commitment to the profession, while at the same time facilitating students' separation from the lay world. As one student candidly remarks:

> Wearing the jacket seems to give you *carte blanche* to just about go anywhere you want in the hospital. People assume that you belong and that you know what you're doing. (Field notes, Second year)

The importance of the white coat as a symbol is reinforced by the faculty and staff who, with the exception of the psychiatry department, mandate that it be worn. As the following incident illustrates, this expectation is rigorously adhered to, and is justified in terms of patients' expectations:

> The rheumatology session tutorial group assembled and walked to the room where Dr. Gordon would be met. Dr. Gordon said, "Well, you know in order to see any of the patients you have to wear a white jacket and a tie." The group was very surprised by his remark and, in fact, John and Ken looked at each other in disbelief.

> JOHN: No, I didn't know that.

> DR. GORDON: Well, you do know that in order to see any of the patients you have to wear a white coat. They expect that. You will agree that they expect that. Wouldn't you agree with that?

JOHN: No, I wouldn't. I mean that hasn't been my experience.

DR. GORDON: Well, have you ever visited any of the patients in the hospital?

JOHN: Yes, for about a year and a half now.

DR. GORDON: Those people who have the white jackets on will be able to visit the patients. Those who don't, won't be able to. (Field notes, Second year)

The separation between "we" and "they" becomes clearer to the students as they learn and adopt the professional system of communication and are absorbed into the medical culture. As they move through the culture, they learn how symbols are used to control and enforce certain definitions of professional situations. From the beginning, in tutorials, readings, demonstrations, and rounds, students are exposed to a language in which they are expected to become facile. A student explains the importance of replacing his lay vocabulary:

When I was just beginning, I would use my own words to describe how a lesion looked or how a patient felt ... because they were more immediate to me and more accessible to me. And on many occasions I was corrected. The way you describe that is such and such because that is the vocabulary of the profession and that is the only way you can be understood. (Interview, Third year)

However, another incident which took place in a tutorial captures the students' difficulties in knowing when use of the new language may be appropriate:

At one point Dr. Smith asked, "What is it, what is the name for this kind of phenomenon that gives this kind of pain?" E.G. volunteered a term and she ended it with a question mark. She was tentatively offering a term. Dr. Smith said, "Just use the plain language, what is the plain everyday word for that?" There was a pause and he said, "Heartburn, that's what everybody calls it and that's good enough." (Field notes, First year)

Students learn how practicing physicians manipulate these symbols and how the ability to use the linguistic symbols of medicine defines members of the profession and creates a boundary that is not easily crossed. Two students reflect on the significance of technical terminology:

So you would talk about things in front of a patient that would totally baffle the patient and keep him unaware of issues that you were discussing. I don't think this is unique to medicine. I think this is a general phenomenon of professionalization. [Learning the language] was a matter of establishing some common ground with people you were going to be relating to on a professional basis for the rest of your life. (Interview, Third year)

You just can't survive if you don't learn the jargon. It's not so much an effort to identify as it is an effort to survive. People in medicine have a world unto themselves and a language unto themselves. It's a world with a vocabulary ... and a vocabulary that, no question about it, creates a fraternity that excludes the rest of the world and it's a real tyranny to lay persons who don't understand it. (Interview, Third year)

In sum, the adoption of special props, costume, and language reinforces the students' identification with, and commitment to, medicine while it enables them to project an image of having adopted a new and special role. Having learned how to manipulate the symbols to reflect audiences' expectations, they can begin to shape and control professional relationships.

The manipulation of symbolic language and props does more than shape and control professional relationships; it actually helps change the neophyte's perception of self. A student thoughtfully comments on the dynamic nature of the relationship existing between the symbol system and his self-image:

When you wore the jacket, especially in the beginning, people were impressed. After all, it told everyone, including yourself, that you were studying to be a doctor.... The other thing about wearing the white jacket is that it does make things more obvious. You know what you are; it is sort of another way of identifying. There were very few ways that people had to identify with the medical profession and one of the ways was to begin to look like some of the doctors. (Interview, Second year)

The Art of Impression Management: Adopting a Cloak of Competence

While appropriate medical accoutrements help the students manage their new roles and are essential to their changing views of self, students are highly sensitive to the necessity of meeting a variety of role expectations. During their rotating clerkship assignments, students are exposed to many different audiences each of which has different expectations about the proper performance of the clerkship role. In fact in the hospital setting, the role itself is ambiguous. The clerk or "clinical jerk" is constantly faced with new situations that do not relate in a clear way to an appropriate role and a "correct" identity.

The variable, often increased, levels of responsibility that come with clerkship are also accompanied by a broader and more intense scrutiny of the student's clinical capabilities. Student descriptions of clerkship experiences highlight the diversity of their audiences and the variability of expectations:

Clerkship, it's difficult because you're under scrutiny all the time. I'm particularly anxious about the staff because they have such conflicting ideas about medicine. You see the thing that we find out is that medicine is not so much a science—it's really much more of an art. (Field notes, Third year)

The taking on of increased responsibility and the concomitant exercise of medical judgment makes clinical clerks accountable to a variety of professionals. While students are generally protected from meeting the expectations of patients, they do face the unpredictable and often critical nature of faculty expectations. Because the teaching staff is responsible for evaluating and determining the progress of students, students attempt to estimate teachers' demands. However, they often find these expectations to be ill-defined and sometimes contradictory. Frequent changes of assignment and the nature of hospital organization combine to ensure a high turnover of audiences for the clerk. There is often considerable ambiguity about which script is appropriate for a particular audience:

> A lot of types of guys [doctors], like certain obstetricians, like their thing done in a certain way. They like their episiotomies done this way, you know. I mean they like them [episiotomies] sewn up in a particular way. You know, there is a certain way to do it, and this is the right way, my way. If you're going to deliver one of my babies, then you've got to do it my way or else you don't do it. (Interview, Third year)

The students' problem is dealing with staff who have widely divergent approaches to the practice of medicine. Faced with a threatening ambiguity, students try to find out the particular biases and special areas of interest of those with whom they must interact (Becker, Geer, Hughes, and Strauss 1961). They soon realize that their evaluators are often totally convinced of the correctness and validity of their own expertise and approach. The students therefore find themselves vulnerable to appraisals by these evaluators, who may remind the students of their incompetence. Students quickly adopt a common perspective for dealing with such uncertainty. When individuals are uncertain about evaluative criteria, including what they should know and how they should apply it, they cover themselves by learning how to deflect questions that may be intended to probe their knowledge or their ignorance (Goffman 1963; Edgerton 1967; Olesen and Whittaker 1968; Haas 1972, 1977; Haas and Shaffir 1977).

This "cloaking" behavior is often accompanied by initiative-taking behavior on the part of students that is intended to impress others (Becker, Geer, Hughes, and Strauss 1961; Bucher and Stelling 1977). In their attempt to control their audiences' impressions of them, students usually use these two broadly based, but intricately related, strategies: the first is "covering up," a strategy intended to provide protection from charges of incompetence; the second is that of taking initiatives to display competence. Both strategies require considerable skills in self-presentation. A student describes one of these strategies, a form of initiative-taking that provides protection from divergent medical approaches taken by senior personnel:

> Like Dr. Jones, who was my advisor or boss for medicine, he always came and did rounds on Tuesday mornings.... His interest was in endocrinology and ...

he was going to pick up that endocrine patient to talk about, and so, of course, Monday night any dummy can read up Monday night like hell on the new American Diabetic Association standards for diabetes or hyperglycemia.... So, the next day you seem fairly knowledgeable.... But I just wonder how much I remember when you try to read over in a hurry and you try to be keen just for the next day. Because that afternoon you forget about it because you figure Wednesday morning hematology people make their rounds and, of course, you have to read hematology Tuesday night. (Interview, Second year)

The constant need to create and manage the image of a competent self through the process of impression management is sometimes at odds with a basic tenet of the school's philosophy, which encourages learning through a problem-solving approach and the complementary development of a questioning attitude. A student expresses his handling of the problem this way:

The best way of impressing others with your competence is asking questions you know the answers to. Because if they ever put it back on you, "Well, what do you think?" then you tell them what you think and you'd give a very intelligent answer because you knew it. You didn't ask to find out information. You ask it to impress people. (Interview, Third year)

Projection of the right image in an evaluative situation is recognized by students as being as important as technical competence. A student referring to the importance of creating the right impression claims:

It's like any fraternity. You've got to know. You've got to have a certain amount of basic knowledge before they think it's worth talking to you. If you display less than that basic knowledge, their reflexes come into play and they think this person is an idiot. Let's find out exactly how much they don't know, rather than building on what you do know. That's a different manoeuvre, being out in the pale, not worth talking to, or within the pale and well worth talking to. There is image management in every profession. (Interview, Third year)

The emphasis upon interactional evaluation in the innovative school contributes to student uncertainty. As Shibutani (1966) notes, in many such situations rumor and gossip are common. When reputations are created and defined in interactional settings, students are concerned about becoming objects of display and discussion:

But here, I mean, you fart and the next day or later that afternoon everybody in the class knows what is going on. Like so and so does so well, and so and so is having problems. And so and so here is really doing great, he is in the library all the time, and he knows all the answers to the questions.... The gossip is unbelievable. (Interview, Second year)

Students generally view impression management as the critical means for avoiding criticism and convincing evaluators or gatekeepers of their competence:

> [In clerkship] how does one person get a good evaluation and another person doesn't. We made this analogy between feathers and black eyes.... If you began in the beginning with too many black eyes, you could never get rid of a black eye. A blue and black eye would always stay there and they would always recognize you with the black eye. It didn't matter how many feathers you got afterwards.... Whereas, if you started off with the feathers and you got enough feathers in the beginning, so you almost had a full hatband of feathers, it doesn't matter what you did. One may fall off every now and then.... And then you'd get to a stage where you'd have all these feathers, shit, a whole roll of feathers, and you couldn't for the life of you, you just couldn't get a black eye. You were invincible. You were the big chief. And that's what clerkship is all about—impressing. And if you impress a person enough, and you impress him at a critical time, then that was it—you got your good evaluation. (Interview, Spring, Third year)

It would appear that nothing succeeds like success and that students gain confidence as they learn that the projection of a successful image is one way to effectively control others' definitions of their developing professionalism. A student describes the importance of impression-management skills in easing relationships with patients, particularly in dealing with the sensitive areas of the physical examination:

> I think it's largely a matter of how you present yourself. Now if I go in all shaky and flushed and nervous about it, the patient is going to pick up on this and is going to respond. So I think you have to go in with a confident manner and know your business and go about it in a very clear-cut way, so the patient does not know you have any fears of the situation and therefore doesn't transfer those fears to himself or herself. (Interview, Third year)

Thus, students anticipate that they can deflect others from evaluating cognitive or performance competence negatively. Another student graphically describes the ambiguous nature of professional evaluation:

> You see the kind of student that they [faculty] want to see is the strong and the assertive-type person. Medical people like to see people who state their position and take a stand ... a go-getter, an individual who can relate, an individual who on their own can lead a tutorial group, who can take patients and follow them through, who can take initiatives.... If they see you being decisive and confident and they see you can do something, then they think you're good. I think it's very easy for you to slide by on personality. Sometimes I think I'm at fault ... because I think I have the personality that I can put others in the situation where they won't go and find out if I'm weak in some areas.

> That's the problem with this place: that they never really separate personality from academics. (Interview, Second year)

The relationship between professional success and the projection of confident performances is further indicated in the following student's comments:

> If you act like you know, they treat you like you know. If you act like you don't know what is happening, then that's the way they treat you. It might sound really strange, but that is the way it is. You've got to let them know that you know what you are doing. (Field notes, Third year)

Confidence is further bolstered by the comparisons that students inevitably make with their peers and practicing professionals. The clerks come to realize that other participants also are involved in the game or art of impression management and that lack of knowledge is easy to hide in a milieu that emphasizes appearances. A student makes this point:

> The comforting thing about clerkship is that you see that specialists and interns and residents don't know everything. That's kind of reassuring to know that first of all you don't have to know everything and secondly, that a lot of people who are beyond you in their training don't know everything. (Field notes, Third year)

Conclusion

The process of professionalization affects newcomer idealism and requires the taking on of a professional approach and role, aiding in the control of definitions of the situation by the use and manipulation of professional symbols and ideas and by acts of impression management. Trustworthy competence is symbolically communicated as part of a necessary process of convincing potentially dubious, but hopeful, audiences and as part of changing one's self-image as a developing professional.

Students soon learn the practical importance of assuming the cloak of competence. Successful negotiations of the trial by ordeal through proper performances helps newcomers gain control or dominance (Freidson 1970), which is basic to professionalism. The cloak, ideally, also allows patients to trust both the health professional and the prescribed treatment. Students thus recognize the importance of appearing authoritative in both professionalizing and professional situations.

The posture of authoritativeness in professional matters is an expected outcome of the trial by ordeal. The special status and role of professional is enveloped in a set of expectations that require special demonstrations of "possessed" competence. Practicing at playing the role eventually results in its adoption and identification. Newcomers model and imitate their mentors and the self-perpetuation of the notion of having an authoritative presence proceeds.

In sum, the students come to realize that, as practicing professionals, they will continue to place emphasis on the communication of competence. Effective reputation-making for practitioners, as well as for students, depends on the successful control and manipulation of symbols, ideas, and legitimators in professional rituals and situations. Donald Light astutely points out the outcome of what amounts to a ritual ordeal in the study of psychiatric residents when he notes:

> By structuring them [training programmes] so that the trainees experience feelings of intense anxiety, ignorance, and dependence, such programmes may be teaching professionals to treat clients as they have been treated. And by exaggerating their power and expertise, mentors establish a model of omnipotence that their students are fated to repeat. To the extent that laymen accept this mythology, omnipotent tendencies become reinforced in daily life. To the extent they challenge it, professionals like physicians or psychiatrists become embattled and defensive. (1980, 307)

The self-fulfilling nature of the conversion process, whereby newcomers attain the higher moral status of a professional through impression management, is captured in two separate interview comments:

> People expect you to be the healer and so you have to act like the healer. (Field notes, Third year)

> You know a large part of our role is a God role. You have to act like God. You're supposed to be like God. If you don't inspire confidence in your patients, they are not going to get better even if you know the correct diagnosis and have the correct treatment. If they don't have faith in you, they are not going to get better. (Interview, Second year)

The process of adopting the cloak of competence is ultimately justified by students as being helpful to the patient. A student summarizes the relationship between acting competently and patients responding to such a performance by getting well, when he says:

> You know the patients put pressure on you to act as if you are in the know. If you know anything about the placebo effect, you know that a lot of the healing and curing of patients does not involve doing anything that will really help them, but rather creating confidence in the patient that things are being done and will be done. We know that the placebo effect, for example, has even cured cancer patients. If they have the confidence in the doctor and what doctor and what treatment they are undergoing, they are much more likely to get well, irrespective of the objective effects of the treatment. (Interview, Second year)

Neophytes and professionals alike are involved in careers and self-images based on reputational control. Indeed, many laypeople are not only aware that the professionals with whom they deal are engaged in playing a part, in projecting the proper image, but they demand it. The interactional basis for this adaptation to a professional role and view of self is summarized by Halmos when he says:

> We must conclude that the role-playing of being a professional is a hard social fact, and a potent behavioral model for the non-professionals, and thus for society at large.... The strange thing is that the world cannot afford to dispense with being systematically conned! Of course, the truth is that the world is not being deceived: it demands the professing of values and their embodiment in a culturally defined style and ritual. (1970, 180–181)

NOTES

1. The data in this paper derive from our study of the professional socialization of students in the McMaster University medical program. Our study involved *participant-observation* and interview research of a class of 80 students over a three-year period. We observed students during the full range of their educational experiences, including tutorials, clinical-skills groups, clerkships, and in informal settings.

Tattoo You: Tattoos as Self-Extensions and Identity Markers

Clint Sanders

Our physical appearance is central in shaping how we think about ourselves and how other people relate to us. Some aspects of appearance—being tall or short, attractive or plain, dark or light complected—are determined rather apart from our overt control. We choose other significant features of how we look. For example, we dress to make a statement to those around us, wear our hair in styles that connect us to certain groups and lifestyles, and decorate our bodies so as to enhance their beauty. In turn other people use appearance to place us into social categories which they employ to decide who we are and how to treat us. Our ongoing experience of other people's responses to us is then used to solidify or alter how we understand ourselves (Cooley 1964 [1902], 97–104). In other words, a person's appearance is central to the elemental social processes of acquiring an identity in the eyes of others, building a self-definition, and managing our relationships with those with whom we interact (Prus 1987, 274–76; 280–81).

Indelible alterations of the body are especially powerful mechanisms for making statements about who we are and they have considerable impact—both positive and negative—upon how other people treat us. In this paper, I want to talk about one such form of voluntarily chosen body alteration—tattooing. The basic point is that the tattoo is a purchased product which graphically extends our social self (Belk 1988). In certain social circumstances it acts as a "mark of affiliation"; the tattoo connects one to other people who value or admire this type of body decoration. In other situations, being tattooed can be stigmatizing. It is seen by some people as symbolizing unconventionality, deviance, or potential danger and thereby leads them to be distrustful of or, in some cases, to discriminate against the tattooed person.

The Research

Fairly early in my academic career I realized that sociology had something special to offer me. It provided what I saw to be a useful and sensible way of seeing things and offered a legitimate context in which to focus on social activities and objects that were of personal interest and sources of private pleasure. Attracted by people and phenomena that are often outside of conventional social boundaries, I have tended to focus on what I have come to think of as the "soft white underbelly of American culture." Among other things, I have researched and written on narcotics police, underground comix (comics), horror film, drug use by GIs in Vietnam, various domestic drug-using subcultures, club performers and other cultural producers, and now tattooing. Since my graduate school experience in the 1960s, I have also been attracted by the experience of doing ethnography. It is a research approach that allows me to work independently (I have usually found interaction with anyone in the role of "boss" to be, at best, annoying), and I find that I possess a certain ability to interact comfortably with a fairly wide range of people. Doing this sort of "lone-ranger" fieldwork in the kinds of social settings I tend to choose has always provided me with a certain measure of adventure and allowed me to escape legitimately from the narrow confines of academia. In general I find myself more at ease interacting with junkies, freaks, night-people, bikers, musicians, and other unsavory sorts, than I am in rubbing shoulders with my colleagues in the university. *Doing* sociology provides me with the opportunity to interact within settings and social networks where I have come to feel comfortable and which are commonly closed to, and therefore unexplored by, my more conventional colleagues. I believe it is important to build an understanding of the complex richness of human behavior from information collected within a *variety* of social settings. My own tastes and experiences have drawn me to employ what skills and knowledge I possess, to participate in the illumination of some of the darker corners of North American culture.

My initial firsthand contact with tattooing came about when I was visiting San Francisco during the summer of 1979. Having a bit of time on my hands, I decided to explore the more obscure museums listed in the "museums" section of the Yellow Pages. Climbing the dingy stairway leading to the Museum of Tattoo Art, I found myself in a new and fascinating social world. After looking at the sizeable collection of tattoo memorabilia, I entered the tattoo studio adjacent to the museum and, like many first-time visitors to tattoo establishments, impulsively decided to join the ranks of the tattooed. After choosing a small scarab (beetle) design from the flash on the wall, I submitted to the unexpectedly painful tattoo experience. Although the resident tattooist was not especially forthcoming in response to the questions I forced out between clenched teeth, I did come to realize that this was a phenomenon that combined my research interests in social deviance, artistic production, and body alteration. It offered, at the same time, a research experience that would provide a much needed escape from the thankless task of writing a textbook in which I had been involved for the last couple of years.

Returning to the east coast I visited a small "street shop" in a "transitional neighborhood" located a few minutes from my office. The owner appeared flattered that a "professor" would want to hang out and listen to him talk about himself and I soon became a regular visitor to the shop, observing the work, talking to the participants and, despite my original vow never again to undergo the pain of indelible body alteration, eventually receiving considerable tattoo "work" from a variety of well-known tattoo artists during the subsequent years.

For the most part, my role in the tattoo studios in which I did my research was that of one of a number of regular hangers-on who either lived in the neighborhood or were friends of the local artist. My participation in the establishment to which I originally gained access was considerably more extensive. In addition to (apparently) just standing around and chatting, I routinely helped with the business of the shop. I made change for the amusement games, provided information about cost and availability of designs, stretched the skin of customers who were receiving tattoos on body areas other than arms or legs, calmed the anxiety of first-time recipients and, in a variety of ways, made myself generally useful.

My understanding of the tattoo as a symbol of both connection to the "tattoo community" and disassociation from conventional society was furthered by my own experience as a tattooed person. Soon after I left the San Francisco studio with that first tattoo, I began to realize that I was now confronted with a new category of routine social decisions—to whom and under what circumstances should I reveal my potentially discrediting decoration? Those with whom I came into contact were now classified on the basis of their anticipated response, ranging from those who would be appreciative and supportive (primarily, close friends and other tattooees) to those who would react negatively (for example, my parents and most of my colleagues). Even such routine decisions as what clothes to wear—particularly during the summer months—were now shaped by new considerations.

My encounters with total strangers in public settings were similarly affected by my personal and professional involvement with tattooing. I regularly began to approach people I saw with tattoos and ask them about where their work had been done and what had led them to choose that particular image. Tattooees accosted in this way initially tended to respond with a certain degree of suspicion and hostility. Their affect changed dramatically, however, when I displayed my own tattoos and could demonstrate some familiarity with the tattooist they had patronized. I was no longer a curious (and, probably, unsympathetic) stranger; we were both members of a select and often stigmatized group. The fact that we would often touch each other—stretching the tattooed skin and feeling the texture of each other's design—was a special indication of the affiliative significance of the tattoo symbol. It was through social encounters such as this that I came to build an understanding of the *meaning* of the tattoo experience beyond that which could have been derived from structured information collected solely through questionnaires and other more conventional sociological techniques.

In the rest of this account I will use my own experience as a tattooed person and as a participant-observer in the social world surrounding tattooing to talk about some central issues. Since whenever I tell people that I have studied tattooing the question of why people get tattooed invariably arises, I will start with a brief discussion of what the people I worked with told me about how they went about deciding to get tattooed, what they presented as their motives (Mills 1940). I will then turn to the effect of acquiring a tattoo on the decorated person's definition of his or her self. Finally, I will present the ways in which wearing a tattoo affects one's interactions and relationships with other people.

Tattoo Motives

Choosing to Get a Tattoo

Becoming tattooed is a highly social act. The decision to acquire a tattoo (and the image that is chosen) is shaped primarily by how the tattoo recipient defines his or her "self." The tattoo becomes an item in the tattooee's personal "identity kit" (Goffman 1961, 20–21) and, in turn, is used by those with whom the person interacts to place him or her into a particular interaction-shaping category.

When asked to describe how they decided to get a tattoo, the vast majority of the people I spoke with referred to another person or group. Family members, friends, business associates, and other people with whom they regularly interacted were described as being tattooed. While tattooees commonly reported having "thought about getting a tattoo for a long time," they usually drifted into the actual tattoo experience when they "didn't have anything better to do," had money to devote to a non-essential (and relatively expensive) purchase, and were, most importantly, in the general vicinity of a tattoo shop.

Typically, the act of getting the tattoo was a social event experienced with close friends or family members. These companions acted as "purchase pals"

(Bell 1967). They provided social support for the decision, helped to pass anxiety-filled waiting time, offered opinions about what design the person should choose and where to put it on the body, and commiserated with, or humorously ridiculed, the recipient during the somewhat painful tattoo experience.

When talking about their initial decision to get a tattoo, people commonly presented themselves as being in the midst of an important transition in their lives. The tattoo was seen as ritually commemorating these changes. For example, one woman going through a divorce described the tattoo as symbolizing the taking back of her body:

> [My friend and I] both talked semi-seriously about getting [a tattoo]. I mentioned it to my husband and he was adamantly opposed—only certain seedy types get tattoos. He didn't want someone else touching my body intimately, which is what a tattoo would involve ... even if it was just my arm. He was against it, which made me even more for it.... I finally really decided some time last year when my marriage was coming apart. It started to be a symbol of taking my body back. I was thinking that about the time I got divorced would be a good time to do it.

Choosing a Design and Body Location

The tattooed people I spoke with commonly described their initial motives for getting a tattoo in fairly general terms. The tattoo connected them to significant others who were similarly marked; it made one unique by separating him or her from those who were bound by convention; it satisfied an aesthetic desire to decorate the body; and, as seen above, it acted to symbolize freedom and self-control. On the other hand, *where* on the body one chose to have the tattoo placed and the *design* they chose were understood and talked about much more specifically. Typically, design choice was related to the tattooed person's connections to other people, his or her definition of self or, especially in the case of women, the desire to enhance and beautify the body. In general people spoke of their choice of a particular tattoo design in terms that could be situated within five overlapping categories of symbolic import.

1. Symbolization of an Interpersonal Relationship. One of the major factors leading people to choose a particular design was to have the same tattoo as was worn by a friend, lover, or family member. This symbolic connection to others was most clear when people chose "vow" tattoos that incorporated the name of the person with whom they had a close relationship. The traditional tattoo with "MOM" inscribed in a heart is an example of this type of tattoo function.

2. Participation in a Group. Involvement with a particular group of people was a common influence on the tattoo chosen. For example, people who were or had been in the military chose service insignia; members of motorcycle gangs chose club symbols; members of sports teams chose designs that represented their team or the sport they favored; and participants in religious groups picked esoteric or conventional religious designs. For these people the tattoo represented their indelible connection to the social group in which an important part of the self concept was centered.

3. Self-Identity. The tattooed person's individual sense of self was also symbolized by the design he or she chose. Many people requested their zodiac sign. Other people chose uniquely meaningful images. For example, one person I spoke with chose a tattoo of an eyeball surrounded by flame because he had very weak eyes. Another tattooee chose a cartoon bee because he was allergic to bee stings. He, half jokingly, believed that the tattooed bee would scare away actual bees. Yet another person chose a more abstractly personal symbol of herself:

> I put a lot of thought into this tattoo. I'm an English major, and I thought that the medieval castle had a lot of significance. I'm an idealist, and I thought that that was well expressed by a castle with clouds. Plus, I'm blond and I wanted something blue.

4. Representation of Important Interests and Activities. People commonly decided on designs that symbolized important personal involvements, hobbies, or occupations. I saw, for example, a rabbit breeder choose a cartoon rabbit, an avid card player select a picture of a hand of cards, and a hunter choose the silhouette of a stag.

5. Decorative/Aesthetic Statements. Many of the people I spoke with responded to my question about what they liked about the tattoo they chose by offering an aesthetic reason. They "liked the colors" or "thought it was pretty." For example:

> I didn't get this tattoo because of being bad or cool or anything like that. It's like a picture. You see a picture you like and you put it in your room or your house or something like that. It's just a piece of work that you like. I like the artwork they do here. I like the color [on my tattoo]. It really brings it out— the orange and the green. I like that—the colors.

This kind of decorative/aesthetic response was most commonly encountered with women who frequently referred to the tattoo as a piece of body jewelry.

The differences between men and women with regard to the designs chosen and the area of the body upon which the person decided to carry the tattoo came to be particularly interesting issues for me. Women typically chose different designs than did men. Rather than selecting the cartoony, death-oriented, or aggressive images typically requested by men, women favored floral pieces, butterflies, gentle mythical beasts (the unicorn and Pegasus were quite popular), and colorful birds such as parrots or peacocks.

While men typically had tattoos inscribed on their arms, women tended to locate tattoos on the breast, back of the shoulder, hip/pubic area, or lower abdomen. These differences in placement were related to differing definitions of the function of the tattoo. Men commonly saw the tattoo as a public symbol whereby they communicated aspects of their social identity to casual acquaintances and strangers in the course of everyday interaction. Women, on the other hand, were more concerned with the perceived unconventionality and possible stigmatization resulting from the tattoo mark. Rather than being a public declaration of self, for the woman, the tattoo was a private decoration—a bodily enhancement meant for personal enjoyment and the private appreciation of those with whom she had intimate relationships.

The Tattoo and the Self-Concept

Acquiring a tattoo changed the ways in which the people I talked with saw themselves. Interviewees commonly said that the tattoo made them feel different or special.

> Having a tattoo changes how you see yourself. It is a way of choosing to change your body. I enjoy that. I enjoy having a tattoo because it makes me different from other people. There is no one in the whole world who has a right arm that looks anything like mine. I've always valued being different from other people. Tattooing is a way of expressing that difference. It is a way of saying, "I am unique."

A tattoo artist expressed a similar understanding of the impact of the tattoo in talking about his clients:

> Tattooing is really just a form of personal adornment. Why does someone get a new car and get all of the paint stripped off of it and paint it candy apple red?... I associate it with ownership. Your body is one of the things you indisputably own. There is a tendency to adorn things that you own to make them especially yours.

Since being tattooed is somewhat painful and most people (at least when they get their first tattoo) are unfamiliar with the tattoo process and have never even been in a tattoo studio, tattooees are often quite anxious when they find themselves confronted by a tattoo artist holding an angrily buzzing tattoo machine. Interviewees often spoke of the pride they felt after having successfully endured the tattoo experience. The tattoo symbolically enhanced their self-definition—they were people who had the necessary courage. One woman, when asked whether she intended to get any other tattoos, spoke of the excitement of the experience as an enticement to acquire future work.

> Oh God! I don't know why but my initial reaction is, "I hope I don't, but I think I'm going to." I think getting a tattoo is so exciting and I've always been kind of addicted to excitement. It's fun. While it hurt and stuff it was a new experience and it wasn't that horrible for me. It was new and different.

This theme of enhancement of the self-concept through enduring a mysterious, painful, and exciting experience was most poignantly expressed by one woman with whom I spoke:

> [In the future] when I'm sitting around and bored with my life and I wonder if I was ever young once and did exciting things, I can look at the tattoo and remember.

The Tattoo and Interaction

As mentioned above, men typically choose to have their tattoos inscribed on "public skin" such as their arms because they understand the tattoo as a public symbolic declaration of themselves and their connections. Women, in contrast, choose "private skin" such as the breast or pubic area because they commonly define the tattoo as an intimate decorative enhancement of their bodies. Women also choose hidden parts of their bodies as the location for tattoos because they are aware that having a tattoo is conventionally defined as more deviant when carried by a woman than it is when carried by a man. This understanding of the stigmatizing effect of having a tattoo was expressed by one woman who wore an unusual tattoo (a snake coiled around a large rose) on what is, for a woman, an unconventional body location—her bicep.

> SANDERS: How did you decide on that particular design?
>
> WOMAN: I wanted something really different and I'd never seen a tattoo like this on a woman before. I really like it but sometimes I look at it and wish I didn't have it.
>
> SANDERS: That's interesting. When do you wish you didn't have it?
>
> WOMAN: When I'm getting real dressed up in a sleeveless dress and I want to look ... uh, prissy and feminine. People look at a tattoo and think you're real bad ... a loose person. But I'm not.

For both the men and the women with whom I talked, this view of the definitional and interactional consequences of the tattoos they had, was not unfounded. Their body decorations, not infrequently, made them the focus of negative and judgmental attention:

> Sometimes at these parties the conversation will turn to tattoos and I'll mention that I have some. A lot of people don't believe it, but if I'm feeling loose enough I'll roll up my sleeves and show my work. What really aggravates me is that there will almost always be someone who reacts with a show of disgust. "How could you do that to yourself!" No wonder I usually feel more relaxed and at home with bikers and other tattooed people.

Because of the judgmental response other people had to the person's tattoos and the negative identity others attributed to the tattooee, individuals with tattoos were often fairly circumspect when making the decision whether or not to reveal their body decorations. This was especially the case when the "other" had power over the tattooed person:

> Usually I'm fairly careful about who I show my tattoos to. I don't show them to people at work unless they are really close friends of mine and I know I won't get any kind of hassle because of them. I routinely hide my tattoos.... I generally hide them from people who wouldn't understand or people who could potentially cause me trouble. I hide them from by boss and from a lot of the people I work with because there is no reason for them to know.

Again, being tattooed is more stigmatizing for women than it is for men. Consequently, many of the women I talked with recounted incidents in which parents, friends, and, especially lovers and spouses reacted badly when they initially became aware of the tattoo:

> He [her husband] said he almost threw up. It grossed him out. I had asked him years ago, "What would you think if ...?" and he didn't like the idea. So, I decided not to tell him. It seemed a smart thing to do. He just looked rather grossed out by the whole thing; didn't like it. Now it is accepted, but I don't think he would go for another one.

Tattooed people commonly used the responses of casual associates or relative strangers as a means of categorizing them. A positive reaction to the tattoo indicated social and cultural compatibility, while negatively judgmental responses were seen as indicating that people were narrow minded or bound by convention:

> I get more positive reactions than I do negative reactions. The negative reactions come from people who aren't like me—who have never done anything astray. It is the straight-laced, conservative person who really doesn't believe that this is acceptable in their set of norms.

We see then that tattooed people commonly protected a valued self-definition (brave, unique, beautiful, and so forth) in the face of negative social responses from others by denigrating the source of these judgmental reactions. Understandably, tattooees were pleased when their decorations met with positive and admiring responses from others. This type of social reaction reinforced the reasonableness of their decision to get tattooed, and supplied information which the tattooed person could use to reinforce a positive self-definition. Further, being tattooed and receiving admiring responses from others made one feel part of what one person referred to as a "special club" of tattooed people:

> Having tattoos in some ways does affect me positively because people will stop me on the street and say, "Those are really nice tattoos," and show me theirs. We kind of ... it is a way of having positive contact with strangers. We have

something very much in common. We can talk about where we got them and the process of getting them and that sort of thing.

Conclusion

Due to its historical and popular cultural connections to sailors, criminals, outlaw bikers, and other disreputable sorts of people, the tattoo is a powerful and potentially degrading symbol. The decision to acquire a tattoo is a decision not only to alter one's physical appearance; it is also a choice to change how the person experiences his or her self and, in turn, how he or she will be defined and treated by others. We live in a culture that both admires and despises unconventionality and since tattoos symbolically set one apart from other "normal" people, the wearing of tattoos is appealing though potentially, somewhat socially dangerous. For some people tattoos enhance their self-definition and social identity in that they overtly demonstrate to themselves and to others that they are willing to flaunt authority and conventionality. As one person colorfully described it, the tattoo is "a poke in the eye to people who don't have them—people who are straights or whatever."

But the tattoo acts as more than a "mark of disaffiliation" (Goffman 1963, 143–47). For the tattooed person the mark symbolically connects him or her to special groups centered around unique interests. Most importantly, the tattoo associates the wearer with other people in the "tattoo community." Other tattooed people view the tattoo as a mark of membership and it helps to provide the tattooee with self-enhancing interactions with an appreciative social audience (Goffman 1963, 23–25).

Contemporary commercial culture provides a number of products such as T-shirts, bumper stickers, buttons, patches, and so forth, which people use to extend their selves to others and solidify or alter their self-concepts. Clothing, jewelry, hairstyle, and other features of personal decoration are used to communicate aesthetic taste and social connection. These modes of self-symbolization are relatively safe because they can be easily changed should they prove to be more socially handicapping than they are worth. In contrast, when choosing to *permanently* alter their bodies, tattooed people voluntarily shape their social identities and enhance their definitions of self in an especially powerful way. Drawn by both the connectedness and unconventionality of the permanent mark, tattooed people have inscribed on their bodies indelible symbols of social identity.

Needing to Know: Adoptees Search for Self Completion

Karen March

The study of adoption reunion offers us a unique opportunity to investigate the strong association that exists between self and identity. Because the institution of adoption in modern Western society denies adoptees access to certain biographical information that others in their society possess, many adoptees experience *identity gaps* that leave them feeling fragmented and incomplete (McWhinnie 1967; Triseliotis 1973; Sorosky, Baran, and Pannor 1975; 1978). A large number of these adoptees have experienced reunion with birth relatives and gained access to this "missing" data (Thompson, Webber, Stoneman, and Harrison 1978; Stoneman, Thompson, and Webber 1980; Simpson, Timm, and McCubbin 1981; Sobol and Cardiff 1983; Haimes and Timms 1985; March 1990). Our study of the role that this biographical information plays for the adoptee's self-concept helps us gain a clearer understanding of the meaning that such knowledge holds for us all.

Self and Identity as Social Products

Mead (1934, 164) noted that the development of self requires an awareness of the existence of others and the ability to continually observe, reflect upon, and take account of these other perspectives. Mead viewed this development of self as a cognitive process whereby an individual makes indications to self, reflects upon those indications, and forms his or her actions accordingly. For Mead, self is a social product that takes its character and form from the symbols and meanings that arise out of the process of social interaction.

In a similar vein Cooley (1964, 183–84) observed that the process of interpreting and applying to self the words and meanings derived from others, results in the formation of a *self-image* (personal identity) that is composed of three interconnected parts. These are: the imagination of our appearance to the other person; the imagination of the other's judgment of that appearance; and some sort of self-feeling such as pride or mortification. This image of self, "the looking glass self," arises from a socially derived understanding of one's individual qualities, attributes, and characteristics as these are evaluated by other members of one's society. It is in this fashion that this intersubjective image of self emerges from the reflected appraisals of others.

At the same time as one takes into account others' opinions of self, one also makes indications to self that are used to direct one's actions. Self can therefore be viewed as having an internalized character that allows people to be objects of their own actions. This view of self, "like other objects ... emerges from the process of social interaction in which other people are defining a person to himself" (Blumer 1969b, 12). That process occurs when people take the role of the other and view self from others' perspective.

Because others certify a person's view of self when they accept the signs and symbols that the individual offers during the course of interaction, each encounter can either sustain, negate, or alter the identity that individuals present. Individuals may therefore imagine or envision their presentation of self before they take action and attempt to modify their behavior and present different parts of self to meet the expectations of the various audiences that they encounter (Goffman 1959). In this way one's personal identity or self-image becomes more complex and diversified as one's universe of social experience unfolds and expands. Identity becomes "situated" in that it reflects a sense of who people are in particular situations (Stone 1962, 93; Alexander and Wiley 1981, 269–89). It becomes an element of people's inter-subjective reality and is formed through social exchange (Berger and Luckmann 1966, 173).

Identity, as understood from this perspective, is not static. It continually evolves as new forms and meanings for self emerge through the passage of time (Strauss 1969, 9). Individuals maintain a somewhat stable sense of identity, however, that evolves from the continuity of community throughout their lives. Shibutani has stated: "The consistency of all such experiences enables each person to integrate them into a unit, a whole, which is also treated as a distinct entity by other people" (1961, 217). In this way people form self-judgments which govern their definitions of past and future action as well as their current definition of the situation. This contributes to an identity that has some uniformity and harmony as well as one that has the capacity for innovation and variety.

Mead (1934, 80–90) viewed this stable sense of identity as an important aspect of one's self-concept, that is, as a person's overarching conception of who they are as an individual and encompassing all of their past experiences. As such, the self-concept acts as the repository of all current and past biographical data. It is less subject to immediate change and modification and provides the individual with a sense of personal coherence and historical continuity. A comprehensive understanding of the circumstances, events, and details that compose one's biography therefore tends to produce a more harmonious and coherent self-concept and a sense of security over one's presentation of self to others. Similarly, lack of biographical information or inaccuracies in one's biographical background will likely produce a sense of uncertainty about self and lead one to question how others perceive them.

In this paper I consider the significance that a complete biography holds for sixty adult adoptees and its impact on their satisfactory presentation of self in social interaction. To my knowledge this is the first study that examines the adopted population's perception of how their community views their social status as adoptees and the difficulties that this social designation causes for the organization of their social world. Although this analysis may be biased by its focus on the perceptions of adoptees who desire search and reunion, rather than an inclusion of those who may not be so inclined, this sample does offer an opportunity to explore the interconnections that exist between biography, identity, and self-concept from a vantage point that gives a better understanding of the meaning that these social processes hold for all of us.

Methodology and Sample Description

The adoptees who are quoted in this paper consist of a randomly selected sample of sixty adoptees who had experienced a reunion with their birth mother (usually) or other birth relatives at least one year prior to their interview for this research project. All of these adoptees are members of the Hamilton chapter of the Canadian self-help search group known as Parent Finders (March 1990). Each research interview lasted approximately two hours and involved an open-ended interview questionnaire followed by a more informal conversation period. Interview questions were based on previous research about search and reunion; a fifteen-month participant-observation period at Parent Finders meetings in both Toronto and Hamilton, Ontario; attendance at public meetings that focused on proposed changes in Ontario's adoption legislation; and anecdotal literature written by reunited adoptees (Paton 1954; Fisher 1973; McKuen 1978; Marcus 1981; Redmond and Sleightholm 1982).

On Being Adopted: The Dilemma of Meeting Others' Expectations

Goffman (1959; 1963) notes that people gather information about others so we may more easily define social situations and know in advance what we may expect of others and what others may expect of us during the social interaction process. Although we use various ways of gathering this type of information, we rely heavily on people's own self-disclosures and documentary evidence as verifiable proofs of the identity that they present to us. In this way we anchor each person as an object for a biography that can be appropriately tested, assessed, and evaluated. We then use this biographical information to assist our own presentation of self when we encounter this person during the process of social interaction.

The informational connectedness of a person's biography is therefore generally very important to us. It lets us assess that person's behavior and our own response more accurately. Individuals who do not offer us complete and precise background information present us with *biographical discontinuities* that can intrude upon the social interaction process and undermine our trust in the social identity that we create of them (Goffman 1963, 62). Each single biographical discontinuity that people possess has the potential to expose them to public ridicule and social embarrassment as people who are pretending to be something or someone they are not. The precariousness of their potentially embarrassing position varies with the number of biographical discontinuities that they maintain; the centrality of any discrediting information; the number of others who know about those discontinuities; and the regularity with which that discrediting information can be drawn into the social interaction process.

Adoptees have limited data on their genetic heritage and generally inadequate accounts of the details surrounding their conception, birth, and relinquishment. Whether intentional or not, simple biographical questions about the adoptee's family of origin, race, ethnicity, or heredity traits raise the potential opportunity for others to discount the identity that the adoptee presents. By denying adoptees a consistent and coherent biography that others may use to assess their social standing, the institution of adoption presents the adoptee with a "spoiled identity" which has the "effect of cutting him off from society and from himself so that he stands as a discredited person facing an unaccepting world" (Goffman 1963, 19).

The reunited adoptees who were interviewed for this study reported a sense of disconnection from others because they were adopted. They believed that this sense of disconnection emerged from their interactions with others who defined them as "different" because of their adoptive status. One adoptee stated, for example, that:

> Those feelings of not belonging that I developed, I don't think that they were necessarily formed on my own. They were inflicted on me from the outside. And that negative message and reaction that you got whenever the topic of adoption was brought up—I soon learned never to volunteer the information that I was adopted to anyone unless I was asked directly. I didn't want to be thought of as different from the rest. (Male, age 35)

Another remarked that:

In the eyes of society adopted children are born in a different way. Plus the fact that some kind people come along and pick up these little waifs and we should be grateful. And other people are waiting for you to go wrong, for the bad blood to show up. My parents, now, they never gave me that message. I was like their own child. This is just something that I learned from others. I learned early that people would react differently to me when they found out that I was adopted. (Female, age 43)

These reunited adoptees also noted many instances in which their lack of biological background information had intruded upon the interaction process and led others to question the identity that they had presented. In such instances their attempt to explain their presentation of self to others usually required that they divulge their adoptive status. It was this status that had given them the "discreditable personal flaw" and the "life-situation" that placed them in opposition to "normals" and separated them from the majority of their community (Goffman 1963, 138). Thus, by drawing their adoptive status into the interaction process, their biographical discontinuites publicly embarrassed them at the same time as it exposed their spoiled identity to others.

For these adoptees then the strong connection that existed between their adoptive status and their lack of background information reinforced their feelings of being separate and apart from others in their community. Since they had derived their adoptive status from their biological parents' initial abandonment of them to the state, they were denied access to information about self that the state believed might be painful, harmful, and traumatizing to them (Garber 1985, 21). At the same time they were labeled as "special" and "chosen" by adoptive parents who had gone to considerable effort to include them as a part of the adoptive family structure. In this way the adoption contract's rule of non-disclosure presented these adoptees with mixed messages about their perceived value to others. These mixed messages, in turn, led them to personally question the dubious genetic background that they actually possessed. To quote one adoptee:

In our society, all that stuff about the chosen child, it only hides the truth— that someone out there didn't choose you. And in order to cover that, they form this romantic ideal of a young mother that had to give you up and suffers in silence and still wants you. That is the story you are told. And *that* you want to believe. But everybody believes differently. They all believe that you weren't wanted. So, to search you are taking a big risk. Because if you find out differently, it's really disappointing. Because then you know that you really were unchosen. (Female, age 43)

These reunited adoptees believed that others' failure to easily accept the lack of a complete biography and the restrictions imposed on them by their adoptive status made adoptees vulnerable to a deliberate process of public scrutiny, which further reinforced the message that they were personally flawed and socially unacceptable. Their ensuing explanations about their adoptive status and the curious inquiries that this knowledge generated from others made it even more difficult for them to adequately manage their presentation of self and gain a feeling of satisfaction from those types of situations. In fact, at times, their inability to fulfil others' demands for this type of information about self became so problematic for some of these adoptees that they were often left feeling powerless and inadequate. For example, one adoptee reported:

> I've had a lot of medical problems in my life. And doctors and medical students always ask about your family background. And when you say that you are adopted, they ask "What difference does that make?" They don't understand. You see, if they're not involved themselves, they don't realize that adoptees can't gain this information. And I haven't got any. Nothing. No family history. And they think it's my fault. (Female, age 41)

Another complained that:

> Not knowing these things about yourself makes it so you don't belong. Like, my nationality. Everybody has a background. They're Italian, English, Jewish or whatever. And I couldn't say what mine was. If anyone mentioned my nationality, then they would start to guess. Because I didn't know. It became a real topic of conversation, a guessing game. Sometimes it would last and last. It wouldn't go away. I wished I knew just so it would stop. (Female, age 36)

It was for this reason that many of these adoptees stated that they would avoid certain social situations which they believed would raise these types of questions and put them in a position of having to consider their adoptive status. Thus, the following adoptee refrained from attending birthday parties and baby showers, sometimes even weddings and other family events.

> People start talking about their children and their relatives. And everyone around you can relate their children and themselves to other members of their family. They say, "He acts like Uncle Joe" or things like that. But I can't do that with myself or with my children. I mean, our heritage was taken away from us for good reasons. But when you take that away from a person, you are taking away a lot that you really don't know about. (Female, age 53)

Another adoptee, however, remarked that such avoidance techniques were ineffective because:

> The issue of adoption is a recurrent theme in your life. And you must deal with it at many different times and in many different places. Like in school when you have to make a family tree. Which one do you use and are you faking it if you use your adoptive parents? Or, when you start to date and you question whether people will think you are loose like your birth mother. Or, when you

have children and you wonder what they will inherit from you. It keeps coming up at different times and at different levels. You could be talking to a neighbor and it might come up. You really never know when. (Female, age 19)

On Being Adopted: The Impact on One's Self-Concept

The reunited adoptees in this study also observed that, like others, they had frequently questioned the legitimacy of their self-presentation and had experienced a sense of uncertainty over the authenticity of the identity that they had presented in these situations. This personal questio ing came from the fact that they themselves could not verify their genealogical heritage or the events that surrounded their birth, relinquishment, and adoption. They, too, lacked the documentary proof that they could use to anchor self as an object of a biography that could be appropriately tested, assessed, and evaluated. This lack of a complete biography left them with a sense of foreboding and apprehension over the events that had led to their adoption and the unknown parts of self that they had inherited from their birth parents. That uncertainty led them to doubt and distrust the identity that they had formed from the data given to them by their adoptive families and the possibility that they might be someone other than the person that they presented. It was for this reason, for example, that one of these adoptees remarked that she repeatedly examined the source of certain ideas she had developed throughout her life and wondered if those thoughts had arisen from parts of self that stemmed from her genetic background. She stated:

> Through my life, I would find myself doing things and thinking a certain way that I know darn well that it wasn't the line of thinking in my family. And I would wonder why was I thinking that way. What was it about me that made me different in that way? I figured I wasn't quite the person that everyone thought me to be. It had to be my heredity. (Female, age 49)

Even such simple information about self as their physical characteristics were problematic for many of these adoptees and created uncertainty about the source of those traits and their integration of that information as a part of self. Thus, one adoptee explained that:

> In a lot of people, there is this need to know, "Why do I look the way I do? Where do I get my characteristics from?" And these things most people take for granted because they can get the answers whenever they want. Without asking. Like, "There's my grandmother and there's my grandfather and she does this and he does that. And, she's like this and he's like that. And I'm like him or her in this way or that." There is this thing called roots. And I would like to know where I got my nose. And, where did I get my teeth? And why do I like carpentry? But adoptees are told they can't have this information. They are told that it is wrong. (Male, age 40)

The practice of non-disclosure became the focus for most of these identity issues because it was that part of the original adoption contract that legally denied these adoptees access to the background information that frequently intruded on their presentation of self. Thus, in describing the effects of their search and reunion on others, these reunited adoptees generally reported that:

> Now, when people ask questions, it's better. Because I can give them answers. And I feel better because I have the answers now. It's a better story when I talk about my adoption. It has an ending. It makes them happy. There isn't a question in their minds. It satisfies their sense of completeness. They aren't satisfied when you say that you don't know because they can't imagine being anyone else than who they are. So, they can't deal with you not knowing. So, knowing makes it better for everyone. (Female, age 33)

However, in describing the effects of their reunion outcome on self, these reunited adoptees would refer more specifically to the personal identity issues that had led them to question self and the sense of instability and lack of cohesion that their biographical discontinuties had created. Like the following adoptee, they would typically state:

> Meeting her gave me roots. Just being able to identify things about myself that I couldn't identify as coming from my mother—my adoptive mother that is. And, in sharing our similarities it gave me the feeling that some of the things that I do, I just didn't invent. Like, I like to drive and so does she. Silly things like that. I hate milk and my mother and I fought about that since the time I was little. She made me drink it and I'd even throw up. Now, my birth mother hates milk and all of the kids in her family do too. It sounds silly but little things like that are important. Like, it was there in the first place. And just being able to say, "I do too." That's the major thing that I got out of meeting her. (Female, age 36)

For the majority of these reunited adoptees then reunion contact with one or more of their birth relatives produced a sense of coherence and personal harmony that arose from:

> This incredible peace that I felt. I looked at her and I thought, "That's who I look like." And, "This is what I am going to look like when I'm old." I was finding out parts of myself that I didn't know. My beginning. It's so elemental but when you are adopted you sometimes feel like you were hatched. There is no information about that aspect of your life. It's mystifying. And I was getting answers about what and who and how it all happened. How it all came about. How I came about. Like, I have a beginning and I know that I'll have an end. I wasn't hatched. I am complete. (Female, age 33)

As a result of the sense of permanence and inner cohesion that these adoptees gained from a more complete knowledge of their genetic background, all of the adoptees in this study reported considerable satisfaction with their reunion outcome. Thus, adoptees whose birth mothers rejected personal contact with them still claimed that:

> Access to background information has given me a better insight into myself, especially emotion-wise. And it has given me a history. It's given me a background, a nationality. And I guess if she was different, we might have had a relationship. But that wasn't what I really set out for anyway. I set out to find out about me. And I am satisfied with that. (Female, age 45)

Similarly, those adoptees who found birth mothers that they considered to be "problematic" or "undesirable" or who discovered background information that might be deemed as "socially unacceptable" such as alcoholism replied:

> Even though the information that I had on her did not look very good, I still had to see her, face-to-face. I had to find out who I looked like and where I came from. I had come too far to back out now. And even though she wasn't that great when I met her, I still feel good because I know what happened and I got the information that I wanted. I don't have any more questions anymore. (Male, age 24)

or,

> I will probably always maintain some kind of contact because I feel very sorry for her. Like, after I first met her I was very happy because I had gotten a lot of family history and I was content with that. And she looked like a woman who did not have a handle on life. I thought that she must had a terrible life to get herself so rundown. She's on welfare and she's slovenly. Like, I am talking about a woman who is 350 pounds. But then she kept calling me and every time I see her I find out more information about myself and my background. And it's important to her. So I will probably always keep some kind of contact. (Female, age 46)

In contrast, those reunited adoptees who failed to get their questions adequately answered by their birth parents reported:

> There was no reason to continue contact with her. If I constantly go there and try to get information and she refuses to give it to me or acts hostile, then why bother? Like, it wasn't a matter of ego. She just didn't open up to me and it was useless. It was like banging my head against a wall. She just wouldn't tell me the truth. (Female, age 24)

Biographical Discontinuities, the Reflections of Others, and a Satisfactory Presentation of Self

The data in this paper demonstrate the important role that a more complete biography plays for the development of self, identity, and social action. Social interaction depends upon a process of deliberation, adjustment, and mutual negotiation among all individuals engaged in the interaction process. This requires a consistent and coherent presentation of self by all actors involved. Goffman (1959, 1) notes, however, that people's presentation of self depends greatly on others' acceptance or rejection of the identity that they offer. Others collect data about people, which they use to construct a biography that they can call upon to assess people's presentation of self. They define people's socioeconomic status, learn about people's attitudes and opinions, establish people's intellectual capabilities, verify people's personal ethics, and so forth. They take cues from people's manner and appearance and apply untested stereotypes to them. They rely on people's personal description of self and the documentary evidence that these people present to support that description. In this way others form a definition of the situation and adjust their interaction patterns to fit that definition. Each individual co-operates in this process "by expressing himself in such a way as to give them the kind of impression that will lead them to act voluntarily in accordance with their own plan" (Goffman 1959, 4).

The adoptees in this study note, however, that they frequently experienced difficulty expressing themselves in accordance with others' expectations because their biographical discontinuties prevented them from offering adequate information about their past identities to others in their present. In their attempt to explain self to others, they were frequently required to reveal their adoptive status and their presentation of self was discredited further as a person who possessed a "spoiled" identity that set them apart from the majority of their community. Because they could not successfully control others' demands for this type of background information about self, these adoptees believed that they could not adequately control the interaction process and were powerless to maintain a consistent and satisfactory presentation of self. Reunion contact with their birth relatives offered them a practical way to resolve their biographical discontinuities and gave them an opportunity to more effectively manage those types of situations. Their reported satisfaction with reunion outcome depended greatly upon the ease with which their birth parents or birth relatives gave them information about their genealogy and the extent of the information that they received. Thus, one adoptee who discovered that his birth mother had died before he had begun his search, expressed some disappointment over this fact, but was still content with his reunion outcome because his birth sisters had answered all the questions he asked of them, thereby removing the biographical discontinuities that he had previously possessed.

The adoptees in this study, however, also noted that they had indicated or made note of the messages that their dissatisfactory presentations evoked from others and had internalized those messages as a part of their self-concept. They, too, had experienced personal doubts and uncertainties about the identity that they presented to others because their lack of genetic information left them questioning the very foundation on which that identity was based. They felt fragmented and incomplete because parts of self remained hidden from them. This questioning about self motivated them to search for, and establish contact with, their birth relatives. By outlining the events of their birth and relinquishment and learning about their genetic heritage, they had removed the sense of uncertainty that their biographical discontinuities had produced for them and also gained a sense of security that comes with the knowledge that their identity was authentic. Even those adoptees who found information about their birth parents that might be considered immoral or corrupt still experienced considerable personal satisfaction because they had removed some of the doubts and anxieties that previously existed for them and they gained a sense of completion by filling in these biographical discontinuities. Thus, one adoptee stated that:

> She was not living in very good circumstances. I really didn't care about that. But I was still shocked to meet her. Like, she's one step up from a hooker. And I was really amazed that I could take it so calmly. But that was her life, not mine. It really didn't have much to do with me. I'm different. And she made me different. She gave me to my parents and gave me that life and made me different from her. She just had answers to questions that I needed to know. And that's the role that she plays for me. (Female, age 39)

Conclusion

The adoptees in this study serve as a prime example of the important role that the definitions of others play for the emergence of self and for the identities that one creates. Before reunion, adoptees' confidence in self and in the identity that they presented to others was negatively affected when their biographical discontinuities intruded upon the interaction process. Since they could not successfully convey this information about self to others, they became insecure about self and lacked confidence in their overall self-presentation. They could not adequately resist unwanted identity imputations from others because they themselves were unclear about their appropriate status, their role, and their identity management. Because these adoptees lacked the ability to selectively convey information about self to others and thereby dispute or combat undesired definitions of self that others attributed to them, they felt flawed, incomplete, disjointed, and deficient. Thus, others' appraisals of them undermined their confidence in self and contributed to the spoiled identity that their adoptive status conveyed.

The many examples that these adoptees gave about others' reactions to their adoptive status and to their lack of complete biographical data clearly demonstrate how others' viewpoints, definitions, and experiences can affect one's identity and how one's continued success or lack of success in negotiating the interaction process can affect one's self-concept. It is for this reason that these adoptees wanted to fill in the identity gaps that their adoptive status produced and learn about the life events that surrounded their conception, birth, and relinquishment. They believed that, by gaining a more complete historical perspective of self, their identities would become more credible and gain more acceptability from others.

Reunion contact helped these adoptees achieve their goal by providing them with historical data about self that they could use to combat many of the unwanted identity imputations that others might attribute to them because of their adoptive status. For the first time in their lives, these adoptees possessed the power to selectively convey and control the release of this type of information about self to others and manage their self-presentations in a more satisfactory manner. After reunion they perceived that others were more satisfied with their accounts of self and the identities that they presented. Thus, they themselves experienced more certainty about self and more confidence in their overall self-presentation. It is this newfound ability to more adequately meet others' expectations that helps explain the sense of satisfaction reported by adoptees who experienced problematic reunion outcomes. The new power that they gained over the release of knowledge about self to others mediated the impact of the negative background information that they had to assimilate. Viewed within this perspective, the adoptee's need for reunion is no longer seen as a deviant act. Self-conceptions, like the rest of our symbolic environment, are constructed through selective perception and imagination as we participate in social groups. Each person's identity is constantly tested, reaffirmed, or discounted by others during the interaction process. Because people are active agents in that process, they reflect upon, and react toward, the messages they receive. The adoptees in this study encountered inconsistent messages about self from others who questioned their adoptive status and the biographical discontinuities that intruded upon the interaction process. They reflected upon those messages and considered the alternatives that were open to them as a means of resolving those unwanted identity imputations. For this particular sample of adoptees, reunion appeared to be a viable option because it presented them with a practical way of gaining access to the background information that they had lost because they had been adopted.

It is in this way that the adoptees in this study offer a forceful example of the impact that others have on the formation of self, identity, and self-concept. Their personal accounts of their quest for more complete biographical information about self demonstrates how the reflected appraisals of others can be internalized and integrated as a part of one's self-concept and how one's perceived expectations of others can affect one's position of negotiation during the interaction process. Because self and identity are shaped and formed through the process of negotiation and interaction with others, we cannot ignore the social context in which these social processes emerge. Any study of self, identity, and self-concept must therefore consider people's perceptions of others' expectations of them and the consequences that those perceptions have on the formation of those social processes. As members of their society, the adoptees in this study knew the social expectations of others. But it is only by examining the relationship between their definition of others' expectations of them and its influence on their self-concept that we can fully understand the meaning that their biographical discontinuities held for them and their need for reunion contact with their birth relatives.

Discoveries of
Self in Illness

Kathy Charmaz

Crises and losses disrupt life, but may result in a changed, more valued self. Having a serious chronic illness can produce sudden crises, unexpected losses, and lasting troubles in adult life. How do chronically ill people overcome losses, resolve feelings, and make discoveries of self? Consider this statement by a young woman whose mysterious, incapacitating symptoms first appeared thirteen years before when she was in college:

> Choosing to believe in myself took a lot of courage. Because what I grew up with was not supporting that in any way, shape, or form.... For me, illness was the gift that brought me together with myself. It was the bridge that helped me do that. So I really see illness as a very profound gift to people, if they take it. They have the choice of using it as an opportunity and they have the choice of not using it, [or] to use it as a scapegoat.... [Previously] I was hiding from who I was. That was when the separation [from self] was the strongest and that was when I felt the most alone. And then what happened gradually, is that I discovered myself in little pieces.... I started interacting with that self that I lost so many years ago. And so I started having fun with myself again and there was somebody there—then all of a sudden, there was somebody home again. And that—that just kept building and building. My illness started a dialogue with myself that I'd lost.

This young woman's sorrow about her declining health had turned to anger when she saw both physicians and family abandoning her. For the first five years of her illness, no one could diagnose why she was so sick. After lengthy testing, the doctors concluded that she suffered from psychosomatic symptoms. Later, a diagnosis of lupus erythematosus validated this woman's view of herself as sick, but her view of herself as a valid *person* remained impaired. The seeds of change began during long nights of immobilizing fevers, while she struggled alone with her symptoms. Unable to do anything but think, her curiosity about her experience was sparked. Previously, she had fought against being sick; now she flowed with it and eventually found her long-past self. This woman's discoveries and development of self took years, but resulted in a stronger, more positive self-concept.

How do people with chronic illnesses create and maintain positive self-images when others dismiss and discredit them? When and how do people discover that they have, in fact, changed? What are the significant turning points in illness? What conditions cause one's views of self to become fiction? How do some people transform sadness and misfortune into personal growth and a stronger self-concept?

The study of chronically ill people provides insights into questions about identity construction and self-concept continuity and change. Serious chronic illness often undermines notions of self and of personal identity that have previously been taken for granted (Charmaz 1973; 1983b; 1987; 1991a; 1991b; Strauss, Corbin, Fagerhaugh, Glaser, Maines, Suczek, and Wiener 1984; Brooks and Matson 1987; Corbin and Strauss 1988). Chronically ill people demonstrate how adults deal with adversity and sometimes turn it to advantage by discovering or creating new aspects of self. Furthermore, examining how images of self founded in daily actions and interactions change, makes the processes contributing to a changed self-concept visible. By looking closely at the situations of chronically ill people, we can discern relationships between the structure of their lives, social meanings, and the self.[1]

Apparent discoveries of self emerge in the face of new demands and new exigencies. Such "discoveries" may actually reflect development of earlier selves or of latent potentials and redirection of self as ill people adapt to their altered bodies and situations. Their self-concepts change as they develop prior hidden strengths, realize how others view them, re-interpret their situations, revise earlier assumptions, and devise new ways of accomplishing their lives. Hence, apparent discoveries result from daily interpretations, choices, and actions. Because much redirection and change of self follows tiny, gradual adaptations to the demands of everyday life, ill people, and often those closest to them, may remain unaware of their changing self-concepts.

Some seriously ill people do not see themselves as different or their lives as changed—at least for a time. Initially, the self in the experience of pain, suffering, and exhaustion may remain an alien, unfamilar one. Moreover, an ill person may disavow that self as reflecting his or her real self (Turner 1976). Thus, experiencing serious illness may not always directly or immediately result in a changed self-concept. Furthermore, when it does, those changes may be subtle and may gradually accrue as the person experiences an altered body and makes sense of events. If so, the person's discoveries of self may occur when he or she defines striking contrasts between past and present.

Ultimately, many people with serious chronic illnesses undergo drastic reconstructions of self during a relatively short period of time. Hence, studying their situations provides us with a distilled version of the changes that occur throughout adult life and accelerate during the later years.

Theoretical Foundations of Self

Symbolic interactionists have long viewed the self as both process and product (Mead 1934; Strauss 1969; Gecas 1982). The self is process in the sense of emergence and change; it is continually unfolding. This process of unfolding occurs as the person interacts with others, feels cultural constraints and imperatives, and evaluates himself or herself relative to experience, situation, others, and society more generally. The self is grounded in sentiment and feeling (Cooley 1902). Thus, the self is both subjective and objective. It is objective in the sense that the person internalizes the language, culture, and meanings of his or her groups. As a result, one makes "objective" appraisals of oneself and one's actions and responses in the same manner as any other object (Mead 1934). Hence, estimations of self-worth affect the unfolding self. Sentiments shape estimations of self-worth and are subject to revision and even reversal when people do not have strong anchors to fixed and stable social organizations, communities, and other individuals.[2] Without firm anchors, the self is more vulnerable to ongoing definition and redefinition. If so these conditions warrant viewing the self as process. This process consists of the continual interpretations of self the individual makes as he or she interacts with others and mentally converses with self.

Conceptions of self as process can complement theoretical views of the self as product, that is, as an organized entity. Following Rosenberg (1979) and Turner (1976) the self-concept is a relatively stable *organization* of attributes, feelings, and identifications that the person takes as defining himself or herself. The self-concept then has boundaries, parts, and elements that are integrated through memory and habit. Because the self-concept is an organized entity, a person does not assume that all of his or her behavior, moods, actions, or experiences reflect his or her self-concept. Rather, someone takes certain behaviors, moods, actions, and experiences as reflecting his or her "real" self (Turner 1976).

The organized and stable nature of the self-concept makes it resistant to change. Furthermore, experience changes more rapidly than the self-concept (Charmaz 1989; 1991a; 1991b). Thus, the self-concept lags behind experience and the possible images of self formed by that experience. It particularly lags when the experience is overwhelming, occurs within an alien setting, and subsequent events differ from the person's ordinary life. Such scenarios take place when sudden, catastrophic illness causes immediate hospitalization with drastic treatment procedures. Then, the experience feels disconnected from one's "real" life and likely, from one's "real" self. Therefore, devastating changes can occur to ill people's bodies without their immediate realization of them or accounting for them within their self-concepts. When ill people persist in subscribing to notions that their old self is their real and true self, others may come to believe that they adopt fictional identities (Glaser and Strauss 1965).

Further, some people who have chronic illnesses neither define illness as adversity nor themselves as sick. If they can continue to function on their own terms, then they may define themselves as "well" for lengthy periods of their illness. Their definitions of the presence or absence of illness, of its projected course and timetable, and of its meanings for everyday life shape which "discoveries" and reconstructions of self they make in illness, how they make them, and when they do so. Their definitions of the meanings of their illness can differ enormously from those of their healthcare practitioners, their families, and their friends. Similarly, definitions of turning points by patients, practitioners, families, and friends may also differ radically. What looks and feels like a forthcoming positive outcome to a patient may stand as a permanent negative turning point to a practitioner. For example, Hoffman (1981) found that stroke patients assumed that they would recover yet, at the same time, their hospital staff defined them as beyond help. Thus, what stands as fact to one may symbolize fiction to the other (Charmaz 1991b).

Until a fictional identity is put to test in the person's ordinary life and usual routines, he or she likely refrains from reconstructing an altered self (Charmaz 1991a; 1991b). In the meantime the person's assumptions about who he or she is, and will become, rapidly become fiction. Further, when the person discovers that the fictions are not founded in fact, initially, he or she is likely to view the discoveries about self as losses rather than gains.

Yet illness can make things more complex. How people interpret meanings of their illness and which actions they take toward it, may reflect their appraisals of a changed situation and of self. If their appraisals and actions do not coincide with the views of others, these ill people might still be thought of as denying their illness and as creating fiction.

Developing a Fictional Identity

Many ill people unknowingly assume a set of beliefs about themselves and project future selves without taking changes caused by disease into account.[3] Here, they assume that their future self will be much like their past self (Olesen 1992). Thus, they may experience symptoms in the present, possibly even serious ones, but they do not infer that the symptoms portend a permanent change in their definitions of self. They take themselves as an object to view, to evaluate, and to compare with others, but they also take that object from long-held assumptions about, and definitions of, self. In short they derive a present self-concept from the past (Charmaz 1989). At this point their taken-for-granted assumptions about their self-concept still remain unchallenged.

When physical changes subsequently indicate a downhill course, ill people's stances about themselves may assume fictional identities. Nonetheless, these fictional identities are not lies, pretense, or manipulations; instead, they actually derive from an understanding of their conditions and situations. *Fictional identities* can reflect lack of awareness, partial knowledge, and the absence of apparent symptoms. They also suggest how changes in self-concept can lag behind lived experience.

The experience of having a chronic illness is often elusive. Meanings of illness and its consequences for daily life typically unfold gradually, rather than becoming immediately apparent. In their struggle to maintain identity and continuity in their lives, ill people usually choose the most promising interpretation of their illness and prognosis (Robinson 1988). For example, a woman who had had surgery and chemotherapy for colon cancer remarked:

> I don't—I don't sit and worry about the cancer reoccurring all the time. They said that I'm a good candidate for reoccurrence and there are statistics and percentages and everything.... But I just say their statistics can go jump in the lake because if it gets me, it gets me, but I'm not going to lay down and let it.

Having access to accurate medical information alone does not neccessarily lead to redefining self as temporarily or permanently ill. Sophisticated people, as well as those lacking medical information, can misread significant signs or symptoms. Ilza Veith (1988, 17), a physician and medical historian, noted encroaching symptoms and dismissed them. She writes:

> To be sure the peculiar symptoms I had been experiencing during the last six weeks would have been reason enough to see a doctor; instead I kept on reading about them in the medical literature and felt that they simply represented symptoms of a transitory disturbance, not serious enough to merit much fuss and bother.

Even tangible disability did not dissuade Ilza Veith of her conviction that her symptoms were inconsequential. Rather than reinterpret these symptoms as serious, she had a ready explanation of them (1988, 24–25):

> When I found one side of myself completely paralyzed, I felt certain that I was a case in line with my researches on hysteria. Initially, I deluded myself that if I admitted the hysterical nature of my hemiplegia to myself and others, it would simply go away. Such was the solution derived from the venerable sources of my research on the history of hysteria.

Whether alternative explanations are sophisticated or simplistic, awareness of one's continuing disability forces some discoveries of self. The *type* of illness certainly shapes meaning, particularly when that illness continues. Some illnesses, like cancer, are laden with negative social meanings, dire images, and immediate medical intervention, and thus, intrude upon daily life more forcefully than others (see also, Swanson and Chenitz 1993). An illness that has immediate consequences, produces visible markers, and forces intrusive regimens certainly affects the individual, at least in the present (Locker 1983; Peyrot, McMurray and Hedges 1987; Pinder 1988). For example, renal (kidney) failure patients often suffer pronounced discomfort after undergoing dialysis. Their dialysis shunt (a surgically created point of entry into the body to permit redirecting the blood into the dialysis machine) is a bodily marker of their changed health status. A dialysis regimen of three times weekly has to be reckoned with. Surely having renal failure would seem, by its very nature, to lead to definitions of self as seriously ill. If ill people take such notable characteristics of their conditions as not only currently salient , but also predictive of the future, then they should logically define themselves as chronically ill. But this does not always occur. Despite their evident illness, sick people may see those same characteristics of illness as temporary—as lasting only until the anticipated transplant, or as only disrupting part of the day or week.

Thus, how someone interprets even severe symptoms and restrictions figures as significantly as the objective disease categories. Should events and others' definitions intervene forcefully, the ill person then has to do more interpretive work to make his or her reality claims stick.

Whether people define themselves as sick depends upon whether the illness remains in the foreground or in the background of their lives. An illness that leaves invisible disabilities may remain masked to the person who has it, as well as to others. If so then illness remains in the background of his or her life as a subliminal possibility rather than as a definitive approaching storm. Further, the routine structure of daily life affects whatever meanings people attach to their illnesses and whether it lurks in the background or looms in the foreground of their lives. Both the overall structure of their lives and specific daily routines can mask or magnify symptoms and images of an ill self. A thirty-eight-year-old graduate student with a heart condition had married a retired widower almost thirty years her senior. Several years before, she had suffered from frightening, intrusive heart symptoms. However, this woman's health had improved markedly after she started heart medications and lost weight. Her husband had severe emphysema and cancer, which had been pronounced as life-threatening when first diagnosed twelve years earlier. In many ways her stance toward him mirrored his toward his first wife to whom he had given care, despite his own declining health. This student said:

> I see my role as caregiver to him and as his wife, I see that as much more problematic than my own health stuff. His health, his needs, our relationship, the fact that he may be dying and I deal with the threat of death every day, I see that as much more problematic than my own health.

This woman's life revolved around the conflicting demands imposed by her marriage, children, work, and graduate school. In addition, the relative control and invisibility of her symptoms kept her own illness in the background and supported her definition of herself as "well." Her husband reinforced her self-definition through his view of her as a vibrant young woman and through his increasing frailty, growing dependence, and multiplying expectations of care. Her identity was a product of interaction with others as well as with self (Mead 1934; Blumer 1969b; Prus 1987).

Although this woman's interactions, actions, and attitudes masked her own condition, they also may have veiled the visibility of her husband's steady decline. Spouses often play a pivotal role in helping their partners to keep illness in the background. Some spouses monitor symptoms, perform daily vital tasks like dressing or driving, and camouflage the ill person's increasing dependency. For many months or even years, a spouse who runs interference for the ill person can render the illness invisible and therefore may sustain the ill person's beliefs (as well as those of others) that he or she remains as before.

Similarly, location and timing can sustain such beliefs. People who have already reduced their reponsibilities and limited their living space may remain remarkably unaware of a gradual decline. As long as they can manage their immediate environment without distressing problems or disquieting realizations, any disparity between their identity claims and emerging self narrows. If a changed body is not put to the test in daily routines, illness may continue to remain in the background of life. Hence, these people see themselves as quite healthy despite their diagnoses (Kelleher 1988; Robinson 1990).

Perhaps the most common reason why people adopt fictional identities is lack of awareness about their condition. They simply do not have sufficient information with which to gauge their situations and to measure themselves using the same yardsticks as professionals do. Hence, exposure to a new identification or new information can cause a sudden jolt of awareness. For example, the response that one doctor got when he mentioned to his male patient that the man's chronic condition would require continuing care was, "A *chronic* condition? Me? Ugh. No." One middle-aged woman who participated in a cardiac rehabilitation program was initially quite complacent about herself and her health status since she had only had an angioplasty. The other patients were all considerably older, less able to do the exercises, and had suffered heart attacks. The attending nurse kept nagging the woman about her regimen. Only after this nurse informed her that medical staff regarded angioplasty as equivalent to having had a heart attack did she take note of the warnings. Until then she had viewed herself as someone with a minor condition from which full recovery would follow (Charmaz 1991b).

Even if someone accepts the medical definition of their illness, that individual may neither know nor follow the subsequent medical prescriptions for dealing with it (Conrad 1985). Limited or compartmentalized knowledge of one's condition dims awareness and understanding of its long-term consequences and furthers the development of idiosyncratic meanings of illness and of what to do about it. For example, one man whose heart condition resulted in bypass surgery declared, "I felt completely free of my problem after the surgery." He openly discussed the fear of open-heart surgery that many prospective patients have and, to help others combat that fear, he served as a volunteer visiting other patients the night before their surgeries. He also made a point of keeping up with technical advances in cardiac care and maintained contact with leading cardiologists in his area through his volunteer activities. He remarked:

> I'm probably much more aware of what's going on with my heart and, things like that [than he had been before surgery]. I'm aware of what's happening in the field and anytime there's something mentioned about the heart, I listen to it; I know about it—you know, that no physician can double-talk me into thinking something different. And I feel I'm up on the latest therapies and techniques and things like that.

This man failed, however, to follow the physical regimen to the satisfaction of his cardiac rehabilitation nurse, but he saw himself as having made significant psychological adjustments and changes in lifestyle—he changed his priorities drastically. For the first twenty-five years of his marriage, work had been the focus of his life. After his heart attack, his family came first. He realized that he could die and his two young sons might grow up without knowing him. But he did not attend systematically to his diet and exercise program. From the professional perspective, he was being negligent; from his own perspective, he was handling his condition and its implications. He said:

> I think I learned to really enjoy myself at this point in time because you don't know if you get a tomorrow.... We take a different attitude, like we take vacations now, always [before] our work came first, and we never took time to enjoy our children, each other, and things like that; we were always too busy working.

Disparate vocabularies of motive give rise to different discourses, divergent actions, and conflicting interpretations between ill people, their families, and healthcare professionals. From this man's perspective, he had taken significant positive steps to deal with his heart and with his life; he believed that he had attended to the real issues. From his nurse's perspective, his rotund physique alone testified to his negligence and to his unwillingness to face the real facts. As far as she was concerned he had ignored the fundamental prerequisites of cardiac care.

Certainly, the patient's firm commitment to full recovery sets into motion the conditions that others can later take as proof of denial and of claims to fictional identities. However, the patient could benefit by gaining both hope and confidence through holding tight to expectations of recovery. During a crisis, the practitioner may encourage views of recovery to spur the patient through it. (Of course at that time, "recovery," to the practitioner, likely means living through it and to the patient, it means fully regaining former function.) Norman Cousins' (1983, 74–75) expectations of recovery smoothed his course through crisis:

> Being free of panic at the start helped to free me of its usual aftermath of uncertainty and dread. I told Dr. Cannon that the dominant emotion, not just at the time of the attack, but during the critical period was curiosity, a sense of challenge and confidence. Every cubit of progress since the heart attack occurred, served as exhilarating evidence that we were en route to recovery.

Practitioners often encourage hopes of recovery during crises like that of Norman Cousins. They view the patient's will to live as pivotal for determining whether or not he or she survives. Afterwards, however, they may turn away from the hope and optimism that they had encouraged during the crisis only to give sobering messages of lasting disability and decline. It is at this point that expectations of recovery may turn against an ill person. Hope for recovery becomes redefined as denial of illness and a fiction (Charmaz 1980; 1991a).

Turning Points and Lessons in Loss

Realizations about a failing body or permanent disability come when people try to live as before and find themselves unable to do so. A bad fall, incapacitating shortness of breath, profound loss of vision, or sudden lack of strength can provide vivid evidence of changes—unwelcome discoveries of self. When ill people finally begin to define the changes as long-term or permanent, they experience lessons in loss. Moreover, their unwelcome discoveries about self constitute turning points for reconstruction of self when they tie these events to their sense of identity.

Turning points often reflect more than just a shift in direction of one's life or discovering new information about self. Rather, they also reflect *emotions* about self. In keeping with Weigert (1991), emotions transform raw experience into meaningful events. Sudden turning points demand reappraisals of self—both of fact and of feeling. In these turning points, the facts one had taken for granted about self are thrown open to question or entirely negated. Long-held feelings about self that had been tied to self-definition are dislodged and perhaps replaced with uncertain self-definitions and subsequent shifting feelings. For example, a middle-aged man with diabetes and a minor heart condition developed ulcers on his leg. After a harrowing episode in intensive care, he related the following story:

> Shortly after I went in, the infection got much worse. The doctor said that he would have to amputate my leg. I could see that it wasn't improving so I could understand that—it wasn't a total surprise. But then a day passed, and another, and another, and the leg still wasn't improving. It didn't seem to be getting worse, but no surgery. I said to the doctor, "What goes?" He said, "We

can't amputate. Your heart isn't strong enough to withstand the surgery. We're going to have to treat you conservatively and just play it by ear." [To me with incredulousness] My heart wasn't strong enough? That was the first I'd heard of that—I had no conception. Oh, I knew I had a heart condition, but it didn't seem very serious. No one made anything of it and it certainly didn't affect anything I did. That was the first time I realized how bad things were. All I had been thinking about was getting the damn infection healed and getting out of there. I expected to be back to work in a week or so and now I don't know if I ever will get back. There's nothing I want more than to go back. There's so much to do and I can't expect the other guys to cover for me. And here I sit, twiddling my thumbs not much good to anybody (he had tears in his eyes).

Perhaps the most telling moments and dramatic turning points occur in interaction with others. Ill people can find themselves being betrayed, stigmatized, exploited, and demeaned. Visible disability invites rude questions and remarks about difference (Albrecht 1992). Invisible disability prompts accusations about failure to maintain sameness or to meet expectations of others. Both can result in unpleasant discoveries of self—devastating discoveries of how one looks and seems to other people. Those with visible disabilities may discover how much illness and disability had defined others' views of them. Shock, sorrow, or shame may follow. For example, Ernest Hirsch (1977), a psychologist who had multiple sclerosis, used a wheelchair. He believed that his colleagues had hardly noticed his illness until, to his shock, he discovered that he would not be permitted to practice psychotherapy because of it. Hirsch's supervisor believed that his disability might cause his patients to feel sorry for him and therefore could interfere with their treatment.

Shock follows such an incident since the nasty surprise uproots one's taken-for-granted assumptions about oneself, relationships, and social location. Ill people come to terms with shock by telling and retelling the event and its meaning—to self and often, to others (Charmaz 1991b). Repeated retelling makes the event real, commits the teller to a definitive point of view, and strengthens that view through audience affirmation. The logic of the story provides the basis for understanding, justifying, and managing the emotions experienced within the event (Sarbin 1986; Hochschild 1990).

Just telling someone else about a shocking diagnosis gives it a new, more obdurate, and irreversible meaning. Conversely, not dwelling upon the shocking event to self, not announcing it to others, and not mentioning it henceforth minimizes its effect, especially if one can also refrain from thinking about it. In this instance, a shocking event becomes less pinned to self. Similarly, the person grants the event less credence for defining future images of self. To the extent that others do not witness the event, or discount its significance if they do witness it, the ill person can more easily detach the event from enduring images of self.

Sorrow complicates and extends the effects of shock. These emotions confirm and extend the loss of prior social meanings (Smith-Lovin 1990). When ill people experience sorrow as well as shock, they accept the social meanings of the event imposed upon them. Moreover, they mourn the lost self that those prior social meanings implied. Ill people may first express shock and then experience sorrow and shame about not having realized how others had actually viewed them all along. For example, one young woman was shocked to discover that her physicians believed she was feigning symptoms. Her shock turned to sorrow when she realized that several nurses and doctors she liked and trusted shared this belief. As she relived earlier events in her mind, she saw that she had overlooked several indications of their actual view of her. Then she felt shame about not being more perceptive and about having trusted them in the first place.

Feelings of sorrow and shame remain once ill people have defined an unalterable turning point into the future. The self of the future will be a different self than known or valued in the past. In both instances a person may feel a sense of self-betrayal as well as betrayal by others (Strauss 1969). The person feels self-betrayal because: (a) he or she now defines and connects earlier cues to present negative identifications; (b) one might share the stigmatized images of illness, but heretofore might not have applied them to self; (c) one's stance has resulted in shame. Betrayal by others is felt because they have ripped away the foundations of oneself. The resulting sorrow then necessitates grieving for the lost self. For example, one woman who had multiple sclerosis discovered that the swimming class her doctor recommended turned out to be for people with severe disabilities. She described herself as intermittently having "a gimp leg, but I'm certainly not a cripple!" She was humiliated that he perceived her to be similar to the people in the class. Her sense of betrayal and shame was intensified because, in her words, "I know it's not right, but I just don't like to be around sick people or the handicapped. Never did."

Feelings of self-betrayal also may rest upon shame for one's prior prejudices and unthinking actions. Occasionally, an ill person revealed as once having had views and feelings such as that of the woman above rejects these feelings after experiencing an illness or handicap themself. Yet without reappraising or condemning oneself in the past, a crucial, negative event alone can elicit shame. The images of self revealed in the event evoke the shame (Cooley 1902). As Lewis (1971) and Scheff (1990) point out, shame signals a threatened bond. Here, the bond may be with another person, but can be to the attachments to self. Acknowledged shame elicits the question: "What kind of person am I?"

Shame intensifies when an embarrassing private event occurs in a public setting. The ill man or woman usually cannot control who witnesses it and their responses to it (Gardner 1991). Even if responses are humane, the knowledge alone that other people *know* about the event affects the person's self-concept. For example, an elderly woman who suffered urinary incontinence at church one day, thereafter avoided public places entirely. Even though other church members ignored the event and later encouraged her to return to church, the memory of this embarrassing event caused her such shame that it became a permanent turning point for her.

Certainly, turning points that ill people define as causing shock, sorrow, and shame require the greatest effort to transcend. When the discovery of self is founded in such profound loss, rebuilding a valued self takes time, effort, and typically, repeated success. In these situations the person links shame to the *self* and not simply to an embarrassing *event* soon to be forgotten or to be retold with humor. Thus, the individual will need many indications of positive value to repair his or her now diminished self.

An earlier devastating turning point can later become redefined as the beginning of a stronger, better self that emerged from struggles and hardships. For example, a thirty-five-year old man who experienced almost total paralysis (Charmaz 1973) had great difficulty in swallowing and was terrified of choking. Worn down by the total care that he expected of her, his first wife left him. His elderly parents brought him into their home and tried to take care of him. Seeing the toll it was taking on them, he reduced his demands and began to swallow his medication and food on his own. To his surprise, he was able to be much more physically independent than he had believed. What had been a struggle, fraught with fear, was the beginning of a series of new achievements.

Moments of insight can pierce despair and become turning points. Arnold Biesser (1988) felt helpless when poliomyelitis left him totally paralyzed. Shortly afterward, his brother suffered from a fatal disease, his stepfather had a stroke, and his mother got the flu. When the irony of it all struck him, he began to laugh and that was the turning point. He writes:

A person can cry only so long without the tears beginning to develop a life of their own. Eventually sadness and tears offer a spurious security by themselves, with the world viewed continuously from a down position. But humor and the laughter it brings allowed me to emerge from despair into the light of day. For a moment I could see with clear eyes again and that allowed for a fresh start. (141–42)

Turning points represent gains when ill people define themselves as having learned and grown. One woman took refuge in her spiritual pursuits, which she believed deepened through her harrowing experiences with illness. She said:

In my mind, I think of myself as a wealthy person—not materially, but I think of myself as a wealthy person.... It [illness] was like being crushed. Someone had a real good analogy—he tried to help me a lot—he'd be phoning me all the time—he said, "Life was like a vise." This lifetime was like a vise, squeezing me.

Resolution, Renewal, and Transcendence

As people learn how intrusive their illnesses are, the discoveries of self that they make are typically first framed in loss (Sarton 1988; Veith 1988). Dealing with physical loss and the hardships that follow it can put relationships, commitments, and self to the test. But simultaneously, ill people may discover that their emerging selves rise to the test. Resolving feelings of loss, hurt, and betrayal take a lot of work and because these feelings often surface precisely when physical distress escalates, resolution can seem like a monumental task. Yet resolution may develop.

Through resolution, ill people are able to put their illness and themselves into a new perspective. The discoveries of self become positive and they view themselves as having grown; they see new strengths in themselves (Sandstrom 1990; Weitz 1991). They re-interpret their feelings and shift their viewpoints. Turning anger outward, for example, instead of inward shifts self-doubt and self-pity into moral outrage. For example, in my second interview thirteen years ago with the woman whose statement opened this article, she described a critical episode of illness that had occurred three years prior to our interview. As mentioned, she felt betrayed by her doctors who had viewed the episode as psychosomatic in origin and by her family and friends who had abandoned her. She recalled:

> I was feeling a lot of anger toward the doctors and toward the whole thing [illness, relatives]. I'm just trying to think if I was feeling angry toward myself. I think that's probably when I stopped feeling angry toward myself.... I think that's the first time in my life that I did that. I think up until then I was just totally feeling angry toward myself.

I asked, "Because?" She said, "For being alive. I thought it was awful. I was always depressed; I thought I was bad. It took the doctors blaming me for me to say, 'No, maybe I'm not the one screwing up here.'"

Like this woman, some people perceive illness as giving them back their perspectives, values, and knowledge that had been lost along the way. One man gained the tools for self-reflection. Several other men gained a deeper appreciation of the value of a loving family. Several women felt that through coming to terms with their feelings about illness they had resolved life-long emotional scars from growing up in alcoholic families. A twenty-three-year-old woman with multiple sclerosis felt that she had learned to experience her feelings. She said:

> But another thing I get from being a child of an alcoholoic is I don't feel a lot of pain; I don't let myself feel a lot of pain which is something that MS gave me back. The ability to pain, to have pain, and to know it's OK. And that's another thing, I thank it [MS] for—I mean it causes problems. I can't walk sometimes; I have problems going pee ... but it's given me back a lot of things, too, the ability to let go.

This woman, like many others, also believed that she had gained a new awareness of control over her feelings and herself in general. She said:

I can change me. And that's about the only control I have left in this life. And I have control over my behavior; I don't have control over yours. Uhm, and I wish I'd known that a long time ago. And I think that MS has helped me [learn that].

Resolving their feelings about illness gives people a sense of strength (Lewis 1985; Pitzele 1985).[4] They are able to believe in themselves and to know that they have met adversity and faced it with courage (Denzin 1987a; 1987b). The woman above avowed, "And I know that I'm very strong now." I asked, "What does strength mean to you?" She replied:

The ability to cope. To know that I can get out of that bed in the morning and drag myself through the day and smile. I can laugh, which again so many can't and that's sad, because there's nothing wrong with them and their bodies. Maybe they should get a disease.

The gains that are made on reaching a state of resolution may make it possible for an ill person to gradually shift into renewal[5] and learn to live with their illness. Experiencing chronic illness may serve to strengthen and develop attributes that the person already possessed. A woman who had disabling arthritis said:

It's made me real receptive to other people's handicaps or illnesses. I always ask how they are, or I try to. So it's like—to me it [illness] has pushed me in a certain direction toward more compassion.

Many people found that experiencing chronic illness gave them a deeper understanding of life and its meaning; it gave them new purposes, new values, new realizations. With that understanding came wisdom that transcended their former self. Chronic illness had both renewed and transformed them. Here, the new discoveries of self can contrast strikingly with past assumptions about self. One young woman had spent four years feeling guilt and self-pity about being ill with colitis. Friends and medical professionals from whom she sought assistance and support could only affirm her feelings of being responsible for her own fate. When she changed locales and made new friends, her feelings of guilt subsided, her spirits lifted, and her illness abated. Old doubts faded and new hopes bloomed. She said, "I was surfacing." Years after her worst episode of illness, she said:

I really think that some of these bad situations [illness, love relationship, situations resulting from illness] … were utilized toward the great growth that I then went through. I feel quite wise. I feel quite emotionally stable. I feel that I am more emotionally stable than most people that I see, but I think that's come out of these great periods of instability.

Renewal brings a revised, not merely restored, self-concept (Le Maistre 1985). Experiencing a sense of renewal follows allowing oneself to experience illness. Though ill people may not accept whatever stigmatized status that illness conferred upon them, these people accept themselves.

Just a few years ago, a middle-aged woman organized her life around making money (lots of it), working out, and dating. After having suffered through a serious illness, she redefined her past life as superficial. She reflected:

> It's when you love all people, that you really love yourself.... I used to be very different. But through being hurt and being sick and stuff, you really learn to change your ways and values. Everybody's wonderful. I've become a better person, more loving really and I've always been a distant, private person. Never really talked about who I was or what I thought.... But you really do have to suffer in order to really find out who you are. And it's a blessing in disguise somehow in finding out that I'm giving up all these other things, but that I'm getting something deeper than I could [before].

Conclusion

The path between creating fictional identities, facing illness, resolving feelings, renewing self, and transcending loss is a slippery one. Clearly, for many chronically ill people, at least initially, what their illness portends is uncertain. Some people intentionally try to keep their self-concepts separate from illness because they wish neither to be in the role of a sick person, nor to have others impose stigmatized identities upon them. They may risk adopting fictional identities, however, by keeping sickness apart from self, they can maintain valued images of themselves and preserve their autonomy. Although such individuals may be aware of their illness, their stance *does* lead them to ignore symptoms, to take risks, and to conceal their infirmities. Because of this, they may ultimately find themselves in a series of spiraling crises which could leave them in an even worse state of health—a person with diabetes might go into insulin shock; someone with heart disease could end up in the emergency room with a full-blown heart attack.

Another scenario concerns people who maintain their fictions, and who insist upon maintaining them, despite the lack of concurrence by their medical care professional. The patients insist that they have an *acute* illness and will prolong this definition for as long as they can—sometimes after the last shred of others' support for their hopes has disappeared. Yearning for recovery, waiting for signs of it, and living a diminished quality of life change anyone's perspective and shrink the boundaries of, and possibilities for, redefinition of self. This process may happen insidiously and without awareness (Sacks 1984); however, when, and if, the person becomes aware of it, the losses of self seem irretrievable. For example, a man who slows down to convalesce finds that he just cannot handle the pace of working even part-time. The shock and depression that follows can further cut into self-definition and thus contribute further to the losses of self.

The balance between allowing definitions of illness to touch and shape the self without becoming inundated by them is difficult to achieve. And people may be able to do so at some point in their illness, but not at others. Similarly, someone may be able to accept an illness when it remains in the background of their life, but not when it springs into the foreground.

In order to gain a sense of resolution and renewal, ill people need be be aware of their illness and appraise its implications upon their emerging selves. Simultaneously, they retain or gain valued attributes of self that transcend illness and the identities accompanying it. To accomplish this, ill people must view essential qualities of self as distinct from their bodies. Likely, too, the person must find value in self that transcends the usual criteria for productivity, achievement, and success. Subsequently, for many ill people, struggling to control the defining images that reconstruct the self becomes a continuous endeavor.

NOTES

1. This paper is drawn from a larger qualitative research project about experiencing chronic illness, which focuses on the effects of illness upon identity (see Charmaz 1987; 1991a; 1991b). The data on which this analysis rests include 120 in-depth interviews with 55 chronically ill people, 20 informal interviews with caregivers and providers, collections of anecdotes and case summaries in addition to published and unpublished autobiographical accounts. I interviewed 26 respondents more than once and followed 16 men and women from seven years to over a decade. The criteria for selecting interview respondents included (a) a diagnosis of a serious, but not terminal, illness; (b) a disease category that posed uncertainty; (c) present or past effects of the condition on the person's daily life; and (d) adult age.

The respondents varied in age, social class, and type of illness. They ranged from 20 to 91 years in age. By class, 31 percent were middle class, 16 percent upper middle class, 13 percent working class and 40 percent lower class. Their illnesses included heart disease, circulatory disease, emphysema, rheumatoid diseases, cancer, kidney failure, multiple sclerosis, and diabetes.

The strategies of grounded theory provided methods of analyzing the data (Glaser and Strauss 1967; Glaser 1978; Charmaz 1983a; 1990; Strauss 1987). In keeping with the grounded theory method, I collected data and analyzed them simultaneously. In later interviews I framed more detailed questions about the self emotions and checked the significance of developing ideas.

2. Sentiments are complex and strong subjective responses that have been consolidated into consistent emotions through cognitive definition. Feelings are more diffuse, immediate sensations and intuitions or effects, which arise in the moment and may be subject to redefinition (Hochschild 1990).

3. To some extent we all develop fictions about ourselves. For example, people may see themselves as undergoing various types of self-improvement, or possessing attributes which others do not see in them (Glassner 1988). But, when the disparity becomes great between our fictions and our experience, the implications for self-concept can become enormous. Other instances in which loss is great include a sudden layoff to a worker who took pride in high performance, or a marital breakup to a spouse who viewed the marriage as strong and stable.

4. A counterpoint process to the ill person's experience can be found in parents reconciling themselves to a son's homosexuality and/or AIDS. Sohier (1993) concludes that parents must first resolve their moral questions about homosexuality before achieving a meaningful closure with their sons.

5. Joanne LeMaistre also discusses renewal as the "hard-won ability to separate yourself from your illness" (1985, 143). In contrast, I use the term to reflect more directly the shifts in emotions and changes in self. Rather than separating oneself from illness, many people develop ways of living with illness. Illness may remain part of them, but they are not ruled by it. Like LeMaistre, I see resolution and renewal as phases, not final states of being. People may be able to resolve their feelings and sense of renewal after suffering certain losses only to experience them again with subsequent losses.

Doing Activity: Accomplishment in Process

Each of the articles in this section is organized around "doing" some activity; in this case, more specifically, doing comedy, the processing of discipline referrals from the classroom, organizing strategies for writing examinations, or negotiating processes for dispute settlement in welfare agencies.

In the first selection, Robert Stebbins examines a particular dimension of the art of the entertainer by focusing both on entertainment magicians and stand-up comics. The analysis focuses on the various stages of acquiring suitable material, organizing the act, and performing it. Never denying the personal and creative dimensions of the entertainer's art, Stebbins concentrates on emphasizing the social side of this phenomenon which is underscored by the necessity of gaining and maintaining audience control.

In the next selection, Robert Emerson investigates a dimension of social control as it operated at the two junior high schools he studied. Specifically, he examines how control specialists, namely counselors, exercise their responsibility for dealing with troubles arising from within the classroom, but which could not be handled within that setting. By processing discipline referrals, these counselors engage in a form of secondary social control as they attempt to determine the meaning to be attributed to particular referrals and in deciding to implement institutionally satisfactory dispositions.

In the third article of this section, Daniel Albas and Cheryl Albas analyze the processes by which university students prepare for examinations. In particular, the authors data shed light on the relationship between students' self-definitions as "aces" or "bombers" and their estimates for probable success and failure. Most significantly, however, we gain insight into how students' developing perspectives and identities influence not only how they execute their actual studying, but also how this is interwoven in their relationships with other students.

The section is rounded out with an article by Gale Miller and James Holstein which analyzes aspects of the disputing process in a type of welfare program. In describing and analyzing the interactional procedures used by the staff members to meet their professional responsibilities, Miller and Holstein focus both on how disputes emerge within staff-client interactions and how they are managed and transformed as more formal dispute processing mechanisms are brought into play. Their analysis suggests that human service organizations may be conceptualized as political arenas where members of the organization formulate and pursue practical interests.

Doing Stand-up: Comedians on Stage

Robert Stebbins

At the very core of any form of stage entertainment lies an art of some sort that makes the entertainment attractive to its audience. In this fundamental respect the commercial stage entertainments are no different from the performing fine arts. Moreover, in some fields, the art of the entertainer is as profound as that of the fine artist even if the latter is valued more highly by the cultural elite than the former. Notwithstanding such snobbery, it takes considerable skill to produce *good* stage entertainment. I put the emphasis on "good," since we must occasionally suffer through mediocre or poor entertainment (and fine art) whose underdeveloped artistry might seem to belie this observation. A principle that is obvious for the entertainment arts, but holds as well for the fine arts, is that they are also fundamentally social endeavors. Nearly all art is created with some public in mind (for possible exceptions, see Becker 1982, 258–69), which means that, at bottom, the artistic process is also sociological. To answer the question, "What is artistic about a particular art?" we must examine, among other things, the social context and social processes surrounding its production. Art is therefore much more than the expression of special personal skills.

What Is Art?

Art, fine and popular, is as social and interpersonal as it is psychological and individual, although this duality is not always recognized. For example, the Italian philosopher Benedetto Croce held that "art is ruled uniquely by the imagination," in contrast to Russian author Leo Tolstoy who believed that "art is not handicraft [but] the transmission of feeling the artist has experienced." The first lodges art in the artist, the second lodges it in the interaction between the artist and his or her public.

Thomas Munro's (1957, 45) definition of art incorporates both dimensions. He notes that an artistic product or production need not be beautiful (aesthetic) or otherwise meritorious to be identified as art. For him, art includes one or more of three skills: (1) making or doing something used or intended to be used as a stimulus for a satisfactory aesthetic experience, aspects of which may include beauty, pleasantness, interest, and emotion; (2) expressing and communicating past emotional and other experience, both individual and social; and (3) designing, composing, and performing through personal interpretation, as distinguished from routine execution or mechanical reproduction. It follows that an artist is someone who holds and expresses one or more of these three skills which, as Howard Becker (1982, 14) has observed, the public sees as special talents, gifts, or abilities. The aim of this paper is to examine the social side of the art of the entertainer by using data from a study of entertainment magicians (Stebbins 1984) and a study of stand-up comics (Stebbins 1990) to illustrate how entertainers sociologically create and express their arts. Representative samples of amateurs and professionals were interviewed on how they produce their form of entertainment. The interviews were supplemented with participant-observation of onstage performances, offstage activities, and after-hour gatherings, and with a sampling of the instructional literature published in the two arts.

How to Be Entertaining

To be entertaining in any art is to develop one or more of Munro's three artistic skills with reference to the chosen form of entertainment. The following discussion of magic and comedy suggests that all three skills are needed to produce a *variety* (entertainment) art. These skills are developed and expressed in the process of producing the art, which can be analyzed as a sequence of stages, each with its distinct social dimension—learning the art, acquiring material, organizing an act, and presenting the act. The sequence repeats itself many times throughout the performing career of the artist, each stage feeding back upon the others. No art is ever completely learned; all artists continually benefit from new learning, material, organization, and onstage experience.

Learning the Art

Most entertainers fall in love with their art through some sort of memorable, abrupt contact with it (Stebbins 1992, chap. 5). To learn it, however, requires more than a single exposure, however impressive. That is, neophytes must come to recognize good and bad expressions of the art and its different styles (particularly the one they would like to emulate), and as well they must recognize exemplars of these two. This is a period of intense reading, watching, listening, and talking with established performers in the art in question as well as with other neophytes who face the same needs to learn.

In magic the initial efforts of the novice are directed toward learning about magic, its history, and its famous personalities and, especially, toward learning tricks. For it is the fascination with how particular tricks are done that lures this individual to the field of magic. But even seasoned professionals spend some of their non-performance time in this manner, since there are always new variations of standard tricks to consider. There is also the sporadic need to vary one's act with new material. Novices are usually keen to demonstrate their newly learned tricks, to perform magic for people who they hope will be both mystified and amused by their descriptions. Thus, they quickly develop an avid interest in the conduct of magic shows, seeking out live and televised performances to aid their learning. Putting together such a show is far from easy; one must first learn the tricks. This is usually done both by reading how to do them and by seeing them performed. Bookstores and community and university libraries stock books on magic; while friends, relatives, magic dealers, local entertainers, and television programs may provide anything from a demonstration of a trick or two to a complete show. As novices penetrate the local magic scene, they also hear of scheduled lectures, magic studio gatherings, nearby conventions, and other events where formal and informal instructions are available. Recently, videotapes have come on the market as an instructional medium (Prus and Sharper 1991, 232). Most beginners are quickly drawn to other magicians, where they can see tricks conducted, learn the shortcuts and special skills pertinent to their art, and gain clarification of printed instructions that are sometimes too sketchy or too complicated. Those who have a flair for magic and want to do it themselves are goaded by an unrelenting curiosity about how certain tricks are conducted, whereas most spectators are content to be entertained and perhaps speculate a bit on how these effects are achieved without their curiosity developing into a passion. Budding magicians, on the other hand, *must* know how the trick was achieved. They are driven, as if by some inner demon, into reflecting on the trick and studying the magic literature. And, being ignorant of the folkways of magic as well as the conduct of tricks, they are especially likely to commit a major gaffe by querying experienced amateurs and professionals with: "How did you do that?" They have yet to learn that this question is an egregious impropriety in the magic world where people are expected to use their imaginations to determine how a trick is done, and refrain from asking performers for their trade secrets (even if those "secrets" are described in books and used by other magicians). Some magic tricks take considerable time to learn, notably those based on manipulative and mental skills, and they can be most difficult to execute. Hence, they claim hours of practice from those who wish to be successful at them. Those hours are as likely to be pieced together with moments snatched from here and there in the day as from specially designated practice sessions. It is common to find amateur magicians who are trying to improve in this area carrying special coins, playing cards, lengths of rope, sponge balls, and other small objects with them so as to be able to exercise their skills whenever the occasion permits (and possibly perform some, too, if appropriate). Sitting before a television set, being interviewed, watching other magicians perform at the open houses at local magic studios, and attending meetings of local magic clubs were among such occasions observed by the author.

Most comics, by contrast, already know something about the nature and history of stand-up comedy through their consumption of the televised and recorded performances of various stars in the art. They had been learning about their art as part of their general socialization in North American popular culture. Thus, for many of the comics who took part in the study, learning their art continued on a more personal level when they were first exposed to live comedy, which was typically at a comedy club. A number of the respondents indicated that the first time they saw live comedy it looked easy. It occurred to them that they could be even funnier than many of the people onstage, and in their naïveté they were inspired to try their hand at it. "It looked like telling jokes with the guys," reflected one professional.

Easy and Fun like any Conversation

By no means did every member of the sample enter into a career in comedy the day after they saw their first live show. More commonly, that decision was delayed for the next few months and was often made after another visit or two to the local comedy club, perhaps reinforced by televised or recorded comedy. But before long the budding comic would be writing lines or assembling lines and jokes heard earlier and beginning to think that it was time to go onstage to see "what it was like." The majority prepared or assembled lines for their first ventures. Only two of the overall sample said they simply went to the club and told street jokes as they came to mind. Sometimes, as I observed in one comedy club, a person would walk in off the street during an open-mike night, mount the stage, and talk extemporaneously to the audience about everyday life in a way that might be interesting, but not especially humorous. Most of the comics made their debut during an amateur night of some kind, mostly in comedy clubs, but sometimes in nightclubs that featured a range of entertainment on amateur nights. A number of the sample had never been to an amateur night and so had little or no idea of what to expect. Up to that point the only live comedy they had observed firsthand was what they had seen in weekend shows. A minority of the respondents performed initially as emcees or, in two cases, as opening acts.

Acquiring Material

When entertainers acquire material, they develop, construct, or purchase one or both of the two principal components of an act or show: *objects* (including substances) and *ideas*. These two components are sometimes linked because the place of objects in an act, when not self-evident, must be explained with gestures or patter (the ideas). For instance, a singer must acquire songs and a juggler bowling pins, both of which have so obvious a relationship to the acts in question that they need no explanation. But a clown will explain by pantomime how he or she intends to use a can of paint, and a magician will talk about the inferiority of the newspaper he or she is ripping apart while performing the torn and restored newspaper routine. As magic and comedy demonstrate, there is much that is sociological about the acquisition of material.

In magic, to acquire material means to obtain magic apparatus and supplies and develop an attractive patter with which to introduce them. For novices the first two may amount to little more than items such as rope, coins, playing cards, or wearing apparel, easily found around the house. Or they may buy, or receive as gifts, a magic set or a couple of commercial tricks, products that can be purchased at a local joke and novelty shop or department store. Finally, they may construct their own props, although this alternative is pursued mostly by those with some performance experience who know what features are desirable in a piece of equipment.

As connections in the world of magic expand, newcomers become familiar with the magic dealers either directly or indirectly through catalogs. At this point they enter a fascinating new world for the dealers' products are not toys (unlike most of the items vended in novelty shops and department stores); they are items designed for serious use in variety theater. At first many amateurs are overwhelmed with the number, diversity, and possible uses of the tricks sold by dealers, an orientation that some of them never completely outgrow. As they read about the trick in a catalog or examine it physically at the studio or convention display booth, they imagine themselves performing it before an admiring audience. They also feel that the excitement of being onstage would be enhanced through the incorporation of this item into their act. The all-encompassing curiosity of how each trick works becomes obsessive. All that remains is for the magician to buy the prop, learn how to work it and, once properly routined, integrate it into his or her act. A young amateur describes his love at first sight with a Svengali deck:

> I'm a sucker. I fall for the easiest things in magic. I'm a magician; things thrill me and I love it. I wanted to know how this thing worked. I was new to magic. This thing could work miracles; I wanted it.

In addition to buying tricks from one another and from dealers, the other main way to acquire them is through construction, an alternative used by amateurs somewhat more than professionals. This may involve little else than the imaginative transformation of everyday objects into vehicles for deceptive entertainment. The need to be entertaining brings out the craftsperson in the magician, as he or she sets out to make such supplies as flash powder or smoke, an illusion or large stage apparatus, or infrequently, a close-up prop. The decision to produce one's own equipment and supplies may stem from necessity; for instance, being unable to afford the manufactured version of the item or being convinced that one can make a prop that is sturdier, more effective, or less gimmicky in appearance. Whatever the motive, building equipment may become a social affair when several magicians collaborate to design, build, and finish a major item, or when one advises another on these procedures. Previously acquired tricks, commercial or homemade, may also be modified by their owners.

One important condition of a good magic act with a verbal accompaniment is an attractive patter. It may be a story, some poetry, an explanation of the moves or procedures of the deception (without disclosing its secrets), a few narrative jokes, a dialogue with a volunteer, or a set of instructions for the audience. Patter locates a trick; it gives that trick a meaningful place not only in the magician's presentation, but also in the spectators' minds. Good patter helps build suspense, set a mood, misdirect audience attention, encourage audience participation, or produce almost any other effect that the magician wishes to achieve.

Developing an imaginative patter is difficult, although some magicians seem to relish the challenge. Without it the verbally based trick is little more than a quaint put-on with limited entertainment value. The trick may actually be impossible to do without the patter, in that the patter justifies bodily movements and positions that shield the magician's deceptive actions. In any event, an original and enjoyable patter is one of the clearest examples of the art of magic. Suggested patters are often enclosed with commercial tricks, although they may not fit the performer's personality or act. Moreover, those instructions may have been written in a foreign language; the trick may have been purchased from a colleague who has lost the original instructions or dialogue; or the performer may have modified the trick to the extent that the original patter is no longer suitable. Hence the occasional need to invent patter is unavoidable.

In "routining" a show, one must also heed its histrionic requirements if good magic is to be the outcome. In variety theater, the term "routine" is also used as a verb, meaning to develop a routine or component of a larger act that the actor regularly performs (Bowman and Ball 1961, 416). Magic is one of the theater arts and magicians are, among other things, actors. But, instead of presenting a role, conjurers present their personalities via their deceptions. Specifically, they do this through their stage business (movements intended to establish atmosphere, reveal character, define a situation), physical effects (sound, lighting, and so forth), makeup, voice projection, and other tricks of the acting trade. The personality presented by these means is the very essence of the show. A routine can be well learned and include an original patter. Yet, if it clashes with the individuality of the performer, its value as entertainment drops markedly. Expressions of personality vary widely; mentalist Phil Goldstein whose countenance is stern, speaks onstage with gravity; Doug Henning's diminutive, boyish physique blends well with his high voice and cheerful demeanor.

In all this, the magician aims to be original. One person's presentation of self onstage is unlikely to suit another so that attempts to imitate him or her are destined to fail. Magicians are advised to watch other's perform and thereby gain a sense of how magic is generally presented, but never to copy them in detail. Nonetheless, in magic, there are standard utterances, gestures, forms of dress, and ways of producing tricks, which are not only widely used by magicians and give them the stamp of being a magician, but are also expected of them by their fellows and by their audiences. One of the problems junior magicians face is precisely where to imitate and where to work for personal interpretation and presentation. In routining an act, one's sense of the audience's capacity is brought into play. To construct deceptive realities that audiences find entertaining, successful magicians, whether they know it or not, imaginatively place themselves in the position of the typical spectator to see how he or she is likely to perceive crucial aspects of the planned routine. Sociologically speaking, they take the role of that person (Prus and Sharper 1991, 304). The fact that individual role-taking abilities vary widely (Stryker 1962; Kinch 1963) helps account for the success of some magicians as entertainers and the relative failure of others. By viewing the act through the eyes of an imagined audience, the magician can determine what will make them laugh, whether they will follow the misdirections, which manipulated objects are most meaningful, and so on. From the adult standpoint, role-taking is generally more difficult to do with youngsters than with adults, since adults are apt to have forgotten their childhood years. For example, the entertainer must see humor where the child sees it, as illustrated in a short patter used by children's entertainer David Ginn:

> "Who knows," Ginn tells his young audience, "you might even win a two-hundred-piece breakfast set." At this point he produces a box of Frosted Flakes. "But that's a cheap gift from the show. It should be a four-hundred-piece set." He then throws the box to the floor and stomps on it.

As magicians go about their role-taking, they work through their own fantasies to create the most amusing routines of which they are capable. Eventually, these are tried on actual audiences whose reactions can be most informative. It is possible that, as a group, amateurs are less tuned to this feedback than professionals are.

Being sensitive to the capacity of an audience also encompasses the ability to know when they have had enough. It is to know how long various types of audiences will enjoy a show; it is to know how much more magic an audience will enjoy before losing interest. Both watching and performing tricks requires concentration. And both spectators and magician need brief respites throughout the act if the magic routines and attention to them are to remain at their peak. Filler routines, such as telling jokes or making balloon animals (for children), serve this purpose. Applause also provides a respite.

Acquiring material in comedy can also include the acquisition of equipment, as in the case of prop comics who use various objects in their acts such as musical instruments, a ventriloquist's doll, and a set of masks. But, in pure stand-up, props are next to non-existent. The most important material to be acquired is the comic line.

A comic searching for new material must first come up with a premise, theme, or subject around which to develop a descriptive monologue of, say, five minutes. For example, he or she might work up a monologue around behavior in elevators or life as a child. In present-day stand-up comedy, the premise is plucked from the everyday experiences and observations of the author, usually as these involve some mishap, person, animal, predicament, or misunderstanding. The new-wave comics of the 1960s and early 1970s were inclined to find their premises in the moral and political spheres. The modern performer finds material as he or she shops, watches television, reads the newspaper, walks around town, attends a concert, drives somewhere, takes an airplane flight, and so on. There is rarely any deep message or sharp controversy in comedy today, only pure entertainment. The comic has a "concept" or "conception" of the premise as, in some way, humorous and worth developing into a monologue. The female comic Charlie in Erika Ritter's (1980, 34) play *Automatic Pilot* provides a short example as she opens her act:

> Hey, I'm in a good mood tonight. I just got my Mensa card. (takes a card from her pocket, shows it) You know what that means? It means I'm insured against ever skipping a period. So ... how do you like my hair? Mr. Doug did it. That's my hairdresser—Mr. Doug.... Mr. Doug told me he was just going to "shape the hair." Notice how they never refer to it as YOUR hair. This is so they can wreck it without either of you feeling personally affected by it.

Writing lines is one of the most difficult aspects of stand-up. Without fail, every respondent in the sample commented on how hard it is to come up with even one line that consistently draws laughs from a range of patrons. "It takes a month to get five minutes of good material," groaned one. Like the playwright, the comic must carefully choose his or her words, their place in the sentence, and the punctuation that guides their eventual delivery onstage. Like any other author, the comic must rewrite several times to create an effective line. Indeed, he or she may shelve a line (and a premise) for six to twelve months or even more because nothing seems to make it work. Clearly, theories of humor play little or no role in the creative process behind stand-up comedy (McGhee and Goldstein 1984).

Of course, some comics buy jokes from a gag writer. Some incorporate street jokes into their acts, steal from colleagues, rely on stock lines, or get them from a friend. But as a performer gains experience and develops a distinctive style, the tendency is to write more and more of his or her own "stuff." As a career peaks, demand may be so great that a star must hire one or more writers to maintain a repertoire of new material (Germain 1988). Bob Hope is said to have six writers, five men and one woman.

Organizing an Act

Learning the art, that is, becoming aware of its good expressions according to style and acquiring the material to perform it, are two main preconditions for organizing an act. Magicians organize their acts by routining them. Having acquired and learned a number of tricks, the fledgling magician is ready to routine them into a short act. An act is organized by arranging jokes, tricks, monologues, and so forth into what is hoped will be an artistic and entertaining sequence. Among beginning entertainers, such sequences typically last no more than fifteen to twenty minutes. Later, with more experience and demand for their services, variety artists extend these acts, sometimes to over an hour. Often, however, even seasoned professionals can offer no more than forty minutes before the audience gets restless. However artistic, variety entertainment is typically superficial, which means that the public quickly grows weary of any single version of it.

A magic show consists of a sequence of tricks, perhaps intermixed with some non-magic filler which, if skillfully arranged, staged, and executed provides entertainment by means of one or more of the five types of magic (stage, close-up, sleight of hand, illusion, and mentalism). The performer's goal is to hold the audience's attention for his or her time onstage, something good magic does and bad magic fails to do.

The production of good magic hinges on a seemingly infinite list of factors, only some of which are possible to cover here. Many of these factors guide the routining of a show where good magic is presented. For instance, one wants to attract and hold audience attention from the moment one steps into the spotlight. Thus, a strong opening routine is desirable. One also wishes to close on a strong note so that the audience will return. In between, variety helps keep the spectators' attention centered on the performer. Tricks with different content may be juxtaposed, such as a sleight of hand card trick and a dove production. Variety is also achieved by a change in pace, lighting, sound, mood, and personnel (volunteers, assistants). Some entertainers build their acts around one or more themes that co-ordinate the sequence of tricks.

In the final analysis the goal of presenting good magic is reached by delivering a "smooth" performance. In such a performance there is an obvious logic to the sequence of tricks that comprise the act. Each trick is routined with meaningful props, bits of stage equipment, and appropriate patter (if trick is verbal), all of which harmonize with the magician's personality. In present-day stand-up comedy, the typical act consists of anecdotes, narrative jokes, one-liners, and short descriptive monologues, which may or may not be related. These must be strung together to make an entertaining sequence. The component monologues also have an internal organization as do the jokes and anecdotes. Basically, each has a three-part structure beginning with the setup, a description of the scene of action—for the comic recognizes that things are funny only within certain contexts (Pollio 1978). In the middle some sort of action unfolds within this context. Finally, the punchline, or payoff, terminates the action. A tag line, or secondary payoff, may be added by the performer (or, rarely, by an audience member) as a sort of entertainment bonus. By way of illustration, consider the lines of Peggy Donacetti (fictitious name) from a monologue about herself and her boyfriend:

> He makes me so mad at times. He's always trying to fondle me in public. One of these days I'm going to buy one of those little round buzzers you get at the joke shops and put it in my bra.

The audience roars, and as the effect of the punchline wears off, Donacetti skillfully follows up with the tag line: "If that doesn't stop him, I'm going to drop one in his pants and grab him."

A comedy veteran presenting a joke with a long middle will supply humor throughout this section to hold attention for the eventual punchline. Certainly the skill and ingenuity this requires exceeds that which goes into stock heckler lines, where the three parts of the joke are contained in one or two sentences.

Performing the Art

The ultimate test of the first three stages comes in publicly performing the act as the artist has organized it. To be sure, polished performances require assiduous rehearsal and practice of skills to the extent that memory and physical movements cannot be overwhelmed by stage fright. But even this is no guarantee of a smooth performance, for numerous problems can arise onstage that could blemish it or challenge the veteran entertainer's ability to cope with adversity. Let us consider some of these problems in comedy where they are possibly more acute than anywhere else in the variety arts.

In pure stand-up comedy, neither props nor scenery exist to distract the audience from a weak act or onstage problems. At the same time, there can be no stand-up comedy without audience participation—interaction with the audience is an essential part of the comic's act. The performer communicates jokes and sketches; the audience indicates, chiefly with laughter, whether these jokes and sketches are funny. Usually, the comic communicates in a conversational manner, using sweeping eye contact and a friendly demeanor while treating familiar subjects. The audience responds with smiles, chuckles, howls, applause, comments to one another and, occasionally, to the performer. From such cues the latter knows that he or she has hit on an effective set of lines with good delivery. Attentive faces, but no smiles or laughs, communicate something too. If laughter is expected under these conditions, then, unless the audience is somehow problematic (drunk, hostile), the comic knows that either the lines or their method of delivery or both must be reworked. In the audience, extended conversation and attention to people, actions, and objects around the room signal boredom.

An artistically strong act may still flop because of certain events or conditions in the room. Some audiences, usually not those in comedy clubs, are present for reasons other than to hear comedy. They might have come to watch a televised baseball game, which an imprudent manager has switched off so the comic could perform. Sometimes comics work for an evening at a nightclub that features dancing as an occasion for single adults to meet. The performer is often seen as obstructing these more important goals. Working at stags can become equally horrific when, for example, tables are served by scantily clad waitresses, a stripper or two circulates through the rooms, poker games are underway, or drunken exchanges break out. Understanding humor requires concentration. A professional looked back on his worst "hell gig":

> The weirdest gig I ever had ... was in Vancouver.... It was like forty dollars to do a hairdressing convention. They had a nice stage, table, and microphone set up for me. But whoever thought of hiring a comedian in the first place, I have no idea. Then they changed everything. "Why not come into the judging room and do your stuff there?" Now I have no microphone, and there's six people, six models sitting down with aprons on and their hair done up. They can't move or laugh. They just have to sit there, and I do my show. There were kids running around and hairdressers and about twenty other people who couldn't figure out why I was there. I began to wonder too. Then I had to give away the door prizes. That's why the rooms [clubs] are the only places where you can just do your stuff. It is no wonder that comics prefer club rooms. (Interview with author)

A weak sound system, rare in comedy clubs, does not help. Poorly designed rooms with a noisy or conspicuous bar, several large posts, or noise from an adjacent room can contribute to a flop. These factors and others only exacerbate such unavoidable distractions as waiters serving tables and patrons traipsing off to the restrooms.

To be sure, no act appeals to all audiences. Most comics are city people whose background is chiefly urban. Comedy clubs are located in medium-sized and large cities. Acts designed to succeed here sometimes fare poorly in small cities surrounded by a large rural hinterland.

And, as Montreal humorist and animateur Yvons Deschamps observed in an interview for this study, different segments of the audience laugh at different lines presented by a particular comic. Research in social psychology demonstrates that men tend to laugh more often than women at aggressive and sexual humor (Groch 1974), whereas women are more amused by the absurd (Brodzinsky, Barnet, and Aiello 1981). The performer is successful if he or she can make a sizeable proportion of the audience laugh. Some comics have noticed that men and women laugh at different places in their acts. One respondent said he gets the most attention and laughter from women when he talks about his girlfriend. In general, men laugh more often and more heartily at off-color material, although this does depend somewhat on the audience. At least one comic has observed that patrons may look at their dates for cues about whether to laugh at a joke.

Moreover, the appearance, bearing, and gender of the comic can affect audience reception to his or her humor. If the audience prefers macho male performers, then a woman or a more effeminate man will draw attention to him or herself and away from the monologue. Such is the preference at the type of satellite room known as the biker bar. The homosexual comedian Simon Fanshaw would likely be given a hard time in such a place and find that his lines drew little laughter. However, when I observed him at Yuk Yuk's urban Yorkville club in Toronto, Ontario, he was a complete success.

Audience Interaction

Friendly humor, in particular, encourages interaction with the humorist. It does so in three ways: (1) when successful, it suggests a willingness on the part of the comic to associate with the audience—the conversational tone abets this tendency; (2) it tells the audience that the performer has a friendly, good-natured disposition and is not angry; and (3) it establishes a sense of equality between comic and audience. Status differences between the patrons and the featured performer, the center of attention, are momentarily overridden by the experience of laughing together.

Unfortunately, most comics do not want spontaneous remarks, questions, and heckling from their audiences (known as calling out). Intrusions interrupt their carefully planned timing, wording, and rhythm. It is like throwing ink onto a painting; the art is destroyed. In comedy when continuity between the set-up and the middle is interrupted, it destroys the punchline. The comic's dilemma therefore is how to deliver a conversational monologue while discouraging responses from the audience. Experienced entertainers know how to make the best of unwanted interaction, for example, by getting two patrons to argue with each other and then assuming the role of referee, a good stance from which to improvise some additional humor.

Perhaps it is true for many forms of stage entertainment that, among other factors, a smooth performance rests on gaining and maintaining audience control (Sanders 1974). By making instantaneous adjustments to audience mood and attention level, by imaginative handling of hecklers, by attractively presenting one's personality, and by establishing eye contact to create in each spectator the feeling of being given special attention, performers keep their audiences tuned into the act and thereby succeed in entertaining them. Only through extensive stage experience can one develop one's ability to control audiences in this fashion.

Control bothers line comics less than monologuists and stand-up comics. Control is achieved partly through audience socialization. Patrons learn from each other and from experience in comedy clubs that active vocal participation is unwelcome. With comedy rooms establishing themselves as a form of urban entertainment, we can expect a more sophisticated clientele in this regard. In the meantime, club managers often announce the norm of non-participation prior to the show. For instance:

> Welcome to Laughable's House of Humor and an evening of terrific comedy entertainment. To enjoy our show to the fullest, we ask that you keep your talking to a minimum and your laughing and applause to a maximum. And now here is your host for the evening, Steve Roth.

If neither socialization nor announcement works and someone gets out of hand, the manager often evicts the offender. By this time, however, a certain amount of damage has already been done.

Certainly these sources of control are helpful. But veteran comics also have their own controls. One is the electronically amplified voice, against which it is difficult for patrons to compete. Talking with energy and enthusiasm is a form of domination in its own right. The same may be said for eye contact and the other principles of good conversation. Of course, the conversational norm of turn-taking in which each person allows the other to have his or her say before responding, must be avoided. The comic raises fewer hackles by sticking with mundane and familiar topics rather than venturing into emotion-laden topics such as politics or the abortion controversy. By sticking with the former, he or she controls the audience's desire to respond.

Another control available to the comic is speaking with confidence and authority. One presents oneself as a formidable target for people who want to call out. Being likeable also appears to reduce heckling, although a likeable comic may inadvertently encourage a comment or question from the audience about what was just said. Some comics control all interventions by ignoring them. Others acknowledge commentary with a brief thank you or "There you are" or, if they are confident, perhaps with a brief impromptu exchange. Still another strategy is to politely, but firmly, remind the offender of comedy club etiquette. Subsequent offenses can bring harsher reactions from the stage, such as "Will you shut up?" The heckler line is the comic's most powerful weapon, and it is frequently brandished. Two of the most commonly used are: "Look honey, I don't come and bounce on the bed when you're working" (for women) and "Hey you're pretty good. Why don't you get yourself a manager? Then you can quit handling yourself" (for men). This weapon (perhaps even some lines themselves) appears to have been borrowed from one prominent predecessor of the stand-up performer, the comic who worked at strip shows (Salutin 1973). The heckler line is almost always an insult and commonly obscene. The hope is that it will silence the target through embarrassment (most likely to succeed if the audience laughs heartily) and defeat—a sense of having been outdone by someone of superior wit. If a series of heckler lines fails to work and a contest still more detrimental to the show develops, a responsible manager will step in and evict or threaten to evict the offending person.

The performance situation is much the same in magic, which is as dependent on an audience as stand-up comedy. In magic, staging conditions can range from poor to excellent with corresponding effects on the show. The same things that affect events in the performance environment and cause competition for the audience's attention in a comedy performance can also affect a magic performance. My observations suggest, however, that magicians may be less subject to heckling than comics, in part because comedy invites interaction whereas magic does not, at least not to the same degree.

Be that as it may, some magicians find that teenage audiences present a unique problem. Many teenagers are reluctant to admit that they have been deceived. Consequently, they may force the performer into the delicate position of having to defend his or her presentation without threatening or embarrassing the heckler. Everyone must save face in such situations. One veteran amateur, for example, was confronted backstage by a teenage boy who maintained he knew how a trick was done. The magician nonchalantly replied: "Good, now go home and practice it," and then returned to directing his assistants on how to pack his apparatus.

An audience filled with children can also present problems (Prus and Sharper 1991, 270–71). They may not even know that they should applaud after each trick, a lack of sophistication that may require special attention. Jody the Magician starts with instructions for the kids:

> "If you see some magic that is really neato, I want you to clap your hands. OK? Let's give it a practice." Several trials of hand clapping are run, in which adults and children reach still louder levels of applause. He continues to arouse their enthusiasm with a waggish patter about his ability to say the ABCs backward. After trifling with the audience for a couple of minutes, he spins around, his back to them, and recites the alphabet. (Performance observed by author)

Conclusions

The art of the entertainer is profoundly social. This quality is evident in the sequential development and expression of commercial stage or variety art as participants cycle through the stages of learning the art, acquiring material, organizing an act, and performing the act. In this sequence we find many manifestations of the three kinds of artistic skills: *making* or *doing* something for a satisfactory aesthetic experience; *expressing* and *communicating* past emotional or other experience; and *designing, composing,* and *performing* through personal interpretation. It is obvious that the art of the entertainer has an individual, personal, creative side, consisting of imaginative and original impulses. No one can deny that, but it is equally obvious that it has a social side, evident in the many ways in which those impulses are generated by the artist, valued by the public, and expressed on the stage. Sociologically speaking, then, we may conclude that Tolstoy's belief that art is the transmission of feeling that the artist has experienced, is a more accurate interpretation than that of Croce, who believed that art is ruled uniquely by the imagination.

Doing Discipline: The Junior High School Scene

Robert Emerson

Social control comprises a key part of the daily operation of all schools. Students are required to behave in orderly ways, and are subject to various penalties if caught when they do not. Teachers learn that they cannot teach effectively unless and until they acquire "classroom control" (Denscombe 1985). Indeed, many schools hire social control specialists whose work involves dealing with a variety of campus troubles on a daily basis—yard supervisors who monitor cafeterias, playgrounds, and bathrooms; and security officers who police and control access to the campus. Schools also rely upon control specialists who are responsible for dealing with troubles arising within the classroom, but which cannot be handled within that setting. These specialists—vice-principals, deans, and counselors—provide backup control for classroom teachers. As a matter of routine they review teachers' complaints about students' classroom misconduct and determine how to respond to those who are involved in such "discipline referrals."

In this sense, deans and counselors represent institutional "troubleshooters," or third parties (Emerson and Messinger 1977), possessing authority to assess and judge the competing claims of teachers and students with regard to these classroom troubles, and to decide upon how to respond to them. Exactly how deans and counselors intervene shapes up what the trouble comes to be—at one extreme, a "real discipline problem" when the counselor accepts and validates the teacher's complaint and intervenes on the side of the teacher; at the other, an "inappropriate referral" when the counselor sides with the student against the teacher. And decisions about *how* to intervene in, and respond to, classroom troubles have important consequences for students' careers within the school; for example, over time a student may become known as a "discipline problem," a status which will narrow and redirect that student's life chances within the school as an institution (Cicourel and Kitsuse 1963; Willis 1977).

This paper will examine how school counselors process discipline referrals from the classroom. It will focus on counselors' decision-making work in determining what referrals involve and in deciding upon and implementing dispositions to complaints about classroom troubles.

Methods and Data

Data for this study derive from a participant-observation research project conducted over a five-month period in 1969 in two northern California junior high schools.[1] This research focused on the discipline practices and decision-making of the schools' administrations and their staffs of dean/counselors. One school, Vincente Junior High, is located in an upper-middle- to middle-class residential area that in the year prior to the study, had been integrated through redistricting to include substantial numbers of black youth; at the time of the study 27 percent of the 1700 students in the school were African-American. The second school, Tijera Junior High, is located in a lower-middle-class heavily white suburb. I have supplemented and updated this research by more occasional interviews with counselors and deans, and by some short-term observation in several junior and senior high schools in southern California in the 1980s.

Both Vicente and Tijera used discipline systems in which counselors handled discipline matters, along with academic and personal counseling.[2] Specific counselors were responsible for discipline referrals from each of the three grades.[3] Procedurally, discipline referrals began with a student reporting to the office of the counselor responsible for his or her particular grade with a *discipline slip* (discipline referral or pink slip) filled out and signed by the complaining teacher. In addition to having the student's name, the date, time, grade, and number of the classroom, pink slips included a space labeled "cause" where the teacher had written a brief description of the incident.[4] After speaking with the student about the incident, the counselor would decide upon some response to the complaint. Possible actions ranged from merely talking to the youth about the incident, to ordering after-school detention(s) with the counselor, to conferences with parents, and possibly, to suspending the student from school for a number of days.[5]

In the following pages I want to examine a number of issues involved in counselors' processing of these sorts of ordinary classroom troubles: How is it that counselors understand "what is going on" in any particular referral? What special knowledge and skills do counselors draw upon to "read the slip" in organizationally informed ways? How do counselors move toward some disposition of particular referrals?

"Backing" the Teacher

The counselor controls access to the major and ultimate sanctions available in the school—detentions, parental contacts, suspensions, and expulsions. Teachers refer classroom discipline problems with the expectation that counselors will invoke these sanctions when needed to sustain classroom order. They expect the counselor to "do something"—to make some significant response to the particular problem. In this sense teachers assume the counselor will "back" their efforts at classroom control. Such "backing" thus provides a fundamental, constraining expectation in the handling of discipline cases: teachers expect the counselor to stand ready to take effective action to reinforce classroom authority when it has encountered challenge or threat.

Counselors in turn acknowledge that discipline referrals should ordinarily be handled in ways that do "back the teacher." When a referral at either of the two sample schools involved "a real discipline problem," counselors felt it was appropriate and necessary to make the sorts of significant responses that comprised "backing." Counselors regarded serious discipline problems to be such "major offenses" (the term used in a document outlining guidelines for appropriate discipline referrals prepared by counselors and administrators and circulated to all teachers at Vincente) as "threat to school personnel," "physical attack on school personnel," "smoking on campus," "use or possession of liquor or narcotics," or "attacking or seriously threatening another student." Such offenses were appropriately referred for disciplinary action. As a counselor at Vincente argued, with some feeling:

> COUNSELOR: I think the disciplinary action should be saved for more important things, for more serious things, so that when you do take disciplinary action, it means something. But how can you discipline for just losing a book or forgetting a book?
>
> INTERVIEWER: What kind of serious things are you—?
>
> COUNSELOR: Fighting, smoking, or the use of abusive language, swearing at a teacher—out and out cussing, using swear words. Or defiance, out and out defiance in a classroom by a student. I think these things then deserve more stringent disciplinary action—calling in the parent or possibly suspension. But for something that has to be disciplined! I don't think that I should have to discipline for this type of thing [forgetting book].

Not only should teachers immediately involve counselors in such incidents (indeed, any report of even potential violence or classroom disruption would find such personnel literally running to the troublespot), but also failure to report such incidents would raise fundamental doubts about the teacher's classroom competence.

On the other hand, counselors regarded too many discipline referrals as inappropriate and unnecessary. Counselors recurrently complained about teachers' tendencies to refer too many "minor" cases, and at Vincente, eventually developed an explicit set of guidelines for discipline referrals that discouraged referrals of "minor offenses that are primarily a teacher's responsibility."[6] Such "minor offenses" included: "pupils coming to class unprepared, without equipment, pencils, books, or homework"; "poor attitude toward class responsibilities"; "gum chewing"; "continuous talking"; and "lack of co-operation." Counselors experienced considerable tension when asked to back the teacher in such "minor" classroom problems.

These various pressures produced a sort of tactical balance between the concerns of counselors and teachers: counselors would back teachers, but expected teachers to make appropriate referrals most of the time. Tensions and struggles between counselors and teachers focused around referrals that the former consider inappropriate, as in the following:

> Art teacher Rockwell sent a ninth grade boy to the counselor for being disruptive in class, asking the counselor to have the boy serve a half-hour detention with him. The counselor felt that Rockwell was trying to pass his work off onto him, and decided to send the youth back to Rockwell after school to serve the detention with him, and to warn the boy that if he missed this detention he would be suspended. He talked to Rockwell about this at lunch, reporting that Rockwell had agreed to it without comment.

Against this background, how did counselors understand and assess particular referrals as "serious" or "minor," "appropriate" or "unnecessary"? To answer these questions requires examination of the actual processes of grasping and responding to referrals, processes that begin with the counselor "reading the discipline slip."

Reading the Slip

Handling a discipline referral begins when the counselor receives the referral slip filled out by the teacher and reads it. But reading a discipline slip is not a simple, straightforward matter. One set of problems arises because the teacher's account of what happened can be very abbreviated and unclear, as in the following referrals: "open defiance," "insolence," "insubordination." The counselor then has to determine what happened in the classroom in the face of such vague and imprecise accounts. To do so she or he must draw upon extensive local knowledge of the school, its teachers and students, and their typical classroom concerns and motives (Stebbins 1970b). This background knowledge allows the counselor to make a variety of inferences about what happened and hence what any particular referral is "really all about."

In this study, I found that counselors often used basic "demographic" information on the slip to make inferences about why the youth was sent out of class. "Time" (in relation to the beginning and ending of class periods) could be significant. Teachers were known to send disruptive or unprepared students out of the classroom at the beginning of a period in order to get rid of them for the duration of that class; youth sent out toward the end of a period are not being referred for this reason.

The identity of the student involved might also allow inferences about what happened. Some students were well known to their counselors, having been regularly referred by all or most of their teachers. For example, a counselor commented on a referral who was "walking in hallway and refused to come back in class without arguing":

> Jim Jefferson—this guy's a real con artist. He's a shrewdie ... a pretty sharp kid. He doesn't apply himself, he likes to play a bit. He knows how to play the game, he's an angler.

Some students were well known because of particular problems with a few teachers or sometimes with one particular class. Others were known not through discipline referrals, but from prior contacts for personal counseling or programming. Here the counselor may well have a more positive anticipation of the youth involved, as in the following instance of a youth referred for "throwing paper and talking loud in the room":

> Nicole Miller, a very good student. This was near the end of the day; it occurred during seventh period. It was the first time I've seen Nicole all year.... The teacher was upset when she wrote this note.... But this wasn't of a serious nature, this particular referral. A very good gal, Nicole.

Similarly, counselors regularly drew upon background knowledge of the classroom discipline procedures and competence of the referring teacher to infer "what was going on." Teachers known to have "good classroom control" and to be conscientious in handling their own discipline problems within the classroom tended to have their discipline referrals viewed favorably and taken seriously. In contrast, counselors assumed that teachers who were ineffective in maintaining classroom order would often use the discipline referral as the quick and easy solution to classroom troubles. Slips from such teachers tended to be regarded with considerable skepticism and even resentment by discipline staff.

Of course, there was a great deal of latitude in assessments of teacher competence, and a variety of extenuating circumstances were recognized. New or inexperienced teachers, for example, were expected to have problems learning how to maintain classroom order and when to turn to counselors for help. In one instance, a counselor commented on a referral slip:

Miss Nielson? Well, she's a first-year teacher. I think she's a good teacher, in my eyes. John is not a problem.... The teacher right here didn't examine the circumstances.

Counselors were well aware that particular classes and students could try any teacher, such that no loss of reputation need occur with frequent referrals. A rash of pink slips from one teacher during a given class period or school day could indicate some immediate problem or just a particularly trying day. While these sorts of inferences might weaken initial presumptions of serious classroom troubles, the teacher's reputation would nevertheless be preserved when the counselor realized that these referrals were an exception to normal practices.

Counselors might also draw inferences from the particular class involved. "Mrs. X's fifth period class" might be known to be particularly unruly, setting up an expectation that referrals would commonly be made from this class. Referrals from "good classes" would raise more question that something unusual was going on.

Questioning the Student

After reading the slip, the counselor generally asks the student directly about what happened in the classroom. Since the accusing party—the teacher—is not present, the student would seem to be in a position to assert and defend his or her "side" or version of what happened. But in fact, counselors in this study carried out this questioning in ways that preserved and honored the teacher's written version of what happened, no matter how vague and imprecise. Consider, for example, the following referral from Mrs. Allen's seventh grade classroom at Tijera. Student James Erikson came in with a slip that read:

> "Constant disturbance yesterday and today. Recommend swats; wasting time, hardly ever uses his class time wisely; distracts other students, making funny faces, etc."
>
> The counselor, after commenting that swats "seem to be quite effective for you," asked "So how did you happen to get sent in?"

> JAMES: I was sittin' there, everybody's talking, a lot of kids are talking. She said, "OK five minutes [detention] after school." So a bunch of us that weren't talking were going to have to stay after school.... So I wrote up on the board, "shut up," you know, in class. She didn't do anything, you know. And then Laura Phillips, she says, "James, quit making faces." Then Miss Allen said, "Alright, James, down the office you go." ... I didn't bother anybody.

> COUNSELOR: Well, that's the teacher's judgment.

JAMES: Yesterday, but not today, I didn't do anything.

COUNSELOR: Well, no, I don't think Mrs. Allen lies. And she says that you're a constant disturbance yesterday and today. That means, all the time.

Here the counselor drew out the student's version of what happened, a version in which he is completely innocent of wrongdoing. But the counselor countered this version by insisting that: (1) the teacher was telling the truth; (2) in her judgment he had bothered others; while (3) linking "yesterday's disturbance" (to which the youth admitted) to "today's."

In general when a student challenged the accuracy or fairness of the teacher's decision to refer, the counselor responded by reasserting the validity of the teacher's version. Counselors, for example, did not accept the argument that because some initial remedy was unfairly meted out, the subsequent remedial process seeking to reinforce and impose that initial sanction should be discounted and ignored. Thus a student sent in for cutting a teacher-assigned detention was not allowed to raise as a defense the unfairness of the teacher's initial reasons for assigning the detention.

Inquiries into Normal Classroom Remedies

Looking at the written content of discipline referrals, it is noteworthy that teachers emphasized that they had persistently tried to remedy the problem within the classroom, but had ultimately failed. Characteristically, discipline slips do not simply list the facts of the present offense. Rather, they locate the present offense in relation to prior efforts to control or remedy the trouble as reflected in the following mundane referrals:

"3rd time not dressed for PE." (Disp: "will serve deten. c coun.")

"Talked, was given detention, still talked." (Disp: "detention w/counselor")

Through such write-ups the present incident is made to appear not as a single, isolated incident, but as one item in a recurring series of such incidents. And indeed, teachers describe many classroom troubles by reference to prior actions that he or she has taken with respect to the student involved (Emerson 1981). In this sense the remedial past of classroom troubles—what has been done, with what consequences in the past—provides a key feature of discipline referrals for both teacher and counselor.[7]

In these terms, the counselor viewed a referral as "minor" in coming to see it as involving a problem that the teacher could and should have handled within the classroom. Counselors discounted such referrals, as reflected in this seventh grade counselor's complaints about a referral for "goofing around":

But I mean, just for a kid—to say "goofing around"—what the hell?... Just how, goofing around? Because he pointed to the wall? Because something was written about him and he pointed to it? Does this constitute goofing off? And why can't you just tell him, "Okay, we'll erase this. Now knock it off, I don't want to see any more about this."[8] Isn't that enough? So you send a kid down here, he's a seventh grader, and you've got "talk, talk, talk, talk, talk." What the hell seventh grader doesn't talk, talk, talk? Can't a teacher handle this problem?

Counselors, however, viewed as "serious referrals," instances in which there had been a consistent effort on the part of the teacher to correct what would ordinarily be a "minor" problem. As the same seventh grade counselor noted:

They [most teachers] have good reasons for sending them down. One of the reasons they send them down here is that they actually cut detentions—several detentions—and they're tardy three, four, five days in a row. These are reasons for action by the dean.[9]

Teachers, of course, routinely anticipated this evaluation criterion and described "what happened" in ways that invoked and sometimes highlighted their prior remedial efforts. Consider the routine slips noted earlier: "3rd time not dressed for PE" emphasizes the recurrence of the misconduct; it can be assumed that with each prior occurrence of the infraction the teacher made some appropriate remedial response. Thus, the current incident indexes and reveals the failure of normal classroom remedies; it is exactly this inference that establishes the seriousness of the current trouble. The second referral, "talked, was given detention, still talked," explicitly documents the sequence of troubles and remedies, the failure of a major classroom sanction (detention), showing the need for action by the counselor. In both cases the teacher provided for the warrant and appropriateness of the referral by making available to the counselor a similar sort of remedial past, one marked by the failure of routine or normal classroom controls.

In other instances teachers may provide very extensive histories of classroom troubles, not only laying out the sequence of prior remedial efforts and their failure, but also explicitly pressuring the counselor to undertake a particularly serious response. For example:

(Seventh grade girl) "Cut detention 2/24 assigned last week for eating potato chips in class. She stated loudly she would not come and did not. Potato chip crumbs and salt were all over her face, so denial is false. The disrespect and rude public refusal must be dealt with. Obviously detention is no solution. She has repeated loudly 'I ain't comin'' whenever mention is made. It can no longer be ignored. Her name has been on board since assigned last week."

In cases where counselors cannot determine from the slip whether normal classroom remedies have been tried and have not worked, they may check directly with the teacher. This is particularly likely where the teacher has a good reputation in discipline matters. For example, a counselor received a slip on a boy, which simply noted: "Does not want to work;

demands too much attention." This complaint was vague and seemed to identify a problem that was the teacher's distinct responsibility. Yet on checking with the teacher, the counselor was able to fill in a persistent series of attempts to deal with the trouble:

> This one yesterday, I went to the teacher and talked to her. She explained what the situation was. It was a continuing thing. He started beginning of the period one thing and then he went to something else. She took it up three or four times. This is why it demands too much attention. I just don't have that kind of time, so I told her I would hold Donald out of class for the rest of the week.

In this way, an incident that appeared minor (and the responsibility of the teacher to handle) became an appropriate discipline matter, meriting serious response once the history of persistent, conscientious remedial efforts by the teacher had been established.

The remedial past of a classroom problem can not only establish the appropriateness of the referral in the ways discussed, but can also provide the point of departure for asserting the adequacy of the counselor's disposition as "backing." That is, real backing requires that the counselor take some action that is more serious than the unsuccessful remedy attempted by the referring teacher. Thus, if the teacher determines that the counselor is doing no more than she or he did in the classroom and feels that something more serious is needed to manage the problem, the counselor's disposition may be criticized as weak or inadequate backing. For example:

> The vice-principal for curriculum came into the office of the vice-principal for student affairs, complaining heatedly: "Here's a discipline problem for you!" An eighth grade teacher had just been in to see him about McDonald, one of the two counselors for the eighth grade. The teacher had given a boy two detentions which not only had he not served, but also for which he had not reported to the counselor with the pink slips. When the counselor had finally been told about the situation by the teacher and had seen the youth, the counselor wrote back to the teacher that the boy would serve the detentions and do some written exercises.
>
> Once he grasped the situation, the student affairs vice-principal responded: "You mean there has been no parent contact? It's clear insubordination! The parents should be called, the youth given a 'sanitary suspension' [unofficially suspended; effectively, not allowed in school] until a conference with the parents can be set up." The academic vice-principal insisted that the counselor be talked to about his lack of action here, and indicated that he was too angry with McDonald to do it himself; student affairs vice-principal agreed to go do it. The academic vice-principal continued to rail angrily against the counselor, saying at one point: "That McDonald! He's sitting on his ass! He didn't do a thing. You call that counseling? Ruth [the teacher] said she didn't get any backing! And she's right!"

Here the counselor had treated the problem as a failure to attend assigned detentions and then informed the teacher that the youth would indeed serve the detentions. He assigned only written exercises as additional punishment (beyond what the teacher had already ordered). But the teacher and both vice-principals saw the youth's behavior—twice failing to report to the counselor with discipline slips—not as the minor peccadillo implied by this trivial punishment (written exercises were regarded as the most minor of sanctions, having less impact even than a detention and rarely used by counselors), but as a major offense, "clear insubordination," requiring the use of major remedies (informal suspension and face-to-face contact with parents). In not responding to the infraction with the severity it deserved (and that the teacher requested), the counselor was criticized for "sitting on his ass" and not "backing the teacher" by undertaking actions that a competent counselor would know are necessary to support the teacher's efforts to deal with student misconduct in the classroom.

Displaying and Elaborating Dispositions

Generally speaking, counselor sensitivity to specific teacher pressures for backing was apparent in the care taken to display to the teacher that something had been done to meet the problem. Counselors emphasized the need to indicate on the "return" part of the discipline slip that some specific action had been taken, vis-à-vis the student. Counselors were very reluctant, for example, to simply write "warned" or "counseled" in communicating their remedial action to the complaining teacher. They preferred to identify some routine action that had been taken, even if it was minimal. For example, while counselors rarely returned students on discipline referrals to the classroom they had been sent out of during that same class period, the following action might be their response: (Eighth grade boy) "Class nuisance; detention Monday too!" Disposition: "Held in office." Or, where in fact nothing other than "counseling" had taken place, the counselor might indicate to the teacher that some explicit action would be taken the next time the trouble occurred with that student. For example, one referral where the teacher explicitly asked for a sanction beyond detention included the following disposition: "one-hour detention with counselor; next referral means two-day suspension."

Even in clear-cut "minor" referrals, counselors were very reluctant to respond in ways that did not provide some support or "backing" to the teacher, however minimal this might be. Thus, in most cases counselors, despite strong feelings about the inappropriateness of such referrals, did keep youths, who had been referred for things such as having no book or pencil, out of class for the rest of the period.

In some instances, however, counselors would send a youth back to class as an explicit message to the teacher not to make such referrals in the future:

Carlos, a Chicano boy frequently in the counselors' office, came into the office early in third period with a discipline slip stating that he had no pencil and had been disturbing the class. Carlos said he had no pencil and had been told to leave. Counselor: "You didn't make any fuss about leaving?" Carlos denied that he had. Then she asked him: "Can you go back without disturbing the class?" Carlos made no comment, but the counselor sent him back to the class for the rest of the period. After the boy had left, the counselor explained to me that it was unusual to send a kid back to class like that. But this teacher sent anyone without a book or pencil to the counselor. "I think he can handle that pencil business as well as I can." But generally, "This is a cardinal rule: You don't send a kid back when he comes in with a pink slip."

Pressure to back the teacher also led counselors to try to expand the range and variety of available sanctions. Counselors frequently complained of a lack of appropriate sanctions or remedies for classroom troubles. In many cases counselors would use the threat of informing parents about a student's conduct and classroom problems. As one counselor commented:

I'll also inform the student, "This is how you're doing, and this is what your mother will be told." So, with this in mind, the student knows that the pressure is on, he or she is being checked, not only by me but as well by the parent, and ... I expect the parent to put more pressure on them.

If, on the face of things, the infraction was not serious enough to warrant suspension and initial remedies such as "detention" or "parental conference" proved ineffective, the counselor was often at a loss as to what to do and hence was also at a loss to convincingly back the teacher's discipline efforts. Intermediate remedies might be needed and sought out or invented. For example, this type of pressure led to an increased use of corporal punishment ("swats"). There was a strong concern with backing teachers as reflected in the following remarks by a vice-principal:

No one likes to swat kids, and it occurs very infrequently, but they had found it useful to give kids who misbehaved a spanking on the rear. "The teacher feels something's been done. The kid knows something's been done. And the parents are usually behind us.... It gives us something else to use—we don't have to suspend them for the first little thing."

Conclusion

Processing discipline referrals is a form of secondary or backup social control. Counselors rarely act as primary social control agents, directly controlling activities in a specific setting; rather, they receive problem cases referred from the key site for such primary control—the classroom. Their typical problems then involve understanding and responding to referrals arising in another setting—the classroom. In so focusing on counselors' discipline work, this paper is concerned with the dynamics of classroom control as "once removed," that is, as classroom control decisions are presented and formulated by those involved (teachers and students) to counselors.

NOTES

1. The Russell Sage Foundation and the Center for the Study of Law and Society at the University of California, Berkeley, supported the research.

2. An alternative way of organizing discipline is to have a dean or vice principal who handles all discipline referrals, freeing counselors of this responsibility.

3. In addition, at Vincente a head counselor closely supervised the school behavior of a small group (25–30) of the "more serious discipline problems"; discipline referrals on any of these students were handled by this counselor irrespective of grade level.

4. The following table shows the frequencies of referral "causes" over a one week period at Vincente Junior High. During this period, teachers made 276 referrals, listing a total of 338 "causes" or "reasons."

"Cause"	Number	Percent
Late to class	44	13
Disturbing class	68	20
No material for class, (book, paper, etc.)	27	8
Chewing gum, eating in class	10	3
Not doing class assignment	26	8
Foul language	18	5
Hitting or fighting	25	8
Cutting detention	42	12
Talking back to teacher (refusing to obey)	43	13
Misc. (smoking, throwing things)	35	10
Total:	338	100%

5. Counselors had other control duties such as supervising the cafeteria during lunch periods. And they received discipline referrals from sources other than classroom teachers; for example, from the student supervisors, when they had apprehended students' misbehaving during lunch or recess. But processing classroom discipline referrals comprised the bulk of a counselor's daily control activities.

Non-classroom discipline referrals were not only less frequent, but also raised different control issues. For example, while a classroom was under the direct control of one teacher, non-classroom spaces—corridors, toilets, and yards/playgrounds—were patrolled by a variety of staff (e.g., deans, yard supervisors, and teachers) with more diffuse responsibility. Furthermore, non-classroom referrals often took a different procedural form: adult staff would typically bring apprehended youth to the counselor in person, that is, *without a written referral*.

6. These guidelines also specified that many "major offenses" were to be referred to counselors only after the teacher had taken prescribed steps to handle the problem.

7. In this sense most classroom troubles that teachers refer to counselors implicitly raise ques-

tions about the adequacy of the formers' past remedial actions; thus, discipline referrals often have implications for the referring agents' routine classroom control procedures.

8. The counselor had sought out and asked the referring teacher exactly what had happened (what did he mean by "goofing around"?) The teacher reported that the youth had been drawing attention to some dirty word written on the blackboard, thereby disrupting class. The counselor shows the trivial nature of the referral by identifying an easily available, but unused remedy to this problem (erase it), thereby emphasizing how the trouble could have been adequately remedied within the classroom.

9. Indeed, Vincente's discipline referral guidelines provided that with tardies "teacher handles through 4th tardy, then refers to counselor"; i.e., only with a pattern of recurring behavior do tardies become "serious." This requirement sought to eliminate teacher use of the discipline referral as the routine response to any and all incidents of coming into class late, making the teacher deal with the problem until it could be shown to be getting out of hand.

Studying Students Studying: Perspectives, Identities, and Activities

Daniel Albas and Cheryl Albas

In his statement on "generic social processes" Prus (in this volume) presents what he regards as the most serious requirements facing ethnography at the present time if it is to flourish and produce. Specifically, there is a need for sharper conceptualization and the use of concepts consistently, cumulatively, and in a codified fashion. He also argues that substantive studies in diverse situations should continue to be carried on with resolute effort to expose parallel processes in the different settings and so establish grounded theory as bridges between these settings. Finally, he offers a useful schema in which what he regards as the most important concepts in the field are set out in a systematic fashion to guide researchers and assure the maximum comprehensiveness of their efforts as they describe and analyze any particular generic social process. To avoid unnecessary repetition, only that part of Prus's schema which shapes our study will be set out.

Specifically, Prus lists as the dimensions of group life: the perspectival, the reflective, the negotiational, the relational, and the processual. He stresses that the processual is the organizing dimension of all the four preceding dimensions. For defining the essence of any activity he lists five processes:

(1) acquiring perspectives, (2) achieving identity, (3) being involved, (4) doing activity, and (5) experiencing relationships.

The present article locates the activity of studying in the student subculture and focuses on preparation for examinations. An attempt is made to paint in the meanings with which students act toward studying. We show how, through reflectivity, they come to regard themselves as *Aces* (superior students), or *Bombers* (less than average students), or *Moderates* (average students), and accordingly estimate their chances of success or failure. In addition we also show how student perspectives and identities affect the ways in which they actually carry out their studying and their relationships to other students (those they perceive as better than, equal to, or worse than themselves).

The data for this paper are drawn from observations, interviews with, and logs obtained from, students in our classes over the last twenty years. The excerpts quoted are types that occur with sufficient frequency to be regarded as validly representative of student experiences.

Before discussing the ways students approach studying, it is important to remember where these perspectives come from: There exists in the university before any contemporary generation of students gets there, a variety of "worlds," or subsocieties, each with its characteristic *geist* (perspective), argot, and organizational principles. Depending upon their academic abilities and social contacts, students become located in one of these worlds and become socialized by, and imbued with, the norms of that particular subsociety (Fine and Kleinman 1979). For our purposes, student perspectives can be subsumed by two extreme types. First, there is the scholar and performer type. Students commonly refer to these people as "Aces," "Keeners," "Sucks," and "Browners." At the other end are low performers, often designated as "Dumb Dumbs."

Although students tend to belong to one or the other of these camps, they are nevertheless constantly being pulled in different directions by the ideologies of the other subcultures and are thus submitted to considerable ambivalence. For example, a Bomber in the fun-oriented culture may admire the academic success of an Ace and so be momentarily tempted to study more, while at the same time finding it necessary to uphold the "fun" norm (you're only young once and you have to enjoy life). Conversely, an Ace who has invested much effort in studying may be tempted to ease up a bit, especially in response to blandishments like, "You owe it to your friends." However, at the same time, most Aces have deeply internalized the dictum that "procrastination is pain postponed." Students between these two extremes (Moderates) are pulled both ways and may at different times occupy the widest range on the scale all the way from Aces to Bombers. In addition these strains set up conflicts of loyalty. For all camps, though not on the basis of the same criteria, there are strong aspirations to be cool and a vigorous striving to defend identity and maintain respectability.

Perspectives

Prus defines perspectives as "the varying meanings with which people act toward phenomena" (in this case, students towards studying). He also states that perspectives are "frameworks or viewpoints for making sense of the world." In these terms, our student protocols reveal that students approach study activity in six somewhat different ways.

Studying as a Necessary Evil

For the vast majority of students, studying is viewed as a "necessary evil"—a comparatively short period of pain necessary for long-term gain realizable first in good grades and eventually in well-paying jobs.

> Just the thought of studying is dreadful. It takes everything I have to actually get to my desk and open my books.... Anything seems more welcoming than hitting the books. I know that it is a necessity, but it's not one that I enjoy.

> Exams and studying are things one must tolerate, somewhat like needles from doctors when you're critically ill.... You don't like them, but you tolerate them in order to get well. In my case I tolerate studying now so that I can get a decent well-paying job in the future.

Studying as a Parent-Teacher Pacifier

Also working within an instrumental perspective some students regard studying as a means of pacifying or pleasing parents and teachers:

> I study mostly to get my parents off my back.

> I find it truly hard to study, but try as best I can to please my parents. My dad, who is a dentist, grew up in a very poor family.... Saying to my father, "I can't [study]" is unheard of.... How can't I, with all my advantages, when he could, when he had none at all.

Studying as a Gift of Love

Sometimes students regard studying as a love gift to their parents in return for their caring:

> My mom has done so much for me. Doing my best in school is what pleases her most. Studying and bringing home good grades are my way of expressing my love and gratitude to her.

> Another kind of love gift is the feeling of some type of a camaraderie of scholarship with the professor. These students recognize that study is a journey in the exploration of knowledge and they regard the teacher as a

leader and comrade along the way. They are spurred to study by the fear that if they don't do well, they will disappoint the teacher.

> The profs I like most make me feel like they and I are exploring a field of knowledge together. If for one reason or another I haven't been able to give their courses my best shot, I feel I let them down.

Studying as an Aesthetic Experience

> I view exams as I view athletic events. Studying is like practicing for the event.... Your competitive results would be dismal if you started to practice only a few days before a sailing competition; it's the same in the case of studying for exams.

> Exams seldom test one's deep understanding of a subject. They measure one's ability to memorize. Since memorization comes easily to me, I find it quite easy to get A's. However, I'm no longer comfortable just getting A's I now spend many extra hours studying for the satisfaction of feeling that I really understand the material.

Studying as an Anti-Professor Weapon

Some perspectives are difficult to classify as either expressive or instrumental because they have elements of both. For example, a few students express their view of studying as an anti-professor weapon. They claim that the effort required to study and do well in exams is somewhat akin to a game or challenge, a way of wreaking vengeance on a long-term tormentor:

> When professors announce the date of an upcoming exam I feel an instant hatred toward them. I make them into a type of enemy that I must beat or they will have the joy of conquering me.

> As exams approach, I feel increasingly antagonistic toward my teachers. Studying becomes a means of accumulating weapons for the battle [exam].

Studying as Status Advancement

Some students view study entirely as a means of status advancement:

> It's gratifying to be at the top of my classes and I study primarily for this satisfaction.

> One of the main reasons I study so hard is to impress my husband. I like to show him that the great academic investment we have made in my coming back to school has really paid off for us.

I positively thrive at exam time because my rewards for all the studying I've done are finally at hand.

A few students were unable to verbalize any sense of meaning in study and preparation for exams. Such students were universally those who, to date, had made no firm career decision. This is a clear demonstration of the symbolic interactionist dictum that the way we act toward something is a function of its perceived utility to us.

In sum, two major facets of meaning emerged from our university student protocols. First, the effect of an all-pervading institutional ethos, called by Becker, Geer, Reisman, and Weiss (1968) "the G.P.A. [Grade Point Average] perspective," clearly influences most students. It consists of the pressure to get good grades in university and subsequently a good, well-paying job. Second, for a minority of students, expressive perspectives of a variety of shades from love gift to anti-professor weapon were noted. The relationship of perspective to subculture is clearly not simply that students who belong to the "scholarship and performance" subculture will have "aesthetic perspectives" and those from the "fun-people" subculture will have the necessary evil perspective.

Accomplishing the Study Activity

As Prus states, all activities acquire meaning and purpose from the perspectives from which they are envisioned and from the identities of the actors. Perhaps the most graphic way of depicting the drama of exam preparation is to examine the contrast between polar opposite types of students, namely, the diligently planning, highly achieving "Aces" and the procrastinating, low achieving "Bombers." Bearing in mind that there are shades of both Bombers and Aces in the middle, an attempt will also be made to sketch a typical accomplishment pattern for the "Moderates."

The accomplishment of the study activity typically comes to a climax in a period of about two weeks before the examination period. A new atmosphere seems to emerge on campus. It manifests itself in pressure for silence in study areas, which become increasingly difficult to find; the formation of study groups; and the seeking out by students of past examination questions. There is an alteration in what Schutz (1962, 1964) calls the "zone of relevance." In our terms the zone of relevance is a time span within which the immediacy of the exam breaks with varying degrees of intensity into the awareness of students. In this context the nearer to exam time, the more sensitive students become to exam-related stimuli and the more intensely they concentrate on study. Furthermore, in contrast to high school settings where there is considerable monitoring and regimenting of students into the study mode, university settings are much "looser"—students are entirely on their own and must rely on their own self-discipline to apply themselves or experience drift—according to their category (Ace or Bomber).

Aces

Keeping "Noses to the Grindstone"

These diligent students are characterized by an awareness of the necessity to keep their "noses to the grindstone." This work discipline is sometimes enhanced by the formation of study groups and by the presence and awareness of others like themselves. They studiously avoid the distractions of itinerant Bombers who ask irrelevant questions and "waste their time."

> As exams approach, those who have not yet begun their preparations always seem to want to start up conversations. Though it might sound impolite I try to discourage them by answering in monosyllables. I hardly look up from my work. It eventually gets through to them that studying is the most important thing to me at that time. If they remark on my less than complete attention to them, I tell them laughingly that after the exam I will talk to them for hours.

Aces tend to view any frivolity or present pleasure as resulting inevitably in future pain. Any guilt they might feel for neglecting their non-academic associates diminishes as their work effort increases. For example, one student states:

> At the beginning of the year I felt guilty if I refused to go out with my friends and instead stayed home to study—it was what I wanted to do for myself. At exam time I would feel even more guilty if I did go out with them.

> During the midterm break my mother said to me "Ease off a little, Lisa." I had to remind her that I was competing with the best for a spot in law school and that the competition was tougher than she could imagine. It left me little room for "easing off."

In another case three very able women students formed a study group. One discussion led to the topic of children. One woman asked the second if she had children. They started to talk about childrearing. At this point the third woman in the group went to the chalkboard, wrote down a formula, and jokingly tapped the board with her piece of chalk: "We got the message ... that was enough chit chat and it was time to get back down to statistics." The pursuit of co-operation in the accomplishment of activity is enhanced to the degree that all people are committed to the same basic goal-developing competence in the subject they are to be tested on. Under such conditions, participants who deviate can be more easily persuaded to keep their "noses to the grindstone." In one study group of premedical students the sense of friendly rivalry was so keen that "even if someone feels he needs a break or has to go to the washroom he'll probably just hang in there to avoid falling behind."

Theoretically, this·is what Blumer (1969b, 8) would lead us to expect because interaction with others produces a result greater than the sum of the individuals involved. This catalytic effect of the group on individual effort was demonstrated experimentally by Triplett (1897). Professional cyclists were tested first against the clock and then against a group of competitors. Performance in the second case was significantly better than in the first.

A Perfectionist Complex

Aces consciously view themselves as overachievers. They are never satisfied with grades below the A level and they blame any faltering in the pursuit of this goal squarely on themselves, not on the stars or any other extraneous source.

> If I get less than a perfect mark I want to see where I went wrong so that I can take it into account for next time.

> Some people can never be satisfied with their best efforts. I am one of those. If I get 95 percent I blame myself for not getting 100 percent.

Careful Scheduling

Study schedules are a function of course difficulty. Aces are predominantly planners and schedulers. They plan systematically and rationally so that the more difficult the course is perceived to be, the earlier the studying begins.

> I don't believe in leaving study until the last minute and then having to cram. I always try to plan things so I can fit in my family and my lifestyle and still have time to prepare thoroughly for every exam.

> I love sociology but I seem to have difficulty with courses in English. Consequently I start studying earliest for English and I have to put my greatest effort into it.

> At one time I scheduled my study with a couple of breaks between each part. I started to realize how susceptible I was to socializing and how much time I wasted. As a consequence, I rescheduled my studying into huge continuous blocks and only after that took a short break.

These last illustrations support Blumer's (1969b, 12–15) point that since we have the capability to view ourselves as social objects we are able to manipulate ourselves in ways that are advantageous to us.

The Cloaks of Competence and Coolness

The Cloak of Competence

A salient, though not universal, characteristic of this group is to flaunt their brilliance by deliberate, overt show:

> If I'm carrying a number of books, I arrange them so that the one with the most impressive title is on the outside. Anyone I encounter on the bus or

wherever will notice the book and type me as someone brilliant who knows what is between those covers.

In what was widely known to be a difficult math course, my friends and I decided to dramatize our superior abilities. We went to the final exam carrying only our ballpoint pens [no pencils or erasers] thus indicating to others that we were so confident that we were unlikely to make any mistakes that might need to be corrected. We were also the first ones to finish the exam and to leave the room. The impression we gave was that the exam offered us little challenge.

Goffman (1959, 30) labels such tactics "dramatic realization." It occurs when individuals infuse their "activity with signs which dramatically highlight and portray confirmatory facts [brilliance] that might otherwise remain unapparent or obscure."

Some Aces do not feel quite up to the standards of their group. Nevertheless they feel it necessary to give the impression that they are every bit as sharp as their peers and so they assume for themselves a cloak of competence:

> The students I associate with are able to read the original works of authors, pick out the major relevant analytical points and present them competently in seminars and in essays. I am unable to do so and I don't want to make my shortcomings apparent to them. I must compensate by relying on secondary sources and even textbooks. However, I present the information as if I took it from the original source.

In sum, there are Aces who are very bright students and who flaunt their abilities and some who are not so bright and have to fake it. Occasionally, even the brightest students must resort to faking it. Student physicians in an innovative medical program at McMaster University in Hamilton, Ontario, are required to interact immediately with patients. There is no long period of anticipatory socialization. In addition, they are constantly appraised and monitored by both their classmates and professors. Faced with meeting such exaggerated expectations, they cope by "behaving as if they are able to accomplish these tasks ... by enveloping themselves in a cloak of competence" (Haas and Shaffir 1987, 207, 222). In effect, they behave as if they are more competent than they in fact are.

The Cloak of Coolness
The characteristic of coolness is highly valued by almost all students. Its essential ingredient is the ability to get good grades with apparently minimum effort. Accordingly, Aces famed for their good grades, quite often study behind closed doors and attempt to give the impression that their accomplishments are 100 percent inspiration and 0 percent perspiration:

> I'm usually able to get the same grades as other A students with less effort than they must expend. The rewards I get from being considered gifted sometimes

lead me to give the impression that I study less than I actually do. At school I am cool. I socialize as much as I can and declare that I do not need to study but when I go home I work my butt off.

Bushnell (1962, 507) found similar tactics used by Vassar students who "have to work quite hard to maintain an impressive grade-point ratio." They devote "considerable effort to presenting the appearance of competence and freedom from academic harassment." Such students attempt to appear more cool than they actually are and, in so doing, they adopt a cloak of coolness.

In sum, coolness and good grades are something admired by everyone. Having to "work your butt off" is the antithesis of coolness, but it might be necessary to get good grades. The ability to achieve both goals (respectability) depends upon audience segregation (Goffman 1959, 49). In turn success at segregating audiences depends upon the ability to "insulate themselves from observability ... and ... the determination of who can hide from whom may be as essential to the workings of a social system as the determination of who has power over whom" (Coser 1961, 39).

Bombers

As stated earlier Bombers are students who procrastinate about studying and even when they do begin, they invest minuscule effort as compared to Aces. A number of behavior patterns characterize Bombers.

Fritters

Perhaps the most typical characteristic of this category of student is their propensity to use fritters as rationalizations for avoiding study. As Bernstein (1976, 375) indicates, "when there is work to be done, students fritter away time." They make use of wise nostrums, self-lulling mantras, and numerous convenient distractions, all of which are directed toward delaying serious study until the very last moment when guilt and fright force them into it. For example:

> The last day of lectures is when the professor ties everything together and says the most important things. It's a waste of time to start studying before then.

> All this studying gives me "bookbrain" [student term for information overload]. If I don't take a break I'll lose my mind.

> The exam is so far down the road that anything I study now I'll just forget by then. Why suffer twice?

> When I start to study, I'm particularly sensitive to the smallest speck of dust on my desk. When I dust that off, it seems necessary to get the whole room in order before I can settle down to study.

> I know that by exam time I will get an incredible burst of intellectual energy, it's worth waiting for.

> I find that I have to start studying either on the hour or at half past it. Starting at any time in-between disorients me.

These rationalizations are typical of the vocabulary of motives that exist in every culture (in this case student culture). They are invoked by people facing problems who must choose one course of action over another and then justify their selections (Mills 1981).

The Antenna Effect

When procrastinating Bombers do decide to get down to work, the decision is made largely as a result of cues, picked up from peers, that everyone is getting serious about studying. Asch (1958) in a group experiment, demonstrates that subjects will yield to cues—even ones provided by stooges—so improbable that they yield even against their better sense.

> When I notice that just about everyone is studying, I begin to feel the effects of the general work attitude.... A kind of panic sets in and it makes me start to study.

Even then, further "dilly-dallying" occurs in the form of long telephone calls to friends to verify that it is indeed "D-day." The conversations almost invariably stray into deviations about non-academic matters.

> The final thing I do before settling down to study is phone my friends who should also be studying. If they're not studying, I feel I don't have to either. The fact that they may be having fun makes me feel even sorrier for myself. When we do the practice questions at the end of the chapter, we frequently encounter uncertainties about the answers. We phone around to our friends to see how they would answer the question. Of course, for politeness sake, it's necessary to chat for a while. If I make more than one call and the answers disagree with each other, I phone back the first person to let him know and we chat a little more. This sometimes happens for every question in the exercise. It makes studying more bearable.

This search for consensus on answers is an example of Sherif's (1936) findings as to how group norms are constructed. Almost all instructors are familiar with the phenomenon of some classes where average grades are unusually high and others where they are unusually low. These clusterings around extreme ends of the grade distribution probably reflect some kind of student consensus as to how much effort needs to be expended for that particular class and, more particularly, reflects the results of group consensus as described above. This search for consensus is, in many ways, parallel to that of teenagers who spend much time and effort consulting with their friends as to what they should wear to a particular party or for a special date.

High Intensity Consumption after Long-Term Delay

There comes a time when Bombers can no longer delay study because the exam is about to occur. At this point they display an intensity of activity that may exceed even that of the Aces. However, it tends to be rather random, impulsive, and even non-rational, relative to its objective. For example, some Bombers say they engage in weight lifting or jogging ("to clear the mind"), while others develop a frantic need to clean house. For yet other Bombers, the imminence of the exam produces the desired result—they open their books with renewed energy, find that they enjoy studying the material and only wish they had a few more days to engage in this newly discovered pleasure! The vast majority of Bombers though will settle for a little "sheer and mere memorization."

The following illustrations represent a composite of quotations from students to demonstrate this point:

> On the Friday evening that lectures ended I realized that exams started on the following Monday and I had yet to crack a book. "Failure" began flashing in my mind. I broke into a cold sweat.

> I suddenly noticed a new keenness, even among my buddies. My textbooks seemed to get bigger and the titles more strident. They even seemed to be looking at me in an accusing way.

> I tried to start studying but nothing made any sense so I went for a walk. When I came back, I tried again to study.... Still no use.... I felt like crying.... I decided to go to sleep and start fresh the next day. Saturday morning I ate a prolonged brunch in order to fortify myself for studying.... When I finally opened my books, I was still in the dark about everything.... I opened the curtains to let in some sunlight. I noticed dust and disorder everywhere. I went into a frenzy of dusting and cleaning and after that I tried to go back to studying.... This time I started to understand one thing and then another.... It kept me motivated. I became so involved that I no longer felt the need to eat or sleep. I began to feel myself capable of achieving even a B in the test. As the day progressed, reality dawned and I realized a C was more likely and a D most realistic.

A few students are so overwhelmed by the immensity of the looming task that they descend into depression. However, most of the procrastinators try to hang in and at this point would be happy to settle for a passing grade. Roy (1952) notes the parallel case of industrial workers. When faced by the challenge of having to perform at an exceptionally high level to make more money in a piece rate system, they chose instead to settle for an hourly rate and a lower income, and consequently avoided the extra effort.

Cloak of Competence

Though it might seem pretentious and unexpected, many Bombers also wear the cloak of competence. In their case it is not to vaunt any competence, but very definitely to hide considerable incompetence. The low grades they do receive probably indicate even more knowledge than they actually possess because the favorite study technique of last minute high-pressure cramming is conducive to short term memory only. That is, once the exam is finished, the knowledge is quickly forgotten because it has not been internalized.

> To me, exams are a lot like defecating. First I gorge myself on food [last minute cramming] and then I go to a room set aside for voiding [room in which the exam is written]. Once I get rid of the stuff [knowledge] I don't think about it any more. In fact, I can't think about it because I never remember a word of it after I get out of the exam room. It has all been flushed away.

This type of situation is similar in many ways to the one described by Edgerton (1967) in his study of institutional retardates. After they were released back into the community, they attempted to hide their disabilities and the fact that they had been institutionalized by enveloping themselves in what he termed "a cloak of competence."

Moderates

As stated earlier this category encompasses by far the largest number of students who reflect the widest variation in abilities, motivation, performance, and lifestyles. These students have multiple roles to enact and consequently are the group most likely to experience problems of role competition. As a result of these complexities, it is very difficult to describe the "typical" Moderate because they range all the way from low Aces to superior Bombers. However, some general characteristics do apply.

An Emphasis on Balance

Moderates are characterized by a non-calculated effort to achieve a sense of balance in their lives.

> I devote less time to study than I might, but I still manage to obtain approximately a C+ average. This way I'm not a zero academically and I also gain a lot of respect and popularity by doing well on the track team. In this way I maintain a nice balance between the social, academic, and athletic aspects of my life. I'm a well-rounded person.

If you can have fun and still get half decent grades, you're in the best position to have a good university life.

I have chosen self-consciously to live a more balanced lifestyle. I take time to enjoy my friends, my family, and my personal interests. I also do a "good job" in my university courses. I am an average student and I am happy with my decision to have a balanced life.

These students represent the numerically largest group at the university and their perspective on student life is the dominant one.

An Emphasis on Avoiding Extremes in Patterns of Association

The focus here is on how Moderates choose their friends and the people with whom they associate. The following two excerpts describe why Moderates do not welcome the company of Aces.

I prefer to socialize with others who are at approximately my level. When I interact with people who get better marks than me, I look like I'm dumb and struggling. When I interact with others on my level it affirms my feeling that it is good to be average.

If a person has read ahead in the assigned readings she/he is not in the same boat as we are and we don't think it is possible for her/him to empathize with us.

The next cases describe why Moderates choose not to interact with Bombers.

It is hard to empathize with people who are too far behind in their work. We have no "common ground" to discuss.

I view students who have not kept up at all with their course work with suspicion and even contempt. Not only are they not responsible they are probably also looking for help—they're leeches!

Interestingly enough, students do not seem to have great difficulty locating themselves in the Moderate subculture as it relates to the extremes of Aces and Bombers. The following quote illustrates one of the techniques used:

Course outlines provide us with a rough estimate of where we ought to be at any given time in the assigned readings and essay assignment. We talk to others to find out where they are and we construct kind of a standard [norm]. Anyone too far ahead or too far behind "disorients" us.

The Moderates make evident how student types define themselves relative to others. They also reinforce Posner's (1976) observation that excellence can be just as stigmatizing as are defects or faults.

An Emphasis on Juggling Roles

Many Moderates, in addition to being students, are also full- or part-time employees, parents, caregivers to parents, friends, lovers, spouses, and members of a variety of organizations. This role competition makes it necessary for them to juggle multiple obligations against their student role, sometimes to its detriment.

The first quote here is from a single mother who is on welfare and has two primary school children. She is a fourth-year student in the faculty of nursing.

> I have to be both mother and dad to my two boys. I slot two to three hours every week night for study. When the work from school piles up faster than I can process it, I put the children to bed earlier than usual so I can have peace and quiet. On weekends I slot one evening for myself.... Once a "highly promising" man asked me for a date. I had to study for an exam and spend some time with my children. It presented a serious conflict.

> Many students like myself have to hold down part-time jobs to get enough money to pay for university.... To spend more time on study than on the job is easier said than done.

Other students make these comments about competing demands:

> I can't study as much as I used to before I met my girlfriend. Now thoughts and feelings about love and desire are constantly on my mind. I've called into work to say I'm sick just so I can spend more time with her.

> It's very seldom that I'm not faced with a decision about whether to spend a night out with friends or a night in with the books.

> I'm on the track team. Training is especially important just before a big competition. I'm caught between an obligation to my coach and an obligation to my professor.

In all of these instances the students indicate that they must ration not only their time, but also their energy. Because Moderates seek to live balanced lives, they lack the clearly established role-identity hierarchies (McCall and Simmons 1978) characteristic of Aces (studying always comes first) and hence must do more juggling to manage their lives.

Accounting for Identity Continuity and Discontinuity

Identity Continuity

Once students are categorized as Aces, Moderates, or Bombers the next question is to account for the continuity of their involvements. Through time, students come to identify themselves with one of these categories and, of course, identity plays an important role in structuring actions. For example, people viewing themselves as Aces who discover that their grades are slipping, typically tend to study harder, consult with the professor, and so on to bring their identity placement in line with their identities. Such an identity is further reinforced through the tendency to adopt "status advancement" and "aesthetic perspectives" on studying. On the other hand, Bombers have a weaker estimation of their academic abilities and do not have much of an academic identity to lose by a weak performance. Indeed, they usually invest considerable pride in their ability to be able to "get by": "Give me a C and let me be free" is their motto. Their identity is further reinforced by the tendency to view studying as a necessary evil. This point was made evident in the earlier discussion of past performance as self-fulfilling present.

Reputation also affects continuity of an identity. As students become known to be Aces, Moderates, or Bombers, others tend to interact with them in such a manner that identities and involvement are promoted (Lemert 1951; 1967). Aces, for example, come to be viewed as "the ones to watch for and compete with" as well as "the ones to get answers from." The selectivity of these interactions reinforces the image of the actor as an Ace. Weinstein and Deutschberger (1963) refer to such interactions as altercasting and they serve to create a self-fulfilling prophecy (Merton 1957). Similarly, a Bomber may be viewed as a "fun person," acted toward by others as such, and eventually transformed into a "party animal." Bombers who are both unable to maintain passing grades and are not accepted by other students frequently end up dropping out of university altogether.

Earlier discussion suggested that families serve as one of our most influential identity-forming groups and how they exert considerable pressure on their student members to perform. Insofar as students take these outside obligations into account in developing their lines of action, they provide another source of continuity in performance level.

Students who share similar identities and orientations tend to be attracted to one another. They find that studying is made easier if they know others like themselves are also studying. They know who to approach if they have a question and they may well become involved in study groups. These working relationships make studying more effective and serve to absorb participants into their respective subcultures. Because the ideologies of these subsocieties tend to be held in opposition to each other, interactions between members of the different subcultures will tend to be held in what Glaser and Strauss (1964) term "a pretense awareness context." That is, students probably know that members of other subsocieties are likely to view them in a less than positive light, but everyone pretends this is not the case. These interactions are frequently anxiety-arousing and require considerable skill and energy in their execution. Conversely, people tend to be attracted to others like themselves because they are able to maintain interactions within an "open awareness context." When people are aware that others share their identities and activities and view them in the same way, then they can relax and just be themselves. These conditions are conducive to the generation of rapport.

In sum, members of the same subsociety become significant reference points, defining reality for each other and thereby promoting continuity.

Identity Discontinuity

Students may also experience pressures to change their student identities. Individuals who have the work habits of one category (Aces, Moderates, or Bombers), but have not yet developed significant ties to others within it, are particularly vulnerable to change if they develop significant relations to others within it who have different perspectives on studying. Such was the case of the solitary, dedicated studier who developed a friendship with a member of the fun subculture. He came to view himself as a "thundering bore" and soon gave up studying so that he could spend more time having fun. Other factors conducive to changing student identities are the taking on of additional roles, for example, a job or a romantic relationship.

There is also a tendency for students to move from a fun to more of a work orientation as they move through their university careers. For many, the shock of receiving low or failing grades on the first set of exams encourages them to either drop out or to study at least enough to get by. As time progresses students also acquire career objectives. Given the keen competition for professional or graduate school admission, studying becomes the only alternative. As was noted earlier, identification with an anticipated status helps to provide energy necessary for the shift. It is not unusual for such students to undergo a "conversion" experience wherein they forego one lifestyle and its accompanying worldview for that of another. Conversions tend to occur most readily and most commonly among people whose present lifestyle is more compatible with the prospective one, for example, from Bomber to Moderate or Moderate to Ace (and vice versa) rather than from the extremes. Furthermore, as students age, studying becomes a more respectable activity.

Conclusion

This paper has examined the ways in which students approach, accomplish, and maintain their study practices in a university setting. While they build on the stock of knowledge required in high school, they also find themselves subjected to a potentially conflicting set of definitions which predate their presence, but characterize the university subculture. Although it varies somewhat with their academic abilities, goals, and fortuitous contacts with other students in this setting, students may find themselves encouraged either to study or not to study as they encounter varying subcultural themes in the university setting. As well, regardless of whether they become and sustain roles as Aces, Bombers, or Moderates, they also become cognizant of the significance of the cloaks of competence and coolness for their day-to-day experiences in this setting.

Although the present study has focused on student roles and may be applicable to student activities in other levels (for example, primary school, high school), the notions of subcultures, identities, and accomplishments as discussed here may have more generic implications for people's involvements in work and recreational settings, as might the cloaks of competence and coolness.

Settling Disputes: Negotiation Processes in Welfare Agencies[1]

James Holstein and Gale Miller

This paper is an analysis of aspects of the disputing process in a Work Incentive Program (WIN). The Work Incentive Program is a United States intergovernmental welfare program that provides help in finding jobs and related social services such as personal counselling and money for baby sitters to selected members of the Aid to Families with Dependent Children (AFDC) population (Miller 1991a). AFDC is intended to aid the children of poor families by providing a financial base for meeting the families' basic subsistence needs and for keeping them together. The WIN program is associated with AFDC because many AFDC clients are required to enroll and participate in WIN in order to receive benefits. Participation for most clients involves looking for a job.

The observations on which the analysis is based were made over a thirteen-month period in a WIN office in a small, industrial city in a midwestern state. They focused on staff members' routine work activities and relationships, including some interactions that occurred out of the WIN office. Detailed notes were taken of staff members' interactions in order to produce nearly verbatim reproductions of the exchanges with others. Such detail is necessary to adequately describe and analyze the interactional procedures used by staff members to organize and accomplish their professional responsibilities. The observations were augmented by informal interviews with staff members and clients about aspects of the WIN program, and their participation in it.

Staff member interviews focused on the practical meanings and procedures associated with WIN activities. They were conducted immediately prior to, or following, the activities in question. Client interviews occurred while they waited for their appointments with staff members and/or completed WIN assignments in the office such as telephoning area employers and participating in workshops. Finally, tape recordings of ninety WIN hearings were provided by the State Hearings Office, and transcribed for analysis. The tapes provided by the State Hearings Office are all of the WIN hearings occurring in the state for a twelve-month period.

The analysis focuses on how disputes emerge within routine staff-client interactions, then are managed and transformed as they are subjected to progressively more formal dispute processing mechanisms. First, we describe the various settings through which WIN disputes emerged and passed on their way to some form of resolution. Then we discuss how the diverse settings shape and transform the disputing process. In the concluding sections, we discuss some of the theoretical implications of the study, particularly how disputing in WIN and similar organizations may be analyzed as micro-political processes. The micro-politics of trouble perspective focuses on the ways in which organization members interactionally define and respond to troubles emergent in their social worlds (Emerson and Messinger 1977).

Conflict and Disputing in a Work Incentive Program

WIN is part of a trend in United States welfare policy that emphasizes the need to hold the poor accountable for their public aid by making it contingent on recipients passing "work tests" (Patterson 1981). Thus, WIN staff members' insistence that their clients look for jobs and fulfill other program requirements is an attempt to enforce a positive orientation to the work ethic (Miller 1991a). One way in which WIN staff members enforce the work ethic, display their commitment to WIN purposes, and fulfill their professional responsibilities in the program is by making complaints to and about clients whom they assess as potentially or actually unco-operative. For staff members, clients were defined as unco-operative when they intentionally failed to fulfill their WIN responsibilities. Staff members' assessments treated aspects of clients' behavior in the WIN office as signs that the clients might be trying to avoid their WIN responsibilities. As in the following exchange, staff members often described such clients as actually or possibly having "bad" attitudes:

STAFF MEMBER: He [a client] has an attitude problem.

OBSERVER: What do you mean, he seems to be co-operating, isn't he?

STAFF MEMBER: Well, yeah, but he doesn't like looking for work. I could tell that by the way he was talking. I'll have to stay on him to keep him looking. I just won't give him too much to do, cause he might get discouraged and give up, but I'll have to keep pushing him. (Miller 1985, 381)

Staff members treated their concerns and complaints about clients' cooperativeness as aspects of a disputing process that might eventually involve formal charges of misconduct against clients. According to staff members, their conflicts with clients became serious disputes when they requested conciliation meetings with clients. Conciliation meetings involved the intervention of two new parties into staff-client disagreements—another WIN staff member and a social worker associated with WIN who specialized in adjudicating staff-client disagreements. Conciliation meetings were serious matters for staff members because they sometimes used the meetings to justify terminating clients from the WIN program. Such action also resulted in a substantial reduction (sometimes elimination) of the client's AFDC support.

Staff members also used the meetings to confront clients with the seriousness of their circumstances, and encourage them to change their attitudes and behavior. As one staff member states:

A lot of these people [unco-operative clients] are like alcoholics. They have to hit bottom to see [that] they have a problem, to feel pain. Then they look at their lives and decide that they hafta make some changes. They'll put it off as long as they can, though. It's only when they don't have any choice that they look at themselves in the mirror. That's what we're doin' here, forcing them to look at their lives and make some changes. (Miller 1991a, 86)

Further disputing occurred when clients, terminated from WIN, appealed the terminations by asking for WIN hearings. The hearings were conducted by attorneys associated with the State Hearings Office, and organized as legal proceedings involving sworn testimony and the presentation of formal evidence to support the adversaries' claims. Based on the evidence presented, hearings officers rendered legally binding decisions that found in favor of one party to the disputes.

In sum, conflict and disputing in WIN involved three major and interrelated settings and contexts: *routine staff-client interactions, conciliation meetings,* and *WIN hearings.* Each setting represented an interactional "dispute domain" within which disputing issues and relationships were structured and transformed. Disputes were structured by the organization of interactants' roles and responsibilities in the settings, and the range and types of trouble definitions and remedies available to interactants in orienting to the disputes at hand. Table 1 summarizes how routine staff-client interactions, conciliation meetings, and WIN hearings may be analyzed as dispute domains.

Disputes in WIN typically emerged in routine staff-client interactions, then were "narrowed" (Mather and Yngvesson 1981) as they were reformulated and renegotiated in conciliation meetings and WIN hearings. They

TABLE 1: Disputes Settings in WIN

	Major Participants	Available Definitions	Available Remedies
Routine Interactions	Complaining staff and accused clients	Client's intentional unco-operativeness or problems beyond client's control	Client promises of future co-operation or adjustment of client's WIN assignments
Conciliation Meetings	Complaining staff, accused clients, and the conciliation team	Client's intentional unco-operativeness	Client promises of future co-operation or termination from WIN
WIN Hearings	Complaining staff, accused clients, hearings officers, and other witnesses	Client's intentional unco-operativeness or staff member's error	Finding in favor of one party over the other

were narrowed because interactants' options in conceptualizing and managing disputes were reduced as the disputes moved through the WIN disputing process. Indeed, the WIN disputing process resembled a funneling operation, whereby the wide array of disputing issues and resolutions that were considered in routine staff-client disputes were reorganized within more limited definitions of trouble and appropriate responses when they were reconsidered in conciliation meetings and WIN hearings.

Disputing in Routine Staff-Client Interactions

According to staff members, conflict was a potential aspect of virtually all their interactions with clients because many clients were primarily interested in avoiding their WIN responsibilities. They stated that one way in which clients tried to avoid their WIN responsibilities was by complaining about WIN policies, procedures, and/or expectations. Indeed, the WIN supervisor anticipated such disputes in the orientation session at which new clients were introduced to WIN expectations and procedures. The supervisor also used her remarks to instruct clients on how to properly complain about staff members. She stated:

> Now in the unions they have a saying, "Work then grieve." Remember that, because if you have a disagreement with your WIN worker about what you are

supposed to do, you can come see me and file a grievance. We'll sit down and try to solve the problem, but you can't just file a grievance and not do anything. You have to work then grieve. That means that you have to do whatever your WIN worker tells you to do and then file your grievance with me. Remember that, work then grieve, just like in the plant [factory]. (Miller 1991a, 111)

Staff members treated most client complaints as excuses and responded by emphasizing the client's responsibilities in solving his or her economic problems. Consider, for example, the following exchange, which occurred in an orientation session intended to introduce new clients to WIN rules and expectations:

CLIENT: [in response to the staff member's description of the conditions under which clients could be required to take jobs] Sounds like communism to me, you have these people workin' for the government who say you [clients] hafta take a job whether you want to or not.

STAFF MEMBER: Well, somebody said that to me the other day too and the only thing I can say to that is that it's more communistic to be livin' off the government. You know, there are some responsibilities that go with being supported by the state. (Miller 1991a, 121)

This exchange illustrates the usual way in which staff members defined clients' troubles and justified organizationally preferred remedies to them. Specifically, staff members described clients' employment troubles as circumstances for which clients should take responsibility, and the best remedy to clients' troubles was the fulfillment of their WIN assignments. Staff members justified their orientation by emphasizing the ways in which clients' characteristics and actions, such as their attitudes toward employment, lifestyles, and employment histories, contributed to clients' difficulties in finding and keeping jobs, and staff members' records of success in helping other, more co-operative clients find jobs.

While staff members usually used their routine interactions with clients to stress clients' responsibilities for solving their employment troubles and fulfilling their WIN responsibilities, they did not always do so. Staff members also considered other possible definitions of, and responses to, the troubles, including the possibility that clients were unemployable and should not be required to participate in WIN. The latter possibility was considered when clients and staff members described clients' troubles as involving circumstances that were beyond clients' control, could not be changed, and made it impossible for clients to keep jobs that would make them economically self-sufficient. As in the following statement, staff members typically justified such a definition of, and response to, clients' troubles by citing clients' severe physical, emotional, or family problems (Miller 1991b).

What am I gonna do with this guy [client]? He shouldn't have been sent [from the welfare department].... I can't do anything for him.... Who's gonna hire [this] guy with that thing, brace, on his arm? They [employers] spot him six blocks away. Employers go, "Oh, you have a disability and a [pending] Workman's Comp [Compensation] suit [against a former employer] too." They don't want him. Injured on the job, they think maybe he's accident prone. He probably isn't, just a guy who had an accident. They [employers] go, "Well, he'll probably slip and hurt himself and he's lawsuit happy too." (Miller 1991a, 143)

More frequently, staff members used definitions of clients' troubles as physical, emotional, or family oriented to justify modifying the clients' WIN assignments. They explained that such responses were warranted because, although the major purpose of WIN is to help clients get jobs, they are also expected to take account of clients' special medical and social service needs. Staff members also treated clients' responses as tests of their willingness to fulfill their WIN obligations. For example, clients who reported serious physical problems were sometimes temporarily excused from their normal WIN assignments and told to get medical treatment for their problems.

Staff members treated clients who failed to seek medical help or follow their treatment programs as intentionally avoiding their WIN responsibilities. Staff members further stated that one of their major professional responsibilities was to hold such clients accountable for their behavior by confronting the clients, asking them to explain their actions, and warning them that further unco-operativeness could result in more severe responses. Staff members responded to clients who continued to act in unco-operative ways by calling pattern-of-behavior meetings, which involved the complaining staff member, the client, and sometimes the WIN supervisor. Staff members and the WIN supervisor used the meetings to emphasize the client's longstanding record of unacceptable behavior, and warn him or her that any subsequent failure to fulfill their WIN obligations would result in conciliation meetings.

Thus, the situational need to reformulate the trouble to meet the demands of a more formal charge led to the production of a "history" of the problem that may not have been previously articulated. The change in setting transformed the terms of the dispute. Staff members also described potential conciliation meetings as serious encounters which might result in the client's termination from WIN and loss of all, or a substantial portion of, the client's AFDC grant. Staff members and the WIN supervisor used the warnings to convey to clients the seriousness of the charges made against them, and give clients "one last chance" to change their behavior. Consider, for example, the following staff-client exchange regarding the consequences of future unco-operativeness:

STAFF MEMBER 1: If you fail to co-operate, then, you'll be cut off of your [AFDC] grant. You'll lose your share and you'll probably be put on Protective Pay....

CLIENT: What's that?

STAFF MEMBER 2: ... It's a procedure to make sure that the money goes for the kids only. You won't get the money to spend on yourself.

CLIENT: You mean, I'll be cut. I'll have less money.

STAFF MEMBER 1: That's right. This is your last chance. If you don't co-operate in the future you'll lose your grant. So its very important that you co-operate.

Pattern-of-behavior meetings were also occasions for narrowing the issues at stake in subsequent staff-client interactions. Staff members defined future interactions as tests of clients' attitudes toward WIN (Miller 1985). In so doing, they cast clients' claims to physical, emotional and/or family problems as excuses which clients used to justify their improper attitudes and unco-operative behavior. Defined as excuses, such claims were no longer matters that staff members were professionally obligated to take into account in responding to clients' troubles. Where a claim of family hardship might have previously been treated as a legitimate problem to be dealt with, it would now be construed as an indication that the client was trying to avoid WIN responsibilities.

Conciliation Meetings

Conciliation meetings changed staff-client relationships in four major ways: (1) staff treated them as occasions for making official complaints against clients; (2) two new officials—the WIN worker in charge of the session and a social worker—were brought into the disputes; (3) the meetings were held behind closed doors and the proceedings were kept confidential; and (4) staff members portrayed the impact of conciliation meetings as more serious for clients than other meetings. As one staff member stated:

> This has more clout. We use more muscle here, psychological muscle. How would you like to be told to co-operate or starve? It's like when a doctor says that you have six months to live. You go, "What!" You change your life, right? That's what we try to do. They have to co-operate or lose their grants and that means starving for most of them, unless they can eat grass. (Miller 1983, 143)

Although this description glosses over other government programs available to many disqualified WIN clients, it highlights a major staff goal in conciliation meetings. Staff stated that part of their responsibilities in conducting conciliation meetings was to create a crisis in clients' lives. In the meetings they also instructed clients on how they might begin to take responsibility for their problems. One of the most important instructions was that clients co-operate with WIN staff in the future. Staff members justified the instruction by describing participation in the WIN program as each

client's job. Viewed this way, clients "earned" their AFDC benefits by participating in WIN, and could be "fired" from their WIN jobs if they failed to
fulfill their WIN assignments.

The following exchange is an example of how staff members sought to
create crises in clients' lives by portraying WIN as a job. It involved a client
who stated that he failed to look for jobs because he had used funds provided
by WIN to cover job seeking expenses to pay family bills:

STAFF MEMBER: This is a job.... It's your job, and like any other job, if you
don't go to work, you'll get fired. Look at it that way.

CLIENT: I don't understand.

STAFF MEMBER: All I'm saying is that you're being paid to co-operate, that's
what your grant is, and so this is your job, to keep appointments and look for
work. (Miller 1983, 148)

Staff members did not expect clients to break down during conciliation
meetings or in some other way openly express feelings of crisis or despera-
tion. A satisfactory conciliation meeting was one in which all of the possible
bases for present and future appeal for another chance or special treatment
were eliminated. In so doing, staff members claimed that they placed clients
in a position of institutional accountability by making them fully responsible
for their future behavior. Staff members accomplished this goal by counter-
ing clients' claims that they did not understand WIN rules and expectations,
and/or suffered from circumstances that made it impossible for them to
fulfill their WIN assignments. Staff members also asked clients to promise
that they would fulfill all of their WIN assignments in the future. Staff
members' interest in obtaining promises of future co-operation was practical
and future-oriented. They sought to create social conditions that they could
use to terminate the clients from WIN should they fail to keep their
promises. Consider, for example, the following exchange:

CLIENT: I thought I was supposed to go out and look for jobs then.

STAFF MEMBER: No, it was explained to you that you were to come here [the
WIN office].

CLIENT: I didn't know that.

STAFF MEMBER: Are you prepared to co-operate now?

CLIENT: Yes.

STAFF MEMBER: Will you come in [to the WIN office] every day in the
morning?

CLIENT: Yes.

STAFF MEMBER: And look for five jobs a day?

CLIENT: Yes. (Miller 1983, 147)

Moving a dispute into a conciliation meeting transformed the interaction by introducing a third party who might take sides in the dispute and by formalizing the troubles at hand. The new circumstances demanded a more structured articulation of the problem—one that was defensible when heard by a third party. This led to the production of the "history" of the problem, as well as the recitation of documents of the problem's seriousness and persistence. As in the following exchange, staff members also used organizational documents to justify their orientations to clients as troublemakers:

CLIENT: He [indicating her WIN worker] has a bad attitude toward us [pause] lower-class people. He doesn't care about us, he thinks he's better than we are.

STAFF MEMBER: Well, let's see what sort of attitude you've had toward WIN. [He reads portions of her WIN record dating back several years. The emphasis is on the times when the client has missed appointments with her WIN worker and failed to complete her WIN assignments.] Now, if I have a bad attitude toward you, it may be because of your record. (Miller 1985, 384)

Conciliation meetings also provided the occasion to put clients on notice that severe formal sanctions were in the offing, thereby foreshadowing a change in the dispute from a matter of interpersonal disagreement or misunderstanding to an instance where compliance could be demanded or benefits would be withheld. The relative positions of the disputants were thus transformed as staff members revealed the substantial organizational resources for extracting client compliance at their disposal, while clients were made aware that their appeals to extenuating circumstances would henceforth be discounted and treated as evidence of unco-operativeness.

WIN Hearings

Clients terminated from WIN could challenge staff members' actions by requesting WIN hearings. These were legal encounters conducted by attorneys (hearings officers) who were unaffiliated with WIN. Hearings officers portrayed themselves as impartial adjudicators who were professionally obligated to hear both sides of the dispute and make decisions based on legal rules and principles. As in the following hearing officer response to a client who stated that he did not understanding the implications of the hearing, hearings officers described the hearings as having two consequences: (1) they could find that staff members' actions were proper and clients should be terminated from WIN for a designated period of time; or (2) clients could be reinstated in WIN and required to co-operate with the WIN staff:

Okay, if I determine, after hearing this case, that you did not co-operate with WIN, then your AFDC grant can be terminated for a period of thiry-four days, or I may determine that that period should be longer or shorter. If I find in your favor, then you will continue to receive your AFDC grant and will be required to co-operate with the WIN program. You will have to do whatever they tell you to do. So, you will either lose your grant for thirty-four days or remain in WIN, okay?

In addition to the involvement of hearings officers, WIN hearings differed from conciliation meetings in three major ways. The differences were further conditions for changing and narrowing staff-client disputes. First, clients, staff members, and other witnesses in the hearings stated their positions by giving sworn testimony and presenting evidence intended to justify their positions in the disputes. They testified by answering questions asked by the hearings officers, WIN representatives, and clients (occasionally clients were represented by attorneys), and offered evidence by submitting official documents to the hearings officers. The requirement that testimony be given in response to questions was significant for WIN staff members and clients because it changed the interpersonal dynamics of the dispute. For example, disputants were no longer arguing with one another, but were answering the questions of a third party.

The demands of this "orchestrated encounter" (Dingwall 1980) also called for argumentation skills and strategies that were unfamiliar to many staff members and clients. Hearings officers aided staff members and clients by reminding them to ask questions and sometimes making suggestions about how they might ask legally permissible questions. They also instructed staff members and (usually) clients who refused or were unable to argue their cases by way of question-answer sequences. Hearings officers explained that it was in staff members' and clients' best interests to ask questions because hearings officers could only consider legally permissible testimony and evidence in making their decisions. The following exchange shows how hearings officers so instructed and managed staff members and clients:

> HEARINGS OFFICER: [To the client] Do you have any questions you wish to ask of this witness [a staff member]?
>
> CLIENT: Yes, I'd like to ask a couple. [pause] Well, they ain't really questions but, uh.
>
> HEARINGS OFFICER: Well, no, now's the time you have to ask questions, you're not under oath and I cannot consider your statements. Do you have any questions you wish to ask of the witness?
>
> CLIENT: Just that, uh, what type of job that he offered me?
>
> HEARINGS OFFICER: [To the witness] Can you, uh, respond to that ...?

The second way in which WIN hearings differed from previous disputing interactions involved the issues at stake in the hearings. Previous interactions focused on the reasons for clients' failure to fulfill their WIN assignments and how to change clients' behavior. WIN hearings were concerned with the legal appropriateness of staff members' decisions to terminate clients from the program. The hearings were challenges to staff members' claims to having acted as competent professionals. Staff members justified their actions and sought to show that they were competent professionals partly by presenting WIN records as evidence that they had followed proper WIN procedures in responding to clients' employment and personal problems and partly by showing patterns of unco-operative behavior. Staff members described the records as accurate and objective portrayals of their own and clients' actions.

In so doing, staff members challenged clients to show that WIN records were not accurate or objective, or to offer alternative and equally credible documents to support their claims and accusations. Clients were seldom able to meet either challenge. The difficulty partly involved the clients' lack of access to alternative documents or failure to bring them to the hearings. It was also related to the ways in which hearings officers and staff members treated the incidents described in clients' WIN records. They organized their questions around the incidents by first citing entries in clients' WIN records that stated that the clients had failed to fulfill their WIN assignments and then asking clients to explain and justify their actions.

This use of documentary evidence was an interactional procedure for narrowing disputing issues by focusing the proceedings on selected instances of client unco-operativeness, rather than on their full record of WIN participation. It also held clients accountable to legal standards of evidence. The following exchange is an example of how WIN records were so used by hearings officers—the hearings officer noted that the client's WIN record showed that he had missed a WIN appointment and asked the client to explain his action:

> CLIENT: Because I had a previous, I had a previous appointment and by the time I got the letter [from WIN] I didn't have enough time to get there [to WIN] and cancel the other one.
>
> HEARINGS OFFICER: What type of other prior appointment did you have?
>
> CLIENT: I was to see the doctor.
>
> HEARINGS OFFICER: And what was the name of the physician?
>
> CLIENT: [pause] I can't remember, it was at [a clinic].
>
> HEARINGS OFFICER: Do you recall what the name of the physician was that you were to see?
>
> CLIENT: No, I don't.
>
> HEARINGS OFFICER: What type of, uh, physician was this that you were to see?
>
> CLIENT: It was about my back. I don't know, they have a ..., I mean, I can't remember what the name of it is....

HEARINGS OFFICER: My question is do you recall whether or not, uh, this individual doctor that you saw was a medical specialist of any kind?

CLIENT: Yes, he was a specialist.

HEARINGS OFFICER: What was the doctor's name?

CLIENT: I can't remember.

Finally, WIN hearings differed from other disputing interactions because staff members treated the hearings as contests in which one side had to win and the other lose. One of the questions asked of staff members by hearings officers was whether they would be willing to conciliate their disputes. Accepting conciliation involved re-admitting clients to WIN and meeting with them to reach mutually agreeable assignments. Of the ninety WIN hearings analyzed for this research, only one WIN representative indicated a willingness to conciliate a dispute. In refusing to conciliate the disputes, staff members cast the hearings as contests in which one party would win and the other lose.

The Micro-Politics of Disputes

The data analyzed here show how WIN and other human service organizations are organized partly as political arenas where individuals bargain and adjust competing interests and perceptions (Handler 1979). When disputes do surface, they emerge from ongoing, routine interactions, and are typically negotiated and resolved in patterned and orderly ways. These interactions involve interpretive and interactional work through which staff and clients organize and voice their competing orientations and interests. Such interactions are both opportunities to formulate and express dissatisfaction as well as constraints on how complaints may be organized and expressed. The disputing process is both implicitly and explicitly political because participants take partisan positions on the issues at hand.

The formulation of the problem, and its solutions—that is, the way a dispute evolves and is settled—may be analyzed as the "micro-politics of trouble" (Emerson and Messinger 1977). From this perspective, organizational disputes involve interactional contingencies that influence and condition how individuals interpret and react to problematic situations. The "micro-politics of trouble" perspective emphasizes how interactants orient to their own and others' disputes as troubled social interactions. In general, disputes are considered to be unsatisfactory aspects of social relations that may result in decisions and/or actions that are also unsatisfactory.

For example, teacher-student conflicts are usually treated as undesirable by teachers, students, and others because they consume time and energy, and depart from preferred images of such relationships as friendly, co-operative, and nurturing. The conflicts are troublesome because the disputants orient to their positions as incompatible and demand that others acquiesce to their positions. To acquiesce, however, involves agreeing to act in dispreferred ways and accept previously unacceptable definitions of the situation and perhaps, of self. (See Emerson in this volume).

The micro-politics of trouble perspective also emphasizes how aspects of organizational disputing are generic social processes (Prus 1987). They are trans-situational aspects of social interaction observable in a diversity of social contexts and settings. As Prus (1987, 251) states, analyses of generic social processes "highlight the emergent, interpretive features of association; they focus on the activities involved in the *doing* or accomplishment of group life." The micro-political activities through which troubles are defined and responded to are trans-situational. While definitions of trouble and remedies used may vary across interactions, the micro-political processes through which the definitions are formulated and tested, and candidate remedies are assessed and applied, are similar across diverse social contexts and settings.

Emerson and Messinger (1977) also highlight the ways in which organizational conflict may involve several inter-related settings and interactions. Disputes are often organized as increasingly formal occasions of disputation involving increasingly severe sanctions for disputants found guilty of wrongdoing, or as appeals and reconsiderations of previous decisions about how to resolve the disputes. The settings may also differ in terms of the parties involved; third parties such as mediators and adjudicators are often asked to intervene in longstanding and/or seemingly unresolvable organizational disputes, changing the dynamics of the conflict process.

Studies of dispute processing in organizations show that disputing issues and relationships may change when they are reformulated and reassessed in different settings. For example, Miller and Sarat (1981) and Felstiner, Abel, and Sarat (1981) suggest that disputes may evolve from prior grievances and claims, then change when disputants present, justify, and negotiate their positions in new settings and for new audiences. Mary Douglas (1986) argues that socially organized settings offer their members typical and routine ways of thinking and talking about social reality.

Thus, one way of analyzing disputes in human service organizations is to consider them as interactions within a series of "dispute domains" which structure the ways in which disputes are organized, negotiated, and resolved. Dispute domains consist of the fundamental assumptions, concerns, and vocabularies of members of particular settings or organizations, and their usual ways of interacting with one another. Client-staff disputes may take place in a variety of settings, but the settings are all bound by organizational parameters. In a sense then an organization constitutes a "dispute domain" that shapes the conduct and outcome of disputes under its auspices.

In another sense, however, organizational disputes may occupy a variety of physical, cognitive, interactional, and procedural domains—all of which may influence the disputing process. For example, diverse "ecologies of knowledge" (Anspach 1987), combined with organizationally, professionally, and situationally embedded ways of thinking and talking about issues of contention form the social contexts within which disputes are formulated and resolved. Clients and staff may occupy different niches, if not different "realities," within the broader organizational context and thus may bring divergent expectations, arguments, and rhetorical styles and resources to their disputes.

The rhetorical domain within which a dispute is conducted—from informal discussions over conflictual matters to formal, legalistic hearings—may facilitate and authorize particular modes or styles of argumentation and promote particular ways of resolving disputes. Thus, the interactional resources available to disputants vary across dispute domains. We conclude by discussing some of the implications of this and other aspects of organizational disputing for future research.

Conclusion

Although the data analyzed in this paper were collected in only one human service organization, the analysis has implications for studies of conflict and disputing in other settings, particularly studies of other human service organizations. For example, the analysis highlights how conflicts are embedded in, and emerge from, routine organizational interactions, and are reorganized as they are processed within varying organizational settings. Put differently, the analysis suggests that human service organizations may be analyzed as inter-related political arenas within which organization members formulate, express, and pursue their practical interests (Handler and Hollingsworth 1971; Handler 1979; Miller and Holstein 1991). The study has two further implications for the analysis of dispute processing as generic social process.

The first issue involves the relationship between trans-situational social processes and the practical settings within which they occur. Conflict and disputing in WIN were generally organized around the trouble-defining and remedy-seeking processes analyzed by Emerson and Messinger (1977) as the micro-politics of trouble. But the range and types of trouble-definitions and remedies considered by WIN staff members and others varied across disputing settings. Thus, studies of disputing might focus on the ways in which trans-situational and micro-political disputing processes are intertwined with, and shaped by, aspects of disputing settings.

The second implication involves the practical consequences of organizational dispute processing for disputants. Disputing in WIN was organized as a "narrowing" process within which the argumentative resources and options available to staff members and clients were transformed and restricted when their disputes were reconsidered in conciliation meetings and WIN hearings. Disputants' options were influenced by the range and types of trouble-definitions and remedies associated with disputing settings and by procedures for properly arguing their positions. The narrowing process was especially problematic for clients.

For example, in conciliation meetings, clients' claims that they failed to fulfill their WIN assignments due to extenuating circumstances were disallowed by staff members who sought to create crises in clients' lives. WIN hearings were problematic for many clients because clients were required to argue their positions by way of question-answer sequences and by the submission of official documents as evidence for their claims. Thus, the social organization of dispute processing has profound implications for how organizational inequalities are organized and sustained.

NOTES

1. Aspects of the research reported on here were supported by a grant from the Fund for Research on Dispute Resolution, Grant #G4-90-32.

2.5

Experiencing Relationships: Bonds, Networks, Communities

In the first selection Patricia Adler and Peter Adler focus on the social world of the upper-level marijuana and cocaine smugglers and dealers. In examining the social organization of this drug world, they consider the various levels of relationship within it, and discuss the nature of their research involvement at each of these levels. While the segment of society they studied encompassed goals, identities, and values that were fundamentally divergent from their own, the authors emphasize not only that, despite these differences, drug dealers' relationships enjoy many features in common with non-deviants, but that researchers, if sensitive to the roles and relationships existing within that world, can enter it for purposes of conducting research.

The second article in this section by Dan Wolf is based on his ethnographic study of a motorcycle club. It is especially organized around an examination of how survival for such an outlaw club requires absolute commitment of its members—to their bikes, their brothers, and to their club—in order to survive in what is perceived as a hostile social environment. His analysis focuses on the club bar and how this setting helps facilitate processes of networking and bonding, which are the cornerstones of their sense of community. Just as important, however, is the fact that the club bar is used by the bikers to demarcate the boundaries between themselves and outsiders and also to allow for their calculated contact with non-members for purposes of possible recruitment.

In the next selection, Dorothy Pawluch, Roy Hornosty, Jack Richardson, and William Shaffir focus on the relations that emerge among undergraduate students enrolled in an innovative university program. In particular they emphasize the dynamics of the student subculture that facilitates the latter's socialization experiences. Faced with uncertain expectations matched by a desire to excel in their academic pursuits, the subculture fosters a set of relations enabling the student body to exercise greater control over the pace and intensity of their university experience.

Nancy Herman's contribution examines the lives of ex-psychiatric patients by focusing on their perceptions of mental illness as a stigmatizing and stigmatizable situation. In particular her analysis investigates how such persons manage such information in the course of social interaction, and the impact of the strategies they adopt for their deviant identities. Her conclusion emphasizes the stigma attached to mental illness even after patients have been discharged from an institution, and suggests that future research must also focus on the families of such ex-patients in terms of both the family's co-operation with the patient as well as the attempts to help re-integrate the patient into society.

Networking Practices among Drug Dealers

Patricia Adler and Peter Adler

The social world of upper-level marijuana and cocaine smugglers and dealers is filled with secrecy, intrigue, and danger. At the same time, it contains many of the same mundane characteristics of ordinary life. While dealers and smugglers spend more money and consume more drugs than the average person, they must reach out to form both social and business relationships. In conducting our research with members of one such community, we experienced the nature of drug traffickers' networks of overlapping relationships. Conducting participant-observation, in fact, required that we become a part of this broad network. In this paper we describe the research we carried out, the nature of the interpersonal and community relationships we found in this dealing community, the way our research involved us in the structure of these relationships, and the effect this had on our data-gathering.

Methods

Our study of drug traffickers was conducted over a six-year period, from 1974 to 1980, and involved daily participant-observation with members of the dealing and smuggling community (Adler 1985). We stumbled onto the community by accident, befriending a neighbor (Dave) who turned out to be a smuggler. Over the years we became close friends with him, his (ultimately ex-) wife, Jean, and their whole world of associates. We spent a great deal of time with Dave, hanging out at his house, testifying at his various trials, visiting him in prison, and taking him into our house to live for nine months after he was released from jail. We also maintained close ties with Jean and the new network she entered after leaving him, working in her legitimate business front, caring for their children, and following her many escapades. Although we did not deal ourselves, we participated in many of their activities, partying with them, attending social gatherings, traveling with them, and watching them plan and execute their business activities. We thus came to know members of this subculture, and formed close friendships with several of them. In addition to observing and conversing casually with these dealers and smugglers, we conducted in-depth, taped interviews, and cross-checked our observations and their accounts against further sources of data whenever possible. After leaving the field, we continued to conduct follow-up interviews during periodic visits to the community for several years and made a follow-up study in 1991 (Adler 1992).

The Social Organization of Drug World Relationships

Southwest County dealers and smugglers lived in a world filled with multiple layers and types of relationships. These expanded concentrically outward around each individual, surrounding him or her with associations that began as highly business oriented, but decreased in their business intensity as they took on an increasingly social nature. *Partnership* bonds were the most closely entwined business relations, being characterized by equality, profit sharing, and self-interest. *Connectional* liaisons were critical to making transactions and often endured over long periods, involving customer-supplier relationships. Beyond these, Southwest County traffickers were associated with others by friendship *networks*, social affiliations with other drug world members that had business overtones. Each individual also belonged to a larger circle of *acquaintances* composed of dealers and smugglers that the individuals knew socially, yet with whom they had no business dealings. Finally, individuals were encircled by a community of other dealers and smugglers known to them by *reputation* only, with whom they had no direct business or social bonds. This pattern of business and social relations surrounded drug traffickers individually, framing and organizing their behavior. While the membership of each person's concentric circles varied, they all partially overlapped.

Partnerships

The closest of all relationships in the drug world are partnering ones, where people work together toward successfully completing each transaction. Contact between partners, often occurring daily, is intense and frequent, requiring the greatest degree of mutual trust. Drug world partnerships are extremely varied in nature: they might endure for long or short periods; they might be augmented by business, social, or familial relations outside the dealing world; and they might be egalitarian or hierarchical in nature. Within Southwest County we found a range of partnering arrangements from working in crews, to groups, to working alone. These varied with the drug involved, the time period of the transaction, and the type of activity conducted.

The first partnering structure incorporated the closest, most enduring, and most intricate set of social relationships. Begun in the 1960s and made nearly obsolete by the mid-seventies, organized "crews" were primarily responsible for importing commercial marijuana. During this time large, stable, and highly specialized groups of individuals were needed to handle international air and local ground transportation, as well as a variety of other supportive roles. Relationships within smuggling crews were very close, involving frequent and intimate contact. The smuggler presided over his crew, supporting them emotionally, picking up the tab for their extensive partying, and mediating disputes. They all associated together on a daily basis, intermingling their business and social contact completely. This could occasionally reach the point of exclusivity, where crew members became drawn into such a tight social circle that they cut off nearly all contact with others. They would then fluctuate in and out of this isolated stance, first expanding their circle to include other drug world members, and later bringing in non-drug friends. Periodically, however, they retreated once again to the security and total drug-using absorption of the crew base.

Beyond the crew structure, it was common for dealers and smugglers to work in "groups." Group partnerships were the most makeshift, fluid, and diverse form of social organization in Southwest County's drug world. Generally ranging from two to four members, group partnerships varied in character along two major dimensions—by the relations that existed between the parties outside the dealing context and by the stability of their relationship.

The most tightly bonded of all dealing and smuggling partnerships were those rooted in the nuclear family. Here, siblings or spouses worked in tandem, living together or in close proximity. Relatives were the most trusted kind of partners because of the familial ties that bound them, augmenting the longevity of the association and ensuring that their interests were overlapping and mutually beneficial. Yet more often partnerships were forged among friends met within the drug world. In lieu of loyalty and trustworthiness, friendship partnerships were rooted in pragmatic, business-oriented bonds centered around specialized divisions of labor.

The final alternative was to operate as an "individual," partnering with no one. Conducting one's business alone occurred frequently among dealers, although as a social form, it was non-existent for smuggling. "Lone Ranger" dealers set personal rules that dictated that they refrain from the type of close affiliation inherent in a partnership. This could be motivated by a combination of pride, greed, mistrust, and fear. One solo dealer elaborated on his feeling about unaffiliated dealing:

I've never trusted anybody completely in my career as a dealer and that's why I never worked with anybody as a partner, not even for one deal. There's an unsaid thing when you're doing a business deal that you're out to get as much as you can for yourself in an amenable arrangement. Having a partner would inhibit that. And also, I know cases of people who dealt with others for months and it turned out that they were narcs, that they ultimately put them in jail. That's why I always work alone.

The extent to which dealers operated as individuals was also tied to the pragmatics of their occupation—the connections and labor involved could be more easily handled by a single person than could the complexities of smuggling. Thus, especially when dealers were trafficking in cocaine or quality marijuana (the less bulky substances), and when they were working in the local area with well-established buying and selling associations, they saw partnering with others as unnecessary.

Connections

Outside the relative intimacy found among smuggling and dealing business partnerships, the next closest form of relationship occurred between connections. While not directly tied together by shared profit, connections were still tightly bonded by money and personal safety each time they came together on different sides of a business transaction. Relations between connections could be extremely friendly and enduring, with people compatibly working together over the course of years, or they might be furtive and short-lived, involving a single sale between people who never saw each other again.

Suppliers (from whom goods were bought) were the most strongly coveted of all drug world connections because access to drugs was the first and most basic requisite of doing business. Individuals' relationships with their suppliers were also critical because these could affect the type of purchase arrangement involved, enabling them to get the goods fronted or forcing them to buy on a cash-only basis. Tom, a multi-kilo marijuana dealer, described his perception of the dealing market as open:

Everybody is always shuffling around, getting new people to buy from, new people to sell to. Sources dry up, people retire. If you stay in the trade pretty actively it's not hard to make new connections. You're always running into somebody who has a good friend; somebody always has a surplus because one of their buyers isn't around and is looking for somebody else they can trust. I'd say that's how you shuffle around quite a bit.

The next mode of connections involved people who operated on a hierarchically equal plane, often buying, selling, and middling back and forth among themselves. People in this type of relationship bonded with similar others into circles, one of the most common forms of dealing associations.

Circles (numbering from four to ten members) were characterized by both intra- and inter-group trading, although dealing within the circle was more predominant. Rob, a pound dealer in cocaine, discussed the nature of his dealing circle:

> Sure, we'd buy and sell from the same people. It would go back and forth, depending on who had the product. There was no hierarchy. That circle of ten people was the hierarchy; we were on the same level with them for quite a bit of time, at least with five of them.... So there were five people with us and the other five right behind us. They were the intermediary, middle people. And the people right above us were the smugglers.

Dealing circles were generally very close, tightly knit groups who were mutually compatible personally, socially, and demographically. They attracted people of roughly the same age, race, and ethnic origin who conducted their business along similar standards of security, reliability, involvement, and commitment. Kerry, another cocaine dealer, commented on the multi-faceted intensity of the relationships within his circle:

> It's good to keep friendships within the circle on both a business and social level because then you're friends on a daily basis; you see them all the time and so you're safe. If you socialize with the people you deal with there's more trust, you're sharing the same traumas. Hell, seventy-five percent of the people I'm involved with now, I was involved with four years ago. Our circle has stayed really tight.

These groups, then, could be fairly steady in membership, often staying together over the full course of each person's involvement in the dealing world. They tended to jell early in dealers' careers and mature with them through the various changes that came with aging through the evolutionary course of the occupation. Members of younger circles, for example, took more risks and were more open to new practices and people than were those in established circles, whose goals narrowed their activities.

Customers (buyers to whom drugs were distributed) formed the third type of connection. Relations with customers were the most transient, being valued less highly than supplier or circle connections. Here a status differential was implied, as high-volume dealers carried more prestige within the community than the low-volume buyers to whom they sold. This relative prestige ranking was based partly (as Best and Luckenbill 1982, 153–54 have noted) on the fact that demand nearly always outstripped supply, giving sellers a position of authority within the transaction. Customer connections were the least sought and most dangerous of all transactional relationships because of the illegality of the product. Dealers' and smugglers' reluctance to seek out new customers was rooted in their awareness of the traditional "buy-bust" procedure, where police try to make a purchase from someone and then arrest him or her once the drugs are sold (Manning 1980).

Therefore, as one dealer explained, people were wary of selling to new faces because this represented the most dangerous form of exchange:

> Trust is a risky business. Dealers get suspicious if a person is overzealous, if he's getting too much out of you too fast. They'll often trust a broke person more than someone who comes running up to you saying, I've got 100 grand, get me something.

Dealers and smugglers varied in their practices concerning the number of customers they maintained and the stringency of the criteria they used for evaluating potential new customers. Smugglers had the strongest preference for selling to the fewest people; their energies were much more directed toward buying and importing drugs than toward maintaining a distribution network. Dealers who had spent many years in the business and those with arrest histories were usually more cautious as well.

Yet some people were more open to having a wide, diversified, and changing group of sales connections. These were either the less reputable dealers who constantly maintained low standards of security (the "vibes dealers"), or those dealers trying to build their business by expanding their range of contacts ("up-and-comers"). Mike, a multi-kilo marijuana dealer, described his basis for establishing trust and doing business with new people:

> I basically operate under the vibes theory of dealing. If I meet someone new, say someone brings him over and introduces him to me, I'll sit down and rap with the guy. If I like what he's saying, like if I feel he's on the level, I'll sell to him.

Networks

Partnering and connection relationships were primarily businesslike in nature, having a social dimension that grew out of mutual occupational concerns. The reverse was true, however, for the next ring of affiliations. Network relationships involved groups of dealers and smugglers who did not regularly deal with each other; rather, members were primarily linked by mutual interests, lifestyles, and friendship. Friendship networks thus cut across the different business niches, linking people who trafficked in different substances, levels, and circles.

Friendship networks did not overlap in the same exclusive way as dealing circles, where each member could list an identical roster of participants for his or her circle. Rather, they corresponded loosely, people sharing some friends in common, but maintaining other close friendships separately. Each individual had his or her own personal friendship network composed of people with whom they socialized, exchanged ideas and favors, and knew fairly intimately. However, because these relationships were within the drug world, business dimensions were never totally absent. Work-related development of network relations took a variety of forms.

For example, a person dealing in one drug could serve as a mentor to someone handling a different drug, offering advice on his or her *modus operandi*, security, and financial diversification. As one marijuana dealer noted:

> I'm very close friends with this guy who's involved in the cocaine market, even though we don't do any business together. I've always respected him because he's the top man, he has everything going for him. He's invested his money in apartments, boats, villas, and legal businesses. Whenever I'm unsure about something, I always discuss it with him. He's a good friend and he gives me a lot of good advice.

Another function of network relations was the exchange of information and aid. Money might be borrowed during financial crises, or loaned from one dealer to another as a short-term, high-interest investment for a particular caper. Ideas could be shared about the latest technological innovations affecting smuggling practices or tips could be exchanged about police practices.

Communication could thus be passed from circle to circle through friendship networks, helping people in other business spheres to stave off arrest. The network system also served as an informal credit rating service, where dealers and smugglers checked out potential connections for a past history of credibility or honesty. When people's network relations were extremely close, they occasionally used them to forge business links, going in on deals together or picking up drugs for each other. Networks served as avenues of occupational mobility as they provided contacts for people to jump from one volume of business to another, or to move from trading in one substance to trading in another.

Acquaintances

Beyond each dealer's and smuggler's close friendship network was a larger group of drug world members with whom they were acquainted. Circles of acquaintances comprised all those people who knew each other personally from seeing each other at various times and events, yet whose relationships had never taken on a more intimate tone. Drug world acquaintances knew each other's business in a general sense, had common friends, and socialized occasionally. Like friendship networks, not everyone's circle of acquaintances could be expected to overlap completely (there must be some inter-relations among different circles of acquaintances), but there had to be a high degree of mutual selection. And like networks, acquaintance relationships were primarily social in nature, but continually infused with the overtones of possible business.

Social interaction among Southwest County dealing acquaintances was enhanced by the nearness of their living and working arrangements—most people lived and operated their legal businesses within a fifteen-square-mile area. They ran into each other semi-regularly at the bars, stores, restaurants, and recreational areas they frequented. More organized socializing occurred either in the context of small, intimate gatherings or at larger weddings, parties, and blowout bashes thrown by Southwest County dealers and smugglers. One marijuana smuggler described such a party:

> I really dig throwing big parties where I try to get everyone loaded to the hilt. I invite all the dealers and smugglers I'm friendly with and they bring their friends. We really get it on with the coke and champagne flowing, a pretty lady on everyone's arm. People in the drug world jokingly refer to these as "dealers' conventions." They're not really for business, but I get to catch up on the latest gossip and prices. Lots of times I meet new people there; I find a connection or try to get someone to work for me. I think this kind of pulls people into the business: they see the lifestyle and they're attracted to it.

Both camaraderie and business affiliation were thus fostered by the closeness, contact, and communication experienced by acquaintances within Southwest County's drug world.

Reputation

Schutz's (1962) concept of *umwelt*, a world of relationships based not on concrete knowledge but on reputation, best describes the final circle of affiliations surrounding each member of Southwest County's dealing community. Someone might have known that Mike was a big dealer in town, that Gregg was behind the recently busted cocaine operation, or that Dave and Phil were the smugglers who owned a local bar and hangout without ever having seen or met any of these people, yet the feeling abounded that everybody at the upper levels knew each other. Drug world acquaintanceships brought many people together, but the bulk of mass relationships was based on reputational association. Dealers might circulate without ever having met, but feel that they are old friends when they finally chance upon each other. One marijuana smuggler offered this example:

> I was down at my real estate broker's office chewing the fat and talking about some property when Marty Morgan came in. I'd never seen him before, but I knew that my broker handled some rental properties for him. You'd never have known that we didn't know each other though, because when the broker introduced us we just said, "Hi, Marty," "Hi, Bill," and smiled, like we saw each other every day. Hell, I know the guy's whole personal history—half the scams he's pulled, who he's dated, and where he's lived for the past three years.

Dealers and smugglers sometimes got an ego boost out of having their reputations precede their entrance. Their feeling of knowing about everybody's business also increased the social solidarity of the community. Yet there were times when the community's intermeshing was disturbing. An ounce dealer in cocaine recounted the following experience with a near stranger:

I was sitting at home in my living room when this guy came in looking for my roommate. I knew his name and that he'd recently started dealing with Cory, but I'd only met him once before. But before I knew it he sat down and started talking to me like we were old friends. He named off all of Cory's and my friends, who they do business with, how they do it, and who was bringing coke across the border. Jeez, it scared the pants off me. If this asshole knows all this stuff I've gotta figure the police know it too.

Thus, despite the obvious need for secrecy, a large amount of personal information permeated the drug world grapevine (Adler and Adler 1980).

Drug world relationships were neither exclusively social nor businesslike in nature, having a reciprocal spillover effect. Combined business and social bonding is characteristic of many deviant groups whose interests, lifestyles, and need for legal isolation do not permit easy social interaction with non-deviants. While these relationships were organized fundamentally around business, they led to the creation of a deviant social world that offered a refuge to its members, providing them with a community and a network of social relationships. It also served as a cocoon, buffering them, in part, from the outside world. Their social relationships fulfilled the function of boundary maintenance, insulating dealers and smugglers from most others and delineating their outer social limits.

Research Relationships

Whenever researchers enter into a social scene to study it, the evolution of their data-gathering will be determined by characteristics of the scene as well as of themselves. Researchers carry different personas, and their unique traits will influence this subjective methodology. Perhaps more importantly, every subculture embodies a variety of different types of social roles into which the members fit. Researchers' roles and their relationships to the members will be determined by the existing roles and relationships in the members' world and the extent to which researchers can fit or be fit into them.

In entering the Southwest County drug world, we adopted and were cast by setting members into the types of relationships already existing in the scene. People defined and treated us according to their (sometimes shifting) perception of us as potential *partners, connections, acquaintances,* or members of their *network* or *reputational* community. This varied from person to person, and greatly influenced our data-gathering.

Partnerships

Our most intimate relationship in the field, our partnership, was always first with each other. Together we shared the common occupational objective of forging and carving relations with subjects, discussing and analyzing these together, and making their findings relevant to a sociological audience. Our bond extended beyond the nature of our work, however, and was based on marital love and trust.

Our relationship with our key informant, Dave, approximated a partnership as well. It was he whom we met early in our stay in Southwest County, who was our neighbor, and who had become our close friend. It was he who drew us into the setting and first agreed to let us carry out the research. We conducted our first taped, life history interview with him, and he sponsored us to his entire circle of friends, introducing us and steering people toward us. He thus became our key informant and associate in the research, read rough drafts of papers that we wrote, and discussed our evolving ideas. As a partner with us in the research, Dave even conducted a "natural experiment" on his own: he picked a lower-level dealer and gave him access to as much supply as he wanted (on a front basis) to see if this would give him upward occupational mobility. When the dealer squandered the drugs and money without moving upward to higher dealing planes, Dave concluded that such market factors were not solely responsible for escalations and declines over the course of dealing careers. He thus became a partner with us in our work life as we became a partner with him in his scene.

In our relationship with Dave, we were the ones he turned to when he had an incriminating letter describing his dealings with some other associates that he needed to place for safekeeping in case something "happened" to him, to whom he turned when he needed someone to testify in his trials, and to whom he came after he was released from jail and needed somewhere to go. So we took him into our house and he lived with us for nine months. During this time he was almost like a family member to us as we supported him, fed him, and housed him. Our contact with him, throughout the years but especially during these months, was frequent and intense, requiring great mutual trust. We talked daily and discussed everything. Our relationship was characterized by great affection and loyalty. He had to trust us not to write anything about him that would harm him, while we had to trust him not to engage in any business dealings under our auspices that would cause us legal exposure or subject us to danger from his associates. We each fulfilled these obligations to the best of our abilities. Our relationship, like many between partners, endured over time. It has now been sixteen years since we first met Dave, and while we do not live near him anymore, we still keep in touch. We would never have been able to do this research without the continuous entrée and sponsorship provided by Dave.

Connections

A second set of relationships with our subjects resembled connections. While they were not as intimate as those with Dave, they were still very close and regular. We held such a relationship with Dave's ex-wife, Jean, and her new husband Jim. After Dave and Jean separated we were conscious not to abandon her. We remained close with Jean, and as she met and fell in love with Jim, we grew to like him as well. We socialized with them regularly, and when they entered the dealing business, they helped us with our research (although not to Dave's extent). But like other drug world connections, our friendship with Jim and Jean was also infused with business overtones. Their legitimate business front was a catering business in which they were partners with another dealing couple. One of us, Patti, joined in this venture with them as an employee and a sometime creator of new recipes. Through this enterprise we were drawn even closer into their social group and found more time to spend together with them, studying the fabric of their complete social world. We became friendly with members of their extended family, spent holidays with them, and cared for their children. They became a major part of our study and opened up entire dealing networks to us that we would not otherwise have known. Like Dave, we have maintained our friendship with Jean over the years (although she and Jim broke up and he disappeared).

Many connectional liaisons are characterized by inequality when one party to the relationship is in a dominant position over the other. We shifted in our relationship with Jean and Jim over the years in this way. There were times when we related as peers, drawn together by mutual friendship and interests. There were times when we felt, however, that our research needs from them put us in a subordinate position, where we could not say what we wanted to without jeopardizing our data-gathering. There were other times when they relied upon us, especially when they went through the personal and occupational roller coaster common to those in the dealing business.

Networks

While our relations with some of the Southwest County dealers were tinged with business dimensions, there were many other people in the community who regarded us as merely members of their social scene. They shared with us a bond of mutual activities, interests, and friends. We revolved in similar circles and saw them at neighborhood and social gatherings. We were closest with Dave's most intimate friends, but we also had special friendships with Jean and Jim, some of their friends, and a few other couples who had drifted away from Dave. We often saw many of these people on a weekly basis, exchanging stories, spending time together, eating, going to the beach, or partying. These were our closest network of drug world friends, and we were often intimate with them in our discussions about our and their selves, families, and various present and future issues. While these relationships were primarily social in character, like other networks in the drug world, they were not without possible business overtones. All of the people in our network knew that we were doing a study of the community as a research project, and helped us with our research whenever possible. This usually only entailed discussing their and others' activities and reflecting on these with us sociologically, as they had all done during taped interviews with us. They, like we, regarded each other as integral members of networks.

Acquaintances

We also fell within Southwest County acquaintanceship circles. These were larger in scope than the more intimate networks, being composed of people who knew each other through casual introduction. We were seen and recognized by drug dealers throughout Southwest County as people who were "in the know," who had been introduced to them by dealer friends. They knew that we recognized them as dealers and they recognized us as friends or roommates of dealers. We would see them at restaurants, at the grocery store, the beach, or the shopping center. We would run into them at mutual friends' houses, with friends, or alone. In encountering them, we would smile and say hello, ask about their recent activities, and chat nonchalantly. We did not ask about their dealing or talk with them intimately, but only joined in conversations with them that included mutual friends. Most of these people did not know we were doing a sociological study, and we did not feel comfortable divulging this information as we did not feel they knew us sufficiently to trust us. Yet even these slight acquaintanceships often provided snippets of data that we would use to gain insight into different people and their styles of operation.

Reputation

The final concentric circle of our research relationships was that formed by the broad community to which we and our subjects jointly belonged. Just as dealers knew of each other by reputation even though they had not met, so too there were those we had heard of without ever encountering them. This group of reputationally recognized others was perhaps even larger for us than for most people, for since we were not dealing, we met a more restricted group of dealers; yet we were more curious to hear about people and their activities than most others, due to our research interests. In this way the drug world grapevine, that proved so vital a reputational credit-rating source for dealers, enhanced our data-gathering purposes as well. There were times when we finally encountered someone whom we had been hearing about for years and felt like we knew all about (we did). Ironically, and countervailing to security needs, the biggest dealers were the most discussed and best known in this shadowy reputational world.

Conclusion

Upper-level drug dealers and smugglers represent a segment of society that is quite different from the norm. While they enter the drug subculture from conventional backgrounds, their lifestyle, motivations, and behavior are set apart from more common patterns. Their relationships are characterized by a mixture of trust and suspicion, insulation and integration, stability and transiency. Studying such a group poses complex problems involving achieving a delicate balance between inquiry and restraint, and between involvement and detachment. It also involves researchers building complex bridges to subjects that may be very unlike them in character. We, for example, would probably never have become as deeply entwined with any of our drug dealer friends had we not chosen to make them subjects of study. And although they enjoyed spending their leisure time in a somewhat similar style to us, their goals, identities, and values were profoundly different from ours. At the most fundamental level, we could never fully grasp how they could "blow their last money on drugs" for partying at night when they knew they had a payment due their connection the next day. They, in turn, could never fully grasp how we could "slave away" at our university teaching assistant jobs for paltry pay and deferred gratification when we knew enough people in the drug community to be easily making twice our monthly salary in one night. These basic differences led to significantly divergent outlooks and made the experience of fieldwork relations difficult.

Yet, drug dealers are still people and, as such, their relationships have other features in common with non-deviants. Creating and sustaining relationships with members of a community of drug dealers, while made more difficult by their extreme present-orientation, the amount of drugs they consume, and the affect this has on their levels of suspicion and paranoia, is not altogether different from experiencing fieldwork relations with members of any subcultural group. To succeed, researchers must come to understand the roles and relationships existing within this world and to fit themselves within these. By consciously adopting the members' repertoire of vocabulary and behavior, researchers can enter into the setting and gather naturally occurring data in an interactive manner.

Brotherhood in
Biker Bars

Daniel Wolf

An outlaw motorcycle club is an experiment in utopian communalism; it is both a personal grasp at self-fulfillment and a collective search for community that rides on wheels amongst the inner city streets and highways of industrial society. In *The Rebels: A Brotherhood Of Outlaw Bikers* (Wolf 1991), I portray the Rebels as a product of urban industrialism, a collective social response to the conditions of alienation as they are experienced by the young men of the working class. Seeking a meaningful personal identity and a genuine sense of community, some of these men join the Rebels Motorcycle Club (MC) and, in doing so, they separate themselves structurally and emotionally from the social mainstream. The Rebels provide an example of a subculture that sets itself up as an alternative, often in opposition to, and sometimes in serious criminal conflict with, the social norms of mainstream North America. What exactly does an outlaw club offer? As a subcultural alternative, the Rebels create a society that provides its members with meaningful participation on three levels of sociocultural reality: *personal, interpersonal,* and *institutional.*

At a *personal* level of participation, an outlaw motorcycle club provides its members with a prerequisite to human social life, a definitive concept of self. The young men who join the Rebels share a biker bond—their attraction to the prestige and power of Harley-Davidson motorcycles, machines that they customize ("chop") into highly personal statements of chrome and steel. Within the outlaw tradition, a man pieces together a system of values and a behavioral style as he moulds himself into a "righteous biker." He will adopt attitudes and learn behaviors that gravitate around focal concerns with independence, freedom, self-reliance, aggressiveness, toughness, impulsiveness, and masculinity, all of which will be embodied in a highly romanticized image of the anti-hero.

At an *interpersonal* level of participation, bonds of shared biker values bring twenty-five men together into a tightly knit social network that behaves like an extended family—they call it "brotherhood." Their interaction is intense and frequent; it includes a wide range of activities that are conducted within an atmosphere of camaraderie and intimacy. The interdependency that develops among the members is the foundation of involvement; it leads to an unflinching commitment based on the very fundamental perception of a shared common fate. A man becomes a "brother" to other bikers, "guys who you know will always be there when it counts."

At an *institutional* level of participation, becoming a Rebel means being part of a tightly knit voluntary association that operates as a secret society. The organizational framework includes a political structure, a financial base, a geographical territory, a chain of command, a constitution, an elaborate set of rules, and internal mechanisms for enforcing justice and compliance from within. These men close their world to the outside, turning to each other for help and guidance. They protect themselves with a rigid code of silence that cloaks their world in secrecy. At its best a veteran club will operate with the internal discipline and precision of a paramilitary organization.

The successful integration of these three levels of participation—personal, interpersonal, and institutional—will result in an outlaw biker community whose activities allow a *patch holder* (member) to act out "the real me" and give him "the freedom to do and be the biker I want to be."

The key to survival for an outlaw motorcycle club is commitment. Patch holders must live an uncompromising commitment to their bikes, their brothers, and their club in order to beat the odds and survive in an often hostile, sometimes fatal, social environment. This extraordinary commitment is based on the universal generic social processes (Prus 1987) of networking and bonding which themselves are the cornerstones of any genuine sense of community. In this paper I will attempt to give you a glimpse of the backstage reality of these processes as they appeared to me in the context of one area of outlaw club life—the club bar.

The image of the outlaw biker is widely recognized. The reality is known only to insiders. In order to bridge the gap between image and reality, I participated in, and observed, the world of the Rebels Motorcycle Club. The Rebels MC is classified by law enforcement agencies as an outlaw club. It began in 1969 as a small group of motorcycle enthusiasts who rode their Harley-Davidsons on the streets of Edmonton, Alberta, a mid-sized city with a population of approximately 700,000 people. Today (1992) the Rebels MC is a federation of three clubs, located in the provinces of Alberta and Saskatchewan, that maintains informal social and political ties with the west coast Hell's Angels MC. My entry into the world of the outlaw biker was not artificial, nor was my participation feigned. I rode, drank, and fought along-side the Rebels for a period of over three years (Wolf 1991). To the Rebels I was Coyote; to me the Rebels were friends and brothers. In my work with the Rebels I was never afforded the luxury of not having to perform or not being able to understand the rules of the outlaw game. Riding with the Rebels meant that I either learned, understood, and performed as well as any other biker who wanted to be a friend of the club, or I left the scene. When I made a mistake, I paid for it. As one novice biker who "wasn't able to cut it" was told by Tramp of the Rebels, "We aren't into babysitting wanna-be bikers."

The Functional Necessity of a Club Bar

The club bar is more than just a stage for "downing cool ones," "smoking rolled ones," "profiling your image," and "hustling sweet things." That's what makes it good times. But there's a hidden agenda there; it covers everything from recruiting new members to gathering information about other clubs. That's what makes the club bar an indispensible part of club life, even though some of the guys would just as soon say "Fuck the bar!" (Coyote, in interview with Ric Dolphin of the Western Report).

Outlaw bikers isolate themselves from the citizens of the society that sur-rounds them. Their social isolation places contradictory demands on the group. The club can defend its integrity only by maintaining clear bound-aries between itself and the community, but the club can perpetuate itself only by crossing those same boundaries in order to attract new members. Outlaw clubs deal with this dilemma by establishing a *club bar*—a public tavern that members use as a regular drinking spot and rendezvous point. The club bar has become an integral part of the outlaw biker tradition. It complements the clubhouse, the location of formal club functions and social activities, by providing an informal place for group gatherings. While the clubhouse is their private domain, the club bar is readily accessible to the public. The otherwise closed social network of the outlaws is exposed to non-members. The club bar becomes a recruiting ground where potential prospects can exhibit their personal prowess, demonstrate their commitment to the ideals of the biker subculture, and experiment with forming ties with club members. In effect, the club bar functions as a point of interface between the outlaw motorcycle club and host society.

Establishing Territory: In Search of a Bar

The search for a club bar involves staking out a territory. Specifically, the Rebels begin the process of converting a hotel tavern (public territory) into a club bar (home territory). While the general public will continue to have access to the bar—the process is never totally exclusionary—the relationship of the Rebels to management and the bar patrons is quite special. In the initial stages, members look for features that are characteristic of many hotel taverns—a large seating capacity, live entertainment in the form of rock bands, pool tables, electronic game tables, and a young peoples' clientele that includes single females. However, a fact of life that bikers have to deal with is that their public image causes the managers of most bars to be less than enthusiastic about the prospect of having motorcycle outlaws as barroom patrons. The club must work out an arrangement with the management of the hotel or bar in order to utilize their tavern as the club bar. In negotiating the parameters of this club-to-management arrangement, it is of vital importance to the club that they not sacrifice their club integrity or independence. Ideally, the club will, over the course of time, come to a common understanding with management and its personnel that the club will employ its own sanctioning devices to control the behavior of its members in the bar. Management's decision as to whether or not to allow club patch holders on their premises as "regulars" will depend on the clientele that the hotel wants to attract and the image they are willing to tolerate. Working in favor of the club is the common knowledge that bikers consume large quantities of draft beer and attract a following of their own.

Upon entering a bar, the Rebels may be asked to leave, a negative sign that is often less than subtle. "A couple of us [Rebels] went to check out the Inn on Whyte [a new bar catering to university students]," recalled Wee Albert. "They told us that we could drink there tonight, but not after that. They said they didn't want their bar to be wrecked." Conversely, management may not say anything when members come to check the bar out, a silence that is interpreted as a positive sign. The club may even receive an overtly positive reception, as when the management of the Corona Hotel put out the welcome mat and actively patronized the Rebels. In this case the managers were not soliciting business as much as they were maneuvering to change their clientele. The Corona's clientele included a volatile collection of junkies, prostitutes, and heavy-handed patrons whose idea of a good time was a barroom brawl. The excessive drunkenness, disorderliness, assaults, stabbings, and drug overdoses led the Alberta Liquor Control Board to shut down the Hotel's beverage services on a regular basis. Based on their past experiences with the Rebels, the Corona management felt that a Rebel presence would alleviate the situation. In addition to making the barroom atmosphere uncomfortable for junkies, an outlaw motorcycle club can effectively curb the amount of violence that the bar management has to deal with. The Rebels exercise stringent self-control and have a ruling that prohibits the initiation of violence in the bar (Book of Rules, Rebels MC):

> They [management] don't mind us coming in there at all. We drink a lot of beer as you know, and that's good for them. We don't go around bothering

everybody. That's the last thing we need; because if the fucking heat [police intervention] comes down, it comes down on us, no questions asked! We sit in that one corner by ourselves and drink beer. (Larry, Rebels MC)

Most barroom brawlers are intimidated by the Rebels' presence and tend to act with a degree of restraint. At the very least, they conduct their disputes in another area of the bar. In this sense the Rebels stabilize potentially volatile situations. When members do become involved in a dispute, it is standard policy to try to settle it without violence, and if violence is required, they settle it as quickly as possible. Members look for inconspicuous solutions; what they want to avoid is a fight inside the bar that involves the bouncers or lands up in the lap of management. If the interaction between an outlaw club and bar management continues over a period of time, it is not uncommon for the working arrangement to become predictable to the extent that mutual co-operation occurs with respect to controlling disorderliness in the bar:

Anybody who had any street smarts realized that there was an arrangement between us [bouncers] and the Rebels. It was a highly visible first name "how's it going?" basis. We provided mutual support for each other. They never stood in line and we always made their favorite tables off limits to other customers. If they ever wanted a guy removed from the bar they'd come up and say: "Look there's this asshole over here. Remove him or we'll do it for you." The guy might have been a flake mouthing off, or he may just have been eyeballin' their woman. It made no difference, either way there were no questions asked, we'd remove the guy. If they ever had to take a guy outside the door [a conflict situation], only the Rebel would return; usually we'd throw both fighters out. For our part we'd use them as our silent partners, and their presence alone would be enough to defuse most situations. (Samuel, a three-year veteran bouncer at the Kingsway Motor Inn)

In effect, the patch holders will take a personal and active interest in maintaining "our club bar." Gypsy, of the Satan's Choice MC, Ontario, recalled that "There used to be a special bar that we would go to. We'd classify it as our bar. We'd act as the bouncers there." The final stage in solidifying this collaboration between the club and management would be the formal hiring of members as part-time bouncers. For example, Dominique, the head bouncer at the Executive House Inn, became a good personal friend of the patch holders and eventually hired Jim and Indian to work as part-time bouncers.

In some instances the relationship between the outlaw club bikers and the bouncers may eventually include a dimension that is hidden from both management and the police. "Smoke and beer went together well for the Rebels," said Samuel who was selling marijuana to the bikers. Samuel periodically gave free samples of grass to the Rebels. In return the Rebels invited Samuel to the occasional party where he would be guaranteed some new sales contacts. Across town, one of the bouncers at the Convention Inn Hotel was selling "chemicals"—MDA that was being produced by a member of a government funded chemistry department—on the premises of the bar:

> My profit margin depended on the Highwaymen MC being in the bar. They'd get rid of the competition. All I'd have to say is: "Sorry fellas, I just can't afford to give you any more freebees [samples] because that guy over there is cutting into my profit margin." I'd wind up carrying my competition out of the washroom after they'd finished with him. Once I had a major deal coming down and I was worried about a rip-off. So I invited the Highwaymen over to my house for a party. I told them that I wanted them to try out some new stuff that I'd gotten hold of. When the wholesaler came over to make the deal, he saw all the bikers in the living room. I knew for sure that when he reached into his briefcase I was going to see chemicals and not a gun. We aren't talking "Miami Vice" here, I was only carrying about $10,000. But people have been ripped off and shot for less, and it only cost me $350 for the grass, booze, and a little chemicals to keep the bikers happy. (Leonard, former bouncer at the Convention Inn Hotel)

Unfortunately for Leonard, the Rebels put Leonard's small business entrepreneurship in jeopardy when they took the Highwaymen MC "off the road." Leonard decided on a career change and became a psychology major at the University of Alberta.

Part of the working arrangement between the club and management is that the responsibility of keeping the members under control is left up to the club itself, especially the sergeant-at-arms. When the sergeant is absent, other members will take it upon themselves to exercise both self and mutual restraint. For example, after having to work all day Saturday, Jim was feeling particularly "raunchy," and became intimidating while drinking at the Kingsway Motor Inn. Jim began by taking a beer tray from a waiter and throwing it at a nearby pool table, completely ruining Caveman's next shot. A few minutes later, he smashed a full beer glass against the wall. One of the members remarked that "When Jimbo starts wasting good brew to wash down the walls, you know something's up." A couple of the Rebels tried to get Jim to sit down and relax. Caveman did his part and invited Jim to join him for a game of pool. Unfortunately, Jim noticed a dirty look from a guy playing pool at an adjoining table. Mindful of the club's ruling on violence, Jim waited till the patron had put down his half-empty beer glass. Then, while the fellow was taking his shot, Jim refilled the glass by urinating into it. Jim's only comment was that "Anybody who's got guts enough to give me a look like that when I'm pissed off, deserves a full glass." Any of the above incidents would have brought a bouncer down on a non-Rebel. But most of the Kingsway's bouncers had gotten to know the Rebels and their style of handling situations. They trusted the discretion of the members:

> They've been drinking here since I started bouncing at the Kingsway, over a year now. And we've got no complaints. Sure, they're rowdy sometimes; they

come on pretty heavy and what have you. But I've never seen them go out of their way looking for trouble. Most times they just sit there by the wall and drink their beer. Not like some of the crazies you get in here. (Mike, bouncer, Kingsway Motor Inn)

Jim crossed the line, however, when he picked up a chair and was about to throw it. At this point a couple of the members intervened and suggested that Jim leave the bar, which he did. Jim was subsequently reported to the sergeant-at-arms by one of the members who had witnessed the performance. Jim appeared before the Rebel executive board and they exchanged views about the incident. After they agreed as to what had happened, the board applied an appropriate sanction: Jim was banned from the bar for a period of one month. It should be kept in mind, however, that as far as the Rebels are concerned, they follow rules that they set, not rules set by management. For instance, Crash was barred from the Executive House Inn by management after he had used his Bowie knife to cut through the band's equipment wires: "Those guys were much too loud. We had to scream to be heard across the table. We asked them to turn it down, but they wouldn't" (Crash, Rebels MC). Unnoticed by those concerned, Crash returned the following evening despite his being "barred for life" by management. Ken, president of the Rebels, commented that "If *we'd* barred Crash, he wouldn't be here now. But they look after their rules, and we look after ours."

Hotel management reciprocates this aspect of bar control by extending special privileges to the club. At any of the club bars, members bypass lineups waiting to get into the bar with no more effort than perhaps an acknowledging glance at the bouncer controlling the lineup. This courtesy is standard practice in outlaw club/hotel management relations. Once inside the bar, the Rebels can expect an occasional free round of beer, or even a free night, from management. They are allowed to join tables together and borrow chairs in a manner that allows the biker community to sit together. Certain bars require bikers to check their helmets—considered potentially dangerous weapons—at the snack bar. The staff working the lunch counters often give them preferential service. The bouncers frequently wander by the Rebels' tables, duck down behind the members, and chug-a-lug a brew, even though it is illegal for a bouncer to drink while on duty. In return for this hidden favor, the bouncers come by the pay-as-you-play pool tables and use their master key to give members free games.

Demarcating Territory: Mixing Booze and Pleasure with Border Markers and Danger

Rebel patch holders go to the club bar to enjoy the exhilaration of "getting high" and have a good time with each other. The Rebels affirm their brotherhood by uninhibited drinking, smoking and eating together, boisterous joking and jostling with one another, "shooting the shit" about Harleys and their performance, telling glory tales about biking, discussing matters related to the club or its members, meeting people who can relate to the outlaw bike scene, playing pool, and hustling young women.

The Rebels park their motorcycles in a group outside the bar. During the course of the evening members will leave their tables on a regular basis in order to "check out the hogs." Most bikers have had their motorcycles tampered with, in one manner or another, while they have been drinking at the bar. This tampering can range from a drunk trying to climb on a chopper and having the machine topple over, to vandalism such as the removal of sparkplug wires or the loosening of brake cables. Some bikers resort to putting warning stickers on their motorcycles: "If you value your life as much as I value this bike, don't fuck with it!" The Rebels attach property stickers (a rectangular decal featuring their skull emblem and the words "Property Of The REBELS Motorcycle Club") to the oil tanks of their Harleys in order to discourage both the overly curious and the foolish. In 1985 the Rebels began the practice of posting a striker on permanent guard duty. However, most members still prefer to conduct their own occasional bike check. These bike checks afford a member an opportunity to escape the sometimes oppressive nature of the intense drinking, noise, and smoke of the bar. He can grab a breath of fresh air, perhaps have a quiet conversation with another member, compare his own motorcycle with those of other patch holders, and make plans, while he draws mental sketches of the work and improvements to his machine that inevitably begin every fall and help pass the cold winter months.

Inside the bar the Rebels engage in a highly stylized behavior that repeats itself night after night in a form of barroom ritual. Together as brothers they share the satisfaction of letting loose in sensual/sexual pleasure. In addition to this sensual element, the barroom ritual has an ideological component; a Rebel performs in a manner that amounts to a public declartion of himself as an authentic biker—the cultural meaning of being an outlaw is shared and articulated. The club bar becomes an important stage for the member in his public articulation of himself as a Rebel. The people a patch holder associates with, the activities he engages in, and the manner in which those activities are performed, will all be in terms of being a Rebel. In return the perfor- mance of those activities and the identity they symbolize is confirmed by the reactions of the general public present.

Outsiders will see the external trappings of the Rebels, but an effective process of insulation prevents penetration of the inner workings of the club. The members mark off a section of the bar by joining together five or six tables in one corner. This is a security precaution that puts their backs to a wall, limits the number of approaches to their tables, and provides some members with an overview of the rest of the bar. This territorial isolation is complemented by the Rebels' practice of draping their leathers on the backs of their chairs. Mounted on the leathers are the club colors—a white skull on a black and red background. To the casual outsider who glances through the smokey haze of the bar, there are no individual faces or features to be made out, only a series of Rebel skull patches draped over leather jackets in a corner of the bar that outsiders seem to warily avoid. The visual effect is a formidable wall of skulls; the message is one of impenetrability. The scene that is presented is much like that in a western movie—hard-faced outlaws in the bar, downing doubles while waiting for the stage coach to arrive. If an uninvited outsider, even a biker, decides to approach these tables, he or she is greeted with a question such as, "Who invited you?" If the outsider is a citizen, the greeting is less than courteous. Only members of the outlaw biker subculture and selected outsiders are allowed to cross the club boundary. This peripheral assemblage of individuals includes friends of the club, unaffiliated bikers or "loners," ol' ladies, and unattatched females. On occasion the Rebels may be joined by visiting patch holders of out-of-town clubs, or members of the Grim Reapers MC who, in tandem with the Rebels, maintain an iron-fisted territorial control over Edmonton, "their city." The larger outlaw biker subculture that is allowed to crystallize around the club provides the Rebels with both material and social resources from the exchange of motorcycle parts to mutual self defense.

For the Rebels, the casual process of drinking at the bar is no longer a personal pastime. The Rebels MC uses the club bar to solidify its social network. Having a club bar effectively draws another area of members' behavior into the sphere of club influence. An outlaw motorcycle club places great emphasis on its members "being around" or "hanging out." This aspect of physical presence by itself reinforces the reality of the informal network of expectations and obligations that bind members together in the brotherhood. When the club's focal activity of "riding in the wind" is temporarily "put in neutral," then "putting down brew" in the club bar becomes a particularly important means of maintaining the ties that bind. In Edmonton from November through March, winter snows silence the big Harley V-twin engines, and drinking at the bar becomes one of the few remaining activities that members can participate in as a collective unit. During the summer "riding season" the bar serves a parallel function for those members who are unable to ride their bikes because of physical injury or loss of driver's license.

The Rebels have their own style for dispatching large quantities of draft and bottled beer. They rarely drink hard liquor and never wine. A patch holder will take it upon himself to call for contributions, and those present will throw a few dollars on the table. The money is collected by a member who then signals to the waiter and orders "another hundred draft." Nobody keeps track of how much each member contributes, but then no one takes advantage of the system either. If a member is in dire financial straits, he will make up for lack of contributions at a later date.

There is a benign relationship between drinking alcohol and the subculture's concern for male prowess. The act of heavy drinking by itself is capable of accentuating the illusion of power. While ethyl alcohol is a sedative depressant drug, it also mobilizes adrenalin in the body, which supplies quick energy. For some individuals, the sensation of increased strength arouses positive feelings of increased personal power. For the outlaw biker these feelings are likely to be expressed in subcultural themes involving strength and daring (from arm wrestling and chug-a-lug contests to hustling at the pool tables), sexual conquests, and high performance motorcycles. Outlaw clubs' preference for draft beer relates to the uninhibited drinking style of their patch holders. Full glasses of draft are often gulped down one after the other, chug-a-lugged by members in seconds. In the loud and boisterous atmosphere of the club bar, the ability of a member to belt down his liquor becomes another aspect of his public presentation of self. It would be difficult for a patch holder to demonstrate his machismo while slowly sipping on a martini decorated with an olive. Food is purchased intermittently at the lunch counter. Chips, spareribs, sausages, and chicken are literally tossed around and shared by the bikers at the tables. The scene as a whole is reminiscent of those consummatory rituals that groups of males—from Vikings of the past to today's F-16 Tomcat fighter pilots—have traditionally engaged in after feats of violence, aggression, or adventure.

Another characteristic feature by which the club distinguishes itself is its use of language. A distinct vocabulary and verbal style marks them as an identifiable group; it implies cohesion and reinforces group solidarity while keeping the public at a respectable distance. In the outlaw motorcycle club subculture, group solidarity and boundary maintenance are verbally achieved through the use of jargon, a distinct verbal style, and nicknames. Verbal competence—being able to speak like a biker—requires that the prospect master biker jargon and the biker verbal style which characterizes the outlaw biker fraternity.

Jargon is is a form of speech, expressing technical terms used for communication between members of a specific group or profession and is strange or meaningless to the general public. The everyday distinctions that are important to the members of a subcultural group are likely to be reflected in their specialized jargon. The conversation of an outlaw patch holder is usually conducted against a background of motorcycles and motorcycling. When a biker speaks of his "chopped hog," he is refering to his customized Harley-Davidson motorcycle. When a biker suggests going for a "run," he wants to ride his motorcycle, not go jogging. A comment made by Larry in the club bar typifies the highly jargonized exchanges between members of the Rebels, much of which would be quite unintelligible to anyone other than a biker:

> Over the winter I'm going to rake the frame and wrench in a stroker kit to juice up the mills of my shovel. (Larry, Rebels MC)

Larry is talking about improving the looks and performance of his motor-cycle. The following is a rough translation:

> Over the winter I'm going to rake the frame [cut a section out of the neck portion of the motorcycle frame, which will allow for the addition of an extended front end without elevating the machine's center of gravity], and wrench in [install] a stroker kit [a customized cylinder head, flywheel, valve, piston, and carburetor system], to juice up the mills [a stroker kit will increase the power of a Harley-74 engine by approximately 15 horse-power], of my shovel [shovel or shovelhead refers specifically to the engine head style, and designates an era of Harley-Davidson motorcycle models, circa 1966–1984].

The collective knowledge represented by those seated around the tables in the club bar provides an immediate reference encyclopedia for any member having any mechanical problems:

> CRASH (REBELS MC): My bike gets this snakey feeling when I'm going into turns.

> STEVE (REBELS MC): Check out your axles. Make sure they're tight. If that doesn't end it, then you'll probably have to fork out a couple of bucks for new wheel bearings. But before you go fucking around with all that shit, make sure you've got proper air pressure in your tires.

The highly technical and arcane knowledge required to engage in these conversations in an intelligent manner is symbolic in its portrayal of the participants as dedicated bikers. Just as these conversations provide a common medium of verbal exchange among bikers, they also serve a converse function as a border marker by setting the group off as a distinct social unit. The blank expressions on the faces of some non-bikers seated at the bar attests to the fact that the purpose of these conversations is not only to enlighten members, but also to exclude "straights." Conversation becomes an exclusionary tool reserved for the already-tenured. Thus, the message of these conversations is not always their content; rather, it may be putting the listener in his place, maintaining non-bikers as mystified outsiders.

Mixed in with tales of motorcycles and motorcycling is dialogue about the club or members themselves. The ties of brotherhood that have formed among members readily facilitate the sharing of personal problems that individuals may be experiencing. These personal problems might include topics such as difficulties at work or a troublesome domestic situation. What will sometimes appear to outsiders as an abusive exchange, is actually a "bare-knuckled" (candid) verbal style acceptable to patch holders by virtue of their intimate comradeship. Excerpts from a conversation carried on by club members at the Airway Motor Inn provide a case in point:

> RON: Hey Renegade, loosen up! You've been acting like a genuine prick lately!

RENEGADE: Look Man, when I'm working on my engine and things aren't going right, I start to burn!

RON: You've gotta let us know. Curse at the fucking thing! Kick in a wall! But let us know. We don't know what's clicking inside of you when you get like that.

DUMP: That guy's like a fucking grenade!

RENEGADE: Just lighten up and give me a little space! I can work things out.

RON: What the fuck! That's what we're here for.

Under the social circumstances of friendship, the semantic intent of abusive terms and obscenities is redefined and the casual use of insults actually becomes a show of solidarity. For example, when patch holders couch their bare-knuckled verbal style within the context of a joking relationship, they are able to criticize aspects of a brother's behavior under amiable circumstances:

DUMP: Randy, you ride like a blind man! Looking here, looking there! Jesus! Watch what you're doing!

RANDY: I'm watching you guys, I don't trust anybody.

RAE: Yeah, now there's a guy who is really on the ball. He likes to keep his eyes on at least eight bikes at once!

DAN: Take it easy Randy. What you don't see won't hurt you.

The joking relationships that exist among members serves to dissipate feelings of anger or frustration that inevitably arise in a small close-knit group. The joking relationship acts as a safety valve. It allows for the expression of negative emotions yet deflects their impact away from the sentiments of brotherhood. The sting of any personal criticism is blunted by the overall style of the joking relationship, which might be best described as a form of light-hearted verbal jousting:

DUMP: Hey! You're getting fat. Look at this love roll!

DAN: What do you expect when you drive a truck [Dan's job]. The only exercise you get is farting.

At this point Dan farted. He had switched his strategy from verbal jousting to non-verbal communication, a none too subtle form of body language.

DAN: Well! There you go. That oughta be worth twenty pushups!

BARRY: Your voice is changing Dan, but you've still got problems with bad breath.

RON: He's the only guy I know that got kicked out of a bar for farting. I don't know how a guy could be so rotten and still walk.

DUMP: I'll get you [Dan] Baxter. I'll drink beer, eat Chinese food and won't shit for a week. Then I'll dump a load on yah!

Conversation that is spiked with storytelling and joking reinforces solidarity in the club. It enables the members to deal with sensitive issues in a manner that strengthens, rather than threatens, their highly personalized relationships.

These biker communication skills are necessary in order to be able to interpret and generate social behavior in a "natural" manner. A stranger unable to develop these skills will never gain the status of having unquestioned access to the group. He or she will remain an awkward and marginal participant, at best, a translator and imitator, but always a stranger in a strange land.

The Vulnerability of Claiming Public Territory: Perils of the Bar

The mood and demeanor of the Rebels while drinking in the bar is noticeably different from drinking sessions held at the clubhouse. This change in style is in response to the ever-present threat of conflict. Putting down brew at the bar becomes more calculated in nature. The patch holders engage in the same behavior, but in a more exaggerated manner that stages their on-guard, defensive posturing. Thus, while some members may become totally "wasted," others will become more reserved and attentive. They constantly survey the bar for potentially threatening situations into which their inebriated brothers may inadvertently fall. These members personify the image of a bygone western era—outlaws waiting for some bounty hunter to make a foolish move:

Once you put on colors you draw heat, sometimes fast, sometimes heavy. The cops you can predict; you learn fast where the lines are and where and when you can cross. But with citizens, you never know when some guy is going to try and waste you by running you off the road. In the bar you've got to expect everything from drunks who don't know what they're doing, to guys in kung fu who do, and can be tough as nails. (Jim, Rebels MC)

The consequence of passing out at the clubhouse might be no more severe than being doused with beer by a member curious to know "why are you leaving the party so early?" On the other hand, a Rebel who gets drunk at a public bar can become the target of assault:

I was so stinking drunk that Dale and my ol' lady carried me out of the bar. This guy wanted to get it on with Shultz, and I said "If you want Shultz you'll have to go through me first!" I was really drunk and I didn't know what I was doing; I took a couple of shots to the head. Then someone grabbed me by the hair, had me down, and was choking me. I bit him in the shoulder; and then Shultz, he took over. (Caveman, Rebels MC)

Two weeks later Larry got Killer out of a similar predicament. Two bar patrons ambushed Killer in the parking lot; one had a tire iron from his truck and the other had an attack dog. Larry, a man of tremendous speed and co-ordination, wrestled the tire iron away from one attacker and used it to silence the dog.

If an outlaw club becomes too lax in maintaining a constant vigil over its motorcycles, the results can be disastrous. Such was the case when a number of the Rebels decided to have a drink at the Executive after the regular Wednesday night meeting. That evening I left the bar early, at about 12:15 AM. Outside the bar I met Onion who was surveying the Rebel "iron" (motor-cycles). I talked with Onion for about five minutes about an upcoming run while taking a picture of the lineup of motorcycles. We had no way of knowing that while I had the bikes in the sights of my camera, someone probably had us in the sights of his rifle. Onion went back inside to have a final brew; I fired up my shovelhead and drove off, perhaps 12:25 AM. At around 12:30 AM someone came running into the bar to tell the Rebels that a truck had run over their bikes. What the Rebels found were eight smashed motorcycles, three of which were jammed under the tires of a four-wheel-drive truck. On top of Jim's motorcycle lay a rifle that one of the men had dropped while abandoning the truck. What caused this incident? Apparently two barroom patrons had been beaten up by two bikers. The bikers had no club affiliation, but they happened to be drinking at the same bar as the Rebels. Members of the Rebels MC realize that the police have no use for them. They were largely on their own in dealing with settlement or retribu-tion: "When we catch them we'll lay their legs over a curb and run over them with a bike" (Killer, Rebels, MC). Over the years a patch holder may have to confront a number of frightening situations. There are no rules to this game of "taking care of business," except for one that all outlaw clubs follow—no cops. Instances of conflict further serve to encapsulate patch holders in the social network of outlaw subculture. Threatening situations and the constant vigil they require reinforce the bikers' perspective that the outside world con-stitutes a threat to themselves and their lifestyle. The Rebels are not naïve about the potential dangers that come with presenting a heavy macho image and "flying outlaw colors." The infamous biker stereotype—"Don't fuck with me!"—becomes as much a necessity as it is a choice of style.

> The way it is now, people stay away from us because they're scared. They stay clear of us, and that's what we want. Now if we were friendly with everybody, they would try and do their best to take advantage of the situation. (Caveman, Rebels MC)

Certainly, the Rebels are not the passive victims of circumstance. Wearing colors into a bar, in conjunction with a highly macho presentation of self, is provocative to many males, especially those whose sense of bravado has been lubricated with alcohol. The Rebels are well aware of the fact that they can evoke violence by their mere presence. In this sense, although the Rebels may not be direct perpetrators, they are often the conscious architects of their dilemma of conflict. The patch holders of an outlaw club are also acutely aware of the fact that they cannot afford to have one of their members beaten in a bar. A public beating would damage the club's reputation and make them appear vulnerable; any apparent weakness in their wall of intimidation would serve to encourage further assaults by outsiders. The structure of the brotherhood will therefore intervene in a manner that protects the patch holder; hence the dictum: "All on one, one on all." Like most outlaw clubs, the Rebels will lend their brother whatever help is necessary to destroy an outsider who starts a fight. If the confrontation is initiated by the club member, the Rebels will mediate and separate the combatants. Citizens will not witness a Rebel being beaten in the bar, however, they also will not witness the beating that the club will administer to the member for starting the fight when they get him back to the isolated confines of the clubhouse—as a patch holder you use the brotherhood, you do not abuse it.

Some Brothers Say "Screw the Bar"

Club patch holders want to attract new members at the bar, and this requires them to make their public presence dramatic enough to impress potential "strikers" or "prospects." But the club bar is a hazardous stage for this kind of performance. The setting is highly unpredictable, and encounters with citizens are often hostile: "You never know what kind of shit is about to come down" (Snake, Rebels MC). A successful performance taxes the varied abilities of club members. Thus, despite the privileges they receive, the good times they have, and the functions the bar serves, not all the Rebels feel that spending time in the bar is a sound idea. In fact some members actively lobby against the club's presence in the bar and question the sanity of trafficking with citizens under any circumstances. As far as Raunch (Rebels MC) was concerned, "They give us privileges and what not, but that's bad in a way because our people start spending too much time in the bar." Some members such as Blues and Terrible Tom, will boycott the bar. Terrible Tom showed up at the club bar only once in three years, and that was to fight alongside his brothers against soldiers from the Canadian Airborne Regiment. Blues periodically avoided the club bar while actively lobbying against members drinking there. On one occasion this lobbying procedure led to a heated argument when Blues suggested that certain members who were "living in the fucking Corona bar" should change their colors to read "Corona MC." Ken, the president and individually most influential Rebel patch holder, likewise found himself in the minority as far as the desirability of frequenting the bar was concerned. While discussing the nature and frequency of contact situations the club had with outsiders, Ken stated that: "The average citizen is mostly the person you see in the bar. And as far as any contact goes, that's where it usually is. Personally, I think the bar is the worst place for a motor-cycle club. And I would like to see it end!" The presence of members in the bar had even been an issue of formal debate at club meetings, but the issue remained both contentious and unresolved:

> There are a few members that don't care for bars themselves. They don't like going to bars. We don't blame them because you can't talk to nobody in them, the damn music is so loud. Its been brought up at club meetings lots of times, trying to get out of the bar. But you can't do it. Let's face it, you've got thirty guys, and a lot of guys, including myself, want to go! (Larry, Rebels MC)

> I've got no use at all for the bar; but it's a good place for wanna be's [prospects] to meet the club. It also helps us collect infomation about what is going on around town. Like if there's a new club that's trying to start up, the bar is where we'll hear about it. There's always debate about going to the bar, but guys keep going there. (Tramp, Rebels MC)

The negative sentiments that some Rebels harbor about the bar revolve around the process of establishing group exclusivity—the preservation of subcultural borders that screen out the infiltration of non-biker values and prevent the formation of non-biker social ties. Some members reason that increased interaction with the public would weaken the club as an integral unit by making it more susceptible to outside influence, and thereby dilute the intensity of the bonds of brotherhood. "I'd just as soon see no contact with them [the public]," said Raunch, "I don't care what they think of us. The more contact you have with them, the looser you are." These Rebels want to tighten up the borders between the club and outsiders by eliminating the one major point of social interface, the club bar.

Balancing Exclusivity and Permeability: Border Guards and Gate Keepers

The Rebels face a paradox. Social integrity requires the maintenance of club boundaries, while social perpetuity requires that those boundaries be crossed. These contradictory needs are met by members who have disparate attitudes toward outsiders and, as a result, enact opposite roles in their presence. I arbitrarily labeled these two groups the "border guards," and the "gate keepers." The guard is comprised of those Rebels who actively manipulate (and thereby advance) the harsh "biker" stereotype imposed by the dominant society; their behavioral style reinforces the boundaries between the club and outsiders. "You never knew what they were up to," observed Walter K., a guitarist who played the bar scene, "They wouldn't enter into the verbal banter or anything; they'd hang back. You would never know what they were saying, thinking, or anything." The rules of boundary maintenance are openly discussed among members:

Yeah we'll talk about it. But its just generally understood that when you're sitting in the bar, you're not supposed to have any straights sitting around the table. If you've got a friend there, and a member doesn't want him there, all he's got to do is say so, and the guy has got to go, no exceptions. (Raunch, Rebels MC)

The border guards can be less than subtle, even in those instances where their brothers are involved:

KILLER (REBELS MC): Hey Snake, what kind of bike does your friend ride?

SNAKE (REBELS MC): He doesn't. He just plays the guitar. He's a close friend of mine.

DANNY (REBELS MC): We don't give a shit! There's no room for him. Tell him to get lost!

Conversely, the gate keepers consist of those Rebels who selectively admit certain outsiders. These more conservative patch holders exoticize their subcultural image and exploit the popular myth of outlaw biker prowess, adventure, and brotherhood in an outgoing approachable fashion.

"I could get along with guys like Clayton, Tiny, and Terrible Tom," commented Walter K., "they'd be entertaining and having fun with you all of the time." In effect, these members are actively selling the club: "You have to remember that before a biker strikes for the club, the club strikes for the biker." (Saint, Rebels MC)

Camouflaging Differences Between Brothers

There are some substantial differences among the Rebels. Members have different perceptions of group goals; they are committed to group goals to varying degrees, and have various personal goals that they hope to achieve by being a patch holder. The ideological and behavioral diversity that results is actually beneficial in that it allows the Rebels to perform disparate and sometimes conflicting organizational tasks. It is this diversity among members that enables the Rebels to establish a point of interface between itself and the larger society in the club bar. In effect differences in members' attitudes toward interacting with outsiders enables the club to maintain an operational balance between *organizational integrity* (border maintenance by "the guard") and *organizational perpetuity* (border crossing allowed by "the gate").

While intermember diversity may be an asset to the Rebels MC, the full recognition of that diversity on the part of members and outsiders may not be. While in the isolated confines of the clubhouse, the reality of intermember diversity often manifests itself in the form of heated debate; it is an accepted fact of the Rebels' political process (Wolf 1983). However, when in the bar, the Rebels continually face unpredictable and potentially threatening situations. Under these conditions, the expression of variability among members can prove to be a costly luxury. Specifically, the exposure of inter-member differences may: (1) be taken as a sign of weakness by hostile outsiders; (2) make the Rebels appear less attractive to potential *strikers* (prospective members); and (3) detract from members' own perceptions of group solidarity by weakening their public image. Thus, in the club bar, the Rebels find themselves walking the razor's edge between group impression management and the authentic expression of personal sentiments.

Processes of collective ritual and symbolism such as "flying the colors," tend to hold in abeyance the otherwise disruptive effects of expressing differences in opinion. This symbolic camouflage allows the intended function of the bar to operate by giving the impression of uniformity to outsiders. "The club is like a safe," confided Wee Albert while we sipped some Canadian Club whisky, "There's a lot of loose change on the inside. But when the tumblers fall into place and the doors to that safe open, Look out! 'cause the Rebels come out as one!"

Even for club members, the effects of internal disagreements are minimized by the sense of mutual empathy—a shared common fate—that bonds individuals who participate in collective risk-taking. In the bar one never escapes this constant awareness of the risk of external threat. Furthermore, the Rebels have guidelines that encourage discretion. As a rule internal conflicts are not aired in the bar and the emphasis shifts to mutual participation in brotherhood-affirming activities. When trouble arises, intermember diversity is transcended by the members' commitment to the club and to one another. Members share all risks, and their collective risk-taking is an important symbolic indicator of the bonds of brotherhood. On occasion brotherhood has to make much more than a symbolic appearance in order to clarify to members the stuff of which these bonds are made. Although the Rebels as a rule do not initiate or welcome violence, an occasional violent encounter with outside society is not without its ancillary benefits. It pulls the club together in a way that other group activities cannot. Group coherence is enhanced and group boundaries made more salient by virtue of the presence of hostile outsiders. Cohesion is especially enhanced by violence.

> When you get right down to it, a good barroom brawl is good for club morale. These days our club reputation means that fights are few and far between. A few weeks ago we got into a real dog fight. We didn't start it, but the guys were sure as hell in an excellent mood after it. (Tramp, Rebels MC)

Violence, whether it is constructive or destructive, is, for the individual, the most intense means of asserting personal identity. When an external threat requires collective violence on the part of the members of a group, individual and group identity are dramatically merged. Nowhere was this clearer than in a barroom battle with members of a Canadian Airborne Regiment (Wolf 1991).

> I looked at all the hardware those guys were carrying, and I thought, "Well this is it! I'm not going to walk for a month!" There must have been at least fifty-five of them. I don't think they expected us to fight against those odds, but we went at them swinging, kicking, clawing with anything we could find. I got a boot in the head and went down with sore ribs, but that was about it. (Onion, Rebels MC)

The Rebels won that brawl and sent thirteen of the soldiers to hospital. But, more importantly, the Rebels had reaffirmed their brotherhood. Each member had taken extreme risks and made personal sacrifices for the group. As a result of extensive media coverage and storytelling by members themselves, from joking references to mutual praise, the "Battle of the Kingsway" became part of Rebel folklore, an historical referent that served to vitalize and confirm a collective identity based upon brotherhood. Loyalty to the club and to one another arises out of the midst of danger, out of the tension and apprehension of possible injury, mutilation, or worse. Whether one considers the process as desperate, heroic, or foolish, really doesn't matter. What does matter is that the brotherhood emerges as a necessary feature of the Rebels continued existence as individuals and as a group.

Conclusion

"If the cops are the Good Guys," writes the representative of an American federal law-enforcement training center, "then it's hard to imagine a more archetypal Bad Guy than the outlaw motorcyclist!" (Ayoob 1982, 26). But, while the content of the *police subculture* (enforcement agents of law and order) and the *outlaw biker subculture* (symbols of antisocial and criminal behavior) are diametrically opposed, many of the underlying processes that make both organizations work are the same. Both organizations revolve around individuals whose self-image is that of a select elite group. Both groups depend on interpersonal commitment based on *esprit de corps* and brotherhood respectively. Members of both organizations have to deal with the problems of juggling intermember commitments with outside ties, such as male-female bonds, that compete for a member's time and attention. Both cops and patch holders attempt to project and manage an authoritarian/intimidating image that is powerful enough to command a degree of control over encounters with outsiders. Both have an argot of their own that simultaneously unifies the members and sets them apart as an identifiable group. The integrity of both groups depends on their members' ability to command access to, and enact exclusion from, territories to which they lay claim. Both groups have to deal with internal personal and political conflicts without giving any hint of these differences to outsiders. However, none of the above similarites would come as a surprise to any reader who has been drawn into a subculture, whether that organization be a military unit or

Kiwanis Club, a fraternity or street gang. While the cultural reality of these groups are fundamentally different, the social processes on which their existence depends, are fundamentally the same. The point being that, if an individual takes it upon himself or herself to understand the sociocultural reality of any group, it is perhaps best to start by first pinpointing those generic social processes (Prus 1987) that are the infrastructural cornerstones that all groups share, and then proceed to fill in the cultural differences in content that make all groups different.

Fostering Relations: Student Subculture in an Innovative University Program

Dorothy Pawluch, Roy W. Hornosty,
R. Jack Richardson, and William Shaffir

A major problem that anyone moving into a new institutional setting faces is understanding and coming to terms with its demands and expectations. In developing a workable "definition of the situation" (Thomas and Thomas 1928, 572) to guide his or her actions, a neophyte may be assisted by others who either have already experienced the transition or currently share a similar situation. Of critical importance is whether the individual experiences the new situation alone or in the company of others—the individual or collective status of the recruits (Becker 1953; Goffman 1961; Becker, Geer and Hughes 1968; Olesen and Whittaker 1968; Glaser and Strauss 1971; Haas and Shaffir 1987; Shaffir 1991b). A related issue is whether the individual has been preceded by others who experienced the transition and who can teach him or her "the ropes" about the setting (Geer, Haas, Vivona, Miller, Woods, and Becker 1968). This distinction is between a serial and disjunctive pattern of socialization, the latter referring to a situation where the recruit is not following in the footsteps of predecessors (Wheeler 1966).

In this paper we examine the socialization experiences of a group of students enrolled in an innovative undergraduate university program—Arts and Science (A and S)—at McMaster University in Hamilton, Ontario. What makes the A and S program unique is its emphasis on providing students with a broadly based education in the sciences, social sciences, and humanities at a time when most university students are following a more specialized course of study (Williams and Schiralli 1991). The program is also unique in its encouragement of social responsibility and involvement, and in the type of institutional support it offers its students. The program, introduced in 1981, was designed to attract students who are academically strong and well-rounded. Though enrollment has remained relatively constant (at approximately 200) by design, the program has steadily grown in popularity as demonstrated by the rising number of applicants each year. Along with increased popularity there has been a steady rise in the average mark required for admission; with a current cut-off average of approximately 90 percent, the A and S program is attracting some of the most capable and gifted of high school graduates.

This paper focuses on how students negotiate the program's specific demands and general expectations. The socialization of A and S students may be characterized as collective and serial; that is, recruits negotiate the transition into their new roles not alone, but together as a collectivity. Moreover, there is a strong, ongoing student culture that assists those already in the program, as well as paving the way for those entering their first year. Therefore, our analysis highlights the role of the student culture and the ways in which it both shapes and directs and is, in turn, shaped and molded by the students' academic and social experiences.

Our study is based on field notes gathered in several ways. Since October of 1990, when the study began, we have been observing and talking to students in a variety of contexts. We have met casually with them in their usual gathering places, including their campus lounge and the student pub. We have attended some of their classes and social events. We have interviewed them both individually and in focus groups ranging in size from three to eight students. We have also spoken with students who have graduated from the program, and with instructors and administrators connected with it.

The Arts and Science Program

The A and S program rests on a clear and well-articulated philosophy that stresses first and foremost, the value of a broadly based and interdisciplinary educational experience. Reacting to what they saw as the liabilities of specialization, and in particular the compartmentalization of knowledge that it entails, the creators of the A and S program attempted to fashion a course of study that would expose students to the strengths of a full range of academic disciplines. They also wanted to give the students a broader understanding of the world and of themselves than they would be likely to get in a specialized program.

Another component of the philosophy is the emphasis on the application of knowledge to the "complex and urgent issues of our time" (Jenkins, Campbell, Carbotte, McCalla, Papageorgiou, Sanders, and Wallace 1980, 2). While the program encourages learning and critical thinking for their own sake, it also fosters the image of educated men and women seeking not only to understand, but to engage the complex, real-world problems of modern society from an interdisciplinary perspective.

These principles are reflected in the way the program is organized. The core curriculum consists of fourteen required full-year courses in the sciences, social sciences, and humanities. The humanities and social science courses, rather than being discipline-based, deal with literature, the creative arts (music, drama, and the graphic arts), and the intellectual history of Western society. Students are also required to take an intensive course in writing and informal logic (or critical reasoning) and a number of specially designed "Inquiry" courses, which focus on themes related to national or international issues, particularly Third World and global environmental problems. Interests in such issues are often pursued by students in optional courses in later years. Despite the load of required courses, the program has some flexibility and leaves enough elective space for students to combine their A and S degree with another major or honors degree if they choose to do so.

The A and S program provides an unusual degree of support for its students. It is both pedagogically and administratively separate from the rest of the university. Besides its own curriculum, it has its own director, degree, and council of instructors (drawn from other departments, but appointed to the council for a specified period of time). Classes are kept small. As a result, discussions, "good talk," and the exchange of ideas are facilitated. Tutorials, seminars, discussion groups, co-operative student projects, interactive teaching, self-directed learning, and thesis or independent study courses all feature prominently. There is extensive student-student and faculty-student interaction not only in classes and seminars, but also in the governance, planning, and development of the program.

Students receive individualized and highly personalized attention with regard to both academic and personal matters. When rules or regulations need to be negotiated to enable students to pursue academically justifiable interests, students can expect to receive support from the director and administrative staff. They also receive a variety of physical supports or "perks" including their own lounge, which provides a comfortable home-base where students can study, meet with other students, relax, and attend to administrative matters. The lounge has a photocopier, a coffee machine, and a refrigerator. Off the lounge there is a small library and a seminar room which is sometimes used for classes or meetings, but is available most of the time for quiet study. Students can sign out their own keys to the lounge and therefore have access to A and S facilities after the building is closed for the day. They also have access to modest research funds and can easily obtain equipment such as video machines, cameras, and tape recorders. All of these features have been carefully thought out and designed with a view to making the students' university experience as enriching and satisfying as possible. They have also contributed, as we later argue, to the evolution of a strong student subculture.

Discovering Expectations and Managing Uncertainty

A major problem faced when moving into a new institutional setting is coming to terms with its demands and expectations. The matters with which A and S students must familiarize themselves are, in many respects, similar to those of undergraduates in the university at large. Initially, they must learn to pace themselves; specifically, to strike an appropriate balance between academic work and the pursuit of leisure activities. One student put it this way:

> I usually go out once during the week, at night. And Saturday night's shot because I'll go out all night, and then Friday night just go out for a bit.... like I organize it that way, otherwise I know I won't get things done.... I don't have any classes today [Friday], so I do errands and stuff like that in the morning.... Saturday is work day, all day. Friday too, which is really good, because research is hard to do in little blocks. You have to spend a lot of time at the library.

Although seemingly unrelated, the matter of pacing is closely connected to students' participation in extra-curricular activities. In high school, the overwhelming majority were involved in a range of such activities; now at university, faced with an even wider choice of events, they must determine whether such intense involvement might adversely impinge upon their academic workload.

The problem of deciding on the extent of their involvement is, for many, related to the program's very content. One first-year course and some popular electives not only focus on Third World countries and specific problems in their development, but the material they read and the discussions they have suggest that solutions to such problems are within the realm of the possible. Their initial idealism about solving national, international, and global problems is maintained and enhanced by the content and focus of the courses they take. Involvement in causes appears to be in tandem with academic pursuits. Many view the program as a promoter of social consciousness which, in conjunction with emphases on inquiry and development of critical thought, challenges them to integrate their academic studies with some measure of social action. A fourth-year student expresses this in the following way:

> I mean so many people in A and S do tend to be involved with a lot of sort of social causes, and whether it's the environment or whether it's sort of native

problems, or development, there just is a lot of awareness of that.... I mean some of the people are sort of the leaders of the groups on campus that are things like ... the Committee for Global Awareness, or the Recycling Initiative, they're all, or many of them are in A and S, for whatever reason.

Another fourth-year student, deeply involved in Third World issues, and clearly aware of this integration states: "There is a continuation between what I'm exploring in class and what I'm doing in my extra-curricular things."

Not all students successfully blend the academic and non-academic sides of university life. For some students, particularly those with well-focused career objectives, there exists a tension in achieving an acceptable balance. As sympathetic as they may be to the pursuits and causes that have attracted their peers, their focus is on career goals, which either precludes or severely constrains their participation in politically based causes and other social activities. A third-year student explains:

> I guess it's just what you choose to spend your time doing. And it's not that I disagree, like, it's not that I don't agree with what all these things [social and political causes] stand for, and I just don't find myself wanting to get heavily involved in all of these groups.... I just don't have the time. I have to think about what my goals are, and the only goal I have in my head right now is to get to graduate school.

A more general problem faced by students is to determine what is expected of them; in short, to learn about the standards that have been set and how these are best met. While this concern is shared with the university's general undergraduate student population, A and S students must, in addition, find their bearings within this specialized program. In reflecting upon the program's first year, a student says:

> First year, people are just like trying to figure out what A and S is and what they're doing here.... What is this program, why am I here? This is what I thought when I came in, this is what I'm seeing, how do they match up? How is this changing me?

The general problem of ascertaining expectations involves, in part, focusing on course requirements and assignment deadlines as the following first-year student reveals:

> I like calculus even though I'm not doing very well so far. I don't have Grade 13 calculus, so it might be that I don't have the background.... I really have to work hard at it. Writing and Informal Logic is O.K. One of the things we have to do for that course is keep a journal. But Inquiry is a killer—"Inquiry hell," everyone calls it. We have these major papers to write, and it's not like high school where you can ... talk around the subject and put pretty well anything down. You have to do library research and have good information.... The first paper's due at Christmas and I'm still having trouble finding a topic.

In addition to allaying their uncertainty regarding the program's over-all objectives, neophytes must also learn to evaluate their academic progress within it. In their study of a university undergraduate program, Becker, Geer, and Hughes, analyzed the perspectives students developed and concluded that:

> Grades are the chief institutionalized valuable of the college.... In this the grading system closely resembles the operation of a money economy, with grades themselves playing a role analogous to that of money or currency in the community (1968, 55).

Our data suggest that while initially measuring their academic progress by relying on grades, the centrality of grades gradually diminishes as students become doctrinally converted (Davis 1968) to the program's objectives and underlying philosophy. One student recalls: "In first year, everyone was so caught up in marks, I guess because we were used to being near the top in high school. But I find that most people have calmed down since then." In fact the importance of grades is gradually substituted by experiences that are deemed to be more personally meaningful. As a fourth-year student comments:

> I think I've gotten a lot out of the program.... I find this year, like it's been a really personally meaningful year.... The courses I have, have been dealing with issues and ideas that are very important to me.

Although their views typically change over time, first-year students' concerns about grades reflects the competition they initially perceive in the program. As one student recalls: "Everyone was, well, not everyone, but quite a few people were just so concerned with their marks.... The competition was unbelievable." Their sense of the program's competitiveness is generally attributed, in retrospect, to their earliest feelings of intimidation and insecurity. Aware that they are part of a select group, many students, nonetheless, questioned whether they were sufficiently equipped to meet the program's rigorous demands and, in comparison to others around them, considered themselves deficient. "Everyone in first year seemed so much smarter than I was during the first few months," one student admits. Another student reflects on similar feelings of inadequacy:

> I know in my case, in first year, and even a little bit in second year, I was a bit intimidated by some of my classmates, my colleagues. I guess because they are very bright. Some of them are extremely bright and intelligent and have a lot of confidence. They come off, they sound as if they know exactly what they're talking about. And I didn't have that feeling about myself and my capabilities, that I knew what I was talking about. And especially in areas that we were studying, some of it was just completely new to me, and some people just seemed to know exactly what some of those things meant, and I'd still be going: "Where do you read this?"

Thus, their insecurity fosters a sense of curiosity regarding their credentials in relation to others and results in a competitive atmosphere:

> I was always kind of personally curious as to how other people were doing, just because I wanted to know how I stacked up.... And I think that kind of curiosity leads to competition because if you're interested in how you stack up, chances are you're interested in stacking up near the top. And, you know, just being able to prove yourself, somehow.

As a result of exposure to the faculty and peers, but especially upper-year students, a transformation occurs with respect to the importance of grades. While it may appear to occur suddenly, it more accurately reflects a confluence of two significant considerations that impact on the individual. First, by getting to know one's fellow students better, the individual's feelings of intimidation are gradually eased. Referring specifically to those students that she believed were markedly brighter than herself, a student remarks:

> After I got to know these people personally, it was a lot easier. I found that these people in the class who seem so confident, as human beings they were interesting persons, and they had all sorts of ideas and that they were human. As soon as I humanized them, it became much more easy to relate to them.

Simultaneously with becoming more familiar with one another, students also learn about themselves. In particular they discover that their original career goals may require some modification, if not complete re-evaluation. The arrival at such an assessment is typically accompanied by the adoption of a new perspective which, to paraphrase one student, maintains that school ought not to interfere with one's education. A consequence of this view is that while preoccupied with grades initially, students generally become critical about their value as reliable markers of education and learning. Two students about to graduate comment:

> I think one thing that I would personally want to see would be to take the focus off the marks, from the beginning. And by that I mean, and this is probably impossible, because that's just the way the university works, but I think that if people are so focused on the fact that everyone got ninety coming in...and so it starts off, first year, everybody's focusing on what their marks were in high school. And I wish that you could somehow take the focus away from what your marks are.

> So you can get in with an eighty-nine, maybe.... It just seems, I don't know, I think that it gets in the way of learning because it doesn't really encourage you to take risks. It encourages you to, I think, learn what you have to do in order to get the cheese in the maze. I'm not concerned about that anymore.

The significance of grades then becomes transformed as students learn to attend more critically to the quality of their educational experiences and recognize that their performance in a course, and their appreciation of it, transcend the immediacy of the specific grade they achieved.

The Dynamics of the Student Subculture

A group that is identified, and identifies itself as different, has the capacity to develop a subculture, enabling its members to compare themselves to others, assess their progress, evaluate their commitment to their specific situation, and to seek solutions to problems. In the A and S program, it is the student culture that provides the benchmarks against which individuals situate their concerns, aspirations, and objectives. In addition the subculture reflects the range of acceptable and appropriate attitudes and behavior regarding the pursuit of academic goals and aspirations and involvement in extra-curricular activities.

A central feature of the student subculture lies in its mitigation of student competition by emphasizing the importance of co-operation and mutual support. In fact the very structure of the program contributes to the development of a perspective among the students that they are all "in the same boat." Although students should strive to do well, the perspective emphasizes that their success ought not to be achieved at the expense of other students. While typically evaluating their performance in relation to their peers, it is expected that they will readily share their information with others. A graduate of the program recalls:

> Everyone is listening to see what everyone else is doing.... Yah, everybody wants to know "Where do I stand?" and you do feel that your standing is relative to other people. But there wasn't anything like "I'm not going to tell you my answers, I'm not going to tell you what I did." We did feel like we were in it together.

Another student about to graduate emphasizes the willingness of students to assist each other:

> I think instead of competition there was a sense of helping one another, especially in physics and calculus. When you didn't understand something there were always people discussing problems.... I can remember second year, Western thought, when I was in residence, the other women who were living in my residence who were in A and S, we would sit around and discuss things. We would help each other that way.... I think people were very good at pointing out each other's strengths.

Our field notes are filled with numerous instances where we observed students discussing their work with others. The guiding ethos was one of mutual support as revealed by the following: "I can think of a number of people in the class that I didn't care for personally, but I can't think of a single instance where if someone came and asked for help, I'd say 'no.'" We observed repeatedly that students offered to lend others books and notes, or to provide each other with information about materials they had read.

Such mutual support was not restricted to others in one's own year. Indeed, students could count on meeting with more senior students either to preview what lay ahead in the program or to seek advice regarding an immediate problem. In fact when students claimed that they compared themselves to others, they referred both to peers in their cohort as well as to more senior students:

> [How do you learn to pace yourself?] Partly you keep your ear to the ground to see who has already started their Inquiry, what they have done, have they gone to all the places in the library, have they sent out for materials from other libraries, have they actually started writing the damn thing up? How many visits have they made to the prof? And you talk to upper years as well, because they've been through it. "Gee, did you start your Inquiry way back in October?" "Well, I didn't do mine till the last minute and I got a C." "O.K. I'd better not do that, I should be starting now." You know, you listen around to know where you should be and what you should do to get there.

For those entering the program, the subculture contains a body of lore that assists them in finding their bearings. For example, tales abound about particular course assignments and some of the more unusual ways in which these were met. Stories prevail about students who left the program, and about the various career trajectories of the program's graduates. For more practical purposes, however, the subculture provides answers to a range of questions such as "What should I expect?" pertaining to courses, quizzes, and assignments.

The student culture is buttressed by a series of institutional supports that set A and S students off from the mainstream of undergraduates. We have discussed some of these in describing the special classes and instructors connected with the A and S program and the special perks that its students enjoy. The program sponsors a number of activities, outside of classes, which bring A and S students together, but at the same time, separate them out from other students. For example, there is an annual fall picnic and a traditional Christmas lecture and reception. Each incoming student has his or her picture taken, and a class picture for each class is distributed not only to the students, but to instructors as well, enabling them to more easily recognize students by name. The significance of the pictures is not lost on the students:

> You know something special about A and S? It's the small number of students and the student-professor ratio. You walk in there and you feel important. People learn your name. They take your photo and put your name to it.... Profs learn your name and they call you by your name. And they smile when they see you and stop to chat with you. Other students know your name.... A

psychology student walks into a big building full of a thousand other faceless people and stares at a video screen.

Several features of the program's structure contribute to the students' sense of self-worth. First, they realize that their application has been carefully screened and that entry into the program is extremely competitive. As well, classes are relatively small, thereby providing opportunities for close and immediate contact with faculty. The significance of student-faculty contacts in the development of identities has been noted in the literature (Newman and Newman 1978; Bean and Kuh 1984). In addition the students are aware that careful attention is directed to the selection of faculty invited to teach in the program. Finally, the program includes two administrative assistants who are committed to helping students solve any academic, administrative, and personal problems that might develop. A third-year student remarks: "I know that if I ever have a problem or get myself in some sort of bind I can run to (an administrator) and it'll get straightened out." "That's what I like about A and S," another student adds: "It's a personal program and you're made to think that you really matter, that someone cares about you." They greatly appreciate the intimate nature of the program. As one student puts it: "You can walk into your classroom or into the office and everyone knows your name. That's nice."

The dynamic of being showcased by the university results in a feedback process whereby students, in recognition of their marked status, become ever more committed to living up to the faculty's expectations:

> We are told we are important. We live up to that. Of course, in an atmosphere like that you flower. You want to do well.... You just feel so much better than you would if you were a number.

One of the program's administrators captures the self-fulfilling nature of this process:

> I don't see these students as thinking of themselves as privileged, that they deserve to be pampered. I think it's enough that they're respected and so they're willing to work. Their professors are giving their work this element of respect, treating them with respect, and that's a level that makes everyone happy. There's a confidence that they can do the work, that they know how to do it. And the things that they have been taught to do are things that are demanded of them. So I think it's a pretty fair deal when you tell them: "This is what you have to do to excel in this program, and this is how you do it, and we're going to help you learn how to do it."

While the program's size, structure, and organization facilitate the formation of a distinctive culture, the students actively shape its contents in the course of interaction in a variety of formal and informal settings. They understand each other, they believe, in ways that others outside of the program probably do not. Like other subcultures, they develop and employ a specialized vocabulary—an argot—consisting of expressions and phrases that help members assess their experiences, facilitate communication, and organize their behavior (Maurer 1964; Letkemann 1977):

> There's a specific language that A and S people use. A shorthand if you will. You can summarize certain ideas with one or two words as they are related to common intense experiences such as Inquiry, which makes it easier for us to talk to each other. Because we go through that intense first-year experience all our common experiences enable us to put together a shorthand that lets us converse more efficiently—pack more information into less words in less time.

The students have created their own association which, among other things, publishes an A and S student newspaper and sponsors a number of social activities throughout the academic year, including talent nights and coffeehouses, pizza parties, and an annual formal dance. A special effort is made to integrate first-year students. For example, since much of the organized activity takes place in campus pubs and involves the consumption of alcohol, and since some first-year students are under the legal drinking age, non-alcohol-related activities such as "milk and cookie" nights are held specifically for them. The student association is also responsible for organizing a buddy system, whereby incoming students are paired with an upper-level student who answers questions, provides guidance, and generally facilitates the integration of the new student into the student culture.

On an informal basis, groups of students—as many as forty in any given week—come together regularly, late on Monday nights at the campus pub. The students also tend to spend a lot of time with each other outside of classes and organized activities. Those who live in residences on campus, even though they may be separated in different buildings and on different floors, will congregate in each other's rooms to study or socialize, eat together, and plan many of their off-campus activities (for example, shopping) together. Many of those who live off-campus share apartments or houses. In fact one of the houses which the students have dubbed "Pooh Corner" has been passed on through several cohorts of A and S students and is generally recognized among the students as an "A and S house."

Flowing from such intense interaction and the sharing of common experiences, students develop a deep appreciation for one another. They recognize one another as being highly motivated, and define this characteristic as the central one that sets them apart from other undergraduates at the university. While they may see themselves as being regarded as superior or elitist by the general student body, they themselves identify their difference as a result of a commitment to the program's opportunities for inquiry and learning to think critically. As one student comments:

> A and S students are different. I don't mean that in an elitist sense. I'm not saying we're better than anyone else. But we have a different attitude toward

learning. We're here because we want to learn, we're curious, and we're not ashamed about following through on our curiosity. There's such a difference between my A and S classes and some of my elective classes. A and S students just really want to get involved. You should see us. People just can't wait to get into the discussion and say their bit. They're really into what they're learning.... And that's just such a great process, such a great way to learn. In my other classes, I don't know, there seems to be more indifference.... They don't always seem that eager to learn. Maybe that's not really how they all feel. But that's the way it looks.

For many, the special bonding formed is akin to the emotional ties within an extended family, and appears to remain even after they have graduated:

[Do you keep in touch with people?] Damn right, I miss them so badly. They were the major part of my socialization. Every time I had an hour or so between classes, I'd hang out in the A and S lounge. My friends were all in A and S. It wasn't a question of elitism, or, you know, "nobody else is good enough for me." These are people like me. They have like interests, they have open minds, they are intelligent. We can discuss anything and have good senses of humor more often than not.

Another student who left A and S after the first year continues to participate in program activities and to spend time in the lounge explaining: "Even after I left the program, I still wanted to be a part of this incredible thing they've got going here."

The students are acutely aware of how their own experience contrasts with that of most other students at the university. One student we interviewed, who roomed with a Business major, makes the following comparison:

Our experiences were as different as night and day. She was absolutely lost. It took her a long time to feel like she was fitting in. There are so many people around, that unless you're taking four or five courses with the same person, there's just not the chance to get to know anyone. But for me, it was different. It was like walking into a family-like situation right away.

Those who take electives outside of the A and S program and find themselves in large classes also have a dramatic point of comparison. One such student notes:

[The closeness in A and S] really sinks in for me when I'm in my computer science class. It's a first-year course and the class is huge. People don't really talk to each other. No one knows you. It's hard to make friends in there.

The intense interaction, familiarity, and personal involvement that students experience call out in them a high degree of responsibility and accountability not only in relation to the program's goals and objectives, but also to each other. Students often spoke about "feeling guilty" for not working as hard as they might or making the contribution they should in class. A third-year student remarks:

> For me the worst part is feeling guilty for not working hard enough. I'm not saying that I'm a slacker, but I know that I could be working. And I sometimes feel guilty that I don't really deserve the high marks I get.

Another third-year student who had missed several classes due to an illness recalls:

> Last month I had pneumonia and had to miss a few classes. And I really felt rotten because there are so few of us to begin with and if anyone misses, it leaves a real hole.

While the close ties between and among the A and S students constrain self-interested individualism, they support and foster self-development and individuality. Students feel free to pursue individual interests, whether they are conventional or uncommon, with considerable support and encouragement from their peers. A fourth-year student who abandoned his initial plans for a career in science because of his intense interest in drama, film, and music, observes that:

> There is a lot of support and interest [in what I've wanted to do]. I guess that over three and a half years I've cultivated a really good close circle of friends, who are just a very supportive group.

Close ties between and among A and S students also facilitate collective efforts to actualize values of social consciousness and responsibility, as evidenced by their degree of involvement in campus and off-campus groups, particularly those centered on environmental and development issues. A and S students make up a large part of the membership, and are often involved in the leadership of such student groups. They are among the most active students at the university. Their record of involvement is one that the students take pride in, whether they themselves participate in these activities or not. One student identified idealism as a distinguishing characteristic of A and S students:

> Understanding the world's problems and wanting to turn things around somehow is so much a part of the way most A and S students think. That makes us different. We're real idealists.

Most students expressed the view that while they entered the program with considerable idealism and confidence in the possibility of finding solutions to the world's major problems, these qualities were enhanced as a result of their experiences in A and S. Those few students who prefer not to become involved in such activities are fully aware that they are not the typical A and S student. A second-year student explains:

I'll be talking to someone in my class on a Monday morning and they'll be telling me about how they spent the weekend raising money for this or that group or meeting about this or that cause. And the question that's hanging in the air is: "And what noble and praiseworthy thing did you do this weekend?" And that makes me feel uncomfortable because [I know it's the A and S thing to do, but] I just don't do that many noble and praiseworthy things.

The defensiveness in how these students sometimes talk about their relative non-involvement demonstrates the power of the informal norm generated within the student subculture.

Conclusion

In contrast to undergraduates for whom the university provides relatively few individualized supportive structures, the distinctive organization of the A and S program enables students to exercise greater control over the direction and pace of their socialization experience. One of the characteristic features of the program is its formation of a web of intense, highly interactive, personal student-student, student-faculty, and student-staff relationships, relationships that are merged with, and buttressed by, a distinctive student culture that provides a collective dimension to the students' experiences. The subculture attenuates competition among the students, provides mutual support for learning, and assists the students in negotiating their way through the university's bureaucracy. As well, it fosters a sense of social responsibility through extra-curricular activities, supports career choices however uncommon they may be, and facilitates personal development. Finally, it encourages idealism, shapes the identities of the students, and develops life-long relationships among them.

Former Crazies in the Community

Nancy Herman

In the name of "humane treatment," I'm on the outside at last
Waiting and watching this damn world fly past
Lying alone in my two by six bed
Wishing and praying to God that I'd soon be dead.
With perpetual visions and nightmares of cruel strangers running through
  my mind
I run, I try to escape, but solace and safety I can't find...
Some of us may be lucky to "make it on the outside," but many of us have
  long since tried
To be normal, to be normal, to blend in the crowd, get to be accepted, to get
  a job, to make life worth living after all.
But many friends and family have forsaken us; our chances for happiness
  grow slim
Our hopes of being normal are growing oh so dim.
We plea, we implore society to dispel your fears and hatred
Help us, oh help us, before it's too late.

POEM WRITTEN BY AN ELDERLY EX-PSYCHIATRIC PATIENT, 1984

Examination of the sociological literature on the stigma of mental illness indicates that much research has focused on: (1) public attitudes toward the mentally ill (Whatley 1959; Nunnally 1961; Farina and Ring 1965; Lamy 1966; Bord 1970; D'Arcy and Brockman 1977; Trute and Loewen 1978; Taylor, Dear, and Hall 1979; Cochrane and Nieradzik 1985); (2) correlates of societal acceptance or rejection of ex-psychiatric patients (Rabinowitz 1982); (3) family acceptance or stigmatization of former mental patients (Kreisman and Joy 1974; Doll, Thompson, and Lefton 1976; Clausen 1981); (4) the stigma experienced by relatives of former patients (Freeman and Simmons 1961; Segal, Baumohl, and Moyles 1980); (5) the stigma of mental illness and available housing (Goldmeir, Shore, and Mannino 1977); (6) the stigma of seeing a psychiatrist (Bar-Levav 1976); and (7) employer responses to psychiatric stigmata (Miller and Dawson 1965; Webber and Orcutt 1982).

Despite the preponderance of sociological research on the stigma of mental illness, few ethnographically based studies have centered on the post-hospital lives of ex-psychiatric patients—largely chronic ex-patients living in halfway homes or boarding houses or involved in specific aftercare treatment programs (Lamb and Goertzel 1977; Reynolds and Farberow 1977; Cheadle, Freeman, and Korer 1978; Estroff 1981). Little systematic attention has been given to the ex-patients' perceptions of mental illness as a stigmatizable/stigmatizing attribute,[1] the ways that such persons manage such discreditable information about themselves in the context of social interaction with others, and the consequences of employing these strategies for altering their deviant identities. It is the purpose of this paper to address this deficit in the sociological literature by presenting ethnographic evidence from a study of 285 Canadian ex-psychiatric patients. First, I begin with a discussion of the sample, settings, and methods used in this study. Second, I analyze the five strategies such persons develop and employ in their "management work." Finally, I address the implications of adopting such stratagems for identity transformation.

Sample, Settings, and Methods

Descriptive data were collected on the nature of deinstitutionalized patient life over a period of four-and-one-half years by means of participant-observation, informal and semi-formal interviewing techniques with 285 non-chronic[2] and chronic[3] ex-psychiatric patients residing in Southern Ontario. A disproportionate, stratified random sample of 300 former mental patients was initially drawn from a list that included: (1) all psychiatric clients discharged between 1975 and 1981 from a provincial psychiatric facility in Southern Ontario; (2) all patients discharged from psychiatric wards in general hospitals; (3) those treated as out-patients in community psychiatric chronic-care units between 1978 and 1981; and (4) all cheats (i.e., those not registered as mental patients) treated privately by a psychiatric team associated with a university teaching hospital.

The sample of 300 was disproportionately stratified[4] to include six subgroups divided by age, chronicity, and type of hospitalization. Comparisons were made, for example, among elderly, middle-aged, and young long-term female and male ex-patients; and among elderly, middle-aged, and young short-term female and male ex-patients.[5]

I initially conducted informal interviews with each of the ex-patients in a mutually agreed upon location such as a coffee shop, their home, a mall, or their place of employment. These interviews lasted from three to five hours, and provided me with a wealth of information about the social worlds of ex-patients; subsequently, I was invited to attend and participate in other aspects of their lives such as self-help group meetings, activist group meetings and protest marches, and therapy sessions. In addition I frequently met ex-patients at their place of employment during coffee and lunch breaks and was afforded the opportunity to observe them interacting with co-workers. I ate lunches and dinners in their homes (as they did in mine)—the former opportunity allowed me to watch them interacting with family members, friends, and neighbors. Each Wednesday afternoon, I met a group of six ex-patients at a local donut shop where they would discuss the problems they were facing "on the outside" and possible remedies.

Mental Illness and Strategies of Information Management

Some studies on *discreditable* attributes (i.e., those not readily or visibly apparent to others) (Edgerton 1967; Humphreys 1972; Ponse 1976) suggest that individuals either disclose their attribute to others or make attempts to actively conceal such information. Other studies, however (Bell and Weinberg 1978; Schneider and Conrad 1980; Veevers 1980; Miall 1986), suggest that being a "secret deviant" is far more complex than either choosing to disclose or not disclose one's "failing." These studies suggest, rather, that individuals *selectively* conceal such information about themselves at certain times, in certain situations, with certain individuals, and freely disclose the same information at other times, in other situations, with other individuals. Concealment and disclosure are contingent upon a "complex interaction of one's learned perceptions of the stigma (of their attribute), actual 'test' experiences with others before or after disclosure, and the nature of the particular relationship involved" (Schneider and Conrad 1980, 39).

The complex reality of how individuals selectively conceal and disclose information was evident in the case of non-chronic ex-psychiatric patients. Examination of their post-hospital worlds revealed that many ex-patients not only faced economic hardships, had problems coping in the community, and experienced adverse side effects from their "meds" (medication),[6] but also that their perception of mental illness as a potentially stigmatizing attribute presented severe problems in their lives. Many lived their lives in states of emotional turmoil, afraid and frustrated, deciding *who* to tell or not tell, *when* to tell and when not to tell, and *how* to tell. Moe, a fifty-two-year-old former postman aptly summed it up for most non-chronics:

> You have no idea how frightening it is and how difficult. It's not a clear-cut thing that you tell everyone or you hide it. You've gotta decide which ones to tell, and which ones not to. And also the reason for doing it. Ever since I got out of the hospital, my stomach has literally been tied in knots. The fear about dealing with people and my mental sickness has given me a perpetual case of diarrhea!

Ex-psychiatric patients learned how, with whom, and under which circumstances to disclose or conceal their discreditable aspects of self, largely through a process of trial and error, committing numerous *faux pas* along the way. Edith, a fifty-nine-year-old widow spoke of the number of mistakes she made in her "management work":

> Since I was discharged three years ago, I've spent a lot of time figuring out exactly how to deal with my "problem" and whether to keep it secret or not, who I should tell or might tell, and the way I'd tell 'em. It's like a baptism by fire—you gotta just jump in and take a chance. Once, I decided to tell some of my congregation because I thought they were Christians and would be charitable, but I was wrong.... Another time, I told my kid's teacher during a parent-teacher meeting. I just blurted it out without really thinking about what I was saying or how. He was just stunned and looked at me!

In fact, even if no *faux pas* were committed, there was no guarantee that others would accept proffered meanings and definitions of self. As Charlie, a twenty-nine-year-old graduate student, hospitalized on three occasions, remarked:

> I'm not a stupid person. I learned how to handle effectively the negative aspects of my sickness—I mean how others view it. I've been doing O.K. now since my discharge, but still, each time I'm entering a new situation, I get anxious; I'm not always a hundred percent sure of whether to tell or not to, especially in the case of dating relationships. Even if you've had success in telling certain types of people, there's always the chance—and it happens more than you think—that people will just not "buy" what you're trying so desperately to "sell" them.

Nearly 80 percent of the non-chronics in this study engaged in some form of information control about their illnesses and past hospitalizations. Specifically, the stratagems adopted and employed by the ex-patients, resembling those observed in other deviant groups (Davis 1961; Levitin 1975; Hewitt and Stokes 1978; Schneider and Conrad 1980; Miall 1986; Miall and Herman 1994), included *selective concealment, therapeutic disclosure, preventive disclosure,* and *political activism*—stratagems adopted by ex-patients in their effort to lessen or avoid the stigma potential of mental illness, elevate self-esteem, renegotiate societal conceptions of mental illness as a discreditable attribute, and alter deviant identities.

Selective Concealment

Selective concealment may be defined as the selective withholding or disclosure of information about selves perceived as discreditable in cases where secrecy is the major stratagem for handling information about an attribute.

Especially during the time-period directly following their psychiatric treatment, the majority of non-chronics had a marked desire to conceal such information about their self from all others. Decisions about disclosure and concealment were made on the basis of their perceptions of others—that is, whether they were "safe others" or "risky others." So, too, were decisions based on prior, negative experiences with certain types of others. Speaking of his classification of others into "safe" and "risky" others, Donald a forty-two-year-old steelworker, institutionalized on four occasions, said:

> After being discharged, I had to seriously consider who I could confide in about my sickness—the safe ones, and those who I should keep it secret from—the risky ones. I thought about all my co-workers, which ones were small-minded and bigoted, and I thought about the church congregation and which people I could entrust.... After much deliberating, I decided only to tell my pastor and "Mrs Smith" and none of the guys at work.

Moreover, there was a hierarchical pattern of selective disclosure based upon the perceived degree of closeness between the individual being told and the ex-patient revealing his or her discreditable attribute. In general such information was most frequently revealed to family members, followed by close friends, and then, acquaintances—a pattern also reflected in the literature on epileptics (Schneider and Conrad 1980) and involuntarily childless women (Miall 1986). As Sarah, a thirty-six-year-old mother of two put it:

> When I was discharged, I didn't automatically hide it from everyone the fact that I was hospitalized for a nervous breakdown again. But I didn't go and tell everyone either. I phoned and told my relatives in "Logenport" and I confided in two of my close, good friends here in town.

Further, selective disclosures to "normal" others were frequently made to test reactions. Similar to Schneider and Conrad's (1980) epileptics, the continued disclosure of one's mental illness was contingent upon responses received to previous disclosures. Maria, a fifty-year-old woman of Italian descent remarked:

> It's really a difficult situation to be in. A long time ago, I decided that I could trust my two best girlfriends, but you should have seen how they reacted to the news. They treated me like I had the plague; they didn't know how to act around me.... After that, I didn't want to tell any of my other friends. Now I'm at the stage where I feel that it's better not to tell anyone because I'm petrified of what they'll think.

In cases where concealment was the dominant strategy of information management, ex-patients usually disclosed only to one or two individuals. As Simon, a twenty-five-year-old ex-patient aptly expressed:

> I decided from the moment that my treatment ended, I would tell as few people as possible about my stay in the psychiatric hospital. I figured that it

would be for the best to "keep it under a lid" for the most part. So, to this day, I've only confided in my friend, Paul, and a neighbor who had a similar illness a while back.

The employment of concealment as a stratagem of information management took the following forms: avoidance of selected "normals," redirection of conversations, withdrawal, the use of disidentifiers, and the avoidance of stigma symbols. Speaking on her redirection of conversations with certain others in an effort to conceal the stigma of her failing, Josie a forty-five-year-old non-chronic explained:

> Sometimes, I think of myself as a traffic director; by that, I mean, sometimes when I'm with a group of people and someone brings up something about mental patients or schizophrenia, I have to do something about it. I try to direct the flow of words—I mean, channel the conversation into another direction, lest myself or one of my children let the truth slip out about me.

For still others, concealment of their discreditable attribute was achieved through withdrawal. Over two-thirds of the ex-patients in this study engaged in withdrawal as a form of concealment, especially during the early months following discharge. Speaking on his use of this technique, Harry, a college junior remarked:

> Sometimes when I'm at a party or some type of gathering with a number of people, I just remain pretty reticent. I don't participate too much in the conversations.... I'm really unsure how much to tell other people. For the most part, I just keep pretty quiet and remain a wallflower. People may think I'm shy or stuck-up, but I'd rather deal with that than with the consequences of others finding out that I'm a mental patient.

A third technique employed by over one-third of the ex-patients to conceal their discreditable aspects of self from certain others, in certain situations, involved the use of *disidentifiers* (Goffman 1963, 44), that is, symbols ex-patients utilized in an effort to prevent "normal" others from discovering their "failing." Studies have shown that homosexuals (Carrier 1976; Delph 1978), unwed parents (Christensen 1953; Pfuhl 1978), and lesbians (Ponse 1976) also frequently make use of disidentifiers in their management work. Specifically, non-chronic ex-patients' disidentifiers took the form of making jokes about psychiatric patients while in the presence of "normal" others, and participating in protests *against* the integration of ex-patients into the community. Mike, a twenty-six-year-old ex-patient, recently released after three hospitalizations, remarked (with some remorse) on the use of this tactic:

> They wanted to use this house down the street for a group home for discharged patients. All the neighbors on the street were up in arms over it. It didn't upset me personally, but the neighbors made up this petition, and to protect myself, I not only signed it, but I also went door-to-door convincing

other neighbors to sign it and "keep those mentals out." ... I felt sort of bad afterwards, but what else could I do?

A final form of concealing information on the part of ex-patients was through the avoidance of *stigma symbols* (Goffman 1963, 43)—signs that would bring into the forefront, or disclose, their discreditable attribute. It is interesting to note that the data presented here on non-chronics and their avoidance of stigma symbols support observations made of other deviant groups, for example, transsexuals (Kando 1973; Bogdan 1974) and unwed fathers (Pfuhl 1978). Among the 146 ex-patients studied, over two-thirds avoided contact with such stigma symbols as other ex-mental patients with whom they had become friends while institutionalized, as well as self-help groups for ex-patients. So, too, did they avoid frequenting drop-in centers, dances and bingos for ex-patients, and, in general, any other places where "patients and ex-patients hung out." For still others, avoidance of stigma symbols entailed not attending post-hospital therapy sessions. Margarette, a stocky middle-aged woman of German descent, explained her avoidance of post-discharge therapy sessions in the following manner:

After I was released, my psychiatrist asked that I make appointments and see him every two weeks for follow-up maintenance treatments. But I never did go because I didn't want someone to see me going into the psychiatric department of "Meadowbrook Hospital" and sitting in the waiting room of the "Nut Wing." Two of my nosey neighbors are employed at that hospital and I just couldn't take the chance of them seeing me there one day.

In sum, ex-patients used selective concealment of their attribute and past hospitalizations as a strategy of information management in an effort to protect themselves from the perceived negative consequences that might result from the revelation of their illness. This became an "offensive tactical maneuver" through which ex-patients attempted (often unsuccessfully) to mitigate the stigma potential of mental illness on their daily rounds. Notably, the employment of concealment as a strategy of information management was a temporary process. The majority of ex-patients employed this strategy primarily during the first eight months following their discharge. During this time in particular they expressed feelings of anxiety, fear, and trepidation. However, as time passed, ex-patients began to test reactions. They encountered both positive and negative responses from certain "normals," and their strong initial desires for secrecy were replaced by alternative strategies.

Therapeutic Disclosure

Therapeutic disclosure may be defined as the selective disclosure of a discreditable attribute to certain trusted, empathetic, supportive others in an effort to renegotiate personal perceptions of the stigma of their "failing."

Similar to Miall's (1986) study on involuntarily childless women and Schneider and Conrad's (1980) study on epileptics, 36 percent of the ex-patients felt that speaking about their mental illnesses and past hospitalizations—getting it off their chests in a cathartic fashion—functioned to alleviate much of the burden. Speaking about the cathartic function served by disclosure to two of his friends, Mitchell, a thirty-nine-year-old ex-patient stated:

> When I finally let it out, it was like a hundred pound weight being lifted off my back. I kept this incredible burden a secret inside of me for so long, my fear, the pain that I had gone through; but once I released these feelings and the truth was known, I felt much better.

Therapeutic disclosure was most often carried out with family members, close friends, and with other ex-psychiatric patients—individuals "sharing the same fate." Ida, a fifty-two-year-old, discussing the circumstances surrounding her disclosure to a neighbor who had also been hospitalized in a psychiatric facility at one time, said:

> At first, I was apprehensive to talk about it. But keeping it inside of you all bottled up is no good either. One day, I walked down the street to a neighbor of mine and she invited me in to have tea. I knew what had happened to her years ago [her deceased husband confided in my husband]. I let out all my anxieties and fears to her that afternoon.... I told her everything and she was so sympathetic.... She knew exactly what I was going through. Once I let it all out, I felt so much better.

Even in cases where ex-patients disclosed to individuals who turned out to be unsympathetic and unsupportive, the disclosure was often considered to be therapeutic:

> A couple of times when I revealed my sickness, I got the cold shoulder. There was a lot of hee-hawing going on. Some people didn't know how to react. They'd fumble around trying to say something, but mostly they'd just stare with their mouths wide open. Others would sometimes try to make a joke of it and that would really hurt my feelings. In one case, the guy told me off and said that he didn't want to have anything more to do with me.... But that's all O.K. because each time I talked about it, it got easier, and I felt better.

Just as therapeutic disclosure functioned to relieve the anxieties and frustrations of ex-patients, it also allowed for the renegotiation of personal perceptions of mental illness as a discreditable attribute. Speaking about the manner by which she came to redefine mental illness in her own mind as a less stigmatizing attribute, Edith explained:

> When I finally opened up and started talking about it, it really wasn't so bad after all. My Uncle John was very supportive and helped me to put my mind at rest, to realize that having mental illness isn't so bad; it's not like having cancer. He told me that thousands of people go into the hospital each year for

psychiatric treatment and probably every third person I meet has had treatment.... After much talking, I no longer think of myself as less human, but more normally.... Having mental illness isn't the blight I thought it was.

In short, ex-patients employed therapeutic disclosure in order to relieve feelings of frustration and anxiety, to elevate their self-esteem, and to renegotiate (in their own minds) personal perceptions of mental illness as stigmatizing.

Preventive Disclosure

Preventive disclosure may be described as the selective disclosure to normals of a discreditable attribute in an effort to influence others' actions and/or perceptions about the ex-patient or about mental illness in general (Schneider and Conrad 1980; Miall 1986). Preventive disclosure of their mental illness and past hospitalizations occurred in situations where ex-patients anticipated future rejection by normal others. In order to minimize the pain of subsequent rejection, 34 percent of the sample decided that the best strategy to employ with certain people was one of preventive disclosure early in their relationships. As Ronald, a thirty-four-year-old musician, put it:

It's not the easiest thing in the world to tell people that you were once institutionalized in the "crazy house." But if you don't tell them, they find out later and reject you, you put yourself through a lot of unnecessary pain. You've wasted all that time building up a friendship for nothing!

Preventive disclosure may have been a way in which ex-patients attempted to prevent a drop in their status in the event that their illness became known at a later date, or a way of testing acquaintances in an effort to establish friendship boundaries.

Just as preventive disclosure was used by non-chronics to avoid future stigma and rejection, so, too, did they employ this strategy in order to influence normals' attitudes about themselves and about mental illness in general. Specifically, in this regard, ex-patients used the following devices: (1) *medical disclaimers* (Hewitt and Stokes 1978; Schneider and Conrad 1980; Miall 1986); (2) *deception/coaching* (Goffman 1963; Schneider and Conrad 1980; Miall 1986); (3) *education* (Schneider and Conrad 1980; Miall and Herman 1994); and (4) *normalization* (Davis 1961, 1963; Cogswell 1967; McCaghy 1968; Scott 1969; Levitin 1975).

Medical Disclaimers
Similar to Schneider and Conrad's and Miall's studies, 52 percent of the ex-patients frequently used medical disclaimers in their management work—"blameless, beyond-my-control medical interpretation(s)" developed in

order to "reduce the risk that more morally disreputable interpretations might be applied by naïve others" discovering their failing (Schneider and Conrad 1980, 41). Such interpretations were often used by ex-patients to evoke sympathy from others and to ensure that they would be treated in a charitable manner. As Dick, an unemployed laborer, put it:

> When I tell people about my hospitalization in a psychiatric hospital, I imme-diately emphasize that the problem isn't anything I did, it's a biological one. I didn't ask to get sick; it was just plain biology; or my genes that fucked me up. I try to tell people in a nice way so that they see mental illness just like other diseases—you know, cancer or the mumps. It's not my parents' fault or my own.... I just tell them, "Don't blame me, blame my genes!"

In a similar vein, Anna, a twenty-nine-year-old waitress, explained her use of medical disclaimers:

> Talking about it is quite tricky. When I tell them about it, I'm careful to emphasize that the three times I was admitted, was due to a bio-chemical imbalance—something that millions of people get. I couldn't do anything to help myself—I ate properly, didn't drink or screw around. It's not something I deserved. When you give people the facts and do it in a clinical fashion, you can sway many of them to sympathize with you.

Moreover, eleven ex-patients revealed their mental illness and past hos-pitalizations as a side effect of another medical problem or disease such as childbirth, stroke, or heart disease, thereby legitimizing what otherwise might be considered a potentially stigmatizing condition. As Sue, a thirty-nine-year-old ex-patient explained:

> When I talk about it to some people, I tell them that the reason I had all those nervous breakdowns was due to childbirth. My husband knocked me up seven times in nine years. Having to deal with so many brats and difficult births where I almost bit the dust it was so painful, caused my breakdowns. I even had toxemia.... Getting mentally sick was an added bonus I hadn't counted on. People really feel for you when you tell them this way.

While Sue achieved a degree of success in influencing others' perceptions about her attribute and mental illness, Lenny lamented his failure with the same strategy:

> Life's not easy for ex-nuts, you know. I tried telling two of my drinking buddies about my schizophrenia problem one night at the bar. I thought if I told 'em that it's a "disease" like having a heart problem that they would understand and pat me on the butt and say it didn't matter to them and that I was O.K. Shit, it didn't work out like I planned; they flipped out on me. Sid couldn't handle it at all and just let out of there in a hurry; Jack stayed around me for about twenty minutes and then made some excuse and left.

In sum, through the use of medical disclaimers, ex-patients hoped to elevate their self-esteem and to renegotiate personal perceptions of mental illness as a stigmatizable attribute.

Deception/Coaching

Deception differed from strategies of concealment in that with the latter, ex-patients readily disclosed their illness and past hospitalizations, but explicitly distorted the conditions or circumstances surrounding it. Similar to Miall's (1986) involuntarily childless women and Schneider and Conrad's (1980) epileptics, about one-third of the ex-patients employed deceptive practices developed with the assistance of coaches. Coaches included parents, close friends, spouses, and other ex-patients sharing the same stigma. Coaches actively provided ex-patients with practical suggestions on how to disclose their attribute in the least stigmatizing manner and present themselves in a favorable light. Sherryl, a twenty-three-year-old ex-patient, recently discharged after her fourth hospitalization, spoke of her parents' "coaching sessions:"

> Pop and mom helped me out—they taught me what to say to people, I mean, word for word spiels or speeches; we'd even rehearse it—I'd try it out on them to see how it sounded. Pop advised me what we'd lie about—the suicide attempts, the wrists—to tone it all down and alter the details to make it sound better.

It is interesting to note that about one-quarter of the ex-patients used deceptive practices together with medical disclaimers. As Benjamin, a sixty-two-year-old ex-patient aptly expressed:

> To survive in this cruel, cold world, you've got to be sneaky. I mean that you've got to try to win people over to your side. Whoever you decide to tell about your illness, you've got to make it clear that you had nothing to do with getting sick; nobody can place blame on anyone.... And you've got to color the truth about how you ended up in the hospital by telling heart-sob stories to get people sympathetic to you. You never tell them the whole truth or they'll shun you like the plague!

Education

A third form of preventive disclosure used by ex-patients to influence others' perceptions of themselves as possessing a stigmatizing attribute and their ideas about mental illness was that of education. Similar to Schneider and Conrad's (1980) epileptics and Miall's (1986) involuntarily childless women who revealed their attribute in an effort to educate others, so too, did 28 percent of the ex-patients reveal their condition for the same educational purposes. Marge, a thirty-nine-year-old ex-patient, speaking about her efforts to educate friends and neighbors stated:

I have this urge inside of me to teach people out there, to let them know that they've been misinformed about mental illness and mental patients. We're not the way the media has portrayed us. That's why people are afraid of us. I feel very strongly that someone has to tell people the truth,… give them the facts…. And when they hear it, they're amazed sometimes and begin to treat me without apprehension…. Each time I make a breakthrough, I think more highly of myself too.

Ex-patients did not automatically attempt to educate everyone they encountered, but rather, based on subjective typification of normals, made value judgments about whom to educate. Alicia, speaking on this matter, explained:

I don't automatically tell everyone I know. That would be suicidal. You learn, you think things through as who should be educated and who you shouldn't bother with—the ones that could probably profit from your discussion…. With some people, the Archie Bunkers of this world, it would be useless to bother. What you got to do is find the Edith Bunker types—the benign but stupid one to talk about it to.

As Goffman (1963, 101) has said, medical disclaimers, deception/ coaching, and education are forms of "disclosure etiquette"; they are formulas for revealing a stigmatizing attribute " in a matter-of-fact way, supporting the assumption that those present are above such concerns, while preventing them from trapping themselves into showing that they are not."

Normalization

A final form of preventive disclosure employed by ex-psychiatric patients to manage stigma (specifically, through the reshaping of others' negative perceptions about mental patients and mental illness) was that of normalization. This concept is drawn from Davis's (1963) study on children with polio and is akin to deviance disavowal (Davis 1961). Normalization is a strategy individuals use to deny that their behavior or attribute is deviant—it "seeks to render normal and morally acceptable that which has heretofore been regarded as abnormal and immoral" (Pfuhl 1986, 163). Similar to observations made on pedophiles (McCaghy 1968), the obese (Millman 1980), the visibly handicapped (Levitin 1975), and paraplegics (Cogswell 1967), about one-quarter of the ex-psychiatric patients employed this strategy. Such persons were firmly committed to societal conceptions of normalcy, and were aware that according to these standards, they were disqualified—that they would never "measure up." Yet, ex-patients made active attempts at rationalizing and downplaying the stigma attached to their failing. So, for example, they participated in a full round of normal activities and aspired to normal attainments. They participated in amateur theater groups, played competitive sports such as hockey and tennis, enrolled in college, and so on.

Ex-patients whose stigma could be considered discreditable would disclose such information for preventive reasons, thereby rendering them *discredited* (visibly apparent or known to others) in the eyes of others. Ex-patients would then attempt to negotiate with normals for preferred images, attitudes, roles, and non-deviant conceptions of self, and definitions of mental illness as less-stigmatizing. Discussing his utilization of this technique, "Weird Old" Larry, a fifty-nine-year-old ex-patient stated:

> The third time I got out [of the hospital], I tried to fit right in. I told some of my buddies and a couple of others about my sickness. It was easier to get it out in the open. But what I tried to show 'em was that I could do the same things they could, some of them, even better. I beat them at pool, at darts; I could out-drink them, I was holding down two jobs—one at the gas station and at K-Mart. I tried to show them I was normal. I was cured! The key to success is being up-front and making them believe you're just as normal as them.... You can really change how they see and treat you.

If successfully carried out, normalization, as a technique of managing stigma, normalized relations between ex-patients and others. This is not to imply, however, that the strategy of normalization worked for all patients in all situations. Similar to Millman's (1980, 78) overweight females who were accepted in certain roles, but who were stigmatized and treated as deviant in others, many ex-patients encountered problems. Frederick, speaking on this problem with respect to co-workers, said:

> It's really tragic you know. When I told the other people at work that I was a manic depressive but was treated and released, I emphasized that I was completely normal in every way.... But they only accepted me normally, part of the time, like when we were in the office.... But they never really accepted me as their friend, as one of "the boys"; and they never invited me over to dinner with their wife and family. They still saw me as an ex-crazy, not as an equal to be worthy of being invited to dinner or playing with their kids.

It is interesting to note that the strategy of normalization was employed by ex-patients whose attribute was discreditable as well as by those with discrediting attributes. Explaining how medication side-effects rendered him discredited, and how he attempted to reduce the stigma of mental illness through normalization, Ross said:

> Taking all that dope the shrinks dish out makes my hands tremble. Look at my shaking legs too. I never used to have these twitches in my face either, but that's just the side effects, a bonus you get. It really fucks things up though. If I wanted to hide my illness, I couldn't; everyone just looks at me and knows.... So, what I do is to try to get people's attention and get them to see my positive side—that I can be quite normal, you know. I emphasize all the things that I can do!

In short by presenting themselves as normals, ex-patients hoped to elicit positive responses from others whose reactions were deemed to be important. From a social psychological perspective, if through this process of negotiation, others accepted and reinforced a non-deviant image of self, the ex-patients could achieve more positive, non-deviant identities.

In many cases ex-psychiatric patients progressed from one strategy to another as they managed information about themselves. Specifically, they moved from a strategy of initial selective concealment to disclosure for therapeutic and preventive reasons. According to the ex-patients, such a progression was linked to their increased adjustment to their attribute as well as to positive responses to the revelation of their mental illness.

Political Activism

Just as ex-psychiatric patients developed and employed a number of individualized forms of information management to deal with the stigma potential of mental illness, enhance self-images, and alter deviant identities, they also employed one collective management strategy[7] to achieve the same ends, namely, joining and participating in ex-mental patient activist groups (Anspach 1979). Such groups, with their goal of self-affirmation, represent what Kitsuse (1980, 9) terms "tertiary deviation," referring to the deviant's conformation, assessment, and rejection of the negative identity embedded in secondary deviation and the transformation of that identity into a positive and viable self-conception.

Political activism served a three-fold function for the ex-patient: first, it repudiated standards of normalcy (standards to which they couldn't measure up) and the deviant labels placed upon these individuals; second, it provided them with a new, positive, non-deviant identity, enhanced their self-respect, and afforded them a new sense of purpose; and third, it served to propagate this new, positive image of ex-mental patients to individuals, groups, and organizations in society. The pay-off from political activism was both personal as well as social.

Similar to such activist groups as the Gay Liberation Front, the Disabled in Action, the Gray Panthers, and the radical feminist movement, ex-mental patient activists, through participation in their group, rejected prevailing societal values of normalcy. They repudiated the deviant identities, the roles and statuses placed on them. Moreover, these individuals flatly rejected the stigma associated with their identities. Sid, a forty-three-year-old unemployed sheet metal worker summed it up for most ex-patient activists when he said:

> I'm rejecting the whole damned thing. I mean, the fact that society has set up a set of rules regarding what is normal and what isn't. It's black and white type of thing—either you're this or you're that. It's too narrow and I don't buy it anymore!

Upon repudiating prevailing cultural values and the deviant identities bestowed on ex-patients, activists collectively redefined themselves in a more positive, non-deviant light according to their own newly constructed set of standards. Speaking about the way she embraced a new non-deviant identity, Susan, a thirty-nine-year-old ex-patient who recently returned to teaching school, said:

> I no longer agree to accept what society says is normal and what is not. It's been so unfair to psychiatric patients. Who are they to say, just because we don't conform that we're rejects of humanity.... The labels they've given us are degrading and make us feel sick.... [They] have a negative connotation to them.... So, we've gotten together and liberated ourselves. We've thrown away the old labels and negative images of self-worth and we give ourselves new labels and images of self-worth—as human beings who should be treated with decency and respect.

In contrast to other ex-patients who employed various individual management strategies to deal with what they perceived to be their own *personal* problems (personal failings), ex-patient activists did not see their problems as personal failings or potentially stigmatizing attributes. Rather, these persons came to see their problems as *societal* problems. The extent to which ex-patients viewed their situations in this manner is directly correlated to their development of more positive self-images. Speaking of this process as one of *stigma conversion*, Humphreys (1972, 142) states:

> In converting his stigma, the oppressed person does not merely exchange his social marginality for political marginality.... Rather, he emerges from a stigmatized cocoon as a transformed creature, one characterized by the spreading of political wings. At some point in the process, the politicized "deviant" gains a new identity, an heroic self-image as crusader in a political cause.

Sally, a neophyte activist, placed the blame on society for her deviant self-image:

> It's not any of our faults that we ended up the way we did. I felt guilty for a long time.... I crouched away feeling that I had something that made me "different" from everyone else, a pock on my life.... But I learned at the activist meetings that none of it was my fault. It was all society's fault—they're the ones who can't deal with anything that is different. Now I realize that having mental illness is nothing to be ashamed of; it's nothing to hide. I'm now proud of who ... and what I am!

Just as political activism, as contrasted with other adaptive responses to stigma, sought, in repudiating the dominant value system, to provide ex-patients with positive, non-deviant statuses, so, too, did it attempt to propagate this new, positive, normal image of ex-psychiatric patient to others in society. Thus, through such activities as attending rallies, demonstrations, protest marches, and conferences on human rights for patients, lobbying politicians and the medical profession, and producing newsletters, ex-patient activists sought to promote social change. Specifically, they sought to counter or remove the stigma associated with their "differentness" and present society with an image of former psychiatric patients as "human beings" capable of self-determination and political action. Abe, the president of the activist group, aptly summed up the aim of political activism during a speech to selected political figures, media personnel, and "upstanding" citizens:

> Simply put, we're tired of being pushed around. We reject everything society says about us, because it's just not accurate. We reject the type of treatment we get ... both in the hospital ... and out. We don't like the meaning of the words [people] use to describe us—"mentals" and "nuts." We see ourselves differently, just as good and worthy as everybody out there.

In sum, through participation in political activist groups, many ex-patients internalized an ideology that repudiated societal values and conventional standards of normalcy, rejected their deviant identities and statuses, adopted more positive, non-deviant identities, and attempted to alter society's stereotypical perceptions about mental patients and mental illness in general.

Discussion and Conclusions: Implications for Becoming an "Ex-Crazy"

When psychiatric patients are discharged from institutions or psychiatric wards of general hospitals, their problems[8] are far from over. In fact numerous problems lie ahead for such persons in their efforts to return to a life of normality or conventionality. As Erikson (1966), Ebaugh (1988), and others have rightly noted in their studies on role exit and the reintegration of deviants into society, there exist virtually no formal rites of passage to mark the ex-deviant's passage out of the deviant identity and role. While society has developed and employed various "degradation ceremonies" (Garfinkel 1956) marking the passage of individuals from "normal" to "deviant" identities and statuses, there are no such comparable ceremonies to reinstate the "transformed" or "ex-deviant." My findings suggested that ex-patients realized not only that no such ritualistic ceremonies existed to "transform them back," but also that they possessed a stigma that severely impeded such a transformation of self as well as their future participation in society. In response to their undesirable post-hospital social situations, non-chronic ex-psychiatric patients employed five strategies that, if successfully carried out, lessened or mitigated the stigma of their failing, enhanced their self-esteem, and allowed for self-transformation and renegotiation of societal conceptions of mental illness as a discreditable attribute.

Strategies of stigma management have important consequences for social identities. Ebaugh (1984), in her study of nuns leaving the convent, speaks of the process of becoming an "ex-" in terms of the concepts of "role exit" and "self-transformation." Specifically, she asserts that ex-roles represent a unique sociological phenomenon in that definitions of self and societal expectations are shaped and often determined by a previous identity. On the one hand, individuals are fighting to leave behind their old identities, statuses, and roles; on the other hand, others are continually taking them into account when interacting. Ebaugh (1984, 156) further points out that there are some ex-roles in our society that are fairly well-defined such as "ex-president," but what we are seeing in society today is an increasing number of ex-roles for which there are few well-defined normative expectations. In these situations, the "ex's" themselves have to create role definitions as they play out their lives. Like ex-nuns' role-exiting experiences—attempting to shake off their old life and create new roles that they negotiate for and proffer to others in an effort to reformulate societal expectations—non-chronic former patients, in their process of self-transformation, struggled to cast off their deviant identity and role. This decision was prompted largely by their perception of mental illness as a stigmatizing attribute. As Goffman (1963, 78) states, "The stigmatized individual tends to hold the same beliefs about identity that we do. His deepest feeling about what he is, may be his sense of being a 'normal' person, a human being like anyone else, a person, therefore, who deserves a fair break. What is desired by the individual is what can be called acceptance." The creation of a new identity of "ex-crazy" or "ex-mental patient," a positive, non-deviant, non-stigmatizing identity, arose then through an ongoing process of negotiations with normals in a bid for acceptance. In particular, ex-patients were successful in transforming their deviant aspects of self when (or if)[9] (a) they began to think of themselves in terms of current, non-deviant roles and began to project such an image to others, and (b) others began to relate to them in terms of their new roles.

In sum, my findings suggest that ex-psychiatric patients are not passive, powerless individuals; rather, they are strategists, expert managers, and nego-tiators who play active (although not always successful) roles in the shaping of deviant outcomes. In other words ex-patients are instrumental in shaping their own social fates; they attempt to elicit desired reactions through their own behaviors, through techniques of stigma management, and through the expectations and images they project. These findings are supported by other research on deviants (Levitin 1975; Hewitt and Stokes 1978; Schneider and Conrad 1980; Miall 1986, among others).

My research also offers new insight into the various strategies that indi-viduals use to manage potentially stigmatizing information about them-selves. Although the strategies employed by the ex-patients have been observed with respect to various other deviant groups, I have documented an interesting difference—specifically, that ex-patients perceived therapeutic disclosure to be helpful and desirable, even in those instances where audiences reacted in a negative, unsupportive manner.[10]

Future research on the stigma of mental illness should also focus on the families of ex-psychiatric patients in terms of the dynamic of family interaction. While some studies (Freeman and Simmons 1961; Lefton, Angrist, Dinitz, and Pasamanick 1962) have concentrated on such family interaction patterns as exclusion and rejection, it would be naïve to conclude that these are the only two responses that develop. Future research needs to examine families' efforts at co-operation with ex-patients, and their efforts at attempting to re-integrate them into society, manage stigma, and so on. So, too, should studies focus on the problems and frustrations experienced by family members in their efforts to cope with ex-patients. Specifically, studies should focus on the perceptions of stigma as it relates to the family and friends of ex-patients—"Do they possess a courtesy stigma?" (Goffman 1963, 30) and if so, how do they deal with it?

Finally, future research should focus on social power, management strategies, and identity transformation. Following Becker's suggestion (1963, 17), presumably, those in positions of power or who have basic resources of social power at their command, will deal with the stigma potential of mental illness in manners different from those without such power. Those with powerful resources will likely be able to achieve more favorable outcomes than those without such resources. Clearly, these factors merit future consideration with respect to ex-psychiatric patients.

NOTES

1. The perceived stigmatized status of individuals and the information management strategies they employ have been well-documented on other groups such as: the retarded (Edgerton 1967); epileptics (Schneider and Conrad 1980); secret homosexuals (Humphreys 1975); involuntarily childless women (Miall 1986); swingers (Bartell 1971); and lesbians (Ponse 1976), among others. See Herman (1986) for discussion with respect to the mentally ill.

2. *Chronicity* for the purposes of this study, was defined not in diagnostic terms, i.e., "chronic schizophrenic"; rather, it was defined in terms of duration, continuity, and frequency of hospitalizations. Specifically, the term *non-chronic* refers to those individuals hospitalized for time-periods of less than two years, on a discontinuous basis, those hospitalized on less than five occasions, or those treated in psychiatric wards of general hospital facilities.

3. The term *chronic* ex-psychiatric patient refers to those institutionalized in psychiatric hospitals for time-periods of two years or more, institutionalized on a continual basis, or on five or more occasions.

4. The decision to stratify the sample by chronicity, was based upon my interests and prior fieldwork activities. My earlier study (Herman 1981) indicated that when we speak of "deinstitutionalized" or "discharged" patients, we cannot merely assume that they are one homogeneous grouping of individuals with like characteristics, similar post-hospital social situations, experiences and perceptions of reality. Rather, prior research led me to believe that I may, in fact, be dealing with distinct subgroups of individuals with varying perceptions of reality and experiences. See Herman (1986) for specific details.

5. In Estroff's (1981) ethnography on chronic ex-mental patients, she points out the catch-22 situation they are in. Ex-patients need to take their medications on a regular basis in order to remain on the outside. However, the situation is ironic because, in an effort to become more like others, "meds" make them "different." The various side effects reinforce their deviant identities.

6. See Herman (1986) for a detailed discussion of such other post-hospital problems.

7. Following Lyman's (1970) typology on deviant voluntary associations, ex-mental patient political activist groups represent an "instrumental-alienative" type of association. It is interesting to note that chronic ex-patients also employed one collective form of stigma management; specifically, they formed and participated in deviant subcultures. See Herman (1987) for details.

8. For a detailed discussion of their problems as pre- and in-patients, see Herman (1986).

9. It is important to reiterate that transforming deviant identities is extremely difficult and complex. The implementation of the various strategies discussed in this paper in no way guaranteed success. Many times, ex-patients were unsure about when to use them, in which situations, with whom, etc. Even if they were used correctly, there was no guarantee that others would react in a positive manner, that is, accept proffered meanings and definitions.

10. One notable exception is Miall's (1986) study on involuntary childless women, but, by and large, this finding has not been noted elsewhere with respect to therapeutic disclosure.

PART 3

In Perspective: Pursuing Intersubjectivity

Although the two articles that conclude this volume are rather different in thrust, both attest to the necessity of developing a social science that is grounded in the ways in which human lived experience is accomplished.

Elvi Whittaker, an anthropologist, comments on the appropriateness of the work of Herbert Blumer for anthropology. This is an important piece for this volume in several respects. First, it provides sociology students with a better appreciation of the status of ethnographic inquiry in anthropology. Second, it alerts readers to some of the differences in emphasis and practices that currently exist between ethnographic inquiry in anthropology and the interactionist ethnographic enterprise. Covering a great deal of material in a short statement, Whittaker also generates some instructive background material on the development of ethnographic inquiry in anthropology and its interlinkages with somewhat parallel practices in sociology. As well, this paper draws attention to some of the debates that have arisen in anthropology with respect to matters of theory and method and the task of "representing" the ethnographic other. Whittaker thus highlights some of the central affinities and disjunctures between anthropological and interactionist approaches to ethnographic research.

While sociologists may gain considerable insight into variations of human lifestyles and practices by examining the anthropological literature, it is also apparent that ethnographers in anthropology may gain much conceptual coherence and clarity by more explicitly attending to the work of Herbert Blumer. Further, although the articles in this volume essentially represent a series of sociological ethnographies depicting facets of people's lived experiences in contemporary North American society, this material may offer much more than a comparative contrast with somewhat parallel inquires that anthropologists may pursue in other cultural settings. As the world becomes increasingly "westernized" on the one hand, and as it becomes more difficult for anthropologists to locate "new" cultural worlds around the globe on the other, we may expect that the works of more ethnographers in anthropology will begin to more closely approximate those of the sociological ethnographers (Daniel Wolf's [an anthropologist] insightful study of outlaw bikers in this volume is a case in point). This means that those engaged in "urban anthropology" may very well find a package of materials of the sort presented here useful in classroom settings or as a general resource.

In more general terms, we should appreciate that the value of Blumer's statement on symbolic interaction is by no means limited to sociologists and anthropologists. Blumer's work is of central significance to social scientists across the board. Indeed, his insistence on the necessity of researchers respecting the nature of the human group in developing theory, methods, and research constitutes the vital synthesizing feature in developing a more sustained analysis of human behavior across the social sciences. In this regard, much more consequential than someone being labeled as a sociologist, an anthropologist, a psychologist, a political scientist, a social historian, and the like, is whether or not the researchers in question attend to the ways in which human group life is acomplished in practice by the people involved in the settings under consideration.

The last article in this volume, "Generic Social Processes: Intersubjectivity and Transcontextuality in the Social Sciences" also builds squarely on Herbert Blumer's notions of symbolic interaction, but focuses on another central aspect of the interactionist approach. Thus, while Blumer's work may be seen to provide the essential impetus for developing a genuine intersubjective social science grounded in human lived experience, Blumer also was very much concerned with developing concepts that would enable researchers to maximize insights with respect to the study of human group life.

Whereas most scholars would acknowledge the exceptional depth and rich insight normally generated through sustained ethnographic inquiry, one of the most common criticisms that ethnographers encounter pertains to the lack of conceptual depth and cumulativeness of what may appear as scattered instances of ethnographic inquiry. Some ethnographers have defended themselves by claiming that each situation they examine is so unique or holistically particular that any attempts to draw comparisons would only destroy the unique configurations or idiographic nature of the lifestyles and practices under consideration. Not all ethnographers are persuaded by this idiographic posture. Still, one might observe that for all the weaknesses associated with ethnographic research, one or two ethnographic inquiries often generate much more instructive understandings of people's life-worlds than that accomplished by conducting piles and piles of survey or experimental research on related topics. As a case in point, one might pit Clifford Shaw's (1930) *The Jack-Roller* and Edwin Sutherland's (1937) *The Professional Thief* against the immense amount of quantitative research that has been conducted in the areas of crime and delinquency over the past century, asking if we have developed any better understanding of involvements in these areas than what these two early ethnographies were able to generate. These sorts of comparisons can generate considerable embarrassment for alternative methods (and those investing considerable time and money in these pursuits). The practical implication is that ethnographic research should be deployed more extensively than has been the case to date. Still, the criticism regarding the lack of conceptual continuity has some merits. If we are to approximate a social science of any type, then more is entailed than achieving better sets of understandings of people's life-worlds than can be accomplished in other manners. We also should give consideration to developing concepts that enable us to transcend particular ethnographic inquiries.

Interestingly, while the criticism pertaining to the lack of conceptual material has often been expressed by outsiders and has been directed at ethnographers in general, the matter of conceptual development has been an element of long-standing concern within the interactionist community. Those working in an interactionist cast derived some early inspiration both from George Simmel's emphasis on the study of forms of association and George Herbert Mead's attempt to develop a processual conceptualization of human group life. As well, since 1931, Herbert Blumer has emphasized the necessity of developing concepts in the social sciences, observing that one can not have a "science without concepts." The question or challenge, however, is not simply to develop concepts, but to generate concepts that accurately and effectively reflect the essence of the phenomenon under consideration. In the case of the social sciences, this means developing concepts that reflect the nature of human lived experience.

While Blumer insists on the pursuit of *intimate familiarity* with one's subject matter through sustained ethnographic inquiry, and also intends to maintain the contextual integrity of the situations being studied, he asks if we might not still be able to locate or define a set of processes that transcend a plurality of contexts. Viewed thusly, each subsequent inquiry into this or that context may be seen as an opportunity with which to assess and redefine current notions of process that appeared viable in other settings.

In contrast to those who would argue for the necessity of remaining at the level of the individual case or idiographic instance—that each context or situation can only be appreciated with respect to itself—Blumer (1928, 349) observes:

> (T)he drawing of abstractions, the formulations of universals, does not annihilate the unique in the sense of transforming its rich individual content into less meaningful general content; rather, the universal is complementary to the individual; instead of subtracting from the individual, it adds to the individual.

Rather than destroying the unique features of situations, concepts represent enabling devices for more fully appreciating both the unique and the more common features of situations by providing comparison points for locating and considering particular practices and viewpoints. Further, by encouraging researchers to be attentive to "what they encounter out there," Blumer notes that each (idiographic and mundane) feature of the situation under consideration may be seen to provide the essential base for developing reformulations, extensions, or alternatives to prevailing conceptual notions.

This emphasis on generic concepts is of central consequence not just to ethnographers in sociology, but would also allow ethnographers in other social sciences to achieve more consequential coherence in what otherwise is apt to remain a set of largely isolated or scattered ethnographic ventures. The generic social processes outlined in the last article have been developed by examining the interactionist/ethnographic literature. As additional research is conducted and the applicability of these notions is explored in this and that setting, these processes should be recast to reflect subsequent inquiries. Even as a working formulation, however, these generic social processes represent an analytical grid for integrating disconnected but essential bodies of ethnographic inquiry, made even more valuable for social scientists by virtue of this communicative medium.

Generic social processes provide a means of comparing and contrasting the various realms of ethnographic ventures, especially those inquiries which have been attentive to the ongoing or dynamic features of human interchange. This conceptual scheme also alerts us to lapses and gaps in the ethnographic literature and consequently to our limitations in understanding human lived experience.

This material may also be seen to constitute a nucleus for reconceptualizing the ways in which social science is pursued in academia. Thus, instead of organizing our knowledge of human group life around "institutions" in a characteristically functionalist manner, we may begin to organize our stock of knowledge around the processes of human interchange. In this way we much better approximate the kind of sociology that Georg Simmel envisioned when he talked about sociololgy as the study of (as)sociation.

The ethnographic inquiries (Parts 2 and 3) in this volume can be seen to move both the field of sociology and the social sciences more generally in the direction Simmel had in mind. Hopefully, other scholars will derive inspiration from these efforts. Hopefully, too, through their own ethnographic inquiries, they will help develop a social science which is both rigorously grounded in the lived experiences of people and attends to the necessity of developing concepts that enable us to develop heightened appreciations of the world of the other.

The Contribution of Herbert Blumer to Anthropology[1]

Elvi Whittaker

Behind the findings, approaches, discoveries, constructions, reportings, and imaginings that anthropologists have offered as truths about the world, an epistemological trend has been obvious for some time. The certainty that was promised by the prospects of an anthropology constructed solely on the model of science has, for the time being, disappeared. What were once thought of as truths, finally uncovered, are now liable to be seen as no more than informed judgments and perceptions. Claims to something called "objectivity," and proclamations titled "conclusions" are now inclined to raise questions rather than dispel them. As more of the comfortable certainties of the past depart from everyday anthropology, more seemingly ambiguous notions replace them. The anthropologist must now contend with "meaning," "experience," "discourse," "narrativity," "representation," "textuality," "interpretation," and "authority." Perhaps all of these issues are better discussed under a gloss term which unifies these concepts—*interpretive anthropology.*

One of the major early figures of North American cultural anthropology, Alfred Kroeber, is known to have observed that betting on a theory is like betting at the races. You can never know which will win. It is in the nature of all theoretical discourses, however, that almost by definition, the end is never reachable. Thus, it is more fruitful to note how the discourse is developed, put to use, criticized, and perhaps how it promotes or contends with the discourses to follow.

For about twenty years anthropology has been developing its own version of interpetive social science. The interpretive paradigm has been a congenial one for a discipline that continually relies on the notion that cultures interpret their worlds differently. So the package of ideas embedded in the interpretive approach seems not only somehow truthful, but inevitable. Perhaps Kuhn (1970) and Schutz (1967a, 1967b) were the theoretical proponents, but the very work of anthropology, its assumptions and practices, support the continuance of the approach. Yet, as with all theoretical discourses, much of the work involves seeking enrichment beyond the boundaries of anthropology, beyond the package of ideas already instituted in the discipline. Theoretical alliances are continually being forged. Thus, the theories in the field are always in process, with a cast of characters that include those already recognized as belonging to anthropology and those who are newcomers. This is where Herbert Blumer comes in.

Blumer is poised in an interesting position. He is obviously an important possible contributor to some of the central and developing questions in the discipline. Moreover, he surely could assume a position in the history of anthropology where at present no position exists. Only the narrowly doctrinaire or the empirically traditional anthropologist would fail to give credence to the kinship.

To some degree Blumer is already known in various anthropological circles. His work is evoked in some centers where anthropologists are trained, and his scholarly contribution is acknowledged sporadically here and there or on this and that issue. This surface exposure, however, suggests that there is good cause to consider his work more extensively. The ongoing attention to interpretive anthropology makes the recognition of Blumer more than a scholarly politeness. It is my intention to suggest an appropriation of Blumer into the abstract world of anthropological reasoning.

The Anthropologist's Blumer: From Scholarly Politeness to Commitment

Anthropology, like all academic disciplines, has been characteristically resistant to venues produced outside its recognized parameters. Though Blumer has not entered the anthropological vernacular to the extent that he deserves, he has claimed a prominent intellectual position at both the Universities of Chicago and Berkeley.[2] These two universities were significant in Blumer's own academic career in that his work began at one in 1925 and ended at the other in 1987.

It was at the University of Chicago in the 1920s and 1930s that Blumer's influence on anthropology was most markedly in evidence. Blumer's doctoral dissertation entitled *Method and Social Psychology* was completed at this university in 1928. It incorporated extensively the perspectives of the pragmatist social philosopher George Herbert Mead, who taught in the philosophy department for many years, and has had a lasting influence on many sociologists.[3] When Blumer assumed a faculty position in 1925, the department was a joint one of sociology and anthropology, established in 1892 and chaired for many years by Albion W. Small, a sociologist. The anthropological concerns were steered by Frederick Starr and generally favored prehistory. On both sides of the department there were obvious attempts to define appropriate boundaries within the broader mandate declared by William Rainey Harper, the president of this major new university, to establish social science. Thus, despite his penchant for physical anthropology and the study of "primitives," Starr had enough interest in ethnography to describe W.I. Thomas as an anthropologist, inspired in this decision by Thomas and Znaniecki's classic work *The Polish Peasant in Europe and America* (Stocking 1979, 15).

The intellectual development of the department continued with the appointments of sociologists Ellsworth Faris and Robert Park. It was Faris who was active in pressing for the development of the anthropological side of the department. He had worked with Bantu languages, was influenced by the Berkeley anthropologist Robert Lowie, and was very critical of Levy-Bruhl's negative evaluations of "primitive mentality" (Murray 1986–87, 80). He managed to bring Ralph Linton, who had a strong interest in culture and personality, to Chicago for a short period and later, upon Starr's retirement, Fay-Cooper Cole was appointed in 1924. This new department member was a student of Franz Boas, the legendary scholar at Columbia University. Small, with prophetic wisdom, had once hoped to appoint Boas to the department at Chicago but failed to do so. With the help of the Laura Spelman Rockefeller Memorial,[4] a linguistic anthropologist and yet another student of Franz Boas, named Edward Sapir, was invited to join the department. Sapir's interests in symbolism, culture, and social psychology were extraordinarily compatible with the legacy of George Herbert Mead and the emergent direction taken by Blumer. After some time in the Chicago department, Sapir is known to have defined his own intellectual goal as the "social psychology of the symbol (Stocking 1979, 17)." With these additions, part of the Boasian tradition with its imperatives of intensive fieldwork, knowledge of language, and attention to the cultural history of Northwest Coast tribes—as against the prevailing concerns with explaining evolution and collecting for museums—was firmly planted in an intellectually nourishing environment.

Robert Redfield was added to the joint department in 1924, making a total of nine. There were predictable problems common to joint departments, where the flexing of disciplinary muscles was a declaration of identity. It is widely reported that the anthropologist Leslie White, on his doctoral orals in anthropology in 1927, was given considerable difficulty by two sociologists, Faris and Park (Stocking 1979, 17; Murray 1986–87, 89–90). It is also widely believed that this particular event led to the separation of the department, proposed by Cole in 1928. Others argue that a stronger reason for the separation was the proposed re-organization of the department into cores such as psychology, social organization, and comparative sociology, which would have split the three anthropologists, Sapir, Redfield, and Cole to three different sections, thereby diluting the possibility of a meaningful anthropological influence (Murray 1986–87, 91). The split was finally effected in 1929. Cole and Faris were the chairs of the new departments.

In 1932 the situation was confused again when Radcliffe-Brown, an anthropologist by training, was invited to come from Sydney, Australia, to join the department. Robert Park quickly asserted that the functionalist paradigm made Radcliffe-Brown's work "nothing more or less than sociology," with only the small qualification that it was concerned with primitive peoples (Stocking 1979, 21). Radcliffe-Brown's theoretical position, his intellectual allegiance to Durkheim, and his professed dedication to the discovery of general laws in the functioning of society seemed to provide a more or less enduring link to sociology. Indeed, so influential was the idea of the seemingly disparate contribution of Radcliffe-Brown's functionalism, that the Department of Anthropology saw itself as composed of five subdisciplines instead of the familiar four that would be recognized in the coming years as "American four-square." The fifth was the interdisciplinary one of social anthropology. This seminal theoretical connection between the two disciplines undoubtedly led one of the most prominent graduates of the Chicago Department of Sociology, Erving Goffman, to dedicate one of his books, *Relations in Public* (1971), a definitive product of the tradition of Mead and Blumer, to the memory of Radcliffe-Brown, "whom on his visit to the University of Edinburgh in 1950 I almost met." The theoretical cohabitation in the Chicago departments was reflected in an actual marriage between Robert Redfield and Margaret Park, the daughter of Robert Park.

Even though housed in different parts of the campus, the frequency of interaction between the sociologists and anthropologists apparently continued uninterrupted. When Redfield assumed the position of Dean of the Division of Social Sciences in 1934, he committed himself to fostering understandings between the various disciplines in his constituency. His published papers reveal that he established committees of social scientists for such undertakings as perusing various published works in order to uncover their methodological virtues. He reports as finding it "curious" that Blumer, in assessing *The Polish Peasant* (1979 [1939]), considered it methodologically unsuccessful in that the propositions advanced were not supported by the facts adduced (1962, 58). Apparently, the committee agreed, but continued to see the Thomas and Znaniecki book as a major work. Moreover, among Redfield's papers is a memorandum written to Blumer in conjunction with a joint seminar of sociologists and anthropologists in 1939. In it he directs his attention to generalizations in ethnography. He refers to what he terms the "internal consistency of culture" (1962, 21), a notion about which Blumer is eventually to reflect in one of his most powerful propositions—*society as symbolic interaction*.

In 1952 Blumer left for Berkeley to chair a department of Sociology and Social Institutions, which had been created several years previously in 1946 (Lyman 1988). He brought the symbolic interactionist tradition to Berkeley.

It was not through the theoretical entrepreneurship of Blumer himself, but through the much more readily accessible and academically popular work of Goffman that symbolic interactionism reached the Anthropology Department. Gerald Berreman, who had come to Berkeley in 1959 from Cornell University, found Goffman's dramaturgical style and concepts such as "impression management" peculiarly insightful in analyzing field experiences in India. Consequently, he produced a classic account of the anthropological experience *Behind Many Masks* (1962). This monograph also became the first self-consciously crafted anthropological work within the emerging symbolic interactionist tradition. The persuasiveness of the theoretical and analytical argument, and the inevitability of its appropriateness for anthropology led Berreman to teach a seminar entitled *Social Interaction*. Many a Berkeley graduate came away from this encounter theoretically and ideologically committed to the interactionist message. Throughout this seminar Blumer's collected work *Symbolic Interactionism* (1969b) was the gateway to an obviously comfortable, if not traditional, anthropological analysis.

Beyond the ordered realms of institutional affiliations such as at Chicago and Berkeley, anthropologists have not been completely ignorant of Blumer's work. Although I do not intend to survey all references to Blumer's thought in anthropology, there are two noteworthy dimensions among these references. The first is where Blumer is sporadically quoted for specific substantive social science contributions, but essentially left untouched for his theoretical message. The second is the growing awakening of selected anthropologists to symbolic interactionism, convinced by the nature of the analysis and seemingly committed to making use of this methodological and theoretical preference.

The first dimension shows professional politeness in acknowledging ownership rights, a move so familiar in the knowledge business as to go virtually unquestioned. These writers cite Blumer's work much in the same light as they would anyone who was closely, or even remotely, involved in the same substantive area. Thus, Weston La Barre, in the process of exploring the problems of psychological disorganization as an explanation for the phenomenon of cargo cults (1971), recognizes Blumer's contribution to social and individual disorganization (1936–37). Mandelbaum (1973), in his analysis of Gandhi within the genre of life histories, recognizes Blumer's attention to life history and to use of personal documents for social science analysis (1979 [1939], 39–47). Sofranko et al. (1977) suggest that their data on the comparative social impacts of technological delivery systems document Blumer's views on the "assimilative response," where the impact of an industrial mode of production is absorbed without any disruption to prevailing value patterns (1964). Willner (1973), in raising the important question of anthropology as a vocation or a commodity, finds it appropriate to cite Blumer's contribution to Horowitz's seminal work on the politics of research *The Rise and Fall of the Project Camelot* (1967). Perhaps most ironically, some anthropologists dealing with topics which eagerly demand a symbolic interactionist analysis, such as the problems of auto-ethnography, turn to Blumer for issues usually seen as peripheral to his major contribution. "To borrow Blumer's (1956) phrase, auto-ethnographers have usually attempted to describe the 'full picture' and breadth of their people" (Hayano 1979, 101). To evoke Blumer as a relevant authority on anthropological holism offers politeness, but misses the most powerful of his contributions to this notion.

There is, however, a small congregation of true believers in anthropology. They see themselves as *bona fide* symbolic interactonists, or as allies of those within a broad paradigmatic conglomeration of perspectives that stand in opposition to positivist analysis. The active opposition itself is already over in the contemporary discipline. Among these practitioners, one scholar might study the interactional formation of meaning, another the cognitive structures of culture, and a third the power of interpretive analysis.

Among those committed to the interactionist vision, Berreman's work has already been singled out. He apparently continues to find interactionist analysis rewarding and is a major anthropological exponent of the method. He openly indicates his preferences (1969, 6), and attests to being liberated from the questions now commonly raised about the power of scientism and the production of mindless anthropology in its image, devoted to the "lifeless description of human life" (1966, 350; 1972). Indeed, his unwavering determination to produce an anthropology committed to humanness and to what he calls "the politics of truth" (1981) is well served by the symbolic interactionist documentation of the world of everyday life and of the meaningful interaction between individuals.[5]

Clearly, some of the practitioners of cognitive anthropology find Blumer and interactionism to their liking. James Spradley, who devoted considerable efforts to laying the foundations for ethnoscience, cognitive anthropology, and culture-as-knowledge, reprints various articles as "interdisciplinary" perspectives in his earliest declarations about cognition and culture—*Culture and Cognition: Rules, Maps, and Plans* (1972). Among these can be found Blumer's powerful exposition of the nature of symbolic interactionism (1969b, 1–21). Spradley credits specific parts of this text with containing "explicit applications" for use by ethnoscience. "It has appeared to me that the data gathered by ethnoscience techniques is sometimes divorced from the reality of social interaction" he notes (1972, 65). On the other hand, he also observes that the studies done in the name of symbolic interactionism:

> often present cogent statements about the way human behavior is organized with reference to meaning, but then resort to sterile research methods. For instance questionnaires which are far removed from the language and

meaning of those studied are often used. In short, ethnoscience appears to be a method in search of a theory, and symbolic interactionism, a theory in search of a method. (1972, 65–66)

In later works Spradley continues to cite and quote from Blumer's writings (1979, 6–7; 1980, 8–9). For Spradley *meaning* must be taken seriously. Objects and events, he maintains, do not imply their own meanings (1972, 65). In this particular statement, he takes on the existing mandates of the most powerful practitioners of cultural anthropology as well as the interpretation of the most favored theories. This is a problem I shall address presently.

Even as Spradley places the aforementioned into print, Norman and Dorothea Whitten explore "social strategies and social relationships" in the introductory volume of the definitive *Annual Review of Anthropology*, and introduce not only several of Goffman's works, but also the crucial quote from Blumer's "Society as Symbolic Interaction":

> The term "symbolic interaction" refers ... to the peculiar and distinctive character of interaction as it takes place between human beings. The peculiarity consists in the fact that human beings interpret or "define" each other's actions instead of merely reacting to each other's actions. Their "response" is not made directly to the actions of one another but instead is based on the meaning which they attach to such actions. Thus, human interaction is mediated by the use of symbols, by interpretation, or by ascertaining the meaning of one another's actions. (1972, 263)

The Meaning Revolution: Blumer as Ancestor and Missing Link

Susan Langer once observed that meaning was the central question of our age. If meaning is the monumental question, then interpretation, which is its obvious manifestation, is equally central to the ongoing endeavor. The preoccupation with the questions of meaning and interpretation is clearly observable in all the humanities and social sciences. It is also evident in the sciences, even in the exact sciences. The usual analytic practice in science of removing the inquiry from the social and political context in which it is embedded, comes under criticism for its epistemological irresponsibility (Whittaker 1981; Hooker 1982). Given this movement away from the certainties and procedures fostered by science, from the moral decisions about how to interpret that science inevitably makes, anthropology has been faced with the thorny question of the nature of meaning. Consequently, some anthropologists have made the decision to work under the auspices of the anthropology of experience; others with narrative anthropology, some with reflexive or interpretive anthropology; and yet others, with the philosophical questions raised by hermeneutics. They are all concerned with meaning, with the ongoing puzzle of how to interpret the meanings held by others, and how to deal with divergent interpretations. As is obvious by now, I am going to argue that the work of Herbert Blumer and interactionism, more generally, constitutes some kind of an ancestor, a missing link in the ongoing theorizing of the many anthropological debates.

The questions raised in the contemporary discourse on meaning are legion. Why does meaning become a question? How is it to be understood? How can an empirically trained discipline study something that emerges from cultural prescriptions, individual experience, and imagination? What connections exist between meaning and behavior? How does a researcher capture and represent it? Moreover, meaning can only be retrieved by reflection, yet reflection itself continually changes the thing being reflected about. How can any representation produced in writing deal adequately with such infinite regress? Indeed, meaning has such elusive properties that regardless of what meanings come under investigation, more meanings are always in production. By definition, meaning and its attendant interpretations are always incomplete and inexact. The awareness of this incompleteness works very well as an understanding for most interpretive anthropologists, but sooner or later it becomes a problem of representation and adequacy in committing matters to text. Indeed these very questions constitute the current debate in anthropology.

Researching and Authoring the Anthropologist and the Natives

Early ethnographies had about them a purity and solemnity. This was made possible by an anthropological consensus, which expected that the final product be presented as removed from any allusions to the toil of the ethnographer. Such strategies are now almost entirely discarded and the ethnographer is as much a part of the ethnography as the peoples being researched. As Geertz noted "we are all natives now" (1983, 151). The notion of faithful replication of data and findings, the idea that different ethnographers in the same setting can or should produce identical data and analysis has departed with the positivistic endeavors of which such replication was an integral part. Obviously, as each ethnographer has different experiences, the knowledge gained reflects these differences. Yet, equally obviously, some observations, some experiences, and some data must synchronize to claim credibility. Ethnographers are now aware that the issues of credibility have changed and the focus has shifted to ethnographic authority (Clifford 1983), ethnographic adequacy (Stoddart 1986), and the political and social problems of representation. Appropriate texts have to be structured to satisfy these mandates. In the new ethnographic enterprise various styles have become distinguishable. One is the anthropological travelogue where the text places the researcher in the narrative as a discoverer (Rabinow 1977; Cesara 1982; Whittaker 1986; Ridington 1988). The positivistically inclined frequently give the derogatory label of "fieldwork confessionals" to these endeavors.

Another ethnographic style opts for presenting the "native's point of view." This deals with the problem of authority, adequacy, and representation by relinquishing these decisions and placing them squarely on those studied. The worldviews and interpretations come in the "voices" of the relevant actors (Leyton 1975; Crapanzano 1986; Whittaker 1986). One specific way of dealing with the issue is through life histories (a familiar method in the discipline), in which anthropologists adjudicate the life story (Radin 1920; Dollard 1935; Shostak 1981; Watson and Watson-Franke 1985; Cruikshank 1990). Many of these works appear as actual direct quotes and usually in the discourse of everyday life. The moral imperative of "giving voice" to those studied is a strong ethic in recent feminist, qualitative, and anthropological methodology. Whatever the ethnographic decision, a dialogue between anthropologist and those being represented must ensue at some time. It is to this all-important mediation, or perhaps "dialogic," to borrow Dwyer's term (1982), that Blumer's negotiation and production of meaning becomes so enriching. In a brilliant passage, written with deceptive simplicity, and now often quoted, he lays bare the questions of meaning and interpretation that have eluded many researchers:

> The first premise is that human beings act towards things on the basis of the meanings that the things have for them.... The second premise is that the meaning of such things is derived from, or arises out of, the social interaction one has with one's fellows. The third premise is that these meanings are handled in, and modified through, an interpretive process used by the person in dealing with the things he encounters (Blumer 1969b, 2).

This is the very process by which meanings are established, albeit momentarily. It is to just such momentary meanings, the talk of people in interview and in participant-observation that, throughout the social scientific tradition, has been referred to as unquestioned "data." The implication is that this so-called data has the efficacy of a movie still chosen from some finite point in a film. It is always a "pregnant moment," which, by definition, is destined to change immediately thereafter. So how is reliable data to be collected? How is any certainty to be accomplished? How are ever-changing meanings to be reproduced into stable text? One way is to consider interviews as negotiated meanings, as constructed narratives (Mishler 1986) and declare, in the words of Rabinow, that these "representations are social facts" (1986). The works of Carlos Castaneda, for example, fall into this tradition (1968).

This new processual style of data, unfixable and thereby seemingly without conclusion, makes disturbing demands of traditional research mores. Some problems of orthodox ethnography and analysis would become essentially irrelevant within this paradigmatic shift. Heider (1988) recently considered one of the enduring problems ethnography is seen to have, namely when two ethnographers report different data from the same field. He notes the reasoning evoked to deal with such threatening diversity—one ethnographer must be wrong, or, in truth, the ethnographers are actually looking at different subcultures. They cannot help but perceive differently because they have different personalities, or values, or they come from different cultures themselves; their orientations and research plans must be different; perhaps their research plans change over time; the lengths of time spent in the field probably differ significantly; they have differing knowledge of the language; or perhaps their previous fieldwork was so different that it affects their present observations. Finally, and especially tellingly, they had different degrees of rapport in the field. The famous Redfield-Lewis debate encapsulates some of these issues (Lewis 1953).

The analysis that comes from symbolic interactionism and especially from its major proponent, Blumer, suggests that these traditional problems are the result of having a static, positivistic, and largely unreflexive notion of what constitutes data. They suggest a poverty in conceptualizing and representing action and process.[6] In particular, two major contributions of the interactionist paradigm, "the definition of the situation," and what Prus (1987) calls "generic social processes" would permit a more enriching analysis of these problems.

The "definition of the situation," the moment in time, the concept which was W.I. Thomas's insightful legacy, proposes an analysis in terms of a cultural and social contextual. The idea, on the whole, is congenial to the thinking of anthropologists and finds itself as an unnamed presence in much recent work. "If men define their situations as real, they are real in their consequences," Thomas wrote. Further Volkart (1951, 30) adds to these crucial ideas the suggestion that facts themselves "do not have a uniform existence apart from the persons who observe and interpret them. Rather, the 'real' facts are the ways in which different people come to define situations" (quoted in Meltzer, Petras, and Reynolds 1975, 27). More recently McHugh (1968) has concentrated upon the idea of the definition of the situation and Goldschmidt (1972) has proposed its adoption into anthropological analysis.

The properties of the situation then shape the knowledge constructed, the facts as they come to be known, and reality itself. The situation constructed between people—that is, the researcher and those to be written about—dictates the interpretation of events, the relevant facts, and reality as it exists for the interactants. The processual nature of these ongoing interpretations suggests a situation in which, as Blumer proposes, there is an "active forging of the social structure." In short, as the sociologist of knowledge would argue, the knower and the context cannot be separated, and the knower and the known cannot be separated. The knowers referred to here include the anthropologist as well as those studied. Thus, the definition of the situation is an ongoing, continually processual ethnographic activity.

Experience, Action, and the Emerging Self

The questions of meaning and reflexivity stalk anthropologists in all endeavors. They replace the old questions that concentrated on the reliability of data, or whether reality had been adequately captured. The group of anthropologists who have rallied to interpretive anthropology, to the anthropology of experience, or to narrative anthropology find themselves advantageously situated to lay to rest nagging expectations about the generalizability of data and the accuracy of analysis. What is particularly intriguing for them is experience, the turning inward, in order then to turn outward. They concentrate on the individual, on person and on self (Whittaker 1992a), and on perceptions, evolving interpretations, and the many avenues to understanding culture. The cast of characters here include Geertz, who is seen as a seminal figure in interpretive anthropology beginning with his monograph *Person, Time and Conduct in Bali* (1966), Edward Bruner, and Victor Turner. Indeed, Victor Turner has almost single-handedly activated notions of cultural performance, symbolic action, and a kind of processual anthropology (1969; 1974; 1979).

As this is a work to extol Blumer rather than Turner, it seems appropriate to consider the former's proposals and how they might enliven the propositions of the latter. What can symbolic interactionism offer to arguments about social structure, about a microsociological set of social practices such as performances, rituals, and the like? Turner's notions about the ritual process, with his van Gennep (1908) type proposals for separation, liminality, and aggregation are now classic and part of mainstream anthropological analysis. His intent could be seen as demonstrating how these processes reveal social structure. Shaped in part by British social anthropology, Turner himself admits that his interests in social structure and performance are enriched by the dramaturgic work of Goffman. Yet from the perspective of symbolic interactionism, his work seems essentially experience-free despite recent attempts to include it within the paradigm of the anthropology of experience. It is distant from involvement in real events, the kind of distance that one has come to associate with structural-functional premises sometimes interestingly known as the very intellectual premises of colonial theory. Yet Turner's work has made an appeal to interactionism. His notion of *spontaneous communitas* (1969, 132) could readily be translated into society as process, society as interaction.

Experience is always a reflexive category, it requires the assumption that a self exists. As Bruner suggests: "We create the units of experience and meaning from the continuity of life (1986, 7)." In other words, the emphasis is on creating, recreating, and reflecting. "Every telling," he continues, "is an arbitrary imposition of meaning on the flow of memory." The anthropology of experience was the organizing label preferred over other possibilities like "processual anthropology." By implication it evokes the elusive concept of the self, which surely is an underlying notion in the very concept of experience and meaning. Yet the anthropology of experience owes too many old debts to classification, categorization, and formalism. This means it is forced into honoring an already ordered social structuralist world, analyzed from a distance, and not from experience-nearness. This world is essentially a static, motionless world, despite such tacit understandings about the nature of experience. In it, action seems to become merely another "unit" of behavior.

The differences about the nature of action in the work of Turner and Blumer essentially make this point. For Turner:

> All human action is impregnated with meaning, and meaning is hard to measure.... Meaning arises when we try to put what culture and language have crystallized from the past together with what we feel, wish, and think about or present ... to see whether and, if so, how tellingly they relate to or illuminate our present individual problems, issues. (1986, 33)

In contrast, for Blumer, as for every symbolic interactionist, there exists a self formed in true Meadian fashion by taking the roles of others with whom one is implicated in the joint activities of life (1969b, 21). One might, of course, argue that the notion of person, as intersubjectively formed and interactively the architect of his or her own destiny, is a curiously North American phenomenon. As such it would not essentially be at all appealing to those with a more traditional, and perhaps functionalist, expectation of anthropology. Blumer's notion of action is predicated, naturally enough, on a highly reflexive notion of person, one that does not usually appear in the anthropological texts:

> The capacity of the human being to make indications to himself gives a distinctive character to human action. It means that the human individual confronts a world that he must interpret in order to act, instead of an environment to which he responds because of his organization. He has to cope with the situations in which he is called on to act, ascertaining the meaning of the actions of others and mapping out his own line of action in the light of such interpretation. He has to construct and guide his action instead of merely releasing it in response to factors playing on him or operating through him. He may do a miserable job in constructing his action, but he has to construct it. (1969b, 15)

The reader is captivated by Turner's ability to make the connection of experience and performance to social structure. Structure is, after all, the mainstay of anthropological analysis from earlier years. Yet it remains curiously distant from everyday experience. The reader is probably more convinced by Blumer's view of "experience" and "performance" in that when checked against his or her experience of the everyday world, these notions become stunningly familiar. It seems inevitable, however, that if the anthropology of experience continues to develop and weds itself to some of the work anthropologists are now producing on the concept of self (Merten and Schwartz 1982; Bruner 1984; Caton 1985; Whittaker 1992a), symbolic interactionism will become increasingly relevant.

Conclusion

In the final analysis, the work of interpretive anthropology owes much, not only to Geertz, its in-house proponent, but also to Alfred Schutz, and to Max Weber's *Verstehendessoziologie* (interpretive sociology). My argument has been that it could be enriched by the contributions of Herbert Blumer who, like Max Weber, has had an undeservedly low profile in anthropology. He would bring to the discipline a lively, symbolic theory of action, a dialectic version of meaning, reflexivity, and contextual analysis. Indeed it is the contribution of Blumer specifically, as of all symbolic interactionists, to offer a theory of action where one at present does not seem to exist. The demand also seems to be that anthropologists not only consider symbolic action, but also account for it in their final texts.

Blumer's claims on the future may have to be tempered by a variety of changes related to the emergence and crystallization of ongoing debates in hermeneutics and postmodernism. The question of anthropological realism, and the unquestioned morality of "the native's point of view," may be considerably transformed when confronted by some recent debates on the reifications in the social sciences (Whittaker 1992b), or eroded beyond recognition under the glare of deconstructivist examination (Whittaker 1987). In an anthropological world, however, which still values theoretical propositions about the experience of "reality," the propositions of Blumer are congenial, familiar, and somehow right. The adoption of Blumer, moreover, does not demand major transformations of anthropological traditions. What is asked, therefore, is for anthropology to provide a place for Blumer in the assembled company of interpretive anthropologists and a seat in the anthropological hall of fame.

NOTES

1. The earlier version of this paper was delivered at the Qualitative Research Conference to honor Herbert Blumer at the University of Windsor, Ontario, May 1988. The help of Stanford Lyman, Bill McKellin, Jay Powell, Robert Prus, Robin Ridington, and Erik Whittaker is gratefully acknowledged.

2. It is of course possible that Blumer's influence on the training of anthropologists may exist in other universities as well. The research to support this possibility is beyond the scope of this essay and I have had to be content with the two obvious academic institutions.

3. An account of Blumer's academic career is summarized in Lyman and Vidich (1988). This work concentrates on the part of Blumer's career which receives less attention than it deserves, namely his work on public philosophy and policy. The nature of sociology at the University of Chicago, the early figures who developed it and the pervasive influence of George Herbert Mead are discussed in Lewis and Smith (1980) and Kurtz (1984).

4. The connections between philanthropic institutions such as the Laura Spelman Rockefeller Memorial and social theory has been ably documented by Fisher (1986). He demonstrates how functionalist theory in Britain was encouraged by this institution.

5. Other symbolic interactionists could be found among Berreman's students, for example Gaines (1978; 1985). There appears to be a loose network among those committed to symbolic interactionism who at one time studied in the anthropology department at Berkeley.

6. A close perusal of Blumer's naturalistic methodology, its many propositions, as well as its shortcomings are discussed in Athens (1984).

Generic Social Processes: Intersubjectivity and Transcontextuality in the Social Sciences[1]

Robert Prus

> *To speak of a science without concepts suggests all sorts of analogies—a carver without tools, a railroad without tracks, a mammal without bones, a love story without love. A science without concepts would be a fantastic creation.*
>
> HERBERT BLUMER, "Science Without Concepts."

As the selections of studies on ethnographic research from this volume indicate, ethnographic research provides an exceptionally rich and viable means of uncovering insights into people's lived experiences. Indeed, since it attends to the interpretive and interactive dimensions, to the intersubjective features of human group life, ethnographic research is essential if one hopes to achieve intimate familiarity with ongoing community life. However, while naturalistic inquiry is invaluable for generating understandings of particular contexts in our own community or in other societies, we might also ask what we may learn about human interchange more generally by examining group life in particular settings. In other words, one of the further tasks of the researcher is that of abstracting (from ethnographic research) concepts which depict central features of people's associations with one another. It is useful and instructive in many ways to accumulate ethnographic studies that carefully describe the perspectives, practices, dilemmas, and interchanges of people in this and that setting. Indeed, there is no better way of achieving a viable understanding of substantive settings than through sustained ethnographic inquiry. Still, we may use this rich textured data as a base for formulating concepts which transcend the particular settings in which the data was gathered.

While there seems an infinite number of ways in which one may approach and analyze settings ethnographically, those assuming an interactionist approach tend to focus most specifically on *activities* (the ways in which people do things and work things out with others). There is a central emphasis on process, or more precisely, on depicting the social processes characterizing people's practices in this or that community or subcultural setting. Thus, while researchers strive for highly detailed accounts of how people view their life-situations, define themselves and others, become involved in particular behaviors, conduct their activities, develop relationships and the like, in practice, there is also an attempt to derive a set of concepts or themes which centrally address the processes characterizing these things. In this manner researchers move from an analysis of more situated or individualized instances of human behaviors to more generalized sets of understandings which, nonetheless, are firmly grounded in the day-to-day practices of those whose activities constitute this or that life-world.

Those presently working within the interactionist tradition are very fortunate in that the researchers who preceded them not only provided some extremely valuable accounts of people's practices in a wide variety of life-worlds, but they have also helped formulate a set of concepts that have great importance for approaching subsequent ethnographic inquiry. As a consequence, not only are we able to define more precisely the assumptions that people make as ethnographers, but also as part of this legacy, we have a body of concepts and a stock of knowledge about the other on which to build in approaching and analyzing subsequent ethnographic projects. Although there is a clear understanding that our findings in the field must maintain priority over our concepts, the availability of this ethnographic literature and the conceptual material that has accompanied it not only provides us with a set of contexts for comparing and contrasting our present inquiries with those developed earlier, but it also means that we can dialogue with, and contribute to, this body of literature in a much more dynamic manner as our inquiries develop.

This statement on *generic social processes* provides readers with a sense of this emphasis on activity. It offers a conceptual framework for approaching ethnographic research and makes reference to a number of ethnographic studies that should have relevance to the study of any community or subcultural setting.

To the extent we are able to delineate concepts with trans-situational or cross-contextual relevance, we may not only be able to tie together a great deal of research that would otherwise remain disconnected or scattered across a range of substantive contexts, but we may also be able to produce a body of concepts that could be used as resources in subsequent ethnographic inquiries. These inquiries could in turn be used as a basis for further assessing, refining, and (if necessary) rejecting concepts pertaining to the study of human group life.[2]

By attending to concepts that are applicable to a wide variety of contexts, researchers working in very different substantive settings (for example, ballet studios, biker clubs, religious communities, schools) may not only benefit from the research that people have done in other settings, but they will find that they have a much broader community of scholars with which to discuss all aspects of their work than would otherwise have been the case.

When researchers are mindful of generic, or trans-situational concepts, every piece of ethnographic research in any realm of human behavior can be used to generate insight into any other realm of human activity. Or, as I sometimes tell my students, these basic or generic social processes are like "magic carpets" or "Open Sesames," for they enable researchers to more quickly, easily, and productively move from one setting to another.

Further, as Blumer (1928, 349) observes, concepts such as generic social processes do *not* destroy the unique or idiographic features of particular instances of human lived experience. Instead, these concepts provide the essential medium through which similarities and differences may be more fully recognized, examined, and appreciated.

For our purposes, *generic social processes* refer to the trans-situational elements of interaction; to the abstracted formulations of social behavior. Denoting parallel sequences of activity across diverse contexts, generic social processes highlight the emergent interpretive features of association. They focus our attention on the activities involved in the "doing" or accomplishing of group life.

Generic social processes address the emerging, sequencing, unfolding, ongoing features of group life. These concepts draw our attention to the shaping, the forging, the forming, the constructing, the implementing, the *ad hocing*, and the building up of human interaction. As Blumer (1969b) notes, *process* encompasses the interpreting, planning, anticipating, doing, experiencing, assessing, and re-adjusting features of action.

Viewed thusly, process does not deny planning or the development of routine practices and recipes for action. Neither does it ignore the *temporal* (historical) or the *organizational* (relational) linkages of action. Rather, it locates activity squarely in these contexts. Process incorporates the perspectives of the participants, as well as people's capacities for reflectivity, their abilities to influence one another, and their tendencies to develop and act upon particularistic relations with others. This notion of process also encompasses the problematic and uncertain features of group life, the dilemmas people experience and their attempts to come to terms with these.

The following listing is offered as a heuristic device for envisioning process in a more concerted fashion. This listing is necessarily tentative, but provides an umbrella for encompassing a great many of the concepts the interactionists and other interpretive sociologists have developed over the years.

The following five processes not only signify key elements of people's involvements in situations, but also define central features of community life. These processes are interdependent and need to be viewed holistically if we are to develop a fuller appreciation of each. In this respect one might opt to put these processes in any number of orderings in a discussion such as this. As well, while individual projects may emphasize one or other of these processes, discussions of any of these five processes rather inevitably entails some consideration of the other processes. Still, each of these generic social processes encompasses several (sub)processes within, and each is amenable to empirical inquiry.

Acquiring Perspectives

> I remember one time when I had just started out with this one top crew. We were playing poker and there was this cripple there. He was deformed and on crutches, but the guy loved to play poker. Anyway, we started to beat him and I felt sorry for the guy. I said, "Leave the guy alone, he's crippled." They looked at me and said, "Are you kidding? His money is just as good as anyone else's!" You see, I wasn't ready to go in there and cheat him, to give the guy a good hand [set him up for a loss]. My guys sensed it and they were getting a little hot. They pulled me aside and said, "Now, look, beat this guy!" Who knows how much money he had on him, he had a stack of twenties. So, even a cripple, if you can beat him, you do it.

> Priests, we beat priests, oh yeah, they're good, they dig into their pocket and blow their money as gracefully as anyone else. When I was starting out, I would say, "I'm a Catholic, I can't beat this priest. Like I had been an altar boy." [road hustler] (Prus and Sharper 1991, 49)[3]

Representing interpretive frameworks or viewpoints (also worldviews, paradigms, versions of reality) for making sense of the world, perspectives provide the substantive content for association. Definitions of fads and fashions are encompassed by the concept of perspective as are traditions, notions of rationality, and political and religious beliefs, as well as language and other symbols. Perspectives (and the object meanings they imply) are very much community products and are built up over time in the course of human association.

As people acquire sets of perspectives or particular versions of reality, they develop stocks of knowledge (Schutz 1962) or an awareness of the generalized other (Mead 1934). It is in attending to, internalizing, and invoking these community-based conceptual frameworks that one becomes "minded" and begins to recognize and locate objects (including other people and oneself) within a meaningful context. These orientational frames may change over time as people attend to various features of their life-worlds, but perspectives draw our attention to the necessity of recognizing that: (a) group interaction precedes individual notions of consciousness and reality; (b) *language* (shared sets of symbols) is essential for generating this sense of the other within oneself; and (c) people's capacities for, and styles of, sense-making activities as well as their notions of reality are grounded in these interactions and awarenesses of the generalized other. Thus, while people may subsequently assess and resist or otherwise modify the viewpoints they have acquired at earlier points in time, they can do so only as a consequence of having acquired some earlier definitions (through language) of their life-worlds. The following statements outline the processes central to "the acquisition of perspectives" as people experience these on an ongoing basis:

- Encountering perspectives (definitions of reality) from others
- Assessing (new, incoming) perspectives and resisting unwanted viewpoints
- Developing images of objects (including images of other people and oneself)
- Learning (cultural) patterns of objects (such as fashion)
- Defining situations (applying perspectives to the "cases at hand")
- Dealing with ambiguity (lapses and limitations in existing explanations)
- Resolving contradictions (dilemmas within and across paradigms)
- Extending or improvising on existing perspectives
- Promoting (and defending) perspectives (and definitions of reality) to others
- Rejecting formerly held viewpoints
- Adopting new viewpoints[4]

Achieving Identity

A lot of people start out imitating someone else's persona and from there they may evolve their own persona. Through their work, they may be able to find something that works for them. And if they're alert, the bright ones, they will start to develop an act around it, when that happens. It's by accident, but something happened, and they have to experience it, and then they might have something unique that the audience likes, whether it's being funny, or sinister, or whatever. [magician] (Prus and Sharper 1991, 249)

As part of the broader process of acquiring a set of perspectives for making sense of the world or developing a mind, people also acquire sets of definitions

pertaining to other people and the self. These identities or self-other definitions are important because they allow people to comprehend others as well as
oneself. While people's identities may vary over time and across contexts, these
identities provide a certain sense of stability in people's lives. They allow
people to anticipate one another and to make ongoing adjustments to the situations at hand. Further, insofar as others act toward objects (including people)
in terms of the meanings that they have for them, people's particularistic identities can affect their subsequent associations, opportunities, and activities.
Indeed, as Lemert (1951; 1967) contends, once people acquire identities or
reputations as certain kinds of people, they may have difficulty avoiding
aspects of the role suggested by those identities even when they wish to do so.
To the extent that others act toward particular people (targets) as if they were
this or that type of person, they encourage these people to assume those identities and act accordingly.

It is important also to note, though, that people generally develop
several or multiple identities or definitions of self as a consequence of the
various groups with which they associate and the differing activities in which
they may engage (even in the same group). Certain of people's identities may
become more dramatized or pronounced in a community context, but their
identities are often situated and reflect the multi-faceted, emergent nature of
human group life.

"Identity work" is contingent on people's capacity for self-reflectivity. It
requires that one become "an object unto oneself"; that one begin to take
oneself into account in developing lines of action. Reflecting the perspectives
one has on the world, people's identities or self-other definitions are not only
situated within those realities, but also are influenced by the ongoing shifts in
perspectives that people normally undergo over time and across situations.
However, in contrast to the more generalized quality of perspectives, identities have a more immediate and personalized ("you and I") focus. Like other
aspects of human group life, identities may become more positively or negatively evaluated in the community at hand, and people may experience
various enhancements or denigrations of self as a consequence of the various
identities imputed to them. When people begin to anticipate that others may
act toward them in more desired or undesired manners as a consequence of
the ways in which they are seen, they may attempt to selectively foster or
resist certain definitions, names, or identities. Thus, we may speak, as does
Erving Goffman (1959; 1963a) of "the [selective] presentation of self in
everyday life" and the problematics of managing disreputable identities.

As products of ongoing community life, people's identities are also fundamentally linked to the identities and activities of their associates, as well
as their own worldviews, other senses of self, and their own activities.
Consequently, identity work reflects ongoing assessments, adjustments, and
negotiations as the parties involved jointly endeavor to work out "self" and
"other" definitions. The following statements on identity work draw our

attention to the human enterprise entailed in the image-making process as this pertains to both definition of the self and definitions of the other:

- Encountering definitions of self from others
- Attributing qualities to self (self definitions)
- Comparing incoming and self-assigned definitions of self
- Resisting unwanted identity imputations
- Selectively conveying information about self to others
- Gleaning information about others
- Assigning identities to others
- Promoting specific definitions of others
- Encountering resistance from others
- Reassessing identities imputed to others[5]

Being Involved

> When you're in sales, the easiest thing to do is to stay in sales. So even if you change companies, or products, you'll still likely end up in sales.... You get known and, of course, that's where your experience is, in sales. If you're in sales, you can get a job almost anyplace. And that makes it easier, because everybody needs somebody to promote their products.... Your sales experience is your ticket. You feel comfortable in sales. It doesn't matter so much what you're selling, within reason. That should be immaterial. You're a salesman! [manufacture-industrial] (Prus 1989a, 283)

"**B**eing involved" denotes the sequencing of people's participation in settings. It draws our attention to the processual nature of human group life. Thus, in contrast to those who focus on *causes* (variables, factors) and *effects*, consideration is given to the ways in which people's experiences unfold over time. In this way we gain a much more viable and comprehensive sense of what people anticipate as they work their ways through settings, how they go about their activities and relate to others they encounter on a here-and-now basis, and how they make sense of, and adjust to, this or that aspect of the situations in which they find themselves along the line.

Emphasizing the *how* (versus the *why*) of involvements, consideration is given to the natural histories (or "careers") of people's participation in particular situations (Becker 1963; Prus 1984). Although researchers typically focus on one involvement at a time, each involvement is best envisioned against a backdrop of people's multiple, shifting, and potentially incompatible involvements in other settings. As well, while each involvement would seem to presuppose a new set of perspectives, identities, activities, and relationships, it should also be appreciated that once people have acquired a working knowledge of the generalized other within the larger community, this stock of knowledge enables people to move somewhat more readily from one subcommunity or subculture within the broader community to another.

Further, while some groups within the community may develop unique (sub)cultural configurations (for example, ideologies, practices), some people may be able to comprehend and accept these viewpoints more readily than others as a consequence of their previous associations with other groups that were more like the new group in this or that regard. Still, even for those coming from rather similar settings, ventures into new realms of the "other" are often characterized by considerable levels of uncertainty and possible disjunctures in perspectives, identities, activities, and relationships. In part, too, the natural history or career approach to involvements alerts us to the problematic and ongoing inter-connectedness of the self with the (intersubjective) other. We become sensitive to the folly of trying to explain individual behavior in reference to individual characteristics. People can and do talk about individual involvements and experiences, but participation in the lifeworlds of others entails some interlinkaging of oneself with the selves of others in the setting. Thus, we would want to be attentive to the ways in which people's lives intersect with others on an ongoing basis.

Not all involvements will realize all stages discussed here (for example, some may never become disinvolved or reinvolved once disinvolved), but four processes are relevant to conceptualizing people's involvements over time—*initial involvements, continuities, disinvolvements,* and *reinvolvements.*[6]

Getting Started (Initial Involvements)

> A number of magicians get into magic through magic sets. A lot of people my age got into magic through Mysto Magic Sets.... These were very instrumental in shaping people's ideas of magic, and then one day, it occurred to me that I could look up magic shops in the phone book. I was like ten years old. I had a Mysto Magic Set and I had gone through all the magic books in the library, and then I looked in the phone book and found six magic shops in town. [magician] (Prus and Sharper 1991, 232)

The ethnographic literature suggests that there are three major ways in which people become initially involved in situations. These reflect notions of "seekership," "recruitment," and "closure."[7] When people pursue situations they define as attractive, interesting, enjoyable, and the like, the concept of "seekership" is applicable. When their involvements are promoted by others who solicit their participation in situations, that constitutes "recruitment." "Closure" comes into play when people engage in activities as a means of realizing pressing obligations. Although any of the following routings (seekership, recruitment, closure) may dominate people's involvements in particular settings, involvements often reflect combinations of these elements. While not pivotal in all cases, any reservations (such as, health, financial, or respectability concerns) people have may deter particular involvements. Initial involvements involve:

- Engaging in seekership (pursuing self-attributed interests)
- Being recruited (others attempt to foster interest, encourage participation)
- Experiencing closure (perceiving pressing obligations, limited choices)
- Managing reservations (overcoming doubts, stigma, risks)

Sustaining and Intensifying Involvements (Continuities)

Okay, say the fellow is not turned off by what he has seen or been through so far and say he can do a few things. Well, he might get connected with a few other guys he finds he can work with, maybe a couple of other men who are more reliable or capable than those he's been associating with. A crew like that, if it stays together for a time, is likely to go places, because when you work together as a unit, it is much easier and your returns are much better. [road hustler] (Prus and Sharper 1991, 27)

Once people have become involved in particular situations, we ask when they are likely to continue (and intensify) their participation in those settings. Continuity may reflect earlier routings of involvement, but people may continue to participate in situations on bases other than those related to their initial involvements. Continuity would appear to depend on the extent to which participants: (a) develop and accept the perspectives (worldviews, definitional frames, justifications) characterizing the group in question; (b) achieve more extensive and exclusive identification as practitioners or participants in particular settings; (c) make larger, more irretrievable investments in the situations at hand; (d) become more adept at accomplishing activities central to the situation; and (e) become more fully involved in ongoing relationships with other participants. As well, (f) where people neglect or curtail other options, they may find that they have little choice but to continue within a particular setting even when they might later wish to detach themselves on these other grounds. Finally, (g) when other people in the setting recognize these bases of continuity and for one or other reasons desire that certain people remain in the setting, they may endeavor to foster continuity on the part of those particular people by providing justifications, encouraging identification, obtaining commitments, facilitating patterns of use, promoting supportive associations, and discouraging alternatives. People's continuities in situations appear to reflect the following dimensions:
- Internalizing perspectives (viewpoints consistent with particular involvements)
- Achieving identity (self and other definitions consistent with particular involvements)
- Accomplishing activities (competence and composure in the focal setting)
- Making commitments (making investments, developing dependencies)

- Developing relationships (experiencing positive bonds with others in the setting)
- Foregoing alternative involvements (neglecting options, "bridge-burning")
- Encountering others who encourage one's ongoing participation

Becoming Disinvolved

We've had to drop a number of suppliers. Sometimes their merchandise isn't moving or, in some cases, the items are not standing up to the usual wear and tear that are required of them. Or you will get some that are very slow in shipping or they are not very careful in their packing and so you have more problems with returns and just delays that way. [wholesale-jewelry] (Prus 1989b, 168)

As with initial involvement and continuity, it is important to envision disinvolvement in process terms. While any reassessment of one's current situation may generate definitions conducive to disengagement, the multiple involvements (and other options) in which people find themselves are especially consequential for disinvolvement from particular situations. Insofar as it is unlikely that people would be highly involved in all of the (prenoted) dimensions of the situation at hand, we may see continuity and discontinuity as closely intertwined. The following suggests some basis on which disinvolvement is more likely, but it should not be assumed that dissatisfaction on any one dimension would necessitate disinvolvement (that is, consider the problems of simultaneous disentanglement on all of these dimensions). The availability of (perceived) feasible options seems central, as do the other elements defining one's participation in a more complete sense:

- Questioning viability of perspectives (facing obstacles, dilemmas)
- Reassessing identity (inconsistent with desired images)
- Finding activities troublesome (boring, unpleasant, cumbersome)
- Being freed-up from existing commitments (free to "relocate")
- Severing relationships (conflict, animosity, exclusion)
- Encountering opportunities for alternative involvements
- Encountering others who discourage participation in that setting[8]

Becoming Reinvolved

To get out, you have to have the money to invest in a business of some sort or a friend or relative who will cut you in on the action. And even then, it's tough because you get so used to that way of life. For so many years you organize your life around this hustling thing and even when you get away from it, okay, for a while you don't miss it, but then you start to think about what the guys are doing. You know the strength of it. You look at the calendar and you think, "There's a good party in ——— tomorrow," and you know that they are going to make money there! And it takes time to get out of it because you are still connected. You can't tell everybody all at once, so people are still calling you and telling you about parties they know of and asking you to come in for a piece of the action. [road hustler] (Prus and Sharper 1991, 132)

Should people's subsequent involvements be found unsatisfactory (*vis-à-vis* perspectives, identities, activities, commitments, relationships), then reinvolvement in an earlier situation appears more likely. Reinvolvement presupposes (re)acceptance of participants by their former associates. And, as with initial involvements, reinvolvements may be sought out by participants (seekership), promoted by people within the group (recruitment), or reflect buyers' assessments that these involvements are the best or only ways to meet pressing obligations (closure). Reinvolvement seems more likely as people begin:

- Defining opportunities for reinvolvements in former situations as more feasible (consider as potentially viable concerns with perspectives, identities, activities, relationships, commitments)
- Noting greater changes to self or situation that would justify reinvolvement (face-saving, reassessments)
- Finding that they have less extensively organized their routines around their present involvements (disentanglement is more easily accomplished)
- Encountering others who encourage reinvolvement

Doing Activity

When you're selling, it's like you're putting on a show for the customer.... Sometimes, I stutter, I get excited, but we've memorized our presentation, all our lines. And it is like being an actor, but you get tested more. And you have to give your version, but you have to watch it. It has to come out more naturally. Not like Sheila. She didn't last because of it. [cosmetics] (Prus 1989a, 66)

Although people's activities have important implications for their subsequent viewpoints and identities, activities acquire their meaning or purposiveness relative to both the perspectives from which they are envisioned and the identities of the people involved. Since the preceding discussions of perspectives and identities have already been cast in action ("do"-ing) terms, our attention turns to four other realms of activity. These include *performing activities, influencing others, pursuing objectives by forming associations with others,* and *making commitments.*

Performing Activities

In every business, there are your winners and your dogs. Now when they come out, you hope you've got a winner. But you don't really determine that, although you can try through your research and your advertising. You hope that at least you're in the running, not losing too much on any line or model. And you can promote it hard, but if people are not buying it that much, then you've got a dog and you better spend your money promoting other things.... That's one thing that discourages you from coming out with many different things. You can spend a lot of money in research and development, and if it's seen as too different, you'll likely take a beating. On the other hand though, you can come out with something that the market research boys weren't so keen on and it can really do well. A new and different product can really hit it big. The timing when you bring it out is a big thing too. [manufacture-industrial] (Prus 1989b, 153)

The "performance of activity" assumes the processes outlined in "getting involved," but highlights the "problematics of accomplishment." It should be noted that no assumption is made about people acting wisely or rationally in any objective sense. Wisdom and rationality are not only matters of definition, but these notions are also apt to be worked out in process (see Prus, 1989b, especially 139–42). Indeed, while people may try to act in manners that they deem wise, rational, and the like, reality is not their's alone to determine. Indeed, matters of ambiguity, uncertainty, and resistance on the part of others can make human endeavor particularly problematic. The processes relevant to performance include:
- Making (preliminary) plans
- Getting prepared
- Managing stage fright (reservations, if any)
- Developing competence (stock of knowledge, tactics, applications)
- Co-ordinating events with others (team members and others)
- Dealing with ambiguity, obstacles, resistances, and distractions
- Conveying images of competence (displaying ability, composure)
- Encountering competition
- Making ongoing assessments and adjustments[9]

Influencing Others

Close-up magic is where you're standing inches from someone. They feel your breath, you feel their breath. You can see their goosebumps, you see their pupils dilate. You can see their hair stand on end when they get frightened.... Close-up magic is very, very intimate! You're practically on top of somebody.... It's the same theatrical principles, but it's toned down, much more subtle, underplayed. In fact, the effect might be ruined if you're trying to relate to ten people instead of three. There's the potential for more complete control, responsiveness, getting them to follow your hands, look up when you want that response. [magician] (Prus and Sharper 1991, 225)

The influence or persuasion process reflects attempts on the part of people to "gain the co-operation or commitment of others" with respect to both one-to-one and more diversified group situations. When dealing with larger groups of people, matters of complexity and ambiguity typically become more noteworthy, as do the greater likelihood of distractions, challenges, and lowered levels of personal accountability. As well, one's opportunities for role-taking are lessened when one faces the task of "pitching" to more generalized audiences as opposed to interpersonal others. This may involve some additional frustration and result in the creation of some unique group-directed tactics, but otherwise the same basic processes appear to hold for these instances as well. Here, we may consider how people go about:

- Formulating (preliminary) plans
- Role-taking (inferring/uncovering the perspectives of the other)
- Promoting interest in one's objectives
- Generating trust
- Proposing specific lines of action
- Encountering resistance
- Neutralizing obstacles
- Seeking and making concessions
- Confirming agreements
- Assessing failures and recasting plans[10]

Pursuing Objectives by Forming Associations with Others

> We want someone [franchisees] who's hardworking, and it would be better if they already had an established business. Then they can add our line to their present business. That way, their immediate overhead is less. Also, for us to let them have a franchise, it should be in a related, but not competing merchandise.... We'll also provide training and support materials to try and make their operation as competitive as possible. Actually, we see our distributors as partners. I know it sounds corny, but they are like family to you. They become like family to you because you end up working so closely with them. [manufacture-appliances] (Prus 1989b, 75)

The notion of forming or generating associations with others typically builds on the aforementioned influence process, but is also contingent on people recognizing the advantages of encompassing the efforts of others into their objectives. These associations can vary greatly in size, duration, formality, and the like, but involve attempts to secure the co-operation of others with respect to ventures people feel unwilling to pursue (or unable to accomplish) on their own. While not all of these ventures will be pursued very far or successfully, three subprocesses seem relevant in a great many cases. These are: *establishing associations, objectifying associations, encountering outsiders.*

Establishing Associations

> If we like his style and he seems solid and fits in with the crew, we might ask him to another party. You try the fellow out, but you don't commit yourself.

Then, if you feel that he is an asset to the crew, you might work him in a little more. If he is willing to learn and digs up a few parties for us, he might become a regular. It depends on his dedication to the crew and how the crew stands at that time. He might work with the crew for quite a while before we tell him anything about our operations. We want to test him—can he work under pressure, is he reliable, is he honest? [road hustler] (Prus and Sharper 1991, 42)

The matter of incorporating others into a collective enterprise or venture (that is, team, side, agency, organization, gang, committee, department, office, crew, mob, band, tribe) can be a quick or very lengthy process. In a more complete sense, it would appear to involve the following activities:
- Recognizing the value of collective enterprise
- Involving others in the venture (recruitment, screening, minimizing reservations)
- Justifying the group (developing perspective, moral viewpoint)
- Defining the team (membership criteria, positions, responsibilities)
- Establishing communication forums (interpersonal, media)
- Pursuing resources for the group
- Arranging member assemblies (encounters, practices)
- Providing instruction for members (perspectives, techniques)
- Monitoring members
- Assessing member performances
- Motivating and disciplining members
- Rejecting and re-instating members
- Facing internal upheaval (splintering, factions, challenges from within)
- Facing generalized loss of interest
- Dealing with dissolution
- Attempting to revitalize co-operative ventures[11]

Objectifying Associations

That's why your name or your label is so valuable. It's what people associate with it. A certain quality, style, a price-range…. If you're buying somebody out, that's something you definitely want to consider, what the label is worth to you. If it's a name that people have a lot of respect for, it could be worth as much as the buildings and the stock and all, over the years. You have a more marketable commodity. [manufacture-clothing] (Prus 1989a, 218)

While the co-ordinators of some groups may plan for their group to remain unnoticed within the larger community, a great many groups appear interested in establishing a prominence that is more obvious to both members and outsiders within the community. Thus, while those groups who wish to "go undercover" for a variety of reasons may adopt certain practices to make their groups appear more "real" to their members, those desiring community-wide objectification may be even more outreaching in their efforts:

- Developing a group identity (name, logo, flag)
- Stipulating justifications for existence and operations
- Creating identity markers for members (uniforms, appearances, signs)
- Defining exclusiveness (selectivity, oaths, codes, jargon)
- Establishing a public presence (publicity, announcements, advertising, rallies, ceremonies)
- Legitimating the group publicly (endorsements, credentials, charters, licences)
- Establishing territorial markers and jurisdictions (buildings, places, locations)[12]

Encountering Others

Audience involvement was a skill learned to entice suckers to play at your game, or bet more money than they should.... And how we did that, of course, was to have them bet more than they should. I've seen it happen so many times. You know, a guy'd be betting, and you would hear from other people, "You've never bet like this before!" You know how they chase that dollar. They'd want to double up. We had so many double ups, and that's how you make your money.... Just let the guy keep going and just keep losing. (Prus and Sharper 1991, 286)

Once established, groups may make contact with a variety of individuals and groups within the community. Some of these people may represent targets (prospects, clients, customers, patrons, cases, suckers, marks, patients, inmates) for the focal group or organization's enterprises; some may be viewed as potential partners of sorts for particular co-operative ventures; some may be seen as adversaries; and others may be viewed more ambiguously or vaguely as part of the community at large. While the focal group's interests in particular individuals and groups can be quite wide-ranging, the following matters tend to be noteworthy more generally:

- Representing the organization's interests
- Making contact with others (establishing co-presence, making the scene)
- Defining the theatre of operation (places, objectives, strategies)
- Defining others (targets, co-operators, adversaries, others)
- Pursuing organizational objectives through the others
- Protecting (sometimes concealing) the organization from the others
- Re-adjusting group routines to more effectively deal with the others[13]

Making Commitments

I used to work on the engraving and the molds [first business] like crazy to pay for the losses in the plastics [second business]. This went on for about two years. I had two people working for me, and meanwhile, I'd be working nights and Saturdays and Sundays on the engraving end to make the money to make expenses. It was tough for the first five years! [manufacture-giftware] (Prus 1989b, 82)

Commitments assume a variety of forms and may include physical investments as well as claims made to oneself or others. Some commitments are clearly desired by the parties making them, but others may be exceedingly tentative or reflect earlier resistance. The processes of "putting one's money down" or "buying into" particular situations have particular consequence for subsequent behavior. To the extent that people acknowledge previous commitments, their choices may be significantly limited (that is, closure). The subprocesses of relevance include:
- Exploring and assessing options
- Dealing with (any) earlier commitments
- Avoiding commitments (elusive targets)
- Minimizing or diversifying investments (hedging bets)
- Organizing routines around particular activities
- Neglecting other options (closure by default)[14]

Experiencing Relationships

When you're selling, you're always on! You have to watch yourself, and you have to watch the customer, be aware of their moods. You have to adjust yourself to them. You have to judge them, see how receptive they are to different styles. Like some people I hardly talk to, and others you can joke around with, and some you'll have to explain things to carefully. This is something you try to do, to adjust yourself to your customers. [women's clothing] (Prus 1989a, 110)

Like the elements preceding, relationships may be largely subsumed by the "doing of activities." However, the selectivity and continuity of association entailed by "bonding" signifies a vital element in social life. Relationships imply perspectives, identities, activities, and commitments; these can be powerful elements shaping the associations that people develop with one another. Since they also entail process, relationships have natural histories or careers (initial involvements, continuities, disinvolvements, reinvolvements), but matters of "intimacy and distancing" become especially prominent here as people try to achieve levels of selectivity and continuity with which they feel comfortable. The following processes seem central to considerations of people's relationships with others:
- Getting prepared for generalized encounters
- Defining self as available for association
- Defining (specific) others as desirable associates
- Making approaches/receiving openings from others
- Encountering (and indicating) rejection/acceptance

- Assessing self and other (for "goodness of fit")
- Developing interactional styles (in each relationship)
- Managing openness and secrecy
- Developing understandings, preferences, loyalties
- Managing distractions (and outside commitments)
- Juggling (multiple) relationships
- Severing relationships (disentanglement)
- Renewing relationships[15]

Conclusion

In discussing *generic social processes*, it is important to appreciate that the study of action has both a *temporal/historical* dimension and a *situated/contextual* dimension. While the temporal dimension draws attention to the interlinkage of past, present, and future behaviors, the situated dimension emphasizes the social production of action in the here-and-now. A recognition that these two dimensions intersect or are interconstituted is vital for the temporal dimension consists of an ongoing or natural history of a series of here-and-now events, while people's situated behaviors must be incorporated into a past and a sense of the future if we are to achieve a viable conceptual grasp of the here-and-now. These notions may be useful in analyzing the data collected in the field, but they may also alert researchers to the two interrelated flows of data that they are apt to encounter in the field. This may result in the collection of more data while in the field, as well as data that is more valuable in later analysis.

When doing field research, ethnographers typically endeavor to open themselves as fully as possible to the situation at hand. Researchers can still use conceptual notions derived from any earlier inquiry (regardless of substantive context) as a source of stimulation in developing material on any research setting, and they can use the material from each new setting to assess the viability of concepts developed in other contexts. First and foremost, however, ethnographers have the objective of achieving intimate familiarity with the life-worlds of the other. The data of human lived experiences must retain primacy over our concepts and that data should be used to reshape and otherwise inform our conceptual developments. In this way, by building a conceptual frame increasingly rigorously grounded in research on people's lived experiences, we may not only become more attentive to the interlinkages of theory, methods, and research, but we may also develop a social science that is genuinely attentive to the ways in which human group life is accomplished and experienced on a day-to-day, moment-to-moment basis:

> The difference is this.... A trick is just a puzzle. That's a pejorative term when I've tricked you.... I could show you something that is puzzling, that you don't understand, but you wouldn't enjoy it. When you're talking about performance,

that's like taking the trick and adding the presentation and making it a dramatic piece. A dramatic piece, it could be funny, but it's dramatic. It has a structure, the audience reacts to it as something more than just an intellectual challenge. So, they're taking part in the effect.... The best magic is a combination of fabulous presentation by a great performer with an interesting effect and a wonderful method. If you get all those things together, it's so enjoyable! You just sit back and enjoy yourself. [magician] (Prus and Sharper 1991, 237–38)

You go out and you talk to so many hundred thousand people on behalf of the client. If you're talking to the right people and you should know that from your research, then you know that if you talk to them in a positive way, that you are going to make an impact and you just keep firing on the impact and then the consumer starts to respond. Believe it or not, it's very hard for a merchant who can put the newspaper ad up on the wall and stick pins in it, to change this kind of thinking around to understand that all he ever bought in the newspaper was impact. [promotions-television] (Prus 1989b, 203)

NOTES

1. A somewhat related earlier version of this paper was published in the *Journal of Contemporary Ethnography* 1987, 16: 250–293. While I have done some "tinkering" with the GSPs generally (and have added more bibliographic references), I would particularly draw readers' attention to the section on *pursuing objectives by forming associations with others* (under the heading "Doing Activity") in the present version. This material addresses a very important theme that was underdeveloped in the earlier statement.

I am indebted to Jim Curtis, Carl Couch, Lorne Dawson, Mary Lorenz Dietz, Scott Grills, Jim Henslin, John Johnson, Lorraine Prus, Howard Robboy, Marvin Scott, and Graham Tomlinson for comments and discussions pertaining to earlier versions of this paper.

2. Although seemingly unaware of much of the literature on which the present statement is built, a somewhat parallel task has been suggested by Noblit and Hare (1988) under the term, "meta-ethnography." Despite this intriguing term, Noblit and Hare provide little direction concerning the ways in which meta-ethnography might be accomplished. The present statement on generic social processes then may be seen as extending their project along more focused, processual dimensions.

3. To better help readers appreciate the generic processes being discussed, I've pulled extracts from some ethnographic studies on which I've worked. One set of materials comes from a study of card and dice hustlers (Prus and Sharper 1977), which in the expanded version (Prus and Sharper 1991) also includes an interrelated study of magicians (two sets of practitioners whose routines are steeped in image work and deception). The other extracts are drawn from a study of marketing and sales activities (Prus 1989a, b). I've just used a single extract on each occasion from one of the two studies. These extracts cannot be expected to convey the full range of the sub-processes entailed in any of the generic social processes under consideration, but may foster a fuller understanding of the trans-situational nature of these processes.

4. Most ethnographies nicely illustrate themes pertaining to "the acquisition of perspectives" and most almost inevitably address notions of identities, involvements, activities, and relationships as well, for these elements are very much interrelated in subcultural lifestyles. Some book-length

ethnographies that do a particularly effective job of conveying the ways in which people become exposed to, and familiar with, particular worldviews include: Anderson (1923), Shaw (1930), Blumer (1933), Sutherland (1937), Becker et al. (1961, 1968), Goffman (1961), Lofland (1966), Scott (1968), Fine (1983), Kleinman (1984), Evans and Falk (1986), Stebbins (1990), Charmaz (1991a) and Wolf (1991b).

5. Ethnographic monographs that are particularly attentive to identity work and self images include: Edgerton (1969), Evans and Falk (1986), Haas and Shaffir (1987), Charmaz (1991a), Sanders (1991) and Wolf (1991b). For reviews of the literature on "identity work" as this pertains to type-casting, public designations, and resisting unwanted imputations, see Prus (1975, 1982). These reviews build centrally on the conceptual work of Lemert (1951, 1967), Goffman (1959, 1963b) and Klapp (1964, 1969, 1971), among others.

6. Among the monographs which more explicitly address involvements or career contingencies in ethnographic inquiries are: Shaw (1930), Cressey (1932), Sutherland (1937), Becker et al. (1961), Goffman (1961), Lofland (1966), Ditton (1977), Lesieur (1977), Fine (1983), Haas and Shaffir (1987), Prus and Irini (1980), Prus (1989a,b), Prus and Sharper (1991), and Wolf (1991b).

7. In a more complete sense, one should also note the existence of "imposed" (e.g., physiological / medical complications) and "inadvertent" (accidental, unwitting) involvements.

8. See Ebaugh (1988) for a review of the literature on "Becoming an Ex," as well as an instructive attempt to formulate the generic social processes constituting disinvolvement. Ray's (1961) article on "abstinence and relapse cycles among heroin addicts" also nicely lends itself to generic applications. As the last point emphasizes, disinvolvement is often accompanied by involvements in other settings. Also see for instance, Denzin's (1987a) account of heavy drinkers becoming involved in Alcoholics Anonymous, as a means of disinvolvement from drinking routines. Thus, all of the processes pertinent to involvement (in activity 2) may intersect with those of disinvolvement (from activity 1).

9. The following book-length monographs provide some of the more focused materials on how people accomplish activities: Anderson (1923), Shaw (1930), Emerson (1969), Hargreaves et al. (1975), Ditton (1977), Lesieur (1977), Letkemann (1977), Athens (1980), Prus and Irini (1980), Ross (1980), Dietz (1983), Fine (1983), Mitchell (1983), Albas and Albas (1984), Powell (1985), Steffensmeier (1986), Prus (1989a, b), Charmaz (1991a), Prus and Sharper (1991), and Wolf (1991b). For detailed illustrations of these particular subprocesses, see Prus (1989b).

10. Notions of persuasion (influence and negotiation processes) are especially evident in the following monographs: Shaw (1930), Sutherland (1937), Festinger (1956), Lofland (1966), Emerson (1969), Wiseman (1970), Prus and Irini (1980), Ross (1980), Fine (1983), Latour (1987), and Prus and Sharper (1991). The subprocesses outlined here are most extensively detailed in an analysis of interpersonal selling activity (Prus 1989a).

11. The following materials ethnographically depict the ways in which people attempt to establish groups or associations of sorts (including screening activities): Sutherland's (1937) professional thieves; Karsh et al's (1953) union organizers; Lofland's (1966) doomsday cult; Prus and Sharper's (1977) road hustlers; Adler's (1985) drug dealers; Prus and Frisby's (1990) party plans; Haas and Shaffir's (1987) medical schools; Wolf's (1991b) outlaw bikers; and Grill's (this volume) political recruitment practices. I have also derived some inspiration from Klapp's (1969) discussion of cults and crusades.

12. For instances of objectification practices of groups wishing to become known in the community at large, see Goffman (1961); Wiseman (1970), and Prus (1989a,b). For examples of objectification practices among those wishing to remain unnoticed in the larger community, see Sutherland (1937), Prus and Sharper (1977). Still other groups may desire or flirt with a semi-public recognition (e.g taxi-dance hall operators [Cressey, 1932]; action bars [Prus and Irini, 1980]; outlaw bikers [Wolf, 1991b]).

13. Those interested in the ways in which groups (organizations) make contact with and deal with outside parties (e.g. targets, clients, suspects, etc.) may wish to examine: Cressey (1932), Sutherland (1937), Goffman (1961), Emerson (1969), Wiseman (1970), Prus and Sharper (1977), Ross (1980), Prus and Irini (1980), Haas and Shaffir (1987), Prus (1989a, b), Prus and Frisby (1990), and Wolf (1991b).

14. For book-length ethnographies which attend more explicitly to the commitment making process, see: Lofland (1966), Lesieur (1977), Prus (1989a,b), and Wolf (1991b).

15. The development and maintenance of relationships is given more explicit attention in the following monographs: Shaw (1930), Waller (1930), Lofland (1966), Wiseman (1970, 1991), Lesieur (1977), Prus and Irini (1980), Fine (1983), Adler (1985), Prus (1989a,b), Prus and Sharper (1991) and Wolf (1991b). Lemert's (1962) analysis of "paranoia and the dynamics of exclusion" deserves special recognition as one of the best accounts of interpersonal relationships.

Reference List

Adler, Patricia A.
1985   *Wheeling and Dealing*. New York: Columbia University Press.
1992   "The 'Post' Phase of Deviant Careers: Reintegrating Drug Traffickers." In *Deviant Behavior* 13, 2 (April–June).

Adler, Patricia A., and Peter Adler
1980   "The Irony of Secrecy in the Drug World." In *Urban Life* 8: 447–65.
1987a   *Membership Roles in Field Research*. Newbury Park, CA: Sage Publications.
1987b   "Role Conflict and Identity Salience: College Athletes and the Academic Role." In *The Social Science Journal* 24: 443–55.
1990   *Backboards and Blackboards: College Athletes and Role Engulfment*. New York: Columbia University Press.
1991   "Stability and Flexibility: Maintaining Relations Within Organized and Unorganized Groups." In *Experiencing Fieldwork*, ed. William B. Shaffir and Robert A. Stebbins, 173–83. Newbury Park, CA: Sage Publications.

Albas, Daniel C., and Cheryl M. Albas
1984   *Student Life and Exams*. Dubuque, IA: Kendall/Hunt.

Albrecht, Gary L.
1992   "The Social Experience of Disability." In *Social Problems*, ed. Craig Calhoun and George Ritzer, 1–18. New York: McGraw-Hill.

Alexander, C. Norman, Jr., and Mary Glenn Wiley
1981   "Situated Activity and Identity Formation." In *Social Psychology: Sociological Perspectives*, ed. M. Rosenberg and R.A. Turner, 269–89. New York: Basic Books.

Altheide, David L.
1980   "Leaving the Newsroom." In *Fieldwork Experience: Qualitative Approaches to Social Research*, ed. W. Shaffir, R.A. Stebbins, and A. Turowetz, 301–10. New York: St. Martin's Press.

Altheide, David L., and E. Pfuhl
1980   "Self-accomplishment Through Running." In *Symbolic Interaction* 3: 127–42.

Anderson, Nels
1923   *The Hobo*. Chicago: University of Chicago Press.
1983   "A Stranger at the Gate: Reflections on the Chicago School of Sociology." In *Urban Life* 11: 396–406.

Anspach, Renée
1987   "Prognostic Conflict in Life-and-Death Decisions: The Organization as an Ecology of Knowledge." In *Journal of Health and Social Behavior* 28: 215–31.

Armstrong, P., and H. Armstrong
1984   *The Double Ghetto: Canadian Women and Their Segregated Work*. Toronto: McClelland & Stewart.

Asch, S.E.
1958 "Effects of Group Pressure Upon the Modification and Distortion of Judgements." In 3d ed., *Readings in Social Psychology,* ed. E.E. Maccoby, T.M. Newcomb, and E.L. Hartley, 174–83. New York: Holt, Rinehart and Winston.

Athens, Lonnie H.
1980 *Violent Criminal Acts and Actors: A Symbolic Interactionist Study.* Boston: Oxford University Press.
1984 "Blumer's Method of Naturalistic Inquiry." In *Studies in Symbolic Interaction* 5: 241–57.

Ayoob, Massad
1982 "Outlaw Bikers." In *Police Product News* 6, 5: 26–30, 63.

Backett, K.
1987 "The Negotiation of Fatherhood." In *Reassessing Fatherhood,* ed. C. Lewis and M. O'Brien. London: Sage Publications.

Barker, Eileen
1984 *The Making of a Moonie: Choice or Brainwashing.* New York: Basil Blackwell.

Barkun, Michael
1972 "Movements of Total Transformation: An Introduction." In *American Behavioral Scientist* 16: 145–51.

Bar-Levav, Reuven
1976 "The Stigma of Seeing a Psychiatrist." In *American Journal of Psychotherapy* 30, 3: 473–82.

Barrett, Stanley R.
1987 *Is God a Racist? The Right Wing in Canada.* Toronto: University of Toronto Press.

Bartell, Gilbert D.
1971 *Group Sex: A Scientist's Eyewitness Report on the American Way of Swinging.* New York: Wyden.

Bean, John P., and George D. Kuh
1984 "The Reciprocity Between Student-Faculty Informal Contact and Academic Performance of University Undergraduate Students." In *Research in Higher Education* 21: 461–77.

Becker, Ernest
1971 *The Birth and Death of Meaning: An Interdisciplinary Perspective on the Problem of Man.* New York: Free Press.

Becker, Howard S.
1953 "Becoming A Marihuana User." In *American Journal of Sociology* 59: 235–42.
1960 "Notes on the Concept of Commitment." In *American Journal of Sociology* 66 (July): 32–40.
1963 *Outsiders: Studies in the Sociology of Deviance.* New York: Free Press.
1970a "Personal Change in Adult Life." In *Social Psychology Through Symbolic Interaction,* ed. Gregory Stone and Harvey Farberman, 583–93. Waltham: Xerox College Publishing.
1970b *Sociological Work: Method and Substance.* Chicago: Aldine.
1973 *Outsiders: Studies in the Sociology of Deviance.* London: Collier Macmillan.
1982 *Art Worlds.* Berkeley: University of California Press.

Becker, Howard S., and Blanche Geer
1957   "Participant Observation and Interviewing: A Comparison." In *Human Organization* 16: 28–32.
1958   "The Fate of Idealism in Medical School." In *American Sociological Review* 23: 50–56.

Becker, Howard S., Blanche Geer, and Everett Hughes
1968   *Making the Grade: The Academic Side of College Life.* New York: Wiley.

Becker, Howard S., Blanche Geer, Everett C. Hughes, and Anselm L. Strauss
1961   *Boys in White: Student Culture in Medical School.* Chicago: University of Chicago Press.

Becker, Howard S., Blanche Geer, David Reisman, and Robert Weiss
1968   *Institutions and the Person.* Chicago: Aldine.

Belk, Russell
1988   "Possessions and the Extended Self." In *Journal of Consumer Research* 15: 139–68.

Bell, Alan, and Martin S. Weinberg
1978   *Homosexualities: A Study of Diversity Among Men and Women.* New York: Simon and Schuster.

Bell, G.
1967   "Self-confidence, Persuasability and Cognitive Dissonance Among Automobile Buyers." In *Risk-Taking and Information-Handling in Consumer Behavior,* ed. D. Cox, 442–68. Boston: Harvard University Graduate School of Business Administration.

Benokraitis, N.
1985   "Fathers in the Dual Career Family." In *Dimensions of Fatherhood,* ed. S. Hanson and F. Bozett. Beverly Hills: Sage Publications.

Berg, B.L.
1989   *Qualitative Research Methods for the Social Sciences.* Boston: Allyn and Bacon.

Berger, Peter, and Thomas Luckmann
1966   *The Social Construction of Reality.* New York: Doubleday.

Bernard, Jessie
1983   "The Good Provider Role: Its Rise and Fall." In *Family in Transition,* ed. A. Skolnick and J. Skolnick, 125–44. Boston: Little, Brown.

Bernstein, S.
1976   "Getting it Done: Notes on Student Fritters." In *Sociology: A Descriptive Approach,* ed. J. Nash and J. Spradley, 384–87. Chicago: Rand McNally.

Berreman, Gerald D.
1962   *Behind Many Masks: Ethnography and Impression Management in a Himalayan Village.* Monograph No. 4, Society for Applied Anthropology.
1966   "Anemic and Emetic Analyses in Social Anthropology." In *American Anthropologist* 68: 346–54.
1969   "Urgent Anthropology in India." In *Transactions of the Indian Institute of Advanced Study* 10: 1–13.
1972   "Anthropology and the Ivory Tower: Bringing It All Back Home." In *Re-Inventing Anthropology,* ed. Dell Hymes, 80–98. New York: Pantheon.
1981   *The Politics of Truth: Essays in Critical Anthropology.* New Delhi: South Asian Publishers.

Best, Joel, and David Luckenbill
1982   *Organizing Deviance.* Englewood Cliffs, NJ: Prentice-Hall.

Biermans, John T.
1986   *The Odyssey of New Religious Movements: Persecution, Struggle,
                Legitimation: A Case Study of the Unification Church.* Lewiston, NY: Edwin
                Mellen Press.

Biesser, Arnold R.
1989   *Flying Without Wings: Personal Reflections on Being Disabled.* New York:
                Doubleday.

Blau, Zena Smith
1973   *Old Age in a Changing Society.* New York: New Viewpoints.

Bloom, Harold
1973   *The Anxiety of Influence.* Oxford: Oxford University Press.

Bloom, Samuel
1973   *Power and Dissent in the Medical School.* New York: Macmillan.

Blumer, Herbert
1928   Method in Social Psychology. Ph.D. diss., University of Chicago.
1931   "Science Without Concepts." In *American Journal of Sociology* 36: 515–33.
1933   *Movies and Conduct.* New York: Macmillan. Reprinted, New York: Arno
                Press, 1970.
1936–37   "Social and Individual Disorganization." In *American Journal of Sociology*
                42: 871–77.
1937   "Social Psychology." In *Man and Society*, ed. Emerson P. Schmidt, 144–98.
                New York: Prentice-Hall.
1939   *Critiques of Research in the Social Sciences: An Appraisal of Thomas and
                Znaniecki's. "The Polish Peasant in Europe and America."* New Brunswick,
                NJ: Transaction Books. Reprinted 1979
1964   "Industrialization and the Traditional Order." In *Sociology and Social
                Research* 48: 129–38.
1966   "Sociological Implications of the Thought of G. H. Mead." *American
                Journal of Sociology* 71: 535–48.
1967   "Threats from Agency-Determined Research." In *The Rise and Fall of
                Project Camelott*, ed. I.L. Horowitz, 153–74. Cambridge: MIT Press.
1968   "Fashion." In *International Encyclopedia of the Social Sciences.* New York:
                Macmillan.
1969a   "Fashion: From Class Differentiation to Collective Selection." In
                Sociological Quarterly 10: 275–91.
1969b   *Symbolic Interactionism: Perspective and Method.* Englewood Cliffs, NJ:
                Prentice-Hall.
1971   "Social Problems as Collective Behavior." In *Social Problems* 18: 298–306.
1980   "Mead and Blumer: The Convergent Methodological Perspectives of Social
                Behaviorism and Symbolic Interactionism." In *American Sociological
                Review* 45: 409–19.

Blumer, Herbert, and Philip Hauser
1933   *Movies, Delinquency and Crime.* New York: Macmillan. Reprinted New
                York: Arno Press, 1970.

Bogdan, Robert
1974   *Being Different: The Autobiography of Jane Fry.* New York: Wiley.

Bord, Richard James
1970   "Rejection of the Mentally Ill: Continuities and Further Developments." In *Social Problems* 18: 490–512.

Boukydis, C.F., and R.L. Burgess
1982   "Adult Physiological Response to Infant Cries: Effects of Temperament of Infant, Parental Status and Gender." In *Child Development* 53: 1291–98.

Bowen, E.S. (pseud.)
1964   *Return to Laughter*. New York: Doubleday.

Bowman, William P., and R.H. Ball
1961   *Theatre Language*. New York: Theatre Arts Books.

Bramson, R.
1973   "The Secularization of American Medicine." In *Hastings Center Studies* 1: 17–28.

Briggs, Jean L.
1970   *Never in Anger: Portrait of an Eskimo Family*. Cambridge: Harvard University Press.

Brodzinsky, David M., Karen Barnet, and John R. Aiello
1981   "Sex of Object and Gender Identity as Factors in Humor Appreciation." In *Sex Roles* 7: 561–73.

Bromley, David G., and Anson D. Shupe Jr.
1979   *"Moonies" in America: Cult, Church, and Crusade*. Beverly Hills: Sage Publications.

Brooks, Nancy A., and Ronald R. Matson
1987   "Managing Multiple Sclerosis." In *Research in the Sociology of Health Care: The Experience and Management of Chronic Illness,* ed. Julius A Roth and Peter Conrad 6: 73–106. Greenwich, CT: JAI Press.

Brownmiller, Susan
1970   "Sisterhood is Powerful." In *Women's Liberation: Blueprint for the Future,* ed. S. Stambly, 141–55. New York: New York Times, 1970.

Bruner, Edward M., ed.
1984   *Text, Play, and Story: The Construction and Reconstruction of Self and Society*. Washington, DC: American Ethnological Society.
1986   "Experience and its Expressions." In *The Anthropology of Experience*, ed. Victor W. Turner and Edward M. Bruner, 3–30. Urbana: University of Illinois Press.

Brymer, Richard A.
1984   "Anthropological and Sociological Approaches to the Study of Deviance: A Critique and Tentative Move to a Theory of Cross-Cultural Deviance." Paper presented at Deviance in a Cross-Cultural Context: An Ethnographic/Interactionist Perspective. University of Waterloo, Waterloo, ON, June 2–5.

Bucher, Rue, and Joan Stelling
1977   *Becoming Professional*. Beverly Hills: Sage Publications.

Burgess, Robert C.
1984   *In the Field: An Introduction to Field Research*. London: George Allen and Unwin.

Bushnell, J.
1962   "Student Culture at Vasser." In *The American College,* ed. N. Sanford. New York: Wiley.

Carden, Marion Lockwood
1974   *The Feminist Movement.* New York: Sage Publications.

Carrier, J.M.
1976   "Family Attitudes and Mexican Male Homosexuality." In *Urban Life* 50: 359–75.

Cassell, Joan
1977   *A Group Called Women: Sisterhood and Symbolism in the Feminist Movement.* Prospect Heights, IL: Waveland Press.

Castaneda, Carlos
1968   *The Teachings of Don Juan: A Yaqui Way of Knowledge.* New York: Ballantine Books.

Caton, Steven C.
1985   "The Poetic Construction of Self." In *Anthropological Quarterly* 58: 141–51.

Caughy, J.
1982   "Ethnography, Introspection and Reflexive Culture Studies." In *Prospects* 7: 115–39.

Cesara, Manda
1982   *Reflections of a Woman Anthropologist: No Hiding Place.* New York: Academic Press.

Charmaz, Kathy
1973   Time and Identity: The Shaping of Selves of the Chronically Ill. Ph.D. diss., University of California, San Francisco.
1980   *The Social Reality of Death.* Reading, MA: Addison-Wesley.
1983a   "The Grounded Theory Method: An Explication and Interpretation." In *Contemporary Field Research,* ed. Robert M. Emerson, 109–26. Boston: Little, Brown.
1983b   "Loss of Self: A Fundamental Form of Suffering in the Chronically Ill." In *Sociology of Health and Illness* 5: 168–95.
1987   "Struggling for a Self: Identity Levels of the Chronically Ill." In *Research in the Sociology of Health Care: The Experience and Management of Chronic Illness,* ed. Julius A. Roth and Peter Conrad 6: 283–321. Greenwich, CT: JAI Press.
1989   "The Self in Time." In *Studies in Symbolic Interaction,* ed. Norman K. Denzin 10: 127–41. Greenwich, CT: JAI Press.
1990   "Discovering Chronic Illness: Using Grounded Theory." In *Social Science and Medicine* 30: 1161–72.
1991a   "Fictional Identities and Turning Points." In *Social Organization and Social Process: Essays in Honor of Anselm Strauss,* ed. David R. Maines, 71–86. New York: Aldine de Gruyter.
1991b   *Good Days, Bad Days: The Self in Chronic Illness and Time.* New Brunswick, NJ: Rutgers University Press.

Charon, Joel
1979   *Symbolic Interactionism: An Introduction, an Interpretation, an Integration.* Englewood Cliffs, NJ: Prentice-Hall.
1992   *Symbolic Interactionism: An Introduction, an Interpretation, an Integration.* 3d ed. Englewood Cliffs, NJ: Prentice-Hall.

Cheadle, A.J., H. Freeman, and J. Korer
1978   "Chronic Schizophrenic Patients in the Community." In *British Journal of Psychiatry* 132: 221–27.

Chodorow, Nancy
1978   *The Reproduction of Mothering: Psychoanalysis and the Sociology of Gender.* Berkeley: University of California Press.

Chow, Esther Ngan-Ling
1987   "The Development of Feminist Consciousness Among Asian American Women." In *Gender & Society* 1 (Sept.): 286–99.

Christensen, Harold T.
1953   "Studies in Child Spacing: I—Premarital Pregnancy as Measured By the Spacing of the First Birth from Marriage." In *American Sociological Review* 18: 53–59.

Cicourel, Aaron V.
1967   "Fertility, Family Planning and the Social Methodological Issues." In *Journal of Social Issues* 23: 57–81.

Cicourel, Aaron V., and Robert J. Boese
1972   "Sign Language Acquisition and the Teaching of Deaf Children." In *Functions of Language in the Classroom,* ed. C. Cazden, V. John, and Dell Hymes, 32–62. New York: Columbia Teacher's College.

Cicourel, Aaron V., and John I. Kitsuse
1963   *The Educational Decision-Makers.* Indianapolis: Bobbs-Merrill.

Clausen, John
1981   "Stigma and Mental Disorder: Phenomena and Terminology." *Psychiatry* 44, 4: 287–96.

Clifford, James
1983   "On Ethnographic Authority." In *Representations* 1: 118–46.

Cochrane, R., and K. Nieradzik
1985   "Public Attitudes Towards Mental Illness—The Effects of Behavior, Roles, and Psychiatric Labels." In *The International Journal of Psychiatry* 31, 1: 23–33.

Cogswell, B.
1967   "Rehabilitation of the Paraplegic: Processes of Socialization." In *Sociological Inquiry* 37: 11–26.

Cohen, T.F.
1987   "Remaking Men." In *Journal of Family Issues* 8: 57–77.

Collins, H.M., and T.J. Pinch
1982   *Frames of Meaning: The Social Construction of an Extraordinary Science.* London: Routledge and Kegan Paul.

Conrad, Peter
1985   "The Meaning of Medications: Another Look at Compliance." In *Social Science and Medicine* 20: 28–37.

Cooley, Charles Horton
1909   *Social Organization: A Study of the Larger Mind.* New York: Shocken.
1922 [1902] *Human Nature and the Social Order.* New York: Shocken.
1926   "The Roots of Social Knowledge." In *American Journal of Sociology* 32: 59–79.

1928   "Case Study of Small Institutions As a Method of Research." In *American Sociological Review* 22: 123–32.

1964 [1902] *Human Nature and the Social Order*. New York: Schocken.

1967   "Looking-Glass Self." In *Symbolic Interaction: A Reader in Social Psychology*, ed. J.G. Manis and B.N. Meltzer, 217–20. Boston: Allyn and Bacon.

Coombs, Robert H.

1978   *Mastering Medicine: Professional Socialization in Medical School*. New York: Macmillan.

Coombs, Robert H., and P.S. Powers

1975   "Socialization for Death: The Physician's Role." In *Urban Life* 4: 250–71.

Cooper, Michael

1988   The Recruitment Process: Sport Recruitment As a Case in Point. Master's thesis, University of Windsor, Windsor, ON.

Corbin, Juliet, and Anselm Strauss

1988   *Unending Work and Care: Managing Chronic Illness at Home*. San Francisco: Jossey-Bass.

Coser, Rose

1961   "Insulation from Observability and Types of Social Conformity." In *American Sociological Review* 26: 28–39.

Cott, Nancy F.

1987   *The Grounding of Modern Feminism*. New Haven, CT: Yale University Press.

Cousins, Norman

1983   *The Healing Heart: Antidotes to Panic and Helplessness*. New York: Avon.

Crapanzano, Vincent

1986   *Waiting: the Whites of South Africa*. New York: Random House.

Cressey, Paul G.

1932   *The Taxi-Dance Hall*. Chicago: University of Chicago Press.

Cruikshank, Julia M.

1990   *Life Told Like a Story*. Vancouver: University of British Columbia Press.

Curtis, James, and William McTeer

1981   "Social Influences in Recruitment to Marathoning." In *Review of Sport and Leisure* 6: 58–82.

Curtiss, Susan

1977   *Genie: A Psycholinguistic Study of a Modern-Day "Wild Child."* New York: Academic Press.

Daniels, Morris J.

1960   "Affect and Its Control in the Medical Intern." In *American Journal of Sociology* 66: 259–67.

D'Arcy, Carl, and Joan Brockman

1977   "Public Rejection of the Ex-Mental Patient: Are Attitudes Changing?" In *The Canadian Review of Sociology and Anthropology* 14, 1: 68–80.

Davis, Fred

1961   "Deviance Disavowal: The Management of Strained Interaction By the Visibly Handicapped." In *Social Problems* 9: 120–32.

1963   *Passage Through Crisis: Polio Victims and Their Families*. Indianapolis: Bobbs-Merrill.

1968	"Professional Socialization as Subjective Experience: The Process of Doctrinal Conversion Among Student Nurses." In *Institutions and the Person*, ed. Howard S. Becker, Blanche Geer, David Reisman, and Robert Weiss, 235–51. Chicago: Aldine.
1973	"The Martian and the Convert: Ontological Polarities in Social Research." In *Urban Life and Culture* 2, 3: 333–43.
1982	"On the 'Symbolic' in Symbolic Interaction." In *Symbolic Interaction* 5, 1: 111–26.
1985	"Clothing and Fashion as Communication." In *The Psychology of Fashion*, ed. Michael Solomon. Lexington, MA: Heath.
1988	"Clothing, Fashion and the Dialectic of Identity." In *Communication and Social Structure*, ed. Carl Couch and David Maines. Springfield, IL: Charles C. Thomas.
1989	"Of Maids' Uniforms and Blue Jeans: The Drama of Status Ambivalences in Clothing and Fashion." In *Qualitative Sociology* 12, 4 (Winter): 337–56.
1991a	"Herbert Blumer and the Study of Fashion: A Reminiscence and a Critique." In *Symbolic Interaction* 14, 1: 1–21.
1991b	"Identity Ambivalence in Clothing: The Dialectic of the Erotic and the Chaste." In *Social Organization and Social Process, Essays in Honor of Anselm Strauss*, ed. David Maines. New York: Aldine de Gruyter.
1992	*Fashion, Culture and Identity.* Chicago: University of Chicago Press.

Davis, Kingsley

| 1949 | *Human Society.* New York: Macmillan. |

de Certeau, Michel

| 1984 | *The Practice of Everyday Life.* Berkeley: University of California Press. |

Deckard, Barbara Sinclair

| 1983 | *The Women's Movement: Political, Socio-Economic, and Psychological Issues.* 3d ed. New York: Harper and Row. |

Delph, Edward W.

| 1978 | *The Silent Community: Public Homosexual Encounters.* Beverly Hills: Sage Publications. |

Denscombe, Martyn

| 1985 | *Classroom Control: A Sociological Perspective.* London: George Allen and Unwin. |

Denzin, Norman K.

1987a	*The Alcoholic Self.* Beverly Hills: Sage Publications.
1987b	*The Recovering Alcoholic.* Newbury Park, CA: Sage Publications.
1989	*The Research Act: A Theoretical Introduction to Sociological Methods.* 3d ed. Englewood Cliffs, NJ: Prentice-Hall.

Diamond, S.

| 1964 | "Nigerian Discovery: The Politics of Fieldwork." In *Reflections on Community Studies*, ed. A.J. Vidich, J. Bensman, and R. Stein, 119–54. New York: Harper and Row. |

Dietz, Mary Lorenz

| 1983 | *Killing for Profit: The Social Organization of Felony Homicide.* Chicago: Nelson-Hall. |
| 1987 | "Accomplishment as Process: Performances as Activity." Paper presented at Canadian Sociology and Anthropology Association Meetings, Hamilton, ON. |

Dietz, Mary Lorenz, and Marjo Callaghan
1985 "Field Observations with Dangerous People: Negotiations and Exchanges in Research with Felons." Paper presented at Qualitative Research Conference, Waterloo, ON.

Dingwall, Robert
1980 "Orchestrated Encounters: An Essay in the Comparative Analysis of Speech-Exchange Systems." In *Sociology of Health and Illness* 2: 151–73.

Ditton, James
1977 *Part-Time Crime: An Ethnography of Fiddling and Pilferage.* London: Macmillan.

Doll, William, Edward Thompson Jr., and Mark Lefton
1976 "Beneath Acceptance: Dimensions of Family Affect Towards Former Mental Patients." In *Social Science and Medicine* 10, 6: 307–13.

Dollard, John
1935 *Criteria for the Life History.* New Haven, CT: Yale University Press.

Donne, John
1980 "Devotions Upon Emergent Occasions." In Bartlett's *Familiar Quotations: A Collection of Passages, Phrases and Proverbs Traced to Their Sources in Ancient and Modern Literature* by John Bartlett, ed. Emily M. Beck, [1624] No. 6. Boston: Little, Brown.

Donnelly, P.
1980 The Subculture and Public Image of Climbers. Ph.D. diss., University of Massachusetts, Amherst.

Douglas, Mary
1986 *How Institutions Think.* Syracuse: Syracuse University Press.

Dubin, R.
1979 "Central Life Interests." In *Pacific Sociological Review* 22: 405–26.

Dubro, James
1985 *Mob Rule: Inside the Canadian Mafia.* Toronto: Macmillan.

Dwyer, Kevin
1982 *Moroccan Dialogues: Anthropology in Question.* Baltimore: Johns Hopkins University Press.

Ebaugh, Helen R.F.
1984 "Leaving the Convent: Role Exit and Self-Transformation." In *The Existential Self in Society,* ed. J.A. Kotarba and A. Fontana, 156–76. Chicago: University of Chicago Press.
1988 *Becoming an Ex: The Process of Role Exit.* Chicago: University of Chicago Press.

Edgerton, Robert
1967 *The Cloak of Competence: Stigma in the Lives of the Mentally Retarded.* Berkeley: University of California Press.

Ellis, Carolyn
1991 "Sociological Introspection and Emotional Experience." In *Symbolic Interaction* 14: 23–50.

Emerson, Joan P.
1970 "Behavior in Private Places: Sustaining Definitions of Reality in Gynecological Examinations." In *Recent Sociology,* ed. Hans P. Dreitzel, 73–97. New York: Macmillan.

Emerson, Robert M.
1969   *Judging Delinquents: Context and Process in Juvenile Court.* Chicago: Aldine.
1981   "On Last Resorts." In *American Journal of Sociology* 87, 1: 1–22.

Emerson, Robert M., ed.
1983   *Contemporary Field Research: A Collection of Readings.* Boston: Little, Brown.

Emerson, Robert M., and Sheldon L. Messinger
1977   "The Micro-Politics of Trouble." In *Social Problems* 25, 2: 121–34.

Erikson, Kai T.
1966   *Wayward Puritans.* New York: Wiley.

Ermarth, Michael
1978   *Wilhelm Dilthey: The Critique of Historical Reason.* Chicago: University of Chicago Press.

Estroff, Sue E.
1981   *Making It Crazy: An Ethnography of Psychiatric Clients in an American Community.* Berkeley: University of California Press.

Evans, A. Donald
1982   The Social Construction of Reality in a Total Institution: An Ethnography of a Residential School for the Deaf. Ph.D. diss., Louisiana State University, Baton Rouge.
1987   "Institutionally Developed Identities: An Ethnographic Account of Reality Construction in a Residential School for the Deaf." In *Sociological Studies of Child Development,* 161–84. Greenwich, CT: JAI Press.
1988   "Strange Bedfellows: Deafness, Language and the Sociology of Knowledge." In *Symbolic Interaction* 11: 235–55.

Evans, A. Donald, and W. W. Falk
1986   *Learning to be Deaf.* Berlin: Mouton Press.

Evans-Pritchard, Edward E.
1974   *The Nuer: A Description of the Modes of Livelihood and Political Institutions of a Nilotic People.* New York: Oxford University Press.

Farina, Amerigo, and Kenneth Ring
1965   "The Influence of Perceived Mental Illness on Interpersonal Relations." In *Journal of Abnormal Psychology* 70: 47–51.

Federico, Ronald
1968   Ballet As An Occupation. Ph.D. diss., Northwestern University.
1983   "The Decision to End a Performing Career in Ballet." In *Performers and Performances: The Social Organization of Artistic Work,* ed. Jack B. Kamerman and Rosanne Martorella, 57–69. New York: Prager.

Felstiner, William L.F., Richard L. Abel, and Austin Sarat
1980–81   The Emergence and Transformation of Disputes: Naming, Blaming, Claiming..." In *Law and Society Review* 15: 631–54.

Festinger, Leon, Henry Riecken, and Stanley Schacter
1956   *When Prophecy Fails.* New York: Harper and Row.

Fetterman, D.
1991   "A Walk Through the Wilderness: Learning to Find Your Way." In *Experiencing Fieldwork: An Inside View of Qualitative Research,* ed. W. Shaffir and R.A. Stebbins, 87–96. Newbury Park, CA: Sage Publications.

Fichter, Joseph H.
1987   *Autobiographies of Conversion.* Lewiston, NY: Edwin Mellen Press.

Fine, Gary A.
1983   *Shared Fantasy: Role Playing Games as Social Worlds.* Chicago: University of
        Chicago Press.

Fine, Gary A., and Sherryl Kleinman
1979   "Rhetoric and Actions in Moral Organizations: Social Control of Little
        Leaguers and Ministry Students." In *Urban Life* 8: 275–94.

Firestone, Shulamith
1970   *Dialectic of Sex: The Case for Feminist Revolution.* New York: Bantam
        Books.

Fisher, Donald
1983   "The Role of Philanthropic Foundations in 'Reproduction and Production
        of Hegemony: Rockefeller Foundations and the Social Sciences.'" In
        Sociology 17: 206–33.
1986   "Rockefeller Philanthropy and the Rise of Social Anthropology." In
        Anthropology Today 2: 5–8.

Fisher, Florence
1973   *The Search for Anna Fisher.* New York: Arthus Fields.

Flugel, J. C.
1930   *The Psychology of Clothes.* London: Hogarth Press.

Forrest, Burke
1986   "Apprentice-Participation: Methodology and the Study of Subjective
        Reality." In *Urban Life* 14: 431–53.

Fox, Renée
1957   "Training for Uncertainty." In *The Student Physician,* ed. Robert K.
        Merton, George G. Reader, and Patricia L. Kendal, 207–41. Cambridge:
        Harvard University Press.

Fredericks, M.A., and P. Mundy
1976   *The Making of a Physician.* Chicago: Loyola University Press.

Freeman, H.D., and O.G. Simmons
1961   "Feelings of Stigma Among Relatives of Former Mental Patients." In *Social
        Problems* 8: 312–21.

Freidson, Eliot
1970   *Profession of Medicine.* New York: Dodd Mead & Company.

Freilich, M., ed.
1970   *Marginal Natives: Anthropologists at Work.* New York: Harper and Row.

Friedan, Betty
1976   *It Changed My Life: Writings on the Women's Movement.* New York:
        Random House.

Friedman, N.
1967   *The Social Nature of Psychological Research.* New York: Basic Books.

Gaines, Atwood D.
1978   "Illness and Interaction: A Case of Paranoia." In *Kroeber Anthropological
        Papers* 53, 54: 71–87.
1985   "Faith, Fashion and Family: Religion, Aesthetics, Identity and Social
        Organization in Strasbourg." In *Anthropological Quarterly* 58: 47–62.

Gans, Herbert J.
1962   *The Urban Villagers: Group and Class in the Life of Italian-Americans.* New York: Free Press.
1968   "The Participant Observer as a Human Being: Observations on the Person Aspects of Fieldwork." In *Institutions and the Person,* ed. H. Becker, B. Geer, D. Reisman, and R. Weiss, 300–317. Chicago: Aldine.

Garber, Ralph
1985   Ministry of Community and Social Services. *Disclosure of Adoption Information.* Report of the Special Commissioner to the Honorable John Sweeney, Minister of Community and Social Services, Government of Ontario, Canada.

Gardner, Carol Brooks
1991   "Stigma and the Public Self: Notes on Communication, Self and Others." In *Journal of Contemporary Ethnography* 20: 251–62.

Garfinkel, Harold
1956   "Conditions of Successful Degradation Ceremonies." In *American Journal of Sociology* 61: 420–24.

Gecas, Viktor
1982   "The Self-Concept." In *Annual Review of Sociology* 8: 1–33.

Geer, Blanche
1970   "Studying a College." In *Pathways to Data,* ed. R. Habenstein, 81–98. Chicago: Aldine.

Geer, Blanche, J. Haas, C. Vivona, S.J. Miller, C. Woods, and H.S. Becker
1968   "Learning the Ropes: Situational Learning in Four Occupational Training Programs." In *Among the People: Encounters With the Poor,* ed. I. Deutscher and E.J. Thompson, 209–33. New York: Basic Books.

Geerken, Michael, and Walter R. Gove
1983   *At Home and at Work: The Family's Allocation of Labor.* Beverly Hills: Sage Publications.

Geertz, Clifford
1966   *Person, Time, and Conduct in Bali: an Essay in Cultural Analysis.* Southeast Asia Studies, New Haven, CT: Yale University Press.
1983   *Local Knowledge: Further Essays in Interpretive Anthropology.* New York: Basic Books.

Gerlach, Luther P., and Virginia H. Hine
1970   *People, Power, and Change: Movements of Social Transformation.* Indianapolis: Bobbs-Merrill.

Germain, Georges H.
1988   "Les mercenaires du rire." In *L'Actualité* (mars) 54–60.

Giddens, Anthony
1976   *New Rules of the Sociological Method.* London: Hutchinson.

Gilmore, S.
1990   "Art Worlds: Developing the Interactionist Approach to Social Organization." In *Symbolic Interaction and Cultural Studies,* ed. H. Becker and M. McCall, 148–78. Chicago: University of Chicago Press.

Giveans, D.L., and Robinson, M.K.
1985   *Dimensions of Fatherhood,* ed. S. Hanson and F. Bozett. Beverly Hills: Sage Publications.

Glaser, Barney, G.
1978   *Theoretical Sensitivity*. Mill Valley, CA: The Sociology Press.

Glaser, Barney G., and Anselm L. Strauss
1964   "Awareness Contexts and Social Interaction." In *American Sociological Review* 29 (Oct.): 669–79.
1965   *Awareness of Dying*. Chicago: Aldine.
1967   *The Discovery of Grounded Theory: Strategies for Qualitative Research*. Chicago: Aldine.
1971   *Status Passage*. Chicago: Aldine-Atherton.

Glassner, Barry
1989   "Fitness and the Postmodern Self." In *Journal of Health and Social Behavior* 30: 180–91.

Glazer, Myron
1972   *The Research Adventure: Promise and Problems of Fieldwork*. New York: Random House.

Goffman, Ervin
1959   *The Presentation of Self in Everyday Life*. New York: Doubleday Anchor Books.
1961   *Asylums: Essays on the Social Situation of Mental Patients and Other Inmates*. New York: Doubleday.
1963a   *Behavior in Public Places*. New York: Free Press.
1963b   *Stigma: Notes on the Management of Spoiled Identity*. Englewood Cliffs, NJ: Prentice-Hall.
1971   *Relations in Public*. New York: Basic Books.
1974   *Frame Analysis*. New York: Harper and Row.

Gold, R.L.
1958   "Roles in Sociological Field Observations." In *Social Forces* 36: 217–23.

Golde, Peggy, ed.
1986   *Women in the Field: Anthropological Experiences*. 2d ed. Berkeley: University of California Press.

Goldmeir, J., M. Shore, and F. Mannino
1977   "Cooperative Apartments: New Programs in Community Mental Health." In *Health and Social Work* 2, 1: 120–40.

Goldschmidt, Walter
1972   "Ethnography of Encounters: A Methodology for the Enquiry into the Relation Between the Individual and Society." In *Current Anthropology* 13: 59–78.

Golenbock, Peter
1990   *Personal Fouls*. New York: Signet.

Goode, W.J.
1982   "Why Men Resist." In *Rethinking the Family*, ed. B. Thorne and M. Yalom, 131–50. New York: Longman.

Gordon, C., C. Gaitz, and J. Scott
1976   "Leisure and Lives: Personal Expressivity Across the Life Span." In *Handbook of Aging and the Social Sciences*, ed. R. Binstock and E. Shanas, 310–41. New York: Van Nostrand Reinhold.

Gordon, David
1974   "The Jesus People: An Identity Synthesis." In *Urban Life and Culture* 3: 159–78.

1987   "Getting Close by Staying Distant: Fieldwork with Proselytizing Groups."
                In *Qualitative Sociology* 10: 267–87.

Gordon, Suzanne
1983   *Off Balance: The Real World of Ballet.* New York: McGraw-Hill.

Green, Pearl
1979   "The Feminist Consciousness." In *Sociological Quarterly* 20: 359–74.

Greil, Arthur L., and David R. Ruby
1984   "Social Cocoons: Encapsulation and Identity Transformation
                Organizations." In *Sociological Inquiry* 54: 260–78.

Griff, Mason
1964   "The Recruitment of the Artist." In *The Arts and Society,* ed. Robert
                N. Wilson, 63–94. Englewood Cliffs, NJ: Prentice-Hall.

Griffin, C.
1991   "The Researcher Talks Back: Dealing with Power Relations in Studies of
                Young People's Entry into the Job Market." In *Experiencing Fieldwork: An
                Inside View of Qualitative Research,* ed. W. Shaffir and R.A. Stebbins,
                109–12. Newbury Park, CA: Sage Publications.

Grills, Scott
1989   Designating Deviance: Championing Definitions of the Appropriate and
                Inappropriate Through a Christian Political Voice. Ph.D. diss., McMaster
                University.

Groch, A.S.
1974   "Generality of Response to Humor and Wit in Cartoons, Jokes, Stories,
                and Photographs." In *Psychological Reports* 35: 835–38.

Gubrium, Jaber
1988   *Analyzing Field Reality.* Newbury Park, CA: Sage Publications.
1991   "Recognizing and Analyzing Local Cultures." In *Experiencing Fieldwork: An
                Inside View of Qualitative Research,* ed. W. Shaffir and R.A. Stebbins,
                131–41. Newbury Park, CA: Sage Publications.

Gurney, J.N.
1991   "Female Researchers in Male-Dominated Settings: Implications for
                Short-Term Versus Long-Term Research." In *Experiencing Fieldwork: An
                Inside View of Qualitative Research,* ed. W. Shaffir and R.A. Stebbins,
                53–61. Newbury Park, CA: Sage Publications.

Haas, Jack
1972   "Binging: Educational Control Among High-Steel Ironworkers." In
                American Behavioral Scientist 16: 27–34.
1977   "Learning Real Feelings: A Study of High-Steel Ironworkers' Reactions to
                Fear and Danger." In *Sociology of Work and Occupations* 4: 147–70.

Haas, Jack, Victor Marshall, and William Shaffir
1981   "Initiation into Medicine: Neophyte Uncertainty and the Ritual Ordeal of
                Professionalization." In *Work in the Canadian Context: Continuity Despite
                Change,* ed. Katherine Lundy and Barbara Warme, 109–23. Toronto:
                Butterworths.

Haas, Jack, and William Shaffir
1977   "The Professionalization of Medical Students: Developing Competence
                and a Cloak of Competence." In *Symbolic Interaction* 1: 71–88.

1978   "Do New Ways of Professional Socialization Make A Difference?: A Study
            of Professional Socialization." Paper presented at the Ninth World
            Congress of Sociology, Uppsala, Sweden.
1980   "Fieldworkers' Mistakes at Work: Problems in Maintaining Research and
            Researcher Bargains." In *Fieldwork Experience: Qualitative Approaches to
            Social Research,* ed. W. Shaffir, R.A. Stebbins, and A. Turowetz, 244–55.
            New York: St. Martin's Press.
1987   *Becoming Doctors: The Adaption of A Cloak of Competence.* Greenwich,
            CT: JAI Press.

Habenstein, Robert W., ed.
1970   *Pathways to Data.* Chicago: Aldine.

Haimes, Erica, and Noel Timms
1985   *Adoption, Identity and Social Policy: The Search for Distant Relatives.*
            London: Gower.

Hall, Gail A.
1977   "Workshop for a Ballerina." In *Urban Life* 6: 193–220.

Hall, Peter M.
1972   "The Negotiation of Identities: Ego Rejects Alter Casting or Who Is a
            Liberal?" In *Perspectives in Political Sociology,* ed. Andrew Effrat, 93–99.
            New York: Bobbs-Merrill.

Halmos, Paul
1970   *The Personal Service Society.* New York: Schocken.

Hammersley, Martyn, and Paul Atkinson
1983   *Ethnography: Principles in Practice.* New York: Tavistock.

Handler, Joel F.
1979   *Protecting the Social Service Client.* New York: Academic Press.

Handler, Joel F., and Ellen Jane Hollingsworth
1971   *The "Deserving Poor."* Chicago: Markham.

Hanna, Judith Lynne
1983   *The Performer-Audience Connection: Emotion to Metaphor in Dance and
            Society.* Austin: University of Texas Press.
1987   *To Dance Is Human: A Theory of Non-Verbal Communication.* Chicago:
            University of Chicago Press.
1988   *Dance, Sex, and Gender.* Chicago: University of Chicago Press.

Hargreaves, David, Stephen Hestor, and Frank Melor
1975   *Deviance in Classrooms.* London: Routledge and Kegan Paul.

Hartsock, Nancy
1981   *Money, Sex, and Power: An Essay on Domination and Community.* New
            York: Longman.

Harvey, A.S., and D.H. Elliott
1983   *Time and Time Again: Explorations in Time Use.* In Vol. 4 Halifax:
            Employment and Immigration Canada.

Hayano, David M.
1979   "Auto-Ethnography: Paradigms, Problems, Prospects." In *Human
            Organization* 38: 99–104.

Heider, Karl G.
1988   "The Rashomon Effect: When Ethnographers Disagree." In *American Anthropologist* 90: 73–81.

Heilman, S.
1992   *Defenders of the Faith: Inside Ultra-Orthodox Jewry*. New York: Schocken.

Heirich, Max
1977   "Change of Heart: A Test of Some Widely Held Theories About Religious Conversion." In *American Journal of Sociology* 83: 653–80.

Herman, N.J.
1981   The Making of a Mental Patient: An Ethnographic Study of the Processes and Consequences of Institutionalization Upon Self-Images and Identities. Master's thesis, McMaster University.
1986   Crazies in the Community: An Ethnographic Study of Ex-Psychiatric Clients in Canadian Society—Stigma, Management Strategies and Identity Transformation. Ph.D. diss., McMaster University.
1987   "'Mixed Nutters and Looney Tuners: The Emergence, Development, Nature, and Functions of Two Informal, Deviant Subcultures of Chronic, Ex-Psychiatric Patients." In *Deviant Behavior* 8: 235–58.

Hess, Robert D., and Gerald Handel
1959   *Family Worlds: A Psychosocial Approach to Family Life*. Chicago: University of Chicago Press.

Hewitt, John P.
1991   *Self and Society*. 5th ed. Needham Heights, MA: Allyn and Bacon.

Hewitt, John P., and R. Stokes
1978   "Disclaimers." In 3d ed. *Symbolic Interactionism*, ed. J. Manis and B. Meltzer, 308–19. Boston: Allyn and Bacon.

Highwater, Jamake
1981   *The Primal Mind: Vision and Reality in Indian America*. New York: Harper and Row.

Higgins, Paul
1980   *Outsiders in a Hearing World: A Sociology of Deafness*. Beverly Hills: Sage Publications.

Hirsch, Ernest
1977   *Starting Over*. Hanover, MA: Christopher.

Hochschild, Arlie
1973   *The Unexpected Community*. Berkeley: University of California Press.
1990   "Ideology and Emotion Management: A Perspective and Path for Future Research." In *Research Agendas in the Sociology of Emotions*, ed. Theodore D. Kemper, 117–44. Albany: State University of New York Press.

Hoffman, Joan Eakin
1981   "Care of the Unwanted: Stroke Patients in a Canadian Hospital." In *Health and Canadian Society*, ed. David Coburn, Carl D'Arcy, Peter New, and George Torrance, 292–302. Don Mills, ON: Fitzhenry and Whiteside.

Hood, J., and Golden, S.
1979   "Beating Time/Making Time: The Impact of Work Scheduling on Men's Family Roles." In *The Family Coordinator* 28: 75–82.

Hooker, C. A.
1982   "Understanding and Control: An Essay on the Structural Dynamics of Human Cognition." In *Man-Environment Systems* 12: 121–60.

Hughes, Everett
1960   "Introduction: The Place of Fieldwork and Social Science." In *Fieldwork: An Introduction to the Social Sciences,* ed. B.H. Junker, iii–xiii. Chicago: University of Chicago Press.

Humphreys, Laud
1970   *Tearoom Trade: Impersonal Sex in Public Places.* Chicago: Aldine.
1972   *Out of the Closets: The Sociology of Homosexual Liberation.* Englewood Cliffs, NJ: Prentice-Hall.
1975   *Tearoom Trade: Impersonal Sex in Public Places.* Enlarged ed. Chicago: Aldine.

Huxley, Aldous
1962   "Words and Their Meanings." In *The Importance of Language,* 1–12. Englewood Cliffs, NJ: Prentice-Hall.

Hymowitz, Carol, and Michele Weissman
1978   *A History of Women in America.* New York: Bantam.

Irwin, John
1977   *Scenes.* Beverly Hills: Sage Publications.

Israel, Joachin
1979   *The Language of Dialectics and the Dialectics of Language.* Atlantic Highlands, NJ: Humanities Press.

Jackson, Philip W.
1968   *Life in Classrooms.* New York: Holt, Rinehart and Winston.

James, A., and R. Jones
1982   "The Social World of Karate-do." In *Leisure Studies* 1: 337–54.

James, William
1902   *The Varieties of Religious Experience.* New York: Longmans, Green, and Company.
1911   *The Energies of Men.* New York: Moffat, Yard and Company.

Jenkins, H.M., D. Campbell, J. Carbotte, D. McCalla, G. Papageorgiou, E. Sanders, and W. Wallace
1980   "Revised Outline: A New Baccalaureate Degree Program in Arts and Science for McMaster University." Hamilton, ON.

Joas, Hans
1985   *G.H. Mead: A Contemporary Reexamination of His Thought.* Cambridge: Polity.

Johnstone, J.W.C.
1983   "Recruitment to a Youth Gang." In *Youth and Society* 14: 281–300.

Jorgensen, Danny L.
1989   *Participant Observation: A Methodology for Human Studies.* Newbury Park, CA: Sage Publications.

Junker, Buford
1960   *Field Work: An Introduction to the Social Sciences.* Chicago: University of Chicago Press.

Kadushin, Charles
1962   "Social Distance Between Client and Professional." In *American Journal of Sociology* 67: 517–31.

Kamens, David H.
1977   "Legitimating Myths and Educational Organization: The Relationship Between Organizational Ideology and Formal Structure." In *American Sociological Review* 42: 208–19.

Kando, Thomas
1973   *Sex Change: The Achievement of Gender Identity Among Feminized Transsexuals.* Springfield: Thomas.

Kanter, Rosabeth M.
1972a *Commitment and Community: Communes and Utopias in Sociological Perspective.* Cambridge: Harvard University Press.
1972b "Commitment and Internal Organization of Millenial Movements." In *American Behavioral Scientist* 16: 219–43.

Kaplan, I. M.
1991   "Gone Fishing, Be Back Later: Ending and Resuming Research Among Fishermen." In *Experiencing Fieldwork: An Inside View of Qualitative Research,* ed. W. Shaffir and R.A. Stebbins, 232–37. Newbury Park, CA: Sage Publications.

Karp, David A., and William C. Yoels
1979   *Symbols, Selves and Society.* New York: Harper and Row.

Karp, I., and M.B. Kendall
1982   "Reflexivity in Fieldwork." In *Explaining Human Behavior: Consciousness, Human Action and Social Structure,* ed. P.F. Secord. Beverly Hills: Sage Publications.

Karsh, Bernard, Joel Seidman, and D.M. Lilienthal
1953   "The Union Organizer and His Tactics." In *American Journal of Sociology* 59: 113–22.

Katz, Jack
1988   *Seduction of Crime: Moral and Sensual Attractions of Doing Evil.* New York: Basic Books.

Kearney, Michael
1984   *World View.* Novato, CA: Chandler and Sharp Publishers.

Kelleher, David
1988   "Coming to Terms with Diabetes: Coping Strategies and Non-Compliance." In *Living with Chronic Illness,* ed. Robert Anderson and Michael Bury, 155–87. London: Unwin Hyman.

Keller, Helen
1902   *The Story of My Life.* New York: Dell.

Kelly, J.
1981   "Leisure Interaction and the Social Dialectic." In *Social Forces* 60: 304–31.

Killian, Lewis
1973   "Social Movements: A Review of the Field." In *Social Movements: A Reader and Source Book,* ed. Robert R. Evans, 9–53. Chicago: Rand McNally.

Kinch, John W.
1963   "A Formalized Theory of the Self-Concept." In *American Journal of Sociology* 68: 481–86.

Kirby, Sandra, and Kate McKenna
1989   *Experience, Research, Social Change: Methods from the Margin.* Toronto: Garamond.

Kirkland, Gelsey, with Greg Lawrence
1986   *Dancing on My Grave.* Garden City, NY: Doubleday.

Kitsuse, John
1980   "Presidential Address." In *Society for the Study of Social Problems* 9: 1–13.

Klapp, Orrin E.
1964   *Symbolic Leaders.* New York: Minerva Press.
1969   *The Collective Search for Identity.* New York: Holt, Rinehart and Winston.
1971   *Social Types: Process, Structure and Ethos.* San Diego: Aegis.

Kleinman, Sherryl
1984   *Equals Before God: Seminarians as Humanistic Professionals.* Chicago: University of Chicago Press.
1991   "Field-Workers' Feelings: What We Feel, Who We Are, How We Analyze." In *Experiencing Fieldwork: An Inside View of Qualitative Research,* ed. W. Shaffir and R.A. Stebbins, 184–95. Newbury Park, CA: Sage Publications.

Klima, Edward, and Ursula Bellugi
1979   *The Signs of Language.* Cambridge: Harvard University Press.

Konvitz, Milton, and Gail Kennedy
1960   *The American Pragmatists.* Cleveland: Meridian.

Kornhauser, William
1962   "Social Bases of Political Commitment: A Study of Liberals and Radicals." In *Human Behavior and Social Processes: An Interactionist Approach,* ed. Arnold Rose, 321–39. Boston: Houghton Mifflin.

Kottack, Philip
1991   *Anthropology: The Exploration of Human Diversity.* New York: McGraw-Hill.

Kreisman, D.E., and V.D. Joy
1974   "Family Responses to the Mental Illness of a Relative: A Review of the Literature." In *Schizophrenia Bulletin* 1, 10: 34–57.

Kuhn, Thomas S.
1970   *The Structure of Scientific Revolutions.* 2d ed. Chicago: University of Chicago Press.

Kurtz, Lester R.
1984   *Evaluating Chicago Sociology: A Guide to the Literature With an Annotated Bibliography.* Chicago: University of Chicago Press.

LaBarre, Weston
1947   "The Language of Emotions and Gestures." In *Journal of Personality* 16: 49–68.
1971   "Materials for a History of Studies of Cargo Cults: A Bibliographic Essay." In *Current Anthropology* 12: 3–44.

Lamb, J., and V. Goertzel
1977   "The Long-Term Patient in the Era of Community Treatment." In *Archives of General Psychiatry* 34: 679–82.

Lamb, Michael E.
1976   "Interaction Between Eight Month Old Children and Their Fathers and Mothers." In *The Role of the Father in Child Development,* ed. M.E. Lamb. New York: Wiley.
1977   "The Development of Father-infant and Mother-infant Attachments in the First Year of Life." In *Child Development* 48: 167–81.
1981   (ed.) *The Role of Father in Child Development.* 2d ed. New York: Wiley.
1986   *The Father's Role: Applied Perspectives.* New York: Wiley.

Lamy, Richard E.
1966   "Social Consequences of Mental Illness." In *Journal of Abnormal Psychology* 70: 47–51.

Lane, Harlan
1976   *The Wild Boy of Aveyron.* Cambridge: Harvard University Press.

Latour, Bruno
1987   *Science in Action.* Cambridge: Harvard University Press.

Lebra, Takie Sugiyama
1972   "Millenarian Movements and Resocialization." In *American Behavioral Scientist* 16: 195–217.

Lefton, Mark, S. Angrist, S. Dinitz, and B. Pasamanick
1962   "Social Class, Expectations and Performance of Mental Patients." In *American Journal of Sociology* 68: 79–87.

LeMaistre, Joanne
1985   *Beyond Rage: The Emotional Impact of Chronic Illness.* Oak Park, IL: Alpine Guild.

Lemert, Edwin.
1951   *Social Pathology.* New York: McGraw-Hill.
1962   "Paranoia and the Dynamics of Exclusion." In *Sociometry* 25: 2–25.
1967   *Human Deviance, Social Problems and Social Control.* Englewood Cliffs, NJ: Prentice-Hall.

Lesieur, Henry
1977   *The Chase.* New York: Anchor Books.

Letkemann, Peter
1977   *Crime as Work.* Englewood Cliffs, NJ: Prentice-Hall.
1980   "Crime as Work: Leaving the Field." In *Fieldwork Experience: Qualitative Approaches to Social Research,* ed. W. Shaffir, R.A. Stebbins, and A. Turowetz, 292–301. New York: St. Martin's Press.

Levitin, T.
1975   "Deviants as Active Participants in the Labelling Process: The Case of the Visibly Handicapped." *Social Problems* 22: 548–57.

Lewis, C., and M. O'Brien
1987   "Constraints on Fathers: Research, Theory and Clinical Practice." In *Reassessing Fatherhood,* ed. C. Lewis and M. O'Brien. London: Sage Publications.

Lewis, Helen Block.
1971   *Shame and Guilt in Neurosis.* New York: International Press.

Lewis, J. David, and Richard L. Smith
1980   *American Sociology and Pragmatism: Mead, Chicago Sociology and Symbolic Interaction.* Chicago: University of Chicago Press.

Lewis, Kathleen
1985   *Successful Living with Chronic Illness.* Wayne, NJ: Avery.

Lewis, Oscar
1953   "Tepoztlan Restudied: A Critique of the Folk-Urban Conceptualization of Social Change." In *Rural Sociology* 18: 121–36.

Leyton, Elliott
1975   *Dying Hard: Ravages of Industrial Disease.* Toronto: McClelland & Stewart.

Liebow, Elliot
1967   *Tally's Corner.* Boston: Little, Brown.

Lief, Harold I., and Renée Fox
1963   "Training for 'Detached Concern' in Medical Students." In *The Psychological Basis of Medical Practice,* ed. H.I. Lief et al., 12–35. New York: Harper and Row.

Light, Donald W., Jr.
1980   *Becoming Psychiatrists: The Professional Transformation of Self.* New York: Harper and Row.

Livingston, Jay
1974   *Compulsive Gamblers.* New York: Harper and Row.

Locker, David
1983   *Disability and Disadvantage.* London: Tavistock.

Lofland, John
1966   *Doomsday Cult: A Study of Conversion, Proselytization, and Maintenance of Faith.* Englewood Cliffs, NJ: Prentice-Hall.
1967   "Notes on Naturalism in Sociology." In *Kansas Journal of Sociology* 3: 45–61.
1971   *Analyzing Social Settings.* Belmont, CA: Wadsworth.
1976   *Doing Social Life: The Qualitative Study of Human Interactiion in Natural Settings.* New York: Wiley.

Lofland, John, and Lyn H. Lofland
1984   *Analyzing Social Settings: A Guide to Qualitative Observation and Analysis.* 2d ed. Belmont, CA: Wadsworth.

Lofland, John, and Norman Skonovd
1981   "Conversion Motifs." In *Journal for the Scientific Study of Religion* 20: 373–85.

Lofland, John, and Rodney Stark
1965   "Becoming a World-Saver: A Theory of Conversion to a Deviant Perspective." In *American Sociological Review* 30: 862–75

Lortie, Dan
1968   "Shared Ordeal and Induction to Work." In *Institutions And The Person,* ed. Howard S. Becker et al., 252–64. Chicago: Aldine.

Luckinbill, David F.
1985   "Entering Male Prostitution." In *Urban Life* 14: 131–53.

Lutwin, D.R., and G.N. Siperstein
1985   "Househusband Fathers." In *Dimensions of Fatherhood,* ed. S. Hanson and F. Bozett. Beverly Hills: Sage Publications.

Lyman, Stanford M.
1970   *The Asian in the West.* Reno/Las Vegas, NV: Western Studies Center, Desert Research Institute.

1988   "LeConte, Royce, Teggart, Blumer: A Berkeley Dialogue on Sociology, Social Change, and Symbolic Interaction." In *Symbolic Interaction* 11: 125–43.

Lyman, Stanford M., and Arthur J. Vidich
1988   *Social Order and the Public Policy: An Analysis and Interpretation of the Work of Herbert Blumer.* Fayetteville: University of Arkansas Press.

Lynn, David B.
1974   *The Father: His Role in Child Development.* Monterey, CA: Brooks/Cole.

MacKinnon, Catharine A.
1982   "Feminism, Marxism, Method, and the State: An Agenda for Theory." In *Feminist Theory: A Critique of Ideology,* ed. Nannerl O. Keohane, Michelle Z. Rosaldo, and Barbara C. Gelpi, 1–30. Chicago: University of Chicago Press.

Maines, David, William Shaffir, and Allan Turowetz
1980   "Leaving the Field in Ethnographic Research." In *Fieldwork Experience: Qualitative Approaches to Social Research,* ed. W. Shaffir, R.A. Stebbins, and A. Turowetz, 261–80. New York: St. Martin's Press.

Mandelbaum, David G.
1973   "The Study of Life History: Gandhi." In *Current Anthropology* 4: 77–96.

Manning, Peter K.
1980   *Narc's Game.* Cambridge: MIT Press.

March, Karen
1990   The Stranger Who Bore Me: Adoptee-Birth Mother Interactions. Ph. D. diss., McMaster University.

Marcus, Claire
1981   *Who is My Mother?* Toronto: Macmillan.

Marshall, Lorna
1976   "Sharing, Talking and Giving: Relief of Social Tensions Among the !Kung." In *Kalahari Hunter-Gatherers: Studies of the !Kung San and Their Neighbours,* ed. Richard B. Lee and Irven DeVore, 349–71. London: Harvard University Press.

Mather, Lynn, and Barbara Yngvesson
1980–81   "Language, Audience, and the Transformation of Disputes." In *Law and Society Review* 15: 775–822.

Matthews, Sarah H.
1979   *The Social World of Old Women.* Beverly Hills: Sage Publications.

Matza, David
1969   *Becoming Deviant.* Englewood Cliffs, NJ: Prentice-Hall.

Maurer, David
1964   *Whiz Mob.* New Haven, CT: College and University Press.

McCaghy, Charles H.
1968   "Drinking and Deviance Disavowal: The Case of Child Molesters." In *Social Problems* 16: 43–49.

McCall, George J., and Jerry. L. Simmons
1978   *Identities and Interactions: An Examination of Human Associations in Everyday Life.* Rev. ed. New York: Free Press.

McCracken, Grant D.
1988   *The Long Interview.* Beverley Hills: Sage Publications.

McGhee, Paul, and Jeffrey Goldstein, ed.
1984   *Handbook of Humor Research.* New York: Springer-Verlag.

McHugh, Peter
1968   *Defining the Situation: The Organization of Meaning in Social Interaction.* Indianapolis: Bobbs-Merrill.

McKuen, Rod
1978   *Finding My Father: One Man's Search for Identity.* New York: Free Press.

McWhinnie, A.M.
1967   *Adopted Children: How They Grow Up.* London: Routledge and Kegan Paul.

Mead, George H.
1932   *The Philosophy of the Present,* ed. Aurther E. Murray. Chicago: Open Court.
1934   *Mind, Self, and Society,* ed. Charles W. Morris. Reprinted Chicago: University of Chicago Press, 1962.
1938   *The Philosophy of the Act,* ed. Charles W. Morris. Chicago: University of Chicago Press.

Mechanic, David
1962   *Students Under Stress: A Study in the Social Psychology of Adaptation.* New York: Macmillan.

Meissner, M., E.W. Humphreys, S.M. Meis, and W.J. Scheu
1975   "No Exit for Wives: Sexual Division of Labour and the Cumulation Household Demands." In *Canadian Review of Sociology and Anthropology* 12: 424–39.

Meltzer, Bernard, and John Petras
1972   "The Chicago and Iowa Schools of Symbolic Interactionism." In 2d ed. *Symbolic Interactionism,* ed. Jerome G. Manis and Bernard N. Meltzer, 43–57. Boston: Allyn and Bacon.

Meltzer, Bernard, John W. Petras, and Larry T. Reynolds
1975   *Symbolic Interactionism: Genesis, Varieties and Criticism.* London: Routledge and Kegan Paul.

Merten, Don, and Gary Schwartz
1982   "Metaphor and Self: Symbolic Process in Everyday Life." In *American Anthropologist* 84: 796–809.

Merton, Robert K.
1957   *Social Theory and Social Structure.* Glencoe, IL: Free Press.
1962   "Foreword," in B. Barber, *Science and the Social Order.* Rev. ed. New York: Collier Books.

Merton, Robert K., George Reader, and Patricia Kendall, ed.
1957   *The Student Physician.* Cambridge: Harvard University Press.

Miall, Charlene E.
1986   "The Stigma of Involuntary Childlessness." In *Social Problems* 33, 4: 268–82.

Miall, Charlene E., and Nancy J. Herman
1994   "Generic Processes of Impression Management: Two Case Studies of Physical and Mental Disability." In *Symbolic Interaction: An Introduction to Social Psychology,* ed. N. Herman and L. Reynolds, 208–23. New York: General Hall.

Micossi, Anita L.
1970   "Conversion to Women's Lib." In *Transaction* 8 (Nov./Dec.): 82–90.

Miller, B., and L. Humphreys
1980   "Keeping in Touch: Maintaining Contact with Stigmatized Subjects." In *Fieldwork Experience: Qualitative Approaches to Social Research*, ed. W. Shaffir, R.A. Stebbins, and A. Turowetz, 212–23. New York: St. Martin's Press.

Miller, Dorothy, and William Dawson
1965   "Effects of Stigma on Reemployment of Ex-mental patients. *Mental Hygiene* 49: 281–87.

Miller, Gale
1978   *Odd Jobs.* Englewood Cliffs, NJ: Prentice-Hall.
1983   "Holding Clients Accountable." In *Social Problems* 31: 139–51.
1985   "Client Attitude and Organizational Process." In *Urban Life* 13: 367–94.
1991a   *Enforcing the Work Ethic.* Albany: State University of New York Press.
1991b   "Family as Excuse and Extenuating Circumstance." In *Journal of Marriage and the Family* 53: 1–13.

Miller, Gale, and James A. Holstein
1991   "Social Problems Work in Street-Level Bureaucracies." In *Studies in Organizational Sociology*, ed. Gale Miller. Greenwich, CT: JAI Press.

Miller, Richard E., and Austin Sarat
1980-81   "Grievances, Claims, and Disputes." In *Law and Society Review* 15: 523–66.

Miller, S.M.
1952   "The Participant Observer and Over-rapport." In *American Sociological Review* 17: 97–99.

Millman, Marcia
1980   *Such a Pretty Face.* New York: Norton.

Mills, C. Wright
1940   "Situated Actions and Vocabularies of Motive." In *American Sociological Review* 5: 904–13.
1981   "Situated Actions and Vocabularies of Motive." In 2d ed. *Social Psychology Through Symbolic Interaction*, ed. Gregory Stone and Harvey Farberman, 325–33. New York: Wiley.

Milner, Christina, and Richard Milner
1972   *Black Players.* Boston: Little, Brown.

Mishler, Elliot G.
1986   *Research Interviewing: Context and Narrative.* Cambridge: Harvard University Press.

Mitchell, Richard G. Jr.
1983   *Mountain Experience.* Chicago: University of Chicago Press.

Morgan, D.H.J.
1975   *Social Theory and the Family.* London: Routledge and Kegan Paul.

Morris, Charles
1970   *The Pragmatic Movement in American Philosophy.* New York: Braziller.

Moskowitz, Breyne Arlene
1978   The Acquisition of Language. *Scientific American,* 239 (Nov.): 92–108.

Moss, P, and J. Brannen
1987   "Fathers and Employment." In *Reassessing Fatherhood: New Observations on Fathers and the Modern Family*, ed. C. Lewis and M. O'Brien. London: Sage Publications.

Munro, Thomas
1957   "Four Hundred Arts and Types of Art." In *Journal of Aesthetics and Art Criticism* 16: 44–65.

Murray, Stephen O.
1986–87   "The Postmaturity of Sociolinguistics: Edward Sapir and Personality Studies in the Chicago Department of Sociology." In *History of Sociology* 6, 2: 75–107.

Nash, J.
1979   "Weekend Racing as an Eventful Experience." In *Urban Life* 8: 199–217.

Newman, Philip R., and Barbara M. Newman
1978   "Identity Formation and the College Experience." In *Adolescence* 13: 311–26.

Noblit, George W., and R. Dwight Hare
1988   *Meta-Ethnography: Synthesizing Qualitative Studies*. Newbury Park, CA: Sage Publications.

Nunnally, J.
1961   *Popular Conceptions of Mental Health*. New York: Holt, Rinehart and Winston.

Olesen, Virginia L.
1992   "Extraordinary Events and Mundane Ailments." In *Investigating Subjectivity: Research on Lived Experience*, ed. Carolyn Ellis and Michael G. Flaherty, 205–20. Newbury Park, CA: Sage Publications.

Olesen, Virginia L., and Elvi W. Whittaker
1968   *The Silent Dialogue: A Study in the Social Psychology of Professional Socialization*. San Francisco: Jossey-Bass.

Olmstead, A.D.
1988   "Morally Controversial Leisure: The Social World of Gun Collectors." In *Symbolic Interaction* 11, 2: 277–87.

Orth, Charles D., III
1963   *Social Structure and Learning Climate: The First Year at the Harvard Business School*. Boston: Division of Research, Graduate School of Business Administration, Harvard University.

Osherson, Samuel
1986   *Finding Our Fathers: The Unfinished Business of Manhood*. New York: Free Press.

Padavic, Irene
1991   "The Re-Creation of Gender in a Male Workplace." In *Symbolic Interaction* 14, 3: 279–94.

Parke, R.D.
1985   "Foreword" in *Dimensions of Fatherhood*. Beverly Hills: Sage Publications.

Parsons, Talcott
1951   *The Social System*. London: Routledge and Kegan Paul.

Parsons, Talcott, and Robert F. Bales
1955   *Family Socialization and Interaction Process*. New York: Free Press.

Paton, Jean
1954   *The Adopted Break Silence.* Acton: Life History Study Centre.

Patterson, James T.
1981   *America's Struggle Against Poverty, 1900–1980.* Cambridge: Harvard University Press.

Paul, Benjamin D.
1953   "Interview Techniques and Field Work." In *Anthropology Today: An Encyclopedia Inventory,* ed. A.L. Kroeber, 430–51. Chicago: University of Chicago Press.

Peyrot, Mark, James F. McMurray Jr., and Richard Hedges
1987   "Living with Diabetes: The Role of Personal and Professional Knowledge in Symptom and Regimen Management." In *Research in the Sociology of Health Care: The Experience and Management of Chronic Illness,* ed. Julius A. Roth and Peter Conrad, 6: 107–46. Greenwich, CT: JAI Press.

Pfuhl, Erdwin H. Jr.
1978   "The Unwed Father: A 'Non-Deviant' Rule Breaker." In *The Sociological Quarterly* 19 (Winter): 113–28.
1986   *The Deviance Process.* 2d ed. Belmont, CA: Wadsworth.

Pinder, Ruth
1988   "Striking Balances: Living with Parkinson's Disease." In *Living with Chronic Illness,* ed. Robert Anderson and Michael Bury, 67–88. London: Unwin-Hyman.

Pitzele, Sefra Kobrin
1985   *We Are Not Alone: Learning to Live with Chronic Illness.* New York: Workman.

Pleck, J.
1983   "Husband's Paid Work and Family Roles: Current Research Issues." In *The Interweave for Social Roles: Jobs and Families,* ed. H. Lopata and J. Pleck, 251–333. Greenwich, CT: JAI Press.
1985   *Working Wives/Working Husbands.* Beverley Hills: Sage Publications.

Pollio, Howard
1978   "Not Work Alone: What's So Funny?" In *New Scientist* 14 (Sept.): 774–77.

Polsky, Howard W.
1972   *Cottage Six.* New York: Sage Publications.

Polsky, Ned
1967   *Hustlers, Beats, and Others.* Chicago: Aldine.

Ponse, Barbara
1976   "Secrecy in the Lesbian World." In *Urban Life* 5: 313–38.

Posner, Judith
1976   "The Stigma of Excellence: On Being Just Right." In *Sociological Inquiry* 46, 2: 141–44.

Powell, Walter
1985   *Getting Into Press.* Chicago: University of Chicago Press.

Prus, Robert
1975   "Labeling Theory: A Reconceptualization and A Propositional Statement on Typing." In *Sociological Focus* 8, 1: 79–96.

1982   "Designating Discretion and Openness: The Problematics of Truthfulness in Everyday Life." In *The Canadian Review of Sociology and Anthropology* 18, 1: 70–91.

1984   "Career Contingencies: Examining Patterns of Involvement." In *Sport and the Sociological Imagination*, ed. N. Theberge and P. Donnelly, 297–317. Fort Worth, TX: Christian University Press.

1987   "Generic Social Processes: Maximizing Conceptual Development In Ethnographic Research." In *Journal Of Contemporary Ethnography* 16, 3: 250–93.

1989a   *Making Sales: Influence as Interpersonal Accomplishment.* Newbury Park, CA: Sage Publications.

1989b   *Pursuing Customers: An Ethnography of Marketing Activities.* Newbury Park, CA: Sage Publications.

1991   "Encountering the Marketplace: Achieving Intimate Familiarity with Vendor Activity." In *Experiencing Fieldwork: An Inside View of Qualitative Research,* ed. W. Shaffir and R.A. Stebbins, 120–30. Newbury Park, CA: Sage Publications.

1992   "Producing Social Science: Knowledge as a Social Problem in Academia." In *Perspectives in Social Problems,* ed. Gale Miller and James Holstein, 3: 57–78. Greenwich, CT: JAI Press.

forthcoming   *Studying Human Lived Experience: Interpretive Roots, Conceptual Themes, and Methodological Issues in Ethnographic Research .*

Prus, Robert, and Lorne Dawson
1961   "Shop 'til You Drop: Shopping as Recreational and Laborious Activity." In *Canadian Journal of Sociology* 16: 145–64.

Prus, Robert, and Wendy Frisby
1990   "Persuasion as Practical Accomplishment: Tactical Maneuverings at Home (Party Plan) Shows." In *Current Research in Occupations and Professions,* ed. Helena Znaniecki Lopata, 5: 133–62. Greenwich, CT: JAI Press.

Prus, Robert, and Styllianoss Irini
1980   *Hookers, Rounders and Desk Clerks: The Social Organization of the Hotel Community.* Salem, WI: Sheffield.

Prus, Robert, and C.R.D. Sharper
1977   *Road Hustler: The Career Contingencies of Professional Card and Dice Hustlers.* Lexington, MA: Lexington Books.

1991   *Road Hustler: Grifting, Magic, and the Thief Subculture.* Expanded ed. New York: Richard Kaufman and Alan Greenberg.

Rabinow, Paul
1977   *Reflections on Fieldwork in Morocco.* Berkeley: University of California Press.

1986   "Representations are Social Facts." In *Writing Culture: The Poetics and Politics of Ethnography,* ed. James Clifford and George E. Marcus. Berkeley: University of California Press.

Rabinowitz, Jonathon
1982   "Shared Ethnicity as a Correlation of Acceptance of the Formerly Hospitalized Mentally Ill." In *Journal of Sociology and Social Welfare* 9, 3: 534–40.

Radin, Paul
1920   "The Autobiography of a Winnebago Indian." In *American Archaeology and Ethnology* 16: 381–473.

Ray, Marsh
1961 "The Cycle of Abstinence and Relapse among Heroin Addicts." In *Social Problems* 9: 132–40.

Raybeck, Douglas
1984 "Anthropology and Labeling Theory: Are Deviants Created or Recognized?" Paper presented at Deviance in a Cross-Cultural Context: An Ethnographic/Interactionist Perspective. University of Waterloo, Waterloo, ON, June 2–5.

Redfield, Robert
1962 *Human Nature and the Study of Society: The Papers of Robert Redfield.* Vol. 1, ed. Margaret Park Redfield. Chicago: University of Chicago Press.

Redmond, Wendy, and Sherry Sleightholm
1982 *Once Removed: Voices from Inside the Adoption Triangle.* Toronto: McGraw-Hill Ryerson.

Reynolds, David K., and Norman Farberow
1977 *Endangered Hope: Experiences in Psychiatric Aftercare Facilities.* Berkeley: University of California Press.

Reynolds, Larry T.
1993 *Interactionism: Exposition and Critique.* 3d ed. New York: General Hall.

Richards, P. M.
1982 "How Should We Approach the Study of Fathers?" In *The Father Figure*, ed. L. McKee and M. O'Brien, 57–71. London: Tavistock.

Richardson, James T.
1980 "Conversion Careers." In *Society* 17: 47–50.

Ridington, Robin
1988 *Trail to Heaven: Knowledge and Narrative in a Northern Native Community.* Iowa City: University of Iowa Press.

Ritter, Erika
1980 *Automatic Pilot.* Toronto: Playwrights Canada.

Ritzer, George
1986 *Social Problems.* New York: Random House.

Ritzer, G., and H. Trice
1970 "On the Problem of Clarifying Commitment Theory." *Social Forces* 48: 530–33.

Roadburg, A.
1980 "Breaking Relationships with Research Subjects: Some Problems and Suggestions." In *Fieldwork Experience: Qualitative Approaches to Social Research*, ed. W. Shaffir, R.A. Stebbins, and A. Turowetz, 281–91. New York: St. Martin's Press.

Robinson, Ian
1988 *Multiple Sclerosis.* London: Tavistock.
1990 "Personal Narratives, Social Careers and Medical Courses: Analyzing Life Trajectories in Autobiographies of People with Multiple Sclerosis." In *Social Science and Medicine* 30: 1173–86.

Rooney, James
1961 "Group Processes Among Skid Row Winos: A Re-evaluation of the Undersocialization Hypothesis." In *Deviance, Reality and Change*, ed. H. Taylor Buckner. Toronto: Random House.

Rooney, John
1980   *The Recruiting Game.* Lincoln: University of Nebraska Press.

Rosaldo, Renato
1989   *Culture and Truth: The Remaking of Social Analysis.* Boston: Beacon Press.

Rosenberg, Morris
1979   *Conceiving the Self.* New York: Basic Books.

Rosenthal, Robert
1966   *Experimenter Effects in Behavioral Research.* New York: Appleton-Century-Crofts.

Ross, H. Lawrence
1980   *Settled Out of Court.* New York: Aldine.

Roth, Julius
1957   "Ritual and Magic in the Control of Contagion." In *American Sociological Review* 22: 310–14.

Rowbotham, Sheila
1974   *Women, Resistance and Revolution.* New York: Vintage.

Roy, Donald
1952   "Quota Restriction and Goldbricking in a Machine Shop." In *American Journal of Sociology* 57: 427–42.

Rucker, Darnell
1969   *The Chicago Pragmatists.* Minneapolis: University of Minnesota Press.

Sacks, Oliver
1984   *A Leg To Stand On.* New York: Summit Books.

Salutin, Marilyn
1973   "The Impression Management Techniques of the Burlesque Comic." In *Sociological Inquiry* 43: 159–68.

Sanders, Clinton R.
1974   "Psyching Out the Crowd: Folk Performers and Their Audiences." In *Urban Life and Culture* 3: 264–82.
1980   "Rope Burns: Impediments to the Achievement of Basic Comfort Early in the Field Research Experience." In *Fieldwork Experience: Qualitative Approaches to Social Research,* ed. W. Shaffir, R.A. Stebbins, and A. Turowetz, 158–71. New York: St. Martin's Press.
1991   *Customizing the Body: The Art and Culture of Tattooing.* Philadelphia: Temple University Press.

Sandstrom, Kent L.
1990   "Confronting Deadly Disease: The Drama of Identity Construction Among Gay Men with AIDS." In *Journal of Contemporary Ethnography* 19: 271–94.

Sapir, Edward
1931   "Fashion." In *Encyclopedia of the Social Sciences.* Vol. 6. New York: Macmillan.

Sarton, May
1988   *After the Stroke: A Journal.* New York: Norton.

Sarbin, Theodore R.
1986   "Emotion and Act: Roles and Rhetoric." In *The Social Construction of Emotion,* ed. Rom Harre, 83–97. London: Basil Blackwell.

Scheff, Thomas J.
1990   *Microsociology: Discourse, Emotion, and Social Structure.* Chicago: University of Chicago Press.

Scheffler, Israel
1974   *Four Pragmatists: A Critical Introduction to Peirce, James, and Dewey.* New York: Humanities.

Schein, Jerome D.
1984   *Speaking the Language of Sign.* Garden City, NY: Doubleday.

Schneider, Joseph W., and Peter Conrad
1980   "In the Closet with Illness: Epilepsy, Stigma Potential and Information Control." In *Social Problems* 28, 1: 32–44.
1983   *Having Epilepsy.* Philadelphia: Temple University Press.

Schutz, Alfred
1962   *Collected Papers I: The Problem of Social Reality.* The Hague: Martinus Nijhoff.
1964   *Collected Papers II: Studies in Social Theory.* The Hague: Martinus Nijhoff.
1967a   *Collected Papers: The Problem of Social Reality,* ed. Maurice Naranson. The Hague: Martinus Nijhoff.
1967b   *The Phenomenology of the Social World.* Evanston, IL: Northwestern University.
1971   *Collected Papers I: The Problem of Social Reality.* The Hague: Martinus Nijhoff.
1973   *Collected Papers I & II.* The Hague: Martinus Nijhoff.

Scott, Lois P.
1981   *Being Somebody: The Negotiation of Identities in a Community Context.* Master's thesis, University of Waterloo.

Scott, Marvin
1968   *The Racing Game.* Chicago: Aldine.

Scott, M., and S. Lyman
1968   "Accounts." In *American Sociological Review* 33: 46–62.

Scott, Robert A.
1969   "The Socialization of Blind Children." In *Handbook of Socialization Theory and Research,* ed. D. Goslin, 1025–45. Chicago: Rand McNally.

Segal, S.P., J. Baumohl, and E.W. Moyles
1980   "Neighborhood Types and Community Reaction to the Mentally Ill: A Paradox of Intensity." In *Journal of Health and Social Behavior* 21: 345–59.

Service, Elman R.
1979   *The Hunters.* Englewood Cliffs, NJ: Prentice-Hall.

Shaffir, William B.
1974   *Life In A Religious Community: The Lubavitcher Chassidim in Montreal.* Toronto: Holt, Rinehart and Winston.
1983   "The Recruitment of the Baalei Tshuval in a Jerusalam Yeshiva." In *Jewish Journal of Sociology* 24–25: 33–46.
1985   "Some Reflections on Approaches to Fieldwork in Hassidic Communities." In *The Jewish Journal of Sociology* 27: 115–34.

1991a   "Conversion Experiences: Newcomers to and Defectors from Orthodox Judaism. (*hozrim betshuvah* and *hozrim beshe'elah*)." In *Tradition, Innovation, Conflict: Jewishness and Judaism in Contemporary Israel*, ed. Z. Sobel and B. Beit Hallahmi, 173–202. Albany: State University of New York Press.

1991b   "Managing a Convincing Self-Presentation: Some Personal Reflections on Entering the Field." In *Experiencing Fieldwork: An Inside View of Qualitative Research*, ed. W. Shaffir and R.A. Stebbins, 72–81. Newbury Park, CA: Sage Publications.

Shaffir, William B., and Robert A. Stebbins, ed.
1991   *Experiencing Fieldwork: An Inside View of Qualitative Research.* Newbury Park, CA: Sage Publications.

Shaffir, William B., Robert A. Stebbins, and Allan Turowetz
1980   *Fieldwork Experience: Qualitative Approaches to Social Research.* New York: St. Martin's Press.

Shaw, Clifford
1961 [1930]   *The Jack-Roller: A Delinquent Boy's Own Story.* Chicago: University of Chicago Press.

Sherif, Murzafer
1936   *The Psychology of Social Norms.* New York: Harper.

Shibutani, Tamotsu
1961   *Society and Personality: An Interactionist Approach to Social Psychology.* Englewood Cliffs, NJ: Prentice-Hall.

1966   *Improvised News: A Sociological Study of Rumor.* Indianapolis: Bobbs-Merrill.

1978   "Reference Groups as Perspectives." In *Symbolic Interaction: A Reader in Social Psychology*, ed. J.G. Manis and B. Meltzer, 108–15. Boston: Allyn and Bacon.

Shostak, Marjorie
1981   *Nisa: The Life and Words of a !Kung Woman.* Cambridge: Cambridge University Press.

Sidel, R.
1989   "But Where Are the Men?" In *Men's Lives*, ed. M.S. Kimmel and M.A. Messner. New York: Macmillan.

Silverman, David
1989   "Six Rules of Qualitative Research: A Post-Romantic Argument." In *Symbolic Interaction* 12: 215–30.

Simmel, Georg
1904   "Fashion." In *International Quarterly*, reprinted in *American Journal of Sociology* 62 (May 1957): 541–48.

1950   *The Sociology of Georg Simmel*, trans. and ed. Kurt H. Wolff. New York: Free Press.

Simpson, Michael
1972   *Medical Education: A Critical Approach.* London: Butterworths.

Simpson, M., H. Timm, and H.I. McCubbin
1981   "Adoptees in Search of their Past: Policy Induced Strain on Adoptive Families and Birth Parents." In *Family Relations* 30: 427–34.

Smith, Dorothy E.
1987   *The Everyday World as Problematic.* Toronto: University of Toronto Press.

Smith-Lovin, Lyn
1990   "Emotion as the Confirmation and Disconfirmation of Identity: An Affect
                Control Model." In *Research Agenda in the Sociology of Emotions,* ed.
                Theodore D. Kemper, 238–70. Albany: State University of New York Press.

Snow, D.
1980   "The Disengagement Process: A Neglected Problem in Participant
                Observation Research." In *Qualitative Sociology* 3: 100–122.

Snow, David A., and Cynthia L. Phillips
1980   "The Lofland-Stark Conversion Model: A Critical Reassessment." In *Social
                Problems* 27: 430–47.

Snyder, Eldon E.
1986   "The Social World of Shuffleboard: Participation Senior Citizens." In
                Urban Life 15, 2: 237–53.

Snyder, Eldon E., and Elmer Spreitzer
1979   "Structural Strains in the Coaching Role and Aligning Actions." In *Review
                of Sport and Leisure* 4: 97–109.
1989   *Social Aspects of Sport.* Englewood Cliffs, NJ: Prentice-Hall.

Sobol, Michael, and Jean Cardiff
1983   "A Sociopsychological Investigation of Adult Adoptees' Search for Birth
                Parents." In *Family Relations* (Oct.): 477–83.

Sofranko, Andrew J., et al.
1977   "A Comparative Analysis of the Social Impacts of a Technology Delivery
                System." In *Human Organization* 36: 193–97.

Sohier, Raphella
1993   "Filial Reconstruction: A Theory of Development Through Adversity." In
                Qualitative Health Research 3: 465–92.

Sorosky, Arthur D., Annette Baran, and Reuben Pannor
1975   "Identity Conflicts in Adoptees." In *American Journal of Orthopsychiatry*
                45: 18–27.
1978   *The Adoption Triangle.* New York: Anchor Books.

Spradley, James P.
1972   *Culture and Cognition: Rules, Maps, and Plans.* San Francisco: Chandler.
1979   *The Ethnographic Interview.* New York: Holt, Rinehart and Winston.
1980   *Participant Observation.* New York: Holt, Rinehart and Winston.

Stark, Rodney
1992   *Sociology.* Belmont, CA: Wadsworth.

Stark, Rodney, and William Sims Bainbridge
1980   "Networks of Faith: Interpersonal Bonds and Recruitment to Cults and
                Sects." In *American Journal of Sociology* 85: 1376–95.

Stebbins, Robert A.
1970a   "Career: The Subjective Approach." In *Sociological Quarterly* 11: 32–49.
1970b   "The Meaning of Disorderly Behavior." In *Sociology of Education* 44: 217–36.
1982   "Serious Leisure." In *Pacific Sociological Review* 25: 251–72.
1984   *The Magician: Career, Culture, and Social Psychology in a Variety Art.*
                Toronto: Irwin.

1990   *The Laugh-Makers: Stand-Up Comedy as Art, Business, and Life-Style.*
            Montreal: McGill-Queen's University Press.
1991   "Do We Ever Leave the Field: Notes on Secondary Fieldwork
            Involvements." In *Experiencing Fieldwork: An Inside View of Qualitative
            Research*, ed. W. Shaffir and R.A. Stebbins, 248–55. Newbury Park, CA:
            Sage Publications.
1992   *Amateurs, Professionals, and Serious Leisure.* Montreal: McGill-Queen's
            University Press.

Steffensmeier, Darrell J.
1986   *The Fence: In the Shadow of Two Worlds.* Totowa, NJ: Rowman and
            Littlefield.

Stocking, George W., Jr.
1979   *Anthropology at Chicago: Tradition, Discipline, Department.* Chicago:
            Joseph Regenstein Library.

Stoddart, Kenneth
1986   "The Presentation of Everyday Life: Some Textual Strategies for 'Adequate
            Ethnography'." In *Urban Life* 15: 103–21.

Stokes, R., and J. Hewitt
1976   "Aligning Actions." In *American Sociological Review* 41: 838–49.

Stoll, Clarice Stasz
1974   *Female and Male: Socialization, Social Roles, and Social Structure.* New
            York: William C. Brown.

Stone, Gregory P.
1962   "Appearance and the Self." In *Human Nature and Social Processes*, ed. A.
            Rose, 20–40. Boston: Houghton Mifflin.

Stoneman, L., J. Thompson, and J. Webber
1980   "Adoption Reunion: A Study of the Effect of Reunion upon Members of
            the Adoption Triad and their Families." Children's Aid Society of
            Metropolitan Toronto.

Strauss, Anselm L.
1959   *Mirrors and Masks: The Search for Identity.* Glencoe, IL: Free Press.
1969   *Mirrors and Masks: The Search for Identity.* San Francisco: The Sociology
            Press.
1987   *Qualitative Analysis for Social Scientists.* Cambridge: Cambridge University
            Press.

Strauss, Anselm L., and Juliet Corbin
1990   *Basics of Qualitative Research.* Newbury Park, CA: Sage Publications.

**Strauss, Anselm, Juliet Corbin, Shizuko Fagerhaugh, Barney Glaser, David Maines,
Barbara Suczek, and Carolyn Wiener**
1984   *Chronic Illness and the Quality of Life.* 2d ed. St. Louis, MO: Mosby.

Stringfellow, William
1966   *My People is the Enemy.* Garden City, NY: Anchor Books.

Stryker, Sheldon
1962   "Conditions of Accurate Role-Taking." In *Human Behavior and Social
            Processes*, ed. A. Rose, 41–62. Boston: Houghton Mifflin.
1980   *Symbolic Interactionism: A Social Structural Version.* Menlo Park, CA:
            Benjamin/Cummings.

Sutherland, Edwin H.
1937   *The Professional Thief.* Chicago: University of Chicago Press.

Sutherland, Edwin H., Donald Cressey, and David Luckenbill
1992   *Principles of Criminology.* New York: General Hall.

Suttles, Gerald D.
1968   *The Social Order of the Slum.* Chicago: University of Chicago Press.

Swanson, Janice M., and W. Carole Chenitz
1993   "Regaining a Valued Self: The Process of Adaptation to Living with Genital
              Herpes." In *Qualitative Health Research* 3: 270–97.

Taylor, S.J.
1991   "Leaving the Field: Research, Relationships, and Responsibilities." In
              Experiencing Fieldwork: An Inside View of Qualitative Research, ed. W.
              Shaffir and R.A. Stebbins, 238–47. Newbury Park, CA: Sage Publications.

Taylor, S.J., and R. Bogdan
1984   *Introduction to Qualitative Research Methods: The Search For Meaning,*
              2d ed. New York: Wiley.

Taylor, S. Martin, Michael Dear, and G. Hall
1979   "Attitudes Toward the Mentally Ill and Reactions to Mental Health
              Facilities." In *Social Science and Medicine* 13: 281–90.

Teft, Stanton K.
1980   *Secrecy: A Cross-Cultural Perspective.* New York: Human Sciences
              Publishers.

Thibaut, John W., and Harold H. Kelley
1959   *The Social Psychology of Groups.* New York: Wiley.

Thomas, William I., and Dorothy Swaine Thomas
1928   *The Child in America: Behavior Problems and Programs.* New York: Knopf.

Thompson, J., J. Webber, A. Stoneman, and D. Harrison
1978   "The Adoption Rectangle: A Study of Adult Adoptees' Search for Birth
              Family History and Implications for Adoption Service." Children's Aid
              Society of Metropolitan Toronto.

Thorne, B.
1979   "Political Activist as Participant Observer: Conflicts of Commitment in a
              Study of the Draft Resistance Movement of the 1960s." In *Symbolic
              Interaction* 2: 73–88.

Travisano, Richard V.
1970   "Alternation and Conversion as Qualitatively Different Transformations."
              In *Social Psychology Through Symbolic Interaction,* ed. G.P. Stone and H.A.
              Farberman, 594–606. Waltham: Xerox College Publishing.

Triplett, N.
1897   "The Dynamogenic Factors in Pacemaking and Competition." In *American
              Journal of Psychology* 9: 507–33.

Triseliotis, J.P.
1973   *In Search of Origins.* London: Routledge and Kegan Paul.

Trute, B., and A. Loewen
1978   "Public Attitudes Toward the Mentally Ill as a Function of Prior Personal
              Experience." In *Social Psychiatry* 13: 79–84.

Turner, Ralph H.
1962   "Role-taking: Process Versus Conformity." In *Human Behavior and Social Processes*, ed. A.M. Rose. Boston: Houghton-Mifflin.
1976   "The Real Self: From Institution to Impulse." In *American Journal of Sociology* 81: 989–1016.
1983   "Figures and Ground in the Analysis of Social Movements." In *Symbolic Interaction* 6: 175–81.

Turner, Victor W.
1969   *The Ritual Process: Structure and Anti-Structure.* Chicago: Aldine.
1974   *Dramas, Fields, and Metaphors.* Ithaca, NY: Cornell University Press.
1979   *Process, Performance and Pilgrimage: A Study in Comparative Symbology.* New Delhi: Concept.
1986   "Dewey, Dilthey, and Drama: An Essay in the Anthropology of Experience." In *The Anthropology of Experience*, ed. Victor W. Turner and Edward M. Bruner, 33–44. Urbana: University of Illinois Press.

Unruh, David R.
1983   *Invisible Lives.* Beverly Hills: Sage Publications.

Van Gennep, Arnold
1960 [1908]   *Rites of Passage.* Chicago: University of Chicago Press.

Van Maanen, John
1988   *Tales of the Field: On Writing Ethnography.* Chicago: University of Chicago Press.
1991   "Playing Back the Tape: Early Days in the Field." In *Experiencing Fieldwork: An Inside View of Qualitative Research*, ed. W. Shaffir and R.A. Stebbins, 31–42. Newbury Park, CA: Sage Publications.

Van Maanen, John, James M. Dabbs Jr., and Robert Faulkner
1982   *Varieties of Qualitative Research.* Beverly Hills: Sage Publications.

Veblen, Thorstein
1899   *The Theory of the Leisure Class.* New York: Macmillan.

Veevers, Jean
1980   *Childless by Choice.* Toronto: Butterworths.

Veith, Ilza
1988   *Can You Hear the Clapping of One Hand?: Learning to Live With a Stroke.* Berkeley: University of California Press.

Vidich, Arthur J.
1955   "Participant Observation and the Collection and Interpretation of Data." In *American Sociological Review* 60: 354–60.

Vidich, Arthur J., and J. Bensman
1964   "The Springdale Case: Academic Bureaucrats and Sensitive Townspeople." In *Reflections on Community Studies*, ed. A. Vidich, J. Bensman, and M.R. Stein, 313–49. New York: Harper and Row.

Visano, Livy
1987   *This Idle Trade.* Ontario: Vita Sana Books.

Volkart, Edmund H., ed.
1951   *Social Behavior and Personality.* New York: Social Science Research Council.

Waller, Willard
1967 [1930]   *The Old Love and the New.* Carbondale: Southern Illinois University Press.

Wallis, Roy
1977   "The Moral Career of a Research Project." In *Doing Sociological Research,* ed. C. Bell and H. Newby, 149–67. London: Allen and Unwin.

Wallis, Roy, and Steve Bruce
1982   "Network and Clockwork." In *Sociology* 16: 102–7.

Warren, Carol A.B.
1988   *Gender Issues in Field Research.* Newbury Park, CA: Sage Publications.

Watson, Lawrence C., and Maria-Barbara Watson-Frank
1985   *Interpreting Life Histories.* New Brunswick, NJ: Rutgers University Press.

Wax, Murray
1967   "On Misunderstanding *Verstehen*: A Reply to Abel." In *Sociology and Social Relations* 51: 323–33.

Wax, Rosalie H.
1952   "Field Methods and Techniques: Reciprocity as a Field Technique." In *Human Organization* 11: 34–37.
1971   *Doing Fieldwork: Warnings and Advice.* Chicago: University of Chicago Press.
1979   "Gender and Age in Fieldwork and Fieldwork Education: No Good Thing Is Done by any Man Alone." In *Social Problems* 26: 509–22.

Webber, Avery, and James D. Orcutt
1982   "Employers' Reaction to Racial and Psychiatric Stigmata: A Field Experiment." Paper presented at the 31st Annual Meeting of the Society for the Study of Social Problems, San Francisco, CA.

Weigart, Andrew J.
1991   *Mixed Emotions: Certain Steps Toward Understanding Ambivalence.* Albany: State University of New York Press.

Weinstein, E., and P. Deutschberger
1962   "Some Dimensions of Altercasting." In *Sociometry* 26: 454–66.

Weitz, Rose
1991   *Life with AIDS.* New Brunswick, NJ: Rutgers University Press.

West, W.G.
1980   "Access to Adolescent Deviants and Deviance." In *Fieldwork Experience: Qualitative Approaches to Social Research,* ed. W. Shaffir, R.A. Stebbins, and A. Turowetz, 31–44. New York: St. Martin's Press.

Westcott, M.
1979   "Feminist Criticism of the Social Sciences." In *Harvard Educational Review* 49: 422–30.

Westin, A.
1964   "The John Birch Society." In *The Radical Right,* ed. Daniel Bell, 239–68. New York: Anchor Books.

Whatley, C.D.
1959   "Social Attitudes Toward Discharged Mental Patients." In *Social Problems* 6: 313–20.

Wheeler, Stanton
1966   "The Structure of Formally Organized Socialization Settings." In *Socialization After Childhood: Two Essays,* ed. Orville G. Brim Jr. and Stanton Wheeler, 53–116. New York: Wiley.

White, Leslie
1949   *The Science of Culture.* New York: Grove Press.

Whittaker, Elvi
1981   "Anthropological Ethics, Fieldwork and Epistemological Disjunctures." In *Philosophy of the Social Sciences* 11: 437–57.
1986   *The Mainland Haole: The White Experience in Hawaii.* New York: Columbia University Press.
1987   "'Buzzing around Emptiness': The Anthropological Pre-occupation with Reality." Paper presented at the Canadian Ethnology Society Meetings, Laval University, PQ.
1992a   "The Birth of the Anthropological Self and Its Career." In *Ethos* 20: 191–219.
1992b   "Culture: The Reification Under Seige." In *Studies in Symbolic Interaction* 13: 107–17.

Whitten, Norman E. Jr., and Dorothea S. Whitten
1972   "Social Strategies and Social Relationships." In *Annual Review of Anthropology* 1: 247–70.

Whorf, Benjamin L.
1962   *Language, Thought, and Reality: Selected Writings of Benjamin Lee Whorf,* ed. John B. Carroll. Cambridge: MIT Press.

Whyte, William F.
1955   *Street Corner Society.* 2d ed. Chicago: University of Chicago Press.
1981   *Street Corner Society: The Social Structure of an Italian Slum.* 3d ed. Chicago: University of Chicago Press.
1984   *Learning From the Field: A Guide from Experience,* (with the collaboration of Kathleen King Whyte). Beverly Hills: Sage Publications.

Williams, T.R. and Martin Schiralli
1991   "Canadian University Presidents' Perceptions of Campus Life Issues." Paper presented at Learned Societies Conference, Queen's University, Kingston, ON.

Willis, Paul
1977   *Learning to Labor: How Working Class Kids Get Working Class Jobs.* New York: Columbia University Press.

Willner, Dorothy
1973   "Anthropology: Vocation or Commodity." In *Current Anthropology* 14: 547–55.

Wiseman, Jacqueline
1970   *Stations of the Lost: The Treatment of Skid Row Alcoholics.* Englewood Cliffs, NJ: Prentice-Hall.
1991   *The Other Half: Wives of Alcoholics and Their Social Psychological Situations.* New York: Aldine de Gruyter.

Wittgenstein, Ludwig
1973   "The Limits of My Language Mean the Limits of My World." In *Rules of Meaning,* ed. Mary Douglas, 201–2. New York: Penguin Books.

Wolf, Charlotte
1975   "Group Perspective Formation and Strategies of Identity in a Post-Threat Situation." In *Sociological Quarterly* 16: 401–14.

Wolf, Daniel R.

1991a   "High-Risk Methodology: Reflections on Leaving an Outlaw Society." In *Experiencing Fieldwork: An Inside View of Qualitative Research,* ed. W. Shaffir and R.A. Stebbins, 211–23. Newbury Park, CA: Sage Publications.

1991b   *The Rebels: A Brotherhood of Outlaw Bikers.* Toronto: University of Toronto Press.

Wolf, Daniel R., and D.E. Young

1983   "The Adaptive Significance Of Intracultural Differences." In *Culture,* 3, 2: 59–71.

Wood, V., and J. Robertson

1978   "Friendship and Kinship Interaction: Differential Effect on the Morale of the Elderly." In *Journal of Marriage and the Family* 40: 367–75.

Yates, Gayle G.

1975   *What Women Want: The Ideas of the Movement.* Cambridge: Harvard University Press.

Zurcher, Louis A., and David A. Snow

1981   "Collective Behavior: Social Movements." In *Social Psychology: Sociological Perspectives,* ed. M. Rosenberg and R. Turner, 447–82. New York: Basic Books.

Contributors

Patricia A. Adler (Ph.D., University of California, San Diego) is Assistant Professor of Sociology at the University of Colorado. She has written and taught in the areas of deviance, social theory, and the sociology of children. She has published *Wheeling and Dealing*, and *The Sociology of Financial Markets*.

Peter Adler (Ph.D., University of California, San Diego) is Associate Professor and Chair of Sociology at the University of Denver. His research interests include social psychology, qualitative methods, and the sociology of sport and leisure. Publications include *Momentum* and *Membership Roles in Field Research*.

Together the Adlers edit the *Journal of Contemporary Ethnography* and *Sociological Studies of Child Development*. Their most recent book, *Backboards and Blackboards*, based on a five-year participant-observation study of college athletes, was published in 1991. Currently, they are researching the culture of elementary school children.

Cheryl Albas (Ph.D., University of Colorado) is Assistant Professor (sessional) at the University of Manitoba. Her research interests include non-verbal cross-cultural communication, family, education, and social psychology.

Daniel Albas (Ph.D., University of Colorado) is Professor of Sociology at the University of Manitoba. His areas of research specialization include social psychology, non-verbal communication, and education.

These two educators have co-authored numerous articles and a monograph detailing the experiences of university student life.

Kathy Charmaz (Ph.D., University of California) is Professor and Chair of the Sociology Department at Sonoma State University in the California State University system. Her research interests include the experience of chronic illness, the development and change of self-concept, and the social psychology of time. She is also interested in qualitative methodology. Her most recent book is *Good Days, Bad Days: The Self in Chronic Illness and Time*. She is also the author of *The Social Reality of Death*.

Michael Cooper (M.A., University of Windsor) received his M.A. in sociology in 1988. His academic interests include social psychology, sociology of sport, criminology, corrections, and deviance. He has worked as a youth counsellor in an open-custody facility.

Kerry Daly (Ph.D., McMaster University) is an Assistant Professor in the Department of Family Studies at the University of Guelph. He is co-editor (with Jane Gilgun and Gerald Handel) of *Qualitative Methods in Family Research*. His qualitative studies of how infertile couples become adoptive parents have been published in journals such as *Qualitative Sociology* and the *Journal of Contemporary Ethnography*. In addition to his work on fatherhood, he is the co-director of the National Adoption Study.

Fred Davis (Ph.D., University of Chicago) was Professor Emeritus at the University of California, San Diego. His research has ranged widely in the fields of medical sociology and the sociology of culture, and he has written on such diverse topics as critical illness, the nursing profession, the social psychology of disability, hippies, nostalgia, and fashion. He is a past president of the Society for the Study of Symbolic Interaction. His most recent book, the genesis of which is described in the contribution to this volume, is *Fashion, Culture, and Identity*.

Mary Lorenz Dietz (Ph.D., Wayne State University) is a Professor at the University of Windsor. In addition to her book, *Killing for Profit*, she has done research on urban lumberjacks, performances, sports, ballet, field research, and visual sociology.

Robert M. Emerson (Ph.D., Brandeis University) is Professor of Sociology at the University of California, Los Angeles. He has written extensively on ethnographic and field research methods, and has published a number of articles using ethnographic methods to examine the work of a variety of social control decision-makers, including juvenile courts, criminal justice prosecutors, and psychiatric emergency teams.

A. Donald Evans (Ph.D., Louisiana State University) is Associate Professor of Sociology and Anthropology at Mercer University in Macon, Georgia, where he has taught since 1971. His research activities have centered on the sociology of language, corrections, and North American Indians. Most of them consist of ethnographic fieldwork among four Indian tribes, six prisons in North America, and two schools for the deaf in the United States. He has taught American Sign Language and the culture of the deaf community for more than twenty years. He has published extensively on the ethnography of deafness.

Scott Grills (Ph.D., McMaster University), Assistant Professor of Sociology at Augustana University College, Camrose, Alberta, specializes in the areas of deviant behavior, religion, and political process. He is currently undertaking an extended study of the processes that accompany the questioning and rejection of faith commitments. Recent articles include "Experiencing Culture Through Artifact" and "Closing the Sale: Political Recruitment as Sales Activity." Professor Grills also serves as a review editor for the interdisciplinary journal *Dianoia*.

Jack Haas (Ph.D., Syracuse University) is Professor of Sociology at McMaster University, Hamilton, Ontario. He has researched and written in the areas of occupations and professions, deviance, qualitative methodology, symbolic-interactionism, education and, more recently, in the areas of the sociology of addictions and recovery. He is presently researching and writing about recovery from addiction and recovery from childhood sexual abuse.

Nancy Herman (Ph.D., McMaster University) is an Associate Professor in the Department of Sociology, Anthropology, and Social Work at Central Michigan University. Her research interests include symbolic interactionism, deviance, social psychiatry, and the institutionalization and de-institutionalization of psychiatric patients. Her recent publications include "Family Caregivers of the Mentally Ill: Negative and Positive Adaptive Responses" in *Michigan Sociological Review*, "The Homeless Mentally Ill in Canada: Dilemmas and Solutions" in *Humanity and Society*, and "The Positive Consequences of Stigma" in *Qualitative Sociology*.

James A. Holstein (Ph.D., University of Michigan) is Associate Professor of Sociology at Marquette University. His research interests include deviance and social control, social problems, family discourse, and dispute processing. He has recently published *Court-Ordered Insanity*, a study of interpretive practice and involuntary commitment. He has also written *What is Family?* and *Constructing the Life Course* (with J. Gubrium), and edited *Reconsidering Social Constructionism and Constructionist Controversies* (with G. Miller).

Roy W. Hornosty (Ph.D., State University of New York at Buffalo) teaches sociology at McMaster University in Hamilton, Ontario, and has taught in the Arts and Sciences Program. In addition to studying the socialization of students in this program, he is presently engaged in research on the professional socialization of pharmacists, the relationship between pharmacy education and practice, and the feminization of pharmacy.

Karen March (Ph.D., McMaster University) is a recent graduate from the Sociology Department at McMaster University in Hamilton, Ontario. She currently holds the position of lecturer at Carleton University in Ottawa where she teaches field research methods and family studies. Her research interests include issues of identity, community studies, network analysis, family roles, and the social construction of motherhood.

Gale Miller (Ph.D., University of Kansas) is Professor of Sociology at Marquette University. His research interests focus on the sociology of work, organizations, and social problems. His studies draw from a number of theoretical perspectives associated with interpretive sociology, particularly those that emphasize the importance of language in everyday life. Miller's most recent book, *Enforcing the Work Ethic*, analyzes how the work of human service professionals is rhetorically organized.

Dorothy Pawluch (Ph.D., McGill University) is currently Assistant Professor of Sociology at McMaster University, Hamilton, Ontario. She teaches and has published in the areas of medical sociology, deviance, and social problems theory.

Robert Prus (Ph.D., University of Iowa) is a Sociologist at the University of Waterloo. He is the author of *Pursuing Customers: An Ethnography of Marketing Activities* and *Making Sales: Influence as Interpersonal Accomplishment*. He also co-authored, with C.R.D. Sharper, *Road Hustler: Grifters, Magic and the Thief Subculture*, and with Styllianoss Irini, *Hookers, Rounders and Desk Clerks: The Social Organization of Hotel Community*. He is presently working on two interactionist ethnographic projects on consumer behavior and the pursuit of corporate investors by cities.

R. Jack Richardson (Ph.D., University of Toronto) is Associate Professor of Sociology at McMaster University, Hamilton, Ontario. His research interests and publications have primarily focused on organizations and their relationship with society. Recently, he has developed an interest in post-secondary education. He is currently Chair of McMaster's innovative graduate program for teachers.

Clint Sanders (Ph.D., Northwestern University) is Professor of Sociology at the University of Connecticut. He is the author of *Customizing the Body: The Art and Culture of Tattooing* and the editor of *Marginal Conventions: Popular Culture, Mass Media and Social Deviance*. Sanders' current research is directed toward building a sociologically informed perspective on human relationships with companion animals and the constitution of animal "mind."

William Shaffir (Ph.D., McGill University) is Professor of Sociology at McMaster University, Hamilton, Ontario. His research has been in the areas of the hassidic communities, qualitative methodology, professional socialization, and religious defection. He is presently continuing his research on hassidic Jews and the sociology of religious defections, and is engaged in a collaborative study on the socialization of gifted students at university. He has also begun a study on the social psychology of messianic revivalism.

Eldon E. Snyder (Ed.D., University of Kansas) is a Professor of Sociology at Bowling Green State University in Ohio. He taught at the public school level and at Kansas State University in Emporia before accepting his present position. His research has been primarily directed toward the social psychological aspects of sport, leisure, and work. He is co-author, with Elmer Spreitzer, of *Social Aspects of Sport*. His recent research interests have focused on the sociology of emotions and sport, using qualitative research methods.

Robert A. Stebbins (Ph.D., University of Minnesota) is Professor in the Department of Sociology at the University of Calgary. He served as President of the Social Science Federation of Canada in 1991–1992, after serving as the President of the Canadian Sociology and Anthropology Association in 1988–1989. His research interests lie in the sociology of work, deviance, serious leisure, and French language maintenance in Canada. His principal publications on qualitative methods and the fine and popular arts include *Amateurs: On the Margin between Work and Leisure; The Laugh-Makers: Stand-Up Comedy as Art, Business, and Life-Style;* and, with William B. Shaffir, *Experiencing Fieldwork: An Inside View of Qualitative Research.*

Elvi Whittaker (Ph.D., University of California, Berkeley) is Professor of Anthropology, University of British Columbia. She works in the areas of contemporary theory, qualitative and feminist methodology, ethics, tourism, and socialization. She is the author of *The Mainland Haole: White Experience in Hawaii,* co-author of *The Silent Dialogue,* and editor of *Odyssey and War.* She has been the president of the Canadian Anthropology Society and of the Social Science Federation of Canada.

Charlotte Wolf (Ph.D., University of Minnesota) is Professor of Sociology at Memphis State University. Her research interests include intergroup relations, group perspective formation, perspectives and responses of oppressed groups, and processes of reality construction. Having published in a number of journals, she has also written books, including *Garrison Community: A Study of an Overseas Military Community* and *Southern Town/Two Communities.*

Daniel Wolf (Ph.D., University of Alberta). Based on his experiences of riding, drinking, and fighting alongside the Rebels Motorcycle Club as "Coyote," Dr. Wolf wrote *The Rebels: A Brotherhood of Outlaw Bikers.* Wolf is presently an adjunct professor with the Department of Sociology and Anthropology, University of Prince Edward Island. His current research interests focus on urban subcultures and international organized crime.